The Princeton Review

Cracking the

PSAT*

NMSQT

2009 Edition

Jeff Rubenstein and Adam Robinson

PrincetonReview.com

Random House, Inc. New York

The Princeton Review, Inc.
2315 Broadway
New York, NY 10024
E-mail: editorialsupport@review.com

ISBN 978-0-375-42866-1
ISSN 1549-6120

Updated by Gary Bedford
Editor: Selena Coppock
Production Editor: Heather Brady
Production Coordinator: Kim Howie

Printed in the United States of America.

10 9 8 7 6 5 4 3 2 1

2009 Edition

Acknowledgments

Thanks to Gary Bedford, John Fulmer, Selena Coppock, Rebecca Lessem, Stephen White, Suzanne Barker, Ryan Tozzi, Kim Howie, Carolyn Curtis, Meave Shelton, Heather Brady, David Ragsdale, Judy Unrein, Christine Parker, Eric Lindblad, Adam Cadre, and the staff and students of The Princeton Review.

Special thanks to Adam Robinson, who conceived of and perfected the Joe Bloggs approach to standardized tests, and many other techniques in this book.

Contents

…So Much More Online!

More Practice…

- Free SAT online demonstration with a full-length practice SAT and interactive lessons

- Daily vocabulary "Word du Jour" with definition and sample sentences

More Good Stuff…

- Chat with other students in our discussion forum

- Tips for a strong essay

- PSAT at-a-glance outline

- Articles on SAT techniques to get you ready for the next step

- E-mail tips for the SAT

…then College!

- Detailed profiles for hundreds of colleges help you find the school that is right for you

- Dozens of Top 10 ranking lists including Quality of Professors, Worst Campus Food, Most Beautiful Campus, Party Schools, Diverse Student Population, and tons more

- Useful information about the admissions process

- Helpful information about financial aid and scholarships

- Cool videos give you a student's-eye-view of many colleges

- Counselor-O-Matic combines your academic and extracurricular history with your school preferences to find the perfect college for you

princetonreview.com/psat

Part I
Orientation

Chapter 1
What Is
the PSAT/NMSQT?

The PSAT/NMSQT—from now on, we'll just call it the PSAT—is a standardized test given primarily to high school juniors to give them a "preliminary" idea of how well they'll score on the SAT. The test is also used to determine which students are eligible for National Merit recognition (as well as scholarships). This chapter will give you a general overview of the test and how it is used, along with the basics to start your preparation.

How Do You Pronounce PSAT/NMSQT, Anyway?

Ah, yes—first thing's first. Well, to be honest, we're not really sure. You can pronounce it *pee-sat-nim-squit* if you want. But we think it's easier just to call it the PSAT.

When Is the PSAT Given?

Keep on Schedule
You'll take the PSAT in the fall of your junior year. Plan to take the SAT in either the spring of your junior year or the fall of your senior year.

The PSAT is officially administered twice each year, on one Saturday and one Wednesday in October. Your school will announce the exact dates at the beginning of the school year, or you can find out on the Web: The Princeton Review at **PrincetonReview.com**, or the College Board at **www.collegeboard.com**.

How Do I Sign Up for the PSAT?

You don't have to do anything to sign up for the PSAT; your school will do all the work for you. Test registration fees can vary from school to school, so be sure to check with your guidance counselor if you have questions about how much the PSAT will cost you.

What About Students with Special Needs?

If you have a diagnosed learning difference, you will probably qualify for special accommodations on the PSAT. However, it's important that you get the process started early. The first step is to speak to your school counselor who handles learning differences. Only he or she can file the appropriate paperwork. You'll also need to gather some information (documentation of your condition) from a licensed practitioner and some other information from your school. Then your school counselor will file the application for you.

Happily, you need to apply for accommodations only once; with that single application you'll qualify for accommodations on the PSAT, SAT, SAT Subject Tests, and AP tests. The one exception to this rule is that if you change schools, you'll need to have a counselor at the new school refile your paperwork.

Does the PSAT Play a Role in College Admissions?

No. The PSAT plays no role in college admissions. It's really just a practice test for the SAT.

The one exception is for that very small group of students, about 4 percent of all students nationwide, whose PSAT scores qualify them for National Merit recognition. (We'll tell you more than you ever wanted to know about that in the next section.) Recognition as a commended scholar, semifinalist, or finalist for National Merit is a fairly impressive addition to your college admissions portfolio, and is something that you should certainly pursue if you're seriously in contention for it.

What Happens to the Score Report from the PSAT?

Only you and your high school will receive copies of your score reports. They won't be sent to colleges.

And What Will Be on It?

The Math sections of the PSAT test only basic arithmetic, algebra, and geometry. The Critical Reading sections test your vocabulary and your ability to answer questions about a passage you've just read. The Writing Skills section, oddly enough, has nothing to do with writing. It tests your ability to recognize a narrow range of errors in English grammar and several points of style. In this book, we'll review the math, vocabulary, and grammar you'll need…and there really isn't much!

So if the PSAT is a test of basic math, vocab, and a few grammar rules, why isn't it just like tests in school? Glad you asked! It's because the test-makers know how Mr. Jones tests you in Math, so when they want to trick you, they do the opposite. If you approach the tricky questions the "school way" you'll take much longer than you should or get totally stuck, but if you know the shortcuts you can be done in seconds, sometimes, or at least know that you're getting the question right. Think about it. When you want to do well on Mr. Jones's math test what do you do? You practice math the way you know he'll test it later. So when it's the PSAT folks giving you the test, practice the way you know they'll test it. The good news is that the test writers don't like to work too hard. They're still using most of the same old tricks they've used since the test was first given, and we've helped generations of students overcome them. In this book, we're going to show you how to avoid the traps and maximize your score.

Who Writes the PSAT, Anyway?

The PSAT is written and administered by Educational Testing Service (ETS), under contract by the College Board. You might think that the people at ETS are educators, or professors of education, or teachers. They're not. The people who work for ETS are average folks who just happen to make a living writing tests. In fact, they write hundreds of tests, for all kinds of organizations. They're a group of "testers-for-hire" who will write a test for anyone who asks.

The folks at ETS aren't really paid to educate; they're paid to write and administer tests. And even though you'll be paying them to take the PSAT, you're not their customer. The people really being served by ETS are the colleges, who get the information they want at no cost. This means that you should take everything that ETS says with a grain of salt and realize that its testing "advice" isn't always the best advice. (Getting testing advice from ETS is a bit like getting first-date advice from your parents.)

Every test reflects the interests of the people who write it. If you know who writes the test, you will know a lot more about what kinds of answers will be considered "correct" answers on that test.

Shortcuts
The Princeton Review's techniques are the closest thing there is to a shortcut to the PSAT. However, there is no shortcut to learning these techniques.

SO THEN WHAT IS THE PRINCETON REVIEW?

The Princeton Review is the nation's leading test-preparation company. In just a few years, we became the nation's leader in SAT preparation, primarily because our techniques work. We offer courses and private tutoring for all of the major standardized tests, and we publish a series of books to help in your search for the right school. If you'd like more information about our programs or books, give us a call at 800-2-Review, or find us on the Web at **PrincetonReview.com**.

HOW TO USE THIS BOOK

This book is divided into two main parts. The first part of the book (Chapters 1–11 and the subsequent Drill Answers) contains both general testing strategies and question-specific problem-solving instruction. The back of the book contains two practice PSATs. The study guide that follows will give you a plan of attack for these things and the rest of the book. There is no single plan that will fit everyone, so be prepared to adapt the plan that appears below to your own needs.

The first practice test will give you an idea of your strengths and weaknesses, both of which can be a source of improvement. If you're already good at something, additional practice can make you great at it; if you're not so good at something, what you should do about it depends on how important it is. If the subject is one that comes up on the test often, you'll want to spend a lot of time on it; if it only comes up once in a while, you'll want to spend very little time working on it and remember that it's something you should put off until you've done easier things or skip entirely.

How do you know what's important? We'll tell you throughout the book when techniques like Plugging In come up, but you can also get an idea from the layout of the book and the structure diagrams on page 32. If you're not so great at Critical Reading or Sentence Completions, you're going to need to work on these things because they represent a lot of questions. If you're not so hot at functions, you can tell that these aren't as important as Plugging In or Math Basics, because they appear in the Advanced section.

A Note about Vocabulary

Vocabulary is an important part of most standardized tests and success in life itself, though in most other ways standardized tests are nothing like real life. This book will give you a lot of techniques and shortcuts that you can use on the PSAT and later when you take the SAT, but while there are useful tools for learning vocab, there are no shortcuts that will magically implant words into your brain, not yet anyway. Important vocab for the PSAT (The Hit Parade in this book) is pretty much the same as it is for the SAT, so if you keep studying it from now until the SAT (and beyond) the task will be far less painful and you'll probably be very pleasantly surprised by how much your reading score improves.

Time Management

To manage your PSAT preparation, make use of the study guide on the following pages. This guide will break down the daunting task of PSAT prep into bite-sized pieces we call sessions. We have mapped out tasks for each session to be sure you get the most out of this book. Sessions will generally take between an hour or two, unless you're taking a practice test. The tests will be the first and last sessions, so you should be sure to plan to have about two and a half hours for these sessions. Most other sessions will last between an hour and two hours, so plan to take a short break in the middle, and if it looks like the session is going to exceed two hours feel free to stop and pick up where you left off on the next day.

When You Take a Practice Test

You'll see when to take practice tests in the session outlines below. Here are some guidelines for taking these tests.

- Time yourself strictly. Use a timer, watch, or stopwatch that will ring, and do not allow yourself to go over time for any section. If you try to do so at the real test, your scores will probably be canceled.
- Take a practice test in one sitting, allowing yourself breaks of no more than two minutes between sections. You need to build up your endurance for the real test, and you also need an accurate picture of how you will do.

- Always take a practice test using an answer sheet with bubbles to fill in, just as you will for the real test. For the practice tests in the book, use the attached answer sheets. You need to be comfortable transferring answers to the separate sheet because you will be skipping around a bit.
- Each bubble you choose should be filled in thoroughly, and no other marks should be made in the answer area.
- As you fill in the bubble for a question, check to be sure you are on the correct number on the answer sheet. If you fill in the wrong bubble on the answer sheet, it won't matter if you've worked out the problem correctly in the test booklet. All that matters to the machine scoring the test is the No. 2 pencil mark.

Managing the Math Sections

After you've taken the practice test, you'll have three scores: math, reading, and writing. There's a lot of math in this book, so you'll need to use your math score to figure out which exact subjects you need the most help in and where your study time will be best spent. The guide that appears below is geared toward someone whose math score is in the middle range, from about the mid 50s to the low 60s, so if your score is lower or higher than this, you'll need to make some adjustments.

If your score is lower than the range mentioned above, your plan should be to spend the three math sessions working only on Chapters 7 and 8 and doing little or nothing in Chapter 9, unless you've got extra time and have thoroughly mastered the two prior chapters, including additional online practice and drills.

If your score is higher than average, you should plan to spend very little time working through Chapter 7, unless you've missed some easy questions on the math sections and don't know why. You'll want to spend most of your time working on Chapters 8 and 9, so skim Chapter 7 for anything that looks unfamiliar and work through those portions then move on to Chapter 8 and work on the math techniques. Working on additional drills on the topics covered in Chapters 8 and 9 will fill out the three sessions devoted to math.

Session-by-Session Study Guide

Session Zero   You're involved in this session right now. Finish reading the first two chapters so you'll know what the test is about, why it is important for you to take, and what to expect from the rest of the book. This step probably won't take you long, so if you've got a couple of hours to devote to a session and you've finished these chapters, you can go on to Session One and take the first practice test.

Session One   Take Practice Test 1 (in the back of this book) and score it. You'll use this result to get an idea of how many questions you should attempt on each section and the parts of the math sections you should concentrate on.

Session Two   Work through Chapters 3 and 4 of the general introduction. Work through Chapter 5, the Sentence Completions, and Week 1 of the Hit Parade. You may want to make flashcards for the Hit Parade vocabulary words.

Session Three   Work through the Math Basics in Chapter 7 and the corresponding drills.

Session Four   Work through the Writing Skills in Chapter 10 and associated drills. Study Week 2 of the Hit Parade.

Session Five   Work through the Critical Reading section in Chapter 6 and associated drills. Study Week 3 of the Hit Parade.

Session Six   Work through Math Techniques, Chapter 8. Techniques like Plugging In are central to doing well on the math sections, so you can't practice them too much. If you've already finished Chapter 8 in Session 3, start Chapter 9 if there's time. Study Week 4 of the Hit Parade.

Session Seven   Work through the Advanced Math Principles in Chapter 9. Study Week 5 of the Hit Parade.

Session Eight   Take Practice Test 2. Use the techniques you've been practicing throughout the book. Score your test and go through the explanations, focusing on where you may have missed the opportunity to use a technique and your decisions about whether you should have attempted a question or not, given your pacing goals and Personal Order of Difficulty.

Some of the terminology in the study guide may be unfamiliar to you now, but don't worry, you'll get to know it soon. Also, you'll want to refer back to this study guide at each session to keep yourself on track.

One important note: In this book, any sample question you see will have a question number that indicates where it would appear on the PSAT. That's why you may see a question 4 followed by a question 14—the question number indicates the PSAT question level instead of its order in the chapter. The discussion on pages 32–33 provides more information about question numbers and order of difficulty.

HOW IS THE PSAT STRUCTURED AND SCORED?

The PSAT has five sections, which are always given in the same order.

Section	Number of Questions	Time
Critical Reading	24	25 minutes
Math	20	25 minutes
Critical Reading	24	25 minutes
Math	18	25 minutes
Writing Skills	39	30 minutes

You'll receive three scores for the PSAT: a Critical Reading score, a Math score, and a Writing Skills score. Each of these scores will be reported on a scale of 20 to 80, where 20 is the lowest score and 80 is the highest score. Your scores will be mailed to your high school principal. He or she will distribute them to you about six to eight weeks after you take the test. If you are homeschooled, your score report will be mailed directly to your house.

HOW DOES THE SAT DIFFER FROM THE PSAT?

The SAT differs significantly from the PSAT in structure, though the questions on the two tests are similar. The SAT has 10 sections for a total of 3 hours and 45 minutes of testing. One of those sections doesn't count toward your score; it's called the Experimental section and its only purpose is to try out questions to see whether they can be used in later tests. The PSAT has no Experimental section.

Here's a breakdown of how the tests differ:

	SAT	PSAT
Structure	10 sections	5 sections
Length	3 hours 45 minutes	2 hours 10 minutes
Purpose	College admissions	NMSQT (see Chapter 2)
Scoring	2400	Selection index out of 240

Here's how an SAT might look, compared to the PSAT. (Remember, though, that the sections on the SAT can appear in a different order.)

SAT		
Section	Number of Questions	Time
Writing	1 essay	25 minutes
Critical Reading	24 multiple-choice	25 minutes
Math	20 multiple-choice	25 minutes
Writing	35 multiple-choice	25 minutes
Critical Reading	24 multiple-choice	25 minutes
Math	18 multiple-choice	25 minutes
Experimental	?? multiple-choice	25 minutes
Math	16 multiple-choice	20 minutes
Critical Reading	19 multiple-choice	20 minutes
Writing	14 multiple-choice	10 minutes

You'll notice that the PSAT is much shorter than the SAT and the SAT includes an essay. However, the multiple-choice question types are the same.

What Does the PSAT Score Mean for My SAT Score?

Very little. Like the SAT, the PSAT gives you a Math score, a Writing score, and a Critical Reading score, using a 20-to-80 scale that is easy to convert to the SAT's familiar 200-to-800 scale. It seems as if you should be able to just add a zero to the end of each score to find out what your future SAT scores will be: a 65 on the PSAT Math section, say, would be a 650 on the SAT Math. Pretty easy, right?

Maybe a little too easy. Think about it like this: World-class sprinters can complete a 100-yard dash in under ten seconds. Going at the same speed, an athlete should be able to run a mile in under three minutes. But has anyone ever run a mile that quickly? Not even close! No one can run at top speed for such a long distance because fatigue sets in. Now consider that the PSAT has five sections and lasts for just over two hours, while the SAT has ten sections and flirts with the four-hour mark. Isn't fatigue likely to be a factor there as well? Many students are disappointed to find that their SAT scores don't match up with their PSAT scores because it's so much harder to stay sharp for four hours than it is to stay sharp for two. Throw in the fact that the SAT has an essay and some slightly more advanced math, while the PSAT doesn't, and you can see that the two tests are actually quite different for the test taker.

How Much Should I Prepare for the PSAT?

Study
If you were getting ready to take a biology test, you'd study biology. If you were preparing for a basketball game, you'd practice basketball. So, if you're preparing for the PSAT (and eventually the SAT), study the PSAT. ETS can't test everything (in fact, they test very little), so concentrate on learning what they *do* test.

If you're in that very small group of students who are in contention for National Merit recognition, it may be worth your while to put in a good deal of time preparing for this test. After all, if you can raise your scores from 71 or 72 to 74 or 76 on one or more of the sections on the PSAT, this may well put you in a better position for National Merit. Otherwise, you should prepare enough so that you feel more in control of the test and have a better testing experience. (Nothing feels quite as awful as being dragged through a testing experience feeling like you don't know what you're being tested on or what to expect—except perhaps dental surgery.) The other reason to prepare for the PSAT is that it will give you some testing skills that will help you begin to prepare for the tests that actually count, namely the SAT and SAT Subject Tests.

The bottom line is: The best reason to prepare for the PSAT is that it will help you get an early start on your preparation for the SAT.

Chapter 2
All About National Merit Scholarships

The NMSQT part of the name PSAT/NMSQT stands for National Merit Scholarship Qualifying Test. That means that the PSAT serves as the test that will establish whether or not you are eligible for National Merit recognition. This chapter will help you figure out what that may mean for you.

How Do I Qualify for National Merit?

To qualify for any National Merit recognition, you must:

- be a U.S. citizen or permanent resident who intends to become a U.S. citizen
- be enrolled full-time in high school
- take the PSAT in the third year of high school (for four-year programs). Slightly different rules apply if you're in a three-year program or other course of study.
- be fully endorsed and recommended for a Merit scholarship by your high school principal
- have a record of strong academic performance throughout high school
- complete the National Merit Scholarship Corporation (NMSC) Scholarship Application
- obtain high scores on the SAT, which you'll take later in the year

The Index

How does your PSAT score qualify you for National Merit? The people at National Merit use a selection index, which is the sum of your Math, Critical Reading, and Writing Skills scores. For instance, if your PSAT scores were 60 Math, 50 Critical Reading, and 60 Writing Skills, your index would be 170.

Math + Critical Reading + Writing Skills = National Merit Index

$$60 \quad + \quad 50 \quad + \quad 60 \quad = \quad 170$$

The Awards and the Process

In the fall of their senior year, about 50,000 students will receive one of two letters from NMSC: either a Letter of Commendation or a letter stating that they have qualified as semifinalists for National Merit.

Commended Students   Roughly two-thirds of these students (about 34,000 total students each year) will receive a Letter of Commendation by virtue of their high scores on the test. This looks great on your college application, so if you have a reasonable chance of getting one, it's definitely worth your time to prepare for the PSAT. Make no mistake, though, these letters are not easy to get. They are awarded to students who score between the 95th and the mid-99th percentiles—that means to the top 4–5 percent in the country.

If you receive this honorable mention from NMSC, you should be extremely proud of yourself. Even though you won't continue in the process for National Merit scholarships, this commendation does make you eligible for special scholarships sponsored by certain companies and organizations, which vary in their amounts and eligibility requirements.

Semifinalists   The other third of these students—those 16,000 students who score in the upper 99th percentile in their states—will be notified that they are National Merit semifinalists. If you qualify, you'll get a letter announcing your status as a semifinalist, along with information about the requirements for qualification as a finalist. These include maintaining high grades, performing well on your SAT, and getting an endorsement from your principal.

Becoming a National Merit semifinalist is quite impressive, and if you manage it, you should certainly mention it on your college applications.

What does "scoring in the upper 99th percentile in the state" mean? It means that you're essentially competing against the other people in your state for those semifinalist positions. Since some states have higher average scores than others, this means that if you're in states like New York, New Jersey, Maryland, Connecticut, or Massachusetts, you need a higher score to qualify than if you live in other states. However, the majority of the indices are in the range of 200–215. (This means approximate scores of 70 Critical Reading, 70 Math, 70 Writing Skills.)

Many students want to know exactly what score they need. Sadly, National Merit is notoriously tight-lipped about these numbers. They release them only on rare occasions and generally don't like to announce them. However, it's not hard to get some pretty reliable unofficial data on what it takes to be a semifinalist. Below you'll find the most up-to-date qualifying scores for the class of 2008 National Merit semifinalists:

Alabama	209	Missouri	211
Alaska	213	Montana	207
Arizona	211	Nebraska	207
Arkansas	201	Nevada	208
California	218	New Hampshire	215
Colorado	213	New Jersey	221
Connecticut	217	New Mexico	208
D.C.	223	New York	219
Delaware	219	North Carolina	214
Florida	212	North Dakota	202
Georgia	214	Ohio	211
Hawaii	213	Oklahoma	207
Idaho	204	Oregon	213
Illinois	213	Pennsylvania	214
Indiana	213	Rhode Island	212
Iowa	209	South Carolina	210
Kansas	212	South Dakota	203
Kentucky	208	Tennessee	213
Louisiana	206	Texas	215
Maine	211	Utah	202
Maryland	221	Vermont	216
Massachusetts	223	Virginia	217
Michigan	209	Washington	215
Minnesota	213	West Virginia	200
Mississippi	202	Wisconsin	208
		Wyoming	200

Note, however, that while these numbers are probably roughly the same from year to year, they do change somewhat. These should be used only to give you a rough idea of the range of scores for National Merit recognition.

Finalists The majority of semifinalists (more than 90 percent) go on to qualify as finalists. Students who meet all of the eligibility requirements will be notified in February of their senior year that they have qualified as finalists. This means that they are now eligible for scholarship money, though it doesn't necessarily mean that they'll get any. In fact, only about half of National Merit finalists actually win scholarships. What determines whether a student gets money or not? There is a final screening process, based on criteria that NMSC doesn't release to the public, to determine who actually gets these scholarships. There are about 8,000 total scholarships awarded, which fall into three groups: National Merit $2,500 scholarships, scholarships sponsored by businesses, and scholarships sponsored by colleges. These scholarships are based on various criteria, and the awards are of varying amounts.

Though the amounts of money are never huge, every little bit helps, and the award itself looks great in your portfolio. So if you think you are in contention for National Merit recognition, study hard. If not, don't sweat it too much, but prepare for the PSAT anyway because it is good practice for the SAT.

But I'm Not a Junior in High School Yet...

If you are not yet a junior, and you're interested in National Merit, you will have to take the test again your junior year in order to qualify.

A certain number of schools give the PSAT to students in their sophomore year—and sometimes even earlier. These schools hope that earlier exposure to these tests will help their students perform better in later years. If you're not yet in your junior year, the PSAT won't count for National Merit scholarship purposes, so it's really just a trial run for you. It's still a good idea to go into the test prepared in order to feel and test your best. After all, there's nothing more unpleasant than an unpleasant testing experience, except maybe having a tooth drilled or watching the sad downward spiral of certain pop stars.

What If I'm in a Three-Year or Other Nonstandard Course of Study?

If you're going to spend only three years in secondary school, you have two options for when to take the PSAT for National Merit purposes: You can take it either in your next-to-last year or in your last year of secondary school. However, our advice is this: If you're in any program other than a usual four-year high school, be sure to talk to your guidance counselor. He or she will consult with NMSC and help ensure that you take the PSAT at the right time. This is important, because not taking the PSAT at the right time can disqualify you for National Merit recognition.

What If I Miss the PSAT Administration My Junior Year?

If you aren't concerned about National Merit scholarships, there's no reason to do anything in particular—except, perhaps, to obtain a few PSAT booklets to practice on, just to see what fun you missed.

However, if you want to be eligible for National Merit recognition, then swift action on your part is required. If an emergency arises that prevents you from taking the PSAT, you should write to the National Merit Scholarship Corporation *immediately* to request alternate testing dates. If your request is received soon enough, they should be able to accommodate you. (NMSC says that this kind of request must absolutely be received by March 1 following the missed PSAT administration.) You'll also need a signature from a school official.

For More Information

If you have any questions or problems, the best person to consult is your school guidance counselor, who can help make sure you're on the right track. If you need further help, contact your local Princeton Review office at 800-2-REVIEW or **PrincetonReview.com**. Or, you can contact National Merit directly:

National Merit Scholarship Corporation
1560 Sherman Avenue, Suite 200
Evanston, IL 60201–4897
(847) 866–5100
www.nationalmerit.org

Chapter 3
General Strategies

In this chapter, we'll discuss some strategies that apply to the PSAT as a whole. Keep these in mind throughout the entire test, and you'll improve your score.

PROCESS OF ELIMINATION

You don't have to know how to solve a problem in order to get the correct answer (or to at least be able to make a good guess). If you can cross off four, or three, or even just two *wrong* answers, you'll be a whole lot closer to finding the *right* one. This technique, called Process of Elimination (which we'll call POE from now on), will be your new best friend. Aggressively using POE will get you points on the PSAT.

1. What is the capital of Malawi?

If you were to see this problem on the PSAT (don't worry, you won't), you'd probably be stuck—not to mention a little upset. But problems on the PSAT usually have answer choices, like the following:

1. What is the capital of Malawi?
   - (A) Washington
   - (B) Paris
   - (C) Tokyo
   - (D) London
   - (E) Lilongwe

Not so bad anymore, is it? By knowing which choices must be wrong, you can often figure out what the answer is—even without knowing *why* it's the correct answer.

Since four of the five choices on any given question are wrong, it's much easier to identify at least some of these and get rid of them. Sometimes, you can even get all the way to the right answer just by using POE, so use POE whenever you can.

_____

5. Although the piranha, <u>a species of</u>
                              A
   carnivorous fish, is <u>native to the waters</u>
                              B
   of the Amazon, <u>they</u> can be seen in aquariums
                   C
   <u>throughout</u> the world. <u>No error</u>
       D   E

Here's How to Crack It

Here's a sample Writing Skills question. Often the correct answer on a Writing Skills question will jump out at you as you read the question; in some cases, however, it won't. This means we should use POE. Let's look at each part in turn. "A species of" is okay, so (A) can't be the answer. "Native to" is the correct idiom, so (B) can also be crossed off. We might have a question about (C): Should the word here be "they" or "it"? If we're unsure, we can leave (C) alone for the moment. How about (D)? "Throughout the world" is okay, so (D) can be eliminated. So now we're down to either (C) or (E). (The answer is (C) because "the piranha" is singular and "they" is plural.)

What's most important is the technique you used, not whether you got the right answer above. You had a one-in-two shot on this problem. Those are fantastic odds, and you should take a guess. In cases where you're not sure of the answer (and this may happen often), immediately think POE. Better guesses mean more points on the PSAT!

Try to answer this question using POE before reading the explanation below.

Be Test-Smart
Many students with good grades get below-average scores because they refuse to guess.

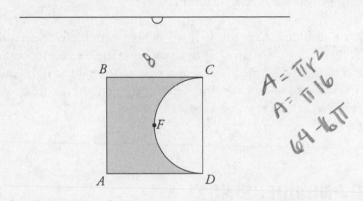

18. If *ABCD* is a square with sides 8, and arc *CFD* is a semicircle, what is the area of the shaded region?

   (A) $16 - 8\pi$
   (B) $16 - 16\pi$
   (C) $64 - 8\pi$
   (D) $64 - 16\pi$
   (E)   64

Here's How to Crack It

Even before we try to solve this problem, let's use POE. We know that the value of π is a little more than 3. If we replace π with 3 in the answers above, what do you notice? Choices (A) and (B) are negative numbers. They can't be right. If we get no further on this problem, we can guess from among (C), (D), and (E), which is a guess that we should take. But what else do we know about the figure? They've told us that the length of the side is 8, so the area is 64, which rules out choice (E), because the shaded area is obviously smaller than the whole square. Already we're down to two, but we seem to be on a roll, so why stop now? Look at the shaded area. Is it more than or less than half? Sure, it's more than half, which is 32. Applying the same trick as we did with choices (A) and (B), we get that choice (C) is about 64 minus 24, or 40, so that works, and choice (D) is around 64 minus 48, which is 12, so that's out, leaving only (C).

Okay, we won't be able to get all the way to the right answer using just POE all of the time. But the question above was a hard question, so if we'd run out of other questions that we knew we could get right and this was what we had left, it would certainly be worth taking a run at with POE on our side.

We know this isn't how you're taught to solve problems and take tests in school. In fact, your geometry teacher would probably have a fit if you were to do most of your work in class like this. That's because in school, what matters is *how* you get a problem right. But this isn't school. It's the PSAT. The only thing that matters on the PSAT is whether you have the correct bubble filled in. How you get that answer right is completely up to you. So don't treat the PSAT like a test in school. Do whatever you need to do (legally!) to get the right answer, and use strategies suited to getting the best score on this test.

POE is a technique that can be used on every multiple-choice problem on the PSAT. By getting rid of answers that you know are wrong, you can improve your chances of guessing correctly and may be able to find the right answer to a question you don't know how to solve. Remember, it doesn't matter how you get to the right answer, as long as you get there.

POE AND GUESSING

So we've talked about POE, but what then? Should you guess if you've gotten rid of one answer? Two? Three? It depends. Technically, if you can eliminate even one answer it is to your benefit to guess, but if you can only get rid of one choice on a particular question, is that really the question you should be working on right then? Maybe. But only if you've got nothing left to attempt that you could work all the way through and get right.

If you get stuck on a question that's harder than you expected and you can eliminate one or more answers, do so quickly and move on. Before you get caught up in a question, though, you should consider whether or not there's something easier to do first, something you can get the whole point for instead of getting bogged down and then rolling the dice.

In the next chapter we'll talk about pacing, which is the number of questions you should attempt to reach your goal score. For now, suffice it to say that it's probably not all of them. If you find that there are enough questions you can do to reach your pacing goal without guessing, then go ahead and do those and keep working on questions you can answer until the time's up. If you run out of questions you can do before you reach your magic number, then you'll need to use POE and guess on a few more questions than you were pacing for.

How the PSAT Is Scored

To generate your final score, ETS first computes your raw score. You get one raw score point for every correct answer and lose one-quarter of a raw score point for every wrong answer on your bubble sheet. Blanks are not counted at all. This raw score is then converted to a scaled score on the 20–80 scale. You can find sample score-conversion tables in the back of this book.

	Raw Points
Correct answer:	+1
Blank:	0
Incorrect answer:	$-\dfrac{1}{4}$

So should you guess? Well, let's look at the scoring system and see how it applies to guessing. The PSAT is a five-option multiple-choice test. If you guess completely randomly on five questions you should—by random chance—get one of these five correct and four of them wrong. Since you'll get one point for the one correct answer and lose one-quarter of a point for each of the four wrong answers, your net raw score will be zero. Thus, random guessing should not help or hurt you on the PSAT. It simply counts for nothing.

So don't waste your time on random guessing. However, if you are working on a problem that you need to answer to meet your pacing goals and you can eliminate even one answer with POE, you should guess! The more answer choices you can eliminate, the better your odds for guessing correctly will be, and the more points will be added to your score.

We've talked a little about POE already, but we'll be talking throughout the book about the kinds of wrong answers you should be on the lookout for in different parts of the test, so keep an eye out for them.

USING YOUR BOOK

At school, you generally aren't allowed to write in your textbooks. (In some cases, they'll even charge you for the book if you do.) But on the PSAT, the booklet is yours—so use it. Even though you will use your calculator for figuring, you should be working extensively in your test booklet, e.g., setting up your calculations, drawing and redrawing figures, and most important, physically crossing off answers—that helps you avoid getting lost as you work through POE.

Don't worry about anyone looking at your booklet and seeing your messy handwriting. Though the proctor will probably collect the booklets at the end of the test for security purposes, nobody will ever look at your booklet after the test.

MAKING THE MATH WORK EASIER

Ballparking

Here's one of those POE tools we promised you. Ballparking means *estimating and eliminating*, that is, using the conditions in the question to get an idea of what the answer should be, then eliminating answers that are too big or too small. If you're stuck or running out of time, you'll need a way to get rid of answers quickly so you can guess and move on. Ballparking is a great tool for quickly rejecting answers on math questions.

Have a look at the following:

---

5. If 12 cans of food can feed 8 dogs for one week, how many cans of food would be needed to feed 6 dogs for 2 weeks?

   (A)   9
   (B)   12
   (C)   16
   (D)   24
   (E)   48

Here's How to Crack It

Before you start to calculate, estimate. If 12 cans will feed eight dogs for one week, and we want to know how many cans we'd need for *two* weeks, the answer is probably larger than 12. So eliminate (A) and (B). But we're only feeding *six* dogs for two weeks, so the answer must be less than 24. Eliminate (D) and (E). Now the only answer left is (C).

———————————————○———————————————

If you're wondering whether it's realistic to expect to be able to Ballpark down to one answer on the test, the answer is: It depends. It's fairly common on easier problems, but in those cases you can often just solve it. So let's try it where it will be useful, on a hard question:

———————————————○———————————————

 16. If the circle with center 0 has a radius of 3, and
$AB = BC$, what is the area of triangle ABC ?

(A) 9
(B) 18
(C) 9π
(D) 18π
(E) 27π

Here's How to Crack It

Since we know that the radius of the circle is 3, we're just a small step away from figuring out the area. The formula for the area of a circle is $A = \pi r^2$, so the area of the circle is 9π, or about 27. We can estimate that the area of the triangle is less than half the area of the circle, so (A) is the only possibility.

———————————————○———————————————

Look Carefully at What the Questions Are Asking For

The test writers know that students are rushed when taking the PSAT. The writers use that to their advantage when designing questions. One of the biggest mistakes students make on the PSAT is working too quickly and making careless mistakes. A common careless mistake is answering the wrong question. You need to know what they're asking for before you can choose the correct answer. Let's look at an example:

---

4. If $6(3p - 2q) = 18$, what is the value of $3p - 2q$?

    (A)   2
    (B)   3
    (C)   4
    (D)   6
    (E)   18

Here's How to Crack It

You might be tempted to multiply out $6(3p - 2q)$ on this problem, which gives you $18p - 12q$. That seems like a logical first step, right? Unfortunately, if you do this, you'll be doing this problem the hard way. Why? Look carefully at what the problem is asking you to solve for. The question doesn't ask for the value of p or q alone; it asks for the value of $3p - 2q$. What's the easiest way to figure that out? Simply divide both sides of the equation by 6, and you get $(3p - 2q) = 3$.

The moral: Always look at what the question is asking for. In math class, you're almost always asked to solve for x or y, but on the PSAT you may be asked to solve for $3x - y$, or $3p - 2q$, or some other strange expression. In these cases, there's usually an easier way to solve the problem than the way you might solve it in math class.

Taking Bite-Sized Pieces

Another common way that the question writers make life difficult for you is throwing a lot of information at you at once to try to confuse you. When this happens, stay calm and take the information in Bite-Sized Pieces. By breaking up a wordy problem, you can transform a long, difficult problem into a few shorter, easier ones. Sound good? Let's look at one together.

---

 12. Lauren and Abbey are performing science experiments in which they each start off with a collection of 6 fruit flies. If Lauren's species of fruit flies triples its population every four days and Abbey's species of fruit flies doubles its population every three days, how many fruit flies will they have if they combine their collections at the end of 12 days?

(A)   96
(B)   162
(C)   192
(D)   258
(E)   324

Here's How to Crack It

Sure, this problem looks like it's going to be a pain, but let's see how difficult it really is when we work through it just a little bit at a time.

Lauren's species of fruit flies triples its population every four days.
She starts with 6.
After 4 days, she has 18.
After 8 days, she has 54.
After 12 days, she has 162.
So Lauren ends up with 162 fruit flies.

Now let's do the same with Abbey.
Abbey's species of fruit flies doubles its population every three days.
After 3 days, she has 12.
After 6 days, she has 24.
After 9 days, she has 48.
After 12 days, she has 96.
Abbey ends up with 96 fruit flies.

Now all we have to do is add Lauren's fruit flies to Abbey's fruit flies. 162 + 96 = 258, so the correct answer is (D). Watch out for the partial answers; 96 and 162 both appear in the list!

Summary

- POE—Process of Elimination—is your best friend on most of the problems on the test. It will help you stay focused on eliminating wrong answers instead of just jumping to pick one, and it will help you guess aggressively to maximize your score.

- Even though you're going to use your calculator for math, it pays to use your test booklet for figuring, POE, and basically anything you need to keep track of.

- If you're stuck on a math question or running out of time, use ballparking to get rid of one or more answers quickly, so you can guess and move on.

- Read the questions carefully to make sure you answer the right question, and take bite-sized pieces to work through each problem step by step. Both will help you avoid choosing trap and partial answers.

Chapter 4
Advanced Strategies

In this chapter, we'll discuss an overall PSAT game plan: figuring out how many problems you should do, which problems you should do, and how to avoid the answers that ETS plants to trap the average student, whom we'll call Joe Bloggs.

WHO IS JOE BLOGGS?

Joe Bloggs is the average test taker. He thinks what works in school will work just as well on the PSAT, so he goes for the obvious answers and uses a typical high-school approach regardless of whether a question is easy or difficult or somewhere in between. The problem with this approach is that ETS knows how things are taught and tested in school, so they can choose to trick him wherever they like, and they write the hard questions to do just that. If you've ever taken a standardized test you've probably noticed that some questions are harder than others. (In fact, most sections start out easy and get harder as you go along, as we'll see on the next page.)

When Joe is faced with an easy question he does fine. That's part of what it means to be easy. When he's faced with a medium question he does all right about half of the time and gets into trouble the other half of the time. When he's confronted with a hard question, he does the same things he would do if he were working on an easy question—but here there are tricks and traps all over the place; consequently, he gets nearly every hard question wrong.

So how can Joe help you do better on the test? If you were walking on a path in the woods behind a friend and your friend tripped on a root, would you trip over it too? Probably not, unless you were filming the latest version of *Dumberer and Dumberer*. Watch for the things that trip Joe up and avoid tripping over them yourself.

PACING

Most students think that you need to do every problem on the PSAT to get a good score. And most students *hurt* their score because they try to do *too many* problems.

Here's what Joe Bloggs does: Joe thinks that he has to finish every problem on the PSAT. In an attempt to do just this, he works as quickly as he can. This means that he rushes through the easy problems—the ones that he should get right—and makes some careless errors, which cost him valuable points. Then he gets to the medium problems. These take more time, are more convoluted, and have a few trap choices in them. Joe gets about half of these right. Then Joe gets to the hard questions. These are designed so Joe will get almost all of them wrong, yet Joe insists on spending lots of time on these problems—for no points at all. What kind of score does Joe get? He gets the average score of about 51.

As you can see, this probably isn't the best strategy. There are two reasons it doesn't make sense to try every problem on the test. First, it's very hard to finish every question while maintaining a high level of accuracy. During timed tests, people naturally rush—and then they make careless errors and lose points. Almost everyone is better off *slowing down*, using the time allotted to work on *fewer* problems, and answering more of those problems correctly. You'll get a higher score if you do only 75 percent of the problems on this test and answer them correctly than if you do all of the problems and answer about half correctly.

Second, not every question is of the same level of difficulty. In fact, most of the problems on this test are arranged in increasing order of difficulty: The earlier questions are easier, and they get gradually harder until the final questions, which are so difficult that only a small percentage of test takers answer them correctly. Hard questions are worth no more than easy questions, so why waste time working on them? Most testers are much better off skipping many of the hard questions and applying all their time to the easy and medium-level questions.

How Many Questions Should I Do?

Only do the number of problems you need for your target score. You're *much* better off doing fewer problems and increasing your accuracy than doing too many problems and getting only a few of them right.

So what should your target score be? Well, your target score should be higher than the score you got on your practice test (now would be a good time to take Practice Test 1 if you haven't already), but should still be reasonable and attainable. If you're currently scoring 50, trying to score a 65 right away will only hurt you, because you would have to rush to finish all the problems you need to do. Try to work your way up in reasonable stages. Pick a score range approximately 5 points higher than the range in which you're currently scoring. If you're currently scoring 50, aim for a 55; when you have reached 55, then you can aim for 60.

The Right Number of Questions for Your Target Score

The pacing charts that follow show you how many problems you need to do in order to get a certain score. You should use all of the time you're given to do only the number of problems indicated by the charts, and answer them as accurately as possible. (The numbers in the charts allow for a small margin of error.) Of course, if you find you have more time after having done this, go ahead and try a few more.

On the Math section, for instance, if you're aiming for a 55, you should just do 15 of the problems in Section 2. Which 15 problems? The 15 that *you* like the best. (More on this to come.) Many of the problems you should focus on will probably be among the first 15; but if you don't like problem number 11, skip it and do number 16 instead.

Math Target Score	Raw Points Needed	Questions to Do on Section 2	Questions to Do on Section 4
35	5	5	5
40	9	8	7
45	14	10	10
50	18	13	11
55	23	15	13
60	27	17	16
65	31	19	17
70	34	all	all
75	36	all	all
80	38	all	all

Below is the pacing chart for Critical Reading. If you're aiming for a 55, you want to do 17 questions on each section (for a total of 34 problems). Which 17? The ones that you like best. There's plenty of Critical Reading to choose from; maybe you like the shorter, paragraph-length passages better than the longer passages. Do you like simple line reference questions or the more general author tone questions?

Critical Reading Target Score	Raw Points Needed	Questions to Do on Section 1	Questions to Do on Section 3
35	7	6	6
40	11	8	8
45	16	11	11
50	21	13	13
55	27	17	17
60	32	19	19
65	38	22	22
70	42	all	all
75	45	all	all
80	47	all	all

Finally, here's the pacing chart for the Writing Skills section:

Writing Skills Target Score	Raw Points Needed	Questions to Do on Section 5
35	5	10
40	9	15
45	13	19
50	17	23
55	21	27
60	25	31
65	28	34
70	32	all
75	35	all
80	38	all

WHICH PROBLEMS SHOULD I DO?

As we mentioned above, you should do whichever problems are the easiest and quickest for *you*.

The Order of Difficulty

Most of the questions on the PSAT are arranged in increasing order of difficulty, as you can see on the charts below. The rest have no order of difficulty (OOD), which means it's up to you to choose the questions that are easiest for you to do.

You should notice in the chart that for sections that have an order of difficulty, approximately the first third of each section is easy, the next third is medium, and the last third is difficult. So you should always pay attention the question number you're working on in these sections, because it will give you important hints about how to approach the question. If it's an easy question, go ahead and use the techniques to answer it and don't second-guess yourself. If it's a medium question, be careful, use POE and the techniques, and watch for the occasional trick. If it's a difficult question, keep in mind that there's something in the question that caused it to be given that high number, a Joe Bloggs answer or two, or maybe it's worded in a tricky way or presents a great deal of information that will be easy to get tripped up in. On hard questions you need to be sure first of all that you should be working on that question at all, a subject that goes beyond order or difficulty and into the next topic, Personal Order of Difficulty.

Your Personal Order of Difficulty

The chart on the previous page shows questions that are considered "easy," "medium," and "hard" by the average test taker. The average number of people who get that question right determines whether a question is easy, medium, or hard by ETS standards.

But for any one test taker, who—for example—might like algebra better than geometry, a question that is usually considered "medium" might be easy. Or vice versa.

This means that you should always answer the questions on the PSAT according to your Personal Order of Difficulty, or POOD—that is, answer the ones that are easiest for you. If you're going to do 14 math questions on a section, you want to find the easiest 14. While it's a good bet that most of the first 14 math questions will be the easiest for you, if you find one or two questions in that group that you don't like, *skip them*. Then find a few other questions elsewhere in the section that look easier for you.

Joe Bloggs Answers

Let's revisit our friend Joe Bloggs and look at another way he can help us on the PSAT. Suppose for a moment that you could look at the page of the tester next to you (you can't). Also, suppose that you know for a fact that every one of your neighbor's answers on the test is wrong. If on problem 20, he marked (C) as his answer, what you do? Eliminate choice (C), right?

Even though you can't look at your neighbor's page, you can use this principle to get points on the test by looking for Joe Bloggs answers. When the folks at ETS write the PSAT, they write it in a very particular way. They write it so that Joe will get most of the easy problems correct, some of the medium problems correct, and none of the hard ones correct.

How do they do this? The test writers are very good at knowing what kinds of answer choices are attractive to the average person. (They've been doing it for more than 40 years.)

Joe Bloggs, the average tester, always picks the answer that first attracts him. Choices that first attract him on math problems have nice round numbers that can be easily derived from other numbers in the problem. Choices that attract him on verbal problems have familiar words that remind him of words in the question or passage.

Joe's Hunches
Should you always just eliminate any answer that seems to be correct? No! Remember what we said about Joe Bloggs:
1. His hunches are correct on easy questions.
2. His hunches are sometimes correct and sometimes incorrect on medium questions.
3. His hunches are always wrong on difficult questions.
On easy multiple-choice questions, pick the choice that Joe Bloggs would. On hard questions, be sure to eliminate the choices that Joe Bloggs would pick.

Question Type	Joe Bloggs Selects	How Joe Does
Easy	What seems right	Mostly right
Medium	What seems right	So-so
Hard	What seems right	All wrong!

What does this mean for you? When you're working on easy problems, pick the choice that seems right to you. When you're working on medium problems, be careful. If you got the answer too quickly, check your work. Medium problems should take more work than easy problems. If you're working on a hard problem, eliminate the choices that first seem attractive; they are almost always traps.

Remember, Joe Bloggs gets the easy problems right. *Only cross off Joe Bloggs answers on the hard problems*. How do you know how hard a question is? By its *question number*.

Take a look at the following example:

20. Michelle rode her bicycle from her house to school at an average speed of 8 miles per hour. Later that day, she rode from school back home along the same route at an average speed of 12 miles per hour. If the round trip took her 1 hour, how many miles long is the round trip?

(A) 8

(B) $9\frac{3}{5}$

(C) 10

(D) $11\frac{1}{5}$

(E) 12

Here's How to Crack It

Which choice do you think seems attractive at first to Joe? When he sees the numbers 8 and 12 and the word "average," he will probably average 8 and 12 to get 10. Therefore, Joe will pick (C).

But now you know better. This problem is number 20, the hardest problem on the section. You know that Joe will get it wrong. So cross off choice (C).

If Joe doesn't pick (C), what else might he pick? He'll pick either (A) 8, or (E) 12, because those are the numbers that appear in the problem. Cross them off as well. Then guess from either (B) or (D). (The answer is (B), but we're not going to spend time on why right now.) If you can quickly cross off a few choices on a hard problem and make a good guess, you'll be in great shape.

Figuring out the right number of problems to do, how to pace yourself, and how to avoid the Joe Bloggs traps are keys to a good PSAT strategy. You're probably eager to get to the rest of the book, but make sure you've taken the time to understand this chapter before moving on. A solid overall approach is crucial to getting your best score on this test.

Summary

- Remember to memorize your pacing goals so that you know exactly how many problems to do—you don't have to do every problem to get a great score.

- The questions on most sections are arranged in Order of Difficulty from easier to harder, which may make it easier to find the problems that are easier for you to do.

- Use your Joe Bloggs instincts on easy and hard problems (according to the test writers' OOD). For easy problems, Joe Bloggs answers tend to be right, while on hard problems, they are almost always wrong.

Part II
Cracking the
PSAT/^{NMSQT}

Chapter 5
Sentence
Completions

A Sentence Completion question will consist of a sample sentence in which one or two words have been replaced by blanks. Below the sentence, you'll find five answer choices, each of which consists of a word or words. This chapter will give you the techniques you need to approach Sentence Completions for maximum accuracy and minimum wasted time and stress.

Solving Sentence Completions relies on two things: First, your ability to figure out what kind of word should go in the blank, and second, your vocabulary. We will focus mostly on technique in this chapter. To work on vocabulary, turn to Chapter 11 for the Hit Parade—The Princeton Review's list of vocabulary words that show up most often on the PSAT.

THE INSTRUCTIONS

Of course, you don't want to take up valuable time during the test to read the directions, so let's learn them now. Here are the instructions for Sentence Completions as you will see them on the PSAT and SAT:

Each sentence below has one or two blanks, each blank indicating that something has been omitted. Beneath the sentence are five words or sets of words labeled A through E. Choose the word or set of words that, when inserted in the sentence, best fits the meaning of the sentence as a whole.

  Example:

   Medieval kingdoms did not become constitutional republics overnight; on the contrary, the change was -------.

   (A) unpopular (B) unexpected (C) advantageous
   (D) sufficient (E) gradual   Ⓐ Ⓑ Ⓒ Ⓓ ●

ETS's answer to this sample question is (E).

ORDER OF DIFFICULTY

Sentence Completion questions will appear on both Critical Reading sections of the PSAT. They will be questions 1–8 in Section 1 and questions 25–29 in Section 3. Their order of difficulty looks like this:

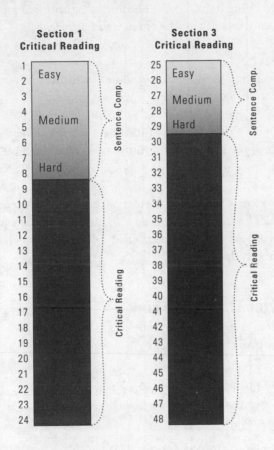

DON'T BE LIKE JOE

Before we talk about the best way to solve Sentence Completions, we should first discuss how *not* to solve them. How does Joe Bloggs, the average student, approach Sentence Completions? The natural way, which seems most intuitive to Joe, is to do the following: He tries to solve these questions by rereading the sentence five times, trying a different word in the blank each time, and hoping to find the one that "sounds right." That is, he does the following:

Joe tries choice (A):

> Medieval kingdoms did not become constitutional republics overnight; on the contrary, the change was *unpopular*.

Joe tries choice (B):

> Medieval kingdoms did not become constitutional republics overnight; on the contrary, the change was *unexpected*.

A Reminder

On easy questions, the answers that seem right to Joe really are right; on hard questions, the answers that seem right to Joe are wrong. In both cases, though, he spends way too much time on them.

Joe tries choice (C):

> Medieval kingdoms did not become constitutional republics overnight; on the contrary, the change was *advantageous*.

Joe tries choice (D):

> Medieval kingdoms did not become constitutional republics overnight; on the contrary, the change was *sufficient*.

Joe tries choice (E):

> Medieval kingdoms did not become constitutional republics overnight; on the contrary, the change was *gradual*.

Unfortunately, while this method is intuitive, it's not a very good strategy. Not only is it a waste of time (why would you want to read the sentence *five times*?), but it's often unreliable, since many of the choices sound pretty good.

What Joe doesn't know is that the correct answer on a Sentence Completion question is not correct because of how it *sounds*, but because of what it *means*. So the best way to solve Sentence Completions is to figure out what the word in the blank should mean. The question is, how?

You're Smarter Than You Think

Try the following exercise: In the following sentence, what word do you think should go in the blank?

> 1. Susan was ------- when the formula, which had worked just yesterday, failed to produce the expected result.

What word did you put in the blank? "Perplexed" or "confused"? Something of this sort has to be the word in the blank.

How about this one:

> 2. Although she was never considered pretty as a child, Margaret grew up to be a ------- adult.

What word did you put in the blank? "Beautiful" or "pretty" or "lovely"? You can figure out what the word in the blank has to mean without looking at the answer choices.

Try it once more:

> 3. Once a cheerful person, the years of fruitless struggle against government waste made him a very ------- man.

Even if you couldn't figure out the exact word that went in the blank, you probably figured out that it had to be a word meaning "unhappy" or "bitter." That will be good enough to get the right answer, or at least to make a very good guess at the right answer.

You see, you're smarter than you think. This is why you should always approach Sentence Completion questions by *speaking for yourself*. Don't look down at the answer choices; if you do, you'll be tempted to use the Joe Bloggs method of trying each word, one at a time, and hoping that one of them sounds right. In fact, you should always approach Sentence Completions the same way we just did: Read the sentence, and put your own word into the blank.

THE METHOD

As you've seen, it's entirely possible to figure out what kind of word goes in the blank just by reading the sentence carefully, and it's much faster than trying every answer choice. To make sure that you speak for yourself, you should actually place your hand over the answer choices so you're not tempted to read them until you've picked your own word for the blank.

Sentence Completion Rule #1
Cover the answer choices until you know what the answer should be.

So here's our method so far for solving Sentence Completions:

1. Cover the answer choices with your hand. This will ensure that you don't do what Joe does, which is to read the sentence five times, trying one of the answer choices each time.
2. Speak for yourself: Read the sentence, and write your own word in the blank.
3. Only after you've put your own word in the blank should you uncover the answer choices and pick the word that comes closest to the word that you came up with.

But how do you know what word to put in the blank? You never have to guess randomly; in fact, ETS always puts clues into the sentences to tell you what sort of word goes in the blank. By learning how to look for these clues, you can reliably figure out what sort of word has to go in the blank, every time.

Speak for Yourself, Part I: The Clue and Trigger Words

To help you speak for yourself, learn to look for the *clue* and *trigger words*.

The Clue

Hold an Audition

If you were directing *Romeo and Juliet* you wouldn't audition everyone for every part, would you? For Juliet you'd only invite teenage girls to audition. With Sentence Completions you can follow a similar procedure; know what you're looking for ahead of time.

We just saw that you could figure out the meaning of the word in the blank without looking at the answer choices. How did you think you were able to know what word went in the blank? Without realizing it, you were using clues in the sentence. There are *always* clues in the sentence that tell you what the word in the blank is supposed to mean.

Let's look back at the first sample problem and see what kind of clues we can find in it.

> 1. Susan was ------- when the formula, which had worked just yesterday, failed to produce the expected result.

How did you know that the word had to be something like "perplexed"? Because this sentence contains a clue: *the formula, which had worked just yesterday, failed to produce the expected result.* This clue tells us how Susan must feel: namely, that she felt "perplexed" or "puzzled." We're going to underline clues, so go ahead and underline the phrase from question 1, italicized above. Remember, it's your book, so write in it and write in your test booklet on test day.

How about in this sentence?

> 2. The park was so ------- that children could play in it for hours without getting bored.

What kind of word would you put in this blank, and why? You probably chose a word like "interesting" or "varied." You probably knew this because the park is described as a place where *children could play for hours without getting bored*. This is the clue that tells us that the park must be a terribly interesting place to be.

The meaning of the word that goes in the blank isn't random—rather, there is always evidence somewhere else in the sentence that tells you what the word in the blank should mean. This evidence is called the clue. *Every sentence has some clue in it. Look for the clue, underline it, and it will help you determine the word that goes in the blank.*

Why Every Sentence Needs a Clue

Every sentence on the PSAT must have some sort of clue in it, or else the question wouldn't have just one correct answer. In that case, the question wouldn't be a good one anymore, and ETS couldn't use it on the PSAT. Let's see why. Take a look at this problem:

1. John made some ------- comments about Marcus's artwork.

    (A) intelligent
    (B) critical
    (C) interesting
    (D) dry
    (E) appreciative

Can you see why this problem would never appear on the PSAT? Because any of the answers might work. There's not enough information in the sentence to make one choice better than any other. Without a clue, the question just won't work. Look at this example:

1. John made some ------- comments about Marcus's artwork, which John thought was fantastic.

    (A) intelligent
    (B) critical
    (C) interesting
    (D) dry
    (E) appreciative

In this case, the word that would best fit would be (E), because of the clue *which John thought was fantastic.* Note that if the clue changes, so does the meaning of the word in the blank.

1. John made some ------- comments about Marcus's artwork, which John thought was the worst he had ever seen.

    (A) intelligent
    (B) critical
    (C) interesting
    (D) dry
    (E) appreciative

In this case, the answer would be (B). By changing the clue, we changed the meaning of the word that should go in the blank.

Suppose you're having trouble identifying the clue, though. There are two questions you can ask yourself to help you find it.

- Who or what is the blank talking about?
- What does the sentence say about that thing?

Let's look at number 1 on page 46 again. Who or what is the sentence talking about? The formula. What does it say about the formula? *That it failed to produce the expected result,* so that's the clue.

It will work for number 2 as well. Who or what was that sentence talking about? The park. What does it say about the park? *That the children could play in it for hours without getting bored,* so that's the clue. Remember to underline it.

Trigger Words

One more important tool for figuring out the meaning of the word in the blank is *trigger words*. These are words in the sentence that tell you how the word in the blank relates to the clue. When you see a trigger word, circle it.

Same or Opposite?

The most common same-direction trigger words are *and, because, so, therefore, since,* and *in fact.*

The most common opposite-direction trigger words are *but, however, yet, although, though, in contrast, rather,* and *despite.* When you see these words, the word in the blank will usually mean the opposite of the clue.

Same-Direction Triggers	Opposite-Direction Triggers
and	but
because	however
so	yet
therefore	although/though
since	in contrast
in fact	rather

Trigger words are words we use every day. For instance, look at the following sentences:

I really like you, *and* _____
I really like you, *but* _____

You already know more or less how these sentences would end, don't you? The first sentence would continue with something positive that goes along with liking someone, such as:

I really like you, *and* I'd like to get to know you better.

In contrast, the second sentence would change direction and end with something not quite so nice, such as:

I really like you, *but* you're really not my type.

Now let's see how trigger words work in a sample sentence. Recall the second example:

2. *Although* she was never considered pretty as a child, Margaret grew up to be a ------- adult.

How did you know that the word in the blank had to be a word like "beautiful"? Because the word *although* told you that there was a change in direction or contrast in the sentence: She was *not pretty as a child*, but she *was* a pretty *adult*.

There are also trigger words that indicate that the word in the blank has the same meaning as the clue. For instance:

4. (Because) Susan could not stand Jim's boorish
   manners, she ------- to be near him at parties.

In this case, what sort of word goes in the blank? The trigger word *because* tells you that the word in the blank will have a similar meaning to the clue *could not stand Jim's boorish manners*. The word in the blank must therefore be something like "hated" or "despised."

Punctuation Triggers

In addition to the words to the right, there are a couple of punctuation triggers. Both colons (:) and semicolons (;) act as same-direction triggers and show us that what follows the colon or semicolon will be an explanation or further description of something that came before. Take a look at this sentence:

2. John's friend was rather ------(:) He never spoke
   unless he was forced to.

In this case, we know that the word in the blank should be a word that means "unwilling to speak"—a word like "quiet" or "taciturn" would do nicely.

Time Triggers

One other, more subtle, kind of trigger, which acts as an opposite-direction trigger, is the time trigger. A time trigger draws a contrast between what used to be true and what is true today. Here's an example:

A Reminder
Circle the triggers!

3. (Once) a cheerful person, the years of fruitless
   struggle against government waste made him a very
   ------- man.

In this case, we know that the word in the blank needs to be a word opposite to "cheerful"—perhaps a word like "gloomy" or "cynical." Why? We know that at one point in the past, this person was cheerful; however, since that time, something has changed. Therefore, the word in the blank should be something that contrasts with "cheerful."

When trying to find the right word for the blank, always look for the clue and trigger words. They will tell you what sort of word you need.

Speak for Yourself—Part II

Here are a few Sentence Completion problems from which we've removed the answer choices. (The complete problems with answer choices follow.) Read the sentence, underline any clues, circle any triggers, then write your own word in the blank using the clues and triggers to guide you. Then use POE to eliminate choices that don't match yours.

1. Many feature films are criticized for their ------- content, even though television news is more often the medium that depicts violent events in excessive detail.

4. In a vitriolic message to his troops, General Patton insisted that he would ------- no further insubordination, no matter how brutal the ensuing engagements might become.

Now that you've identified the clues and triggers, let's crack these problems.

1. Many feature films are criticized for their ------- content, even though television news is more often the medium that depicts violent events in excessive detail.

   (A) discretionary
   (B) graphic
   (C) dramatic
   (D) artistic
   (E) honest

Here's How to Crack It

The clue in this sentence is *depicts violent events in excessive detail*. The word in the blank should mean something like "violent" or "violence in detail." You can often "recycle" the clue, that is, the word or words you fill in the blank don't have to be fancy, they just need to complete the meaning of the sentence. So feel free to recycle the word violent and use it as your own word.

Now let's use POE to get the answer. Does discretionary mean violent? Nope. Cross it off. (Oops, what if we don't know what discretionary means? Then we should keep it for the time being. If it's the only answer left then we'd pick it, but if we find a better match we'd pick that instead.) Does graphic mean violent? Seems pretty close, so keep it for now. Does dramatic mean violent? Nope. Cross it off. Does artistic mean violent? Definitely not. Finally, does honest mean violent? No. So, we're left with (B). Go ahead and pick it.

Ok, ready for the next one?

———————————○———————————

4. In a vitriolic message to his troops, General Patton insisted that he would ------- no further insubordination, no matter how brutal the ensuing engagements might become.

(A) impede
(B) brief
(C) denote
(D) brook
(E) expose

Here's How to Crack It

The clues here are *insisted* and *no further insubordination, no matter how....* Did you pick a word like "tolerate" or "stand for" in this case? That's exactly the meaning of the correct answer. The words in the answer choices are hard, but eliminate what you can, keep the words you don't know, and take a good guess. The answer is (D).

———————————○———————————

Two Blanks: Twice as Easy

Some of the Sentence Completion questions will have two blanks rather than just one. To solve these questions, do them one blank at a time. Pick one blank or the other, whichever seems easier to you, and figure out what word should go in the blank. (Hint: Often, but not always, the second blank is easier to figure out.) Then cross off all of the choices that don't work for that blank.

If more than one choice remains, then pick a word for the other blank, and see which of the remaining answer choices works best.

Shoe Store
If you were shopping for shoes and one didn't fit, you wouldn't bother trying on the other one, would you? Half wrong is all wrong. If one answer doesn't fit, cross out the whole choice.

Have a look at these examples:

---

2. The scientific community was ------- when a living specimen of the coelacanth, which ichthyologists had feared was -------, was discovered by deep-sea fishermen.

    (A) perplexed . . common
    (B) overjoyed . . dangerous
    (C) unconcerned . . exterminated
    (D) astounded . . extinct
    (E) dismayed . . alive

Here's How to Crack It

The clue for the second blank is that a *living specimen* was found, which the scientists *feared was....* So the second blank must mean something like "dead." Only choices (C) and (D) are possible, so we can eliminate the others. Now look at the first blank. How did the scientists feel about the discovery? They were probably happy about it. Of (C) and (D), which choice works with the first blank? Choice (D).

Let's do another:

---

5. Chang realized that she had been ------- in her duties; had she been more -------, the disaster may well have been avoided.

    (A) unparalleled . . careful
    (B) irreproachable . . aware
    (C) derelict . . vigilant
    (D) arbitrary . . interested
    (E) neglectful . . insensible

Here's How to Crack It

The clue for the second blank is that the *disaster may well have been avoided*, so the second blank must be a word like "careful." This will allow us to eliminate (D) and (E). The word in the first blank must be a word like "neglectful," since Chang failed to do her duty. The only remaining choice that works for the first blank is (C).

Here's one more:

---

5. Although Jane's professors reproached her as a ------- during her first year in college, she became attentive and ------- once she found a major that interested her.

   (A) neophyte . . assiduous
   (B) sycophant . . critical
   (C) malingerer . . focused
   (D) beginner . . average
   (E) candidate . . distracted

Here's How to Crack It

Remember to cover the answers before reading the sentence! Although we know that the first blank is probably a bad thing (because Jane's professors *reproached* her), we don't have great clues. So let's move on to the second blank. The clue for the second blank is *attentive*, so we can recycle it and use attentive as our own word. Then we can eliminate (B), (D), and (E), because they don't mean anything close to *attentive*.

Now we have a better idea of what goes in the first blank. Because of the trigger *although*, the first blank means a person who is the opposite of *attentive*. Perhaps we would write down *slacker*. Our two remaining answer choices are (A) and (C). If you don't know what *neophyte* means, remember to leave it there—it could be correct. (C) does mean *slacker* though, so that's our best answer

---

Relationship Between the Blanks

Remember we said that all questions have clues? Well, in some tricky questions the clues may be pretty unclear or missing altogether because one blank is the clue for the other blank. In this case we'll have to do things a little bit differently, namely, use the relationship between the blanks to eliminate answers that don't have that some relationship. For example, take a look at the question that follows:

---

5. Because their new album is more ------- than previous ones, the band may alienate their fans who like ------- music.

If you tried to fill in the blanks with your own words, you might come up with something like *traditional* for the first blank and *experimental* for the second. But you could just as easily switch those words in the blanks and the sentence would still make sense, so we can't do this one blank at a time. The word that goes in the first blank is dependent on the word in the second blank, and vice versa. So the key is to focus on the *relationship between the blanks*—whether they're the same or different.

In this sentence, we're pretty clearly looking for words that are different. So we would eliminate any answer choices with words that were the same or that didn't have any relationship at all.

Let's try another one. Keep in mind that triggers can really help you because they tell you about the relationship between clues and blanks.

---

4. The author is reliably -------; every book he writes is more ------- than the one before.

   (A) dull . . inspired
   (B) exceptional . . hackneyed
   (C) artistic . . informed
   (D) imaginative . . creative
   (E) original . . lackluster

Here's How to Crack It
The sentence doesn't have clues for the individual blanks, so let's look for triggers that will tell us whether the relationship between the blanks is the same or different. First, there is a semicolon, which tells us the two parts of the sentence go in the same direction. Also, the words *reliably* and *every book he writes* are clearly describing a relationship of similarity between the blanks. So we would note that the words should be the same, and go through our answer choices. (A), (B), and (E) are clearly opposites, and the words in (C) don't really have a relationship, so we're left with (D) as our best answer.

Final Words
As the questions get harder, you'll probably find harder words in the answer choices. Although you'll have a word of your own to compare to the answers and use POE, you might find many or most of the answer choices are words you don't know. When this happens, get rid of whatever you can quickly and take a guess. If you can't come up with your own word using the two questions we discussed earlier, then you should skip that question altogether. For example, some harder questions might also use a tough vocabulary word in the clue. If you don't know what the clue means you won't be able to fill in the blank with your own word and you're most likely going to get it wrong. If it's a two-blank question and you can fill in one of the blanks, you might try to eliminate a few and guess, but only if you've worked through the whole section and have run out of questions you can do with certainty.

Summary

○ The first step on Sentence Completion questions is to cover the answer choices with your hand.

○ Next, speak for yourself: Read the sentence, and put your own word in the blank.

○ To help you figure out the meaning of the word that goes in the blank, find the clues in the sentence. Also, pay close attention to trigger words.

○ Only after you've come up with your own word for the blank should you look down at the answer choices. Pick the word that comes closest to the word that you created. Be sure to use POE and evaluate every answer choice.

○ On two-blank questions, just do one blank at a time.

Chapter 6
Critical Reading

Although the entire section is called Critical Reading, it includes Sentence Completions as well. This chapter deals only with passage-based reading questions. You'll see a passage followed by questions about the content of the passage. These questions are supposed to measure how well you understand what you read, but in reality they mostly measure how efficiently you can locate specific pieces of information. There are two types of passages—long ones and short ones—and we're going to look at them both.

LONG PASSAGES—WHAT TO EXPECT

Critical Reading long passages are generally from 40 to 100 lines, with six to twelve questions for each passage. The questions will be numbered 13–24 on Section 1 and 34–48 in Section 3. Unlike Sentence Completions, passage-based reading questions are not arranged in a set order of difficulty, so it will be up to you to identify which questions will be easiest for you to do. But don't worry; we'll show you what to expect and how to pick the best questions for your skills.

AN OPEN-BOOK TEST

Answering passage-based reading questions is like taking an open-book test; all of the information that you could be asked about is sitting right in front of you, so you never have to worry about any history, chemistry, or literature that you may (or may not!) have learned in school. Although you'll have to use the passage to answer the questions, there isn't really time to read the passage thoroughly, master all its details, and then painstakingly select the one choice that answers the question perfectly. What you need is a way to get in and out of this section with as little stress and as many points as possible.

If someone were to give you a ten-volume encyclopedia and ask you in what year Louis Pasteur invented pasteurization, would you begin reading at the A's and work all the way through to the P's? Probably not. You'd go right to the entry on Pasteur and read only the few lines that you needed to. That's how to approach passage-based reading questions on the PSAT.

THE METHOD
1. Read the blurb
2. Quickly read for the main idea
3. Choose a question and paraphrase it
4. Read what you need to answer the question
5. Answer in your own words
6. POE

Step 1: Read the Blurb

Long passages usually begin with a short introduction in italics which will give you a little background about the passage. If you see one, read it! It will give you some good context before you start reading the passage.

Step 2: Quickly Read for the Main Idea

Now take a minute to skim the passage. We're looking for the main idea here, so we don't want to get bogged down in the details. (We'll be coming back to the passage to answer the questions in step 4; we'll focus on the details then.) As we're reading we should be thinking about what the author is getting at; what's the big idea?

We're not just looking for this information so we can answer a main idea question later. In fact, knowing the main idea is central to answering all sorts of questions about the passage. Everything in the passage is there to support the main idea, so any time we start asking why the author did something, said something, or made some choice about what to say or what not to say, he or she did it because it has something to do with the main idea

Once again, though, don't get wrapped up in the details of the passage. If something is confusing, leave it for now and stay focused on the big picture. There may not be any questions about that part of the passage anyway, and even if there are questions about it, they're probably going to be good questions to skip or save for last.

Passage Types

Critical Reading passages come from four broad subject areas:

1. Science: Discoveries, controversies, or other topics in physics, chemistry, astronomy, biology, medicine, botany, zoology, and the other sciences.
2. Humanities: Excerpts from essays about art, literature, music, philosophy, or folklore; discussions of artists, novelists, or historical figures.
3. Social sciences: Topics in politics, economics, sociology, or history.
4. Narrative: Usually excerpts from novels, short stories, or humorous essays. (We have yet to see a poem on the PSAT.)

ETS usually includes a passage involving a historically overlooked community or social group. This passage is usually either a social science or humanities passage.

Step 3: Choose a Question and Paraphrase It

All points are created equal, but not all questions are. The math sections and the sentence completions have an order of difficulty to help you make POOD decisions before you even read the question, but the reading passages don't give you this hint. You're going to have to use your judgment as you go along, taking into consideration such things as how long or complicated the question stem is and whether or not the things it asks about in the passage are hard to understand.

If the question is easy to understand, and therefore to paraphrase, then it may be a good question to attack right away. Questions that you have to spend time just trying to interpret and paraphrase should be put off until later. Or if the part of the passage that you need to read in order to answer the question is particularly difficult, then you should probably put off that question until later or skip it altogether. But if the reading is a breeze (or at least pretty straightforward), you probably want to do it now.

The question can still be tough if there are tricks in the answer choices, but we'll talk about what to watch out for when we get to POE.

Now that we've chosen a question it's time to paraphrase it. We'll do this so that we know what we're looking for when we go to the passage. We need to know this because we want to read actively, which means we're going to be actively searching for the information we need and thinking about it, not just passively letting photons hit our eyeballs as we daydream about sunny days at the beach.

Take a look at the following question:

> The author mentions the Israeli-Palestinian conflict
> in the last paragraph (lines 92-97) in order to

This question is asking us for the purpose of something, in other words, why did the author talk about something? What's the something? The Israeli-Palestinian conflict. When we read we're going to want to know what the author says about this and why, so the question is *Why does the author talk about the Israeli-Palestinian conflict?*

That was pretty simple, but we broke it into pieces anyway. This helps us to keep in mind how we'd paraphrase it if it were more complicated and to stay focused on the fact that we're trying to figure out why the author talks about something, not just what he says about it.

Remember back in step 2 we talked about getting the main idea of the passage? Here's where it starts to come in handy, because we know in most cases when we paraphrase a question like the one above, we really want to know what the thing we're being asked about has to do with the main idea of the passage.

Take a minute to read the questions below and think about what they're asking you to find out, then paraphrase them.

42. According to the passage, the parrot became uncooperative because

43. The author's use of irony in line 55 suggests that

44. The primary purpose of the passage is

45. The argument about crows in the third paragraph would be most strengthened if which of the following were true?

Explanations

42. The question is asking why the parrot became uncooperative, so we can paraphrase it as, *Why did the parrot become uncooperative?* How easy was that? Just make it into a question by starting with one of the "W" words. This question looks pretty simple, as it's not asking us to think about anything beyond what the passage says, so this is a question we'd certainly want to try on our first pass through the questions.

43. *What does the author's use of irony in line 55 tell us?* Questions that ask about what's *suggested* or *implied* can be pretty tough, because we don't really know what the question is after; it could be a number of things. Paraphrasing the question as above will get us focused on looking for whatever information is given on the topic in the passage, but we're going to have to focus on the answers and use POE carefully here. This would be a good question to hold off on for now and maybe come back to later.

44. *What is the primary purpose of the passage?* Another way to think about this question is, *Why did the author write this passage?* He's trying to get something across or convince us of something, so we should focus on trying to figure out what that is. We should probably hold off on general questions like this until we've worked more specific questions and therefore have more background.

45. This question is asking us to go outside of the information given in the passage. The answer must still be something we can derive from the passage or logically infer, but it's probably going to be pretty tough. The answer choices are going to present new information. Notice that the question stem says *if which of the following were true.* This is definitely a question to do last and only if we're going to attempt every question. To paraphrase it, we'll actually want to try to break it down into a few questions, rather than just one, as follows: *What is the third paragraph trying to convince us of about crows?* and *What kind of information would make this more likely?*

If you have to do this question, be sure to use bite-sized pieces to figure out what steps you'll need to take to answer the question. In fact, any time there's more than one question hidden in the question, see if you can break it down into a couple of questions, and don't forget to make one of them about how the main idea is related to whatever the question is asking about.

Step 4: Read What You Need to Answer the Question

The PSAT is a standardized test. That means that the answers can't just be a matter of opinion. If the folks at ETS are going to put a question on the test and say that the answer is (D), they need to be able to prove that (D) actually *is* the best answer and that no one who truly understood the question and the passage could disagree. They need to be able to point to a line in the passage and say, "See that sentence there? That means the answer *has* to be (D)." And because the test is designed this way, you absolutely cannot leave out Step 4. If you're about to pick an answer choice and you haven't found a line or lines in the passage that you can point to and prove that you've picked the right one, then you haven't picked the right one. Don't just choose based on your memory or on your gut. Don't depend on things you've learned in school, and under no circumstances should you make stuff up. ("Yeah, I guess the War of 1812 could've been fought against the Australians...") *FIND* the answer in the passage. It's in there!

Step 5: Answer in Your Own Words

Remember how we covered our answers and jotted down our own words for Sentence Completions, so we wouldn't be distracted by ETS's answer choices? The same goes for passage-based reading questions. It does you no good to know that the answer is in line 39 if you have no idea what line 39 means! You must translate the answer into your own words before you go to the choices. This often means taking a long-winded paragraph and condensing it down to a handful of words. (ETS often uses exact words from the passage to trick you into picking wrong answers, which is another good reason to substitute your own wording.) As you read the following paragraphs, consider what the key ideas are and how you might boil them down into a sentence or two.

1. We are told that the trouble with Modern Man is that he has been trying to detach himself from nature. He sits in the topmost tiers of polymer, glass, and steel, dangling his pulsing legs, surveying at a distance the writhing life of the planet. In this scenario, Man comes on as a stupendous lethal force, and the Earth is pictured as something delicate, like rising bubbles at the surface of a country pond, or flights of fragile birds.

2. When in the course of human events it becomes necessary for one people to dissolve the political bands which have connected them with another, and to assume among the powers of the earth the separate and equal station to which the Laws of Nature and of Nature's God entitle them, a decent respect to the opinions of mankind requires that they should declare the causes which impel them to the separation.

Answers

1. *Some say that the Earth is delicate and that Modern Man's detached from it and can really mess it up.*

2. *When people declare independence, they'd better tell the world why.*

Note that these answers are *short!* If you found yourself copying phrases such as "surveying at a distance" or "the course of human events," you are missing the point. Copying long phrases means that you don't understand them. You can't go to the choices and expect to get the right answer unless you comprehend what you've read.

Step 6: POE

Process of Elimination is the single most important step. After all, what good is understanding the passage and finding the correct answer if you don't fill in the correct little bubble? None, according to ETS; there is no partial credit on the PSAT. So you need to know what makes a good answer and what makes a bad answer in ETS-land. Some things to keep in mind:

PSAT Do's and Don'ts

- **Evaluate every answer choice.** The directions tell you to pick the "best" answer, and you can only do that if you've read through each one. Remember, ETS knows how to write answers that sound great but are actually wrong, and you're much more likely to avoid those traps if you work through each question completely.

- **Be aggressive.** There will be lots of things wrong in the answer choices, and if part of an answer choice is wrong, the whole thing is wrong. The "best" answer does not have to sound good or make you happy—it just has to be free of error, which means it's supported by the passage and answers the question, but may not be particularly impressive.

- **It's all about the passage.** If you know more about the War of 1812 than the author of the passage does, that's great…but it's not necessarily going to help you on the PSAT. Any answer choice that requires you to know outside information is wrong—everything you need is in the passage.

Cross It Off
On passage-based reading questions, it is very likely that you may need to read a few of the answer choices more than once. To avoid confusion, be sure you cross off each answer entirely when you eliminate something. That way, if you have two or three choices you are considering, you can easily tell which choices are left in the running and which you have eliminated.

POE Tips

- **Beware exact phrasing.** ETS often uses exact words from the passage in the wrong answers because they sound familiar and, therefore, test takers are likely to pick them. But correct answers to specific questions are usually *paraphrases* of information in the passage.

- **For General questions, pay attention to scope.** For example, if a passage gives a brief overview of the effects of the Industrial Revolution on city growth in England and you are asked for the primary purpose, you might find incorrect answers such as "detail the Bessemer process of steel manufacturing" (too specific) or "chart the spread of the Industrial Revolution throughout Europe" (too broad). Often, answers that are too specific are just mentioned once or twice in the passage, and answers that are too broad simply cannot be accomplished in 100 lines or fewer.

- **Avoid extremes and give no offense.** Last but certainly not least, ETS does not make extreme or offensive answer choices correct on its tests. If you see an answer choice that's extreme or potentially offensive to a certain group of people, eliminate it. The reason for this is simple: The more extreme an answer choice is, the easier it is to prove that answer choice wrong. The more offensive a passage is, the more likely it is that ETS will get sued. ETS doesn't like to be proven wrong or get sued, so "best" answers are wishy-washy and offend no one.

Buzzwords

Avoid answer choices that contain the following words:
must
always
impossible
never
cannot
each
every
totally
all
solely
only

Here are some examples of extreme or offensive answer choices:

> Everyone believes that Shakespeare was the greatest writer in history.

> Nineteenth-century scientists were foolish and ignorant to believe in the existence of ether.

> The judges deliberately undermined the constitution in the landmark case.

In the first example, the passage would have to say that every single person in the world believes Shakespeare is the greatest, but if they wrote that in the passage this question would be pretty easy to answer, wouldn't it? Besides, how would they know? Can they read your mind? So it comes down to what can be supported by the passage once again.

In the second and third examples, an observation is made about some group that they (or their grandchildren) would probably be offended by. PSAT passages are very reasonable and wishy-washy, so offensive answers wouldn't be consistent with the passage.

Likewise, PSAT passages are usually not extreme in tone, so you can eliminate answer choices in questions that ask about the author's tone using extreme words like *condemnation, ridicule, adulation,* and *cynicism.*

Try It Yourself

Now that you know the steps for Critical Reading passages, it's time to try them out. Remember to look back to The Method on page 58 if you need a reminder of how to do something!

The following passage comes from a nineteenth-century British novel, The Picture of Dorian Gray, *about the influence of one member of the idle rich upon another. In the opening paragraph, Dorian Gray is speaking to Lord Henry Wotton about a portrait that's recently been painted of himself by another friend, Basil Hallward.*

"Dear Basil! I have not laid eyes on him for a week. It is rather horrid of me, as he has sent me my portrait in the most wonderful frame, specially designed by himself,
Line
and, though I am a little jealous of the picture for being a
5   whole month younger than I am, I must admit that I delight in it. Perhaps you had better write to him. I don't want to see him alone. He says things that annoy me. He gives me good advice."

Lord Henry smiled. "People are very fond of giving
10 away what they need most themselves. It is what I call the depth of generosity."

"Oh, Basil is the best of fellows, but he seems to me to be just a bit of a Philistine. Since I have known you, Harry, I have discovered that."

15 "Basil, my dear boy, puts everything that is charming in him into his work. The consequence is that he has nothing left for life but his prejudices, his principles, and his common sense. The only artists I have ever known who are personally delightful are bad artists. Good artists
20 exist simply in what they make, and consequently are perfectly uninteresting in what they are. A great poet, a really great poet, is the most unpoetical of all creatures. But inferior poets are absolutely fascinating. The worse their rhymes are, the more picturesque they look. The mere
25 fact of having published a book of second-rate sonnets makes a man quite irresistible. He lives the poetry that he cannot write. The others write the poetry that they dare not realize."

"I wonder is that really so, Harry?" said Dorian Gray,
30 putting some perfume on his handkerchief out of a large, gold-topped bottle that stood on the table. "It must be, if you say it. And now I am off. Imogen is waiting for me. Don't forget about tomorrow. Good-bye."

As he left the room, Lord Henry's heavy eyelids
35 drooped, and he began to think. Certainly few people had ever interested him so much as Dorian Gray, and yet the lad's mad adoration of some one else caused him not the slightest pang of annoyance or jealousy. He was pleased by it. It made him a more interesting study. He
40 had been always enthralled by the methods of natural science, but the ordinary subject-matter of that science had seemed to him trivial and of no import. And so he had begun by vivisecting himself, as he had ended by vivisecting others. Human life—that appeared to him the
45 one thing worth investigating. Compared to it there was nothing else of any value. It was true that as one watched life in its curious crucible of pain and pleasure, one could not wear over one's face a mask of glass, nor keep the sulphurous fumes from troubling the brain and making the
50 imagination turbid with monstrous fancies and misshapen dreams. There were poisons so subtle that to know their properties one had to sicken of them. There were maladies so strange that one had to pass through them if one sought to understand their nature. And, yet, what a great reward
55 one received! How wonderful the whole world became to one! To note the curious hard logic of passion, and the emotional coloured life of the intellect—to observe where they met, and where they separated, at what point they were in unison, and at what point they were at discord—
60 there was a delight in that! What matter what the cost was? One could never pay too high a price for any sensation.

13. Dorian's statement about Basil in lines 6-8 ("I don't ... good advice.") implies that Dorian

(A) wishes to avoid Basil
(B) believes that Basil's advice does not apply to him
(C) is jealous of Basil's skill as a painter
(D) would prefer not to be reminded of his faults
(E) does not wish to be without Sir Harry

Here's How to Crack It

This looks like a pretty straightforward inference question, which, hopefully, you would choose to do in your first pass through the questions. First, we'll paraphrase it: What is it asking? What does Dorian's statement tell us about him? This is kind of open-ended; we don't know exactly what we're looking for, so we'll go to the passage and, as we read, pay attention to the things we know for sure about Dorian based on what he's said and what he may be responding to in the context.

Remember, we want to read about five lines above and below the indicated lines, so we should start at the beginning of the passage and continue through the next couple of exchanges of dialogue. In fact, the statement in quotes can pretty much stand alone in this case. In the dialogue after the quote, Lord Henry doesn't really address Dorian's statement in a way that tells us anything about Dorian, so there's not much to be found there. In the statements themselves, Dorian says something a little surprising, doesn't he? Basil says things *that annoy him,* but what sort of things are these? Not advice of just any kind, but *good advice.* So Dorian is annoyed by good advice.

Let's take a look at the answers now. On our first pass through the answers, remember, we want to get rid of the answers that are just bad and then slow down and be a bit more careful once we're down to two. Also, because it's an inference the key part of the process is the one we're engaged in now, that is, we need to use POE to eliminate answers that are not supported by the passage. To think of it another way, we need to cross out answers that don't have to be true. (A) says Dorian wishes to avoid Basil. Does this have to be true? Not really. In fact, this is answer is a bit deceptive: Dorian says he *doesn't want to see him alone.* (B) also doesn't have any support in the passage. (C) is another deceptive answer; he says he's jealous of the painting, not of Basil. (D) looks pretty good, right? We decided that Dorian didn't like good advice. (E) has nothing to do with anything we read. So the answer is (D). There wasn't a close second, so we didn't need to slow down and agonize over the choice on this question. This is another indication that it was an easier question, but, of course, we didn't know that until after we'd finished.

14. The statement in lines 9-11 ("People are ... generosity.") implies that Sir Henry believes

(A) that Basil is uncommonly generous
(B) that Dorian should take Basil's advice
(C) that Basil would benefit from some good advice
(D) that giving advice is a foolish endeavor
(E) one is not constrained from giving advice to others even if one needs it oneself

Here's How to Crack It

Here we want to figure out what Lord Henry believes about something or other. This is another inference question, so we want to pay attention to the evidence the passage gives us and try to decide for ourselves ahead of time, if we can. Although we read this part of the passage when we did number 17, we should read about five lines above and below again because now we're trying to answer a different question and we need to look for that answer. If you lost a sock and a favorite pen somewhere in your house and you searched for and found the sock in a corner of the living room, you might have to search that same area again when you started looking for the pen, because that's not what you were searching for before.

As we read, we can ask ourselves things about what we're reading, like who or what is Lord Henry talking about? He's talking about Basil. In fact, the whole subject of discussion here is Basil, so it's a good bet that this will be what the belief is about. What does he *say or imply* about Basil? In response to Dorian's observation about advice, Lord Henry says that *people are very fond of giving away what they're most in need of.* What people? He must mean Basil. This implies that Basil could use some of what he's giving away, which is *good advice.*

Let's take a look at the answers. Choice (A) is deceptive, the reference to generosity is there to tempt us. (B) is out because Lord Henry's belief appears to be about Basil, not Dorian. (C) looks pretty close to what we said. (D) is not supported, but might look tempting because Lord Henry's tone implies skepticism toward something, though we don't really know what he thinks of advice. What the heck is (E) trying to say? It seems like it could be relevant because it's talking about giving advice, but it's hard to tell how it relates to the passage.

15. Sir Henry's observation in lines 21-28 ("A great poet ... dare not realize.") depends most on the distinction between

(A) the temporary and the permanent
(B) subjective reflections and observations of others
(C) great poetry and the poet's writing ability
(D) one's social persona and the character of one's work
(E) relevant and irrelevant considerations

Remember to Read What You Need
to answer the question. This is usually about five lines above and below the lines they send you to, but if it doesn't seem like you have much information relevant to answering the question, then you probably haven't read enough.

Here's How to Crack It

This question should strike you as being a bit harder than some of the others we've seen. The question of what distinction something depends on is pretty abstract, as we'll need to think not only about what Sir Henry said and what he might have meant by it or what the author might have meant by it, but also what the underlying logic of his thought process was. We're going to need to paraphrase this using smaller bites rather than just one big gulp. First of all, what observation did he make? Let's plan to characterize or describe what the main idea of this part of the passage is. Then we'll need to think about what sorts of things he's comparing. Let's look at the first question. Reading just the lines in question is definitely not going to be enough context. To get at what Lord Henry is really talking about we're probably going to need to read the whole paragraph or so. As we read we should keep in mind what we're looking for, which, as we decided above, is the main idea of this paragraph. This sort of information is often stated directly somewhere in the vicinity of the lines we're interested in, just not necessarily in the lines the test sends us to. This is why reading enough context is so important at this point.

What is Lord Henry trying to convince us of in this paragraph? The information is in the first few sentences of the paragraph (where main ideas often appear), and it says that Basil puts all that's good about himself into his work, so there's nothing left for his personality. Then he goes further and says this is true of poets in general, that *the great ones are unpoetical,* whatever that means, while *the inferior ones are fascinating.* So the distinction is between work and personality.

Let's take a look at the answers. Choice (A) is totally irrelevant. Choice (B) seems to mean something, but we might not be sure what, so keep it for now. Choice (C) looks like it might be on target, it's talking about poetry and poetic abilities, that was certainly in what we were reading. Choice (D) talks about personality and work, that was what we decided was relevant to the answer in our analysis above. Choice (E) isn't related to anything we read in the passage, though it might look tempting because how could relevant things not be relevant to some distinction.

All right, we haven't managed to get all the way to the answer, so we're going to need to slow down and try to get rid of some of the answers we have left. Choice (B) looks pretty confusing, so let's leave it for now. When an answer is weird or unintelligible or uses garbled language, leave it alone for the time being. If there's nothing else left, we'll pick it, otherwise, we'll try to find a better answer. We're going to take a close look at choices (C) and (D), so if we can, we want to compare them and only pay attention to the parts that are different. The two have hardly anything in common, so we're going to want to focus instead on trying to find something wrong with each of the two remaining answers. Choice (C) we said was relevant, so let's take it apart and see if we can find a flaw. The question is about making a distinction, so every answer has two main parts; let's look at one side at a time. The first part says *great poetry*. That was definitely something that was being compared to something else, so it's probably okay. The right side says *the poet's writing ability*. Was that something that was under comparison in this paragraph? Take a look back at the paragraph. There are things that are kind of like that in there, but it's not about how they're different from poetry, it's really the same thing as the great poetry, so (C) is out. Notice, also, that this means that choice (C) doesn't answer the question. Choice (D) matched our expectation of what we were looking for, so we'll give it a quick check just because we still have that weird answer choice (B) lingering in the background. The first part of the answer talks about *one's social persona*, that means someone's outward personality in society, so that looks pretty good. The second part says *the character of one's work*, which seems to mean what kind of work someone does, good, bad, whatever, and that is what Lord Henry contrasts with personality, so this answer is both supported by the text and answers the question. We'll ignore the confusing answer (B) and pick choice (D).

This was a tough one. Take a closer look at what made it tough and remind yourself of what to look for when you see questions like these on the test. We'd definitely want to leave this question for later and only do it if our pacing goals said we were attempting nearly all of the questions in the section. Notice also that we didn't abandon POE when we were down to two and just pick something on a hunch. If we were really stuck we would have, but the possibility of getting stuck on a hard question and having to guess is part of the reason we'd save this one for last.

16. Dorian Gray's attitude toward Lord Henry can best be described as one of

   (A) concealed distrust
   (B) ironic irreverence
   (C) sincere respect
   (D) morbid fearfulness
   (E) paralyzing awe

Here's How to Crack It

Questions about tone often have an extreme answer or two, and this one is no exception. There are a couple of answers we could get rid of almost without reading the passage. We're not going to do that if we can do the question, of course, and this question doesn't look too bad, but if we were totally out of time and had run out of any easier questions, we could get rid of (D) and (E) because they're pretty over the top. They use language like *morbid,* which means dying, and *paralyzing,* which would mean that Dorian is stunned frozen like a deer caught in headlights. We'd need some real evidence in the passage to justify something that extreme, but we're not going to find it.

To approach the question we need to look for something Dorian says or does that shows us how he feels about Lord Henry. In line 13 he suggests that Basil is a *philistine* compared to Lord Henry. Maybe we don't know what this means exactly, but, it sounds bad and in the surrounding lines Lord Henry and Dorian were criticizing Basil. In lines 31-32, Dorian acknowledges that *if you say something it must be true,* so it looks like he obviously has a positive view of Lord Henry. We can get rid of choices (A) and (B) because they don't match, and we're left with (C), so let's pick it.

17. The fact that Lord Henry's "eyelids drooped" indicates that

    (A) he has grown tired due to the extensive conversation
    (B) his attitude has become thoughtful
    (C) he would like to join Dorian at the theater
    (D) he is irritated that Dorian has become involved with an actress
    (E) he is interested in what will occur when he and Dorian meet with Basil again

Here's How to Crack It

Why did Lord Henry's *eyelids droop*; what is the author trying to tell us about Lord Henry by telling us about this gesture? (Remember: everything in the passage is there for a reason.) It's right there in the same sentence, *he began to think.* Checking out some more context we find Lord Henry doing a bunch more thinking. Let's take a look at the answers. (A) suggests he's grown tired, but we really have no evidence for this; this answer is there to trap people who don't go back and read the appropriate part of the passage. (B) looks like a match. There's no support for answers (C), (D), or (E), so get rid of them. (B) is the only answer left, so let's pick it and move on.

Now let's try a more complex question:

18. Lord Henry's reaction to Dorian's "mad adoration" implies that he views his relationship to Dorian as most akin to that of

(A) an audience member to an actor in a play
(B) a scientist to a laboratory animal
(C) a detective to a criminal at large
(D) an attorney to his client
(E) a storyteller to the romantic hero

Here's How to Crack It

This question should set off some alarm bells. It's got the word *implies* in it, and it's asking us to compare something in the passage to some new information that might seem to have very little to do with the subject matter of the passage. A glance at the answer choices shows that we're being asked about some kind of weird analogy. We don't want to focus on the answers, but a glance can give us some useful information when we're confronted with a weird question or one in which we're really unsure of what the question is asking. The first thing we want to know here is, what *is* Lord Henry's reaction to Dorian's "mad adoration"? Then we'll need to characterize it in the abstract, that is, what *sort* of reaction is it? This way we'll be able to match it to the abstractness of the answers. In the passage we find that Lord Henry is untroubled by Dorian's fling, and for some reason likes that he doesn't mind. Then he goes on to talk about science and psychology and why people are interesting to study and a bunch of other tough language that has something to do with science. We really have to focus on looking for information about how Lord Henry thinks of Dorian in the last paragraph, and we're probably going to need to read the whole thing because not a lot of it seems to answer our question. Some things we can notice about the structure of the passage might help us, though—namely, that it starts with Lord Henry thinking about Dorian, and then turns to Henry's thoughts on science and studying things. What things? *Human life.* Choices (C) and (D) have nothing to do with this, so we can get rid of them. (A) is also unsupported, but if you happen to have read the book *The Picture of Dorian Gray*, by Oscar Wilde, you might remember that his crush is an actress. Outside information isn't necessary, and besides, Lord Henry is not a passive observer, as choice (A) implies. Choice (E) might look tempting because of the deceptive reference to Dorian's adoration of someone else, but that's a trick. Choice (B) matches what we've been looking for, so let's pick it.

19. To Lord Henry, "the mask of glass" and the "sulphurous fumes" most nearly represent

(A) a window to look through and a veil that obscures
(B) a defense and a danger
(C) objects to be studied
(D) tools of the scientific trade
(E) things that trouble the mind

Here's How to Crack It

This question might be on the complicated side because it asks us what something *represents*, not merely what it *means*, as in a vocab-in-context question. We probably don't want to do this one on the first pass through the questions, but we might need to pick it up on the second pass, depending on what we need to reach our pacing goals. As we read, we'll want to consider what sort of things the objects mentioned are and what they're intended for. Once we've figured this out, we may have enough information to answer the question. The part of the passage that talks about this is pretty tough, as it turns out. There's some kind of extended metaphor being used and these objects are part of it. If this part of the passage is totally bewildering, we might want to bail at this point, especially if there are other easier questions to do. If we do decide to ditch this one we can cross out (A), (D), and (E), because they're all too literal for a question about a part of the passage that's this intensively figurative. (C) is deceptive, because we're not interested here in the things to be studied, but rather the reaction of the person doing the studying. (B) is supported because the mask of glass refers to something to protect someone's face and the sulphurous fumes, since they trouble the mind, are a danger, so the answer is (B).

Vocabulary or Not Vocabulary?

Some Go-Fetch questions, which we'll call "Vocab-in-Context" questions, ask you for the meaning of a word in the passage. Here's an example:

> The word "domestic" (line 43) most nearly means

Vocab-in-Context questions come in two flavors: Either they'll ask about difficult words (so you don't already know the meaning) or about secondary definitions of simple words (so you'll be tempted to pick a meaning that you're already familiar with). You should treat Vocab-in-Context questions like Sentence Completions questions—pretend the word is a blank and think about how to fill it based on the context of the sentence. So while it looks like these questions test your vocabulary, you're much better off depending on the context surrounding the word—again, it's an open-book test.

20. The quote in lines 51-52 ("There were poisons... sicken of them.") most likely indicates an attempt to convey which of the following beliefs held by Lord Henry

    (A) the study of life can be sickening and therefore not worth it

    (B) there are things about man that are disturbing to consider and these qualities make him repellent

    (C) the understanding of some complex subjects may require one's immersion in the subject

    (D) some toxic chemicals have been found to be useful for study in the natural sciences

    (E) there are dangers in the study of any subject, but those that occur in the natural sciences are not worth the risk

Here's How to Crack It

Here's another inference question in disguise. We need to figure out what Lord Henry believes, based on something stated in the passage, so we'll need to think about what we know from the passage and be sure to read enough context. The line in question refers to certain poisons as being subtle, but the passage really isn't about poisons, so there's a metaphor in use here. (In fact, the language is pretty tough in this part of the passage, so this is another question we should be doing later, during our second pass through the questions.) How did this come up in the first place? In the lines before, he's thinking about the fact that the study of people is the only interesting things to study when he says in lines 44-45, *human life - that appeared to him the one thing worth investigating*. In fact, this is the main point of the paragraph, and we've come back to it a few times to answer our questions about what he's thinking or why he brings up something else in the paragraph. But how is this related to the idea of poison and getting sick? It's not necessarily easy to figure this out, but notice in the sentence before that he says that *as one watched life ... one could not wear over one's face a mask of glass*. What would a mask do? It would protect. In the line we're asked about, he says that *to know the poisons ... one had to sicken of them*. So in general he seems to be saying that we can't be protected and would have to take the poison. He's talking about studying people, after all, so he must be saying that if you're going to study people, you're going to have to get involved and it might hurt. Whew! That was rough.

Let's check out the answers. Choice (A) looks pretty poor, since he clearly says at the end of the paragraph that any price is worth paying. Choice (B) is not supported, as he doesn't make any judgments about people in this section of the text. Choice (C) looks like it might be relevant, but it's not clear how, so keep it for now. Choice (D) is far too literal for something this figurative. Choice (E) might look tempting if you hadn't read carefully, but this part of the passage wasn't about the natural sciences, it was about the study of man, so get rid of this deceptive answer and pick (C). Fortunately, we didn't really have to figure out exactly what it meant, but if we had, we'd see that it's saying just what Lord Henry was getting at, that you can't stay apart from what you study sometimes.

21. The "great reward" referred to in line 54 is most likely

(A) good sensations
(B) a curious logic of the passions
(C) the knowledge of man's troubled nature
(D) a life of the imagination untroubled by monstrous dreams
(E) the keen understanding of human nature

Here's How to Crack It

The question is asking us *What's the great reward?* Reading that part of the passage we find a bunch of evidence in subsequent sentences like *to note* the curious hard logic of passion and *to observe* where they met and that *one can never pay too high a price for any sensation.* So the reward has something to do with *noting* and *observing* and *sensation.* Watch out for choice (A), that's a bit obvious and it doesn't give the full picture. Choice (B) should look suspicious because it just repeats something from the passage, that's deceptive and almost certain to be wrong. (C) looks all right, as it refers to knowledge, which is kind of what we're looking for. (D) is another deceptive answer that quotes the text, so let's get rid of that. (E) also looks like what we were looking for, so let's keep that as well. The two answers we have left, (C) and (E), are pretty similar, so let's compare them. How are they different? (C) refers to man's nature as *troubled,* but is otherwise nearly the same as (E), while (E) says a *keen understanding.* Does Lord Henry think of man's nature as troubled? He might. He does refer to poisons, maladies, and high prices to be paid, but is this the whole story? Let's leave it for the moment and take a look at choice (E). Certainly an understanding of human nature is supported and the same as the majority of choice (C), but what about a *keen* understanding? Going back to the portion of the passage that we read to get an answer of our own, we find that it spends several sentences describing the nature of the understanding that would be gained, as in, *to observe where they met, and where they separated, at what point they were in unison, and at what point they were in discord,* so the keen understanding seems to be pretty well supported. It might look like we're stuck now, but we have one more tool to try. Remember, the answer choice has to answer the question being asked. Does choice (C) do that? Not really, because the knowledge of man's troubles would only be half of the reward of understanding, whereas some of the paragraph clearly indicates that his reward would be an understanding of good *and* bad things, as, for example, *the emotional coloured life of the intellect,* and, of course, the passage also mentions that when one has the reward, *how wonderful the whole world became,* which does not match the tone of choice (C) either.

22. In line 56, "curious" most nearly means

    (A) paradoxical
    (B) interesting
    (C) thoughtful
    (D) excessive
    (E) overly emotional

Here's How to Crack It

This is a vocab-in-context question, and we'll approach it the same way as a sentence completion. We'll go to the passage, cross out the word "curious," and use the evidence in that sentence (and the surrounding sentences, if necessary) to fill in a word of our own. Then we'll use POE to get rid of answers that don't match our word and, hopefully, pick the one remaining answer. Remember, when the word is an "easy" word, like curious, watch out for answers that are too obvious. What's too obvious? A lot of the time, Joe Bloggs doesn't bother to go back to the passage for his answers, so what would he pick if he just wanted something that means curious? Choices (B) and (C) look pretty suspicious now, don't they? We're not going to cross them out until we attempt the question, though. If we were to get stuck we could cross these two out, guess, and move on, but we want to use the approach if it's possible, especially in an easy question like this.

When we go back to the passage and cross out curious, we find it followed by the phrase *the hard logic of passion.* What do logic and passion have to do with each other? Isn't this a bit of a contradiction? So maybe we should use a word like *contradictory* or *paradoxical.* Hello! Paradoxical is there, so that looks pretty good. Check the other answers quickly, and if nothing else works, we'll pick (A). We had already decided to be wary of options (B) and (C), but *interesting* and *thoughtful* don't mean *contradictory*, so they're out. Neither *excessive* nor *overly emotional* means *contradictory* either, so we can get rid of them too. So (A) is the answer.

Notice, if we didn't know what paradoxical meant, we could still get the answer because we can POE our way there. Remember, if you don't know a word or understand an answer choice, you should keep it for the time being; it might be the right answer.

SHORT PASSAGES—WHAT TO EXPECT

About eight of the Critical Reading questions will be based on short, paragraph-long passages. They generally will not have a blurb or any introductory material, and they will usually be followed by only one or two questions per passage. But the object is the same: Answer the questions correctly, using as little time and effort as possible.

The Method

1. Read the passage for the general idea
2. Paraphrase the question
3. Read what you need to answer the question
4. Answer in your own words
5. POE

As you can see, the approach to the Short Reading is very similar to what we've been doing on the Long Reading. The key idea is that you're never reading the passage just to see what's there; you're always looking for the answer to the question you're working on. Let's try a couple:

Parkinson's disease is an incurable, progressive, degenerative brain disease that affects the way nerves control muscles. Since the disease has no cure, it

Line becomes more severe over time, and causes the gradual

5 deterioration of cells in the brain. Generally, Parkinson's disease is thought to be caused by a combination of unknown environmental and genetic factors. However, recent studies have linked some cases of early-onset Parkinson's (a rarer form of the disease that strikes

10 patients under the age of 50) to specific genes shared by sufferers. No such link has been found in patients over 50.

9. The author mentions "recent studies" in line 8 in order to

(A) explain a possible difference of one form of a disease

(B) to suggest that environmental factors are irrelevant

(C) highlight an error in common scientific wisdom

(D) connect two divergent theories on what factors cause a disease

(E) strengthen a controversial argument

Here's How to Crack It

The main point of this passage is that some ideas about Parkinson's may not apply to a particular form of the disease. We'll probably need to read most of the passage to get some context, because the question is asking us why the author talks about something, so we'll need to figure out how that something—*the recent studies*—relates to his main idea. Thankfully, we have a pretty good tool for getting a quick approximation. Remember we talked about trigger words in the sentence completions section? Well, they're equally useful in the passage reading sections. Notice the trigger word *however* in the beginning of the phrase *however, recent studies have linked...*. That's just the thing we're interested in and it's telling us that there's a change in direction, so the new studies must tell us about an exception or a difference. We can get rid of (B), (C), and (E) on this basis. Now compare choices (A) and (D): what's different? Choice (D) mentions connecting the different things while (A) does not. Was there any mention of a connection between the two? No. So, (D) is out and the answer is (A).

Notice also that the use of the word *irrelevant* in choice (B) is too strong and the word *common* in choice (C) is not supported by the passage. Even if you don't figure out the magic bullet to answer the question every time, stay on the lookout for ways to get rid of answers. POE is king in the Critical Reading section.

---

9. It can be reasonably inferred from the discussion of the causes of Parkinson's disease that

(A) the factors that cause Parkinson's disease in patients over 50 are only environmental

(B) "degenerative" refers to a disease that becomes less severe over time

(C) research has been done on the causes of early-onset Parkinson's

(D) the cure for Parkinson's disease will eventually be found through genetic research

(E) early-onset Parkinson's patients are exposed to the same environmental factors as patients over 50

Here's How to Crack It

We have another inference question here. Do we really have to see how each answer choice maps onto the passage? Nah. Remember, POE is your best friend! It tells you that it's safe to get rid of (A), because the phrase "only environmental" is too extreme to be a correct answer on the PSAT. (D) predicts the future, which is never a good idea—who says that a cure *will* be found? What if the planet gets hit by a comet first? Now we can go to the passage and discover that (B) is contradicted by the passage, which says that Parkinson's "becomes more severe over time," and (E) is not supported by the passage. But (C), on the other hand, must be true if recent studies have made discoveries about early-onset Parkinson's, as the passage indicates, and *must be true* is what we want on inference questions. (C) it is!

BEYOND THE BASICS

In addition to the techniques we've discussed so far, we have a few final points to round out our repertoire.

Literary Terms

There may be one or two questions on the test that ask about the literary devices the author uses to make a point. These aren't anything to be afraid of; they're usually relatively simple once you know the terminology, but they can be skipped if you're very uncomfortable with this question type. ETS tends to stick to the basics, so let's do some review:

- A **simile** (not to be confused with a smiley) is a comparison using "like" or "as." *The smoke curled out of the chimney like a snake being charmed out of its basket.*

- A **metaphor** is a figure of speech that is technically false but that suggests a likeness or analogy. When Romeo says that *Juliet is the sun*, he doesn't mean that she is literally a big ball of hydrogen gas 93 million miles away; he means that she *resembles* the sun in that she is radiant and makes him feel warm all over and stuff.

- An **extended metaphor** occurs when a metaphor is, you guessed it, extended to cover several comparisons. *From the top of the building, the people below were ants, scurrying to and fro with their parcels, stopping briefly to touch antennae in greeting, and disappearing back into their tunnels to continue their work.*

- **Personification** is the treatment of something inanimate as if it were alive. *The sun smiles down upon the trees and flowers.*

- **Hyperbole** is deliberate exaggeration. *I beat your PSAT score by about a trillion points.*

- **Verbal irony** occurs when there is a discrepancy between what someone says and what the situation indicates the speaker meant. *You dropped your car keys into the sewer? Smooth move!* Sarcasm is probably the most common type of verbal irony: It's verbal irony used to hurt someone's feelings.

- **Situational irony** occurs when people plan for events to turn out one way, but they turn out another. Contrary to the Alanis Morissette song, rain on your wedding day isn't ironic. It's a bummer, but there's no reason not to expect it. On the other hand, moving your wedding from Seattle to Phoenix to avoid the chance of rain, and then having a downpour in Phoenix on your wedding day while it's clear and sunny in Seattle—*that's* ironic.

- A **paradox** is a statement that looks like a contradiction, yet is actually true in a sense. *Less is more.*

Dual Passages

You will probably see one or more dual passages, which are passages that relate to each other somehow with questions that cover both of them. Dual passages can be short or long passages, and there will always be some differences in how the authors view the topic. Dual passages can have questions that ask about only one passage in addition to questions that ask about both passages; the questions that ask about both passages are usually more difficult, so the best strategy is:

1. Work passage 1 and the questions that ask about only passage 1.
2. Work passage 2 and the questions that ask about only passage 2.
3. Work the questions that ask about both passages.

It's especially important in dealing with the third step to get your own answers and write them down; just like two-blank Sentence Completions, these can be tricky if you try to deal with too much information at once.

Down to 2

Last but certainly not least, one final word about POE: Just about all test takers get to a point, particularly on passage-based reading questions, at which they're going back and forth between two answers, trying to decide which is better. At this point, stop yourself from arguing FOR each answer choice (I like this one because...) and start actively finding a reason to eliminate one or the other. You can use the following steps in any order, together or separately, to help you get down to one answer choice.

- **Find the bad part.** Four out of five answer choices have *something* in them that makes them wrong, whether it is a word that's too extreme, a small phrase that's not supported by the passage, or something that's outside the scope of the passage. And usually, you're tempted to pick that answer choice anyway because the rest of it is exactly what you think the correct answer is. But you wouldn't buy a pair of shoes in which one fits really well and the other doesn't fit at all, would you? Well, the same goes for Critical Reading answer choices—find one part that's bad, and you can eliminate the whole answer choice.

- **Find the difference.** ETS won't put two identical answer choices on the PSAT. Either the answers will say different things, or they will say nearly the same thing in different ways; for example, one is phrased in a more extreme way than the other. Focus on the differences between the answers and you'll have an easier time figuring out which one is better supported by the passage and which one has the flaw. Don't be afraid to go back to the passage and look for flaws: Is the information really there? Does it answer the question?

Summary

- Long Passages
  - Read the blurb
  - Quickly read the passage for the main idea
  - Choose a question and paraphrase it
  - Read what you need to answer the question
  - Answer in your own words
  - POE

- Short Passages
  - Read the passage for the general idea
  - Paraphrase the question
  - Read what you need to answer the question
  - Answer in your own words
  - POE

- Dual Passages
  - First, attack questions about Passage 1 only
  - Next, do questions about Passage 2 only
  - Last, attempt questions about both passages

- Down to 2
  - Eliminate based on a careful reading of each answer to try to find the "bad part"
  - Eliminate based on the differences between the remaining answers

- Literary Terms
  - Remember to study them, even if it's just to be familiar enough to skip them!

Chapter 7
Math Basics

One of the more humiliating aspects of the PSAT (and the same applies to its big brother, the SAT) is that ETS claims that the Math section tests only sixth- to ninth-grade math. While this may be technically true—you'll see no trigonometry or calculus, only concepts that you'll have learned in algebra and geometry—what they don't tell you is that they will use these concepts in very sneaky ways. This chapter will help you lay the foundation to avoid the test writers' traps.

HOW TO CONQUER PSAT MATH

So what do you need to do? There are three important steps:

1. **Know the basic content.** Obviously you do need to know the basics of arithmetic, algebra, and geometry and to know this stuff cold. We'll cover what you need to know in this chapter.
2. **Learn some PSAT-specific problem-solving skills.** Since these basic concepts appear in ways you're probably not used to from math class, you need to prepare yourself with a set of test-specific problem-solving skills designed to help you solve PSAT Math problems. We'll cover the most important ones in the next chapter.
3. **Have a sound overall testing strategy.** This means knowing the order of difficulty of questions, and having a plan to pace yourself to get the maximum number of points in the time allotted. Be sure to read carefully the material in Chapter 4, to make sure you're using the strategy that will get you the greatest number of points in the time you have.

ORDER OF DIFFICULTY

The Math sections on the PSAT are Sections 2 and 4. Section 2 contains 20 multiple-choice questions. Section 4 is divided into multiple-choice and grid-in question types. Note that the order of difficulty goes from easy to hard within each of these types. For instance, on Section 4, number 28, the last multiple-choice question will be hard, but number 29, the first grid-in question, will be easy. This means that if you're going to skip some problems in Section 4, it's likely that you'll want to skip some of the questions numbered 27–28 and 36–38.

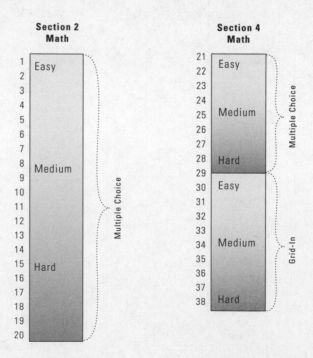

USING YOUR CALCULATOR

You are allowed to use a calculator on the PSAT, and you should definitely do so. You can use any graphing, scientific, or plain old four-function calculator, provided that it doesn't have a keyboard, a tape printout, or make any funny bleeping noises during the test. (This tends to annoy proctors, as well as your fellow testers.)

There are a few simple rules to remember when dealing with your calculator:

1. Use the calculator you're most comfortable with. You definitely don't want to be trying to find the right button on test day. Ideally, you should be practicing with the same calculator you'll use on test day.
2. Change your batteries the week before the test. If they run out during the test, there's nothing you can do about it.
3. Be sure to hit the "clear" or "on/off" button after each calculation to reset the calculator after an operation. A common mistake to make when using your calculator is to forget to clear your last result.
4. Your calculator is very good at calculating, but watch out for mis-keying information. (If you type the wrong numbers in, you'll get the wrong result.) Check each number on the display as you key it in.
5. Remember that, while it's nice to have all those funky scientific functions (like sine, cosine, etc.), you'll never need them on the PSAT. The most you'll need is the basic operations of addition, subtraction, multiplication, and division; the ability to convert fractions to decimals and vice versa; and the ability to do square roots and exponents.
6. Then, there's one really big, important rule whenever you think about using your calculator:

> A calculator can't think; it can only calculate.

What does this mean? It means that a calculator can't think through a problem for you. You have to do the work of understanding and setting up the problem correctly to make sure you know what the right calculation will be to get the answer. Only then can you use the calculator to calculate the answer. A calculator can't replace good problem-solving skills. It can only help make sure that you do basic calculations correctly.

Also, your calculator can't help you set up a problem in the way pencil and paper can. You should always be sure to set up the problem in your test booklet—writing it down is still the best method—this will help you catch any errors you might make and allow you to pick up where you left off if you lose focus.

That doesn't mean you won't use your calculator, though…far from it. Once you have set up a math problem, move quickly to your calculator to chug your way through the arithmetic, and be careful to enter each number and operator correctly. Remember, using your calculator is already saving you time—don't rush and lose the advantage that it gives you.

Drill 1

DEFINITIONS

One of the reasons that good math students often don't get the credit they deserve on the PSAT is that they've forgotten one or more of these definitions—or they read too fast and skip over these "little" words. Be sure you know them cold and watch out for them!

Match the words with their definitions, and then come up with some examples. Answers can be found in Part III.

1. integers

2. positive numbers

3. negative numbers

4. even numbers

5. odd numbers

6. factors

7. multiples

8. prime numbers

9. distinct

10. digit

11. consecutive numbers

12. divisible

13. remainder

a. numbers that a certain number can be divided by, leaving no remainder
Examples: _____

b. numbers in a row
Examples: _____

c. the result of multiplication
Examples: _____

d. numbers that are greater than zero
Examples: _____

e. having a different value
Examples: _____

f. integers that can be divided by 2 evenly (with no remainder)
Examples: _____

g. the result of addition
Examples: _____

h. a number's distance from zero; always a positive value
Examples: _____

i. numbers that can be divided by a certain number with no remainder
Examples: _____

14. sum

15. product

16. difference

17. quotient

18. absolute value

j. a figure from 0 through 9 that is used as a placeholder
    Examples: _____

k. numbers that are less than zero
    Examples: _____

l. a whole number that is left over after you divide
    Examples: _____

m. the result of subtraction
    Examples: _____

n. can be divided with no remainder
    Examples: _____

o. numbers that have exactly two distinct factors: themselves and one
    Examples: _____

p. integers that cannot be divided evenly by 2
    Examples: _____

q. the result of division
    Examples: _____

r. numbers that have no fractional or decimal parts
    Examples: _____

Finding Factors

The easiest way to find the complete list of the factors of a number is to begin trying all the integers beginning with 1, and see which of the integers go into that number without remainders. For instance, let's find the factors of 36.

Factor List:
Does 1 go into 36? Yes, 1 times 36.
Does 2 go into 36? Yes, 2 times 18.
Does 3 go into 36? Yes, 3 times 12.
Does 4 go into 36? Yes, 4 times 9.
Does 5 go into 36? No.
Does 6 go into 36? Yes, 6 times 6.

Once you get to an integer that you've already seen in the factor list (in this case, 6) you know you're finished. So the factors of 36 are 1, 2, 3, 4, 6, 9, 12, 18, and 36.

Let's try this once more. What are all the factors of 40?

Does 1 go into 40? Yes, 1 times 40.
Does 2 go into 40? Yes, 2 times 20.
Does 3 go into 40? No.
Does 4 go into 40? Yes, 4 times 10.
Does 5 go into 40? Yes, 5 times 8.
Does 6 go into 40? No.
Does 7 go into 40? No.

We don't have to try 8, since the number 8 has already appeared in our list of factors. So the factors of 40 are 1, 2, 4, 5, 8, 10, 20, and 40.

> Having trouble remembering the difference between *factors* and *multiples*? Try this mnemonic:
>
> *Factors are Few, Multiples are Many.*
>
> Twelve is a number that has a relatively large number of *factors*, but it still has only six of them. The *multiples* of 12, on the other hand, go on forever. Every number has an infinite number of multiples.

Negative Land
Think of integers as steps on a staircase leading up from the cellar (the negatives), through a doorway (zero), and above the ground (the positives). Five steps down (–5) is farther below ground than four steps down (–4) because you're one step farther away from the cellar door (0). Integers are like stairs because when climbing stairs, you can't use a fraction of a step.

Remember
Every positive integer is its own greatest factor and least multiple.

Prime Factors

When you need to find the **prime factors** of a number, you can make a prime factor tree. Let's say you need to find the prime factors of 60.

Start by writing down the number you're going to factor.

Then factor out the primes one at a time. The first prime number is 2, so that's where we'll start. 60 divided by 2 is 30, so we can draw branches for the 2 and 30.

Now let's move on to 30. 30 is also divisible by 2 ($30 \div 2 = 15$), so we can draw branches for 2 and 15.

Fifteen is not divisible by 2, so we move on to the next prime number: 3. Fifteen divided by 3 is 5, so we can draw branches for 3 and 5.

Five is prime, so we're done! The prime factors of 60 are 2, 2, 3, and 5. Remember, though, if a problem asked for the *distinct* prime factors of 60, your answer would be 2, 3, and 5.

Managing Multiples

One type of question you'll see frequently on the PSAT involves finding common multiples. The easiest way to find a common multiple is to start listing out the multiples of the numbers you're given until you find which ones they have in common.

Here are some examples.

4. If a number p is a positive multiple of both 3 and 8, p must also be a multiple of

   (A) 5
   (B) 11
   (C) 12
   (D) 14
   (E) 18

Here's How to Crack It

Let's start by listing the multiples of 3: 3, 6, 9, 12, 15, 18, 21, 24, 27…. Now let's list the multiples of 8: 8, 16, 24, 32, 40….

Which numbers belong to both groups? 24 does. So the numbers that are multiples of both 3 and 8 must be multiples of 24. Of course, 24 itself isn't listed as an answer (that would be too easy.) But 24 (and every multiple of 24) will have a factor of 12 in it, so the answer is (C).

5. How many integers between 1 and 100 are multiples of both 4 and 6 ?

   (A)   8
   (B)   12
   (C)   18
   (D)   22
   (E)   24

Here's How to Crack It

Let's start by listing the multiples of 4: 4, 8, 12, 16, 20, 24, 28…. Now the multiples of 6: 6, 12, 18, 24, 30….

After just a few multiples, you should be able to see the pattern. The numbers 12 and 24 (and likewise, every multiple of 12: the numbers 36, 48, etc., will also work) are the common multiples of both 4 and 6. So the real question is, how many multiples of 12 are there between 1 and 100? That's not too difficult to figure out. We can list them out with the help of a calculator: 12, 24, 36, 48, 60, 72, 84, 96. So there are a total of 8, and that's (A).

Drill 2

Answers can be found in Part III.

a. What are 3 consecutive odd integers whose sum is 15?
_____ _____ _____

b. What are the factors of 10? _____ _____ _____ _____

c. What are the prime factors of 10? _____ _____

d. What are the factors of 48? _____ _____ _____ _____ _____ _____
_____ _____ _____ _____

e. What are the prime factors of 48? _____ _____

f. What are the first 7 positive multiples of 6? _____ _____ _____
_____ _____ _____ _____

g. What are the first 7 positive multiples of 4? _____ _____ _____
_____ _____ _____ _____

h. Numbers that are multiples of both 6 and 7 are also multiples of
_____.

i. The product of two positive integers x and y is 30 and their sum is 11.
What are x and y? _____ and _____

j. The product of two positive integers x and y is 30 and their difference
is 13. What are x and y? _____ and _____

1. Which of the following does NOT have a remainder
   of 1 ?

   (A) $\dfrac{15}{7}$

   (B) $\dfrac{17}{8}$

   (C) $\dfrac{51}{3}$

   (D) $\dfrac{61}{4}$

   (E) $\dfrac{81}{10}$

2. Which of the following numbers has the digit 4 in
   the thousandths place?

   (A) 4000.0
   (B)   40.0
   (C)   0.4
   (D)   0.04
   (E)   0.004

3. Which of the following numbers is NOT prime?

(A) 11
(B) 23
(C) 27
(D) 29
(E) 31

4. Which of the following is the least of 3 consecutive integers if their sum is 21 ?

(A) 4
(B) 5
(C) 6
(D) 7
(E) 8

5. If a, b, c, d, and e are consecutive even integers, and $a < b < c < d < e$, then $d + e$ is how much greater than $a + b$?

(A) 10
(B) 12
(C) 14
(D) 16
(E) 18

6. All numbers divisible by both 3 and 14 are also divisible by which of the following?

(A) 6
(B) 9
(C) 16
(D) 28
(E) 32

Exponents and Square Roots

Exponents are just a shorthand for multiplication. Instead of writing $3 \times 3 \times 3 \times 3$, you can write 3^4. Thus, you can handle exponents by expanding them out if necessary.

$$y^2 \times y^3 = y \times y \times y \times y \times y = y^5$$

$$\frac{y^4}{y^2} = \frac{y \times y \times y \times y}{y \times y} = y \times y = y^2$$

However, you can also multiply and divide exponents that have the same base using a shortcut called MADSPM. MADSPM also helps you remember how to deal with raising exponents to another power. Let's see the breakdown:

- **MA** means when you see a MULTIPLICATION sign, ADD the exponents. So $y^2 \times y^3 = y^{2+3} = y^5$.
- **DS** means when you see a DIVISION sign (or fraction), SUBTRACT the exponents. So $\frac{y^5}{y^2} = y^{5-2} = y^3$.
- **PM** means when you see an exponent raised to a POWER, MULTIPLY the exponents. So $(y^2)^3 = y^{2 \times 3} = y^6$. (This is really easy to confuse with multiplication, so watch out!)

Be careful, because the rules of MADSPM don't work for addition and subtraction. For example, $3^2 + 3^5$ does NOT equal 3^7. (Crunch it on your calculator if you want to prove it.)

Here are some additional rules to remember about exponents:

- Anything to the zero power equals 1: $3^0 = 1$. Mathematicians argue about whether 0^0 is 1 or is undefined, but that won't come up on the PSAT.
- Anything to the first power equals itself: $3^1 = 3$.
- 1 to any power equals 1: $1^{3876} = 1$.
- A negative exponent means to take the reciprocal of what would be the result if the negative weren't there: $2^{-2} = \frac{1}{2^2} = \frac{1}{4}$.
- A fractional exponent has two parts (like any other fraction), the numerator, which is the power the base is raised to, and the denominator, which is the root of the base. For example, $8^{2/3} = \sqrt[3]{8^2} = \sqrt[3]{64} = 4$

Remember that in calculating the value of a root, you're looking for what number multiplied by itself results in the number under the radical. In the above example, $\sqrt[3]{64} = 4$ because 4 x 4 x 4 = 64.

When you see the square root sign, that means to take the positive root only. So, $\sqrt{9} = 3$, but not −3.

Square roots work just like exponents: You can *always* multiply and divide roots, but you can only add and subtract with the *same* root.

Multiplication and Division:

$$\sqrt{8} \times \sqrt{2} = \sqrt{8 \times 2} = \sqrt{16} = 4$$

$$\sqrt{\frac{1}{4}} = \frac{\sqrt{1}}{\sqrt{4}} = \frac{1}{2}$$

$$\sqrt{300} = \sqrt{100 \times 3} = \sqrt{100} \times \sqrt{3} = 10\sqrt{3}$$

Addition and Subtraction:

$$2\sqrt{2} + 3\sqrt{2} = 5\sqrt{2}$$

$$4\sqrt{3} - \sqrt{3} = 3\sqrt{3}$$

$2\sqrt{3} + 3\sqrt{2}$ *Cannot be added without a calculator since the terms do not have the same root.*

Drill 3

Answers can be found in Part III.

a. $3^3 \times 3^2 = \underline{\hspace{2cm}}$

b. $\dfrac{3^3}{3^2} = \underline{\hspace{2cm}}$

c. $\left(3^3\right)^2 = \underline{\hspace{2cm}}$

d. $x^6 \times x^2 = \underline{\hspace{2cm}}$

e. $\dfrac{x^6}{x^2} = \underline{\hspace{2cm}}$

f. $\left(x^6\right)^2 = \underline{\hspace{2cm}}$

3. If $3^4 = 9^x$, then $x =$

(A) 2
(B) 3
(C) 4
(D) 5
(E) 6

5. If $\left(3^x\right)^3 = 3^{15}$, what is the value of x ?

(A) 3
(B) 5
(C) 7
(D) 9
(E) 12

11. If $x^y x^6 = x^{54}$ and $\left(x^3\right)^z = x^9$, then $y + z =$

(A) 10
(B) 11
(C) 12
(D) 48
(E) 51

Equations and Inequalities

An **equation** is a statement that contains an equals sign, such as $3x + 5 = 17$.

To solve an equation, you want to get the variable x alone on one side of the equals sign and everything else on the other side.

The first step is to put all of the variables on one side of the equation and all of the numbers on the other side, using addition and subtraction. As long as you perform the same operation on both sides of the equals sign, you aren't changing the value of the variable.

Then you can divide both sides of the equation by the *coefficient,* which is the number in front of the variable. If that number is a fraction, you can multiply everything by its reciprocal.

For example: $3x + 5 = 17$

$$
\begin{array}{rcl}
3x + 5 & = & 17 \\
\underline{-5 \quad\quad -5} & & \qquad \text{Subtract 5 from each side.} \\
3x & = & 12 \\
\underline{\div 3 \quad\quad \div 3} & & \qquad \text{Divide each side by 3.} \\
x & = & 4
\end{array}
$$

Always remember the rule of equations:

Whatever you do to one side of the equation, you must also do to the other side.

An **inequality** is any statement with one of these signs:

<	(less than)
>	(greater than)
≤	(less than or equal to)
≥	(greater than or equal to)

You can solve inequalities in the same way you solve equations, with one exception: Whenever you multiply or divide an inequality by a negative value, you must change the direction of the sign: < becomes >, and ≤ becomes ≥.

For example: $3x + 5 > 17$

$$
\begin{array}{rcl}
3x + 5 & > & 17 \\
-5 & & -5 \\
\hline
3x & > & 12 \\
\div 3 & & \div 3 \\
\hline
x & > & 4
\end{array}
$$

Subtract 5 from each side.

Divide each side by 3.

In this case, we didn't multiply or divide by a negative value, so the direction of the sign didn't change. However, if we were to divide by a negative value, we would need to change the direction of the sign.

$$
\begin{array}{rcl}
-4x + 3 & > & 15 \\
-3 & & -3 \\
\hline
-4x & > & 12 \\
\div -4 & & \div -4 \\
\hline
x & < & -3
\end{array}
$$

Subtract 3 from each side.

Divide each side by -4.

Simultaneous Equations

Simultaneous equations occur when you have two equations at the same time. They're easier to deal with than they appear. All you have to do is stack the equations, and then add or subtract them.

———————○———————

12. If $x - 2y = 10$ and $3x + 4y = 5$, then $4x + 2y =$

   (A)   5
   (B)   9
   (C)   15
   (D)   24
   (E)   30

Here's How to Crack It

Just stack the equations, making sure that all the x variables are lined up, all the y variables are lined up, and all the numbers are lined up.

$$
\begin{array}{r}
x - 2y = 10 \\
3x + 4y = 5 \\
\end{array}
$$

Now you need to decide whether to add the two equations together or subtract one from the other. The question is asking for $4x + 2y$ in this case, so that tells you to add, since $x + 3x = 4x$ and $-2y + 4y = 2y$.

$$
\begin{array}{r}
x - 2y = 10 \\
+ \quad 3x + 4y = \ 5 \\
\hline
4x + 2y = 15
\end{array}
$$

That's your answer: 15. The question doesn't ask for the values of each variable, so you don't need to worry about figuring out anything else.

Let's try one more.

9. If $3x + 2y = 7$ and $2x + 2y = 9$, what is the value of x ?

    (A) -2
    (B)   2
    (C)   7
    (D)   9
    (E)   16

Here's How to Crack It
Again, stack your equations.

$$
\begin{array}{l}
3x + 2y = 7 \\
2x + 2y = 9
\end{array}
$$

This time the question asks for the value of x. Would adding the equations or subtracting them give you x alone? Subtracting the second equation from the first one would, because the coefficients for y are the same.

$$
\begin{array}{r}
3x + 2y = \ 7 \\
- \quad 2x + 2y = \ 9 \\
\hline
x \qquad \ = -2
\end{array}
$$

The y variables cancel out, and you get -2 for your answer.

GEOMETRY DEFINITIONS

Lines and Angles

Common sense might tell you what a line is, but for this test you are going to have to learn the particulars of a line, a ray, and a line segment.

A **line** continues on in each direction forever. You need only two points to form a line, but that line does not end at those points. A straight line has 180 degrees on each side.

A **ray** is a line with one distinct endpoint. Again, you need only two points to designate a ray, but one of those points is where it stops—it continues on forever in the other direction. A ray has 180 degrees as well.

A **line segment** is a line with two distinct endpoints. It requires two points, and it is the length from one point to the other. A line segment has 180 degrees.

Whenever you have angles on a line, remember *the rule of 180*: The angles on any line must add up to 180. In the figure below, what is the value of x? We know that $2x + x$ must add up to 180, so we know that $3x = 180$. This makes $x = 60$.

If two lines cross each other, they make *vertical angles*. These angles will always have the same measure. In the figure below, we know that z must equal 50, since $130 + z$ must equal 180. We know that y is 130, since it is across from the angle 130. We also know that x is 50, since it is across from z.

Any time you have two parallel lines and a line that crosses them, you have two kinds of angles: big angles and small angles. All of the big angles have the same measure, and all of the small angles have the same measure. In the following figure, angles a, d, e, and h all have the same measure; angles b, c, f, and g also all have the same measure.

Four-Sided Figures

Thinking Inside the Box
Here's a progression of quadrilaterals from least specific to most specific:
quadrilateral = 4-sided figure
↓
parallelogram =
a quadrilateral in which opposite sides are parallel
↓
rectangle =
a parallelogram in which all angles equal 90°
↓
square =
a rectangle in which all sides are equal

Parallelogram   Rectangle   Square

A figure with two sets of parallel sides is a **parallelogram**. In a parallelogram, the opposite angles are equal, and any adjacent angles add up to 180 degrees. (In the figure above, $x + y = 180$ degrees.) Opposite sides are also equal.

If all of the angles are also right angles, then the figure is a **rectangle**. And if all of the sides are the same length, then the figure is a **square**.

The *area* of a square, rectangle, or parallelogram is *length* × *width*. (In the parallelogram above, the length is shown by the dotted line.)

The *perimeter* of any figure is the sum of the lengths of its sides. A triangle with sides 3, 4, and 5 has a perimeter of 12.

Triangles

The sum of the angles inside a triangle must equal 180 degrees. This means that if you know two of the angles in a triangle, you can always solve for the third. Since we know that two of the angles in the following figure are 90 and 60 degrees, we can solve for the third angle, which must be 30 degrees.

An **isosceles triangle** is a triangle that has two sides that are equal. Angles that are opposite equal sides must be equal. In the figure below, we have an isosceles triangle. Since $AB = BC$, we know that angles x and y arc equal. And since their sum must be 150 degrees (to make a total of 180 degrees when we add the last angle), they each must be 75 degrees.

The **area** of a triangle is $\frac{1}{2}$ *base* $\times$ *height*. Note that the height is always perpendicular to the base.

$$\text{Area} = \frac{1}{2} \times 10 \times 4 = 20 \qquad \text{Area} = \frac{1}{2} \times 6 \times 4 = 12$$

An **equilateral triangle** has all three sides equal and all of its angles equal to 60 degrees.

Circles

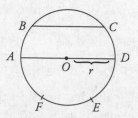

The **radius** of a circle is the distance from the center to the edge of the circle. In the figure above, *OD* is a radius. So is *OA*.

The **diameter** is the distance from one edge, through the center, to the other edge of the circle. The diameter will always be twice the measure of the radius and will always be the longest line you can draw through a circle. In the figure above, *AD* is the diameter.

A **chord** is any line drawn from one point on the edge of the circle to the other. In the figure above, *BC* is a chord. A diameter is also a chord.

An **arc** is any section of the circumference (the edge) of the circle. *EF* is an arc in the figure above.

The **area** of a circle with radius *r* is πr^2. A circle with a radius of 5 has an area of 25π.

The **circumference** is the distance around the outside edge of the circle. The circumference of a circle with radius *r* is $2\pi r$. A circle with radius of 5 has a circumference of 10π.

Area = 9π

Circumference = 6π

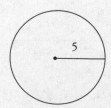

Area = 25π

Circumference = 10π

The Coordinate Plane

You'll probably see one or two questions on the PSAT that involve the coordinate plane. The biggest mistake that people make on these questions is getting the x- and y-axes reversed. So let's just review:

The x-axis is the horizontal axis, and the y-axis is the vertical axis. Points are given on the coordinate plane with the x-coordinate first. Positive x-values go to the right, and negative ones go to the left; positive y-values go up, and negative ones go down. So point A (3, 1) is 3 points to the right on the x-axis and 1 point up from there. Point B (2, –1) is two points to the right on the x-axis and 1 point down from there.

Slope is a measure of the steepness of a line on the coordinate plane. On most slope problems you need to recognize only whether the slope is positive, negative, or zero. A line that goes up and to the right has positive slope; a line that goes down and to the right has negative slope, and a flat line has zero slope. In the figure below, line 1 has positive slope, line 2 has zero slope, and line 3 has negative slope.

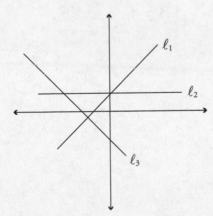

If you do need to calculate the slope, and the graph is drawn for you, here's how: slope = $\dfrac{y_2 - y_1}{x_2 - x_1}$. The *slope* of a line is equal to $\dfrac{rise}{run}$. To find the slope, take any two points on the line and count off the distance you need to get from one of these points to the other.

In the graph above, to get from point x to point y, we count up (rise) 3 units, and count over (run) 3 units. Therefore, the slope is $\frac{rise}{run} = \frac{3}{3} = 1$. Always remember to check whether the slope is positive or negative when you use $\frac{rise}{run}$.

If you're not given a figure and you can't draw one easily using the points given, you can find the slope by plugging the coordinates you know into the slope formula. The slope formula is $slope = \frac{y_2 - y_1}{x_2 - x_1}$. Just remember to plug the numbers into the formula carefully!

Drill 4

Answers can be found in Part III.

a. What is the area of square *ABCD* above? _____

b. What is the area of triangle *XYZ* above? _____

c. If the area of the triangle above is 400, what is the length of *AC*? _____

d. What is the area of the circle above with center *O*? _____

e. What is its circumference? _____

f.   If *ABCD* is a rectangle, *x* = _____ *y* = _____

g.   What is the perimeter of rectangle *ABCD* ? _____

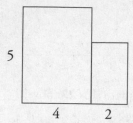

h.   If the above figure is composed of two rectangles,
     what is the perimeter of the figure? _____

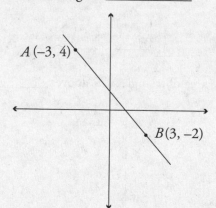

i.   How many units do you count up (rise) to get from point *B* to point *A* ?
     _____

j.   How many units must you count over (run) to get from point *A* to
     point *B* ? _____

k.   What is the slope of the line above? _____
     (Remember, the line is going down to the right so it must have a
     negative slope.)

17. If *ABCD* is a square, what is the area of the square?

(A)   2
(B)   4
(C)   20
(D)   25
(E)   36

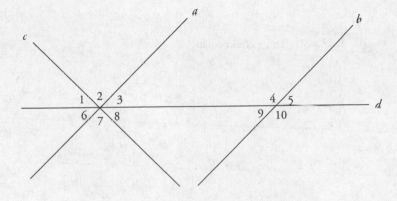

10. In the figure above, lines *a* and *b* are parallel. Which of the following pairs of angles must have equal degree measures?

   I. 1 and 5
   II. 2 and 7
   III. 3 and 9

(A)   None
(B)   I only
(C)   II only
(D)   III only
(E)   II and III only

$$x + 2y = 12$$
$$2x + y = 9$$

19. Given the system of equations above, what is the value of $x + y$?

(A) 3

(B) 7

(C) $\dfrac{21}{2}$

(D) 21

(E) It cannot be determined from the information given.

10. If $x^{\frac{5}{2}} = 8x$, then x could equal

(A) 2
(B) 4
(C) 6
(D) 8
(E) 12

Grid-Ins: The Basics

You will see 10 questions on the PSAT that ask you to bubble in a numerical answer on a grid, rather than answer a multiple-choice question. These questions are arranged in order of difficulty and can be solved according to the methods outlined for the multiple-choice problems on the test. Don't worry that there are no answer choices—your approach is the same.

The only difficulty with grid-ins is getting used to the way in which you are asked to answer the question. For each question, you'll have a grid like the following:

We recommend that you write the answer on top of the grid to help you bubble, but it's important to know that the scoring machine only reads the bubbles. *If you bubble incorrectly, the computer will consider the answer to be incorrect.*

Here are the basic rules of gridding:

1. If your answer uses fewer than four boxes, you can grid it anywhere you like.
   To avoid confusion, we suggest that you start at the leftmost box. For example:

Keep Left

No matter how many digits in your answer, always start gridding in the leftmost column. That way, you'll avoid omitting digits and losing points.

2. You can grid your answer as either a fraction or a decimal, *if* the fraction will fit.

You can grid an answer of .5 as either .5 or $\frac{1}{2}$.

or

3. You do not need to reduce your fractions, *if* the fraction will fit.

If your answer is $\frac{2}{4}$, you can grid it as $\frac{2}{4}$, $\frac{1}{2}$, or .5.

or

or

4. If you have a decimal that will not fit in the spaces provided, you *must grid as many places as will fit.*

   If your answer is $\frac{2}{3}$, you can grid it as $\frac{2}{3}$, .666, or .667 but .66 is *not* acceptable.

   You do *not* need to round your numbers, so we suggest that you don't. There's no reason to give yourself a chance to make a mistake if you don't have to.

5. You cannot grid mixed numbers. Convert all mixed numbers to ordinary fractions.

   If your answer is $2\frac{1}{2}$, you must convert it to $\frac{5}{2}$ or 2.5, otherwise the computer will read your 2 1/2 as 21/2.

Don't Mix
Never grid in a mixed number. Change it into an improper fraction or decimal.

6. You can't grid π, square roots, variables or negative numbers, so if you get an answer with one of those terms, you've made a mistake. Check your work.

Drill 5

Answers can be found in Part III.

Note: Figure not drawn to scale.

33.   In triangle *ABC* above, if *AB* = *BC*, then *x* =
(Disregard the degree symbol when gridding your answer.)

34.   The sum of five consecutive integers, arranged in order from least to greatest, is 100. What is the sum of the next four consecutive integers?

35.   If $5x^2 = 125$, what is the value of $5x^3$?

36.   What is the sum of the distinct prime factors of 140 ?

33.

	⊂/⊃	⊂/⊃	
⊂.⊃	⊂.⊃	⊂.⊃	⊂.⊃
	⊂0⊃	⊂0⊃	⊂0⊃
⊂1⊃	⊂1⊃	⊂1⊃	⊂1⊃
⊂2⊃	⊂2⊃	⊂2⊃	⊂2⊃
⊂3⊃	⊂3⊃	⊂3⊃	⊂3⊃
⊂4⊃	⊂4⊃	⊂4⊃	⊂4⊃
⊂5⊃	⊂5⊃	⊂5⊃	⊂5⊃
⊂6⊃	⊂6⊃	⊂6⊃	⊂6⊃
⊂7⊃	⊂7⊃	⊂7⊃	⊂7⊃
⊂8⊃	⊂8⊃	⊂8⊃	⊂8⊃
⊂9⊃	⊂9⊃	⊂9⊃	⊂9⊃

34.

	⊂/⊃	⊂/⊃	
⊂.⊃	⊂.⊃	⊂.⊃	⊂.⊃
	⊂0⊃	⊂0⊃	⊂0⊃
⊂1⊃	⊂1⊃	⊂1⊃	⊂1⊃
⊂2⊃	⊂2⊃	⊂2⊃	⊂2⊃
⊂3⊃	⊂3⊃	⊂3⊃	⊂3⊃
⊂4⊃	⊂4⊃	⊂4⊃	⊂4⊃
⊂5⊃	⊂5⊃	⊂5⊃	⊂5⊃
⊂6⊃	⊂6⊃	⊂6⊃	⊂6⊃
⊂7⊃	⊂7⊃	⊂7⊃	⊂7⊃
⊂8⊃	⊂8⊃	⊂8⊃	⊂8⊃
⊂9⊃	⊂9⊃	⊂9⊃	⊂9⊃

35.

	⊂/⊃	⊂/⊃	
⊂.⊃	⊂.⊃	⊂.⊃	⊂.⊃
	⊂0⊃	⊂0⊃	⊂0⊃
⊂1⊃	⊂1⊃	⊂1⊃	⊂1⊃
⊂2⊃	⊂2⊃	⊂2⊃	⊂2⊃
⊂3⊃	⊂3⊃	⊂3⊃	⊂3⊃
⊂4⊃	⊂4⊃	⊂4⊃	⊂4⊃
⊂5⊃	⊂5⊃	⊂5⊃	⊂5⊃
⊂6⊃	⊂6⊃	⊂6⊃	⊂6⊃
⊂7⊃	⊂7⊃	⊂7⊃	⊂7⊃
⊂8⊃	⊂8⊃	⊂8⊃	⊂8⊃
⊂9⊃	⊂9⊃	⊂9⊃	⊂9⊃

36.

	⊂/⊃	⊂/⊃	
⊂.⊃	⊂.⊃	⊂.⊃	⊂.⊃
	⊂0⊃	⊂0⊃	⊂0⊃
⊂1⊃	⊂1⊃	⊂1⊃	⊂1⊃
⊂2⊃	⊂2⊃	⊂2⊃	⊂2⊃
⊂3⊃	⊂3⊃	⊂3⊃	⊂3⊃
⊂4⊃	⊂4⊃	⊂4⊃	⊂4⊃
⊂5⊃	⊂5⊃	⊂5⊃	⊂5⊃
⊂6⊃	⊂6⊃	⊂6⊃	⊂6⊃
⊂7⊃	⊂7⊃	⊂7⊃	⊂7⊃
⊂8⊃	⊂8⊃	⊂8⊃	⊂8⊃
⊂9⊃	⊂9⊃	⊂9⊃	⊂9⊃

Summary

o   The Math sections are arranged in Order of Difficulty, which can make it easier to spot the less difficult problems. However, remember that the test writers' idea of "easier" problems is not necessarily the same as your idea. Let your Personal Order of Difficulty be your guide.

o   Write in your test booklet to set up problems, and then use your calculator for figuring. And remember to type carefully—your calculator won't check for mistakes.

o   Review basic definitions again before the test to make sure you don't get stuck on the "little words."

o   To tell the difference between factors and multiples, remember that Factors are Few and Multiples are Many.

o   When you have to manipulate exponents, remember your MADSPM rules.

o   Inequalities can be worked just like equations, until you have to divide by a negative. Then you need to flip the inequality sign.

o   Got several equations to work with at once? Just follow the guidelines of Simultaneous Equations: Stack the equations and add or subtract to get what you're looking for.

o   Be sure to review your basic geometry rules before the test; often, problems hinge on knowing that vertical angles are equal or that a quadrilateral has 360 degrees.

o   When doing Grid-Ins, be sure to keep to the left, and don't bother reducing fractions if they fit.

Chapter 8
Math Techniques

In the previous chapter, we mentioned that one of the keys to doing well on the PSAT is to have a set of test-specific problem-solving skills. This chapter discusses some powerful strategies, which—though you may not use them in school—are specifically designed to get you points on the PSAT. Learn them well!

PLUGGING IN

One of the most powerful problem-solving skills on the PSAT is a technique we call Plugging In. Plugging In will turn nasty algebra problems into simple arithmetic and help you through the particularly twisted problems that you'll often see on the PSAT. There are several varieties of Plugging In, each suited to a different kind of question.

Plugging In Your Own Numbers

The problem with doing algebra is that it's just too easy to make a mistake.

> Whenever you see a problem with variables in the answer choices, PLUG IN.

Start by picking a number for the variable in the problem (or for more than one variable, if necessary), solve the problem using your number, and then see which answer choice gives you the correct answer.

Take a look at the following problem:

When to Plug In
- Phrases like "in terms of k" in the question
- Variables in the answers

2. If x is a positive integer, then 20% of $5x$ equals

(A) x
(B) $2x$
(C) $5x$
(D) $15x$
(E) $20x$

Here's How to Crack It

Let's start by picking a number for x. Let's plug in a nice round number such as 10. When we plug in 10 for x, we change every x in the whole problem into a 10. Now the problem reads:

2. If 10 is a positive integer, then 20% of 5(10) equals

(A)   10
(B)   2(10)
(C)   5(10)
(D)   15(10)
(E)   20(10)

Look how easy the problem becomes! Now we can solve: 20 percent of 50 is 10. Which answer says 10? (A) does.

That was a number 2, which means it was an easy problem. Let's try it again on a harder question.

———————————————○———————————————

8. If $-1 < x < 0$, then which of the following has the greatest value?

(A) x

(B) x^2

(C) x^3

(D) $\dfrac{1}{x}$

(E) $2x$

Here's How to Crack It

This time when we pick a number for x, we have to make sure that it is between -1 and 0, because that's what the problem states. So let's try $-\dfrac{1}{2}$. If we make every x in the problem equal to $-\dfrac{1}{2}$, the problem now reads:

8. If $-1 < -\dfrac{1}{2} < 0$, then which of the following has the greatest value?

(A) $-\dfrac{1}{2}$

(B) $\left(-\dfrac{1}{2}\right)^2$

(C) $\left(-\dfrac{1}{2}\right)^3$

(D) $\dfrac{1}{-\dfrac{1}{2}}$

(E) $2\left(-\dfrac{1}{2}\right)$

> **Plugging In Quick Reference**
> - When you see *in terms of* and variables in the answers choices, you can plug in.
> - Pick your own number for an unknown in the problem.
> - Do the necessary math to find the answer you're shooting for, or the target. Circle the target.
> - Use POE to eliminate every answer that doesn't equal the target.

Now we can solve the problem. Which has the greatest value? Choice (A) is $-\dfrac{1}{2}$, choice (B) equals $\dfrac{1}{4}$, choice (C) equals $-\dfrac{1}{8}$, choice (D) equals -2, and choice (E) equals -1. So choice (B) is the greatest.

———————————————○———————————————

Plugging In is *such* a great technique because it turns hard algebra problems into medium and sometimes even easy arithmetic questions. Remember this when you're thinking of your POOD and looking for questions to do among the hard ones; if you see variables in the answers, there's a good chance it's one to try.

Don't worry too much about what numbers you choose to plug in; just plug in easy numbers (small numbers like 2, 5, or 10 or numbers that make the arithmetic easy like 100 if you're looking for a percent). Also, be sure your numbers fit the conditions of the questions (if they say $x \leq 11$, don't plug in 12).

What If There's No Variable?

Sometimes you'll see a problem that doesn't contain an x, y, or z, but which contains a hidden variable. If your answers are percents or fractional parts of some unknown quantity (total number of marbles in a jar, total miles to travel in a trip), try using Plugging In.

Take a look at this problem:

8. In a certain high school, the number of seniors is twice the number of juniors. If 60% of the senior class and 40% of the junior class attend the last football game of the season, approximately what percent of the combined junior and senior class attends the game?

(A) 60%
(B) 53%
(C) 50%
(D) 47%
(E) 40%

Here's How to Crack It

What number, if we knew it, would make the math work on this problem incredibly easy? The number of students. So let's plug in a number and work the problem. Suppose that the number of seniors is 200 and the number of juniors is 100.

If 60% of the 200 seniors and 40% of the 100 juniors go to the game, that makes 120 seniors and 40 juniors, or 160 students. What fraction of the combined class went to the game? $\frac{160}{300}$, or about 53%. So the answer is (B).

Try another one.

---

10. Paolo sells cars at a certain dealership. On Monday, Paolo sells one-third of the cars on the lot. On Tuesday, Paolo sells one-fourth of the remaining cars. If Paolo sells half of the cars left on the lot on Wednesday, and no new cars were added to or taken from the lot, what percent of the original cars did Paolo sell?

   (A)   4.2%
   (B)   65%
   (C)   75%
   (D)   85%
   (E)   95.8%

Here's How to Crack It

Clearly Paolo is selling his share of cars, but notice that you're missing a very important piece of information in the problem: How many cars are on the lot? That's your hidden variable!

In a problem that deals with fractions, you can find a good number to plug in by multiplying the denominators in the problem. Since we're taking $\frac{1}{3}$ of the number, then $\frac{1}{4}$ of it, and then $\frac{1}{2}$ of it, we want something that will divide evenly by 3, 4, and 2. Whatever we get when we multiply 3 by 4 by 2 will certainly fit the bill! This turns out to be 24. This quick technique can save you a lot of headaches once you get to the math.

Now let's work through the problem, using 24 for the number of cars on the lot:

First, Paolo sells one-third of the cars on the lot. If we start with 24 cars, that's 8 cars Paolo sold and 16 cars left on the lot. On Tuesday, Paolo moves one-fourth of what's left, or 4 cars; that raises Paolo's tally to 12 cars and leaves 12 on the lot. Finally, Paolo sells half of the remaining cars. That equals 6 cars and brings Paolo up to 18 cars sold for the week. To figure out the percentage, divide the cars Paolo sold (18) by the total number of cars on the lot (24). Thus, 18 ÷ 24 is .75, or 75%, which is answer choice (C).

Drill 1

12. Jodi has x dollars in her bank account. She withdraws $\frac{1}{6}$ of the money in her account to pay her rent and another $\frac{1}{6}$ of the money in her account to make her car payment. Jodi then deposits her paycheck of y dollars into her account. A week later, she withdraws $\frac{1}{2}$ of the money in her account to spend on a new set of knives. In terms of x, how many dollars are left in Jodi's account?

(A) $\dfrac{(4x-3y)}{6}$

(B) $\dfrac{(3x-5y)}{6}$

(C) $\dfrac{(2x+2y-3)}{6}$

(D) $\dfrac{(3x-y)}{6}$

(E) $\dfrac{(2x+3y)}{6}$

4. On Tuesday, Martha does $\frac{1}{2}$ of her weekly homework. On Wednesday, she does $\frac{1}{3}$ of the remaining homework. After Wednesday, what fractional part of her homework remains to be done?

(A) $\dfrac{1}{6}$

(B) $\dfrac{1}{5}$

(C) $\dfrac{1}{4}$

(D) $\dfrac{1}{3}$

(E) $\dfrac{1}{2}$

14. If $a = \dfrac{b}{c^2}$ and $c \neq 0$, then $\dfrac{1}{b^2} =$

(A) ac^2

(B) $a^2 c^4$

(C) $\dfrac{1}{ac^2}$

(D) $\dfrac{1}{a^2 c^4}$

(E) $\dfrac{a^2}{c^4}$

12. If $p \neq 0$, then $\dfrac{\dfrac{1}{8}}{2p} =$

(A) $\dfrac{1}{4p}$

(B) $\dfrac{p}{4}$

(C) $\dfrac{4}{p}$

(D) $\dfrac{4p}{3}$

(E) $4p$

Plugging In the Answers

You can also plug in when the answers to a problem are actual values, such as 2, 4, 10, or 20. Why would you want to do a lot of complicated algebra to solve a problem, when the answer is right there on the page? All you have to do is figure out *which* choice it is.

How can you tell which is the correct answer? Try every choice *until you find the one that works*. Even if this means you have to try all five choices, PITA is still a fast and reliable means of getting the right answer.

But if you use your head, you almost never have to try all five choices. When you plug in the answer choices, begin with choice (C), the middle number. If choice (C) works, you're done. If choice (C) doesn't work because it's too small, try one of the larger numbers. If choice (C) doesn't work because it's too big, try one of the smaller numbers. You can almost always find the answer in two or three tries.

Let's try PITA on the following problem.

---

4. If the average (arithmetic mean) of 8 and x is equal to the average of 5, 9, and x, what is the value of x ?

   (A) 1
   (B) 2
   (C) 4
   (D) 8
   (E) 10

Here's How to Crack It

Let's start with choice (C) and plug in 4 for x. The problem now reads:

4. If the average (arithmetic mean) of 8 and 4 is equal to the average of 5, 9, and 4 . . .

Does this work? The average of 8 and 4 is 6, and the average of 5, 9, and 4 is also 6. Therefore, (C) is the answer.

Neat, huh? Of course, (C) won't always be the right answer. Let's try one more.

———————◯———————

10. If $(x - 2)^2 = 2x - 1$, which of the following is a possible value of x ?

(A)   1
(B)   2
(C)   3
(D)   6
(E)   7

Here's How to Crack It

If we try plugging in (C), 3, for x, the equation becomes 1 = 5, which is false. So (C) can't be right. If you're not sure which way to go next, just pick a direction. It won't take very long to figure out the correct answer. If we try plugging in (B), 2, for x, the equation becomes 0 = 3, which is false. If we try plugging in (A), 1, for x, the equation becomes 1 = 1, which is true. There's no need to try other answers, because there are no variables; only one answer choice can work. So the answer is (A).

———————◯———————

Plugging In More Than Once

Some Problem Solving questions will require you to plug in more than once. They look like regular Plugging In problems, usually with variables in the answer choices, but they also have the word *must* or *always* in the question. You can treat these problems like normal Plugging In problems, but you will probably have to plug in more than one number before you can get down to the correct answer choice.

What you should do first is plug in an easy number and eliminate any answer choices that contradict what the question is looking for. Plugging in easy numbers will usually rule out two or three answer choices, but to get down to the just one, we'll probably have to resort to something less obvious, like the weird numbers in the box.

Let's give it a try.

---

7. If $f < g < h$, which of the following must be true?

   (A) $fg < h$
   (B) $f < gh$
   (C) $fgh > 0$
   (D) $h - g > 0$
   (E) $fg < gh$

Here's How to Crack It

There are variables in the answers and the word *must* in the question, so be prepared to plug in more than once!

For the first pass, we'll use easy, small numbers: $f = 2$, $g = 3$, and $h = 4$. Now we'll plug those values into each choice. (A) gives us $(2)(3) < 4$, which is false. Get rid of (A). (B) works out to $2 < (3)(4)$, which is true, so we'll keep that one around for the time being. (C) says that $(2)(3)(4) > 0$, which is also true, so (C) sticks around. (D) claims that $4 - 3 > 0$, and rightly so. (D) stays. And (E) states that $(2)(3) < (3)(4)$, which is true. (E) survives to the second round.

Hmm, looks like we only got rid of one choice. That means it's time to break out the weird numbers. How about if we make $f = -5$, $g = 0$, and $h = 1$? Back to the choices! (A) is already gone, so we go straight to (B): $-5 < (0)(1)$. That's still true, so (B) still survives. But (C) now says that $(-5)(0)(1) > 0$, which is false. Eliminate (C). (D) now works out to $1 - 0 > 0$, which is true, so (D) sticks around, but (E) says that $(-5)(0) < (0)(1)$, which is false: they're equal. Eliminate (E).

At this point you might be tempted to choose between (B) and (D) by flipping a coin (in your head—if you actually flip a coin during the PSAT, the proctor may kick you out). But we haven't tried all of our weird numbers. Nothing in the problem says these numbers have to be integers! What if we tried $f = 0.5$, $g = 0.6$, and $h = 0.7$? Now (B) works out to $0.5 < (0.6)(0.7)$, which is false, because $(0.6)(0.7)$ is only 0.42! Eliminate (B), and that just leaves (D), which still works: $0.7 - 0.6$ is greater than 0. Select (D), and you're done.

Plugging In on Geometry

You can also plug in on geometry questions, just as you can for algebra. Any time that you have variables in the answer choices, or hidden variables, plug in! As long as you follow all the rules of geometry while you solve, you'll get the answer.

Take a look at this problem.

8. In the figure above, what is the value of $x + y$?

    (A) 120
    (B) 140
    (C) 180
    (D) 190
    (E) 210

Here's How to Crack It

We could solve this problem using algebra, but why? We can plug in whatever numbers we want for the other angles inside the triangle—as long as we obey the rule of 180, and make sure that all the angles in the triangle add up to 180 degrees. So let's plug in 60 and 90 for the other angles inside that triangle. Now we can solve for x and y: If the angle next to x is 60 degrees, then x will be equal to 120. If the angle next to y is equal to 90 degrees, then y will be equal to 90. This makes the sum $x + y$ equal to $120 + 90$, or 210. No matter what numbers we pick for the angles inside the triangle, we'll always get the same answer, (E).

Drill 2

8. If $3^{x+2} = 243$, what is the value of x ?

(A) 1
(B) 2
(C) 3
(D) 4
(E) 5

14. If $\dfrac{24x}{4} + \dfrac{1}{x} = 5$, then $x =$

(A) $-\dfrac{1}{6}$

(B) $\dfrac{1}{6}$

(C) $\dfrac{1}{4}$

(D) $\dfrac{1}{2}$

(E) 2

15. In the figure above, what is the value of b in terms of a ?

(A) $30 - a$
(B) $30 + a$
(C) $60 + a$
(D) $80 - a$
(E) $90 + a$

THE AVERAGE PIE

You probably remember the average formula from math class, which says:

Average (arithmetic mean) = $\dfrac{\text{total}}{\text{\# of things}}$. However, the PSAT rarely will ask you to take a simple average. Of the three parts of an average problem—the average, the total, and the number of things—you're usually given two of these parts, but often in tricky combinations.

Therefore, the most reliable way to solve average problems is always to use the average pie:

What the pie shows you is that if you know any two of these parts, you can always solve for the third. Once you fill in two of the elements, the pie shows you how to solve for the third part. If you know the total and the number, you can solve the average (total divided by number); if you know the total and the average, you can solve for the number (total divided by average); if you know the number and average, you can solve for the total (number times average).

Let's try this example.

⎯⎯⎯⎯⎯⎯⎯⎯⎯○⎯⎯⎯⎯⎯⎯⎯⎯⎯

4. The average (arithmetic mean) of 3 numbers is 22 and the smallest of these numbers is 2. If the remaining two numbers are equal, what are their values?

   (A) 22
   (B) 32
   (C) 40
   (D) 64
   (E) 66

Here's How to Crack It

Let's start by filling in our average pie. We know that 3 numbers have an average of 22. So we can fill in our pie, and the pie shows us that the sum total of these numbers must be 22 × 3, or 66.

We know that one of the numbers is 2, so we can subtract it from the total we've just found, which leaves 64. What else do we know from the question? That the remaining two numbers are equal, so 64/2 = 32. So the answer is (B).

Try one more.

8. Caroline scored 85, 88, and 89 on three of her four
    history tests. If her average (arithmetic mean) score
    for all four tests was 90, what did she score on her
    fourth test?

    (A) 90
    (B) 93
    (C) 96
    (D) 98
    (E) 99

Here's How to Crack It

Let's start with what we know: We know that the average of all 4 of her tests was 90. So we can fill in an average pie with this information:

Now the pie tells us that the sum total of the scores on these 4 tests will be 4 × 90, or 360. Since 3 of these tests have a sum of 85 + 88 + 89, or 262, we know that the score on the fourth test must be equal to 360 − 262, or 98. This makes the answer (D).

MEDIAN AND MODE

There are two more terms you should know: median and mode. You'll see at most one question on the PSAT that tests these ideas, but you might as well get it right.

The **median** of a group of numbers is the number in the middle, just as the "median" is the large divider in the middle of a road. To find the median, here's what you do:

- First, put the elements in the group in numerical order from lowest to highest.
- If the number of elements in your group is *odd*, find the number in the middle. That's the median.
- If you have an *even* number of elements in the group, find the two numbers in the middle and calculate their average (arithmetic mean).

Try this on the following two problems:

---○---

11. If the 5 students in Ms. Jaffray's math class scored 91, 83, 84, 90, and 85 on their final exams, what is the median score for her class on the final exam?

    (A) 84
    (B) 85
    (C) 86
    (D) 88
    (E) 90

Here's How to Crack It

First, let's place these numbers in order from lowest to highest: 83, 84, 85, 90, 91. The number in the middle is 85, so the median of this group is 85 and the answer is (B).

---○---

The **mode** of a group of numbers is the number that appears the most. (Remember: *Mode* sounds like *most*.) To find the mode of a group of numbers, simply see which element appears the greatest number of times.

Finding a Median
To find the median of a set containing an even number of items, take the average of the two middle numbers after putting the numbers in order.

33. If the 7 students in Ms. Holoway's math class scored 91, 83, 92, 83, 91, 85, and 91 on their final exams, what is the mode of her students' scores?

Here's How to Crack It

Since the number 91 is the one that appears most often in the list, the mode of these numbers is 91. Pretty simple!

PERCENTS

Percent just means "divided by 100." So $20\% = \dfrac{20}{100} = \dfrac{1}{5}$ or $.2$.

Likewise, $400\% = \dfrac{400}{100} = \dfrac{4}{1} = 4$.

Any percent question can be translated into algebra—just use the following rules:

Percent	$\div\ 100$
Of	$\times$
What	x (or any variable)
Is, Are, Equals	$=$

Take a look at some examples of phrases you might have to translate on the PSAT:

8 percent of 10		$.08 \times 10 = .8$
10 percent of 80		$.1 \times 80 = 8$
5 is what percent of 80?	becomes	$5 = \dfrac{x}{100} \times 80$
5 is 80 percent of what number?		$5 = \dfrac{80}{100} x$
What percent of 5 is 80?		$\dfrac{x}{100} \times 5 = 80$

Percent Increase or Decrease

$Percent\ Increase$ or $Percent\ Decrease = \dfrac{change}{original\ amount} \times 100.$

For example: If an $80 item is reduced to $60 during a sale, the percent decrease is the change in price ($20) divided by the original amount ($80), or 25%.

RATIOS AND PROPORTIONS

Ratios

Ratios are about relationships between numbers. Whereas a fraction is a relationship between a part and whole, a ratio is about the relationship between parts. So, for example, if there were 3 boys and 7 girls in a room, the fraction of boys in the room would be $\dfrac{3}{10}$. But the ratio of boys to girls would be 3 : 7. Notice that if you add up the parts, you get the whole. 7 + 3 = 10. That's important for PSAT ratio problems, and you'll see why in a moment.

Ratios vs. Fractions

$Fraction = \dfrac{part}{whole}$

$Ratio = \dfrac{part}{part}$

Ratio problems usually aren't difficult to identify: the problem will tell you that there is a "ratio" of one thing to another, such as a 2 : 3 ratio of boys to girls in a club. When you see a ratio problem, drawing a ratio box will help you organize the information in the problem and figure out the correct answer.

For instance, suppose a problem tells you that there is a ratio of 2 boys to 3 girls in the physics club, which has 40 members total. Here's how you would put that information in a ratio box so that you can answer the question being asked:

Boys		Girls		Whole	
2	+	3	=		← Ratio
×		×		×	
	=		=		← Multiplier
=		=		=	
	=		=	40	← Actual #s

The first line of a ratio box is where you put the *ratio* from the problem. These are parts of the whole; they're not actual numbers of people, animals, books, or anything else. By themselves, they don't tell you *how many* of anything you have.

The second line of a ratio box is for the **multiplier**. The multiplier tells you how much you have to multiply the ratio by to get an actual number of something. The multiplier is the same all the way across; it doesn't change from column to column. And usually, the multiplier isn't in the problem; you have to figure it out yourself.

The third line is for *actual numbers*, so when the problem gives you a number of people (or animals, books, or whatever), that information goes in the third line.

One more thing to notice: See how there's a column for "whole"? This is where you add up the numbers in the ratio row and actual numbers row. Don't forget to add a column for the whole—it's usually key in figuring out the problem.

Now that you know some information from the problem and you know how the ratio box works, you can fill in the rest of the box.

Boys		Girls		Whole	
2	+	3	=	5	← Ratio
×		×		×	
8	=	8	=	8	← Multiplier
=		=		=	
16	+	24	=	40	← Actual #s

The first step is adding the ratio columns to find the whole, which is 5. Then you can find the multiplier by figuring out what you need to multiply 5 by to get 40. Once you fill in 8 for the multiplier all the way across the middle row, finding the actual number of boys and girls in the club is a snap.

Now you can answer all kinds of questions about the membership of the physics club. There are 16 boys and 24 girls. Take the $\frac{part}{whole}$ from the ratio row to figure out that $\frac{3}{5}$ of the members are girls. That means $\frac{2}{5}$, or 40%, of the members are boys.

Try this one.

Gridding In
A ratio is usually expressed as 2 : 3 or 2 to 3, but if you need to grid a ratio, grid it as $\frac{2}{3}$.

---

3. If a certain kind of lemonade is made by mixing water and lemon juice in a ratio of $3\frac{1}{2}$ cups of water for every $\frac{1}{2}$ cup of lemon juice, how many cups of lemon juice will there be in 24 cups of lemonade?

   (A)   3
   (B)   8
   (C)   16
   (D) $16\frac{1}{2}$
   (E)   21

Here's How to Crack It

Water		Lemon	Whole
$3\frac{1}{2}$	+	$\frac{1}{2}$	4
×		×	×
6		6	6
=		=	=
21		3	24

Let's set up our ratio box. We have $3\frac{1}{2}$ cups of water and $\frac{1}{2}$ cup of lemon juice, which makes a total of 4 cups of lemonade; that's our "whole." Now we need to figure out how much lemon juice is in 24 cups of lemonade, so if we put 24 into the box, we can see that we need to multiply each part by 6. This means that there will be a total of 3 cups of lemon juice in 24 cups of lemonade. This makes (A) the correct answer.

―――――――――○―――――――――

Direct Proportion/Variation

Direct Proportion problems generally ask you to make a conversion (such as from ounces to pounds) or to compare two sets of information and find a missing piece. For example, a proportion problem may ask you to figure out the amount of time it will take to travel 300 miles at a rate of 50 miles per hour.

> To solve proportion problems, just set up two equal fractions. One will have all the information you know, and the other will have a missing piece that you're trying to figure out.

$$\frac{50 \; miles}{1 \; hour} = \frac{300 \; miles}{X \; hours}$$

Be sure to label the parts of your proportion so you'll know you have things in the right place; the same units should be in the numerator on both sides of the equal sign and the same units should be in the denominator on both sides of the equal sign. Notice how using a setup like this helps us keep track of the information we have and to find the information we're looking for, so we can use bite-sized pieces to work through the question.

Now we can cross-multiply and then solve for x: $50x = 300$, so $x = 6$ hours.

Let's try the following problem.

―――――――――○―――――――――

2. John receives $2.50 for every 4 pounds of berries he picks. How much money will he receive if he picks 90 pounds of berries?

    (A) $27.00
    (B) $36.00
    (C) $42.25
    (D) $48.50
    (E) $56.25

Here's How to Crack It

To solve this, set up a proportion.

$$\frac{\$2.50}{4 \ pounds} = \frac{x}{90 \ pounds}$$

Now we can cross-multiply. $4x = 2.50 \times 90$, so $4x = 225$, and $x = 56.25$. The answer is (E).

Occasionally, you may see a problem that tells you there are two equal ratios. For example, if a problem says that the ratio of 24 to 0.6 is equal to the ratio of 12 to y, you can solve for y by setting up a proportion. A proportion, after all, is really just two ratios set equal to each other.

$$\frac{24}{0.6} = \frac{12}{y}$$

Then you can cross-multiply and solve to get 0.3 for your answer.

Indirect Proportion/Variation

Indirect Proportion is simply the opposite of a direct, or ordinary, proportion. In a direct proportion when one variable increases, so does the other; however, in an indirect variation or proportion, when one variable *increases*, the other variable *decreases*, or vice versa. These types of problems are generally clearly labeled and all you have to do is apply the indirect variation formula:

$$x_1 y_1 = x_2 y_2$$

Once you memorize the formula, applying it will become second nature to you.

Other Names
Indirect Proportion is sometimes called Inverse Proportion or Inverse Variation.

Now try this one.

─────────────────○─────────────────

18. On a particular survey, the percentage of people answering a question with the same response is inversely proportional to the number of the question. If 80% of the people surveyed answered the same response to the eighth question, then, approximately, what percentage of the people surveyed answered the same answer to the 30th question?

(A) 3%
(B) 13%
(C) 18%
(D) 21%
(E) 36%

Here's How to Crack It

The problem tells us that the numbers are inversely proportional, so we need to figure out what to put into the formula. The first piece of information is that 80 percent of the people answered the eighth question correctly; we need to know the percent of people who answered the 30th question correctly. Let's make x the percent and y the question number. Your equation should look like this:

$$(80)(8) = (x_2)(30)$$

When you solve the equation, you should end up with $\frac{640}{30}$ or $21\frac{1}{3}$, which is answer choice (D) (remember, when the problem says "approximately," you'll probably have to round up or down).

─────────────────○─────────────────

Drill 3

a. If a student scores 70, 90, 95, and 105, what is the average (arithmetic mean) for these tests? _____

b. If a student has an average (arithmetic mean) score of 80 on 4 tests, what is the total of the scores received on those tests? _____

c. If a student has an average of 60 on tests, with a total of 360, how many tests has the student taken? _____

d. If the average of 4 and x is equal to the average of 2, 8, and x, what is the value of x? _____

e. What percent of 5 is 6? _____

f. 60 percent of 90 is the same as 50 percent of what number? _____

g. Jenny's salary increased from $30,000 to $33,000. By what percent did her salary increase? _____

h. In 1980, factory X produced 18,600 pieces. In 1981, factory X only produced 16,000 pieces. By approximately what percent did production decrease from 1980 to 1981? _____

i. In a certain bag of marbles, the ratio of red marbles to green marbles is 7 : 5. If the bag contains 96 marbles, how many green marbles are in the bag? _____

4. The average (arithmetic mean) of 4 numbers is 80. If two of the numbers are 50 and 60, what is the sum of the other two numbers?

	/	/	
.	.	.	.
	0	0	0
1	1	1	1
2	2	2	2
3	3	3	3
4	4	4	4
5	5	5	5
6	6	6	6
7	7	7	7
8	8	8	8
9	9	9	9

11. 60% of 80 is equivalent to 40% of what number?

    (A) 100
    (B) 105
    (C) 110
    (D) 120
    (E) 140

14. A group of 30 adults and 20 children went to the beach. If 50% of the adults and 80% of the children went swimming, what percent of the group went swimming?

    (A) 30%
    (B) 46%
    (C) 50%
    (D) 62%
    (E) 65%

Sets

Sets are basically lists of distinct numbers. The numbers in a set are called **elements** or **members**.

For example, if a problem asks for the set of even integers greater than 0 but less than 12, the set would be {2, 4, 6, 8, 10}.

Let's try one.

———————————————◯———————————————

4. If set $X = \{2, 3, 5, 7\}$ and set $Y = \{3, 6, 8\}$, then which of the following represents the union of X and Y?

   (A) {3}
   (B) {2, 3}
   (C) {2, 3, 5, 7}
   (D) {3, 6, 7, 8}
   (E) {2, 3, 5, 6, 7, 8}

Here's How to Crack It

The question asks for the union of the two sets, so you need to combine the elements into one big set, as in (E). Watch out for (A), which is the tricky answer; it's the intersection, not the union.

———————————————◯———————————————

Summary

- The test is full of opportunities to use arithmetic instead of algebra—just look for your chances to use Plugging In and Plugging In the Answers.

- If a question has *in terms of* or variables in the answer choices, it's a Plugging In problem. Plug in your own number, do the math, find the target, and use POE to get down to one correct answer.

- If a question doesn't have variables but asks for a fraction or a percent of an unknown number, you can also plug in there. Just substitute your own number for the unknown and take the rest of the problem step by step.

- If a question has an unknown and asks for a specific amount, making you feel like you have to write an equation, try Plugging In the Answers instead.

- When plugging in with geometry problems, remember to use your knowledge of basic geometry rules, e.g., there are still 180 degrees in a triangle when you're using Plugging In.

- The Average Pie can help you tackle any question about the average (arithmetic mean)—just fill what you know from the problem into the correct spots for *Total*, *Number of Things*, and *Average*.

- Use the ratio box on questions that ask about a ratio. Fill in the ratio box with information from the problem, calculate the missing piece, then solve for whatever the problem is asking for.

- Remember that there's a difference between direct and indirect (inverse) proportions. First, figure out which one you're dealing with, and then set up the correct formula and fill in the information the problem gives you.

- Sets are groups of distinct numbers.

Chapter 9
Advanced Math Principles

So far we've covered basic knowledge and some PSAT-specific problem-solving skills. Now we'll look at some of the more advanced skills tested on the PSAT.

FUNCTIONS

The first of our topics takes us back to school. While much of this test isn't based on the math you've seen in high school recently, this is one topic that you'll most likely recognize. The functions on the PSAT mostly look like this:

$$f(x) = x^2 + 6x + 24$$

Just Follow the Instructions
Functions are like recipes. Each one is just a set of directions for you to follow. ETS provides the ingredients and you work your magic.

Most questions of this type will give you a specific value to plug in for x and then ask you to find the value of the function for that x. Each function is just a set of instructions that tells you what to do to x—or the number you plug in for x—in order to find the corresponding value for $f(x)$ (a fancy name for y). Just plug your information into that equation and follow the instructions.

Let's try an easy one.

---

5. If $f(x) = x^2 + 3x - 3$, then $f(7)$ equals

   (A) 14
   (B) 20
   (C) 32
   (D) 67
   (E) 83

Here's How to Crack It

Function questions are just trying to see if you can follow the directions, so follow them! The instructions, in this case, are in the equation. So plug 7 into the equation and it should look like this: $f(7) = 7^2 + 3(7) - 3$. Do the math and $f(7) = 67$. Therefore, the answer is (D).

FUNCTIONS WITH WEIRD SYMBOLS

If you ever see a strange symbol on the PSAT—& or @ for example—don't worry. There are no special symbols you should have learned in school that the PSAT requires you to know. What you're looking at is another type of function problem.

> A function problem is just ETS's way of testing whether you can follow directions. And the key is always to plug in numbers.

For instance, you might see a question like this one:

If $@x = 2x + 2$, what is the value of $@3$?

What ETS is asking you to do is to plug in the number that follows the @ symbol everywhere you see the variable x. So to solve for $@3$, you plug in 3 for x in the expression $2x + 2$, and get $2(3) + 2$, or 8.

To figure out the value of a function, all you have to do is plug in a value for x and solve.

Try the following:

---

5. If $x \# y = 4x - y$, what is the value of $3 \# 4$?

    (A)   6
    (B)   8
    (C)   10
    (D)   12
    (E)   14

Here's How to Crack It

In this case, we need to plug in whatever is to the left of the # for x, and whatever is to the right of the # for y. This means that we plug in 3 for x and 4 for y. So $3 \# 4$ will be equal to $4(3) - 4$, or 8. This makes (B) the answer.

EXPANDING, FACTORING, AND SOLVING QUADRATIC EQUATIONS

Ah, factoring. You're likely to see at least one problem on the PSAT that asks you to do this sort of complex algebraic manipulation. It may have been a little while since you've done this, so let's review.

Expanding

Most often you'll be asked to expand an expression simply by multiplying it out. When working with an expression of the form $(x + 3)(x + 4)$, multiply it out using the following rule:

FOIL = First Outer Inner Last

Start with the *first* figure in each set of parentheses: $x \times x = x^2$

Now do the two *outer* figures: $x \times 4 = 4x$

Next, the two *inner* figures: $3 \times x = 3x$

Finally, the *last* figure in each set of parentheses: $3 \times 4 = 12$

Add them all together, and we get $x^2 + 4x + 3x + 12$, or $x^2 + 7x + 12$

Factoring

If you ever see an expression of the form $x^2 + 7x + 12$ on the PSAT, there is a good chance that factoring it will be the key to cracking it.

The key to factoring is figuring out what pair of numbers will multiply to give you the constant term (12, in this case) and add up to the coefficient of the x term (7, in this question). (It could be more complicated if the x^2 term had a coefficient, but that rarely happens on the PSAT.)

Let's try an example:

Step 1: Draw two sets of parentheses next to each other and fill an x into the left side of each. That's what gives us our x^2 term.

Step 2: 12 can be factored a number of ways: 1 x 12, 2 x 6, or 3 x 4. Which of these adds up to 7? 3 and 4, so place a 3 on the right side of one parenthesis and a 4 in the other.

Step 3: Now we need to figure out what the correct signs should be. They should both be positive in this case, because that will sum to 7 and multiply to 12, so fill plus signs into each parenthesis.

$$x^2 + 7x + 12$$

$$(x \quad)(x \quad)$$

$$(x \quad 3)(x \quad 4)$$

$$(x + 3)(x + 4)$$

If you want to double-check your work, try expanding out $(x + 3)(x + 4)$ using FOIL and you'll get the original expression.

Now try the following problem.

---

13. If $\dfrac{x^2 + 5x - 6}{x - 1} = 2$, then what is the value of x ?

    (A) −4
    (B) −1
    (C)   5
    (D)   6
    (E)   8

Here's How to Crack It

Since we know we can factor $x^2 + 5x - 6$, we should do so. When we factor it, we get $\dfrac{(x-1)(x+6)}{(x-1)} = 2$. Now we can cancel the $(x - 1)$ and we're left with $x + 6 = 2$. If we solve for x, we find $x = -4$ and our answer is (A).

Don't forget that we can also just Plug In the Answers!

Solving Quadratic Equations

Sometimes you'll want to factor to solve an equation. In this case, there will be two possible values for x, called the roots of the equation. To solve for x, use the following steps:

Step 1: Make sure that the equation is set equal to zero.

Step 2: Factor the equation.

Step 3: Set each parenthetical expression equal to zero. So if you have $(x + 2)(x - 7) = 0$, you get $(x + 2) = 0$ and $(x - 7) = 0$. When you solve for each, you get $x = -2$ and $x = 7$. Therefore, -2 and 7 are the solutions or roots of the equation.

Try the following problem.

14. If $x^2 + 2x - 15 = 0$, then the possible values of x are

(A) 2 and 4
(B) −13 and −4
(C) 5 and −4
(D) −5 and 3
(E) 6 and 3

Here's How to Crack It

Let's try the steps:

Step 1: The equation is already set equal to zero.

Step 2: We can now factor the left side of the equation, to get $(x + 5)(x - 3) = 0$.

Step 3: When we set each parenthetical expression equal to zero, we get $x = -5$ and $x = 3$. Therefore, the answer is (D).

13. In triangle *ABC* above, $x =$

(A) 30
(B) 40
(C) 50
(D) 60
(E) 70

Here's How to Crack It

We know that the angle adjacent to the 100-degree angle must equal 80 degrees since we know that a straight line is 180 degrees. Fill it in on your diagram. Now, since we know that the sum of the angles contained in a triangle must equal 180 degrees, we know that $80 + 60 + x = 180$, so $x = 40$. That's (B).

Being Aggressive on Geometry Problems

The most important problem-solving technique for tackling PSAT geometry is to learn to be aggressive. This means, whenever you have a diagram, ask yourself: *What else do I know?* Write everything you can think of on your booklet. You may not see right away why it's important, but write it down anyway. Chances are good that you will be making progress toward the answer, without even knowing it.

ETS is also fond of disguising familiar figures within more complex shapes by extending lines, overlapping figures, or combining several basic shapes. So be on the lookout for the basic figures hidden in complicated shapes.

Drill 1

Be Aggressive! Answers can be found in Part III.

a. What is the sum of 30 and x? _____
b. What is the value of x? _____

c. What is the value of x? _____ y? _____ z? _____

d. What is the sum of 60, 40, and x? _____
e. What is the value of x? _____

f. What are all of the angles in the above diagram?

4. In the figure above, what is the value of *x* ?

(A) 25
(B) 30
(C) 35
(D) 40
(E) 50

Note: Figure not drawn to scale.

6. In the figure above, if *AB* and *CD* are lines, what is the value of *y* ?

(A) 60
(B) 70
(C) 75
(D) 80
(E) 85

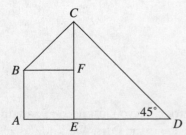

13. If the area of square *ABFE* = 25, and the area of triangle *BCF* = 10, what is the length of *ED* ?

(A)   7
(B)   8
(C)   9
(D) 13
(E) 14

THIRD SIDE RULE

Suppose you don't know anything about a triangle except the lengths of two of its sides. You can also then figure out that the third side must be between certain values, that is, the length of the third side must be less than the sum of the other two and greater than the difference.

> *The third side of a triangle is always less than the sum of the other two sides and greater than the difference between them.*

Why? Consider a triangle that looks like this:

The shortest distance between two points is a straight line, right? And yet in this figure, the straight-line distance from A to C is 9, yet the scenic route from A to B to C is…8? That can't be right! And it isn't. The crooked path must be longer than the straight path, and thus any two sides of a triangle added together must be longer than the third side. In this example, $2 < AC < 8$.

No Figures?
Draw one before you do anything else.

14. Which of the following is a possible perimeter of a triangle with sides 5 and 8 ?

 (A) 15
 (B) 16
 (C) 17
 (D) 26
 (E) 30

Here's How to Crack It

To find the perimeter of a triangle, you just need to add up the sides of the triangle, so let's see what we know about the sides. We know that the two given sides add up to 13, so the perimeter will be 13 + the third side. The third side will be between the sum and difference of those other two sides. $8 + 5 = 13$ and $8 - 5 = 3$, so the third side will be greater than 3 and less than 13. Add these to the sum of the sides we already know (13), and the perimeter must be between 16 (13 + 3) and 26 (13 + 13). The only answer choice that fits the bill is (C).

THE PYTHAGOREAN THEOREM

Whenever you have a right triangle, you can use the Pythagorean theorem. The theorem says that the sum of the squares of the legs of the triangle (the sides next to the right angle) will equal the square of the hypotenuse (the side opposite the right angle).

Pythagorean Theorem: $a^2 + b^2 = c^2$, where c is the hypotenuse of a right triangle. Learn it, love it.

$$a^2 + b^2 = c^2$$

Two of the most common ratios of sides that fit the Pythagorean theorem are $3 : 4 : 5$ and $5 : 12 : 13$. Since these are ratios, any multiples of these numbers will also work, such as $6 : 8 : 10$, and $30 : 40 : 50$.

Try the following example.

33. If *ABCD* is a rectangle, what is the perimeter of triangle *ABC* ?

Here's How to Crack It

We can use the Pythagorean theorem to figure out the length of the diagonal of the rectangle—since it has sides 6 and 8, its diagonal must be 10. (If you remembered that this is one of those well-known Pythagorean ratios, you didn't actually have to do the calculations.) Therefore, the perimeter of the triangle is 6 + 8 + 10, or 24.

2	4		
	⊂/⊃	⊂/⊃	
⊂•⊃	⊂•⊃	⊂•⊃	⊂•⊃
	⊂0⊃	⊂0⊃	⊂0⊃
⊂1⊃	⊂1⊃	⊂1⊃	⊂1⊃
⊂2⊃	⊂2⊃	⊂2⊃	⊂2⊃
⊂3⊃	⊂3⊃	⊂3⊃	⊂3⊃
⊂4⊃	⊂4⊃	⊂4⊃	⊂4⊃
⊂5⊃	⊂5⊃	⊂5⊃	⊂5⊃
⊂6⊃	⊂6⊃	⊂6⊃	⊂6⊃
⊂7⊃	⊂7⊃	⊂7⊃	⊂7⊃
⊂8⊃	⊂8⊃	⊂8⊃	⊂8⊃
⊂9⊃	⊂9⊃	⊂9⊃	⊂9⊃

SPECIAL RIGHT TRIANGLES

There are two specific right triangles, the properties of which may play a role in some harder PSAT math problems. They are the right triangles with angles 45-45-90 and 30-60-90.

An isosceles right triangle has angles that measure 45, 45, and 90 degrees. Whenever you have a 45-45-90 triangle with sides of x, the hypotenuse will always be $x\sqrt{2}$. This means that if one of the legs of the triangle measures 3, then the hypotenuse will be $3\sqrt{2}$.

This right triangle is important because it is half of a square. Memorizing the 45-45-90 triangle will allow you to easily find the diagonal of a square from its side, or find the side of a square from its diagonal.

Here's an example.

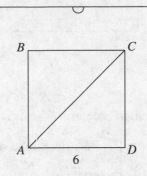

13. In square ABCD above, what is the perimeter of triangle *ABC* ?

(A) $6\sqrt{2}$

(B) 8

(C) $12 + \sqrt{2}$

(D) $12 + 6\sqrt{2}$

(E) 18

Here's How to Crack It

Remember we mentioned disguised figures a few pages back? Here's an example. This question looks like a question about a square, and it certainly is, in part, but it's really more about the two triangles formed by the diagonal.

In this square, we know that each of the triangles formed by the diagonal *AC* is a 45-45-90 right triangle. Since the square has a side of 6, using the 45-45-90 right triangle rule, each of the sides is 6 and the diagonal is $6\sqrt{2}$. Therefore, the perimeter of the triangle is $6 + 6 + 6\sqrt{2}$, or $12 + 6\sqrt{2}$ and the answer is (D).

The other important right triangle to memorize is the 30-60-90 right triangle.

A 30-60-90 triangle with a short side of x will have a hypotenuse of $2x$ and a middle side of $x\sqrt{3}$. If the smallest side (the x side) of the triangle is 5, then the sides measure 5, $5\sqrt{3}$, and 10. This triangle is important because it is half of an equilateral triangle, and it allows us to find the height of an equilateral triangle.

Try the following.

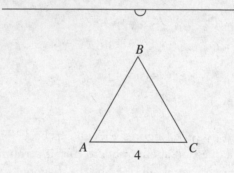

13. Triangle *ABC* above is equilateral, with sides of length 4. What is its area?

    (A)   3
    (B) $4\sqrt{2}$
    (C) $4\sqrt{3}$
    (D)   8
    (E) $8\sqrt{3}$

To find the area of the triangle, we need to know the base and the height. The question tells you that the base (line segment AC) is 4; now we need to find the height, which is *perpendicular* to the base. You can create a height by drawing a line from angle B straight down to the base, as you can see in the drawing above. Now you have two 30-60-90 triangles, and you can use the rules of 30-60-90 triangles to figure out the height. Half of the base would be 2, and that's the side across from the 30 degree angle, so you would multiply it by $\sqrt{3}$ to get the height.

Now we know that the base is 4 and the height is $2\sqrt{3}$, so plugging those numbers into the formula for area of a triangle, we get $A = \dfrac{1}{2} \times 4 \times 2\sqrt{3}$, which equals $4\sqrt{3}$. Thus, (C) is the correct answer.

OVERLAPPING FIGURES

Very often on a harder geometry problem you'll see two figures that overlap: a triangle and a square, a triangle and a circle, or a square and a circle.

> The key to solving overlapping figure problems is figuring out what the two figures have in common. This may be something you have to draw in yourself.

Take a look at the following problem.

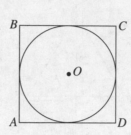

16. In the figure above, the circle with center O is drawn
in square $ABCD$. If the area of square $ABCD$ is 36,
what is the area of circle O ?

(A) 18
(B) 24
(C) 9π
(D) 12π
(E) 36π

Here's How to Crack It

Go ahead and draw a diameter in the figure through point O and parallel to the
base. We mentioned earlier that we want to write down things we know about the
figure, so let's write the formulas for both of the figures we've been given. The questions mentions the area of the square and the area of the circle, so write $A = s^2$
for the square and $A = \pi r^2$ for the circle.

Now let's take the information we've been given and take bite-sized pieces to crack
it. Since we know that the area of the square is 36, we can solve the first equation
and to get $s = 6$, so $d = 6$ as well. Let's take that information to the other formula,
that of the circle, which is what we're being asked to find. The radius is half of the
diameter, so $A = \pi 3^2 = 9\pi$, so that's our answer, choice (C).

Let's try another one.

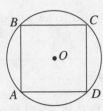

19. In the figure above, *ABCD* is a square drawn in the circle with center *O*. If the area of the circle is 16π, what is the area of square *ABCD* ?

(A)   4
(B)   16
(C) $16\sqrt{2}$
(D)   32
(E) $32\sqrt{2}$

Here's How to Crack It

What do the square and the circle have in common? A diagonal of the square is a diameter of the circle. Go ahead and draw that on the figure now. Once again, we have two formulas we might need here, $A = s^2$ for the square and $A = \pi r^2$ for the circle. We know something about the circle, so let's use that information to take the next bite: subbing in 16π for the area, we can solve and get $r = 4$. This tells us that the diameter is 8 and so is the diagonal of the square. What now? We could use the Pythagorean theorem to solve for the sides, but if you remember your special right triangles, you might remember that when you draw a diagonal in a square it divides it into two 45-45-90 triangles. Since we multiply the length of the side by $\sqrt{2}$ in these special right triangles to find the diagonal, we can just divide by $\sqrt{2}$ to find the side, which gives us $8/\sqrt{2}$ as the length of a side of the square. We won't bother getting the decimal equivalent or rationalizing because if we put this right into the formula we get $\left(8/\sqrt{2}\right)^2 = 64/2 = 32$, which is the answer, so we'll pick choice (D).

Quick Review
- An interior angle is an angle formed by two radii.
- A sector is the portion of the circle between the two radii.

PROPORTIONALITY IN A CIRCLE

Here's one more rule that plays a role in more advanced circle problems.

> Arc measure is proportional to interior angle measure, which is proportional to sector area.

This means that whatever fraction of the total degree measure is made up by the interior angle, the arc described by that angle is the same fraction of the circumference, and the pie piece created has the same fraction of the area.

Take a look at the figure below:

If angle x is equal to 90 degrees, which is one-quarter of 360 degrees, then the arc AB is equal to one-quarter of the circumference of the circle and the area of the sector of the circle enclosed by radii OA and OB is equal to one-quarter of the area of the circle.

To see how this works in a question, try number 18.

18. The circle above with center O has a radius of 4. If $x = 30$, what is the length of arc AB ?

(A) $\dfrac{\pi}{6}$

(B) $\dfrac{2\pi}{3}$

(C) 3

(D) $\dfrac{3\pi}{2}$

(E) 3π

Here's How to Crack It

Since the interior angle x is equal to 30 degrees, which is $\dfrac{1}{12}$ of 360 degrees, we know that the arc AB will be equal to $\dfrac{1}{12}$ of the circumference of the circle. Since the circle has radius 4, its circumference will be 8π. Therefore, arc AB will measure $\dfrac{1}{12} \times 8\pi$, or $\dfrac{2\pi}{3}$, choice (B).

11. Points A and B lie on a circle with center O such that the measure of $\angle OAB$ is 45°. If the area of the circle is 64π, what is the perimeter of $\triangle AOB$?

(A) $8 + 8\sqrt{2}$
(B) $16 + 8\sqrt{2}$
(C) $16 + 16\sqrt{2}$
(D) $32 + 16\sqrt{2}$
(E) $64 + 16\sqrt{2}$

Here's How to Crack It

This time a diagram isn't given, so drawing the circle should be your first step. Since points A and B lie on the circle, $\overline{OA}$ and $\overline{OB}$ are both radii, and equal in length, making $\triangle AOB$ isosceles. The problem indicates that $\angle OAB$ is 45 degrees, which means that $\angle OBA$ is also 45 degrees, which makes $\triangle AOB$ a 45-45-90 triangle (remember those special right triangles?).

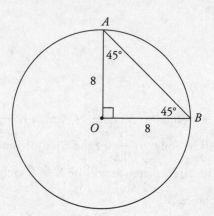

Given the circle's area of 64π, the radii of the circle (which are the legs of the isosceles right triangle) are 8, and the hypotenuse is $8\sqrt{2}$, making the perimeter $8 + 8 + 8\sqrt{2}$, or $16 + 8\sqrt{2}$, which is answer choice (B).

TANGENTS TO A CIRCLE

A tangent is a line that intersects the edge of a circle at exactly one point. A radius drawn to the point of tangency forms a 90 degree angle with the tangent line. This comes up occasionally on hard problems, so take a look at the example below. As you work through this question, if you're thinking that you'd never know how to do it yourself, there's still a valuable lesson here, and it's that this question is not in your POOD, so you should look instead for a plug in or something you're more familiar with, even if it's a number 19 or 20.

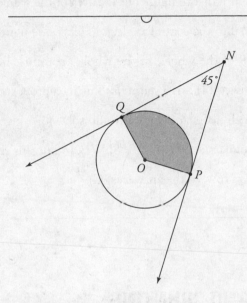

18. In the figure above, $\overrightarrow{NP}$ and $\overrightarrow{NQ}$ are tangent to the circle with center O at points P and Q, respectively. If the area of the shaded region is 24π, what is the circumference of the circle?

   (A) 8π
   (B) 12π
   (C) 16π
   (D) 40π
   (E) 64π

Here's How to Crack It

The key is remembering that any line or line segment drawn tangent to a circle is perpendicular to a radius drawn from the center of the circle to that tangent point; this means both $\angle OQN$ and $\angle OPN$ equal 90 degrees. With $\angle QNP$ given as 45 degrees, that leaves the central $\angle QOP$ of quadrilateral $QNPO$. Since all quadrilaterals contain 360 degrees and since 45 of the remaining 180 degrees are accounted for, that remaining angle must be 135 degrees. As all circles contain 360 degrees of arc, this means the shaded area represents $\frac{135}{360}$ or $\frac{3}{8}$ of the area of the entire circle.

Remember, we want to write down the formulas for quantities the question talks about, so that's $A = \pi r^2$ and $C = 2\pi r$. So far we don't have anything we can put directly into a formula, so what do we know? We're told that the area of the shaded sector is 24π, so we can use that to figure out the area of the whole circle, because we know it's proportional to the central angle. In fact, we've figured out that this part of the circle is 3/8 of the whole, so the whole area must be 8/3 times the sector, so $8/3 \times 24\pi = 64\pi$ (This is a shortcut to using a proportion, which looks like this: $\frac{3}{8} = \frac{24\pi}{x}$, which if we cross-multiply and solve for x gives us 64π.) Now we can use the first formula and solve for $r = 8$. We can put this right into the second formula and get $C = 16\pi$, so the answer is (C).

PROBABILITY AND COUNTING

Probability refers to the chance that an event will happen, and is always given as a fraction between 0 and 1, inclusive. A probability of 0 means that the event will never happen; a probability of 1 means that it is certain to happen.

$$\text{Probability} = \frac{\text{number of outcomes you want}}{\text{number of possible outcomes}}$$

For instance, if you have a die with faces numbered 1 to 6, what is the chance of rolling a 2? There is one face with the number 2 on it, out of 6 total faces. Therefore, the probability of rolling a 2 is $\frac{1}{6}$.

What is the chance of rolling an even number on one roll of this die? There are 3 faces of the die with an even number (the sides numbered 2, 4, and 6) out of a total of 6 faces. Therefore, the probability of rolling an even number is $\frac{3}{6}$, or $\frac{1}{2}$.

Let's try one.

───────────○───────────

7. In a jar there are 3 green gumballs, 5 red gumballs, 8 white gumballs, and 1 blue gumball. If one gumball is chosen at random, what is the probability that it will be red?

(A) $\frac{5}{17}$

(B) $\frac{5}{16}$

(C) $\frac{1}{17}$

(D) $\frac{1}{12}$

(E) $\frac{1}{10}$

Here's How to Crack It

To solve this problem, we take the number of things we want (the 5 red gumballs) and place it over the number of possible things we have to choose from (all 17 gumballs in the jar). This gives us choice (A).

───────────○───────────

1, 2, 3, ... , 1000

Some questions may ask you how many ways something can happen. The trick here is to draw an underline representing each of the spots you need to fill, then for each spot, write in the number of things that could fill that spot. When you're done with all the spots, multiply them.

Let's take a look at an example:

_____◯_____

14. Ms. Grady will choose one boy and one girl from her class to be the class representatives. If there are 3 boys and 7 girls in her class, how many different pairs of class representatives could she pick?

(A) 10
(B) 13
(C) 21
(D) 23
(E) 25

Here's How to Crack It

How many spots do we need to fill? Ms. Grady wants a pair of representatives, so we need to fill two spots. One will be a boy and the other a girl, so we need to fill one spot with the number of boys that we have to choose from and the other with the number of girls we have to choose from, then multiply them, so it's $3 \times 7 = 21$, which is choice (C).

_____◯_____

Let's try another.

_____◯_____

12. Sandra has six trophies, but only has room for three of them on her mantle. How many possible ways can she arrange three of the six trophies on her mantle?

(A) 18
(B) 54
(C) 80
(D) 120
(E) 216

Here's How to Crack It

How many places does Sandra have on her mantle in which she can put trophies? She has three, so draw that many underlines. How many choices does she have for what to place in the first spot? She has six, so fill a six into the first underline. Then she has five left to choose from for the second spot and four left to choose from for the last spot; we'll fill in the spots and multiply, $6 \times 5 \times 4 = 120$, so the choice is (D).

_____◯_____

Drill 2

Answers can be found in Part III.

Ice Cream	Toppings
Chocolate	Peanuts
Vanilla	Hot Fudge
Strawberry	Chocolate Chips
Wild Berry	
Coffee	

14. Kim is going to buy an ice cream sundae. A sundae consists of one flavor of ice cream and one topping. If she can choose from the kinds of ice cream and toppings shown in the chart above, how many different sundaes could she create?

    (A)   8
    (B)   12
    (C)   15
    (D)   18
    (E)   24

15. At the school cafeteria, students can choose from 3 different salads, 5 different main dishes, and 2 desserts. If Isabel chooses one salad, one main dish, and one dessert for lunch, how many different lunches could she possibly choose?

    (A)   15
    (B)   30
    (C)   45
    (D)   60
    (E)   80

16. If a drawer contains 6 white socks, 6 black socks, and 8 red socks, what is the probability that a sock drawn at random from the drawer will be red?

(A) $\dfrac{1}{8}$

(B) $\dfrac{2}{5}$

(C) $\dfrac{1}{2}$

(D) $\dfrac{2}{3}$

(E) $\dfrac{4}{5}$

8. Jennifer wants to visit 4 different cities on her vacation. If she will visit them one at a time, in how many different orders can she visit the four cities?

(A) 4
(B) 16
(C) 24
(D) 30
(E) 36

17. A bowl of marbles contains 8 blue marbles, 6 green marbles, 10 red marbles, and 1 white marble. If one marble is drawn at random from the bowl, what is the probability that it will be either blue or green?

(A) $\dfrac{8}{25}$

(B) $\dfrac{9}{25}$

(C) $\dfrac{14}{25}$

(D) $\dfrac{3}{5}$

(E) $\dfrac{4}{5}$

Summary

o   On Functions questions, just take the formula they give you and plug in the numbers they give you. Anyone adept at Plugging In will do great, whether the problem has $f(x)$ or weird symbols.

o   Quadratics generally require that you *expand* or *factor*—the general rule is, if you see a quadratic in one form, switch it to the other.

o   On all geometry problems, draw figures out and aggressively fill in everything you know.

o   The third side rule says that any side of a triangle must be between the sum and the difference of the other two sides.

o   There is no trigonometry on the PSAT—Pythagorean Theorem, common right triangles (such as 3 : 4 : 5 and 5 : 12 : 13), and Special Right Triangles (45-45-90 and 30-60-90) are the only tools you need to figure out angles and lengths in a right triangle.

o   When you see overlapping figures, figure out which measurement the two figures have in common.

o   Circles that show an interior angle (an angle that extends from the center of the circle) have proportionality. The interior angle over the whole degree measure (360 degrees) equals the same fraction as the arc enclosed by that angle over the circumference. Likewise, both of these fractions are equal to the area of the segment over the entire area of the circle.

o   When you see a line that is "tangent to" a circle, remember two things:
   • The line intersects the circle at exactly one point.
   • The radius of the circle that intersects the tangent line is perpendicular to that tangent line.

o   Probability is always a fraction between 0 and 1 (inclusive), and it is equal to the number of outcomes the question is asking for divided by the total number of possible outcomes.

Chapter 10
Writing Skills

For some of you, taking a test of your writing skills would be a good thing; for others, it's not so appealing. But don't worry—there is no essay. What this section really tests is a few grammar rules and your skill at correcting sentences using those rules. Even if you haven't had much grammar in school, this chapter will teach you what you need to know and help you approach the Writing Skills section like a pro.

WHAT TO EXPECT

The Writing Skills section contains 39 questions, including 14 Error Identification questions, 20 Improving Sentences questions, and 5 Improving Paragraphs questions. If these questions don't sound like anything you've studied in school about writing, you're not mistaken. The Writing Skills section is much more about test-taking skills than it is about actual writing skills. It will be the last section of the PSAT, and you will be allotted 30 minutes to complete it.

PSAT Grammar

The grammar ETS chooses to test on the PSAT is pretty basic. Even if you haven't done much grammar in school, don't sweat it; learning just a few rules will take you a long way. While we can't cover every single scenario that you might see on test day, ETS is actually quite predictable and likes to test the same few rules over and over. We'll cover those rules in this chapter, and if you need more in-depth work in any of the areas covered here, pick up a copy of The Princeton Review's *Grammar Smart* for a more comprehensive review.

How to Do Well
- Review/learn PSAT grammar
- Know how to attack each question type
- Know which questions to do and which ones to skip

Question Strategy

Every question type on the PSAT can be cracked, and the Writing Skills questions are no exception. While reviewing the basic grammar you need, you will also learn how to crack Error ID and Improving Sentences questions. After you solidify your approach to these question types, you'll learn how to crack Improving Paragraphs questions by employing the grammar and skills you've already mastered.

To Do or Not To Do

The Writing Skills section is arranged in a rough order of difficulty, with the exception of the Improving Paragraphs questions, which are the last five questions of the section. As usual, this means that the early questions will have fairly obvious answers that you shouldn't second guess, the middle third will be fairly straightforward but will contain some tricks, while the last third should be approached with caution. The Writing Skills sections are a little different than the other two sections, though, because they're more about knowing the rules that are tested and less about having to think hard about how to solve something or what the passage means.

If you spot the mistake in a sentence right off the bat, you're already close to getting the answer. Stay focused on what kind of error ETS is testing in that question, and use POE. If you don't spot an error, you'll have to proceed more carefully; don't trust your ear, especially on the later (hard) questions.

SNEAK PREVIEW

Error IDs

Before we begin reviewing ETS's grammar, let's take a peek at the two main question types you'll see on the Writing Skills section.

21. This is an <u>example</u> of an Error ID
      A   B
   question <u>that</u> <u>has</u> no error. <u>No error</u>
           C D   E

An Error ID question gives you a sentence that has four words or phrases underlined, each with a corresponding letter underneath. At the end of each sentence will be "No error"—choice (E). There are some important things you need to know about Error IDs:

- There is never more than one error per sentence.
- If there is an error, it's always underlined.
- Approximately 20 percent of all Error ID questions are correct as written, so don't be afraid to pick choice (E).
- Error IDs are short and therefore quick; you should usually be able to eliminate at least one answer choice, so you should plan to attempt most Error ID questions, but be extra careful or skip the last couple of questions.

Improving Sentences

15. This is an example of an Improving Sentences question <u>that does not contain</u> an error.

   (A) that does not contain
   (B) that has not been containing
   (C) which has not been contain
   (D) which is not being with
   (E) about which there is nothing to indicate it being with

Improving Sentences questions give you a sentence, part or all of which is underlined. The underlined part may or may not contain a grammatical error. There are some important things you need to know about Improving Sentences questions:

- Answer choice (A) always repeats the underlined portion exactly as it appears in the initial sentence. Thus, you never need to read answer choice (A)—you already did when you first read the sentence.

- Approximately 20 percent of the sentences will be correct as written, so don't be afraid to choose answer choice (A) if you've eliminated the other choices.
- The non-underlined portion of the sentence is always correct. Make sure to read it carefully. Many students focus only on the underlined part since that's where the error has to be (if there is one); however, often you can only find the underlined error by focusing carefully on the sentence as a whole.
- Don't try to revise the sentence in your head; you never know how ETS is going to fix it, and your perfect revision probably won't be listed. Work with the answer choices they give you and look for the *best* answer.

THE METHOD

There are many similarities in the way we approach Error IDs and Improving Sentences. Here are some things to keep in mind for both question types:

- **Don't make decisions based on sound.** One of the biggest ways the test writers try to trip you up is to use an error that sounds correct to you because you hear it so often in everyday life. For example, the sentence "Everyone should bring their own lunch" sounds perfectly normal, yet it contains a grammatical error (pronoun agreement, which you'll hear more about later). Alternatively, ETS can put in words that sound odd because you're not used to hearing them, but are, in fact, perfectly correct. The important thing is to move beyond "It sounds bad" or "It sounds okay" as the sole reason you eliminate or choose an answer choice. Learn the rules ETS tests, and look for them.
- **Use POE aggressively.** Focus on eliminating everything you can, based on the rules of grammar, not on picking something that stands out as a "good" sentence.
- **Trim the fat.** One technique that will help you decide if an answer choice contains an error is "trimming the fat." This means taking a sentence and getting rid of the extraneous words and phrases that are just there for distraction. For example, take the following sentence: "Japan, since the early part of the 1980s when Japanese products became popular with consumers, have been able to export the high-quality technology demanded by foreign markets." There is a long, distracting phrase separating *Japan* and *have* so that it's easy to forget that these two words have to agree in number to be correct—and they don't. It should be *Japan...has,* because Japan is *one* country. So when you see prepositional phrases or phrases offset by commas, ignore them while you figure out if the surrounding words are correct. You can even cross them off, but don't make it so that it's hard to read; you may need to see those words later.

Error IDs

When you first read an Error ID, one of two things will happen: Either you will spot an error immediately, or you won't. It doesn't really matter if you do or not; there are ways to get the correct answer regardless.

Plan A: If You Spot an Error Immediately

1. Try to articulate to yourself what the error is, so that you avoid picking an answer solely by using your ear. For instance, say to yourself, "There is a subject/verb agreement error, because *Japan* is singular and *have* is plural."
2. Check the other answers just to be safe.
3. Select your original answer if you're confident it truly is an error.

Plan B: If You Don't Spot an Error Immediately

1. Check each underlined portion individually, thinking about the grammar rules that might apply to it. For example, if the word *everyone* is underlined, say to yourself, "*Everyone* is a pronoun, so I need to check for agreement, ambiguity, and case."
2. Eliminate answers that you know are grammatically correct.
3. Select the answer that violates a rule, or (E) if there is no error.

Improving Sentences

Again, when you first read the sentence, either you will spot an error or you won't. What you *don't* want to do, above all, is read the sentence five or six times, replacing the underlined portion with each of the answer choices. This is a huge waste of time and will end in your picking an answer based on what you remember sounding the best —not a great way to go through these problems. Remember, ETS knows how to trick your memory and your ear.

Plan A: If You Spot an Error Immediately

1. Again, try to articulate to yourself what the error is, so that you avoid picking an answer solely by ear. If you're confident it's an error, then eliminate (A) and any answer choices that make the same error.
2. Compare the remaining answer choices and note how they differ. Eliminate any answer choices that contain new errors or change the intended meaning of the original sentence. If you get down to two answers that both seem grammatically correct, pick the more concise (usually shorter) answer.
3. Repeat Step 2 until you're down to one answer choice, and pick it.

Plan B: If You Don't Spot an Error Immediately

1. Compare the answer choices and note how they differ. Eliminate any answer choices that contain errors.
2. Repeat Step 1 until you have one answer choice left.

Now that we've talked about how to do each question type, we're going to move on to reviewing the grammar. We'll do problems as we go along to practice the techniques.

Grammar? Ugh!

To do well on the Writing Skills section, you need to remember some basic grammar rules. Now, don't get worked up about being tested on grammar. PSAT grammar is not difficult, nor is it extensive. In fact, the PSAT really tests only five basic grammatical concepts:

1. verbs
2. nouns
3. pronouns
4. prepositions
5. other little things

These are the five areas in which a sentence can "go wrong." They will function as a checklist for you—every time you read a sentence, you will look at these five areas to find the error. If you don't find one after checking these five things, then there probably isn't one.

No Error?

As we've mentioned, about 20 percent of Error ID questions and Improving Sentences questions contain no error. If you've used your checklist and can't find a mistake, chances are there isn't one. Don't be afraid to pick *No error*—choice (E) on Error ID or choice (A) on Improving Sentences questions.

VERBS

A **verb** is an action word. It tells what the subject of the sentence is doing. There are three types of errors you can see with verbs:

*   agreement
*   parallelism
*   tense

Agreement

> Verbs must always *agree* in number with the subjects with which they are paired: singular with singular, plural with plural.

Subject-verb agreement is heavily tested on the PSAT, so whenever you see a verb in the underlined portion of a sentence make sure it agrees in number with the subject it refers to. That is, plural with plural, singular with singular. Remember, the subject is the thing the sentence is talking about. If you are given a singular subject (*Jake, the car, she, Europe*), it must be paired with a singular verb (*is, was, plays, rocks*). Singular verbs generally have an *s* on the end, like plural nouns.

Let's look at a question.

---

1. The statistics released by the state department <u>makes the economic situation look bleaker than it really is</u>.

    (A) makes the economic situation look bleaker than it really is
    (B) makes the economic situation look bleaker than they really are
    (C) make the economic situations look bleaker than it really is
    (D) make the economic situation look bleaker than it really is
    (E) make the economic situation look more bleak than they really are

Here's How to Crack It

The verb *makes* appears in the underlined portion of the sentence, so we need to check the subject. This sentence is about *the statistics*, so the subject is plural. Don't be confused by all of the other words that appear after it, *released by the state department,* they're just there to distract us. We're only interested in the simple subject, which is plural. The verb *makes* is singular, though, so there's a problem with the sentence as it's written. Let's go ahead and cross out choice (A) now. Remember, we don't need to read it because it repeats the underlined portion of the sentence exactly. Let's also cross out (B) right away because it repeats the error.

Answer choices (C) and (D) are identical except for the words *situation* and *situations*. Which is correct? The verb it is paired up with is *is*, which is singular, so the singular *situation* is correct. We can eliminate (C). Comparing (D) and (E) we find that (E) uses *they...are,* which is plural, so we can get rid of that and choose (D).

Sometimes, though, you will have to do more work to figure out if the subject of the sentence is plural or singular. Here are some things to watch out for:

Collective Nouns

These can be a little tricky, but they have one thing in common: They are all *groups* of people, places, or things. Therefore, they are singular and take singular verbs.

> The *family* is
> The *jury* is
> The *group* is
> The *audience* is
> The *company* is
> The *government* is
> The *United States* (or any other country) is

Compound Subjects

Subjects joined by *and* are plural: Bill and Pat *were* going to the show. However, subjects joined by *or* can be either singular or plural (the same is true for *nor*). If the last noun given is singular, then the sentence takes a singular verb; if the last noun given is plural, it takes a plural verb.

The following pronouns also take singular verbs:

> Either *is*
> Neither *is*
> None *is*
> Each *is*
> Anyone *is*
> No one *is*
> Everyone *is*

Let's try a question.

---

27. Pam Cruise and Jim Braswell, neither of whom takes the
                                   A   B
    bus to work, is secretly plotting to take over the world.
             C   D
    No error
    E

Here's How to Crack It

If you don't immediately spot the error, go through each answer choice and eliminate anything that contains no error. Answer choice (C) gives us the singular verb *is*. When we Trim the Fat to get rid of the phrase between the subject and the verb, we see that *is* has been paired up with a plural subject here: *Pam Cruise and Jim Braswell.* Therefore, the correct answer is (C).

Parallelism

> The next thing you need to check when you see a verb is whether it is *parallel* to the other verbs in the sentence.

In other words, do the verbs use the same form? For example, *to run, to walk,* and *to sing* are in the same form, whereas *to walk* and *singing* are not. Be particularly careful to watch for parallelism when you see lists of verbs.

Now let's try out a question that tests our skills.

---

8. As a competitor in the Iron Man competition, Paula was required to swim 2.4 miles, bike 112 miles, and <u>running the last 26 miles</u>.

   (A) running the last 26 miles
   (B) to run the last 26 miles
   (C) run the last 26 miles
   (D) ran the last 26 miles
   (E) she had to run the last 26 miles

Here's How to Crack It

We can tell from comparing the answer choices that it all boils down to which form the verb *run* should be in, so let's look at the sentence for clues. The first verb in the list is *to swim*, and the second one is *bike*. When a list starts with *to*, the rest of the verbs can start with *to*, or the rest of the verbs can leave off the *to*, like *bike* does in this sentence. *Running, to run,* and *ran* aren't parallel to *swim* and *bike*, so (A), (B), and (D) can be eliminated. (E) just repeats a lot of words from the sentence unnecessarily, so it can go too, leaving (C) as our best answer.

Just the Answer, Please
Remember, when solving Error ID questions, all you have to do is identify the error. Don't worry if you don't know exactly how to fix an error—ETS only cares if you can identify it.

Tense

Finally, verbs need to be in the proper *tense,* such as past, present, or future. Verb tenses should generally be consistent in a sentence unless the meaning requires different tenses.

Let's try an example:

Throughout the Middle Ages, women work
        A   B

beside men, knowing that the effort of men and
      C

women alike was essential to survival. No error
                        D   E

Here's How to Crack It

The verb *work* refers to something that happened *throughout the Middle Ages,* according to the sentence, and the Middle Ages definitely happened in the past. *Work,* though, is in the present tense, so it's erroneous, and (B) is the correct answer.

That's Just Perfect

If you see the verbs *have, has,* or *had* paired up with other verbs on the PSAT, you're probably looking at verbs in a *perfect* form, such as the past perfect or present perfect. Here's how and when you use those forms:

Past perfect verbs describe something in the past that took place *before another event in the past.* It uses the word *had,* then the verb. For example:

I *had sung* all night until my neighbor called the police.
Leigh *had skied* every day before she broke her leg.

Present perfect usually tells you about an event that started in the past and is continuing through the present. It can also refer to an event that happened at an unspecified time in the past. Present perfect uses the words *have* or *has,* depending on whether a singular or plural verb is needed, and then the verb. For example:

> The dogs *have sung* along with me before.
> My neighbor *has glared* at me ever since.

Verbs in the perfect form have to be constructed properly when used (*have sung* instead of *have sang*), and they should be used only if needed for the above situations; it's not okay to substitute them for simple past, present, and future verbs.

NOUNS

Nouns are words that indicate a person, place, thing, or idea. Anything you can touch, talk about, discuss, or think about is a noun in that context. PSAT sometimes tests noun agreement. When two or more nouns in a sentence refer to each other, they need to agree in number: singular with singular and plural with plural.

Give this question a try:

───────────○───────────

26. If your friends <u>are</u> not good students <u>now</u> <u>they will</u>
            A   B   C
   probably not be <u>a good student</u> in college. <u>No error.</u>
                     D   E

Here's How to Crack It

Did you see an error? In the first part of the sentence it says *students,* while in the later part of the sentence it says *student.* Are we to believe that your friends will morph into one person when they go to college? Maybe if they're headed to Comic Book University. The answer is (D).

───────────○───────────

PRONOUNS

Pronouns are words that take the place of nouns. As with verbs, there are three types of errors that pronouns can have:

- agreement
- ambiguity
- case

Agreement

> **Pronouns** must agree in number with the nouns they replace. Singular pronouns replace singular nouns; plural pronouns replace plural nouns.

After all the time we've spent on verb agreement this may seem obvious, but there are some additional tricks that ETS especially likes to pull with pronouns. To learn how to get around them, first we're going to look at some pronouns that are *always* singular.

> Either *is*
> Neither *is*
> Each *is*
> Anybody *is*
> No one *is*
> Everyone *is*
> Everything *is*

Pronouns starting with *any* and *every* can be tricky because the words *any* and *every* seem to imply that there are several people or things, but just remember: If you see *one*, *body*, or *thing* at the end of the word, it's singular. Also, the word *none* can be singular or plural, but ETS prefers to treat it as singular, so you should too.

ETS also likes to write questions with the word *their* used as a singular pronoun, like many people do in everyday speech: *Everyone should clean up their stuff.* However, in ETS-land, *their* is still always considered plural. If it's being used to replace a singular pronoun (like *everyone*), it's wrong. (This is another way the test writers will try to trick you if you're using your ear, but it's easy to spot once you know about it!) Don't worry about whether *their* should be replaced with *his, his or her,* or some other option—you won't have to choose for the PSAT. You just need to know that *their* is plural and should replace only plural subjects, such as *the students, Al and Susan,* or *voters.*

Try this question.

———————○———————

Everyone <u>on the softball</u> team <u>who came up to bat</u>
          A   B
squinted <u>at the pitcher</u> in order to keep the sun's
          C
glaring rays out of <u>their eyes.</u> <u>No error</u>
                  D   E

Here's How to Crack It

Is there an underlined pronoun late in this sentence? There sure is: *their eyes*. Whose eyes are being referred to? Let's Trim the Fat to check this sentence:

> "*Everyone*…squinted…to keep the sun's…rays…out of *their* eyes."

> *Everyone* is singular, but *their* is plural, so it cannot replace *everyone*.

The answer is (D).

———————○———————

Ambiguity

> When you see a pronoun in a sentence on the PSAT, you should make sure it's perfectly clear what the pronoun replaces.

For example:

> *After looking over the color samples, Mary agreed with Martha that her porch should be painted green.*

Whose porch is being painted green? Mary's or Martha's? This sentence has a problem with pronoun *ambiguity*, which means you can't tell which noun the pronoun is supposed to replace.

Whenever you spot a pronoun, especially late in a sentence, look to see what the pronoun is referring to. If there's more than one possibility, the pronoun has an ambiguity error. If it's perfectly clear what noun (or pronoun) the pronoun replaces, move on to checking for agreement and case. Let's try one:

The director <u>told</u> the star of the production that <u>he</u> was
        A   B
making far too much money <u>to tolerate</u> such nasty
                                  C
<u>treatment from</u> the producer. <u>No error</u>
      D   E

Here's How to Crack It

When you identify answer choice (B) as a pronoun, you should immediately try to figure out which noun (or pronoun) it is referring to. Here, who is making too much money—the director or the star? From the sentence there's no way to tell, so (B) has a pronoun ambiguity error and is the correct answer. You might think the sentence would make more sense if the word *he* referred to the director—or the star. However, the sentence itself doesn't give you any clues pointing to either one, so the pronoun is ambiguous.

Subject Pronouns

Singular	**Plural**
I	we
you	you
he	they
she	they
it	they
who	who

Object Pronouns

Singular	**Plural**
me	us
you	you
him	them
her	them
it	them
whom	whom

Case

Pronouns come in two "flavors," or cases: **subjective** and **objective**. The subject is the person or thing performing the action in the sentence. The object is the person or thing *receiving* the action. Think of it this way: An object just sits there. It doesn't *do* anything—things are done to it. The subject, however, *does* something.

Subjects and objects are represented by different pronouns. For example, *I* is a subject pronoun, as in the sentence "I did it," while *me* is an object pronoun, as in "It happened to me." See how the subject does something, and the object has something done to it?

Try the following example:

---○---

The leading roles in the widely acclaimed play, a modern
                          A
version of an Irish folktale, were performed by Jessica
        B   C
and him. No error
    D   E

Here's How to Crack It

Look at the pronoun that comes at the end of the sentence. *Him* is in the object case, so we need to know if that's correct. In this case, *performed by...him* is correct. You'd need the subject case if you were going to say *he performed*, but as it stands, the pronoun is correct. The rest of the underlined portions of the sentence also check out, so the answer is (E).

---○---

The I/Me Thing

Are you always getting corrected on your use (or misuse) of *I* or *me*? When in doubt about whether a pronoun needs a subject or object case, Trim the Fat to figure out whether it is acting or being acted upon. Which of the following sentences is correct?

> *The book belongs to Jerry and I.*
> *The book belongs to Jerry and me.*

Let's trim the fat and take out *Jerry and*. Now we're left with *The book belongs to _____*. What goes in the blank, *I* or *me*? *Me* is correct, because *to* is a preposition (more on those in a moment) and we need an *object* pronoun to come after the preposition. Let's look at a trickier one:

> *Clare is more creative than I.*
> *Clare is more creative than me.*

Be careful. This may look as if the pronoun is an object, but actually the sentence is incomplete. What the sentence really says is, "Clare is more creative than I am." The *am* is understood. When in doubt, say the sentence to yourself, adding *am, is,* or *are*. If any form of *be* makes sense, the sentence requires a subject pronoun.

PREPOSITIONS

Prepositions add information about a noun, generally to give one noun's relationship to something else, either in time or space. (For example: *over, under, around, along, by, to, beside, near, with, beyond, before, after, at, in, on*, etc.)

Prepositions are *always* followed by a noun or pronoun, which is called the *object* of the preposition. In the sentence "I threw the ball to him," *to* is the preposition and *him* is the object. (Notice that *him* is an *object* pronoun.) Together they create the prepositional phrase *to him*. It's important to recognize prepositional phrases because they often appear as distractions on the PSAT, and you'll want to get rid of them when you trim the fat.

DRILL 1

Identify the prepositions and their objects in the following sentences: Answers can be found in Part III.

1. Lina walked over the bridge.
2. The ball went beyond the green.
3. Please shelve the dictionary with the other reference books.
4. I want to return the movie to her.

DRILL 2

Another reason prepositions are important is that some words have to be paired with certain prepositions. These word pairs are called *idioms,* and unlike subject/verb agreement and pronoun ambiguity, you won't have certain rules to fall back on to solve an idiom problem on the test; you'll just have to memorize them. Here are some questions involving idioms that are commonly tested on the PSAT; fill in the blanks, check your answers, and make flash cards to memorize any that you don't know. Answers can be found in Part III.

1. I am *indebted* _____ you.
2. I am *resentful* _____ you.
3. I am *delighted* _____ you.
4. I am *jealous* _____ you.
5. I am *worried* _____ you.
6. I am *astounded* _____ you.
7. The women had a *dispute* _____ politics.
8. You have a *responsibility* _____ take care of your pet.
9. My friends are not so *different* _____ your friends.
10. Scott is *considered* _____ the best composer at the conservatory.

Try an Error ID example:

------------------○------------------

28. Despite the poor weather, my sister and I were
$\qquad$ A $\qquad$ B $\qquad$ C
planning on attending the festival. No error
$\qquad$ D $\qquad$ E

Here's How to Crack It
Though we may hear similar sentences every day and not realize there is a grammar mistake, the word *planning* is part of an idiom: *planning to*. A correct use would read *planning to attend*, so (D) has an error and is the correct answer.

------------------○------------------

OTHER LITTLE THINGS
The final area of grammar we're going to cover is Other Little Things—some areas that are tested on the PSAT but don't fall into our other categories. The areas are:

- faulty comparisons
- misplaced modifiers
- adjectives/adverbs
- voice
- active/passive

Faulty Comparisons
Whenever you see a PSAT question that makes a comparison, check for these types of errors.

Apples to Apples
One type of error is comparing things that can't actually be compared. A correct comparison compares apples to apples, not apples to banana pudding. For example, look at the following sentence:

> *Larry goes shopping at Foodtown because the prices are better than Shop Rite.*

Even though it's pretty common to hear sentences like this in everyday speech, it's actually wrong and you will probably see something like this in a couple of test questions. This one can be tricky to spot for the very reason we stated above, that lots of people talk this way and we know what they mean, so we give them the benefit of the doubt and assume they're speaking correctly. But we can't do that on the PSAT. Remember, don't trust your ear; when you see comparison words like *like, as, compared to,* and so on, check to see if the things being compared are actually the same sort of thing. The two things being compared are *Foodtown's prices* and *Shop Rite,* instead of *Foodtown's prices* and *Shop Rite's prices.* Even though we would assume the speaker was comparing prices to prices if we heard that sentence on television, the comparison has to be made more clearly on the PSAT. Better sentences would read:

> *Larry goes shopping at Foodtown because the prices are better than Shop Rite's prices.*

or even

> *Larry goes shopping at Foodtown because the prices are better than Shop Rite's.*

Do You Count?

While we're on the subject of grocery stores, you've probably seen a sign that says *10 items or less* about a thousand times. Guess what? It's grammatically wrong. When items can be counted, the word *fewer* should be used instead of *less.*

For example:

> If you eat *fewer* French fries, you can use *less* ketchup.

Similar word pair include *many* (can be counted) versus *much* (can't be counted)...

> *Many* hands make *much* less work.

...and *number* (can be counted) versus *amount* (can't be counted).

> The same *number* of people ate different *amounts* of pudding.

Two's Company, Three or More Is...?

Finally, different words must be used when comparing two things versus comparing three or more things. The following examples will jog your memory:

- *More* (two things) versus *Most* (three or more things)
  Given vanilla and strawberry as ice cream flavor options, I think vanilla is the *more* appealing option.
  In fact, of all the flavors I've tried, I like vanilla the *most.*

- *Less* (two things) versus *Least* (three or more things)
  I am *less* likely to be chosen than Judy is.
  I am the *least* likely person to be chosen from the department.
- *Better* (two things) versus *Best* (three or more things)
  My math teacher is *better* than the one I had last year.
  My Princeton Review teacher is the *best* teacher I have ever had.
- *Between* (two things) versus *Among* (three or more things)
  Between you and me, I never liked her anyway.
  Among all the people here, no one likes her.

Misplaced Modifiers

A modifier is a descriptive word or phrase inserted in a sentence to add dimension to the thing it modifies. For example:

Talking in his sleep, Mr. Ed was a unique horse.

"Talking in his sleep" is the modifying phrase in this sentence. It describes a characteristic of Mr. Ed. Generally speaking, a modifying phrase should be right next to the thing it modifies. If it's not, the meaning of the sentence may change. For example:

Walking down the road, my mood shifted from bitter to relaxed.

What is walking down the road? *My mood,* because that's what comes right after the comma. Questions about this mistake can be tricky because we know what the sentence is trying to say and we're likely to give it the benefit of the doubt, but when you see a descriptive phrase in the beginning of a sentence and it's underlined, take a look at what comes after the comma to see if that's really what it's talking about.

Try the following example:

17. <u>Perhaps the most beautiful natural vegetation in the world</u>, the west of Ireland explodes each spring with a tremendous variety of wildflowers.

   (A) Perhaps the most beautiful natural vegetation in the world
   (B) In what may be the world's most beautiful natural vegetation
   (C) Home to what may be the most beautiful natural vegetation in the world
   (D) Its vegetation may be the world's most beautiful
   (E) More beautiful in its natural vegetation than anywhere else in the world

Here's How to Crack It

Is the west of Ireland a kind of vegetation? No, so cross off (A). We need an answer that will make the opening phrase modify *the west of Ireland*. Answer choice (B) is still modifying the vegetation, so cross it off. All three other choices fix the problem, but (C) does it the best. (D) makes the sentence a bit awkward, and (E) actually changes the meaning of the sentence by saying that the west of Ireland definitively has the most beautiful vegetation while the original sentence says *perhaps*. ETS's answer is (C).

Adjectives/Adverbs

Misplaced modifiers aren't the only descriptive errors ETS will throw at you. Another way they try to trip you up is by using adjectives instead of adverbs and vice versa. Remember that an **adjective** modifies a noun, while an **adverb** modifies verbs, adverbs, and adjectives. The adverb is the one that usually has *–ly* on the end. In the following sentence, circle the adverbs and underline the adjectives:

> The stealthy thief, desperately hoping to evade the persistent
> police, ran quickly into the dank, dark alley after brazenly
> stealing the stunningly exquisite jewels.

First, let's list the adjectives along with the nouns they modify: *stealthy* thief, *persistent* police, *dank* alley, *dark* alley, *exquisite* jewels. Now for the adverbs with the words they modify: *desperately* hoping (verb), ran (verb) *quickly*, *brazenly* stealing (verb), *stunningly* exquisite (adjective).

Now try the following Improving Sentences example:

---

15. Movie cameras are no longer particularly costly, but film, development, and editing equipment <u>cause the monetary expense of making a film to add up tremendous</u>.

    (A) cause the monetary expense of making a film to add up tremendous
    (B) add tremendously to the expense of making a film
    (C) much increase the film-making expenses
    (D) add to the tremendous expense of making a film
    (E) tremendously add up to the expense of making a film

Here's How to Crack It

Here we have an adjective/adverb error. What should the last word in the sentence be? Tremendous*ly*. Cross off (A) and also (D), since it doesn't fix the error and changes the meaning of the sentence. (C) is way out there, so cross it off too. In (E), the placement of the *tremendously* is awkward and slightly changes the meaning of the sentence. ETS's answer is (B).

Active/Passive Voice

Last but not least, ETS prefers sentences written in the active voice to sentences written in the passive voice. In the **active voice**, the subject of the sentence is doing something. In the **passive voice**, the main actor becomes the object, and is being acted upon. The word *by* often (but not always) highlights passive voice.

Active:	She took the PSAT.
Passive:	The PSAT was taken *by* her.

Passive voice isn't wrong, but when you see it in a PSAT question, there will generally be a choice that uses that active voice, so if that choice is grammatical, pick it.

TECHNIQUE REVIEW

Before we go to Drill 3, let's review some techniques.

For Error ID questions, read the sentence and determine whether you spot an error. If you do spot an error, try to articulate that error to yourself to make sure you're not basing your decision simply on sound. Check the other answers against the grammar rules you've learned, and if you're still sure your original error is the correct answer, pick it.

If you don't spot an error right off the bat on an Error ID question, check all answer choices against the grammar rules. Eliminate any choices that stand up to scrutiny until you find an error or until only (E) is left.

For Improving Sentences questions, read the sentence and ask the same question— do you spot an error? If you do, try to articulate it to yourself, and if you decide it violates one of the rules we've discussed, eliminate (A) and any answer choice that repeats the error. Compare the remaining answer choices, eliminating errors until you are down to one.

If you don't spot an error immediately on an Improving Sentences question, move straight to comparing answer choices. The differences among the answer choices give you clues to what rules are being tested, and you can eliminate answers based on the rules you've learned. Repeat until only one answer choice is left.

Drill 3

Before we move on to Improving Paragraphs questions, try putting together what you've learned. Do the following Error ID and Improving Sentences questions using your grammar checklist. Remember to trim the fat and use POE. On Improving Sentences, do not hesitate to check out the answer choices for a clue to help you spot the error. You may wish to jot down your grammar checklist before you begin. Answers can be found in Part III.

1. When the student council announced its intention to elect a minority representative, <u>neither the principal nor the superintendent were willing to comment on the issue</u>.

   (A) neither the principal nor the superintendent were willing to comment on the issue
   (B) neither the principal or the superintendent were willing to comment on the issue
   (C) neither the principal nor the superintendent was willing to comment on the issue
   (D) neither of the principal nor the superintendent was willing to comment on the issue
   (E) neither the principal or the superintendent was willing to comment on the issue

2. Artists can offer startling representations of the world <u>but with their responsibility</u> to elevate humanity.

   (A) but with their responsibility
   (B) with the responsibility
   (C) having also the responsibility
   (D) but ought also
   (E) their responsibility being as well

3. The patient began his difficult postsurgery <u>recovery, but he was</u> able to recover from the psychological effects of the injury.

   (A) recovery, but he was
   (B) recovery, where he was
   (C) recovery only when he was
   (D) recovery only when being
   (E) recovery, also he was

4. <u>It is a more difficult task to learn to type than mastering a simple word-processing program.</u>

   (A) It is a more difficult task to learn to type than mastering a simple word-processing program.
   (B) It is more difficult of a task to learn to type than mastering a simple word-processing program.
   (C) It is a more difficult task to learn to type than to have mastered a simple word-processing program.
   (D) It is a more difficult task to learn to type than simply to master a word-processing program.
   (E) It is a more difficult task to learn to type than to master a simple word-processing program.

5. <u>In 1962 Jackie Robinson gained admission to the National Baseball Hall of Fame, he was the first Black baseball player in the major leagues.</u>

   (A) In 1962 Jackie Robinson gained admission to the National Baseball Hall of Fame, he was the first Black baseball player in the major leagues.
   (B) In 1962 Jackie Robinson, the first Black major-league baseball player, gained admission to the National Baseball Hall of Fame.
   (C) In the National Baseball Hall of Fame in 1962, Jackie Robinson, the first Black baseball player in the major leagues, was admitted to it.
   (D) With admission to the National Baseball Hall of Fame in 1962, he was the first Black major-league player to do it, Jackie Robinson.
   (E) The first Black major-league player was when he was Jackie Robinson, admitted to the national Baseball Hall of Fame in 1962.

6. A well-organized person can go through the day efficiently, <u>wasting little time or they waste none at all</u>.

   (A) wasting little time or they waste none at all
   (B) wasting little or no time
   (C) wasting little time or wasting none at all
   (D) wasting either little time or none
   (E) either little or no time being wasted

7. When Michelle Shocked recorded her *Arkansas Traveler* album, <u>regional American folk songs were used as inspiration, but it was never copied exactly by her</u>.

   (A) regional American folk songs were used as inspiration, but it was never copied exactly by her
   (B) regional American folk songs were used as inspiration, but she never copied them exactly
   (C) regional American folk songs were used as inspiration by her and not copied exactly
   (D) she used regional American folk songs, but they were not exactly copied
   (E) she used regional American folk songs as inspiration, but never copied them exactly

8. Educators and parents agree that a daily reading time will not only enhance a child's education <u>but also will encourage the child to read independently</u>.

(A) but also will encourage the child to read independently

(B) but also encouraging the child to read independently

(C) but encourage the child to read independently too

(D) but encourage children to read independently

(E) but also encourage them to read independently

21. Eric's new CD <u>were destroyed</u> when Paula Ann,
$$\text{A}$$
running <u>quickly</u> <u>through the office</u>, stepped on <u>it</u>.
$$\text{B}\text{C}\text{D}$$
<u>No error</u>
$$\text{E}$$

22. Because <u>their</u> <u>class</u> was going on a field trip that day,
$$\text{A}\text{B}$$
James and Alice <u>each</u> needed a <u>lunch</u> to bring to
$$\text{C}\text{D}$$
school. <u>No error</u>
$$\text{E}$$

23. None <u>of the students</u> on the review board <u>is qualified</u>
$$\text{A}\text{B}$$
to ascertain <u>whether</u> the money was <u>well spent</u>.
$$\text{C}\text{D}$$
<u>No error</u>
$$\text{E}$$

24. Just <u>between</u> you and <u>I</u>, *Borat* was the
$$\text{A}\text{B}$$
dumbest movie I <u>have</u> ever <u>seen</u>. <u>No error</u>
$$\text{C}\text{D}\text{E}$$

25. If you <u>had looked</u> at the prices <u>closely</u>, you'll see that
$$\text{A}\text{B}$$
the "economy size" of detergent is <u>actually</u> more
$$\text{C}$$
expensive than the <u>smaller</u> trial sizes. <u>No error</u>
$$\text{D}\text{E}$$

26. The <u>new</u> course schedule worked out <u>splendid</u> for all
$$\text{A}\text{B}$$
<u>of those students</u> who <u>had been</u> concerned. <u>No error</u>
$$\text{C}\text{D}\text{E}$$

27. <u>Many</u> young adults find it extremely difficult to <u>return</u>
$$\text{A}\text{B}$$
home from college and <u>abide with</u> the rules <u>set down</u>
$$\text{C}\text{D}$$
by their parents. <u>No error</u>
$$\text{E}$$

28. I <u>recently</u> heard an <u>announcement where</u> the Rangers
$$\text{A}\text{B}$$
<u>will be playing</u> a game at home <u>this</u> weekend. <u>No error</u>
$$\text{C}\text{D}\text{E}$$

29. Just <u>last month</u>, two weeks after the announcement
$$\text{A}$$
<u>of elections</u> in Kazakhstan, 92-year-old Fydor
$$\text{B}$$
has cast his first vote <u>in 70 years</u>. <u>No error</u>
$$\text{C}\text{D}\text{E}$$

Improving Paragraphs

Questions in the Improving Paragraphs section are not just about grammar, but also about the logical flow of the passage and its support of the main idea.

The five Improving Paragraphs questions require you to make corrections to a "first draft" of a student's essay. You will be given a passage composed of approximately three paragraphs. Each paragraph contains numbered sentences. Your job is to "edit" the rough draft to make it better. You're not going to be asked lots of tough questions about the content of the passage, so take about 30 seconds to skim it before going to the questions.

Here is a sample passage for you to skim:

> (1) Conservation and ecology are the hot topics at our school. (2) Students used to just throw everything out in one big garbage pail. (3) Sure, it was easy. (4) It wasn't good for the environment.
>
> (5) I volunteered to head up the conservation team. (6) My friends and I decided to map out our strategies. (7) First we needed to get students to become aware of the problem. (8) Educating was important. (9) A thing to do was implement a recycling program. (10) We checked with the local town government. (11) They would supply the recycling bins. (12) We had to supply the people who'd be willing to recycle. (13) The most important thing students had to learn to do was to separate their garbage. (14) Glass in one container. (15) Plastic in another.
>
> (16) Our final step was to get the teachers and administrators involved. (17) Paper can be recycled too. (18) We ran a poster contest. (19) The winners are hanging in our halls. (20) Reuse, recycle, renew. (21) That's our school's new motto.

Now, before you get out your red pencil and jump in, there are a few more things you need to know. Your passage may consist of 15 or more sentences, each potentially containing some kind of error. However, you will be asked only five questions. Don't spend time fixing errors for which there are no questions.

The Questions

There are three basic types of questions that you will be asked:

- **Revision questions:** These questions ask you to revise sentences or parts of sentences in much the same way as Improving Sentences questions do.
- **Combination questions:** These questions ask you to combine two or more sentences to improve the quality and/or flow of the paragraph.
- **Content questions:** These questions ask you about passage content, typically by asking you to insert a sentence before or after a paragraph.

Revision Questions

As we mentioned, these questions are very similar to Improving Sentences questions. Therefore, you can follow the same basic approach. One warning: There is normally no such thing as "No error" on Improving Paragraphs questions. Do not assume that (A) is merely a repeat of the given sentence.

Even though the sentence you are revising is provided for you, you may still need to go back to the passage to gain some context when trying to fix a sentence. Before going back, however, use POE. If you have spotted an error in the given sentence, cross off answers that don't fix it. Also, cross off answer choices that contain obvious errors. After doing some POE, go back and read a few sentences before and after the given sentence in the passage. This should be enough context for you to determine the best edit.

Try the following revision question, referring back to the sample passage.

---

37. In context, what is the best way to revise sentence 9 (reproduced below)?

    A thing to do was implement a recycling program.

    (A) Next, we needed to implement a recycling program.
    (B) Implementing a recycling program was a thing to do.
    (C) A recycling program needed to be implemented.
    (D) Implementing a program for recycling was the step that would be next.
    (E) A program would need to be implemented next for recycling.

Here's How to Crack It

The correct revision will be concise and unambiguous. It will also flow well. We can get rid of choices (B), (D), and (E) before going back to the passage. Choice (B) is as clunky as the given sentence; choices (D) and (E) are awkwardly written.

That leaves (A) and (C). Choice (C) is in the passive voice, which is a reason to be very wary of choosing it. But choice (A) also seems to have a problem: It starts with the word *Next*, and if we don't consider the surrounding context, that looks a little weird. But if we *do* consider the surrounding context, it makes perfect sense. Go back to line 7: "First, we needed to…" Oh, so this is a list! First we did this, and next we did that, and finally we did the other thing. All righty then. (A) it is.

Combination Questions

Combination questions are revision questions with a twist: You are working with two sentences instead of one. The sentences are almost always reprinted for you underneath the question. As with revision questions, go back to the passage to get context and a sense of flow first.

To combine sentences you will need to work with conjunctions. If the sentences are flowing in the same direction, look for an answer with words like *and*, *since*, *as well as*, etc. If the sentences seem to be flowing in opposite directions, look for trigger words in the answer choices such as *however*, *but*, *on the contrary*, etc.

Try the following question:

---

38. Which of the following represents the most effective way to combine sentences 20 and 21 (reproduced below)?

Reuse, recycle, renew. That's our school's new motto.

(A) Reuse, recycle, renew and you know our school's new motto.

(B) The new motto of our school is that: "Reuse, recycle, renew."

(C) "Reuse, recycle, renew" are the new motto of our school now.

(D) The new motto of our school is reusing, recycling, and renewing.

(E) "Reuse, recycle, renew" is our school's new motto.

Here's How to Crack It

First, the sentences are moving in the same direction. Your job is to find a clear, concise way to combine them. (A) and (B) are out because they are poorly worded. (C) is a trap: "Reuse, recycle, renew" *is* a motto. Don't be fooled into thinking you need a plural verb simply because there is no "and" in answer choice (C). Choice (D) changes the quoted portion, and therefore the meaning. ETS's answer is (E).

Try another:

---

36. Which of the following represents the best revision of the underlined portions of sentences 7 and 8 (reproduced below)?

First we needed to get students to become aware of the <u>problem. Educating was important</u>.

(A) problem for educating was important
(B) problem of educating. It was important
(C) problem to educate was important
(D) problem: education was important
(E) problem for education was important to us

Here's How to Crack It

Again, we have a same-direction combination going on. We need something that flows. (A) and (C) use the wrong prepositions, which slightly change the meaning of the sentence. Cross them off. (B) is as awkward or more awkward than the original sentence. (E) uses the wrong preposition and adds extra awkward stuff. ETS's answer is (D). The colon is a nice, neat way to continue a thought without using two sentences.

Content Questions

ETS will occasionally ask you a question regarding the content of the passage. These questions may ask:

1. Which sentence should immediately follow or precede the passage?
2. Which sentence should be inserted into the passage?
3. What is the best description of the passage as a whole?

If you are asked the third question, you will need to read the whole passage. However, you will more likely be asked one of the first two questions. To answer these, you will need to read the relevant paragraph.

Try this example using the sample passage from earlier in this section:

———————◯———————

35. Which of the following sentences, if added after
sentence 4, would best serve to link the first
paragraph to the second paragraph?

(A) Unfortunately, the environment suffered.
(B) Clearly, we had to make a change.
(C) Easy things are often not good for the
      environment.
(D) However, people can be very lazy.
(E) The school was against any change.

Here's How to Crack It

The question wants us to link the first two paragraphs together, which makes
sense only if there's currently a gap between them. So let's look for the gap. The
first paragraph is about the wasteful practices that used to be in vogue at this
writer's school. Then we hit the second paragraph and all of a sudden we find that
the writer has "volunteered to head up the conservation team." What conservation
team? Did a conservation team just drop out of the sky? Something's missing! It
looks like the link we need to make is between realizing that there are problems
and deciding to take action.

If we look at the choices, we find that (A), (C), and (D) all just talk more about the
problems with how people at the school dispose of their trash. Those choices don't
make the transition to taking action. For that matter, neither does (E), which hints
that trying to change the way students throw away their trash will be a futile effort.
Only (B) gets us from seeing the problem to doing something about it, so pick (B).

———————◯———————

Time Is of the Essence

Now, keep in mind that this is the end of a 30-minute section at the end of a
two-hour test. You may not have the time or the energy to do all the Improving
Paragraphs questions. Therefore, do the shorter, easier questions first. Then, if you
have the time, do the longer questions.

Drill 4

Try the following Improving Paragraphs drill to practice what you have learned. Answers can be found in Part III.

(1) Censorship in the media had been an extremely important issue throughout the twentieth century. (2) In the 1950s television programs and movies had to comply with codes that enforced strict standards of propriety. (3) Couples were shown sleeping in separate beds, and the concept of nudity or verbal profanity was unheard of. (4) In reaction to them, in the 1960s and 1970s the media abandoned the codes in favor of more realistic representations of relationships and everyday life. (5) Filmmakers and songwriters were able to express themselves more honestly and freely. (6) The idea that in the early 1960s the Rolling Stones had to change their lyrics from "let's spend the night together" to "let's spend some time together" seemed almost unlikely by the end of the decade.

(7) Yet in the mid-1980s a period of conservative reaction occurred, turning the cycle around. (8) Explicit song lyrics began to be censored. (9) Warning labels were added to the covers of albums. (10) The labels indicated that some of the language might be "offensive" to the consumer. (11) It is unfortunate that people feel the need to blame the media for societal problems instead of realizing that the media only brings to light the problems that already exist.

(12) Hopefully, our reactions will ultimately break free of all previous patterns. (13) Yet until this happens we must remain content to know that the good parts of the past, as well as the bad, repeat themselves.

35. In context, what is the best version of the underlined portion of sentence 1 (reproduced below)?

    Censorship in the media had been an extremely important issue throughout the twentieth century.

    (A) (as it is now)
    (B) was extremely
    (C) was an extremely
    (D) has been extreme as an
    (E) will be an extremely

36. Which of the following would be the best subject for a paragraph immediately preceding this essay?

    (A) The types of movies most popular in the 1950s
    (B) The changing role of the media over the last ten years
    (C) The ways in which the economy affects society's political views
    (D) The role of the media in European countries
    (E) The roots of media censorship

37. The author wishes to divide the first paragraph into two shorter paragraphs. The most appropriate place to begin a new paragraph would be

    (A) between sentences 1 and 2
    (B) between sentences 2 and 3
    (C) between sentences 3 and 4
    (D) between sentences 4 and 5
    (E) between sentences 5 and 6

38. What word could best replace "unlikely" in sentence 6?

    (A) strange
    (B) conventional
    (C) unpopular
    (D) inconceivable
    (E) unbearable

39. Which would be the best way to revise and combine the underlined portions of sentences 9 and 10 (reproduced below)?

    Warning labels were added to the covers of __albums__. __The labels indicated__ that some of the language might be "offensive" to the consumer.

    (A) albums, indicating
    (B) albums, which indicated
    (C) albums, and they indicated
    (D) albums, the indication being
    (E) albums, being indicative

Final Words of Wisdom

As with all the sections of the PSAT, don't be afraid to do some POE and guess. You will almost always be able to eliminate some answer choices, so always try to knock out the questions you know you can do in your first run through the questions. If you need a couple more points to reach your pacing goals or if you've started to answer the question but gotten stuck, eliminate whatever you can *quickly*, guess, and move on.

Summary

- About one-fifth of all Improving Sentences and Error ID questions are correct as is—(A) for Improving Sentences and (E) for Error ID.

- Resist using your ear to pick a right or wrong answer. You can use it to guide you toward possible errors, but you should always make the decision to keep or eliminate an answer choice based on grammar rules.

- Remember to use Plan A or Plan B on all Improving Sentences and Error ID questions, based on whether you spot an error immediately after reading the sentence.

- Verbs have to agree in number, be parallel, and be in the proper tense to be correct.

- Pronouns have to agree, be in the proper case, and not be ambiguous in order to be correct.

- Prepositions are always followed by a noun or pronoun and have to be idiomatically correct, meaning that some words go together just because.

- Comparisons must equate two (or more) things that can really be compared, use the correct comparison word based on whether the things being compared can be counted (*less* vs. *fewer*), and must use the correct words based on how many things are being compared (*more* vs. *most*).

- Modifiers must be placed directly next to the words they are modifying, so check to see that the placement of a modifier makes sense (and isn't "misplaced").

- Adjectives modify only nouns, whereas adverbs modify verbs, adjectives, or other adverbs.

- The test writers prefer active voice over passive voice, so if an answer choice says that something was done by someone, look for a better answer.

Chapter 11
Vocabulary

As you've seen, vocabulary can be an important issue in the Critical Reading sections of the PSAT, particularly in Sentence Completions. This chapter is intended to help you further develop your vocabulary.

How to Learn Vocabulary

First, let's talk about how NOT to learn vocabulary. Some people assume that you should take a dictionary, and learn each word, one at a time, starting with the letter *A*. This, of course, is not a very well thought-out plan. The kind of vocabulary that appears on the PSAT is actually a fairly narrow range of what is considered by the test writers to be those words that a well-educated college student should know. These are the words that are typically used by good writers of English prose, scholars, and scientists (when they're writing for the public and not in scientific jargon).

To help with learning vocabulary, it's extremely important that you carry a pocket dictionary with you all the time so you can look up unfamiliar words. You can find inexpensive paperback dictionaries at any used bookstore. Carry one with you from now until the test!

The Hit Parade

The Princeton Review's Hit Parade is a list of the words that commonly appear on the PSAT and SAT. It starts on page 203 of this book. This list is useful not only because some of these words are likely to appear on your test, but also because it shows you what *kinds* of words are typically tested on the PSAT and SAT. These are the sorts of words that you should pay particular attention to when you're doing your daily reading. Write them down and learn them!

Flash Cards

Some people like using flash cards as a way to help them learn vocabulary. Flash cards are useful, but be sure to write down not only the word and its definition, but also an example sentence in which you use that word. If you need help, ask a teacher, parent, or friend to help you come up with a sentence.

Some Daily Reading

While you are preparing for these tests, it's important that you get in the habit of reading. This will not only help you on the reading passages, but also will help you improve your vocabulary. Make sure to set aside 20–30 minutes *every day* to do some reading.

What should you read? Anything. Everything. Pick your favorite magazine or book. Ideally, read something that is above, but not too much above, your current reading level, but *read something every day*. While you're reading, circle any words that you don't understand, and look them up. Then add them to your list of words to learn. In fact, you should start a vocab journal and plan to update and maintain it from now until after the SAT, at least.

Using These Words

One great way to learn vocabulary is to be annoying. No kidding! Here's how you do it:

Pick 5–10 words each day. Write them down, along with their definitions, on a small note card, which you can refer to if your memory fails you. Now go about your daily business, but use these words every chance you get. Instead of *outgoing*, use the word *gregarious*. Instead of *funny*, use the word *mirthful*. You will really annoy your friends, but you will certainly learn those words.

Mnemonics

Another great technique for learning words is to find a mnemonic device. *Mnemonic* is from the Greek word *mneme*, which means "memory," so a mnemonic device is something that is so stupid or funny that it's unforgettable, and will help remind you of the meaning of a word. (By the way—what other common English word comes from that same Greek root *mneme*? We'll tell you in a minute.)

For instance, for the word *excavate*, which means "to make a hole by digging," you can think of the word *cave*. A cave is a hole underground and part of the word excavate.

How about another one? Let's try the word *paramount*, which means "of chief importance." You can remember this word because it's like a **mount**ain—it's the biggest and most important thing on the horizon.

Try making mnemonics for each of the following words:

prosaic

flagrant

clandestine

timorous

Once you've made your own mnemonics for the above words, read our examples on the following page.

Prosaic
Rebecca made a **prosaic mosaic**—it consisted of only one tile.

Flagrant
Burning the **flag** shows **flagrant** disrespect for the country.

Clandestine

The **clan** of spies planned a **clan**destine maneuver that depended on its secrecy to work.

Timorous

Tiny **Tim** was **tim**orous; he was afraid that one day a giant would crush him.

And the answer to the earlier question: What other common English word has the same root (*mneme*) as the word *mnemonic*? *Amnesia* (the prefix *a-* meaning "without," the word itself means "without memory").

If you want more help with mnemonics, check out some other books by The Princeton Review: *Word Smart, Word Smart II, Illustrated Word Smart, More Illustrated Word Smart,* and *How to Remember Everything.* All of them contain some great drills, visuals, or mnemonics to help you memorize more words.

The Hit Parade

Here is a list of the words most commonly found on the PSAT. We've grouped them by topic, so they'll be easier to memorize. Happy studying!

Pronunciation Guide

A is pronounced like the *a* in *hat*

AH is pronounced like the *a* in *father*

AI and AY are pronounced like the *a* in *game*

AW is pronounced like the *aw* in *law*

E is pronounced like the *e* in *hem*

EE is pronounced like the *e* in *me*

I and IH are pronounced like the *i* in *icky*

IE and Y (as a vowel) are pronounced like the *ie* in *lie*

J is pronounced like the *j* in *jam*

O is pronounced like the *o* in *home*

OO is pronounced like the *oo* in *boot*

OR is pronounced like the word *or*

OW is pronounced like the *ow* in *cow*

S is pronounced like the *s* in *sad*

U and UH are pronounced like the *u* in *hum*

ZH is pronounced like the *ge* in *garage*

WEEK 1

ARE YOU TALKIN' TO ME?

candid   KAN did
> *completely honest, straightforward*
>
> Candace's candidness overwhelmed her business colleagues, who were not used to such honesty.

conjecture   kun JEK chur
> *inference; guesswork*
>
> At this point, Kimaya's hypothesis about single-cell biorhythms is still conjecture; she doesn't have conclusive evidence.

didactic   die DAK tik
> *instructive*
>
> The tapes were entertaining and didactic; they both amused and instructed children.

euphemism   YOO fuh miz um
> *a mild, indirect, or vague term substituting for a harsh, blunt, or offensive term*
>
> "To pass away" is a common euphemism for dying.

extrapolate   ek STRAP uh layt
> *to infer or estimate by extending or projecting known information*
>
> Seeing the wrecked bike and his daughter's skinned knees, Heath extrapolated that she had had a biking accident.

incoherent   in ko HAIR unt
> *lacking cohesion or connection*
>
> Maury's sentences were so incoherent that nobody understood a word.

insinuate   in SIN yoo ayt
> *to introduce or communicate stealthily*
>
> Sean insinuated that Grace stole the arsenic, but he never came out and said it.

lucid   LOO sid

easily understood; clear

> Our teacher provides lucid explanations of even the most difficult concepts so that we can all understand them.

rhetoric   RET uh rik

the art of using language effectively and persuasively

> Since they are expected to make speeches, most politicians and lawyers are well versed in the art of rhetoric.

WHAT'S UP, TEACH?

acumen   AK yoo men

quickness, accuracy, and keenness of judgment or insight

> Judge Ackerman's legal acumen was so well regarded that he was nicknamed the "Solomon of the South."

adroit   uh DROYT

dexterous; deft

> An adroit balloon-animal-maker, Adrianna became popular at children's parties.

ascertain   as er TAYN

to find out, as through investigation or experimentation

> The private investigator had long suspected my dog; before long, he ascertained that Toto was indeed the murderer.

astute   uh STOOT

shrewd; clever

> Stewart is financially astute; he invests wisely and never falls for scams.

circumspect   SER kum spekt

careful; prudent; discreet

> Ned's circumspect manner makes him a wise appointment to the diplomatic corps.

disseminate   dis SEM uh nayt

   to scatter widely, as in sowing seed

     The news about Dave's embarrassing moment at the party disseminated quickly through the school; by the end of the day, everyone knew what had happened.

erudition   er yuh DISH un

   deep, extensive learning

     Professor Rudy's erudition was such that she could answer any question her students put to her.

husbandry   HUZ bun dree

   the application of scientific principles to agriculture, especially to animal breeding

     After years of practicing animal husbandry, Marsha's husband was able to create a breed of dog that actually walked itself.

pedantic   puh DAN tik

   excessively concerned with book learning and formal rules

     Pedro's pedantic tendencies prompted him to remind us constantly of all the grammatical rules we were breaking.

perspicacious   per spih KAY shus

   shrewd; clear-sighted

     Persephone's perspicacious mind had solved so many cases that the popular private investagator was able to retire.

pragmatic   prag MAT ik

   practical

     Never one for wild and unrealistic schemes, Matt took a pragmatic approach to research.

precocious   pre KO shus

   exhibiting unusually early intellectual aptitude or maturity

     Bobby Fisher's precocious intellect made him one of the world's best chess players before he could even drive.

prospectus   pro SPEK tus
formal proposal

> Before writing my thesis, I had to submit a detailed prospectus to the department for approval.

rudimentary   roo duh MEN tuh ree
basic; elementary; in the earliest stages of development

> Josh's rudimentary golf skills were easily overpowered by Tiger Woods's amazing performance on the green.

WHEN THE GOING GETS TOUGH

abstruse   ab STROOS
difficult to understand

> Abby found her professor's lecture on non-Euclidian geometry abstruse; she doubted anyone else in class understood it either.

callous   KAL us
emotionally hardened; unfeeling

> Callie's callous remark about her friend's cluttered room really hurt his feelings.

convoluted   kon vo LOO tid
intricate; complex

> The directions were so convoluted that we became hopelessly lost.

enigma   en IG ma
a puzzle, mystery, or riddle

> The emu was an enigma; you could never tell what it was thinking.

inscrutable   in SKROOT uh bul
difficult to fathom or understand; impenetrable

> The ancient poet's handwriting was so inscrutable that even the most prominent Latin scholars could not read the manuscript.

reticent   RET uh sint

> *inclined to keep silent; reserved*

>> Rosanna's reticent behavior caused the interviewer to think her incapable of conversing with other students.

staid   STAYD

> *unemotional; serious*

>> Mr. Estado was well known for his staid demeanor; he stayed calm even when everyone else celebrated the team's amazing victory.

CULTURAL ARTIFACTS

arcane   ar KAYN

> *known or understood by only a few*

>> The dusty archive includes an arcane treasure trove of nautical charts from the Age of Discovery.

assimilate   uh SIM uh layt

> *to absorb or become absorbed; to make or become similar*

>> Keisha assimilated so quickly at her new school that she was named head of the social committee a month after enrolling.

autonomy   aw TAHN uh mee

> *independence; self-determination*

>> Candice gained autonomy upon moving out of her parents' house into her own apartment.

cosmopolitan   koz mo PAHL i tun

> *worldly; widely sophisticated*

>> Inga was surprisingly cosmopolitan considering that she had never left her tiny hometown in Norway.

derivative   duh RIV uh tiv

> *something that comes from another source*

>> *Special Victims Unit* and *Criminal Intent* are derivatives of the original *Law & Order* drama series.

entourage   AHN ter azh

> *a group of attendants or associates; a retinue*

>> Top celebrities travel with extensive entourages, which often include security guards, assistants, stylists, managers, publicists, and more.

esoteric   es oh TAIR ik

> *intended for or understood by only a small group*

>> Esme's play is extremely esoteric; someone not raised in Estonia would find it difficult to follow.

gaffe   GAF

> *a clumsy social error; a faux pas*

>> Geoff committed the gaffe of telling his date that he'd gone out with her sister the night before.

idiosyncrasy   ID ee oh SINK ruh see

> *characteristic peculiar to an individual or group*

>> She had many idiosyncrasies, one of which was washing her socks in the dishwasher.

insular   IN suh ler

> *isolated; narrow or provincial*

>> The family was so insular that no one else could get near them.

orthodox   OR thuh doks

> *adhering to the traditional and established, especially in religion*

>> My father held an orthodox view of baseball; he believed that the field should be outside and made of real grass.

potentate   PO tun tayt

> *one who has the power and position to rule over others; monarch*

>> An omnipotent potentate is a person to be reckoned with; great power in the hands of a great leader is a powerful combination.

CAST OUT

castigate   **KAS tih gayt**

to scold, rebuke, or harshly criticize

Mr. Castile preferred not to castigate student misbehavior publicly; instead, he would quietly send the troublemaker to the principal's office.

censure   **SEN shur**

to issue official blame

In recent years the FCC has censured networks for the provocative antics of Super Bowl halftime acts; what goes on during the game, however, usually escapes the organization's notice.

denounce   **duh NOWNTS**

to condemn openly

In many powerful speeches throughout his lifetime, Martin Luther King, Jr. denounced racism as immoral.

reclusive   **ree KLOO siv**

seeking or preferring seclusion or isolation

Our neighbors were quite reclusive, hardly ever emerging from behind the closed doors of their home.

relinquish   **ree LING kwish**

to retire from; give up or abandon

Ricky relinquished his career in order to search for the source of the world's best relish.

renounce   **ree NOWNTS**

to give up (a title, for example), especially by formal announcement

Nancy renounced her given name and began selling records under the moniker "Boedicia."

vituperative   **vie TOOP ur uh tiv**

marked by harshly abusive condemnation

The vituperative speech was so cruel that the members left feeling completely abused.

THERE'S NO WAY AROUND IT

circumscribe   SER kum skryb
> *to draw a circle around; to restrict*
>
> The archeologist circumscribed the excavation area on the map.

contiguous   kun TIG yoo us
> *sharing an edge or boundary; touching*
>
> The continental United States consists of 48 contiguous states.

WEEK 2

I'LL BE THE JUDGE OF THAT!

conciliatory   kon SIL ee uh tor ee
> *appeasing; soothing; showing willingness to reconcile*
>
> After arguing endlessly with them for weeks, Connie switched to a more conciliatory tone with her parents once prom season arrived.

credible   KRED uh bul
> *capable of being believed; plausible*
>
> The shocking but credible report of mice in the kitchen kept Eddie up all night.

exonerate   eg ZON er ayt
> *to free from blame*
>
> Xena was exonerated of all charges.

incontrovertible   in kahn truh VERT uh bul
> *indisputable; not open to question*
>
> The videotape of the robbery provided incontrovertible evidence against the suspect—he was obviously guilty.

indict   in DITE
> *to officially charge with wrongdoing or a crime*
>
> President Nixon was indicted during the Watergate scandal.

litigious   luh TIJ us

   prone to engage in lawsuits

      Letitia was a litigious little girl; at one point, she tried to sue her dog.

partisan   PAR tiz un

   devoted to or biased in support of a party, group, or cause

      Today's partisan politics are so antagonistic that it's difficult to reach a successful compromise on any issue.

parity   PA ruh tee

   equality, as in amount, status, or value (antonym: disparity)

      The judges at the Olympics must score each athlete's performance with parity; such impartial treatment is hard since one always wants to root for one's own country.

rectitude   REK ti tood

   moral uprightness; righteousness

      Thanks to his unerring sense of fairness and justice, Viktor was a model of moral rectitude; his hometown even erected a statue in his honor.

remiss   ree MISS

   lax in attending to duty; negligent

      Cassie was remiss in fulfilling her Miss America duties; she didn't even come close to ending world hunger.

repudiate   ree PYOO dee ayt

   to reject the validity or authority of

      I repudiated the teacher's arguments about Empress Wu Zetian's reputation by showing him that the reports of her cruelty were from unreliable sources.

sanctimonious   sank ti MO nee us

   feigning piety or righteousness

      The sanctimonious scholar had actually been plagiarizing other people's work for years.

scrupulous   SKROO pyoo lus

principled, having a strong sense of right and wrong; conscientious and exacting

> Evan's scrupulous behavior began to annoy his friends when he called the cops on them for toilet papering their teacher's house.

solicitous   so LIS it us

concerned

> The parents asked solicitous questions about the college admissions officer's family.

sophistry   SAHF is tree

plausible but misleading or fallacious argument

> The professor's sophistry misled the sophomore into incorrect beliefs.

substantiate   sub STAN shee ayt

to support with proof or evidence; verify

> The argument was substantiated by clear facts and hard evidence.

veracity   vuh RA si tee

adherence to the truth; truthfulness

> Since Vera was known for her veracity, it came as a complete shock when her family found out she'd lied on her application.

vindicate   VIN dih kayt

to free from blame

> Mrs. Layton was finally vindicated after her husband admitted to the crime.

FLATTERY WILL GET YOU NOWHERE

cajole   kuh JOL

to urge with repeated appeals, teasing, or flattery

> The sweet-talking senior cajoled an impressionable junior into seeing *Lord of the Rings* for the tenth time.

chicanery   **chik AY ner ee**

trickery

The candidate accused his debate opponent of resorting to cheap chicanery to sway the electorate.

obsequious   **ob SEEK wee us**

fawning and servile

Kevin was so obsequious that even his teachers were embarrassed; as a result, his sucking up rarely led to better grades.

sycophant   **SIK uh fent**

insincere, obsequious flatterer

Siggie is such a sycophant; he slyly sucks up to his teachers and reaps the rewards of his behavior.

ONE PERSON CAN CHANGE THE WORLD

altruism   **AL troo iz im**

unselfish concern for the welfare of others; selflessness

Alta, a model of altruism, gave her movie ticket to someone who needed it more.

eminent   **EM uh nent**

distinguished; prominent

Emeril Lagasse is one of the most eminent chefs working today; every TV-watcher knows how well known and highly regarded he is.

empathetic   **em puh THET ik**

identification with and understanding of another's situation, feelings, and motives

Emily is one of my most empathetic friends; she can always relate to my emotions.

extol   **ek STOL**

to praise highly

Tollivan extolled the virtues of the troll while his teacher looked on amazed.

laudatory   **LAW duh tor ee**

full of praise

The principal's speech was laudatory, congratulating the students on their SAT scores.

magnanimous   **mag nan IM it ee**

courageously or generously noble in mind and heart

The magnanimous prince cared deeply for his country and its people.

philanthropic   **fil un THROP ik**

humanitarian; benevolent; relating to monetary generosity

Phil was a philanthropic soul, always catering to the needy and the underprivileged.

reciprocate   **ree SIP ro kayt**

to mutually take or give; to respond in kind

The chef reciprocated his rival's respect; they admired each other so much that they even traded recipes.

GET RID OF IT

defunct   **duh FUNKT**

no longer existing or functioning

The theory that the world was flat became defunct when Magellan sailed to the West and didn't fall off the earth.

eradicate   **er RAD i kayt**

to get rid of as if by tearing it up by the roots; abolish

Radcliffe did her best to eradicate the radishes from her farm.

expurgate   **ek spur GAYT**

to remove objectionable content before publication or release

The Chinese government expurgates nearly all obscene matter from the nation's Internet.

extirpate   **ek stir PAYT**

to destroy

While the family was on vacation, the termites practically extirpated the house.

quell   **KWEL**

    to put down forcibly; suppress

       Nell quelled the fight over the quiche by throwing it out the window—
       she had long given up on reasoning with her sisters.

raze   **RAYZ**

    to level to the ground; demolish

       It is difficult to raze a city building without demolishing other structures
       around it.

squelch   **SKWELCH**

    to crush as if by trampling; squash

       Sam wanted to keep squash as pets, but Quentin squelched the idea.

supplant   **suh PLANT**

    to usurp the place of, especially through intrigue or underhanded tactics

       The ants prepared to supplant the roaches as the dominant insect in the
       kitchen; their plan was to take the roaches by surprise and drive them
       out.

stymie   **STY mee**

    to thwart or stump

       Stan was stymied by the Sudoku puzzle; he just couldn't solve it.

IF YOU CAN'T SAY ANYTHING NICE

abase   **uh BAYS**

    to lower in rank, prestige, or esteem

       Bayard's withering restaurant review was an attempt to abase his former
       friend, the owner.

deride   **duh RIDE**

    to mock contemptuously

       Derrick was derided for wearing two different colored socks, but he
       couldn't help it—it was laundry day.

derogatory **duh RAH guh tor ee**

insulting or intended to insult

The unethical politician didn't just attack his opponent's views; he also made derogatory remarks about the other candidate's family and personal hygiene.

disparage **dis PAR uj**

to speak of negatively; to belittle

Wanda disparaged Glen by calling him a cheat and a liar.

effrontery **eh FRON ter ee**

brazen boldness; presumptuousness

The attorney's effrontery in asking such personal questions so shocked Esther that she immediately ran from the office.

ignominy **IG nuh mi nee**

great personal dishonor or humiliation; disgraceful conduct

Ignacio felt great ignominy after the scandal broke.

impugn **im PYOON**

to attack as false or questionable

Instead of taking the high road, the candidate impugned his opponent's character.

mar **MAR**

to damage, especially in a disfiguring way

The perfect day was marred by the arrival of storm clouds.

pejorative **puh JOR uh tiv**

disparaging, belittling, insulting

Teachers should refrain from using pejorative terms as *numbskull* and *jackass* to refer to other teachers.

vex **VEKS**

to annoy or bother; to perplex

Bex's mom was vexed when Bex was very vague about her whereabouts for the evening.

vindictive　　　　　　　　　　　　　　　　　　　**vin DIK tiv**

　　disposed to seek revenge; revengeful; spiteful

　　　Vincenzo was very vindictive; when someone hurt him, he responded by vigorously plotting revenge.

WEEK 3

OVERKILL

bombastic　　　　　　　　　　　　　　　　　　**bom BAS tik**

　　given to pompous speech or writing

　　　The principal's bombastic speech bombed in the eyes of the students; it only furthered their impression of him as a pompous jerk.

ebullience　　　　　　　　　　　　　　　　　　**eh BOO li ents**

　　intense enthusiasm

　　　A sense of ebullience swept over the lacrosse fans crowd when their team won the game.

exorbitant　　　　　　　　　　　　　　　　　　**eg ZOR bit int**

　　exceeding all bounds, as of custom or fairness

　　　I wanted to buy a Porsche, but the price was exorbitant, so instead I purchased a used mail truck.

exuberant　　　　　　　　　　　　　　　　　　**eg ZOO bur ent**

　　full of unrestrained enthusiasm or joy

　　　William was exuberant when he found out that he'd gotten into the college of his choice.

embellish　　　　　　　　　　　　　　　　　　**em BELL ish**

　　to ornament or decorate; to exaggerate

　　　One can never trust that Anwar's stories are realistic; his details are almost always embellished so that his experiences sound more interesting than they really are.

flagrant   FLAY grent
> *extremely or deliberately shocking or noticeable*
>> Burning the flag shows flagrant disrespect for the country.

gratuitous   gruh TOO uh tus
> *given freely; unearned; unnecessary*
>> The film was full of gratuitous sex and violence inessential to the story.

lavish (adj)   LAV ish
> *extravagant*
>> Lavanya's wedding was a lavish affair.

lugubrious   luh GOO bree yus
> *mournful, dismal, or gloomy, especially to an exaggerated or ludicrous degree*
>> Lucas's lugubrious eulogy for his pet lobster quickly became ridiculous.

opulent   OP yoo lent
> *displaying great wealth*
>> The ophthalmologist's opulent home was the envy of his friends; the crystal chandeliers, marble floors, and teak furniture must have cost a fortune.

ornate   or NAYT
> *elaborately decorated*
>> The wood carvings were so ornate that you could examine them many times and still notice things you had not seen before.

penchant   PEN chent
> *a strong inclination or liking*
>> Penny's penchant for chocolate-covered ants led her to munch on them all day.

redundant   ree DUN dint
> *needlessly repetitive*
>> The author's speech was terribly redundant, repeating the same phrases, saying the same thing over and over, and constantly reiterating the same point.

ubiquitous   yoo BIK wit us

being or seeming to be everywhere at the same time; omnipresent

Kenny had a ubiquitous little sister; wherever he turned, there she was.

THROUGH SOMEONE ELSE'S EYES

vicarious   vie KA ree us

felt or undergone as if one were taking part in the experience or feelings of another

Stan, who was never athletic but loved sports, lived vicariously through his brother, a professional basketball player.

vignette   vin YET

a short scene or story

The poodle vignette in my new film expresses the true meaning of Valentine's Day.

LOTS 'N' LOTS

amalgam   uh MAL gum

a combination of diverse elements; a mixture

The song was an amalgam of many different styles, from blues to hip hop to folk.

inundate   IN un dayt

to overwhelm as if with a flood; to swamp

The day after the ad ran, Martha was inundated with phone calls.

multifarious   mul ti FAYR ee us

diverse; various

The multifarious achievements of Leonardo da Vinci, ranging from architecture and painting to philosophy and science, are unparalleled in our century.

multiplicity   mul tuh PLI sit ee

state of being various or manifold; a great number

A multiplicity of views is essential to a healthy multicultural democracy.

IT'S GETTING BETTER ALL THE TIME

alleviate   **uh LEE vee ayt**

to ease a pain or burden

> Alvin meditated to alleviate the pain from the headache he got after taking the SAT.

ameliorate   **uh MEEL yor ayt**

to make something better; improve

> Winning a silver medal quickly ameliorated Amelia's angst at losing the gold.

beneficial   **ben uh FISH ul**

producing or promoting a favorable result; helpful

> According to my doctor, tea's beneficial effects may include reducing anxiety.

curative   **KYUR uh tiv**

able to heal or cure

> The aloe had a curative effect on my sunburn; within hours, the flaking had stopped.

palliative   **PAL lee uh tiv**

relieving or soothing the symptoms of a disease or disorder without effecting a cure

> Watching professional polo on TV became a palliative for the screaming child; it was the only thing that would quiet him.

therapeutic   **thair uh PYOO tik**

having or exhibiting healing powers

> The therapeutic air of the Mediterranean cured Thomas of his asthma.

MODEL BEHAVIOR

complement   KOM plem ent
    something that completes, goes with, or brings to perfection

      The lovely computer is the perfect complement to the modern furnishings in Abby's apartment.

epitome   ep IT o mee
    a representative or example of a type

      She is the epitome of selflessness; no matter how much or little she has, she always gives to others.

felicitous   fuh LIH sih tus
    admirably suited; apt

      Jamie Foxx made a felicitous speech when he won his Oscar.

LIAR, LIAR, PANTS ON FIRE

belie   bee LIE
    to misrepresent

      He smiled in order to belie his hostility.

debunk   duh BUNK
    to expose untruths, shams, or exaggerated claims

      The university administration debunked the myth that bunk beds are only for children by installing them in every dorm on campus.

dubious   DOO bee us
    doubtful; of unlikely authenticity

      Jerry's dubious claim that he could fly like Superman didn't win him any summer job offers.

duplicitous   doo PLIS uh tus
    deliberately deceptive

      The duplicitous man duplicated dollars and gave the counterfeits to unsuspecting vendors.

fabricate   FAB ruh kayt

to make up in order to deceive

Fabio fabricated the story that he used to play drums for Metallica; he has never actually held a drumstick in his life.

fallacy   FAL uh see

a false notion

The idea that there is only one college for you is a fallacy.

mendacious   men DAY shus

lying; untruthful

John's mendacious statements on the stand sealed his fate; he was found guilty of lying to the court about his role in the crime.

specious   SPEE shus

having the ring of truth or plausibility but actually false

Susie's specious argument seemed to make sense, but when I looked more closely, it was clearly illogical.

SITTIN' ON THE FENCE

ambiguous   am BIG yoo us

open to more than one interpretation

Big's eyes were an ambiguous color: in some lights they looked brown, and in others, green.

ambivalent   am BIV uh lint

simultaneously feeling opposing feelings; uncertain

Amy felt ambivalent about her dance class: On one hand, she enjoyed the exercise, but on the other, the choice of dances bored her.

apathetic   ap uh THET ik

feeling or showing little emotion

The apathetic students didn't even bother to vote for class president.

capricious   kuh PREE shus

impulsive and unpredictable

The referee's capricious behavior angered the players; he would call a foul for minor contact, but ignore elbowing and kicking.

equivocal   **e KWIV uh kul**

open to two or more interpretations and often intended to mislead; ambiguous
(antonym: unequivocal)

> The politician made so many equivocal statements during the scandal
> that no one could be sure what, if anything, he had admitted to.

erratic   **e RAT ik**

markedly inconsistent

> Erroll's erratic behavior made it difficult for his friends to predict what
> he would do in a given moment.

impetuous   **im PET choo us**

suddenly and forcefully energetic or emotional; impulsive and passionate

> Mr. Limpet was so impetuous that we never knew what he would do
> next.

impetus   **IM pit us**

an impelling force or stimulus

> A looming deadline provided Imelda with the impetus she needed to
> finish her research paper.

sporadic   **spo RAD ik**

occurring at irregular intervals; having no pattern or order in time

> Storms in Florida are sporadic; it's hard to predict when they're going
> to occur.

vacillate   **VA sil ayt**

to sway from one side to the other; oscillate

> The cook vacillated between favoring chicken and preferring fish; he
> just couldn't decide which to prepare.

whimsical   **WIM zi kul**

characterized by whim; unpredictable

> Egbert rarely behaved as expected; indeed, he was a whimsical soul
> whose every decision was anybody's guess.

I JUST CAN'T TAKE IT ANYMORE

flag   FLAG

to decline in vigor or strength; to tire; to droop

After several few days climbing mountains in pouring rain, our enthusiasm for the hiking trip began to flag.

jaded   JAY did

worn out; wearied

Jade's experiences had jaded her; she no longer believed that the junk stacked in her garage was going to make her rich.

WEEK 4

SHE'S CRAFTY

ingenuous   in JEN yoo us

lacking in cunning, guile, or worldliness (antonym: disingenuous)

Janine was so ingenuous that it was too easy for her friends to dupe her.

subterfuge   SUB ter fyoozh

a deceptive stratagem or device

The submarine pilots were trained in the art of subterfuge; they were excellent at faking out their enemies.

surreptitious   sir up TISH us

secretive; sneaky

Sara drank the cough syrup surreptitiously because she didn't want anyone to know that she was sick.

JUST A LITTLE BIT

dearth   **DERTH**

scarce supply; lack

There was a dearth of money in my piggybank; it collected dust, not bills.

modicum   **MAHD ik um**

a small, moderate, or token amount

A modicum of effort may result in a small score improvement; in order to improve significantly, however, you must study as often as possible.

paucity   **PAW sit ee**

smallness in number; scarcity

The struggling city had a paucity of resources and therefore a high level of poverty.

squander   **SKWAN der**

to spend wastefully

Kerri squandered her savings on shoes and wasn't able to buy her apartment.

temperate   **TEM per ut**

moderate; restrained (antonym: intemperate)

Temperate climates rarely experience extremes in temperature.

tenuous   **TEN yoo us**

having little substance or strength; shaky

Her grasp on reality is tenuous at best; she's not even sure what year it is.

I WILL SURVIVE

diligent   DIL uh jint

marked by painstaking effort; hard-working

With diligent effort, they were able to finish the model airplane in record time.

maverick   MAV rik

one who is independent and resists adherence to a group

In the movie *Top Gun*, Tom Cruise played a maverick who often broke rules and did things his own way.

mercenary   MUR sin air ee

motivated solely by a desire for money or material gain

During the war, Mercer was a mercenary; he'd fight for whichever side paid him the most for his services.

obstinate   OB stin it

stubbornly attached to an opinion or a course of action

Despite Jeremy's broken leg, his parents were obstinate; they steadfastly refused to buy him an XBox.

proliferate   pro LIF er ayt

to grow or increase rapidly

Because fax machines, pagers, and cell phones have proliferated in recent years, many new area codes have been created to handle the demand for phone numbers.

tenacity   te NAS uh tee

persistence

With his overwhelming tenacity, Clark was finally able to interview Brad Pitt for the school newspaper.

vigilant   VIJ uh lent

on the alert; watchful

The participants of the candlelight vigil were vigilant, as they had heard that the fraternity across the street was planning to egg them.

CONNECT THE DOTS

extraneous   **ek STRAY nee us**

irrelevant; inessential

The book, though interesting, had so much extraneous information that it was hard to keep track of the important points.

juxtapose   **JUK stuh pohz**

to place side by side, especially for comparison or contrast

Separately the pictures look identical, but if you juxtapose them, you can see the differences.

superfluous   **soo PUR floo us**

extra; unnecessary

If there is sugar in your tea, honey would be superfluous.

synergy   **SIN er jee**

combined action or operation

The synergy of hydrogen and oxygen creates water.

tangential   **tan JEN chul**

merely touching or slightly connected; only superficially relevant

Though Abby's paper was well written, its thesis was so tangential to its proof that her teacher couldn't give her a good grade.

I WRITE THE SONGS

aesthetic   **es THET ik**

having to do with the appreciation of beauty

Aesthetic considerations determined the arrangement of paintings at the museum; as long as art looked good together, it didn't matter who had painted it.

aural   **AW rul**

of or related to the ear or the sense of hearing

It should come as no surprise that musicians prefer aural to visual learning.

cacophony   kuh KAH fuh nee

discordant, unpleasant noise

Brian had to shield his ears from the awful cacophony produced by the punk band onstage.

dirge   DERJ

a funeral hymn or lament

The dirge was so beautiful that everyone cried, even those who hadn't known the deceased.

eclectic   uh KLEK tik

made up of a variety of sources or styles

Lou's taste in music is quite eclectic; he listens to everything from rap to polka.

incongruous   in KAHN groo us

lacking in harmony; incompatible

My chicken and jello soup experiment failed; the tastes were just too incongruous.

sonorous   SAHN ur us

producing a deep or full sound

My father's sonorous snoring keeps me up all night unless I close my door and wear earplugs.

strident   STRY dent

loud, harsh, grating, or shrill

The strident shouting kept the neighbors awake all night.

DUDE, THIS SUCKS!

debacle   duh BAHK ul

disastrous or ludicrous defeat or failure; fiasco

Jim's interview was a complete debacle; he accidentally locked himself in the bathroom, sneezed on the interviewer multiple times, and knocked over the president of the company.

debilitate   duh BIL i tayt

impair the strength of; weaken

Deb ran the New York City marathon without proper training; the experience left her debilitated for weeks.

tumultuous   tum UL choo us

noisy and disorderly

The tumultuous applause was so deafening that the pianist couldn't hear the singer.

IT'S ALL IN THE TIMING

anachronistic   ah nak ruh NIS tik

the representation of something as existing or happening in the wrong time period

I noticed an anachronism in the museum's ancient Rome display: a digital clock ticking behind a statue of Venus.

archaic   ar KAY ik

characteristic of an earlier time; antiquated; old

"How dost thou?" is an archaic way of saying "How are you?"

dilatory   DIL uh tor ee

habitually late

Always waiting until the last moment to leave home in the morning, Dylan was a dilatory student.

ephemeral uh FEM er ul

lasting for only a brief time

The importance of SAT scores is truly ephemeral; when you are applying, they are crucial, but once you get into college, no one cares how well you did.

redolent RED uh lint

fragrant; aromatic; suggestive

The aroma of apple pie wafted into my room, redolent of weekends spent baking with my grandmother.

temporal TEM per ul

of, relating to, or limited by time

One's enjoyment of a mocha latte is bound by temporal limitations; all too soon, the latte is gone.

WHO CAN IT BE NOW?

onerous O ner us

troublesome or oppressive; burdensome

The onerous task was so difficult that Ona thought she'd never get through it.

portent POR tent

indication of something important or calamitous about to occur; omen

A red morning sky is a terrible portent for all sailors—it means that stormy seas are ahead.

prescience PRE shens

knowledge of actions or events before they occur; foreknowledge; foresight

Preetha's prescience was such that people wondered if she was psychic; how else could she know so much about the future?

BOOORING

austere   **aw STEER**

without decoration; strict

The gray walls and bare floors of his monastery cell provided an even more austere setting than Brother Austen had hoped for.

banal   **buh NAL**

drearily commonplace; predictable; trite

The poet's imagery is so banal that I think she cribbed her work from *Poetry for Dummies.*

hackneyed   **HAK need**

worn out through overuse; trite

All Hal could offer in the way of advice were hackneyed old phrases that I'd heard a hundred times before.

insipid   **in SIP id**

uninteresting; unchallenging; lacking taste or savor

That insipid movie was so predictable that I walked out.

prosaic   **pro ZAY ik**

unimaginative; dull (antonym: poetic)

Rebecca made a prosaic mosaic consisting of identical, undecorated tiles.

soporific   **sah puh RIF ik**

inducing or tending to induce sleep

The congressman's speech was so soporific that even his cat was yawning.

vapid   **VAP id**

lacking liveliness, animation, or interest; dull

Valerie's date was so vapid that she thought he was sleeping with his eyes open.

WEEK 5

IT ALL CHANGES SO FAST

brevity   **BRE vi tee**

the quality or state of being brief in duration

Brevity = briefness. (You can't get any shorter than that!)

expedient   **ek SPEE dee ent**

appropriate to a purpose; convenient; speedy

It was more expedient to use FedEx than to use the post office.

transient   **TRAN zhent**

passing quickly in time or space

Jack Dawson enjoyed his transient lifestyle; with nothing but the clothes on his back and the air in his lungs, he was free to travel wherever he wanted.

FULL ON

augment   **awg MENT**

to make greater, as in size, extent, or quantity; to supplement

The model Angele Franju is rumored to have augmented her studies in chemistry with a minor in German literature.

bolster   **BOWL ster**

to hearten, support or prop up

The class bolstered Amelia's confidence; she had no idea she already knew so much.

burgeon   **BER jun**

to grow and flourish

The burgeoning Burgess family required a new house because its old one had only one bedroom.

copious   **KO pee us**

plentiful; having a large quantity

She took copious notes during class, using up five large notebooks.

distend   dis TEND

to swell out or expand from internal pressure, as when overly full

The balloon distended as it was filled with helium, much like Mike's stomach after Mike ate an entire turkey on Thanksgiving.

grandiose   gran dee OHS

great in scope or intent; grand

The party was a grandiose affair; hundreds of richly dressed guests danced the night away.

prodigious   pruh DIJ us

enormous

Steven Spielberg's prodigious talent has made him the most successful film producer and director of our time.

profundity   pro FUN di tee

great depth of intellect, feeling, or meaning

The actor's profundity surprised the director, who had heard that he was a bit of an airhead.

redouble   ree DUB ul

to make twice as great; to double

Rita redoubled her efforts to become president of her class by campaigning twice as hard as before.

scintillating   SIN til ay ting

brilliant

The writer's scintillating narrative diverted Izabel's attention away from her other guests.

DON'T MAKE WAVES

averse | uh VERS

strongly disinclined

Ava proved so averse to homework that she would break out in hives at the mere mention of it.

conspicuous | kun SPIK yoo us

easy to notice; obvious (antonym: inconspicuous)

The red tuxedo was conspicuous among all the classic black ones. What was he thinking?

demure | duh MYUR

modest and reserved

Muriel was the most demure girl in the class, always sitting quietly in the back of the room and downplaying any compliments she received.

diffidence | DIF uh dins

timidity or shyness

Lea's diffident nature often prevented her from speaking out in class.

docile | DAHS i ul

submissive to instruction; willing to be taught

The SAT class was so docile that the teacher wondered if she was in the right room.

innocuous | in NAHK yoo us

having no adverse effect; harmless

The plants were as innocuous as they looked; we suffered no ill effects from eating their leaves.

placid | PLAS id

calm or quiet; undisturbed

Lake Placid was the place to go for those in need of a quiet vacation.

quiescent | kwee ES sint

quiet, still, or at rest; inactive

Quinn's quiescent behavior made him an ideal roommate.

DO YOU AGREE?

concord   **KON kord**

agreement (antonym: discord)

The class was in concord about the necessity to perform *Hamlet*, rather than *King Lear*, in the spring show.

concur   **kun KUR**

to agree

The board concurred that the con artist who had stolen their money had to be convicted.

dogmatic   **dog MAT ik**

stubbornly attached to insufficiently proven beliefs

Avik was dogmatic in his belief that the power lines were giving his dog headaches.

fastidious   **fas TID ee us**

carefully attentive to detail; difficult to please

Kelly, always so fastidious, dramatically edited our group's report.

intransigence   **in TRAN zi jents**

refusal to moderate a position or to compromise

Jeff was so intransigent in his views that it was impossible to have a rational debate with him.

jocular   **JOK yoo ler**

characterized by or given to joking

Yung-Ji's jocular disposition helped him gain popularity.

meticulous   **muh TIK yoo lus**

extremely careful and precise

Since Kelly was so meticulous, we asked her to proofread our group's report.

OFFICER FRIENDLY

affable   AF uh bul

easy going; friendly

My mom always said that the key to being affable is the ability to make others laugh.

alacrity   uh LAK ruh tee

promptness in response; cheerful readiness; eagerness

I was so happy when I got the acceptance letter from the University of Alaska that I sprinted home with great alacrity to share the good news.

amiable   AY mee uh bul

friendly; agreeable; good-natured

Mr. Amis was so amiable that he let us call him "Big A."

benign   be NINE

kind and gentle

Uncle Ben is a benign and friendly man who is always willing to help.

sanguine   SAN gwin

cheerfully confident; optimistic

Harold's sanguine temperament kept him cheerful, even through somber times.

NASTY BOYS

belligerent   buh LIH jer int

eager to fight; hostile or aggressive

The prosecutor was reprimanded for his belligerent cross-examination of the witness, who had dissolved into tears.

byzantine   BIZ un teen

extremely complicated or devious

I gave up trying to understand the byzantine tax code and had an accountant file my taxes for me.

cantankerous   kan TANK er us

ill-tempered and quarrelsome; disagreeable

The dog hid under the tank as a result of the cat's cantankerous disposition.

contentious   kun TEN shus

quarrelsome

The contentious debate over science class content is increasingly making the news.

deleterious   dil uh TER ee us

having a harmful effect

It was only once he started his test that Murray realized the deleterious effects of one too many Red Bulls; he couldn't concentrate, and his hands were shaking so much he could barely write.

exacerbate   eg ZA ser bayt

to increase the severity, violence, or bitterness of; aggravate

Alan's procrastination problems were exacerbated by the monkeys who kept throwing bananas at him while he tried to concentrate.

flippant   FLIP ent

disrespectfully humorous or casual

Flap's flippant remarks to the teacher got him sent to the principal's office.

insolent   IN suh lint

insulting in manner or speech

The insolent prime minister stuck her tongue out at the queen.

nefarious   nuh FAYR ee us

flagrantly wicked; vicious

Dorothy's kindness and bravery triumphed over the nefarious antics of the Wicked Witch of the West.

pernicious   per NISH us

extremely or irrevocably harmful; deadly

The fertilizer's pernicious effects were not immediately obvious, but researchers became suspicious when all their petunias died.

rancorous   RANK er us

> *marked by bitter, deep-seated ill-will*

> They had such a rancorous relationship that no one could believe that they had ever gotten along.

repugnant   ree PUG nent

> *arousing disgust or aversion; offensive or repulsive*

> The pug's behavior at the dog park was repugnant, causing other dogs to avoid him altogether.

tawdry   TAW dree

> *gaudy and cheap*

> Connor's tawdry attire embarrassed his snooty host.

EARTH, WIND, AND FIRE

arboreal   ar BOR ee ul

> *relating to or resembling a tree or trees*

> The Rocky Mountain National Forest will celebrate its arboreal splendor with an Arbor Day concert.

invocation (n)   in vo KAY shun

> *a call (usually upon a higher power) for assistance, support, or inspiration*

> The group invoked the god of war as their protector on the field of battle.

stratify   STRAT i fy

> *to layer or separate into layers*

> Jonas studied the stratified bedrock and was able to see which time periods went with which layers.

variegated   VAR ee ih gay tid

> *having streaks, marks, or patches of a different color or colors; varicolored*

> The wood's markings were so variegated that Mr. Vargas assumed they had been painted on.

verdant   VUR dent

> *green with vegetation*

> The garden was verdant after the rain.

Summary

- To learn vocabulary for the PSAT, it's best to take things in daily doses.

- Flash cards are a great way to learn vocabulary; customize yours with funny sentences and mnemonics to help you remember words you have trouble with.

- For more help with vocabulary, check out the *Word Smart* series of books. They're all focused on the words found most often on standardized tests such as the PSAT.

Part III
Drill Answers and
Explanations

CHAPTER 7

Drill 1 Answers

Question	Answer	Explanation
1	r	Examples: –7, 0, 1, 8
2	d	Examples: .5, 2, 118
3	k	Examples: –.5, –2, –118
4	f	Examples: –4, 0, 10
5	p	Examples: –5, 1, 17
6	a	Examples: *Factors* of 12 are 1, 2, 3, 4, 6, and 12. Factors of 10 are 1, 2, 5, and 10.
7	i	Examples: *Multiples* of 12 include –24, –12, 0, 12, 24, and so on. Multiples of 10 include 20, –10, 0, 10, 20, 30, and so on.
8	o	Examples: 2, 3, 5, 7, 11, and so on. There are no negative *prime numbers*, and 1 is not prime.
9	e	Examples: 3 and 4 are *distinct* numbers. –2 and 2 are also distinct.
10	j	Examples: In the number 274, 2 is the *digit* in the hundreds place, 7 is the digit in the tens place, and 4 is the digit in the ones place.
11	b	Examples: –1, 0, 1, and 2 are *consecutive* numbers. Be careful—sometimes you will be asked for *consecutive even* or *consecutive odd* numbers, in which case you would use just the odds or evens in a consecutive list of numbers.
12	n	Examples: 6 is *divisible* by 2 and 3, but not by 4 or 5.
13	l	Examples: When you divide 26 by 8, you get 3 with a *remainder* of 2 (2 is left over). When you divide 14 by 5, you get 2 with a remainder of 4 (4 is left over).
14	g	Examples: When you add 2 and 3, you get a *sum* of 5. When you add –4 and 1, you get a sum of –3.
15	c	Examples: When you multiply 2 and 3, you get a *product* of 6. When you multiply –4 and 1, you get a product of –4.
16	m	Examples: When you subtract 2 from 3, you get a *difference* of 1. When you subtract –4 from 1, you get a difference of 5.
17	q	Examples: When you divide 2 by 3, you get a quotient of $\frac{2}{3}$. When you divide –4 by 1, you get a quotient of –4.
18	h	Examples: The absolute value of –3 is 3. The absolute value of 41 is 41.

Drill 2 Answers

Question	Answer	Explanation
a	3, 5, 7	
b	1, 2, 5, 10	
c	2, 5	
d	1, 2, 3, 4, 6, 8, 12, 16, 24, 48	
e	2, 2, 2, 2, 3	
f	6, 12, 18, 24, 30, 36, 42	
g	4, 8, 12, 16, 20, 24, 28	
h	42	
i	5 and 6 or 6 and 5	
j	15 and 2 or 2 and 15	
1	C	51 can be divided evenly by 3 with no remainder.
2	E	The thousandths place is the third to the right of the decimal.
3	C	27 can be divided by 3 and 9.
4	C	The three consecutive integers must be 6, 7, and 8. The least of them is 6.
5	B	If the numbers are 2, 4, 6, 8, and 10, then 8 + 10 = 18 and 2 + 4 = 6. The last two numbers are 12 greater than the first two. (Don't forget that the numbers have to be consecutive and even!)
6	A	While this problem can be solved by listing multiples of 3 and 14, you end up having to list a lot of multiples to get to the answer! When this happens, you can factor instead. 14 can be factored into 2×7, so any number divisible by 3 and 14 must be divisible by 3, 2, and 7. That means it must be divisible by 6 since $2 \times 3 = 6$. Thus, choice (A) is the correct answer.

Drill 3 Answers

Question	Answer	Explanation
a	3^5	
b	3^1	
c	3^6	
d	x^8	
e	x^4	
f	x^{12}	
3	A	If $3^4 = 9^x$, then $81 = 9^x$. Therefore, $x = 2$. You could also rewrite 3^4 as $3 \times 3 \times 3 \times 3 = 9 \times 9$.
5	B	If $(3x)^3 = 315$, then by the rules of MADSPM, $3x = 15$, and $x = 5$.
11	E	Let's take the two equations separately, using the rules of MADSPM. If $x^y \times x^6 = x^{54}$, then $y + 6 = 54$, and $y = 48$. If $(x^3)^z = x^9$, then $3z = 9$, and $z = 3$. Now we know that $y = 48$ and $z = 3$, so $y + z = 51$.

Drill 4 Answers

Question	Answer	Explanation
a	36	
b	24	
c	20	
d	16π	
e	8π	
f	10, 5	
g	30	
h	22	
i	6	
j	6	
k	−1	
17	D	Because this is a square, the two sides are equal. Therefore, $2x + 1 = x + 3$. Solve for x, and you get that x must be 2. Therefore, a side equals $x + 3$ or $2x + 1 = 5$, so the area equals 25.

Question	Answer	Explanation
10	E	Here are four lines; a and b are parallel, d intersects a and b, and c does not intersect both parallel lines. In statement I, angles 1 and 5 do not have to be equal because a side of angle 1 is line c, which has nothing to do with the parallel lines. Thus, the angles in statement I do not have to be equal, and you can eliminate (B). The angles in statement II have to be equal because angles 2 and 7 are opposite angles (two angles made up of the same two lines) and opposite angles must be equal. Eliminate (A) and (D). The angles in statement III must be equal because angles 3 and 9 are made up of the same line (line d) and one of the parallel lines. In fact, 3, 6, 5, and 9 are all the same "small angle," so eliminate (C). Therefore, statements II and III are true, and the correct answer is (E).
19	B	This question involves simultaneous equations, so the trick is to stack and combine them. You're being asked for $x + y$, so even getting the same number of x variables as y variables would be useful. Let's see what happens when we add the equations: $x + 2y = 12$ $2x + \ y = \ 9$ $3x + 3y = 21$ Now all we need to do is divide both sides of the equation by 3 to get the expression we're being asked for, $x + y$, and we end up with the answer, 7.
10	B	When we simplify the fractional exponent, we get $\sqrt{x^5} = 8x$. Squaring both sides gives us $x^5 = 64x^2$. We can divide by x^2 on each side to get $x^3 = 64$ (remember your MADSPM rules!). Finally, taking the cube root of both sides gives us $x = 4$.

Drill 5 Answers

Question	Explanation
33	Because the triangle is isosceles, with $AB = BC$, we know that angles A and C must have the same measure. So angle A must also be 40 degrees. Angles A and C have a combined measure of 80 degrees, and we need 180 total degrees in the triangle. Therefore, x must measure 100.

Question	Explanation
34	If five consecutive integers have a sum of 100, they must be 18, 19, 20, 21, and 22. The next four consecutive integers are 23, 24, 25, and 26. Their sum is 98.
35	Because $5x^2 = 125$, we know that $x^2 = 25$ and $x = 5$. Therefore, $5x^3 = 5 \times 125 = 625$.
36	Remember your prime factor tree? The prime factors of 140 are 2, 2, 5, and 7, but the *distinct* prime factors are 2, 5, and 7. Add them up and you get 14.

CHAPTER 8

Drill 1 Answers

Question	Answer	Explanation
12	E	Variables in the answer choices? Absolutely! So let's plug in our own numbers: for x (Jodi's account), plug in $18 (hey, who said Jodi had to be rich?). With $18 in her account, $\frac{1}{6}$ for rent is $3 and the car payment is also $3. Subtract that from the $18, and Jodi's got $12 left in her account. Now we have to plug in for y (the amount Jodi deposits); let's make that $8, bringing her account balance to $20. Well, she now purchases a set of knives for $10 ($\frac{1}{2}$ the amount in her account) and has $10 left. Go through all of the answer choices, using $x = 18$ and $y = 8$ and see which one gives you $10. The only one that works is (E).
4	D	Let's plug in a number for the amount of homework Martha has. Let's say she has 12 pages of work to do. If she does half of this on Tuesday, she does 6 pages, and there are 6 pages left. If, on Wednesday, she does one-third of the remaining 6 pages, that means she does 2 more pages. So she has 4 pages left over from the original 12. What fractional part is left over? $\frac{4}{12}$ or $\frac{1}{3}$.
14	D	Let's pick numbers for a, b, and c such that $a = \frac{b}{c^2}$. We can pick $4 = \frac{16}{2^2}$. Now the question becomes, what is $\frac{1}{b^2}$ or $\frac{1}{16^2}$? The answer is $\frac{1}{256}$. When you work through all of the answer choices using $a = 4$, $b = 16$, and $c = 2$, which choice says this? Choice (D) does.
12	B	Let's pick a number for p. How about 2? Now the problem reads $\dfrac{\frac{1}{8}}{2(2)} =$ and the answer is $\frac{1}{2}$. Which choice says $\frac{1}{2}$? When you plug $p = 2$ into the answers, (B) turns out to be right.

Drill 2 Answers

Question	Answer	Explanation
8	C	Let's begin by plugging in the middle number, 3, for x. Does $3^5 = 243$? Yes. So the answer is (C).
14	D	If we try plugging in (C), $\frac{1}{4}$, for x, the equation becomes $\frac{6}{4} + 4 = 5$, which is false. If we try plugging in (D), $\frac{1}{2}$, for x, the equation becomes $\frac{12}{4} + 2 = 5$, which is true.
15	B	This is another great example of Plugging In. Let's plug in a number for a. How about 90, just to make the math easy? If $a = 90$, then the other angle inside the triangle must be equal to 60. Therefore, b must be equal to 120. What choice says 120, remembering that $a = 90$? (B) does.

Drill 3 Answers

Question	Answer
a	90
b	320
c	6
d	$x = 8$
e	120
f	108
g	10%
h	$\frac{2,600}{18,600}$ = approximately 14%
i	40
4	210

Question	Answer	Explanation
11	D	60% of 80 translates as $\dfrac{60}{100} \times 80$, which is the same as 48. So the problem now reads: 48 is the same as 40% of what number? We can translate this question as $48 = \dfrac{40}{100}x$. Then we solve for x, which equals 120, which is choice (D).
14	D	50% of the adults = 15, and 80% of the children = 16, so 31 total people went swimming. 31 out of 50 is 62%.

CHAPTER 9

Drill 1 Answers

Question	Answer	Explanation
a	180	
b	150	
c	$x = 135$, $y = 45$, $z = 135$	
d	180	
e	80	
f		
4	A	We know that the third angle in the triangle with 45 and x must be 110. Because the other two angles in the triangle with x are 45 and 110, then x must be 25.
6	D	We know that the three angles labeled x are on a straight line and, therefore, must make 180. Since $3x = 180$, $x = 60$. Because the unlabeled angle is opposite an x, it too must be 60. And 60, y, and 40 lie on the same line, so $60 + y + 40 = 180$. Therefore, y must be 80.
13	C	If the area of the square $ABFE$ is 25, then each of its sides must be 5. Since BF is 5, and the area of triangle BCF is 10, then side CF must be 4, making EC equal to 9. Since ECD has one angle that is 90, and one angle that is 45, the other angle must be 45. This makes ECD an isosceles triangle. If EC is 9, so is ED.

Drill 2 Answers

Question	Answer	Explanation
14	C	Because there are 5 kinds of ice cream and 3 toppings to choose from, the number of different sundaes will be 5 × 3, or 15.
15	B	The number of possible combinations is the product of the number of things Isabel can choose from: in this case, 3 different salads × 5 different main dishes × 2 different dessert options = 30 possible combinations.
16	B	The total number of socks in the drawer is 6 + 6 + 8 = 20. The number of socks we want (the red ones) is equal to 8, so the chance of drawing a red sock is 8 out of 20, which reduces to $\frac{2}{5}$.
8	C	This question asks in how many different orders can Jennifer visit 4 cities. So we're really *arranging* the cities from first to last, which means this is a permutation. We have four slots to fill, corresponding to the cities she visits first, second, third, and fourth. _____ × _____ × _____ × _____ She has 4 options for which city to visit first, then 3 options for the second slot, then 2, and then 1 for the final slot. 4 × 3 × 2 × 1 = 24, so the correct answer is (C).
17	C	The total number of marbles is 8 + 6 + 10 + 1 = 25. The number of marbles that are blue or green is 8 + 6 = 14. Therefore, the chance of drawing either a blue or a green is 14 out of 25.

CHAPTER 10

Drill 1 Answers

Question	Explanation
1	*Over* is the preposition, and *the bridge* is the object.
2	*Beyond* is the preposition, and *the green* is the object.
3	*With* is the preposition, and *the other reference books* is the object.
4	*To* is the preposition, and *her* is the object. Be careful—*to* also appears in this sentence in front of the verb *return,* but it's not being used as a preposition. *To return* is the whole verb; if *to* were being used as a preposition, it would be followed by a noun. (A verb like *to peel, to writhe,* or *to expire* is said to be in the *infinitive* form.)

Drill 2 Answers

Question	Answer
1	to
2	of
3	for
4	of
5	about, for, by
6	by
7	over
8	to
9	from
10	No preposition is needed after considered.

Drill 3 Answers

Question	Answer	Explanation
1	C	One thing that splits the answer choices is the *were* versus *was*; it's not easy to see because it's in the middle of each choice, but it is there. *Neither* follows the same rules as *either* when connecting two subjects: The second subject determines whether we need a singular or plural verb. *The superintendent* is singular, so *was* is correct, and we can eliminate (A) and (B). Of the remaining answer choices, we can eliminate (D) because it adds in the word *of* unnecessarily, and we can eliminate (E) because when *neither* is used, it should always be followed by *nor*, not *or*. That leaves (C) as our best answer.
2	D	As written, the sentence lacks a verb, so it's not a sentence at all, but a fragment. Get rid of (A) and anything else that repeats this error, which rules out choices (B), (C), and (E), so the answer is (D), the only choice that contains a verb.
3	C	The word *but* in the underlined portion indicates a change of direction, but that doesn't make sense in the sentence. Eliminate (A). (B) is out because *where* can only refer to a location. (D) has *being*, which nearly always makes a sentence awkward and wordy. Cross it out. (E) doesn't makes sense with the meaning of the sentence and uses a comma incorrectly to connect what should be two separate sentences. Eliminate it. (C) contains no errors and has the right meaning, indicating that the physical recovery was contingent upon the psychological one.

Question	Answer	Explanation
4	E	If you don't spot an error right off the bat, look at the answer choices. One main difference is the form of the word *master*. Answer choices (A), (B), and (C) aren't parallel with the verb *to learn*, so we can eliminate those. (D) changes the meaning of the sentence by using *simply* instead of *simple*, so it's gone too. (E), the best answer, keeps the verbs parallel and doesn't create any new errors.
5	B	The original sentence is trying to connect two separate sentences with a comma, so (A) is wrong. (C) is constructed in a very confusing way, leaving an *it* at the end that doesn't clearly refer to one noun, so it can be eliminated. In choice (D), the phrase between the commas is a complete sentence, so it needs to be marked off with a semicolon or period instead of a comma. Choice (E) says *when he was Jackie Robinson*, which is nonsense (unless the question is about reincarnation). (B) is straightforward and doesn't introduce new grammatical errors, so it is the best answer.
6	B	The *they* in the underlined portion doesn't agree with *A well-organized person*, so (A) is out. (B) doesn't appear to have any new problems and it fixes the pronoun agreement error, so we can keep it. (C), (D), and (E) fix the pronoun agreement error, but are needlessly wordy, so (B) is correct.
7	E	The original sentence contains a pronoun agreement problem, because *it* is singular and the *folk songs* it refers to is plural. Get rid of (A). (C) uses the wrong conjunction, as we should have a change in direction, rather than the same direction. (D) changes the intended meaning of the original. (B) and (E) both look all right grammatically, but (B) is passive, so (E) is the right answer because ETS likes the active voice better.
8	A	The answer choices again provide great places to start if an error isn't immediately apparent. When a sentence uses *not only*, it must be followed with *but also*, so answer choices (C) and (D) are out. One difference in the remaining answer choices is the form of the verb *encourage*. It should be parallel to the verb *enhance*, so (B) can be eliminated. (E) uses *them* to refer to *a child*, which is a mismatch, leaving (A) as the best answer.
21	A	The verb *was* is singular, but its subject is *CD*, an abbreviation for the phrase "compact disc," which is singular. Thus, we have a subject/verb agreement error in (A).
22	E	There is no error in the sentence.
23	E	There is no error in the sentence. Remember, ETS likes to use *none* as a singular pronoun, so *is* agrees.
24	B	*You* and *I* are objects of the preposition *between*, so they must be in the object case. *I* is subject case, so it is erroneous and (B) is the best answer.
25	A	The past perfect verb *had looked* doesn't match with the other tenses in the sentence, and there's no reason to use the past perfect since we don't have another action in the past. (A) is the error.

Question	Answer	Explanation
26	B	*Splendid* is an adjective and it's being used to modify *worked,* a verb. An adverb, such as *splendidly,* would be better. The correct answer is (B).
27	C	*Abide with* is incorrect; the correct idiom is *abide by.* (C) is the correct answer.
28	B	*Where* can only be used to describe a location, and an announcement is not a location. *That* would be better, so (B) is the best answer.
29	C	The present perfect *has cast* is not necessary, because there is no continuous action. The correct form is the simple past *cast,* so the correct answer is (C).

Drill 4 Answers

Question	Answer	Explanation
35	C	Because there's no event in the past that this sentence comes before, past perfect cannot be correct. Let's eliminate (A). (D) and (E) completely change the meaning of the sentence (and when we get some context from the passage, we can see that this paragraph is a discussion of censorship in the past), so they are gone. (B) leaves out an important word, *an,* which makes the sentence not make sense, so (C) is the best answer.
36	E	This essay follows a chronological order in its discussion of media censorship, so it would make the most sense to precede it with something that comes before the censorship of the 1950s. Therefore, (E) is the most logical choice.
37	C	Sentence 4 changes direction, because it starts talking about a reaction to the standards described in the first three sentences. This change of topic makes (C) the best answer.
38	D	This question can be done just like a Vocab-in-Context or Sentence Completion question. Reading sentences 5 and 6 for context, we learn that artists were expressing themselves very freely in reaction to earlier codes of censorship, so we can replace *unlikely* with something like *unthinkable.* (D) is the closest answer.
39	A	Remember that there is no "correct as is" unless explicitly stated in the answer choices. (D) and (E) add *being,* which is awkward. (C) includes the pronoun *they,* which is ambiguous because it could refer to either the albums or the warning labels. (B) also doesn't make clear whether it was the albums or the labels that indicated something. (A) is the best choice.

Part IV
The Princeton Review Practice Tests and Explanations

Chapter 12
Practice Test 1

SECTION 1

Time — 25 minutes
24 Questions

Directions: For each question in this section, select the best answer from among the choices given and fill in the corresponding oval on the answer sheet.

Each sentence below has one or two blanks, each blank indicating that something has been omitted. Beneath the sentence are five words or sets of words labeled A through E. Choose the word or set of words that, when inserted in the sentence, <u>best</u> fits the meaning of the sentence as a whole.

Example:

Medieval kingdoms did not become constitutional republics overnight; on the contrary, the change was -------.

(A) unpopular (B) unexpected (C) advantageous
  (D) sufficient (E) gradual

1. Though many people are willing to ------- saving the environment when speaking in public, they are often not willing to ------- their lifestyles to help protect the earth.

   (A) promote . . maintain
   (B) condone . . justify
   (C) advocate . . alter
   (D) denounce . . adjust
   (E) champion . . substantiate

2. Due to his ------- personality, Prince Klemens von Metternich dominated the Congress of Vienna after the defeat of Napoleon.

   (A) amiable (B) pleasant (C) commanding
    (D) duplicitous (E) sympathetic

3. The floor of the forest is enlivened by ------- hues whenever the lush canopy is ------- by the strong rays of the sun.

   (A) vibrant . . blemished
   (B) muted . . overwhelmed
   (C) threatening . . enveloped
   (D) mellow . . blanketed
   (E) vivid . . pierced

4. The reclusive nature of the iguana helps to explain the longstanding ------- of fruitful investigations of its behavior in the wild.

   (A) constancy (B) notoriety (C) necessity
    (D) paucity (E) probity

5. The aim of the governor's plan was to make more housing available for middle-income families, but unfortunately she only ------- the problem by making such housing even more scarce.

   (A) repealed (B) exacerbated (C) abolished
    (D) hoisted (E) ingratiated

6. Many people consider Dana ------- because of her friendly and honest manner, but she is actually a ------- negotiator.

   (A) trustworthy . . relaxed
   (B) gullible . . shrewd
   (C) taciturn . . decisive
   (D) vigilant . . lenient
   (E) eccentric . . secluded

7. When jazz was first introduced to Europe, many musicians were greatly ------- it and tried to ------- its free-form style.

   (A) drawn to . . emulate
   (B) impressed by . . reject
   (C) attracted to . . originate
   (D) opposed to . . adopt
   (E) afraid of . . accept

8. The senator's aide claimed that even though the United States was established by rebellion, it is now inclined to view ------- in other nations with -------.

   (A) reactionaries . . adoration
   (B) misers . . disdain
   (C) insurgents . . animosity
   (D) autocrats . . malevolence
   (E) revolutionaries . . indifference

GO ON TO THE NEXT PAGE

The passages below are followed by questions based on their content; questions following a pair of related passages may also be based on the relationship between the paired passages. Answer the questions on the basis of what is <u>stated</u> or <u>implied</u> in the passage and in any introductory material that may be provided.

Questions 9-10 are based on the following passage.

The Oulipo, short for *Ouvroir de Littérature Potentielle*, is a literary group that was founded in Paris in 1960. It has met for monthly meetings without fail for over forty years.
Line The products of this group are not the novels or short stories
5 that other writing groups churn out. Rather, the business of the Oulipo is to collaboratively produce "constraints," or procedures, usually mathematical in nature, which must be followed in constructing a text. Although it might seem like following rules would limit what is possible to write,
10 these constraints function as a recipe for anyone to produce interesting, if not always sensible, texts. Among Oulipian inventions are many methods of word replacement; ways of restricting certain words or letters of the alphabet; and various methods of combining texts. Following these
15 techniques is not so different from using the centuries-old rules for haikus or sonnets. That poems, novels, and stories are actually created using the Oulipo's methods is almost beside the point. The group considers its product to be the *potential* writing that might be created using its methods.

9. The author brings in the examples of the haiku and the sonnet in order to

(A) create a rhythmic flow in the text of the passage
(B) point out that the Oulipo's methods are completely unoriginal
(C) demonstrate the potential writing produced by Oulipo's "constraints"
(D) connect a new way of writing with long-practiced traditions
(E) indicate the international demographic of the Oulipo

10. The use of the phrase "churn out" in sentence 3 implies that the author

(A) is unenthusiastic about the work of some literature groups
(B) has little use for the writing methods of the Oulipo
(C) is placing the narrative in a bucolic setting
(D) demands tremendous production from her writing group
(E) is disgusted at the training received at writing schools

Questions 11-12 are based on the following passage.

The Gulf of Tonkin Resolution, passed on August 7, 1964, empowered President Lyndon Johnson to resolve a brewing conflict with the North Vietnamese using whatever means he deemed necessary. Five days prior to Congress's
Line
5 approval of the resolution, the U.S.S. *Maddox*, a naval destroyer, was patrolling the waters in the Gulf of Tonkin near Hon Me, a North Vietnamese island. Three North Vietnamese torpedo boats encountered the U.S.S. *Maddox*, forcing the American vessel to flee. Two days later, the
10 U.S.S. *Maddox* returned to the Gulf of Tonkin accompanied by the U.S.S. *Turner Joy*, another naval destroyer. Suspiciously, that evening the *Turner Joy* picked up three high-speed vessels on its radar, but the *Maddox* did not. The U.S.S *Turner Joy* sought and attacked these ships.
15 Some have hypothesized that President Johnson, who had been quite vocal about the need for an increased military presence in the area, may have manufactured this crisis, but there is no evidence to support such claims.

11. The structure of the passage could best be described as the presentation of a historical event that is

(A) elaborated upon and a possible controversy downplayed
(B) explained, and its repercussions enumerated
(C) cited, and the character of one participant attacked
(D) noted, and its cultural significance elaborated upon
(E) explained, and its validity questioned

12. The argument that President Johnson did not have any inappropriate involvement with the Gulf of Tonkin incident would be best supported by

(A) a statement from crewmen on the U.S.S. *Maddox* stating that they did not see any high-speed vessels the night of August 4th
(B) a report stating that many destroyers at that time had difficulty locating and tracking high-speed vessels
(C) several North Vietnamese soldiers testifying that they were not in the Gulf of Tonkin on the night in question
(D) a report stating that the U.S.S. *Maddox* had no mechanical problems with its radar
(E) a poll of Americans stating that the majority believed President Johnson

GO ON TO THE NEXT PAGE ➡

Questions 13-24 are based on the following passages.

The process of changing wild animals into tame ones is known as domestication, an important development in the course of human cultural history. Two reasons for the domestication of animals are explored here.

Passage 1

The geographer Eduard Hahn (1896), in a series of writings at the turn of the century, posed the basic questions involved in the study of the domestication of cattle. These are the questions still raised today, and they are still answered by culture historians substantially in the way he answered them. Hahn pointed to the exceptional position of cattle among animals that have been domesticated. In the case of some animals, domestication may have come about spontaneously. For example, the ancestor of the dog as well as that of the domestic pig probably, as scavengers, sought out man, and gradually man assumed the leadership in the relationship. One may indeed ask, "Who then initially domesticated whom?" Domestication, again, may have been furthered by instincts which make us cherish our own infants and which are aroused by young mammals of somewhat similar bodily proportions. Piglets and dog pups are nursed by women in some primitive societies. But the domestication of wild cattle cannot be explained as an inadvertent process. Wild cattle presumably did not seek human company, and the initiative must have come from man. Furthermore, man must have had a strong motivation since the wild urus was a powerful, intractable animal of whom it is said in Job (Job 3:9–10): "Will the urus be willing to serve thee, or abide by thy crib? Canst thou span him into a plowing harness or will he harrow the valleys after thee?"

Eduard Hahn has postulated that the motive for capturing and maintaining the urus in the captive state was to have available a supply, for sacrificial purposes, of the animal sacred to the lunar mother goddess worshipped over an immense area of the ancient world. The economic uses of the animal would then have been a by-product of a domestication religious in origin. Why the urus was selected as the animal sacred to the deity is uncertain, but this was probably because its gigantic curved horns resembled the lunar crescent. Studies in prehistoric and early historic religion have shown that the bovine was early regarded as an epiphany of the goddess or her consort and was slain in the ritual reenactment of the myth of her death. This myth involves the notion of the death and resurrection in new life of the deity. Of course, if cattle were domesticated because the horns of the urus resembled the moon's crescent, it is possible that other horned animals such as sheep and goats were also domesticated for their horns. For example, it is possible that an unsuccessful attempt to domesticate crescent-horned gazelles was made for this reason.

Passage 2

Man probably entered into a state of beneficial mutualism with certain animal species because, to put it in very general terms, the animals were already socially and psychologically preadapted to being tamed without loss of reproductive abilities. A second factor was that the human culture milieu had evolved to a state of organization such that the animals could be controlled and maintained, generation after generation, in a condition of dependence. At least to some degree these animals had to be protected from predators and provided with food—the latter perhaps only in time of scarcity. The detailed pattern of the process leading to domestication naturally varied with both the particular species and the human culture that were interacting; certainly the domestication of the wolf to the dog by the Maglemosian hunter-collectors of northwestern Europe was different in detail from the domestication of the hoofed food animals by the post-Natufian cultivators. Unfortunately, we know nothing of the details of either process, partly because of our inability to reconstruct the behavior and cultural environment of the people involved and partly because of our ignorance of the psychology of the various wild animals involved.

With the exception of one of the most recently domesticated mammals, the laboratory rat, we know little enough about the behavior patterns of our common domestic animals, but we know much less about the behavior of their wild progenitors. Furthermore, detailed comparative observations of wild and domestic *Rattus norvegicus* emphasize the tremendous behavioral changes undergone by a species during domestication. Thus, psychological studies on domesticates probably cannot yield the total behavior pattern of the wild ancestors. It was, however, these wild ancestors that man first tamed and reared.

The social enzyme that activated the union of man and beast was undoubtedly the human proclivity, not only of children but of women also, to keep pets, although purposeful capture of young animals by men, to serve as hunting decoys, may well have been another avenue toward domestication.

The psychological factor of "imprinting," explored particularly by Lorenz in a notable series of animal experiments, was undoubtedly a major influence in the domestication of birds with precocial young (chickens, ducks, geese, turkeys, and so on). *Imprinting* refers to the tendency, most pronounced in such precocial birds, to recognize and psychologically to attach themselves to the most frequently seen and heard living thing during an early and short "critical period." Typically this would be the mother, and we have thus an instinctive mechanism for recognition of the parent by an active newborn.

GO ON TO THE NEXT PAGE

13. The author's primary purpose in Passage 1 is to

    (A) provide an argument as to why the horns
        of cattle, sheep, and goats had religious
        significance
    (B) explain a religious motivation for the
        domestication of cattle and other horned
        animals
    (C) detail the anatomical differences between wild
        animals and their domesticated counterparts
    (D) discuss the scavenger nature of wild cattle and
        how that led them into domestication
    (E) examine the domestication of pigs and dogs
        based on the similarities of their body
        proportions to man's

14. The quote in lines 13-14, "Who then initially
    domesticated whom?" refers to

    (A) the nursing of piglets and puppies by women in
        some primitive societies
    (B) man's strong motivation to domesticate cattle
    (C) the exceptional position of cattle among animals
        that have been domesticated
    (D) the theory that pigs and dogs, as scavengers,
        sought out man
    (E) the controversy inspired by Hahn's cultural
        history

15. In line 20, the word "inadvertent" most nearly
    means

    (A) motivated
    (B) accidental
    (C) sacrificial
    (D) difficult to domesticate
    (E) intractable

16. The myth discussed in lines 37-42 revolves around

    (A) the gigantic curved horns of the urus
    (B) the economic uses of early cattle
    (C) the cow as an incarnation of the moon goddess
    (D) ritual sacrifice of gazelles
    (E) prehistoric reenactments of the creation of the
        moon

17. The author of Passage 2 uses the term "beneficial
    mutualism" in lines 49-50 to characterize

    (A) a harmony of needs between man and some
        species that leads to the domestication of those
        species
    (B) the domestication experiments with the musk ox
    (C) a process opposed to imprinting as a means for
        offspring to recognize their mother
    (D) the reproductive abilities of tamed species
    (E) man's protection from predators and
        provision of food for animals that have been
        domesticated

18. The author of Passage 2 compares the
    domestication of the wolf by Maglemosian hunter-
    collectors to the domestication of hoofed food
    animals by post-Natufian cultivators in order to

    (A) reconstruct the behavior and cultural
        environment in which domestication occurred
    (B) show how ignorant we are of the psychology
        of wild animals and the peoples who
        domesticated them
    (C) suggest that the process of domestication
        varied with the species but not with
        the human culture
    (D) support the notion that the process of
        domestication is dependent upon both the
        species and the human culture
    (E) imply that the process of domestication was a
        process independent of both the species and
        the human culture

19. The studies mentioned in Passage 2 with regard to
    Rattus norvegicus revealed

    (A) the behavior patterns of wild progenitors of
        hoofed animals
    (B) psychological insights into the laboratory rat
    (C) how man first tamed and reared wild animals
    (D) that observing a domestic animal can lead to an
        understanding of its wild counterpart
    (E) dramatic differences in behavior between wild
        and domesticated rats

GO ON TO THE NEXT PAGE

20. Lorenz's experiments with birds and imprinting are used by the author to support the contention that

(A) imprinting is the method by which young birds recognize and attach themselves to a parent

(B) hunting decoys may have been an avenue of domestication for some species

(C) chickens, ducks, geese, and turkeys are birds that have precocial young

(D) imprinting was a major influence in the domestication of birds

(E) the mother is the parent to which most young attach themselves

21. The authors of the two passages would most likely agree that

(A) the human proclivity to keep pets is the single most important factor in domestication

(B) domestication of some species, such as the wolf-dog, occurred because both man and the species benefited from the arrangement

(C) a combination of imprinting and religious mythology shaped the process by which cattle were domesticated

(D) the purposeful capture of young animals for use in religious ceremonies was a critical stage in the domestication of cattle

(E) women felt sorry for the young animals used as hunting decoys and turned them into pets

22. Which of the following statements best characterizes the main difference between the two passages?

(A) The first focuses on religious motivations for the domestication of cattle, but does not exclude other factors for the domestication of other species, whereas the second covers a variety of motivations for domestication, yet does not rule out religion.

(B) The first presents the hypothesis that religious motivations were responsible for domestication of many species, while the second argues that religious motivations were totally absent in the process of domesticating birds.

(C) The first explores in detail how the scavenger nature of dogs and pigs led to their domestication, and the second argues against that proposition, offering a hypothesis for dog and pig domestication based on a desire for pets and social enzymes.

(D) The first suggests that only horned animals had religious significance, but the second focuses on the use of hoofed animals for food.

(E) The second implicitly criticizes the first for ignoring the importance of psychological insights into wild animal behavior that can be gleaned from studying laboratory rats and birds with precocial young.

GO ON TO THE NEXT PAGE

23. The authors of both passages would be LEAST likely to agree with which of the following statements?

(A) The bison, a large herbivore with crescent-shaped horns, was probably domesticated initially for religious reasons and then for economic reasons (food and products derived from the animal).

(B) The cat, a scavenger with body proportions similar to humans, probably insinuated itself into human culture, which was able to adapt and accept the animal for the advantages it gave in terms of rodent control.

(C) Reptiles have not been domesticated since they are not scavengers, not a valued food source, lack body proportions similar to humans, and are a species that does not imprint.

(D) The urus is an example of a hoofed and horned food animal that may have been originally domesticated for religious purposes (such as a supply for sacrifice), but whose economic importance led to its continued role and domestication in human society.

(E) *Rattus norvegicus* is an example of a scavenger with body proportions similar to humans, which was probably domesticated through the purposeful capture of the young to use as hunting decoys.

24. The "social enzyme" noted in Passage 2 is most closely associated with which of the following quotations from Passage 1?

(A) "... the exceptional position of cattle among animals that have been domesticated"

(B) "Will the urus be willing to serve thee?"

(C) "Piglets and dog pups are nursed by women in some primitive societies."

(D) "... the motive for capturing and maintaining the urus ... was to have available a supply, for sacrificial purposes ..."

(E) "... the ancestor of the dog as well as that of the domestic pig probably, as scavengers, sought out man ..."

STOP

If you finish before time is called, you may check your work on this section only. Do not turn to any other section in the test.

SECTION 2

Time — 25 minutes
20 Questions

Directions: This section contains two types of questions. You have 25 minutes to complete both types. For questions 1-20, solve each problem and decide which is the best of the choices given. Fill in the corresponding oval on the answer sheet. You may use any available space for scratch work.

---

1. If $12b - 4 = 0$, then $b =$

   (A) 4

   (B) 3

   (C) 0

   (D) $\dfrac{1}{3}$

   (E) $\dfrac{1}{4}$

---

2. If an oil tank contains 60 gallons of fuel and is $\dfrac{5}{12}$ full, how many gallons does the tank hold when full?

   (A)   72
   (B)   84
   (C)   128
   (D)   144
   (E)   720

3. If the area of rectangle $ABDE$ is 16 square inches, and C is the midpoint of $\overline{BD}$, what is the area, in square inches, of $\triangle ACE$?

   (A)   2
   (B)   4
   (C)   6
   (D)   8
   (E)   16

GO ON TO THE NEXT PAGE

4. An integer that is a multiple of 32 must also be a multiple of which of the following integers?

(A) 11
(B) 9
(C) 8
(D) 5
(E) 3

5. In $\triangle ABC$ above, what is the value of x ?

(A) 18
(B) 23
(C) 32
(D) 38
(E) 42

6. If x, y, and z are consecutive integers and $x < y < z$, what is the sum of y and z in terms of x ?

(A) $2x + 6$
(B) $2x + 4$
(C) $2x + 3$
(D) $2x - 2$
(E) $2x - 1$

7. If $(2^a)^b = 64$, then $ab =$

(A) 2
(B) 3
(C) 4
(D) 5
(E) 6

8. $6\sqrt{18} + 4\sqrt{72} - \left(\sqrt{8} + 10\sqrt{32}\right) =$

(A) -1
(B) 0
(C) 1
(D) $2\sqrt{2}$
(E) $6\sqrt{2}$

9. In the 6-sided regular polygon above, how many diagonals can be drawn that have negative slope?

(A) 0
(B) 1
(C) 2
(D) 3
(E) 4

10. If a certain number is 3 more than 7 times itself, what is the number?

(A) -3

(B) $-\dfrac{3}{2}$

(C) $-\dfrac{1}{2}$

(D) $-\dfrac{3}{8}$

(E) $\dfrac{1}{2}$

GO ON TO THE NEXT PAGE

11. Which of the following is equivalent to
$-12 \le 3b + 3 \le 18$?

(A) $-5 \le b \le 5$
(B) $-4 \le b \le 6$
(C) $-5 \le b \le 6$
(D) $3 \le b \le 5$
(E) $5 \le b \le 5$

12. If x is an odd integer divisible by 3, which of the following must be divisible by 4 ?

(A) $x + 1$
(B) $x + 2$
(C) $x + 3$
(D) $2x$
(E) $2x - 2$

13. If $\overline{AC} \cong \overline{BC}$ in the figure above, what is the perimeter of $\triangle ABC$?

(A) 14
(B) 15
(C) 16
(D) 18
(E) $10 + 3\sqrt{3}$

5, 11, 29, . . .

14. If the nth term in the sequence above is defined by $2 + 3^n$, what is the sum of the 5th and 7th terms?

(A) 40
(B) 245
(C) 2,189
(D) 2,434
(E) 2,920

15. A bottle containing c ounces of juice can be emptied to fill g identical glasses. How many such bottles would be needed to fill n of these glasses with juice?

(A) $\dfrac{gn}{c}$

(B) $\dfrac{cn}{g}$

(C) $\dfrac{g}{n}$

(D) $\dfrac{n}{g}$

(E) $\dfrac{c}{n}$

$A = \{-1, 0, 1, 2\}$

$B = \{0, 1, 2, 3\}$

$C = $ Intersection of A and B

$D = $ Union of A and B

16. Sets A, B, C, and D are shown above. A set is said to be "interior" if, for any two numbers x and y in the set, xy is also in the set. Which of the following is an interior set?

(A) A
(B) B
(C) C
(D) D
(E) A union C

GO ON TO THE NEXT PAGE

17. A large cubical block of cheese measures 8 inches on each edge. If a small rectangular solid measuring 4 inches by 2 inches by 2 inches is cut out and thrown away, the volume of the remaining block of cheese is what fraction of its original volume?

(A) $\dfrac{1}{32}$

(B) $\dfrac{3}{4}$

(C) $\dfrac{7}{8}$

(D) $\dfrac{15}{16}$

(E) $\dfrac{31}{32}$

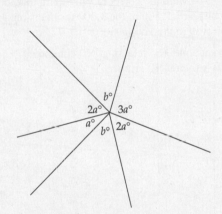

Note: Figure not drawn to scale.

18. In the figure above, what is the value of b in terms of a ?

(A) $90 + 2a$
(B) $180 - 4a$
(C) $180 - 8a$
(D) $360 - 8a$
(E) $360 - 12a$

19. If x and y are integers and $y = 4x$, which of the following could be the average (arithmetic mean) of x and y ?

(A) −36
(B) −35
(C) 4
(D) 12
(E) 28

20. If y is directly proportional to the square of x, and $x = 3$ when $y = 18$, then when $y = 2$, $x =$

(A) $\dfrac{1}{3}$

(B) 1

(C) 3

(D) 9

(E) 81

STOP

**If you finish before time is called, you may check your work on this section only.
Do not turn to any other section in the test.**

SECTION 3

Time — 25 minutes
24 Questions

Directions: For each question in this section, select the best answer from among the choices given and fill in the corresponding oval on the answer sheet.

Each sentence below has one or two blanks,
each blank indicating that something has been omitted.
Beneath the sentence are five words or sets of words labeled A through E. Choose the word or set of words that, when inserted in the sentence, <u>best</u> fits the meaning of the sentence as a whole.

Example:

Medieval kingdoms did not become constitutional republics overnight; on the contrary, the change was -------.

(A) unpopular (B) unexpected (C) advantageous

(D) sufficient (E) gradual

Ⓐ Ⓑ Ⓒ Ⓓ ●

25. While its unique eating habits make the mountain gorilla a fascinating subject for observation, its small population and its shyness serve to ------- many potential studies.

(A) inspire (B) release (C) fortify
(D) hinder (E) extenuate

26. Originally designed as work clothes for miners, jeans are now worn by all segments of society, their appeal ------- by their comfort and affordability.

(A) overwhelmed (B) corroded (C) broadened
(D) lessened (E) complicated

27. While many consumer electronics are ------- in a very short time by newer technologies, it will be many years before the home computer becomes -------.

(A) supplanted . . obsolete
(B) popularized . . uncommon
(C) noticeable . . forgotten
(D) discovered . . disparaged
(E) replaced . . remembered

28. Although many believed that the problems of the community were -------, the members of the governing council refused to give up and devised several ------- solutions.

(A) insoluble . . ingenious
(B) intractable . . inconsequential
(C) exorbitant . . promising
(D) irrelevant . . lofty
(E) obscure . . meager

29. So ------- were the voters of Winesburg that, despite the blizzard, 2,500 of the 3,200 residents made their way to the voting sites.

(A) endemic (B) relenting (C) ephemeral
(D) resolute (E) erratic

GO ON TO THE NEXT PAGE

The passages below are followed by questions based on their content; questions following a pair of related passages may also be based on the relationship between the paired passages. Answer the questions on the basis of what is <u>stated</u> or <u>implied</u> in the passage and in any introductory material that may be provided.

Questions 30-33 are based on the following passages.

Passage 1

It is often said that history is written by the winners, and for good reason. Contrary to the revisionist teachings of some "new historicists," history is not by nature an
Line interpretive discipline. Facts are facts are facts, after all.
5 New interpretations of Woodrow Wilson's isolationist policies do not change the fact that the United States entered World War I later than its European counterparts, or that the United States was instrumental in winning that particular war. Trying to rewrite our understanding of U.S.
10 policy does a grave disservice to the facts of history.

Passage 2

History is by nature a discipline of interpretation. The bigger issue is the bias of the interpreter. Much of a historian's job is related to distinguishing relevant information from extraneous material. For too long, the
15 contributions of racial minorities, women, and other groups have been deemed inessential to an understanding of history. Recognizing the vital role of African American soldiers in a segregated military or the factory work of women in World War II will give us a more complete
20 picture of America, both in the past and in the present.

30. On what point would the authors of both passages agree?

    (A) History is based on irrefutable facts.
    (B) Revisionist history is antithetical to historical analysis.
    (C) Historical analysis requires a basis of factual information.
    (D) Military victories are the most important part of history.
    (E) Interpretation is essential to an understanding of history.

31. Unlike Passage 2, Passage 1 contains

    (A) vocabulary specific to the discipline of history
    (B) references to historical events
    (C) an international perspective
    (D) a partisan judgment
    (E) a reference to historical bias

32. The conflict between the passages can be most accurately described as that between the importance of

    (A) military history and social history
    (B) domestic history and international history
    (C) objectivity and subjectivity
    (D) fact-based analysis and limited interpretation
    (E) bias and accuracy

33. The author of Passage 2 is most concerned that

    (A) the segregationist policies of the American military were wrong
    (B) history cannot be accurately analyzed
    (C) historians cannot be trusted
    (D) factual analysis is impossible
    (E) traditional historical analysis ignores minority groups

GO ON TO THE NEXT PAGE

Questions 34-39 are based on the following passage.

The following excerpt is from an essay by a leading scientist and professor of paleontology. In it he describes how an experience in one field—choral music—led to a revelation about himself.

Thirty years ago, on April 30, 1958, to be exact, I sat with 250 students facing one of the most formidable men of our generation—Peter J. Wilhousky, director of
Line music in the New York City Schools and conductor of the
5 New York All-City High School Chorus. As the warm, and primarily parental, applause receded at the concert's end, Wilhousky returned to the podium of Carnegie Hall, gestured for silence, and raised his baton to conduct the traditional encore, "Madame Jeanette." Halfway through,
10 he turned and, without missing a beat (to invoke a cliché in its appropriate, literal sense), smiled to acknowledge the chorus alumni who stood at their seats or surrounded the podium, singing with their current counterparts. These former members seemed so ancient to me—though none
15 had passed forty, for the chorus itself was by then only twenty years old—and their solidarity moved me to a rare fit of tears at a time when teenage boys did not cry in public.

"Madame Jeanette" is a dangerous little piece, for it
20 ventures so near the edge of cloying sentimentality. It tells the tale, in close four-part a cappella harmony, of a French widow who sits at her door by day and her window by night. There she thinks only of her husband, killed so many years before on the battlefield of St. Pierre, and
25 dreams of the day when they will be reunited at the cemetery of Père Lachaise. With 250 teenagers and sloppy conducting, "Madame Jeanette" becomes a maudlin and embarrassing tearfest. Wilhousky, ever the perfectionist, ever the rationalist, somehow steered to the right side of
30 musicality, and ended each concert with integrity and control.

"Madame Jeanette" was our symbol of continuity. For a very insecure boy, singing second bass on the brink of manhood, "Madame Jeanette" offered another wonderful
35 solace. It ends, for the basses, on a low D-flat, just about as far down the scale as any composer would dare ask a singer to venture. Yes, I knew even then that low did not mean masculine, or capable, or mature, or virile, but that fundament resonated with hope and possibility, even in
40 pianissimo.

We lived, thirty years ago, in an age of readier obedience, but I still marvel at the discipline that Wilhousky could maintain with his mixture of awe (inspired) and terror (promulgated). He forged our group
45 of Blacks from Harlem, Jews from Queens, and Italians from Staten Island into a responsive singing machine. He worked, in part, through intimidation by public ridicule. One day, he stopped the rehearsal and pointed to the tenor section, saying: "You, third row, fourth seat, stand up.
50 You're singing flat. Ten years ago, Julius La Rosa sat

in the same seat—and sang flat. And he's still singing flat." (Memory is a curious trickster. La Rosa, in a recent *New Yorker* profile, states that Wilhousky praised him in the same forum for singing so true to pitch. But I know what
55 I heard. Or is the joke on me?) Each year, he cashiered a member or two for talking and giggling—in public, and with no hope of mercy or reinstatement.

But Peter Wilhousky had another side that inspired us all and conveyed the most important lesson of intellectual
60 life. He was one of the finest choral conductors in America, yet he chose to spend every Saturday morning with high school kids. His only rule, tacit but persuasive, proclaimed: "No compromises." We could sing, with proper training and practice, as well as any group in America; nothing
65 else would be tolerated or even conceptualized. Anything less would not be worth doing at all. I had encountered friendliness, grace, kindness, animation, clarity, and dedication among my teachers, but I had never even considered the notion that unqualified excellence could
70 emerge from anything touched or made by students. The idea, however, is infectious. As I worked with Wilhousky, I slowly personalized the dream that excellence in one activity might be extended to become the pattern, or at least the goal, of an actual life.

34. The author's main purpose in writing the passage is to

(A) urge students to participate in music
(B) worship a gifted individual
(C) analyze a particular piece of music
(D) relate an incident from his childhood
(E) trace the development of a particular attitude

35. The author describes "Madame Jeanette" as a "dangerous little piece" (line 19) because

(A) it can appear trite and melodramatic when performed under less than ideal conditions
(B) it contains seditious material
(C) it has a profoundly moving effect on most audiences
(D) it evokes harrowing images of death and violence
(E) it is a technically difficult piece for most choirs to perform

GO ON TO THE NEXT PAGE

36. It can be inferred from the third paragraph that performing "Madame Jeanette" filled the author with a feeling of

    (A) masculinity
    (B) insecurity
    (C) optimism
    (D) melancholy
    (E) embarrassment

37. In the context of the passage, the term "readier" (line 41) most nearly means

    (A) more prepared
    (B) more willing
    (C) more complete
    (D) more clever
    (E) more punctual

38. The authors includes the anecdote of the student in the "third row, fourth seat" (line 49) in order to

    (A) provide an example of how Wilhousky maintained discipline in the chorus
    (B) suggest that Wilhousky had lied about Julius La Rosa
    (C) show how cruel and arbitrary Wilhousky could be at times
    (D) illustrate how unreliable the human memory can be
    (E) imply that Wilhousky liked to trick his students into obeying him

39. The passage suggests that Wilhousky inspired the author to

    (A) strive for excellence in all of his endeavors
    (B) pursue a career in music
    (C) devote himself to helping high school students
    (D) attend future performances of the chorus as an alumnus
    (E) never resort to compromising with anyone

GO ON TO THE NEXT PAGE

Questions 40-48 are based on the following passage.

The following passage discusses the differing paths of China and India after World War II and offers explanations for the disparity.

The Japanese surrender aboard the U.S.S. *Missouri* ignited a series of events which radically changed the shape and destiny of Eastern and Southern Asia.
Line Within two years, India had gained independence from
5 Britain. Within four, Mao Tse Deng's communists had established the People's Republic of China. At the end of the twentieth century, China and India were the two largest nations in the world. Both were nuclear powers, both were still ruled by the regimes which had founded
10 them and both had embarked on daring reform programs in order to modernize their economies. This is where the similarities end. While China experienced wild success in industrializing, in India, for both political and economic reasons, the process stagnated.
15 Politically, China was successful because its political system was conducive to the high levels of centralized control required for the scale of development that it was attempting. Economically, China was successful because it was patient. It expanded its economy slowly, only entering
20 new sectors when it had the resources to be successful in them. For example, China only attempted to develop high-tech manufacturing after its initial reforms had taken effect.
What made India so different? Like China, India
25 was established after World War II as an independent country. However, unlike China, the new government was a parliamentary democracy. This factor is essential to understanding why seemingly similar reforms had radically different effects.
30 India's reforms were quite different from China's in result if not in shape. After its independence from Britain in 1947, India established large State Owned Enterprises (SOE's) that were given generous protections by the government to promote growth. India operated
35 for years under policies that attempted to foster domestic manufacturing of formerly imported goods. Unfortunately, these policies resulted in consumers paying a higher price for and receiving a lower quality of goods than they had previously. SOEs were given protections under the
40 assumption that being free from competition, they could improve their products, increase their business experience, and make their operations more efficient. Unfortunately, India, unlike rigidly communist China, had no way of truly enforcing these policies. China could quash any dissent
45 with few repercussions for government. India's parliament, however, had to seek reelection. This proved a disincentive for "rocking the boat" too much. While everyone wanted more efficient businesses, no one wanted to tell the voters back home that jobs would be lost to cut costs.
50 So what went wrong in India? China was able to successfully reform because it acted in stages and acted

fully. India never actually changed the system enough to promote development. Its politicians remained too dependent upon reelection to make sweeping reforms.
55 Its financial sector was not developed enough to foster growth independent of the government. Its political system remained in question; even today assassination remains a popular way to voice dissenting opinions. In order for India to industrialize fully and develop a level of economic
60 depth comparable to China's, it must reevaluate its priorities and set truly national goals. Given its democratic system, India's task is harder than China's was, but it is not so hard as to be impossible.

40. It can be inferred from the passage that prior to World War II India and China were

(A) both behind other countries in modernizing their economic systems
(B) the two largest nations in the world
(C) the victims of continual bloody and destructive political revolutions
(D) competitors in various economic and martial arenas
(E) concerned with setting truly national goals

41. Which of the following facts, if true, would most call into question the author's claims about the reasons for China's relative success?

(A) The Chinese government had the resources to enter the high-tech market a decade before it actually did.
(B) India had been a British colony while China had remained nominally sovereign.
(C) Many far-flung provinces felt free to ignore the mandates of China's central government.
(D) China also used a version of SOEs in order to encourage national manufacturing rather than foreign imports.
(E) India actually has more natural resources per capita than does China.

GO ON TO THE NEXT PAGE

42. The author would be most likely to agree with which of the following statements about parliamentary democracies?

(A) They are highly preferable to forms of rule such as communism.
(B) They must be abolished if a country is to flourish economically.
(C) They tend to make reform difficult because leaders must worry about the approval of their constituents.
(D) They were the best possible option for Eastern and Southern Asian countries after World War II.
(E) They can be risky because they encourage countries to make economic moves for which they are not fully ready.

43. SOEs were put into place in India for all of the following reasons EXCEPT

(A) to discourage foreign manufacturing
(B) to increase business experience
(C) to cultivate domestic manufacturing
(D) to improve the quality of products
(E) to increase efficiency in manufacturing

44. As used in line 45, "repercussions" most closely means

(A) returning
(B) loud noises
(C) labors
(D) consequences
(E) new laws

45. The line "So what went wrong in India?" (line 50) serves as

(A) a request for information
(B) a move to summation
(C) a shift in focus
(D) an unanswerable complaint
(E) a flippant rejoinder

46. Suppose that India, rather than trying to move directly into free trade, had implemented reform in stages. The author would most likely argue that

(A) India would certainly have been more successful than it is today
(B) the process would have fostered revolution, which would have been disastrous considering India's nuclear capabilities
(C) such a move would lead to a reevaluation of priorities and national goals
(D) changing the shape of the reforms would certainly lead to different results
(E) there might need to be a simultaneous centralization of governmental power to achieve positive results

47. According to the passage, in order to be economically successful, India must

(A) abolish its democratic system and move to totalitarian communism
(B) promote the use of SOEs
(C) vote out current leaders and elect new ones who are willing to "rock the boat"
(D) let go of old beliefs and offer reforms aimed at changing the priorities of the country as a whole
(E) cut jobs in order to reduce costs

48. The author's attitude toward China can best be described as

(A) awed reverence
(B) measured admiration
(C) guarded dislike
(D) disdainful pity
(E) politic respect

STOP

**If you finish before time is called, you may check your work on this section only.
Do not turn to any other section in the test.**

SECTION 4

Time — 25 minutes
18 Questions

Directions: This section contains two types of questions. You have 25 minutes to complete both types. For questions 21-28, solve each problem and decide which is the best of the choices given. Fill in the corresponding oval on the answer sheet. You may use any available space for scratch work.

Notes

1. The use of a calculator is permitted.
2. All numbers used are real numbers.
3. Figures that accompany problems in this test are intended to provide information useful in solving the problems. They are drawn as accurately as possible EXCEPT when it is stated in a specific problem that the figure is not drawn to scale. All figures lie in a plane unless otherwise indicated.
4. Unless otherwise specified, the domain of any function f is assumed to be the set of all real numbers x for which $f(x)$ is a real number.

Reference Information

$A = \pi r^2$
$C = 2\pi r$

$A = lw$

$A = \frac{1}{2}bh$

$V = lwh$

$V = \pi r^2 h$

$c^2 = a^2 + b^2$

Special Right Triangles

The number of degrees of arc in a circle is 360.

The sum of the measures in degrees of the angles of a triangle is 180.

---

21. What is the value of z if $3z + 4z + 7z = -42$?

(A) 3

(B) $\frac{1}{3}$

(C) $-\frac{1}{3}$

(D) -3

(E) -588

22. If 10 pecks are equivalent to 2.5 bushels, then 4 bushels are equivalent to how many pecks?

(A) 1
(B) 4
(C) 10
(D) 12.5
(E) 16

23. What is the y-intercept of the line with equation $2x + 3y = 12$?

(A) 4

(B) 3

(C) 2

(D) $\frac{1}{4}$

(E) $-\frac{2}{3}$

GO ON TO THE NEXT PAGE

24. For $x \neq 0$, $\dfrac{a}{x^2} + \dfrac{7}{x} =$

(A) $\dfrac{a+7x}{x}$

(B) $\dfrac{a+7x}{x^2}$

(C) $\dfrac{a+7}{x^2+x}$

(D) $\dfrac{a+7}{x^2}$

(E) $\dfrac{a+7}{x^2}$

25. If $y = 6x + 3$ and $y = cx + 3$ are the equations of perpendicular lines, then what is the value of c ?

A) -6

(B) $-\dfrac{1}{6}$

(C) $\dfrac{1}{6}$

(D) $\dfrac{1}{3}$

(E) 6

26. The positive difference between -5 and p is the same as the positive difference between -1 and 2.5. Which of the following could be the value of p ?

(A) -8.5
(B) -6.5
(C) -2.5
(D) 6.5
(E) 8.5

27. If $f(x) = x^{-\frac{2}{3}}$, what is the value of $\dfrac{f(8)}{f(3)}$?

(A) $\dfrac{3}{4}$

(B) $\dfrac{4}{\sqrt[3]{9}}$

(C) $\dfrac{8}{3}$

(D) $\sqrt{\dfrac{512}{27}}$

(E) $\dfrac{\sqrt[3]{9}}{4}$

28. The figure above represents a circular amusement park ride with 6 seats, labeled a through f. If two students are to sit next to each other, leaving the other seats empty, how many such arrangements of the two students are possible?

(A) 3
(B) 6
(C) 10
(D) 12
(E) 30

GO ON TO THE NEXT PAGE

Directions: For Student-Produced Response questions 9-18, use the grids at the bottom of the answer sheet page on which you have answered questions 1-8.

Each of the remaining 10 questions requires you to solve the problem and enter your answer by marking the circles in the special grid, as shown in the examples below. You may use any available space for scratch work.

Answer: $\frac{7}{12}$

Write answer in boxes. → Fraction line

Grid in result.

Answer: 2.5 → Decimal point

Answer: 201
Either position is correct.

Note: You may start your answers in any column, space permitting. Columns not needed should be left blank.

- Mark no more than one circle in any column.

- Because the answer sheet will be machine-scored, **you will receive credit only if the circles are filled in correctly.**

- Although not required, it is suggested that you write your answer in the boxes at the top of the columns to help you fill in the circles accurately.

- Some problems may have more than one correct answer. In such cases, grid only one answer.

- No question has a negative answer.

- **Mixed numbers** such as $3\frac{1}{2}$ must be gridded as 3.5 or 7/2. (If [3 1 / 2] is gridded, it will be interpreted as $\frac{31}{2}$, not $3\frac{1}{2}$.)

- **Decimal Answers:** If you obtain a decimal answer with more digits than the grid can accommodate, it may be either rounded or truncated, but it must fill the entire grid. For example, if you obtain an answer such as 0.6666..., you should record your result as .666 or .667. **A less accurate value such as .66 or .67 will be scored as incorrect.**

Acceptable ways to grid $\frac{2}{3}$ are:

29. What is the value of $\left|-10\right| - \left|3\right|$?

30. If 20 percent of n is 36, what is 0.2 percent of n ?

GO ON TO THE NEXT PAGE →

31. In $\triangle RST$, $\overline{RS} \cong \overline{ST}$. If the measure of $\angle S$ is 20°, then what is the degree measure of $\angle T$?

32. If all of the angles in the figure above are right angles, what is its perimeter?

33. If $x - 8 = 5y$ and $x = 23$, then what is the value of $x - y$?

34. What is the product of all the positive integer factors of 20 ?

35. Marcia can type 18 pages per hour, and David can type 14 pages per hour. If they work together, how many <u>minutes</u> will it take them to type 24 pages?

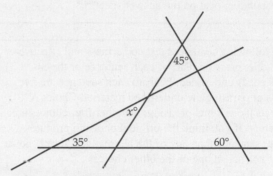

Note: Figure not drawn to scale.

36. What is the value of x in the figure above?

37. If $f(x) = x^2 - x + 4$, a is non-negative, and $f(a) = 10$, then what is the value of a ?

38. A box contains only large marbles and small marbles. There are twice as many large marbles as small marbles in the box. The large marbles are all either blue or red, and there arc 5 times as many large blue marbles as large red marbles. If one marble is drawn from the box at random, what is the probability that it will be a large blue marble?

STOP
**If you finish before time is called, you may check your work on this section only.
Do not turn to any other section in the test.**

SECTION 5

Time — 30 minutes

39 Questions

Directions: For each question in this section, select the best answer from among the choices given and fill in the corresponding oval on the answer sheet.

The following sentences test correctness and effectiveness of expression. Part of each sentence or the entire sentence is underlined; beneath each sentence are five ways of phrasing the underlined material. Choice A repeats the original phrasing; the other four choices are different. If you think the original phrasing produces a better sentence than any of the alternatives, select choice A; if not, select one of the other choices.

In making your selection, follow the requirements of standard written English; that is, pay attention to grammar, choice of words, sentence construction, and punctuation. Your selection should result in the most effective sentence—clear and precise, without awkwardness or ambiguity.

EXAMPLE:

Laura Ingalls Wilder published her first book and she was sixty-five years old then.

(A) and she was sixty-five years old then
(B) when she was sixty-five
(C) at age sixty-five years old
(D) upon the reaching of sixty-five years
(E) at the time when she was sixty-five

1. After visiting their friends in Paris, my parents told me that in France they sometimes do not wear bathing suits on the beach.

(A) in France they sometimes
(B) in France some people
(C) some French people
(D) in France there are some who
(E) in France, men and women

2. Today's computers are becoming not only more varied and powerful, but also less expensive.

(A) are becoming not only more varied and powerful, but also less expensive
(B) not only are becoming more varied and powerful, they cost less
(C) become not only more varied and powerful, they become less expensive
(D) becoming more varied and powerful, but also less expensive
(E) become more varied and powerful, not only, but also less expensive

3. Getting off the chairlift, Neil adjusted his boot buckles, polished his goggles, and skied down the slope.

(A) Getting off the chairlift, Neil adjusted his boot buckles, polished his goggles, and skied down the slope.
(B) He got off the chairlift, Neil adjusted his boot buckles, polished his goggles, and skied down the slope.
(C) After getting off the chairlift, Neil adjusted his boot buckles, polished his goggles, and then he went skiing down the slope.
(D) Neil, after getting off the chairlift, adjusted his boot buckles, polished his goggles, and was skiing down the slope.
(E) After he got off the chairlift, Neil adjusted his boot buckles, polished his goggles, and skied down the slope.

GO ON TO THE NEXT PAGE

4. Since they have been told not to do so in their school books, students often hesitate to write in their personal books; yet, circling an unknown word or underlining an important phrase <u>is critically when one wishes to learn something.</u>

   (A) is critically when one wishes to learn something
   (B) is critically being as one might wish to learn something
   (C) is critical when one wishes to learn something
   (D) is critical when you want to learn that something has been
   (E) can only be seen as critical when one wishes to learn something

5. <u>One of Humphrey Bogart's earlier movies, Samuel Spade is a detective trying to solve the mystery of his partner's death in *The Maltese Falcon*.</u>

   (A) One of Humphrey Bogart's earlier movies, Samuel Spade is a detective trying to solve the mystery of his partner's death in *The Maltese Falcon*.
   (B) One of Humphrey Bogart's earlier movies, *The Maltese Falcon* is a movie in that Samuel Spade, detective, tries to solve the mystery of his partner's death.
   (C) One of Humphrey Bogart's earlier movies, *The Maltese Falcon* is a mystery in which Samuel Spade tries to solve his partner's death.
   (D) In *The Maltese Falcon*, one of Humphrey Bogart's earlier movies, Samuel Spade is a detective trying to solve the mystery of his partner's death.
   (E) In *The Maltese Falcon*, one of Humphrey Bogart's roles is that of Samuel Spade, a detective trying to solve the mystery of his partner's death, and it was also one of his earlier movies.

6. <u>While Boudin's own paintings have never been held in the highest regard, he is seen as having played a critical role in the education of Impressionist painter Monet.</u>

   (A) While Boudin's own paintings have never been held in the highest regard, he is seen as having played a critical role in the education of Impressionist painter Monet.
   (B) While Boudin's own paintings were never regarded highly, Monet is seen as having been one of his most educated students.
   (C) It is seen that Boudin's critical role in educating the Impressionist painter Monet was held in higher regard than his paintings.
   (D) Since Boudin's own paintings have never been held in that high regard, he has been seen as having played a critical role in the education of Impressionist painter Monet.
   (E) Since Boudin's own paintings, which were never held in that high regard, were seen as having played a critical role in the education of Impressionist painter Monet.

7. Although everyone was forewarned about the upcoming exam, <u>yet only three students out of the entire class</u> passed it.

   (A) yet only three students out of the entire class
   (B) only three students out of the entire class
   (C) only three students, which was out of the entire class,
   (D) yet only three students that were forewarned out of the entire class
   (E) but only three students out of the entire class

8. The committee chairpersons agreed <u>to return to their respective committees and they would discuss</u> the proposals made by the executive board.

   (A) to return to their respective committees and they would discuss
   (B) upon return to their respective committees, thereby discussing
   (C) to return to her respective committees and discuss
   (D) to return to their respective committees discussing
   (E) to return to their respective committees and discuss

GO ON TO THE NEXT PAGE ⟹

9. The clog has come back into fashion recently, yet few people know that originally it was called the sabot, made by hollowing a single piece of wood, and was worn by peasants in Europe.

   (A) it was called the sabot, made by hollowing a single piece of wood, and was worn by peasants in Europe
   (B) it was called the sabot, making it by hollowing a single piece of wood, and worn by peasants in Europe
   (C) it was called the sabot, made by hollowing a single piece of wood, and worn by peasants in Europe
   (D) it was called the sabot, making it by hollowing a single piece of wood, and was worn by peasants in Europe
   (E) it was called the sabot, and the pesants made it by hollowing a single piece of wood, and wore it in Europe

10. Many say that, after inventing an explosive more powerful than any then known, Alfred Nobel instituted the Nobel Peace Prize to atone for his "accomplishment" and relieve his conscience.

   (A) after inventing an explosive more powerful than any then known
   (B) after inventing an explosive that was more powerful than any that were then known
   (C) after he invented an explosive more powerful than he or any others had then known
   (D) after he invented an explosive, it being more powerful than any then known
   (E) after inventing an explosive more powerful then any than known

11. For many a brilliant actor, being free to interpret their character as they wish is more important than being well paid.

   (A) being free to interpret their character as they wish
   (B) being free to interpret his or her character as they wish
   (C) being free to interpret their character as they wishes
   (D) being free to interpret his or her character as he or she wishes
   (E) being free to interpret his or her character as he or she wish

12. On Sunday afternoons, Omar and his family enjoy playing Monopoly with the neighbors, and they always win.

   (A) and they always win
   (B) even though they always win
   (C) even though the neighbors always win
   (D) and the neighbors, they always win
   (E) it being that the neighbors always win

13. Known for graduating from college despite being blind and deaf, the fact that Helen Keller spent over six decades fighting for socialist causes is often left out of accounts of her life.

   (A) the fact that Helen Keller spent over six decades fighting for socialist causes is often left out of accounts of her life
   (B) accounts of Helen Keller's life often leave out that she spent over six decades fighting for socialist causes
   (C) many people are unaware that Helen Keller spent over six decades fighting for socialist causes, as this fact is often left out of accounts of her life
   (D) six decades were spent by Helen Keller fighting for socialist causes, though this fact is often left out of accounts of her life
   (E) Helen Keller spent over six decades fighting for socialist causes, a fact often left out of accounts of her life

14. After getting her driver's license, Jenny used her father's car as often as possible, and her father said to put less miles on it by walking to school and work.

   (A) as often as possible, and her father said to put less miles on it
   (B) as often as possible; eventually her father told her to put fewer miles on it
   (C) as often as possible, but then eventually her father told her to be putting fewer miles on it
   (D) as often as possible; eventually her father told her to put less miles on it
   (E) as often as possible, and her father said to be putting less miles on it

GO ON TO THE NEXT PAGE

15. The French classical composer, <u>Maurice Ravel, has enlisted as an ambulance driver</u> during World War I.

(A) Maurice Ravel, has enlisted as an ambulance driver

(B) Maurice Ravel, was to be enlisted as an ambulance driver

(C) Maurice Ravel, was enlisting as an ambulance driver

(D) Maurice Ravel, enlisting to be an ambulance driver

(E) Maurice Ravel, enlisted as an ambulance driver

16. <u>The art of carving totem poles with fantastic animal figures were practiced by Pacific Northwest Native American tribes.</u>

(A) The art of carving totem poles with fantastic animal figures were practiced by Pacific Northwest Native American tribes.

(B) The art of carving totem poles with fantastic animal figures was practiced by Pacific Northwest Native American tribes.

(C) The art of carving totem poles with fantastic animal figures were being practiced by Pacific Northwest Native American tribes.

(D) Pacific Northwest Native American tribes were practicing the art of carving totem poles with fantastic animal figures.

(E) Pacific Northwest Native American tribes practiced the art of carving totem poles with fantastic animal figures.

17. <u>The bristlecone pine, regarded to be one of the varieties of longest living trees, is native to the American West.</u>

(A) The bristlecone pine, regarded to be one of the varieties of longest living trees, is native to the American West.

(B) The bristlecone pine, regarded to be one of the varieties of longest living trees, are native to the American West.

(C) The bristlecone pine, regarded as one of the varieties of longest living trees, are native to the American West.

(D) The bristlecone pine, regarded as one of the longest-lived varieties of trees, is native to the American West.

(E) The bristlecone pine, regarded as being one of the varieties of longest living trees, is native to the American West.

18. Scholars of popular culture have found that <u>the mainstream music of one decade often originates from the most obscure</u> underground music of the previous decade.

(A) the mainstream music of one decade often originates from the most obscure

(B) the mainstream music of one decade often originates from the more obscure

(C) the mainstream music of one decade often originates in the most obscure

(D) the mainstream music of one decade often originates with the more obscure

(E) the mainstream music of one decade often originates with the more obscure

19. <u>P. T. Barnum catered to the taste of the public</u> with such circus acts as Major Tom Thumb and Jumbo the elephant.

(A) P. T. Barnum catered to the taste of the public

(B) P. T. Barnum catering to the taste of the public

(C) P. T. Barnum catering for the taste of the public

(D) P. T. Barnum catered for the taste of the public

(E) P. T. Barnum, having catered to the taste of the public,

20. <u>In the early 1900's, Enrico Caruso was America's finest operatic tenor, more recently opera fans have enjoyed the talents of Plácido Domingo and José Carreras.</u>

(A) In the early 1900s, Enrico Caruso was America's finest operatic tenor, more recently opera fans have enjoyed the talents of Plácido Domingo and José Carreras.

(B) In the early 1900s, Enrico Caruso was America's finest operatic tenor; more recently, opera fans have enjoyed the talents of Plácido Domingo and José Carreras.

(C) In the early 1900s, Enrico Caruso was America's finest operatic tenor: more recently, opera fans have enjoyed the talents of Plácido Domingo and José Carreras.

(D) In the early 1900s, Enrico Caruso was America's finest operatic tenor; but more recently, opera fans have enjoyed the talents of Plácido Domingo and José Carreras.

(E) In the early 1900s, Enrico Caruso was America's finest operatic tenor, however, more recently, opera fans have enjoyed the talents of Plácido Domingo and José Carreras.

GO ON TO THE NEXT PAGE

The following sentences test your ability to recognize grammar and usage errors. Each sentence contain either a single error or no error at all. No sentence contains more than one error. The error, if there is one, is underlined and lettered. If the sentence contains an error, select the one underlined part that must be changed to make the sentence correct. If the sentence is correct, select choice E. In choosing answers, follow the requirements of standard written English.

EXAMPLE:

The other delegates and him immediately accepted
     A   B   C
the resolution drafted by the neutral states. No error
           D   E

(A) ● (C) (D) (E)

21. Revered as one of the world's most versatile geniuses,
     A
Leonardo da Vinci excelled in every endeavor
                 B
he attempted and serving as a prototype for the
               C   D
Renaissance man. No error
             E

22. The twins wanted to be a member of the team, but the
                A   B
captain had already made her selections. No error
      C   D   E

23. Of the nominees for the Nobel Prize in Literature
 A   B
this year, few are as qualified as the English novelist
        C   D
Anthony Powell. No error
          E

24. The recent production of Arthur Miller's *A View from*
              A
the Bridge exemplifies the strength of this unsung
masterpiece and demonstrates that the work has been
            B   C
ignored unjust. No error
   D   E

25. Yoga is more than simply a series of stretches and
      A   B
poses; it is a means of centering oneself spiritually
and focus in such a way as to put one's life in order.
    C   D
No error
 E

26. Prior to the Industrial Revolution, children and parents
     A
spend a great deal of time working together to meet the
  B   C
needs of the family. No error
    D   E

27. Neither the president nor the CEO of the three
           A
sister companies was able to determine why the last
         B
quarter's financial reports were so inconsistent with
             C
previous years. No error
    D   E

GO ON TO THE NEXT PAGE ⟹

28. If one is interested <u>in</u> learning more about Jacob
         A
Lawrence, <u>you should</u> visit the Metropolitan Museum
              B
of Art when next <u>his</u> work <u>is exhibited</u>. <u>No error</u>
                  C   D   E

29. <u>Despite</u> the dangerous road conditions
         A
<u>after the blizzard</u>, the company <u>insisted on</u> <u>its</u>
        B   C   D
employees be on time. <u>No error</u>
                          E

30. While in training, each member of the team <u>were</u>
                                                A
required to focus exclusively on the tasks associated

<u>with</u> <u>her</u> position, and therefore had little sense of the
 B   C
functioning of the team <u>as a whole</u>. <u>No error</u>
                            D   E

31. The gift that Karen and Mary ultimately purchased for

<u>her</u> mother <u>was</u> much <u>less</u> expensive than the gift they
 A   B   C
originally intended <u>to purchase</u>. <u>No error</u>
                        D   E

32. Deciding to follow his conscience and not <u>give in to</u>
                                                A
the <u>pressure to conform</u>, the local worker was a <u>vocal</u>
        B   C
<u>critic toward</u> the regional vice president. <u>No error</u>
    D   E

33. Many scholars <u>agree</u> that there <u>has been</u> no greater
                     A   B
contributor to the advancement <u>of architecture</u> in the
                                   C
twentieth century than <u>that</u> of Frank Lloyd Wright.
                          D

<u>No error</u>
   E

34. Constructing a fence <u>ought not</u> to be seen as an
                            A
insurmountable task; <u>rather</u>, it should be viewed as a
                        B
challenge <u>that</u> can be accomplished by a
             C
<u>combination of</u> perseverance and patience. <u>No error</u>
    D   E

GO ON TO THE NEXT PAGE

Directions: The following passage is an early draft of an essay. Some parts of the passage need to be rewritten.

Read the passage and select the best answers for the questions that follow. Some questions are about particular sentences or parts of sentences and ask you to improve sentence structure or word choice. Other questions ask you to consider organization and development. In choosing answers, follow the requirements of standard written English.

Questions 35-39 are based on the following passage.

(1) Our town needs to make more of an effort to make its museums accessible to children. (2) Raised with frequent exposure to sculpture and paintings, it is much more likely that young people will mature into artists and patrons of the arts.

(3) It is often quite easy to accomplish a great deal simply. (4) Placed slightly lower on the walls, paintings become more visible to children. (5) But extensive programs to encourage children to appreciate art are often not a necessity. (6) Children have a natural enjoyment of art. (7) A museum is an excellent place for a child. (8) We must only understand that these young museum patrons can not help acting like them. (9) Children should not be asked to be silent, or spend long periods of time in front of any one piece. (10) If necessary, museums should set up special "children's times" during which young people may roam through the building, enjoying the artwork in their own way. (11) A wonderful learning experience! (12) Children can have a great time, and at the same time gain an appreciation of art. (13) Precautions could be taken to make sure that no damage was done.

(14) This is necessary because places like museums must be available for everyone. (15) These changes cannot happen overnight, but if we volunteered and were helping to make these changes in our town's museums, we can realize the goal of making them accessible to people of all ages.

35. Which version of the underlined portion of sentence 8 (reproduced below) provides the most clarity?

We must only understand that these young museum patrons can not help acting like them.

(A) (as it is now)
(B) like it
(C) as if they were
(D) like what they are
(E) like children

36. After sentence 13, the writer's point would have been strengthened most by the inclusion of

(A) a description of possible damage
(B) an explanation of the precautions to be taken
(C) a historic precedent
(D) an extension of her argument to include other institutions
(E) an explanation of the mission of a museum

37. Which of the following represents the best version of sentence 4 (reproduced below) ?

Placed slightly lower on the walls, paintings become more visible to children.

(A) (As it is now)
(B) Placing them slightly lower on the walls, the paintings become more visible to the children.
(C) For example, placing paintings slightly lower on the walls makes them more visible to children.
(D) For example, when placed slightly lower on the walls, children can see the paintings better.
(E) Placed paintings that are lower on the walls are more visible to children.

GO ON TO THE NEXT PAGE ⟶

38. Which of the following is the best way to revise sentences 10 and 11 (reproduced below)?

If necessary, museums should set up special "children's times" during which young people may roam through the building, enjoying the artwork in their own way. A wonderful learning experience!

(A) To avoid disrupting everyone else, create "children's times" in the museum, during which children could roam throughout the building, enjoying the artwork in their own way and a wonderful learning experience.

(B) Museums should set up "children's times." This would be a wonderful learning experience. Children could roam through the museum. Children could enjoy the artwork in their own way.

(C) If necessary, museums should set up a wonderful learning experience called "children's times." During it, young people could roam throughout the building, enjoying the artwork in their own way.

(D) To enjoy artwork in their own way, children should be given the freedom to roam throughout the building. This would be a wonderful learning experience, and it could be called "children's times."

(E) To avoid disrupting other museum-goers, museums should set up special "children's times." During these times, children would be allowed to roam throughout the building and enjoy the artwork in their own way. What a wonderful learning experience!

39. In context, sentence 14 could be made more precise by changing the phrase "This is" to which of the following?

(A) That is

(B) These changes are

(C) The reasons for these changes is that they are

(D) It is

(E) These changes, as mentioned above, are also

STOP

**If you finish before time is called, you may check your work on this section only.
Do not turn to any other section in the test.**

PRACTICE TEST 1 ANSWERS

Section 1	Section 2	Section 3	Section 4	Section 5	
1. C	1. D	25. D	21. D	1. B	31. A
2. C	2. D	26. C	22. E	2. A	32. D
3. E	3. D	27. A	23. A	3. E	33. D
4. D	4. C	28. A	24. B	4. C	34. E
5. B	5. B	29. D	25. B	5. D	35. E
6. B	6. C	30. C	26. A	6. A	36. B
7. A	7. E	31. A	27. E	7. B	37. C
8. C	8. B	32. C	28. D	8. E	38. E
9. D	9. D	33. E	29. 7	9. C	39. B
10. A	10. C	34. E	30. .36	10. A	
11. A	11. A	35. A	31. 80	11. D	
12. B	12. E	36. C	32. 14	12. C	
13. B	13. C	37. B	33. 20	13. E	
14. D	14. D	38. A	34. 8,000	14. B	
15. B	15. D	39. A	35. 45	15. E	
16. C	16. C	40. A	36. 40	16. E	
17. A	17. E	41. C	37. 3	17. D	
18. D	18. B	42. C	38. $\frac{5}{9}$	18. C	
19. E	19. B	43. A	or	19. A	
20. D	20. B	44. D	.555	20. B	
21. B		45. B	or	21. C	
22. A		46. E	.556	22. A	
23. E		47. D		23. E	
24. C		48. B		24. D	
				25. C	
				26. B	
				27. D	
				28. B	
				29. C	
				30. A	

You will find a detailed explanation for each question beginning on page 292.

SCORING YOUR PRACTICE PSAT

Critical Reading

After you have checked your answers against the answer key, you can calculate your score. For the two Critical Reading sections (Sections 1 and 3), add up the number of correct answers and the number of incorrect answers. Enter these numbers on the worksheet on the next page. Multiply the number of incorrect answers by .25 and subtract this result from the number of correct answers. Then round this to the nearest whole number. This is your Critical Reading "raw score." Next, use the conversion table to convert your raw score to a scaled score.

Math

Figuring your Math score is a bit trickier, because some of the questions have 5 answer choices (for these, the incorrect answer deduction is .25), and some are Grid-Ins (which have no deduction for wrong answers).

First, check your answers to all of the problem-solving questions on Sections 2 and 4. For Section 2 and questions 21–28 of Section 4, put the number of correct answers and the number of incorrect answers into the worksheet on the next page. Multiply the number of incorrect answers by .25 and subtract this total from the number of correct answers. For questions 29–38 of Section 4, the Grid-In questions, simply put in the number of correct answers. Now, add up the totals for both types of math questions to give you your total Math raw score. Then you can use the conversion table to find your scaled score.

Writing Skills

The Writing Skills section should be scored just like the Critical Reading sections. Add up the number of correct answers and the number of incorrect answers from Section 5, and enter these numbers on the worksheet on the next page. Multiply the number of incorrect answers by .25 and subtract this result from the number of correct answers. Then round this to the nearest whole number. This is your Writing Skills raw score. Next, use the conversion table to convert your raw scores to scaled scores.

WORKSHEET FOR CALCULATING YOUR SCORE

Critical Reading

	Correct	Incorrect	

A. Sections 1 and 3 _____ – (.25 × _____) =

$\boxed{}$
A

B. Total rounded Critical Reading raw score

$\boxed{}$
B

Math

			Correct	Incorrect

C. Section 2 and Section 4—Problem Solving _____ – (.25 × _____) =

$\boxed{}$
C

D. Section 4—Grid-Ins_____ =

$\boxed{}$
D

E. Total unrounded Math raw score (C + D)

$\boxed{}$
E

F. Total rounded Math raw score

$\boxed{}$
F

Writing Skills

Section 5 _____ – (.25 × _____) =

$\boxed{}$

Total rounded Writing Skills raw score

$\boxed{}$

SCORE CONVERSION TABLE

Math Raw Score	Math Scaled Score	Critical Reading Raw Score	Critical Reading Scaled Score	Writing Skills Raw Score	Writing Skills Scaled Score
0	26	0	25	0	29
1	29	1	27	1	30
2	30	2	29	2	31
3	32	3	30	3	32
4	34	4	32	4	33
5	35	5	33	5	35
6	36	6	34	6	36
7	38	7	36	7	37
8	39	8	37	8	39
9	40	9	38	9	40
10	41	10	39	10	41
11	42	11	40	11	43
12	43	12	41	12	44
13	44	13	42	13	45
14	45	14	43	14	46
15	46	15	44	15	48
16	47	16	45	16	49
17	48	17	46	17	50
18	50	18	47	18	51
19	51	19	48	19	52
20	52	20	49	20	54
21	53	21	50	21	55
22	54	22	51	22	56
23	55	23	52	23	57
24	57	24	53	24	59
25	58	25	54	25	60
26	59	26	54	26	62
27	60	27	55	27	63
28	61	28	56	28	65
29	62	29	57	29	66
30	64	30	58	30	68
31	65	31	59	31	69
32	66	32	60	32	71
33	68	33	61	33	73
34	70	34	62	34	74
35	72	35	62	35	76
36	74	36	63	36	77
37	77	37	64	37	78
38	80	38	66	38	80
		39	67	39	80
		40	68		
		41	69		
		42	71		
		43	72		
		44	74		
		45	76		
		46	78		
		47	80		
		48	80		

Chapter 13
Practice Test 1:
Answers and
Explanations

Section 1

Question	Answer	Explanation
1	C	It's probably easier to start with the second blank on this question. The clue *protect the earth* indicates that we can fill in the blank with something like *change*. That eliminates answer choices (A), (B), and (E). The trigger *though* tells us that the first part of the sentence goes in a different direction than the second (which tells us that people are not willing to change), so we can write down something like *promote*. That eliminates answer choice (D), so only (C) is left.
2	C	All we know about Prince Klemens von Metternich is that he *dominated* the Congress of Vienna, so he probably had a *dominating* personality. Only answer choice (C) comes close.
3	E	The first blank has the clues *enlivened* and *by the strong rays of the sun,* so *lively* would be a good word to write down. (B), (C), and (D), therefore, can go. The second blank is talking about the canopy, which typically covers the forest floor; if the forest floor now has sun shining on it, the canopy must have been *broken through.* (E) is much closer than (A).
4	D	If the iguana is *reclusive,* then fruitful investigations are probably hard to get. So *rarity* would be a good word to fill in the blank. Answer choice (D) is closest.
5	B	The governor wanted *more housing,* but she ended up making housing *even more scarce.* That means she *worsened* the problem. The only answer choice that means *worsened* is (B).
6	B	The clues *friendly and honest manner* tell us we can replace the first blank with *friendly and honest,* so we can eliminate (C), (D), and (E). We have a trigger, *but,* which tells us the second part of the sentence goes in the opposite direction, so we can write down *not friendly and honest* for the second blank. The closest answer is (B).
7	A	Because we don't have clues for each blank here, we should go by the relationship between the blanks. The blanks here have a relationship of similarity; either the musicians loved it and wanted to promote it, or they hated it and wanted to get rid of it. So we would write down *same.* (A) has a relationship of similarity, so we can keep it. (B), (D), and (E) are going in opposite directions, and (C) has no relationship, so we can eliminate those.
8	C	The first blank can be replaced with something like *rebellion,* based on the clue *rebellion* in the sentence. That eliminates (B) and (D). We can see now in the answer choices that the first words in each pair are actually people, but that doesn't matter—following the technique, we're still right on track. The triggers *even though* and *now* tell us that the second blank is going to have a negative word in it; the United States now views rebels as *bad.* That eliminates (A), which has a positive word, and (E), which has a neutral word, leaving only (C).

Question	Answer	Explanation
9	D	Answer choice (D) is correct because the passage states that the *centuries-old rules* are *not so different* from Oulipo techniques. (B) is extreme, (C) can be eliminated as the group has been meeting only since 1960, and neither (A) nor (E) is supported by evidence from the passage.
10	A	Answer choice (A) is correct because *churn out* indicates quantity instead of quality. (B) is incorrect because the phrase is not a reference to Oulipo. There is no evidence for (C) or (D) in the passage, and (E) is extreme—ETS isn't going to include a passage by an author who is "disgusted."
11	A	Answer choice (E) is too ambitious, as no historical event is really explained in the passage. Cultural significance is not mentioned, so we can eliminate answer choice (D). There is no explanation to support (B), and President Johnson's character is not attacked, as (C) says. As for (A), there is in fact a possible controversy downplayed: The contention that President Johnson manufactured the Gulf of Tonkin crisis is waved away in the last sentence. So (A) is a good fit.
12	B	The argument would be strengthened by a report explaining the discrepancy between the two destroyers. Which answer choice says this? (C) and (E) are not relevant to the scope of the passage. (A) and (D) don't resolve the discrepancies between the two destroyers, so they actually weaken the argument. But (B) makes the argument stronger by explaining how it could be that the U.S.S. *Maddox* did not pick up the other ships on its radar. Be careful when dealing with weaken/strengthen questions, as the opposite answer to what you're looking for will generally be in the answer choices.
13	B	This is a primary purpose question, so we want an answer choice that describes what the author was trying to accomplish in Passage 1. (C) is clearly outside the scope of the passage. (D) confuses cattle with pigs and dogs as to which species are scavengers. (A) and (E) are too narrow. (B) is a nice summary of the argument at the end of the passage, so it's the best choice.
14	D	Here we have a line reference question, so go back to the quote and read above and below it. The quote refers to the interactive nature of the domestication of species such as pigs and dogs. Thus, (B), (C), and (E) are not correct. (A) refers to the same general notion, but it is too narrow, leaving us with answer choice (D).
15	B	This is a Vocab-in-Context question. We want to come up with our own word based on the context of the passage. We might come up with something like *unplanned*. (A), (C), (D), and (E) are all distracters based on the language of the passage. (B) is the closest thing to our word.

Question	Answer	Explanation
16	C	Another line reference question, so go back to the passage and read about 5 lines above and 5 lines below. The myth is described as the life and death of the moon goddess. (A) misses the focus, so it's out. (B) is out of context. Gazelles are mentioned later, as an afterthought, so (D) is incorrect. (E) is a distracter that garbles the words of the paragraph. (C) is the best option.
17	A	The passage indicates that the animals were susceptible to domestication, and the human culture was evolved enough to control the animal. The correct answer needs to reflect both elements. (D) and (E) focus on one side or the other. (B) is out of context. (C) is not even in the ballpark. Knowing the vocabulary helps a lot: We're looking for an answer choice that reflects a *mutually beneficial* relationship. (A), with its mention of "harmony," fits the bill.
18	D	This is a lead word question. Look for the word *Maglemosian* and you'll find it in line 63. Then read 5 lines up and 5 lines down to find the answer. The author is emphasizing that we don't really know what happened, but domestication clearly differed with respect to both species and human culture. Since the author gives no details, (A) is clearly not the answer. While (B) is probably true, it's not the answer to the question. (C) is out, as the point of mentioning both cultures was to indicate that culture is important. (E) is gone for basically the same reason; culture and species are important. Only (D) says this.
19	E	This is a Lead Word question. Go find where the passage talks about *Rattus norvegicus* and see what the studies revealed. The passage states that "the tremendous behavioral changes undergone by a species during domestication…cannot yield the total behavior pattern of the wild ancestors." Only (E) reflects that statement. (A) is a distracter based on confusion about what *Rattus norvegicus* is. (B) is a distracter based on the language of the passage, but the passage doesn't say that psychological insights were learned. (C) and (D) are the direct opposites of the implication of the paragraph.
20	D	Another Lead Word question, so go hunt down where the passage talks about Lorenz's imprinting experiments. Looks like the fourth paragraph tells us that imprinting helped domesticate birds. (A), (B), (C), and (E) are all true, but none answer the question. The question is, "What is the author saying about the role of imprinting in domestication?" (D) answers that question.
21	B	Here we need to pick an answer that is consistent with the views of both authors. (A) has extreme language: *the single most important factor*, so cross it out. Imprinting applies mainly to birds and not to mammals, so (C) is incorrect. (D) is wrong because capturing animals for ceremonies is a possible stage, not a critical stage. (E) presents what we perhaps would like to think, but it is neither stated nor implied in the passage.

Question	Answer	Explanation
22	A	The difference in the two passages is really one of emphasis, based in part on the species discussed. The two are closest in terms of dogs and pigs, but neither rules out what the other describes about the domestication of various species. (B) is incorrect since Passage 1 deals mainly with the religious significance of cattle, not other species. (C) is incorrect since Passage 1 treats dogs and pigs in passing; cattle are the focus of Passage 1. (D) is too narrow a construction of both passages. (E) is incorrect because Passage 1 doesn't deal with studying lab rats and birds. (A) is our best choice.
23	E	Here we need an answer choice that shows a difference between the authors' views or something that states an idea they both reject. (A), (B), (C), and (D) combine ideas from each passage that the authors would agree on. (E) garbles the hypotheses: Lab rats weren't used as hunting decoys!
24	C	The "social enzyme" has to do with the "proclivity…to keep pets." Neither passage notes the roles of cattle as "pets," so (A), (B), and (D) are incorrect. The scavenger behavior has to do with dogs and pigs seeking out man, not man keeping them as pets, so (E) is incorrect.

Section 2

Question	Answer	Explanation
1	D	To solve for b, our first move should be to move the 4 to the other side of the equation by adding 4 to both sides. This will give us $12b = 4$. Now we divide each side by 12, and get $b = \frac{1}{3}$.
2	D	Before doing any math on this problem, we should ballpark and eliminate answers we know are wrong. The question tells us that 60 gallons represents $\frac{5}{12}$ of the full tank—or a little less than half. So the full tank will need to be a little more than twice 60 gallons, or something a little larger than 120. This makes choices (A), (B), and (E) unreasonable, so let's eliminate those choices. The answer has to be either (C) or (D). To figure out which, let's try plugging in the answer choices. Is $\frac{5}{12}$ of 128 equal to 60? Nope, that's equal to 10.67. So let's try choice (D). Is $\frac{5}{12}$ of 144 equal to 60? Yes, so (D) is the answer.

Question	Answer	Explanation
3	D	To make this problem easier, let's plug in some numbers for the sides of this rectangle. We can pick whichever numbers we want, as long as they make the area equal to 16. So let's assume that the rectangle has dimensions 8 and 2. This makes the base of the triangle 8 and the height 2, so the area of the triangle will be $\frac{1}{2} \times 8 \times 2$ or 8. (Even if we made the dimensions of the rectangle 16 and 1, we'd still get the same answer!) You may also know the rule that a triangle inscribed in a rectangle will have exactly half the area of that rectangle; but even without knowing the rule, by plugging in some values we can figure it out.
4	C	The first multiple of 32 is 32, so the correct choice must divide evenly into 32. In other words, 32 must be a multiple of the correct choice. Is 32 a multiple of 11? No; nor is it a multiple of 9, 5, or 3. So we can eliminate (A), (B), (D), and (E).
5	B	This looks like a good opportunity to Plug In the Answers. If we plug in (C), 32, we find that angle A is 32, angle B is 94, and angle C is 90—which adds to way more than 180, the number of degrees in any triangle. This eliminates (C), (D), and (E). When we try (B), 23, we get a triangle whose angles measure 23, 67, and 90. Perfect!
6	C	Since we've got variables in the answer choices, we should plug in. We can plug in whatever consecutive numbers we want for x, y, and z, provided that we obey the rule that $x < y < z$. Let's choose 2 for x, 3 for y, and 4 for z, since those are easy numbers. The question then asks: What is the sum of y and z? Using our numbers, the answer will be $3 + 4$, which makes 7. Now the question is: Which of the answer choices gives 7, using our value of 2 for x? Answer choice (C) gives $2(2) + 3$, which equals 7.
7	E	This question looks nasty, but if we remember our MADSPM rules, it won't be too bad. Whenever we raise an exponent to another exponent, it is the same as multiplying the exponents together. So $(2^a)^b$ is the same thing as $2^{a \times b}$. Using a calculator we can figure out that $64 = 2^6$, so $a \times b$ must be equal to 6.

Question	Answer	Explanation
8	B	Let's remember our rules for adding and subtracting roots: We can only add or subtract if the number under the radical sign is the same. So first, we have to simplify the expressions. $6\sqrt{18}$ can be rewritten as $6\sqrt{9 \times 2}$. Since we have a perfect square under the radical sign, we can square root it and pull it out, giving us $6 \times 3\sqrt{2}$, or $18\sqrt{2}$. $4\sqrt{72}$ equals $4\sqrt{36 \times 2}$, which becomes $4 \times 6\sqrt{2}$ or $24\sqrt{2}$. $\sqrt{8}$ equals $\sqrt{4 \times 2}$, which equals $2\sqrt{2}$. $10\sqrt{32}$ equals $10\sqrt{16 \times 2}$, which equals $10 \times 4\sqrt{2}$, which becomes $40\sqrt{2}$. So finally we have $18\sqrt{2} + 24\sqrt{2} - (2\sqrt{2} + 40\sqrt{2})$. Now all of our roots have been simplified to something $\sqrt{2}$, so we can add and subtract normally. Starting inside the parentheses, $2\sqrt{2} + 40\sqrt{2} = 42\sqrt{2}$. $18\sqrt{2} + 24\sqrt{2} - 42\sqrt{2} = 0$. Of course, you can also just do this problem on your calculator.
9	D	A line with negative slope is one that you can draw going down and to the right from any starting point. Lines $\overline{AE}$ and $\overline{BD}$ won't count, since they have no slope. The only ones we can draw are $\overline{AC}$, $\overline{FD}$, and $\overline{AD}$. Don't be thrown off by the coordinates given for points A and B—they're just there to assure you that segments AB and DE actually are parallel to the x-axis.
10	C	You can Plug In the Answers here, but in this case translation is a little bit easier: Once we have $x = 3 + 7x$, we can subtract $7x$ from both sides to leave us with $-6x = 3$. Divide both sides by -6 and we find that x is equal to 3 divided by -6, which equates to choice (C).
11	A	Like many problems on the PSAT, this question will be difficult if we try to do it all at once. Instead, let's break it down into bite-sized pieces. Let's start with just part of the inequality, $-12 \le 3b + 3$. Remember that we can solve inequalities just like equations—provided that if we multiply or divide by a negative value, we swap the direction of the inequality sign. To solve this part of the inequality, though, we just need to subtract 3 from each side (giving us $-15 \le 3b$) and then divide each side by 3, which leaves us with $-5 \le b$. Now we can eliminate several choices that we know won't work: (B), (D), and (E) don't have -5 in them. Now let's take the other part of the inequality: $-3b + 3 \le 18$. If we subtract 3 from each side and then divide by 3, we get $b \le 5$. Now we can cross off (C), and we're left with (A).

Question	Answer	Explanation
12	E	Let's start by plugging in a number for x. We need an odd integer divisible by 3, so let's pick $x = 9$. The question asks us which of the following must be divisible by 4. (A) says $x + 1$, or 10, which is not divisible by 4. (B) says $x + 2$, or 11, which is also not divisible by 4. This allows us to eliminate (A) and (B). (C) says $x + 3$, or 12, which is divisible by 4, so we should leave (C) in. (D) says 18, which is not divisible by 4, so we can eliminate this choice too. (E) says 16, which can be divided by 4, so we should leave it in. Now we're down to (C) and (E). Let's pick another number for x and keep working. How about $x = 15$? In this case, (C) gives us 18, which is not divisible by 4. This knocks off (C), so the answer must be (E).
13	C	To find the perimeter, we need to find the lengths of each of the sides of this triangle. Side AB is fairly easy, since we can just count the points: from $(0, 4)$ to $(6, 4)$ is a length of 6. However, finding sides $\overline{AC}$ and $\overline{BC}$ is a little more difficult. The problem tells us that $\overline{AC} \cong \overline{BC}$, so we know that point C must be on the x-axis right in between points A and B—which places it at coordinate $(3, 0)$. Now to find the length of $\overline{AC}$, we can look at the triangle formed by A, C, and the origin. This triangle has a base of 3, since point C is at $(3, 0)$, and a height of 4, since point A is at $(0, 4)$. This makes a right triangle with sides 3 and 4, so side $\overline{AC}$ must be equal to 5. We can do the same thing to solve for side $\overline{BC}$. So we know that the sides of this triangle are 6, 5, and 5 for a total perimeter of 16.
14	D	Let's plug 5 and 7 in for n to find the 5th and 7th terms. The 5th term is $2 + 3^5 = 2 + 243 = 245$. The 7th term is $2 + 3^7 = 2 + 2,187 = 2,189$. The sum of the 5th and 7th terms is $245 + 2,189 = 2,434$.
15	D	Since we have variables in the answer choices, we should plug in on this problem. To make the math work easily, let's pick 5 for c, 10 for g, and 20 for n. If 1 bottle containing 5 ounces will fill 10 glasses, then how many bottles will be needed to fill 20 glasses? Two bottles. So now 2 is our target answer. Using 5 for c, 10 for g, and 20 for n, (A) equals 40, which is too large. (B) gives 10, which is also too large. (C) gives .5, which is too small. (D) gives 2, which is our target, but let's remember to do POE completely and check the remaining answer choice. (E) gives .25, which is too small.
16	C	First, let's figure out sets C and D. Set C is the intersection of sets A and B, so its elements are the elements that are in both sets: 0, 1, and 2. Set D is the union of A and B, so we figure out its elements by taking all the distinct elements from each set: -1, 0, 1, 2, and 3. So $C = \{0, 1, 2\}$ and $D = \{-1, 0, 1, 2, 3\}$. Now we can work through the answer choices and eliminate any that don't fit the description of an "interior" set. In answer choice (A), if we multiply -1 by 2, we would get a product of -2. -2 is not in set A, so we can eliminate (A). In (B), we can multiply 2 and 3 for a product of 6, which isn't in set B, so (B) can be eliminated too. (D) also has a 2 and 3 but no 6, so we can eliminate it. In (E), the union of A and C is $\{-1, 0, 1, 2\}$. Since -1 and 2 give a product of -2 and there is no -2 in the set, (E) is also not correct.

Question	Answer	Explanation
17	E	This question is testing volume. The volume of the original block of cheese is $8 \times 8 \times 8$, or 512. The piece that we cut out measures $4 \times 2 \times 2$, so its volume is 16. If we take away 16 from 512, so we get 496. The fractional part that remains will be $\dfrac{496}{512}$, or $\dfrac{31}{32}$.
18	B	This figure is not drawn to scale, so we won't be able to trust our eyes on this one. We can, however, still plug in, since we have variables in the answer choices. Let's plug in 30 for a and see what happens. If we make $a = 30$, then we will have values for four of our angles: angle a (30), angle $2a$ (60), angle $3a$ (90), and the other angle that measures $2a$ (60). This makes a total of 240 degrees out of 360. This means that the other angles, b and b, must add up to 120. So b must be equal to 60. The question asks us for the measure of b, so 60 is our answer. Now we just see which choice (remembering that $a = 30$) gives 60. This shows us that (B) is the answer.
19	B	If we're averaging two numbers x and y, then this average will always be half of the sum of these numbers. Let's try some values for x and y and see what kind of numbers we get. Since $y = 4x$, if $x = 5$ then $y = 20$, and their sum is 25. If $x = 6$ then $y = 24$, and their sum is 30. If $x = 7$ then $y = 28$, and their sum is 35. It looks like the sum of x and y will always be a multiple of 5. Now let's look at the choices we have, starting with (C). If the average of x and y is 4, then their sum will be 8. But we know that the sum of x and y will always be a multiple of 5, so (C) can't be right. Likewise for answer choices (D) and (E): If the average is 12, the sum of x and y will be 24; if their average is 28, their sum would have to be 56. So neither of these could be right. The only answer choice that would give us a sum of x and y as a multiple of 5 is choice (B).
20	B	To solve direct proportion questions, just set up a proportion. In this case, $\dfrac{y_1}{(x_1)^2} = \dfrac{y_2}{(x_2)^2}$ becomes $\dfrac{18}{(3)^2} = \dfrac{2}{(x_2)^2}$. Cross-multiplying and solving gives you $x_2 = 1$.

Section 3

Question	Answer	Explanation
25	D	The sentence mentions *small population* and *shyness*, which are both factors that would *hurt* studies, so *hurt* is a good word to fill in the blank. Only (D) comes close to the same definition.
26	C	*All segments of society* provides a good clue to tell us that something like *increased* or *made popular* would be a good replacement for the blank, making (C) the best answer choice.

Question	Answer	Explanation
27	A	It looks like we can start with the first blank easily enough: What happens to old technology when new technology comes along? It gets *replaced*, which allows us to eliminate (B), (C), and (D). A trigger helps us nail down the second blank: *While many* consumer electronics are replaced, apparently the home computer is an exception, and it will be many years before it becomes…*useless*, maybe? That allows us to eliminate (E). (A) still works, so pick (A).
28	A	Let's work on the first blank. We have the clue *refused to give up* and the trigger word *although* which means that a good word for the first blank would be something like *insurmountable*. That eliminates (C), (D), and (E). For the second blank, we know that we're looking for something positive, perhaps *good* or *clever*. That eliminates (B), so (A) is correct.
29	D	Wow, if 2,500 out of 3,200 residents made their way through a blizzard to vote, they must have been pretty *determined*. (D) has the closest definition.
30	C	Answer choice (C) is correct; both passages mention the importance of facts or relevant information. (A) and (B) are incorrect; only Passage 1 supports those answers. (D) is extreme. (E) is wrong because only the author of Passage 2 would agree with the answer.
31	A	Answer choice (A) is correct; Passage 1 mentions *new historicist*, revisionism. (B) is wrong because both passages mention historical events. (C) is incorrect because both passages are focused on U.S. history, and both mention one of the world wars. (D) is wrong because both passages are partisan—one toward conservative historical analysis, one toward revisionist history. (E) is never mentioned.
32	C	Answer choice (C) is correct; Passage 1 claims that *facts are facts*, while Passage 2 admits the possibility of bias. (A) is wrong because both passages mention military history. (B) is wrong because both deal with U.S. history. (D) is wrong because Passage 2 deals with bias, not limited interpretation. (E) is wrong because both passages believe that their approach to history is the most accurate one.
33	E	Answer choice (E) is correct; the second passage is concerned that historians overlook the contributions of minority groups. (A) is too narrow. (B) and (D) are extreme. (C) is extreme and offensive.
34	E	The author's main purpose in writing the passage, as can be seen in the last paragraph, is to show how his experiences with the choir affected his approach to other areas of his life. While (C) and (D) occur in the passage, neither adequately summarizes the entire passage. In (B), *worship* is too strong. (A) is never mentioned in the passage. Therefore, (E) is the best answer.

Question	Answer	Explanation
35	A	Here's a line reference question, so let's go back to the passage and read enough to get the context. In describing "Madame Jeanette," the author uses terms such as *cloying sentimentality*, and states that, when performed by teenagers under the guidance of *sloppy conducting*, it becomes *maudlin* and an *embarrassing tearfest*. (B) and (D) are never mentioned in the passage. (C) is incorrect because the piece becomes compelling and poignant only under the guidance of a director of Wilhousky's caliber. While (E) might look tempting, the reader is never told that the piece is technically difficult for most choirs, and we are never told that this is a reason for it to be considered "dangerous." Therefore, (A) is the best answer.
36	C	In lines 34–35, the author states that performing the piece was a *wonderful solace for an insecure boy of his age*, and later in the paragraph he refers to its ability to fill him with a sense of *hope and possibility*. This makes (C) the best answer.
37	B	Here's a Vocab-in-Context question, so let's come up with our own word. The author states in line 42 that he *still marvels* at the level of obedience Wilhousky was able to command, which implies that children at that time were quite obedient to begin with. So perhaps *more common* will work. While (A), (C), (D), and (E) could be considered plausible definitions of the word *ready*, only (B) is close to our word. Thus, it is the best answer.
38	A	This question asks us why the author included a particular detail. The author introduces the anecdote of the boy in the third row immediately after discussing how Wilhousky instilled discipline "through intimidation by public ridicule," and the boy's story serves as an example of this. (B) is incorrect because the author himself confesses that he is uncertain about what was really said, so we can't be sure that Wilhousky was really lying. This also eliminates (E), since we can't be sure that he's really trying to *trick* his students. (D) is incorrect because while the author does mention the human memory, this is not the purpose of the anecdote. While the author suggests that Wilhousky was a disciplinarian, it's hard to find evidence in the passage that the author would go so far as to call him *cruel*, which eliminates (C). Therefore, (A) is the best answer.
39	A	In the last paragraph, the author states that, as a result of working with Wilhousky, the author "slowly personalized the dream that excellence in one activity might be extended to become the pattern, or at least the goal, of an actual life." (B), (C), (D), and (E) are never mentioned. Therefore, (A) is the best answer.

Question	Answer	Explanation
40	A	We're being asked to infer something here, so we need something that stays close to the passage, even if it's not literally mentioned. The passage states that China and India both "embarked on daring reform programs in order to modernize their economies," making (A) a solid inference. (B) describes the situation at the end of the twentieth century, not before World War II. There is nothing in the passage to support (C) or (D). (E) is what the author says India must do now to gain economic success.
41	C	The author argues that "China was successful because its political system was conducive to the high levels of centralized control"; (C) would most hurt this claim. (A) would support the argument that China was economically patient. (B) and (E) are both irrelevant to the author's arguments about politics and economics. India's SOEs were ineffective, but the fact that China also had them would not hurt the author's argument about why China was more successful, making (D) incorrect.
42	C	The author states that the fact that India had a parliamentary democracy made all the difference in terms of the effects of its reforms and then goes on to discuss how Indian leaders were hampered by their fear of *rocking the boat* and losing the ability to get elected, making (C) the best answer. (A) and (D) both take a far more positive stance toward parliamentary democracies than the author does. (B) is too extreme. (E) is not supported by the passage; parliamentary democracies and economic patience are not discussed in conjunction with each other.
43	A	This is a weird question with an EXCEPT for us to deal with. We need to find which answer choices have support and which don't. The odd one out will be our answer. India wanted to decrease the country's dependence on *formerly imported goods*, not to discourage foreign manufacturing in and of itself. Thus, (A) is the only answer not supported by the passage. (B), (C), (D) and (E) can all be found in the fourth paragraph.
44	D	Vocab-in-Context. From the context, it is clear that "repercussions" are negative effects; the author contrasts India's leaders, who would have to get reelected, to those in China, making (D) the credited answer. (A) and (B) attempt to trick the readers with words that remind one of the original word. The sentence does not go into how much work would be involved, making (C) incorrect. The sentence does not suggest that India would need to change laws to quash rebellion, making (E) incorrect.
45	B	The final paragraph serves to reiterate India's difficulties in modernizing and point to a future path, making (B) the correct answer. The author offers answers about what happened to India, so (A) and (D) are not correct. The final paragraph follows the tone and direction of the rest of the passage, making (C) incorrect. (E) is not a possible answer; there is nothing lighthearted about the passage.

Question	Answer	Explanation
46	E	This is a weird, hypothetical question. We need the answer most consistent with the author's argument. The author asserts that India would have needed both development in stages and the capability to enforce changes fully, making (E) the credited answer. (A) and (D) are drawing too strong a conclusion since they deal with only half of the equation. There is nothing in the passage to support (B). (C) is not correct; it is what the author insists India must do now to foster success.
47	D	The passage states that India "must reevaluate its priorities and set truly national goals," as in (D). (A) is not correct; the passage argues for changes within India's democratic system. SOEs were one of the reasons India did not succeed, so (B) is incorrect. While the passage argues that India's leaders are ineffective because they will not rock the boat, voting them out, as in (C), is not suggested as a solution. (E) is not correct: The fact that no one is willing to cut jobs is simply offered as one of the current problems with India's system.
48	B	This is a tone question, so we need to focus on how the author talked about China. Throughout the passage, the author emphasizes China's strengths, making (B) the credited answer. (A) is too extreme. (C) and (D) both suggest a negative attitude toward China not found in the passage. (E) indicates that the author's admiration for China is because of the need to keep a good relations with the country; the passage does not support this reading.

Section 4

Question	Answer	Explanation
21	D	We can add the like terms to find $14z = -42$. Divide by 14 to find $z = -3$.
22	E	This question is asking us to compare pecks and bushels, so let's make a proportion: $\frac{10\,\text{pecks}}{2.5\,\text{bushels}} = \frac{x\,\text{pecks}}{4\,\text{bushels}}$. Then we can cross-multiply and solve for x, which results in $x = 16$.
23	A	The slope-intercept form of the equation of a line is $y = mx + b$, where m is the slope, and b is the y-intercept. So we would manipulate this equation to solve for y. Subtracting $2x$ from both sides of the equation and then dividing both sides by 3 gives us $y = -\frac{2}{3}x + 4$, so the y-intercept is 4.

Question	Answer	Explanation
24	B	We've got variables in the answer choices, so let's plug in. Try $a = 3$ and $x = 2$. The expression turns into $\frac{3}{4} + \frac{7}{2}$, which equals $\frac{17}{4}$, our target number. Now we can replace a with 3 and x with 2 in the answers to see which hits our target. Only (B) does.
25	B	The slope-intercept form of the equation of a line is $y = mx + b$, where m is the slope and b is the y-intercept. So the slope of the line given by the first equation is 6. To find the slope of a perpendicular line, we would take the negative reciprocal. So $c = -\frac{1}{6}$.
26	A	Positive difference just means the absolute value of the difference. So for $|-1 - 2.5|$, the difference is 3.5. Plug in the answer choices to find the one with the difference of 3.5: $$\|(-5) - (-8.5)\| = 3.5$$
27	E	Negative exponents mean to take the reciprocal of the positive exponent. For example, $y^{-2} = \frac{1}{y^2}$, and $2^{-3} = \frac{1}{2^3}$. For fractional exponents, the denominator tells us what root of the number to take and the numerator acts as a normal exponent. So, $f(x)$ is $\frac{1}{\sqrt[3]{x^2}}$. First, let's find $f(8)$: $\frac{1}{\sqrt[3]{8^2}} = \frac{1}{\sqrt[3]{64}} = \frac{1}{4}$. Next, let's find $f(3)$: $\frac{1}{\sqrt[3]{3^2}} = \frac{1}{\sqrt[3]{9}}$. Put these values in for $\frac{f(8)}{f(3)}$. So, $\frac{\frac{1}{4}}{\frac{1}{\sqrt[3]{9}}} = \frac{1}{4} \div \frac{1}{\sqrt[3]{9}} = \frac{1}{4} \times \sqrt[3]{9} = \frac{\sqrt[3]{9}}{4}$. Remember to look at the answer choices so you don't keep trying to simplify when there's no need to.
28	D	The first student has 6 choices of where to sit. For each place the first student sits, the second student has 2 choices of where to sit—only on either side of the first student. (So, if the first student sits in seat b, the second student can sit in seat a or seat c.) Thus, the total number of possible arrangements is $6 \times 2 = 12$.
29	7	The vertical bars around a number mean absolute value, which tells us to find the distance on the number line between that number and zero. To find the absolute value of a negative number, simply remove the negative sign. The absolute value of $|-10|$ is 10, and the absolute value of $|3|$ is 3. So, $10 - 3 = 7$.

Question	Answer	Explanation
30	.36	Let's start with the first part of the question. Twenty percent of n is 36. If we translate this into math, it becomes $\frac{20}{100}n = 36$. Now we can solve for n by reducing $\frac{20}{100}$ to $\frac{1}{5}$ and by multiplying each side by 5. $\frac{1}{5}n = 36$, so $n = 36 \times 5$. This gives us $n = 180$. Now we translate the other part and plug in 180 for n. What is .2 percent of 180 becomes: $x = \frac{.2}{100} \times 180$. Now we solve for x, and get $x = .36$.
31	80	When we draw it, we see that triangle RST is isosceles, with angle R equal to angle T. Since there are 180 degrees in a triangle, and we are told that angle S is 20 degrees, angles R and T must add up to 160 degrees. Since R has the same measure as T, each is 80 degrees.
32	14	While we don't know the exact lengths of the bottom or right side of the figure, we don't need to know them. We know that the edges unknown horizontal edges must have a total length of 3, and the unknown vertical edges must have a total length of 4. Therefore, we know that the total perimeter of the object is 4 + 3 + 4 + 3 = 14. You can also simply make up values for the missing side lengths, so long as the horizontal ones add up to 3 and the vertical ones add up to 4.
33	20	Since the problem tells us the value of x, which is 23, we can put this into the equation and solve for y. $23 - 8 = 5y$, so we know that $15 = 5y$ and $3 = y$. Now we know the value of y. However, on this problem, let's not forget that we're not just solving for y; we're solving for $x - y$. So the correct answer is $23 - 3$, or 20.
34	8,000	Let's start by finding all of the positive integer factors of 20. We can factor 20 into 1 × 20, 2 × 10, and 4 × 5. The question asks for the product of these numbers, which will be 1 × 20 × 2 × 10 × 4 × 5, or 8,000.

Question	Answer	Explanation
35	45	If Marcia types 18 pages per hour, and David can type 14 pages per hour, then together they will be able to type 18 + 14, or 32 pages per hour. To see what fraction of an hour it will take them to type 24 pages, we can set up a proportion: $$\frac{32 \; pages}{1 \, hour} = \frac{24 \; pages}{x \; hours}$$ If we solve for x, we can see that they can type 24 pages in .75 of an hour. But that isn't our answer! The question asks for the answer in minutes. Three-quarters of an hour is equal to 45 minutes, so the answer is 45.
36	40	When it's difficult to tell where to start on a geometry question, it's best to just start filling in what you know. Since we know that the angles in a triangle always add up to 180, we can figure out the third angle of the triangle with angles 45 and 60. The sum of these angles is 105, so the third angle must measure 75. This means that the angle next to it on the line must also measure 105. Now in the triangle on the left, we have angles 105 and 35. Together these angles make 140, so we know that the third angle (marked with an x) is equal to 40.
37	3	Since the problem tells us that $f(a) = 10$, and that $f(x) = x^2 - x + 4$, we can say plug a into the function for x so $f(a) = a^2 - a + 4$, and $10 = a^2 - a + 4$. Now we need to factor to solve for a. If we subtract 10 from both sides of the equation, we get $a^2 - a - 6 = 0$ which we can factor as $(a - 3)(a + 2) = 0$. The value of a could be 3 or -2, but since the question tells us that a is non-negative, the value of x must be 3.
38	$\frac{5}{9}$ or .555 or .556	When the problem asks for relationships between numbers (read: fractions, percents, ratios, probabilities) but doesn't give any actual numbers, it's time for us to plug in! Let's start with the large blue and large red marbles and work our way out: Say there are 2 large red marbles and 10 large blue marbles. That means there are 12 large marbles, so there must be 6 small marbles, giving us a total of 18 marbles. Therefore, the probability of picking a large blue marble out of the whole box is $\frac{10}{18}$ which won't fit in the grid, so we can reduce it to $\frac{5}{9}$ or divide it out to get .555 or .556.

Section 5

Question	Answer	Explanation
1	B	*They* is an ambiguous pronoun—does it refer to the French, the friends, or the parents (yuck)? (B) is the only answer that fixes the pronoun problem without changing the meaning of the sentence.
2	A	The sentence is correct as written. It's a little awkward, but none of the answers improves the sentence.
3	E	Neil couldn't possibly have done all of those things at the same time. (C), (D), and (E) fix that problem, but only (E) fixes it in a way that doesn't introduce parallelism errors.
4	C	*Critically* is an adverb, but the sentence needs an adjective to modify *circling* and *underlining*. (Yes, they look like verbs, but they are the subjects of the second part of the sentence, so we treat them like nouns.) (A) and (B) are gone, then, and (E) adds way too many redundant words, so we can eliminate it, too. The first difference between (C) and (D) is *one* versus *you*. *One* stays in the same voice as the other subjects in the sentence, and *you* does not. (D) also has some extra words on the end, so it's out anyway, and (C) is correct.
5	D	The sentence has a misplaced modifier; Samuel Spade is not a movie. (And you don't have to be a film buff to know that— even the sentence says that Samuel Spade is a detective and the movie is *The Maltese Falcon*.) So (A) can be eliminated, and so can (E), which doesn't fix the misplaced modifier. (B) mentions that *The Maltese Falcon* is a movie twice, so it's redundant, and also the phrase "Samuel Spade, detective" is awkward. (C), like (B), is missing a comma after *The Maltese Falcon*. (D) fixes the misplaced modifier problem without adding new errors, so it is the best answer.
6	A	The sentence is correct as written.
7	B	The sentence has a redundant conjunction; *yet* is unnecessary because there is already an *although* at the beginning. So we can eliminate (A), as well as (D) and (E), which don't solve the problem. (B) and (C) say the same thing, but (B) is short and sweet while (C) is awkward and wordy, so (B) is correct.
8	E	The pronoun *they* in the underlined portion is ambiguous—we don't know whether it refers to the chairpersons or the committees—so (A) is gone. (B) unnecessarily introduces *thereby*, and both (B) and (D) change the verb form, so we can eliminate them. (C) replaces *their* with *her*, which does not agree with the subject, *chairpersons*. Only (E) fixes the error without creating new ones.
9	C	The verbs in the underlined portion are not parallel, so (A) can be eliminated. (B) and (D) don't fix the parallelism problem. (E) changes the meaning slightly, so (C) is our best answer.
10	A	The sentence is correct as written.

Question	Answer	Explanation
11	D	The word *actor* is singular, so *their character* is wrong; *his or her character* is correct. Eliminate (A) and (C). For the same reason, *as they wish* is wrong, so eliminate (B), and *as he or she wish* has an agreement error that you can spot without even referring back to the rest of the sentence, so eliminate (E). That leaves (D).
12	C	*They* is an ambiguous pronoun; we don't know whether it refers to *Omar and his family* or *neighbors*. (B) repeats the problem. (D) fixes the ambiguity but is redundant, and (E) adds awkwardness by adding *being* unnecessarily.
13	E	This one is easier than it might look. Who was known for graduating from college despite being blind and deaf? Helen Keller was: not *the fact*, not *accounts*, not *many people*, and not *six decades*. Eliminate (A), (B), (C), and (D). Only (E) fixes the error, so you can stop there.
14	B	Miles can be counted, so the comparison word *less* is incorrect; therefore, we can eliminate (A), (D), and (E). The *to be putting* in (C) is awkward, which typically happens when an *–ing* verb is added, so (B) is the best answer.
15	E	The verb *has enlisted* is in present perfect tense, but the action happened in the past and does not continue to the present. Only (E) has the correct verb tense.
16	E	(A) and (C) both have the verb *were*, which doesn't agree with the subject, *art*. (B) is passive, and (D) has the progressive tense *were practicing*, which changes the meaning. (E) is in active voice with no grammatical errors.
17	D	There is a clear split between the answer choices, so we can use that to determine the first thing being tested. (A) and (B) have *regarded to be*, and (C), (D), and (E) have *regarded as*. Which idiom is correct? *Regarded as* is correct, so we can eliminate (A) and (B). Now let's look for differences in the remaining answer choices. (C) has the plural verb *are*, while (D) and (E) have the singular verb *is*. Since the subject *the bristlecone pine*, *is* is correct we can eliminate (C). (E) adds an unnecessary *being*, making the answer choice awkward and wordy, so (D) is the best answer.
18	C	The correct idiom here is *originates in*, not *originates from* or *originates with*. The only choice with the correct form is (C).
19	A	The sentence is correct as written.
20	B	The sentence uses a comma to connect two independent clauses. We need a period, a semicolon, or a conjunction here, so we can eliminate (A). (C) joins the clauses with incorrect punctuation, as a colon should introduce an example or examples of what came before it. (D) is incorrect because we don't want a semicolon *and* a conjunction. (E) adds a *however*, which should come only after a semicolon. Only (B) joins the independent clauses correctly, with a semicolon.
21	C	The verb *serving* is not parallel to *attempted*. *Served* would be correct.
22	A	*A member* doesn't agree with *twins*. *Members* would be correct.
23	E	The sentence is correct as written.

Question	Answer	Explanation
24	D	*Unjust* is an adjective, yet it is modifying the verb *ignored*. The adverb *unjustly* would be correct.
25	C	The verb *focus* is not parallel to *centering*. *Focusing* would be correct.
26	B	The verb *spend* is in the wrong tense in the context of the sentence. *Spent*, which is in past tense, would be correct.
27	D	*Previous years* is being compared to *last quarter's financial reports*, creating an incorrect comparison. *Previous years' reports* or *those of previous years* would be correct.
28	B	The pronoun *you* is being used to replace *one*, which is in a different form. *One* would be correct.
29	C	*Insisted on* is an incorrect idiom. *Insisted that* would be correct.
30	A	*Were* is paired up with the singular pronoun *each*, but a singular verb is needed. *Was* would be correct.
31	A	The possessive pronoun *her* doesn't agree with the subject that it's replacing, *Karen and Mary*. *Their* would be correct.
32	D	*Critic toward* is an incorrect idiom. *Critic of* would be correct.
33	D	*That of* is being compared to *contributor*, which is an apples-and-oranges comparison. Leaving out *that of* entirely would be correct.
34	E	The sentence is correct as written.
35	E	The answer choice that provides the most clarity would be the one that identifies who *them* is. (E) is the only answer choice that does that.
36	B	(B) is the answer choice that is most relevant to the passage; all the other answer choices are too far out of scope.
37	C	(C) and (D) provide the best transition from sentence 3 with the addition of *for example*, but (D) and (A) have misplaced modifiers—are the children going to be placed on the walls? (E) is passive and (B) is very awkward. Therefore, (C) is the best answer.
38	E	Though most of (A) flows well with no errors, it has a missing verb at the end that makes it incorrect. (B) has no transitions between each short, choppy sentence, so there is no logical flow. (C) and (D) change the meaning of the sentence. Only (E) keeps the meaning, has a good flow, and doesn't introduce new errors.
39	B	A good replacement for *This is* would agree with (and make clear) what's being referred to. (A), (C), and (D) do not do that. (E) introduces the redundant *as mentioned above*, so (B) is the best answer.

Chapter 14
Practice Test 2

SECTION 1
Time — 25 minutes
24 Questions

Directions: For each question in this section, select the best answer from among the choices given and fill in the corresponding oval on the answer sheet.

Each sentence below has one or two blanks, each blank indicating that something has been omitted. Beneath the sentence are five words or sets of words labeled A through E. Choose the word or set of words that, when inserted in the sentence, <u>best</u> fits the meaning of the sentence as a whole.

Example:

Medieval kingdoms did not become constitutional republics overnight; on the contrary, the change was -------.

(A) unpopular (B) unexpected (C) advantageous

(D) sufficient (E) gradual

1. Unlike her award-winning first book, Roberta's new volume can only be considered a ------- effort.

   (A) significant (B) mediocre (C) whimsical
   (D) feasible (E) laudable

2. Most animals respond to ------- with excessive violence; in contrast, some remain ------- when facing serious physical danger.

   (A) kindness . . calm
   (B) peril . . aggressive
   (C) sympathy . . impassive
   (D) neutrality . . belligerent
   (E) threats . . placid

3. Unfortunately, many of Aristotle's works are ------ to us, since they were ------- along with the ancient library at Alexandria.

   (A) unknown . . promoted
   (B) lost . . destroyed
   (C) meaningless . . investigated
   (D) important . . chastised
   (E) clear . . suppressed

4. Engineers attribute the building's ------- during the earthquake, which destroyed more rigid structures, to the surprising ------- of its steel girders.

   (A) obliteration . . strength
   (B) damage . . weakness
   (C) survival . . inadequacy
   (D) endurance . . suppleness
   (E) devastation . . inflexibility

5. Prior to the discovery of one intact ancient burial site in Central America, it had been thought that all of the Mayan tombs had been ------- by thieves.

   (A) levitated
   (B) exacerbated
   (C) inculpated
   (D) delayed
   (E) desecrated

6. Although the first viewers of *Waiting for Godot* jeered and called the play -------, later audiences came to recognize the ------- of the piece, and it soon became one of the classics of world theater.

   (A) abominable . . impenetrability
   (B) complicated . . fickleness
   (C) lenient . . unpleasantness
   (D) melancholy . . exultation
   (E) preposterous . . subtlety

7. In his later works, Langston Hughes's discussions of ethnic issues in America became increasingly -------, as he relied less on veiled criticism and more on direct confrontation.

   (A) concrete (B) coherent (C) forthright
   (D) confused (E) delineated

8. Few would call the company president ------- ; in fact, he would often ------- the ideas of his subordinates, alleging that they were his own.

   (A) xenophobic . . exemplify
   (B) original . . expropriate
   (C) innovative . . inculcate
   (D) duplicitous . . arrogate
   (E) egregious . . steal

GO ON TO THE NEXT PAGE

The passages below are followed by questions based on their content; questions following a pair of related passages may also be based on the relationship between the paired passages. Answer the questions on the basis of what is <u>stated</u> or <u>implied</u> in the passage and in any introductory material that may be provided.

Questions 9-12 are based on the following passages.

Passage 1

Medicine as a discipline is focused on the concept of "complete benevolence": that is, the purpose of medicine is to heal patients. This idea has been
Line espoused by doctors and other medical professionals
5 since time immemorial. The Hippocratic Oath—conceived by doctors in ancient Greece and still used today— reinforces this idea: according to the oath, the first job of a medical worker is to "do no harm" to the patient. Complete benevolence is the highest moral
10 standard of science and should be the focus of every doctor's practice and decision-making ability.

Passage 2

Patient care is a large part of medicine; this fact cannot be denied. However, medicine is a science, and as such its primary goal is a quest for knowledge.
15 Without the use of human subjects in laboratory experiments, doctors would still be using leeches to cure their patients. The use of humans as well as lab animals to further science has led to the development of vaccines, cures for common aliments, and the
20 introduction of revolutionary drug therapies. Doctors are healers, but care for their patients should never interfere with the process of scientific discovery.

9. The difference between the two passages' views on the purposes of medicine can best be described as the difference between an emphasis on

(A) research on human subjects and research on animal subjects
(B) subjective care and objective care
(C) sympathy and practicality
(D) patients' rights and doctors' rights
(E) patient care and science

10. Which of the following would the author of Passage 1 most likely claim in order to weaken the author of Passage 2's assertion that scientific discovery is paramount in medicine?

(A) Scientific discovery is impossible without practical tests.
(B) Biology may be a research-based science, but medicine is applied knowledge.
(C) More patients die under the care of surgeons than under family doctors.
(D) Humans use scientific discovery to destroy life as well as preserve it.
(E) Preliminary research often reaches inaccurate conclusions.

11. The author of Passage 1 refers to the Hippocratic Oath in order to

(A) support the claim that patient care has been a primary concern of doctors for millennia
(B) highlight changes in ancient Greek medicine and modern medicine
(C) disprove the usefulness of modern laboratory experiments
(D) allude to a higher standard of medicine than the one currently used
(E) differentiate between medicine and research

12. On which of the following points would the authors of both passages most likely agree?

(A) Patient care and scientific discovery are sometimes incompatible.
(B) Patients are essential to the practice of medicine.
(C) Patient care and research can coexist for the good of the patient.
(D) Medicine is a science of discovery.
(E) Medicine has always valued patients over everything else.

GO ON TO THE NEXT PAGE

Questions 13-24 are based on the following passages.

The following passages both concern ecological conservation. Passage 1 discusses the Serengeti, one of the last remaining African nature preserves, while Passage 2 discusses a specific conservation study there.

Passage 1

There is no other plain in the world comparable to the Serengeti. Wild animals still graze in obscure corners of the African continent from Cape Town to Chad, but as
Line civilization moves in, the animals are quickly crowded
5 out; in Botswana, for example, the northwest corner was said to hold abundant game up until 1973, but now the diamond industry is preparing to drill wells for its mines and the Okovanggo Basin, which sustained the game, may be drained out. Every major civilization has eventually
10 destroyed its wildlife, and civilization is fast overtaking Africa.

The Serengeti remains the great anachronism, its survival maintained through an odd, almost mystical series of countervailing conditions that have thus far managed
15 to tip a fragile balance slightly to the side of the animals: population increases vs. drought and famine; cattle proliferation vs. pestilence and disease; land pressure for cultivation vs. tourist income; scientific research vs. the vagaries of nature.
20 The Serengeti's agonies are local and for the most part unrealized by the rest of the world; its importance as a cultural resource for the world community, however, is unchallenged. Scientists see it as a sort of an ecological paradise regained, however briefly, and not only for its
25 importance as the last gathering place for the rich diversity of African wildlife but as well for the light it may shed on the larger question of man's survival.

"The Serengeti is basic to the concerns of conservation," says William Conway, director of the Bronx Zoo. "If
30 animals can live there, so can man; if not, man cannot. It is the case of what is often referred to as the canary simile—the miners in Wales took canaries into the pits to serve as an early-warning system; when the foul air killed the canaries, the miners knew it was time to get out. There
35 are practical aspects to all this. The production of the Salk vaccine required the destruction of 600,000 wild monkeys over a three-year period. Between the United States and Japan, science is currently using them up at the rate of 100,000 a year." Peter Jackson, director of information at
40 the World Wildlife Fund, says, "All our domestic crops and animals have been bred from wild stock, and especially among plants it is the genetic resources available in the wild which have helped to produce new wild yields." Conway asks, "Do we save animals for themselves or for
45 ourselves? Will man set aside for tomorrow something he can use today? It hasn't happened yet. Does man truly want wildlife on Earth, and is he willing to make the sacrifices necessary to keep it here?"

Passage 2

Of all his projects, John Owen's decision to establish a
50 scientific observation in the midst of the Serengeti Plain was his most inspired. In 1961, the wildebeest appeared to be overgrazing the grasslands of the Serengeti. Owen felt he ought to find out if this was so; and if it was, what should be done about it. Soon, in characteristic
55 fashion, he virtually backed the new government into the establishment of an observatory station.

In order to answer Owen's early question of whether the wildebeest were overgrazing the Serengeti, the scientists first had to establish the relationship of the wildebeest
60 to their food supply. In 1958, the Michael Grzimek Laboratory had counted 99,000 wildebeest. In 1963, Lee and Martha Talbot counted 240,000. By 1969, there would be more than half a million. It appeared that, in fact, the wildebeest were not overgrazing the Serengeti; by the
65 mid-1960s some of the reason for this would become clear. There was a severe drought in 1960-1961 that had since ended. However, although the grasses feeding the wildebeest within the park had become thick and healthy, the land surrounding the Serengeti, which fed cattle, was
70 overgrazed. Inexplicably, as the cattle outside the park were starving, the wildebeest inside were flourishing.

The fact that the wildebeest population was increasing is significant. More important, however, is the fact that a principal regulating mechanism tended to keep their
75 numbers below levels that would have damaged their habitat. In other words, even though the high rainfall throughout the 1960s produced more food for more animals, there were never too many animals for the grass that was there. Thus, the wildebeest population
80 was regulated by a symmetrical relationship between the wildebeests' birth and death rates, the number of animals adjusted by the death rate—starvation as a form of control even in a time of abundance.

What had now become apparent to the scientists of the
85 Research Institute was that the grasslands of the Serengeti formed a self-sustaining ecological system. Everything, they found, was interdependent—fire, rain, soil, grass, the host of animals. Each living thing depended on the other, each flourished because of the other. The Serengeti, with
90 its extraordinary residents, was at a stage, still undisturbed, of an evolutionary process that had been going on for hundreds of thousands of years.

GO ON TO THE NEXT PAGE

13. Passage 1 implies which one of the following about the northwest corner of Botswana?

   (A) All of its wildlife will be destroyed through increasing encroachment by civilization.

   (B) After 1973, it was no longer home to as much wildlife as it had previously been.

   (C) Its problems are local concerns and have no effect on the world ecology.

   (D) The world must study its ecological destruction in order to prevent similar tragedies.

   (E) The Okovanggo Basin was drained to make room for diamond mines.

14. The author of Passage 1 believes that we should study the problems of the Serengeti plain because

   (A) many other regions of the world share similar concerns

   (B) of the disappearance of certain types of wildlife

   (C) the natural balance may be now tipping toward mankind

   (D) the results of this study may assist humanity in its quest for survival

   (E) of increasing development in the region

15. The author of Passage 1 quotes Conway (lines 28-39) in order to

   (A) point out the distinction between survival and conservation drawn in the previous paragraph

   (B) show why current conservation methods have failed to achieve the desired results

   (C) provide further support for the claim that conservation assists humans as well as animals

   (D) discuss conservation methods from earlier centuries

   (E) support the position that the Serengeti is no longer an interesting subject of study

16. The word "yields" (line 43) most nearly means

   (A) reservations
   (B) claims
   (C) output
   (D) traffic
   (E) difficulties

17. The examples of the miners in Wales and the Salk vaccine (lines 32-37) provide support for which one of the following claims?

   (A) Animals may in some cases be able to help humans live longer and happier lives.

   (B) Wherever people can live, animals can live there also.

   (C) The natural competition between animals and humans in the wild is detrimental to humans.

   (D) Animals that cannot be tamed are of no use to humans.

   (E) Advances in medical science will be impossible without the continued use of animals for scientific experimentation.

18. The author of Passage 2 mentions that prior to John Owen

   (A) there had been no attempt made to study the Serengeti

   (B) the national government was reluctant to support any scientific research

   (C) there had been some investigation of the wildlife on the Serengeti

   (D) the Serengeti was a natural habitat virtually unknown to humans

   (E) other scientists had unsuccessfully attempted to enlist governmental support for their studies

19. The author of Passage 2 discusses the three studies that counted the number of wildebeest (lines 60-63) in order to

   (A) show that many scientists were working on the same problem of wildebeest populations

   (B) support the claim that the Serengeti was not being overgrazed

   (C) discuss the effects of a severe drought on animal populations

   (D) demonstrate the importance of cattle in the Serengeti ecosystem

   (E) show the dramatic climatic changes that occurred during the 1960s

GO ON TO THE NEXT PAGE

20. The phrase "principal regulating mechanism" in line 74 refers to

   (A) the natural limit placed on population growth by the food supply
   (B) the way in which the wildebeest were harmful to the environment
   (C) the difference between wildlife on the Serengeti and wildlife just outside the Serengeti
   (D) the effect of humanity's attempts to control disease in wildlife
   (E) the interaction of different types of wildlife in the Serengeti

21. According to the author of Passage 2, the primary conclusion of the Research Institute was that

   (A) the wildebeest was an isolated and unique case of wildlife population growth
   (B) humans were in danger of disturbing the ecological balance on the Serengeti
   (C) the Serengeti was a good example of a breakdown in a natural food chain
   (D) the Serengeti was a complex ecosystem with each member closely linked to the rest of the structure
   (E) the evolution of life on the Serengeti was coming to an end

22. For which of the following claims made in Passage 1 does Passage 2 provide the strongest evidence?

   (A) "Between the United States and Japan, science is currently using them [wild monkeys] up at the rate of 100,000 a year." (lines 37-39)
   (B) "Scientists see it as sort of an ecological paradise regained . . . for the light it may shed on the larger question of man's survival." (lines 23-27)
   (C) "Every major civilization has eventually destroyed its wildlife, and civilization is fast overtaking Africa." (lines 9-11)
   (D) "'All our domestic crops and animals have been bred from wild stock . . .'" (lines 40-41)
   (E) "The Serengeti remains the great anachronism, its survival maintained through an odd, almost mystical series of countervailing conditions that have thus far managed to tip a fragile balance slightly to the side of the animals." (lines 12-15)

23. The author of Passage 1 would most likely argue that if the Serengeti continues to develop according to recent trends, it will probably

   (A) eventually no longer be able to support wildlife
   (B) remain relatively stable for the foreseeable future
   (C) push back against the encroachment of civilization and regain lost territory
   (D) rapidly evolve new species of plants and animals that are better adapted to coexisting with civilization
   (E) be destroyed by researchers

24. Both authors would agree that the success of the Serengeti in maintaining its ecosystem is due in part to

   (A) a variety of different counterbalancing elements, both natural and artificial
   (B) humanity's lack of interest in the development of the plain
   (C) conservation efforts focusing on maintaining the fragile ecosystem
   (D) the fear of animals that keeps most people away from the Serengeti
   (E) the success of certain species in fully utilizing the abundant natural resources

STOP

**If you finish before time is called, you may check your work on this section only.
Do not turn to any other section in the test.**

NO TEST MATERIAL ON THIS PAGE.

SECTION 2
Time — 25 minutes
20 Questions

Directions: This section contains two types of questions. You have 25 minutes to complete both types. For questions 1-20, solve each problem and decide which is the best of the choices given. Fill in the corresponding oval on the answer sheet. You may use any available space for scratch work.

1. If each of the 12 small squares in the figure above has a side of length 2, what is the perimeter of rectangle *WXYZ* ?

(A) 28
(B) 32
(C) 36
(D) 46
(E) 56

2. If z is an even integer, which of the following must be an odd integer?

(A) $3z$
(B) $3z - 1$
(C) $2z$
(D) $2z - 2$
(E) $z + 2$

GO ON TO THE NEXT PAGE

3. If 16 feet of a 96-foot-tall tree are below ground, approximately what percent of the tree is above ground?

    (A) 16.6%
    (B) 20%
    (C) 25%
    (D) 33.3%
    (E) 83.3%

4. The number of holiday cookies sold at a certain bakery in the month of December varies directly with the day of the month. If 24 holiday cookies are sold on the 4th day of December, how many holiday cookies are sold on the 20th day of December?

    (A) 72
    (B) 108
    (C) 120
    (D) 144
    (E) 176

5. If $x = \dfrac{5n}{20}$, what is the value of n in terms of x ?

    (A) $\dfrac{x}{40}$

    (B) $4x$

    (C) $40x$

    (D) $100x$

    (E) $200x$

6. If $f(x) = 4x^2 + 3x + 8$, then $f(x) - 4 =$

    (A) $x^2 + 3x - 4$
    (B) $x^2 - x - 8$
    (C) $2x^2 + x + 8$
    (D) $4x^2 - x + 4$
    (E) $4x^2 + 3x + 4$

7. Eighty students went on a class trip. If there were 14 more boys than girls on the trip, how many girls went on the trip?

    (A) 66
    (B) 47
    (C) 40
    (D) 33
    (E) 26

8. If the area of one face of a cube is 36, what is the volume of the cube?

    (A) 18
    (B) 36
    (C) 64
    (D) 72
    (E) 216

Bake Sale Results	
Item	**Number Sold**
Cupcakes	33
Cookies	68
Small cakes	w
Large cakes	z
Doughnuts	24

9. At a bake sale, a total of 260 items were sold, as shown in the table above. If four times as many small cakes as large cakes were sold, what is the value of z ?

    (A) 22
    (B) 27
    (C) 32
    (D) 39
    (E) 135

GO ON TO THE NEXT PAGE

10. For which of the following lists is the average (arithmetic mean) less than the median?

(A) 1, 2, 6, 7, 8
(B) 2, 4, 6, 8, 11
(C) 4, 4, 6, 8, 8
(D) 4, 5, 6, 7, 8
(E) 4, 5, 6, 11, 12

11. During a sale, for every three shirts purchased at regular price, a customer can buy a fourth at 50% off. If the regular price of a shirt is $4.50, and a customer spent $31.50 on shirts, how many shirts did the customer purchase?

(A) 5
(B) 6
(C) 7
(D) 8
(E) 9

12. If $\dfrac{x^2 - x - 12}{2x^2 - 10x + 8} = \dfrac{5}{2}$, what is the value of x ?

(A) $\dfrac{1}{2}$
(B) 2
(C) $\dfrac{5}{2}$
(D) 3
(E) 5

13. If the value of x is at most 10 less than twice the amount by which z is greater than y, which of the following expresses x in terms of y and z ?

(A) $x \le 2(z - y - 10)$
(B) $x \le 2(z - y) - 10$
(C) $x \le 10 - 2(z - y)$
(D) $x \ge 10 - 2(z - y)$
(E) $x \ge 2(z - y) - 10$

14. Which of the following is the product of two consecutive multiples of 3 ?

(A) 240
(B) 255
(C) 270
(D) 285
(E) 300

15. What are the coordinates of the midpoint of the line segment with endpoints (6, −3) and (6, 9) ?

(A) (3, 3)
(B) (3, 6)
(C) (6, 1)
(D) (6, 3)
(E) (6, 6)

16. The ratio of a to b is 4 : 7 and the ratio of c to d is 2 : 5. Which of the following is equivalent to the ratio of bc to ad ?

(A) $\dfrac{8}{35}$
(B) $\dfrac{7}{10}$
(C) $\dfrac{1}{2}$
(D) 2
(E) $4\dfrac{3}{8}$

GO ON TO THE NEXT PAGE

17. A student took five tests. He scored an average (arithmetic mean) of 80 on the first three tests and an average of 90 on the other two. Which of the following must be true?

    I. The student scored more than 85 on at least one test.

    II. The average (arithmetic mean) score for all five tests is less than 85.

    III. The student scored less than 80 on at least two tests.

(A) I only
(B) II only
(C) I and II
(D) II and III
(E) I and III

18. The figure above shows two semicircles inscribed in a square. If the square has a side of length 10, what is the area of the shaded region?

(A) $50 - 75\pi$

(B) $50 - 25\pi$

(C) $100 - 25\pi$

(D) $\dfrac{100 - 25\pi}{2}$

(E) $\dfrac{100 - 75\pi}{2}$

19. If x is a positive integer such that $\dfrac{x}{4}$ is an odd integer and $\dfrac{x}{3}$ is an even integer, which of the following statements must be true?

    I. $\dfrac{x}{4} - \dfrac{x}{3}$ is odd.

    II. x is odd.

    III. $\left(\dfrac{x}{3}\right)^2$ is even.

(A) I only
(B) II only
(C) I and II
(D) I and III
(E) I, II, and III

20. A circle and a triangle have equal areas. If one base of the triangle has length 9, and the altitude to that base has length 8, what is the radius of the circle?

(A) 6

(B) 6π

(C) $\dfrac{6}{\sqrt{\pi}}$

(D) $\sqrt{72\pi}$

(E) 72

STOP

If you finish before time is called, you may check your work on this section only. Do not turn to any other section in the test.

SECTION 3

Time — 25 minutes
24 Questions

Directions: For each question in this section, select the best answer from among the choices given and fill in the corresponding oval on the answer sheet.

Each sentence below has one or two blanks, each blank indicating that something has been omitted. Beneath the sentence are five words or sets of words labeled A through E. Choose the word or set of words that, when inserted in the sentence, <u>best</u> fits the meaning of the sentence as a whole.

Example:

Medieval kingdoms did not become constitutional republics overnight; on the contrary, the change was -------.

(A) unpopular (B) unexpected (C) advantageous
    (D) sufficient (E) gradual

Ⓐ Ⓑ Ⓒ Ⓓ ●

25. Though he is usually very ------- at such occasions, John was surprisingly quiet at his engagement party.

(A) reserved (B) outgoing (C) successful
    (D) irreverent (E) vague

26. Although a few critics loved Isabel's new play, it never achieved the ------- success necessary for a long run in the theaters.

(A) intellectual (B) eccentric (C) persuasive
    (D) dignified (E) popular

27. Despite their very ------- cultural and religious backgrounds, the leaders of the civil rights march were able to put their differences behind them and fight for a ------- goal.

(A) diverse . . common
(B) different . . poetic
(C) similar . . joint
(D) indifferent . . unified
(E) incompatible . . remote

28. The ------- water made it extremely difficult for the divers to search for the sunken treasure, as they could see no more than a few feet in front of their faces.

(A) transparent (B) murky (C) malodorous
    (D) turgid (E) noxious

29. She was a very ------- student; she checked every reference in her papers and always used the correct form in her footnotes.

(A) prodigious (B) supercilious (C) punctilious
    (D) acute (E) inspirational

GO ON TO THE NEXT PAGE

The passages below are followed by questions based on their content. Answer the questions on the basis of what is <u>stated</u> or <u>implied</u> in the passage and in any introductory material that may be provided.

Questions 30-31 are based on the following passage.

Elizabeth Cady Stanton, along with her more famous colleague Susan B. Anthony, was one of the architects of the Women's Suffrage Movement. An avid diarist, she
Line frequently recorded events in her journal. Of her historic
5 first meeting with Miss Anthony in May 1851, she wrote these words: "How well I remember the day! . . . There she stood, with her good earnest face and genial smile, dressed in gray delaine, hat and all the same color, relieved with pale blue ribbons, the perfection of neatness and sobriety.
10 I liked her thoroughly, and why I did not at once invite her home with me to dinner I do not know . . ."

30. Stanton writes "How well I remember the day!" primarily to emphasize

   (A) the vividness with which she can recall this significant meeting
   (B) the beauty of the fall afternoon in her small town
   (C) the fact that Susan B. Anthony later claimed to have no recollection of their first meeting
   (D) the excitement she felt in meeting a famous person like Susan B. Anthony
   (E) the paramount importance this meeting had in furthering the suffrage movement

31. The author uses the word "relieved" in line 8 to mean

   (A) pleased
   (B) calmed
   (C) contrasted
   (D) replaced
   (E) reassured

Questions 32-33 are based on the following passage.

Studies have shown that male scientists tend to formulate their most influential theories while they are still fairly young. Albert Einstein, for instance, published
Line his breakthrough work on relativity at the tender age of 26.
5 One recent theory explains this phenomenon by contending that young male scientists, like young criminals, are subconsciously motivated by the desire to attract a mate. Most male criminals commit crimes in their late twenties and early thirties; most male scientists make the greatest
10 impact in their respective fields during the same period in their lives. After these scientists have found mates, according to this theory, their predilection for pursuing momentous scientific discoveries declines. In a similar vein, the severity and frequency of illegal activity among
15 male criminals generally diminishes after they marry. Both types of men have already attained the ultimate goal: a spouse.

32. In context, the word "predilection" in line 12 most nearly means

   (A) natural curiosity
   (B) strong dislike
   (C) intellectual ability
   (D) financial compensation
   (E) underlying preference

33. The primary argument of the "recent theory" in line 5 is that

   (A) young male scientists are essentially criminals
   (B) the main goal of momentous scientific discoveries is for the scientist to attract a mate
   (C) criminals commit crimes in their late twenties in order to attract a mate
   (D) people should make great discoveries if they seek a mate
   (E) the actions of one group of individuals are analogous to those of another in that the unconscious purpose of each is the same

GO ON TO THE NEXT PAGE

Questions 34-39 are based on the following passage.

The passage below is a short story written in 1982 that focuses on the reliability of an individual's perceptions of the outside world. The author investigates the psychology of several characters as they respond to a situation in their town.

One night a terrible screaming sounded through the city. It sounded so loudly and piercingly that there was not a soul who did not hear it. Yet when people turned to
Line one another in fear and were about to remark "Did you
5 hear it, that terrible screaming?" they changed their minds, thinking: "Perhaps it was my imagination, perhaps I have been working too hard or letting my thoughts get the upper hand" (one must never work too hard or be dominated by one's thoughts); "perhaps if I confess that I heard this
10 terrible screaming others will label me insane, I shall be hidden behind locked doors and sit for the remaining years of my life in a small corner, gazing at the senseless writing on the wall."

Therefore no one confessed to having heard the
15 screaming. Work and play, love and death, continued as usual. Yet the screaming persisted. It sounded day and night in the ears of the people of the city, yet all remained silent concerning it, and talked of other things. Until one day a stranger arrived from a foreign shore. As soon as he
20 arrived in the city he gave a start of horror and exclaimed to the Head of the Welcoming Committee, "What was that? Why, it has not yet ceased! What is it, that terrible screaming? How can you possibly live with it? Does it continue night and day? Oh, what sympathy I have for you
25 in this otherwise fair untroubled city!"

The Head of the Welcoming Committee was at a loss. On the one hand the stranger was a Distinguished person whom it would be impolite to contradict; on the other hand, it would be equally unwise for the Head of the Welcoming
30 Committee to acknowledge the terrible screaming. He decided to risk being thought impolite.

"I hear nothing unusual," he said lightly, trying to suggest that perhaps his thoughts had been elsewhere, and at the same time trying to convey his undivided attention
35 to the concern of the Distinguished Stranger. His task was difficult. The packaging of words with varied intentions is like writing a letter to someone in a foreign land and addressing it to oneself; it never reaches its destination.

The Distinguished Stranger looked confused. "You hear
40 no terrible screaming?"

The Head of the Welcoming Committee turned to his assistant. "Do you perhaps hear some unusual sound?"

The Assistant who had been disturbed by the screaming and had decided that very day to speak out, to refuse to
45 ignore it, now became afraid that perhaps he would lose his job if he mentioned it. He shook his head.

"I hear nothing unusual," he replied firmly.

The Distinguished Stranger looked embarrassed. "Perhaps it is my imagination," he said apologetically. "It is
50 just as well that I have come for a holiday to your beautiful city. I have been working very hard lately."

Then aware once again of the terrible screaming he covered his ears with his hands.

"I fear I am unwell," he said. "I apologize if I am unable
55 to attend the banquet, in honor of my arrival."

"We understand completely," said the Head of the Welcoming Committee.

So there was no banquet. The Distinguished Stranger consulted a specialist who admitted him to a private rest
60 home where he could recover from his disturbed state of mind and the persistence in his ears of the terrible screaming.

The specialist finished examining the Distinguished Stranger. He washed his hands with a slab of hard soap,
65 took off his white coat, and was preparing to go home to his wife when he thought suddenly, "Suppose the screaming does exist?"

He dismissed the thought. The Rest Home was full, and the fees were high. He enjoyed the comforts of civilization.
70 Yet supposing, just supposing, that all the patients united against him, that all the people of the city began to acknowledge the terrible screaming? What would be the result? Would there be a complete panic? Was there really safety in numbers where ideas were concerned?
75 He stopped thinking about the terrible screaming. He climbed into his Jaguar and drove home.

The Head of the Welcoming Committee, disappointed because he could not attend another banquet, yet relieved because he would not be forced to justify another item of
80 public expenditure, also went home to his wife. They dined on a boiled egg, bread and butter and a cup of tea, for they both approved of simple living.

Then they went to the bedroom, switched out the light and enjoyed the illusion of uncomplicated dreams.
85 And outside in the city the terrible screaming continued its separate existence, unacknowledged. For you see its name was silence. Silence had found its voice.

GO ON TO THE NEXT PAGE

34. What is the purpose of the parenthetical statement in lines 8-9 ?

   (A) It signals that the narrator disapproves of the informal tone of the people's thoughts.

   (B) It offers advice directly to the reader of the story.

   (C) It suggests that people tend to rationalize decisions that might be questionable.

   (D) It indicates that the people in the story are suffering from schizophrenia.

   (E) It emphasizes how surprising the people found the scream.

35. With which of the following statements would the author most likely agree?

   (A) Trust the perceptions of those around you rather than obsessing about your own ideas.

   (B) It is important to fall in with the beliefs of others.

   (C) Insanity always spreads most quickly at night.

   (D) People should never agree with the sensory perceptions of those surrounding them.

   (E) The fear of speaking out allows evil to be perpetuated.

36. As used in line 20, the word "start" most nearly means

   (A) sympathetic stare

   (B) quick beginning

   (C) sudden jump

   (D) pleased surprise

   (E) endless scream

37. It can be inferred from the passage that the author believes that the "packaging of words with varied intentions" (line 36)

   (A) guarantees the reception of those words

   (B) needs to be translated for those from other countries

   (C) always conveys several different meanings according to the listener

   (D) should be used by dignitaries dealing with foreign visitors

   (E) is inherently unlikely to convey the ideas behind the words, regardless of what those ideas are

38. According to the passage, one reason the Rest Home specialist dismisses the thought that the screaming might exist is that

   (A) the status quo affords him a lifestyle replete with material possessions

   (B) acknowledging the screaming would certainly lead to complete panic

   (C) if the screaming were real, the Rest Home would have to begin admitting more patients

   (D) such a conclusion would go against his professional training

   (E) he cannot accept that a foreigner such as the Distinguished Stranger might be right

39. This story can best be described as

   (A) a fable about how fears of job security lead to cowardice

   (B) an allegory that illustrates the pernicious effects of fear

   (C) a metaphor for insanity

   (D) a trivialization of the crippling effects of silence

   (E) a symbol of the benefits of modernity

GO ON TO THE NEXT PAGE

Questions 40-48 are based on the following passage.

Though slang may appear on the surface to be unworthy of serious study, Mario Pei in his 1954 book All About Language *offers an astute examination of the history of slang and its significance in modern society.*

Dialects are a matter of geography. Slang is nationwide. There are some who think that only poorer and less educated people use slang. This is not necessarily true. A little bit of slang, in fact, is used by practically everybody.
Line
5 Slang is a departure from standard, accepted language, but it may easily turn into standard language if it meets with enough favor. Or it may die out and leave little or no trace.

English is a language very rich in slang, but the mortality among slang words is very high. People who
10 make up our dictionaries usually admit slang expressions on probation. They are either placed in a separate section of the dictionary, or marked "colloquial" or "vulgar" or "slang." If they survive a certain number of years, the label is removed, and they are admitted on a basis of equality
15 with other words. If they disappear from use, they vanish also from the dictionaries.

In a many good cases, slang words and uses can be traced to one individual. Dizzy Dean, of baseball fame, is responsible for "goodasterous" as the opposite
20 of "disastrous," and "slud" as the past of "slide." Walter Winchell started the expression "making whoopee," and Shakespeare himself was the first to use, at least in writing, "beat it" and "not so hot." But far more often the creator of the slang expression is unknown.

25 Slang as we said before is nationwide. The expressions we see would be understood pretty much anywhere in America. Dialect is local, as where sections of the Midwest use "mango" in the sense of "green pepper." Two other items that call for discussion are cant and jargon.
30 Jargon is a form of speech current in a given class or profession and hardly understood on the outside. Cant, the language of the underworld, is a variety of jargon. A French poet of the fifteenth century, François Villon, used in many of his poems a type of Paris underworld cant that
35 cannot be understood today. American and British cant has been mysterious in the past, but today large segments of it are known, having been spread by detective stories, and many of its expressions have become general slang and even regular language. "Sawbuck" for "$10" and
40 "grand" for "$1,000" are generally understood and even used, though they are not the best language in the world. Other cant expressions that have acquired a measure of respectability are "take the rap," "take for a ride," "throw the book at," "blow one's top," "frisk," and "gat." But
45 there are many others not so well known, like "quizmaster" for "District Attorney."

There are jargons of the various professions and trades, even jargons of the sexes and age-levels. Bankers, lawyers, and doctors will talk among themselves in specialized
50 languages that people on the outside have difficulty

following. So do scientists, technicians, teachers, and scholars in every field. But it is not only the intellectual professions that have jargons; it is also the manual trades and occupations. From them, too, many words have come
55 into the general language. Shipboard terminology is very extensive and complicated, as you know if you have read stories about ships, particularly the old sailing vessels. When you speak of "knowing the ropes," "keeping on an even keel," "keeping a weather eye open," "giving
60 plenty of leeway," you are using sailors' expressions that have become general. But there are many more such expressions that have not entered the general language and that you have to look up in the dictionary if you want to understand all the details of a sea story.

65 There is a jargon for the military, railroad workers, rodeo people, truck drivers, and soda fountain attendants. In short, there is no occupation that doesn't have its own special terminology that baffles outsiders. Though linguists might condemn the investigation of slang as
70 unworthy of legitimate study, there is certainly the possibility that its widespread use might cause some of it to become part of the standard language sooner than they think.

40. In line 1, the phrase "Slang is nationwide" refers to the view that

(A) the use of slang is not restricted to a particular group of people
(B) slang is considered equivalent to standard English
(C) dictionary writers often accept slang on a trial basis
(D) the controversy over slang's popularity is not just a local problem, but also a national concern
(E) jargon is something that both professional and nonprofessional people have in common

41. In line 8, the word "rich" most nearly means

(A) wealthy
(B) abundant
(C) entertaining
(D) seasoned
(E) productive

GO ON TO THE NEXT PAGE

42. In the third paragraph, the author refers to Dizzy Dean and Shakespeare in order to

(A) present the reader with some of the more amusing examples of slang
(B) show how slang became popular both in sports and literature
(C) illustrate how both men shared similar phrases in their everyday speech
(D) explain that slang can usually be traced back to a single person
(E) offer examples of single individuals who were responsible for certain expressions

43. It can be inferred that "cant," as mentioned in line 31, was most popularly used by

(A) criminals
(B) French aristocracy
(C) Midwestern farmers
(D) bankers and doctors
(E) the military

44. It can be inferred from the passage that François Villon provides an example of

(A) how slang adds a unique quality to any piece of literature
(B) why certain slang expressions seem to enter into standard, accepted language
(C) how some expressions pass out of use over time
(D) how slang can make the difference in a writer's career
(E) why the French underworld during the fifteenth century was able to thrive for so long

45. The author describes certain examples of cant as "not the best language in the world" in line 41 so as to

(A) convey his opposition to the popular belief that cant has become one of the most accepted dialects
(B) describe the overwhelming popularity that cant seems to possess
(C) find a reason that cant is generally understood and even used
(D) communicate that such speech is not universally regarded as proper
(E) imply his distaste for the use of cant in society

46. The word "measure" in line 42 most nearly means

(A) rhythm
(B) meter
(C) degree
(D) melody
(E) regulation

47. The author mentions "shipboard terminology" in line 55 in order to illustrate

(A) that slang evolved within manual trades as well as intellectual fields
(B) the intellectual background that inspired such general terms as "keeping on an even keel"
(C) the complications that often followed sailors who worked on old sailing vessels
(D) the distinction between complicated nautical terms and more general terms like "knowing the ropes"
(E) the importance of understanding phrases like "keeping a weather eye open" in order to become an accomplished sailor

48. The author is primarily concerned with

(A) defining the importance of jargon in intellectual professions
(B) explaining the origins of slang and its different variations
(C) tracing the history of slang
(D) discussing how certain professions have been affected by the popularity of cant
(E) describing the effect that a single individual can have on slang

STOP

**If you finish before time is called, you may check your work on this section only.
Do not turn to any other section in the test.**

SECTION 4
Time — 25 minutes
18 Questions

Directions: This section contains two types of questions. You have 25 minutes to complete both types. For questions 21-28, solve each problem and decide which is the best of the choices given. Fill in the corresponding oval on the answer sheet. You may use any available space for scratch work.

1. The use of a calculator is permitted.

2. All numbers used are real numbers.

3. Figures that accompany problems in this test are intended to provide information useful in solving the problems. They are drawn as accurately as possible EXCEPT when it is stated in a specific problem that the figure is not drawn to scale. All figures lie in a plane unless otherwise indicated.

4. Unless otherwise specified, the domain of any function f is assumed to be the set of all real numbers x for which $f(x)$ is a real number.

Reference Information

$A = \pi r^2$
$C = 2\pi r$
$A = lw$
$A = \frac{1}{2}bh$
$V = lwh$
$V = \pi r^2 h$
$c^2 = a^2 + b^2$

Special Right Triangles

The number of degrees of arc in a circle is 360.

The sum of the measures in degrees of the angles of a triangle is 180.

---

21. A certain computer downloads 4 files of equal size per second. How many files of the same size will it download in 2 <u>minutes</u>?

(A) 6
(B) 8
(C) 120
(D) 240
(E) 480

22. In $\triangle ABC$, $AB = BC = CA$. If $\triangle ABC$ is congruent to $\triangle DEF$ then what is the measure of $\angle D$?

(A) 180°
(B) 150°
(C) 120°
(D) 90°
(E) 60°

23. Three roommates share their monthly rent payment in a ratio of 7 : 8 : 10. If the monthly rent is $1,200, then what is the amount of the <u>greatest</u> share?

(A) $336
(B) $360
(C) $384
(D) $400
(E) $480

GO ON TO THE NEXT PAGE

24. If $qs \neq 0$, then $\dfrac{2p}{q} - \dfrac{r}{2s} =$

(A) $\dfrac{4ps - qr}{2qs}$

(B) $\dfrac{2p - r}{2qs}$

(C) $-\dfrac{pr}{qs}$

(D) $\dfrac{2p - r}{q + 2s}$

(E) $\dfrac{2p - r}{q - 2s}$

25. If $abcd \neq 0$, $c = ab^{-2}$ and $d = a^{-1}b^4$, what is the value of cd in terms of a and b ?

(A) $\dfrac{1}{ab^8}$

(B) $a\sqrt[8]{b}$

(C) b^2

(D) $\left(\sqrt{a}\right)\left(\sqrt[5]{b}\right)$

(E) $\dfrac{a}{b}$

26. If $a = 9x^2 + 4$ and $b = 3x + 2$, what is a in terms of b ?

(A) $b^2 - 4b + 8$
(B) $b^2 - 4b + 4$
(C) b^2
(D) $9b^2 - 36b + 72$
(E) $9b^2 + 36b + 72$

27. In a group of 15 integers, the probability of randomly selecting an even number is $\dfrac{1}{3}$. Based on this information, which of the following can be determined?

   I. The probability of selecting an odd number
   II. The probability of selecting a number that is not the mode
   III. The average (arithmetic mean) of the greatest and least numbers in the group

(A) None
(B) I only
(C) II only
(D) III only
(E) I and II only

Note: Figure not drawn to scale.

28. In the figure above, the circle with center C is tangent to $\overleftrightarrow{AB}$ at point A. If $AB = 12$ and the length of segment $\overline{BC}$ (not drawn) is 13, what is the area of the circle with center C ?

(A) 10π
(B) 25π
(C) 144π
(D) 169π
(E) 313π

GO ON TO THE NEXT PAGE

Directions: For Student-Produced Response questions 9-18, use the grids at the bottom of the answer sheet page on which you have answered questions 1-8.

Each of the remaining 10 questions requires you to solve the problem and enter your answer by marking the circles in the special grid, as shown in the examples below. You may use any available space for scratch work.

Answer: $\frac{7}{12}$

Answer: 2.5

Answer: 201
Either position is correct.

Write answer → in boxes.

← Fraction line

← Decimal point

Grid in → result.

Note: You may start your answers in any column, space permitting. Columns not needed should be left blank.

• Mark no more than one circle in any column.

• Because the answer sheet will be machine-scored, **you will receive credit only if the circles are filled in correctly.**

• Although not required, it is suggested that you write your answer in the boxes at the top of the columns to help you fill in the circles accurately.

• Some problems may have more than one correct answer. In such cases, grid only one answer.

• No question has a negative answer.

• **Mixed numbers** such as $3\frac{1}{2}$ must be gridded as

3.5 or 7/2. (If [3 1 / 2] is gridded, it will be

interpreted as $\frac{31}{2}$, not $3\frac{1}{2}$.)

• **Decimal Answers:** If you obtain a decimal answer with more digits than the grid can accommodate, it may be either rounded or truncated, but it must fill the entire grid. For example, if you obtain an answer such as 0.6666..., you should record your result as .666 or .667. **A less accurate value such as .66 or .67 will be scored as incorrect.**

Acceptable ways to grid $\frac{2}{3}$ are:

29. In the figure above, what is the value of $x + y$?

30. If x is a negative integer and $|x| < 3$, what is one possible value of $|x|$?

GO ON TO THE NEXT PAGE

31. Two numbers have the property that their sum is equal to their product. If one of these numbers is 4, what is the other number?

32. If $\frac{1}{2}a$, $\frac{1}{2}a$, and a are the degree measures of a triangle, what is the value of a?

$$5, 11, 29, 83, \ldots$$

33. In the sequence above, the nth term can be expressed as $2 + 3^n$. What is the value of the 8th term?

34. What is the greatest of 4 consecutive integers whose sum is 414?

35. What is the area of a square with a diagonal of length $3\sqrt{2}$?

36. If n is a prime number greater than 3, then $6n$ has exactly how many positive integer divisors?

GO ON TO THE NEXT PAGE

37. If $x + y = 5$ and $x^2 - y^2 = 16$, what is the value of $x - y$?

38. Sally, Abdul, and Juanita have volunteered to stuff a certain number of envelopes for a local charity. Working by herself, Sally could stuff all the envelopes in exactly 3 hours. Working by himself, Abdul could stuff all the envelopes in exactly 4 hours. Working by herself, Juanita could stuff all the envelopes in exactly 6 hours. If Sally, Abdul, and Juanita work together at these rates to stuff all the envelopes, what fraction of the envelopes will be stuffed by Juanita?

STOP
If you finish before time is called, you may check your work on this section only.
Do not turn to any other section in the test.

SECTION 5
Time — 30 minutes
39 Questions

Directions: For each question in this section, select the best answer from among the choices given and fill in the corresponding oval on the answer sheet.

The following sentences test correctness and effectiveness of expression. Part of each sentence or the entire sentence is underlined material. Choice A repeats the original phrasing; the other four choices are different. If you think the original phrasing produces a better sentence than any of the alternatives, select choice A; if not, select one of the other choices.

In making your selection, follow the requirements of standard written English; that is, pay attention to grammar, choice of words, sentence construction, and punctuation. Your selection should result in the most effective sentence—clear and precise, without awkwardness or ambiguity.

EXAMPLE:

Laura Ingalls Wilder published her first book <u>and she was sixty-five years old then</u>.

(A)   and she was sixty-five years old then
(B)   when she was sixty-five
(C)   at age sixty-five years old
(D)   upon the reaching of sixty-five years
(E)   at the time when she was sixty-five

1. A large predatory snake, the muscular body of a boa constrictor can reach over 10 feet in length.

   (A)   the muscular body of a boa constrictor
   (B)   a boa constrictor whose muscular body
   (C)   a boa constrictor's muscular body
   (D)   the boa constrictor has a muscular body that
   (E)   as well as having a muscular body, the boa constrictor

2. The audience's response was better than Martin could possibly have <u>expected, having received</u> a standing ovation and great cheers from the crowd.

   (A)   expected, having received
   (B)   expected; and so he was receiving
   (C)   expected; he received
   (D)   expected: including the reception of
   (E)   expected, he was receiving

3. Watering your plant too often is as unhealthy <u>than if you do not water it</u> often enough.

   (A)   than if you do not water it
   (B)   as not watering it
   (C)   as if one were not to water it
   (D)   than not watering
   (E)   as for not watering it

4. Not only did the ancient Egyptians know about the North Pole, <u>but they also knew in precisely which direction it lay</u>.

   (A)   but they also knew in precisely which direction it lay
   (B)   but they had also known in precisely which direction it lay
   (C)   also knowing its precise direction
   (D)   also precisely knowing its direction
   (E)   but knowing its precise direction as well

GO ON TO THE NEXT PAGE

5. The Luna space probes were the first to enter solar orbit and photograph the far side of the moon, in 1959 they were launched.

(A) The Luna space probes were the first to enter solar orbit and photograph the far side of the moon, in 1959 they were launched.
(B) Launched in 1959, the Luna space probes were the first to enter solar orbit and photograph the far side of the moon.
(C) In 1959, the first solar orbit and photograph of the far side of the moon was taking place when the Luna space probes were launched.
(D) The launching of the Luna space probes was in 1959, the solar orbit was entered and the far side of the moon was photographed.
(E) The first solar orbit was when the Luna space probes were launched in 1959, and the first photograph of the far side of the moon was taken as well.

6. Perhaps the best-known of all southern American writers, William Faulkner's famous books include *The Sound and the Fury* and *As I Lay Dying*.

(A) William Faulkner's famous books include
(B) William Faulkner's books are famous for including
(C) William Faulkner has included among his famous books
(D) William Faulkner is famous for such books as
(E) William Faulkner is famous for including such books as

7. When the coach of the basketball team spoke, new uniforms for all the players were implied, but it was not promised by him.

(A) new uniforms for all the players were implied, but it was not promised by him
(B) new uniforms for all the players were implied, but he did not actually promise it
(C) new uniforms for all the players were implied by him and not actually promised
(D) he implied new uniforms for all the players, but they were not actually promised by him
(E) he implied, but did not actually promise, that he would get new uniforms for all the players

8. When Michelle was younger, she was hired by a local furniture store to watch the store in the mornings as well as cleaning the windows.

(A) as well as cleaning the windows
(B) and she also cleaned the windows
(C) as well as to clean the windows
(D) the cleaning of windows also being done by her
(E) together with cleaning the windows

9. Jason was nervous about the race he had to run, this nervousness gave him the energy to run even faster than he had expected.

(A) this
(B) furthermore
(C) but this
(D) for which
(E) that

10. The earliest design for a helicopter drawn by Leonardo da Vinci, the Italian artist and inventor, more than four hundred years ago.

(A) The earliest design for a helicopter drawn by Leonardo da Vinci
(B) Among the earliest designs for a helicopter by Leonardo da Vinci
(C) Leonardo da Vinci drew the earliest design for a helicopter
(D) Leonardo da Vinci, creator of one of the earliest design for a helicopter
(E) The earliest design for a helicopter was drawn by Leonardo da Vinci

11. After reading Mary Shelley's masterpiece *Frankenstein*, I couldn't hardly believe that she was only nineteen when she wrote it.

(A) I couldn't hardly believe
(B) I could hardly not believe
(C) I could not hardly believe
(D) I could hardly believe
(E) I could hardly be believing

12. Both Caleb and Joy seem like they are intending to become doctors.

(A) like they are intending to become doctors
(B) like they are intending to become a doctor
(C) to be intending to become doctors
(D) to be intending on becoming doctors
(E) like their intent is of becoming a doctor

13. Hydrogen, in combination with oxygen, forms the molecule we call water.

(A) in combination with oxygen
(B) in its combining with oxygen
(C) in the combination of it and oxygen
(D) having combined itself with oxygen
(E) with oxygen in combination

GO ON TO THE NEXT PAGE

14. Neither a broken leg nor an upset stomach <u>has prevented Jason to play</u> the flute in this year's concert.

(A) has prevented Jason to play
(B) have stopped Jason playing
(C) have prevented Jason from playing
(D) has prevented Jason from playing
(E) have stopped Jason in his playing

15. Zora Neale Hurston, author of *Their Eyes Were Watching God*, <u>is considered as one of the finest writers in</u> the Harlem Renaissance.

(A) is considered as one of the finest writers in
(B) is considered one of the finest writers of
(C) is considered to be one of the finest writers among
(D) considered as one of the finest writers of
(E) is the consideration of one of the finest writers of

16. Since Jonas Salk and Albert Sabin created protective vaccines, <u>Americans are no longer concerned with the spread of polio</u>.

(A) Americans are no longer concerned with the spread of polio
(B) Americans are no longer concerned with spreading polio
(C) Americans have no longer been concerned about the spread of polio
(D) Americans are no longer concerned about the spreading polio
(E) Americans are no longer concerned in the spreading of polio

17. The Brothers Grimm collected, <u>wrote, and published a book of fairy tales, they also wrote the first comprehensive German dictionary</u>.

(A) wrote, and published a book of fairy tales, they also wrote the first comprehensive German dictionary
(B) wrote, and published a book of fairy tales; but were also writing the first comprehensive German dictionary
(C) wrote, and published both a book of fairy tales and the first comprehensive German dictionary
(D) wrote and published a book of fairy tales; and the first comprehensive German dictionary
(E) wrote and published a book of fairy tales, they were also writing the first comprehensive German dictionary

18. The age-old practice of <u>extracting syrup from maple trees provides a natural source of sugar that has been done for many years</u>.

(A) extracting syrup from maple trees provides a natural source of sugar that has been done for many years
(B) extracting syrup from maple trees provides a natural source of sugar, and it has been done for many years throughout history
(C) extracting syrup from maple trees provides a natural source of sugar
(D) extracting syrup from maple trees, providing a natural source of sugar
(E) extracting syrup from maple trees providing a natural source of sugar has been done over time for many years

19. <u>If all citizens would take a more proactive stance on environmental issues,</u> Americans could look forward to a future of cleaner air and water.

(A) If all citizens would take a more proactive stance on environmental issues,
(B) Were all citizens to take a more proactive stance on environmental issues,
(C) Were all citizens taking a more proactive stance on environmental issues,
(D) If all citizens would be taking a more proactive stance on environmental issues,
(E) If all citizens would have taken a more proactive stance on environmental issues,

20. Children attending Camp Northwoods need to <u>bring a stamp</u> for <u>the letters they will write home to their parents</u>.

(A) bring a stamp for the letters they will write home to their parents
(B) bring a stamp for the letters he or she will write home to their parents
(C) bring stamps for the letters he or she will write home to their parents
(D) bring stamps for the letter they will write home to their parents
(E) bring stamps for the letters they will write home to their parents

GO ON TO THE NEXT PAGE

The following sentences test your ability to recognize grammar and usage errors. Each sentence contain either a single error or no error at all. No sentence contains more than one error. The error, if there is one, is underlined and lettered. If the sentence contains an error, select the one underlined part that must be changed to make the sentence correct. If the sentence is correct, select choice E. In choosing answers, follow the requirements of standard written English.

EXAMPLE:

The other delegates and him immediately
    A   B   C
accepted the resolution drafted by the
                     D
neutral states. No error
         E

Ⓐ ● Ⓒ Ⓓ Ⓔ

21. The actors were exhausted, but each was able to
          A   B
remember all the complicated lines on opening night.
        C   D
No error
  E

22. Mary Anne was indebted with her mother for all the
                 A   B
hard work her mother had done in preparation for the
        C   D
party. No error
     E

23. One way to determine the accuracy of reference books
          A
is to check the credentials of its editorial board.
B C   D
No error
  E

24. It is more convenient to reply to email at one's own
     A   B   C
convenience than answering the phone every time it
            D
rings. No error
     E

25. The works of Stephen King are similar to Peter Straub,
             A   B
a fact that is not surprising since the two men are
              C
friends and have even collaborated on two novels.
              D
No error
  E

26. In flight, a flock of geese encounters scarcely no wind
                 A   B
resistance because of the "v" formation it employs.
        C   D
No error
  E

27. Vital to any analysis of the causes of the Russian
            A
Revolution are an understanding of the many alliances
        B   C
between political parties in the early 1900s. No error
     D   E

28. Many of the players were professionals who, in prior
      A   B   C
years, had received gold medals. No error
     D   E

GO ON TO THE NEXT PAGE

29. A recent conducted poll shows that people are littering
     ___A___   ___B___
   less frequently, a development that reflects a great
                                   ___C___
   change in the public's attitude toward the environment.
                                   ___D___
   No error
   ___E___

30. Neither the giant alligator or the tiny lizard is the cause
     ___   ___A___   ___B___   ___C___
   of Joey's nightmares. No error
   ___D___   ___E___

31. Marjorie, the newest of the two violinists who
              ___A___
   have recently joined the symphony, has excellent tone
   ___B___   ___C___
   and a marvelous command of her instrument. No error
                           ___D___   ___E___

32. The more you read the early works of Michel Tournier,
     ___A___   ___B___
   the more they begin to provoke an emotional reaction.
   ___C___   ___D___
   No error
   ___E___

33. Although they are widely used, standardized test
              ___A___
   scores are not a reliant indicator of a student's
              ___B___   ___C___   ___D___
   academic potential. No error
                       ___E___

34. Since 1960, less than three graduates from our school
                 ___A___   ___B___
   have won the Rhodes Scholarship. No error
   ___C___ ___D___   ___E___

GO ON TO THE NEXT PAGE

Directions: The following passage is an early draft of an essay. Some parts of the passage need to be rewritten.

Read the passage and select the best answers for the questions that follow. Some questions are about particular sentences or parts of sentences and ask you to improve sentence structure or word choice. Other questions ask you to consider organization and development. In choosing answers, follow the requirements of standard written English.

Questions 35-39 are based on the following passage.

(1) I used to have an irrational fear of bees. (2) Anytime I heard a buzzing sound, my heart would start to beat faster and faster. (3) Sometimes breathing was hard.

(4) I've always loved working in my garden. (5) But once spring came around, all the bees came out. (6) I was terrified of going outside. (7) My garden began to wither away. (8) Finally, I decided to do something about it. (9) I called up my friend Anne. (10) Her uncle happens to be a beekeeper. (11) I wanted to ask if I could meet him. (12) Anne's uncle agreed to take me to his hives the next day. (13) From the second I woke up that day, I was petrified, but luckily, Anne's uncle was very understanding. (14) He suited me up in beekeeping gear so that I couldn't get stung, and then he showed me his bee hives.

(15) To my surprise, I found myself fascinated by them. (16) Anne's uncle described how they are organized in castes, how they act as pollinators, and how they make honey. (17) I was so interested by what he said that I went to the library that very night and researched bees for hours. (18) And now—now I can't keep away from bees. (19) Each morning, I have visited Anne's uncle, helping out with the hives, while in the afternoon, I devote my time to my garden surrounded by bees.

35. Which of the following sentences, if added after sentence 3, would best link the first paragraph with the rest of the essay?

(A) It seems that I have had this fear of bees for an eternity.
(B) There were even times that I couldn't move my body, so intense was my fear of bees.
(C) Unfortunately, I couldn't ignore my fear of bees, because I have a garden.
(D) Usually, gardening is a pleasurable experience.
(E) I try not to be afraid of bees, but in my garden it's impossible.

36. Which of the following is the best way to revise and combine sentences 6 and 7 (reproduced below) ?

I was terrified of going outside. My garden began to wither away.

(A) Being terrified of going outside, my garden began to wither away.
(B) Though going outside terrified me, my garden began to wither away.
(C) Since going outside did terrify me, it was then my garden began to wither away.
(D) Going outside terrified me, and as a result, my garden began to wither away.
(E) My garden, withering away, as I was terrified of going outside.

37. The phrase "to do something about it" in sentence 8 can best be made more specific by being rewritten as which of the following?
(A) to make my garden grow again
(B) to learn more about bees
(C) to get in touch with a beekeeper
(D) to combat my fear of bees
(E) to reconsider my feelings

GO ON TO THE NEXT PAGE

38. Which of the following versions of sentence 15 (reproduced below) is most effective?

To my surprise, I found myself fascinated by them.

(A) (As it is now)
(B) To my surprise, I found myself fascinated by it.
(C) To my surprise, they have been very fascinating to me.
(D) To my surprise, I found myself fascinated by the bees.
(E) Fascination was surprisingly found by me in them.

39. In the context of the third paragraph, which of the following is the best version of the underlined portion of sentence 19 (reproduced below) ?

Each morning, I have visited Anne's uncle helping out with the hives, while in the afternoon, I devote my time to my garden surrounded by bees.

(A) (as it is now)
(B) I visit Anne's uncle to help out
(C) having visited Anne's uncle and helping out
(D) visiting Anne's uncle to help out
(E) visiting Anne's uncle has helped out

STOP
**If you finish before time is called, you may check your work on this section only.
Do not turn to any other section in the test.**

PRACTICE TEST 2 ANSWERS

Section 1	Section 2	Section 3	Section 4	Section 5	
1. B	1. A	25. B	21. E	1. D	31. A
2. E	2. B	26. E	22. E	2. C	32. E
3. B	3. E	27. A	23. E	3. B	33. C
4. D	4. C	28. B	24. A	4. A	34. A
5. E	5. B	29. C	25. C	5. B	35. C
6. E	6. E	30. A	26. A	6. D	36. D
7. C	7. D	31. C	27. B	7. E	37. D
8. B	8. E	32. E	28. B	8. C	38. D
9. E	9. B	33. E	29. 139	9. C	39. B
10. B	10. A	34. C	30. 1 or 2	10. E	
11. A	11. D	35. E	31. $\frac{4}{3}$ or	11. D	
12. B	12. B	36. C	1.33	12. C	
13. B	13. B	37. E	32. 90	13. A	
14. D	14. C	38. A	33. 6563	14. D	
15. C	15. D	39. B	34. 105	15. B	
16. C	16. B	40. A	35. 9	16. C	
17. A	17. C	41. B	36. 8	17. C	
18. C	18. D	42. E	37. $\frac{16}{5}$ or	18. C	
19. B	19. D	43. A	3.2	19. B	
20. A	20. C	44. C	38. $\frac{2}{9}$ or	20. E	
21. D		45. D	.222	21. E	
22. E		46. C		22. A	
23. B		47. A		23. D	
24. A		48. B		24. D	
				25. B	
				26. B	
				27. B	
				28. E	
				29. A	
				30. B	

You will find a detailed explanation for each question beginning on page 346.

SCORING YOUR PRACTICE PSAT

Critical Reading

After you have checked your answers against the answer key, you can calculate your score. For the two Critical Reading sections (Sections 1 and 3), add up the number of correct answers and the number of incorrect answers. Enter these numbers on the worksheet on the next page. Multiply the number of incorrect answers by .25, and subtract this result from the number of correct answers. Then round this to the nearest whole number to get your Critical Reading "raw score." Next, use the conversion table to convert your raw score to a scaled score.

Math

Figuring your Math score is a bit trickier, because some of the questions have 5 answer choices (for these, the incorrect answer deduction is .25), and some are Grid-Ins (which have no deduction for incorrect answers).

First, check your answers to all of the problem-solving questions on Sections 2 and 4. For Section 2 and questions 21–28 of Section 4, put the number of correct answers and the number of incorrect answers into the worksheet on the next page. Multiply the number of incorrect answers by .25, and subtract this total from the number of correct answers. For questions 29–38 of Section 4, the Grid-In questions, simply put in the number of correct answers. Now, add up the totals for both types of math questions to give you your total Math raw score. Then you can use the conversion table to find your scaled score.

Writing Skills

The Writing Skills section should be scored just like the Critical Reading sections. Add up the number of correct answers and the number of incorrect answers from Section 5, and enter these numbers on the worksheet on the next page. Multiply the number of incorrect answers by .25 and subtract this result from the number of correct answers. Then round this to the nearest whole number. This is your Writing raw score. Next, use the conversion table to convert your raw scores to scaled scores.

WORKSHEET FOR CALCULATING YOUR SCORE

Critical Reading

	Correct	**Incorrect**	
A. Sections 1 and 3	_____	– (.25 × _____) =	[____] A
B. Total rounded Critical Reading raw score			[____] B

Math

	Correct	**Incorrect**	
C. Section 2 and Section 4—Problem Solving	_____	– (.25 × _____) =	[____] C
D. Section 4—Grid-Ins	_____ =		[____] D
E. Total unrounded Math raw score (C + D)			[____] E
F. Total rounded Math raw score			[____] F

Writing Skills

Section 5 _____ – (.25 × _____) = [____]

Total rounded Writing Skills raw score [____]

SCORE CONVERSION TABLE

Math Raw Score	Math Scaled Score	Critical Reading Raw Score	Critical Reading Scaled Score	Writing Skills Raw Score	Writing Skills Scaled Score
0	26	0	25	0	29
1	29	1	27	1	30
2	30	2	29	2	31
3	32	3	30	3	32
4	34	4	32	4	33
5	35	5	33	5	35
6	36	6	34	6	36
7	38	7	36	7	37
8	39	8	37	8	39
9	40	9	38	9	40
10	41	10	39	10	41
11	42	11	40	11	43
12	43	12	41	12	44
13	44	13	42	13	45
14	45	14	43	14	46
15	46	15	44	15	48
16	47	16	45	16	49
17	48	17	46	17	50
18	50	18	47	18	51
19	51	19	48	19	52
20	52	20	49	20	54
21	53	21	50	21	55
22	54	22	51	22	56
23	55	23	52	23	57
24	57	24	53	24	59
25	58	25	54	25	60
26	59	26	54	26	62
27	60	27	55	27	63
28	61	28	56	28	65
29	62	29	57	29	66
30	64	30	58	30	68
31	65	31	59	31	69
32	66	32	60	32	71
33	68	33	61	33	73
34	70	34	62	34	74
35	72	35	62	35	76
36	74	36	63	36	77
37	77	37	64	37	78
38	80	38	66	38	80
		39	67	39	80
		40	68		
		41	69		
		42	71		
		43	72		
		44	74		
		45	76		
		46	78		
		47	80		
		48	80		

Chapter 15
Practice Test 2:
Answers and
Explanations

Section 1

Question	Answer	Explanation
1	B	Since Roberta's first book was award-winning but her second is unlike it, we could fill in the blank with a word that means not award-winning. Only (B) comes close.
2	E	If we do the second blank first, the trigger in contrast tells us the blank will be opposite from our clue, *excessive violence*. So, *not violent* would be a good word to write down for the blank, and we can eliminate (B) and (D). Our clue for the first blank is *serious physical danger*, because that's what the animals we're comparing here are responding to. So a good word for the first blank would be *danger*. Out of (A), (C), and (E), the only one that fits is (E). Remember, don't waste your time checking the first word in (B) or (D) because we've already eliminated them!
3	B	We don't have very specific clues for the individual blanks, so we can work on relationship between the blanks. The word *since* tells us there is a cause/effect relationship between the first and second blanks, which will be a relationship of similarity. (We also know that the words will probably be negative because of the clue *unfortunately*, but we may not even need that information.) Only (B) has a relationship of similarity.
4	D	We know that other structures were destroyed during the earthquake, so *survival* might be a good word for the first blank. That lets us eliminate (A), (B), and (E). Remember, even if we see our exact word in the answer choices, we still need to finish the process because it could be paired with a word that doesn't fit in the other blank. If more rigid buildings were destroyed and the girders had a surprising quality, it's probably *flexibility*, the opposite of *rigidity*. That allows us to eliminate (C), and only (D) fits.
5	E	The clue *intact* and the time trigger prior tell us to fill in the blank with an opposite word, such as *destroyed*. Only (E) means the same thing as *destroyed*. Remember, if you don't know what a word in the answer choices means, leave it! It could be correct.
6	E	The clue *jeered* tells us that the first viewers didn't like the play, so we could write down something like *terrible* for the first blank. That gets rid of (B), (C), and (D). The trigger word *although* tells us the sentence is going to change directions, and the clue *classics of world theater* also tells us that the second blank is going to be a positive word, so perhaps we could write down *quality* for the second blank. *Impenetrability* doesn't come close, so the correct answer is (E).
7	C	The clue *relied more on direct confrontation* tells us that *confrontational* is a good replacement for the blank. (C) is the closest fit.
8	B	Let's do the second blank first, since we have better clues for it. *Alleging that they were his own* tells us that a word like *steals* would be a good replacement for the blank. That gets rid of (A) and (C). Now let's look at the first blank. Because he steals ideas, few people would call the company president ethical or creative or anything positive. That eliminates (D) and (E), leaving us with (B).

Question	Answer	Explanation
9	E	The first passage puts patients first; the second puts the quest for knowledge first. (E) is closest to that idea. (A) is incorrect because only Passage 2 deals with both animal and human lab subjects. (B) is wrong because subjective care is never mentioned. (C) is wrong because we're never told which approach is more practical. (D) is wrong because the conflict is between care and knowledge, not doctors and patients.
10	B	A distinction between research (biology) and patient care (medicine) would weaken Passage 2's assertion that research is the most important part of medicine. (A) strengthens Passage 2 rather than weakening it. (C) is irrelevant. (D) is out of scope. (E) is irrelevant to the argument.
11	A	The author draws parallels between ancient and modern medicine to emphasize the importance of patient care in medicine. (B) and (D) are incorrect because the author does not mention a change in priorities or make a value judgment about modern medicine. (C) is never indicated by the passage and is extreme. (E) is not mentioned in the passage, so (A) is the only supported answer.
12	B	Both passages mention the importance of patients in the practice of medicine. (A) is wrong because scientific discovery is not mentioned in Passage 1. (C) is out of scope. (D) is only the opinion of Passage 2. (E) is wrong because Passage 2 does not indicate the primacy of patient care.
13	B	Here we have to infer something about the northwestern corner of Botswana. The passage tells us in lines 5–6 that "the northwest corner was said to hold abundant game up until 1973." The author wouldn't have added that "until 1973" tag unless something had changed in 1973! This makes (B) the best choice. (A) is too extreme ("All of its wildlife will be destroyed"). (C) is also too extreme ("no effect") and wrong to boot. (D) argues that the world "must" do something, which is almost never right. (E) says the basin "was drained" when the passage says only that it "may be drained" (lines 8–9).
14	D	Why does the author of the first passage believe that we should study the Serengeti? The Serengeti is, according to the third paragraph, important because of the "light it might shed on man's survival." (A), (B), and (E) are not supported by the passage, and (C) is the opposite of information stated in the passage. (D) is a nice paraphrase of the passage, making it the correct answer.
15	C	This question is asking for the purpose of a quote. The quote shows how the animals' survival is linked to man's survival. (C) is the answer closest to this. (A), (B), (D), and (E) are not mentioned in the passage.
16	C	Vocab-in-Context. The clue produces tells us we can replace yields with something like products, making (C) the best answer.

Question	Answer	Explanation
17	A	Go back to lines 31–37 and read for context. The canaries are used to help save human lives, as are the wild monkeys used to create the Salk vaccine. (B) is reversing information stated in the passage. (C) and (D) are not supported by the passage, and (E) is extreme.
18	C	Here we have a Lead Word question. We should find where the passage mentions John Owen and read before that. The author mentions that the wildebeest had appeared to be overgrazing and that they had been counted in 1958; therefore, there had been some prior study of them. That's what (C) says. (A) and (B) are extreme. (D) and (E) are unsupported by the passage.
19	B	Line reference question. Go back to lines 61–64, read above and below, and think why the author discusses the three studies. The studies show that the wildebeest were not overgrazing, as their population was increasing. This is what (B) says. (A), (C), (D), and (E) are not supported by the passage.
20	A	The "principal regulating mechanism" was the way in which the wildebeest population was naturally controlled through starvation, birth, and death. (B) is not supported by the passage, and (C), (D), and (E) are not even mentioned in the passage.
21	D	What did the Research Institute conclude? According to the last paragraph, the Serengeti consists of a system of interdependent relationships. (D) is an excellent paraphrase of this. (A), (C), and (E) are not supported by the passage. (B), while it is a logical conclusion to make with outside information, is not mentioned in the passage.
22	E	Passage 2 shows how the animals in the Serengeti have maintained their survival, supporting the claim made in (E). (A), (B), (C), and (D) are not affected by the information presented in Passage 2.
23	B	The author of Passage 1 says that the Serengeti is an exception among many areas in that conditions have thus far favored animals over human development. (A) is the opposite of this claim. (C), (D), and (E) are not supported by the passage. (B) is the best answer.
24	A	Both authors recognize the system of interdependencies present in the Serengeti. (B), (C), (D), and (E) are not supported by both passages. (A) is.

Section 2

Question	Answer	Explanation
1	A	We can see that the perimeter of this rectangle is made up of 14 segments—four sides each on top and bottom, and three each on the left and right sides. Each of these segments has length 2, so the whole perimeter will be 14 times 2, or 28.
2	B	Let's try plugging in a number for z to solve this problem. What if we try making $z = 2$? (Remember that we have to obey the rule in the question, which says that z must be an even integer.) If $z = 2$, then (A) becomes 6, (B) becomes 5, (C) becomes 4, (D) becomes 2, and (E) becomes 4. Since the question asks which of the following must be an odd integer, we can eliminate any of the choices that are not odd integers. This means we get to eliminate (A), (C), (D), and (E). This leaves us only with (B), which must be our answer.
3	E	If 16 feet of the tree are below ground, then the other 80 feet of the tree must be above ground. Thus, the fraction of the tree that is above ground is $\frac{80}{96}$. Now we can divide on the calculator to get .883 or 83.3%.
4	C	To solve a direct variation problem, set up a proportion. If 24 cookies are sold on the 4th of the month, finding the number sold on the 20th sets up as $\frac{\text{Day 4}}{24 \text{ cookies}} = \frac{\text{Day 20}}{x \text{ cookies}}$; cross-multiplying the proportion gives 120 cookies.
5	B	This question has the words "in terms of" and variables in the answer choices in it, so we know this is a good Plugging In problem. Let's try plugging in a nice easy number for n. If we make $n = 2$, then we can solve so that x must be equal to $\frac{1}{2}$. The question then asks for the value of n. According to the numbers we picked, $n = 2$. So let's write that number down and circle it—that's our target. Now whichever answer choice equals 2 (remembering that $x = \frac{1}{2}$) will be our answer. (A) is equal to $\frac{\frac{1}{2}}{40}$, which does not equal 2. (B) is equal to $4 \times \frac{1}{2}$, which *does* equal 2. Let's check the other choices to be sure; (C) equals 20, (D) equals 50, and (E) equals 100, so (B) is correct.
6	E	Admittedly, this is a trick question, designed more to test our ability to read and pay attention than much about functions. The "minus 4" given here is outside the notation $f(x)$, indicating that the function $4x^2 + 3x + 8$ should simply have 4 subtracted from it, leaving $4x^2 + 3x + 4$. (This is very different from asking what $f(x - 4)$ would equal, which is an easy mistake to make if we're not reading carefully.)

Question	Answer	Explanation
7	D	This is a great Plugging In the Answers problem, but let's do some Ballparking first to narrow down the answer choices we have to work with. Since there are 80 students on the trip and there were more boys than girls, the number of girls has to be less than 40. Cool—that eliminates (A), (B), and (C)! Now we can start with either of the remaining answer choices and PITA. Let's start with (D): If there are 33 girls, we can add 14 for a total of 47 boys. Does 33 + 47 equal 80? Yes, so (D) is the correct answer.
8	E	This question is testing whether we understand how to calculate the volume of a cube. Remember that the volume of any object is equal to the base times the height times the depth. Since each of these is the same on a cube, we can just take any one side and cube it (or multiply it by itself, and then by itself again) to get the volume. But first we need to figure out the length of the sides. Since the area of a square face is 36, and the area of a square is equal to one side squared, we know that each side must measure 6. Therefore, the volume of the cube will be $6 \times 6 \times 6$, or 216.
9	B	Because this problem gives us actual amounts (no ratios, variables, etc.) in the answer choices, and it's structured to tempt us to write an equation, it's a great Plugging In the Answers problem. Let's start with (C) and say that z equals 32. Then w would equal four times that, or 128. Add those numbers to the 125 items already in the chart (33 cupcakes + 68 cookies + 24 doughnuts), and we get 285. The problem said our total was 260, so (C) is too large—which means we can also eliminate (D) and (E). Moving on to (B), we get z equals 27, so w equals 108. Add 27 and 108 to the 125 items already in the chart, and we get 260—bingo!
10	A	For this problem, you'll have to remember the meaning of "median," which is the middle number in any group of numbers when they have been put in order. In this case, you'll notice that the median of each group of numbers is 6. So the question is: Which group has an average that is less than 6? Of course, one way to solve this is to find the average of each group using your calculator. With a little test-taking logic, though, we can narrow down the choices. Choices (C) and (D) have numbers that are evenly spaced around the middle number (6), so you can probably tell at a glance that their averages will both be 6. Choices (B) and (E) have numbers to the right of 6 that are farther from 6 than the numbers on the left, so their averages will be greater than 6. Verify your work by finding the average of the numbers in choice (A)—it's the only one with an average less than 6.

Question	Answer	Explanation
11	D	This is another great question for PITA—Plugging In the Answers. Let's start with (C). If a customer buys 7 shirts, then the total bill will be: shirt 1 4.50 shirt 2 4.50 shirt 3 4.50 shirt 4 (50% off) 4.50 shirt 5 4.50 shirt 6 4.50 shirt 7 4.50 Total: $29.25 This is a bit smaller than the $31.50 that we know the customer spent, so (C), (B), and (A) can be eliminated and we should try a larger number. How about (D)? For 8 shirts, the total would be: shirt 1 4.50 shirt 2 4.50 shirt 3 4.50 shirt 4 (50% off) 4.50 shirt 5 4.50 shirt 6 4.50 shirt 7 4.50 Total: 31.50 Our total is $31.50, so (D) is correct.
12	B	Let's factor the top and bottom of the expression to try to find something to cancel out. Starting with the top: $x^2 - x - 12 = (x - 4)(x + 3)$. Next, we factor the bottom: $2x^2 - 10x + 8 = 2(x^2 - 5x + 4) = 2(x - 4)(x - 1)$. So, the equation is now $\dfrac{(x-4)(x+3)}{2(x-4)(x-1)} = \dfrac{5}{2}$. The $(x - 4)$ cancels out of the top and bottom. So, $\dfrac{(x+3)}{2(x-1)} = \dfrac{5}{2}$. Multiply both sides by 2, to get $\dfrac{(x+3)}{(x-1)} = 5$. Multiply both sides by $(x - 1)$ to get $x + 3 = 5x - 5$. Subtract x from both sides and add 5 to both sides to get $8 = 4x$. Divide by 4 to get $x = 2$.

Question	Answer	Explanation
13	B	This could be done with Plugging In because there are variables in the answer choices, but translating English to Math is also a great way to go—do whatever works better for you. Let's try translating: *Is at most* means *the greatest value x could be*, which in math terms means ≤. So $x \leq$ something. Already, we can get rid of (D) and (E). *10 less* means we have to subtract 10. (A) and (B) look promising because they both have −10 in them. *The amount by which z is greater than y* means $z - y$, and twice that is $2(z - y)$. The −10 should be outside the parentheses, so the only answer that completely matches is (B).
14	C	Instead of figuring out all the factors of each of the answer choices and looking for consecutive multiples of three, let's just take consecutive multiples of three and multiply them until we get in the ballpark of the answer choices. 3 and 6 have a product of 18, which is way too small, so let's move up a bit. 12 and 15 have a product of 180, so that's closer, but still too small. 15 and 18 have a product of 270, which is answer choice (C).
15	D	If the line segment is defined by points (6, −3) and (6, 9), we know that the *x*-coordinate (6) doesn't change. The line, therefore, goes from −3 to 9 vertically through 6 on the *x*-axis. This is a distance of 12 units, so halfway will be 6 units from each end. This places the midpoint at 3 on the vertical line. So, the final coordinates of the midpoint will be (6, 3). (We could also have made a quick sketch to help us visualize the problem.)
16	B	If the ratio of *a* to *b* is 4 : 7 and the ratio of *c* to *d* is 2 : 5 then we can simply plug in the numbers 4 for *a*, 7 for *b*, 2 for *c*, and 5 for *d*. This makes the ratio of *bc* to *ad* equal to (7)(2) to (4)(5), which is a ratio of 14 : 20. This reduces to 7 : 10, which is answer choice (B).
17	C	Notice the word *must* in the question? Let's plug in so that we can work with real numbers, and because the word *must* is in the problem, we can expect to plug in more than once. Because we want to use numbers that are easy to work with, let's use 78, 80, and 82 for the first three tests and 88 and 92 for the last two. That makes I true, II true, and III false. Since the question asks for what must be true, and we've seen an example in which III is false, we can eliminate any answer choice that contains III. Good-bye, (D) and (E)!

Question	Answer	Explanation
18	D	First, let's do some Ballparking. Since the square has a side of length 10, the area of the square is 100. The shaded region is pretty small in comparison—maybe about 10 or 12. Only (D) comes close to that approximation; (A), (B), and (E) are negative! (Remember, π is about 3.)

If we want to check our Ballparking with math, we would again start with 100 as the area of the square. Now let's remove the area of the circle to get the size of the remaining area (which includes the shaded region, and the identically shaped area just below it). Since these are each semicircles, together they will make one complete circle, with a radius of 5. (We know the radius is 5 because it's half of one side of the square.) This means that the area of the circle will be 25π. So once we remove the area of the circle, what is left is $100 - 25\pi$. Now the shaded region is only half of this, so we need to divide by two, and the area of the shaded region will be $\frac{100 - 25\pi}{2}$. |
| 19 | D | We know from the *must* in this problem that we should be prepared to plug in more than once. The value of x has to be divisible by both 3 and 4, because $\frac{x}{4}$ and $\frac{x}{3}$ are both integers. So we can try 12 for x; 12 gives us an odd integer for $\frac{x}{4}$ and an even integer for $\frac{x}{3}$. Now we can go down to the Roman numerals.

Roman numeral I is true, because 3 – 4 is odd. In fact, since the problem tells us directly that $\frac{x}{4}$ is odd and $\frac{x}{3}$ is even, and an odd number minus an even number will always be odd, we can eliminate any answer choice that doesn't have I in it—goodbye, (B).

Roman numeral II isn't true this time, because 12 isn't odd. So we can eliminate any remaining answer choices that have II in them, and (C) and (E) go away.

Now we just have to figure out if III *must* be true. It's true with the first number we plugged in, because $\left(\frac{12}{3}\right)^2 = 16$, which is even. In fact, since we know from the problem that $\frac{x}{3}$ is always even, the square of $\frac{x}{3}$ will always be even, so III is correct. That leaves us with only answer choice (D). |

Question	Answer	Explanation
20	C	Let's start by finding the area of the triangle. We know that the triangle has a base of 9 and a height of 8, so its area will be $\frac{1}{2} \times 9 \times 8$, or 36. Now, we know that the triangle and the circle have equal areas, so the circle must also have area 36. To solve for the radius of the circle, remember the formula for the area of a circle, which is $a = \pi r^2$. We know the area is 36, so we know that $36 = \pi r^2$. To solve for the radius r we first need to divide each side by π, which gives us $\frac{36}{\pi} = r^2$. Now we take the square root of each side: $$\sqrt{\frac{36}{\pi}} = r, \ \text{so}$$ $$\frac{6}{\sqrt{\pi}} = r$$ This is answer choice (C).

Section 3

Question	Answer	Explanation
25	B	The clue *quiet* and triggers *though* and *surprisingly* tell us that we need to fill in the blank with an opposite word from *quiet*, such as *talkative*. Answer choice (B) comes closest.
26	E	The trigger *although* and clue *a few critics* indicate that Isabel needed something more than a few critics' support, so *broad* would be a good replacement for the blank. Only (E) fits that definition.
27	A	The clue *differences* tells us that *different* would be a good word for the first blank, allowing us to eliminate (C) and (D). We need something opposite for the second blank, since they put their differences *behind them*, so *same* is a good word to write down for the second blank. That eliminates (B) and (E), so only (A) is left.
28	B	Since the divers *could see no more than a few feet in front of their faces*, the water was *opaque* or even *not see-through*. (B) comes closest to our word.
29	C	The clues are *checked every reference* and *always used the correct form*, so *careful* or *thorough* are good words for the blank. That allows us to eliminate all answer choices except (C).
30	A	The quote emphasizes what a strong impression meeting Susan B. Anthony had on the author, and is supported by the author's ability to recollect the event in detail. (B), (C), and (E) are not even mentioned in the passage, and (D) is not supported.

Question	Answer	Explanation
31	C	The pale blue ribbons would *stand out* against the gray clothes, making (C) the best answer.
32	E	*Predilection* can be replaced with a word such as *tendency,* based on the context of the passage. The closest answer choice is (E).
33	E	The theory says that both scientists and criminals are driven to achieve in their own fields by the prospect of attracting mates, which is best described by answer choice (E). (A) and (D) are not supported by the passage, and (B) and (C) state the theory incompletely. Furthermore, (B) is too strong by suggesting that finding a mate is the *main* goal of scientific discoveries.
34	C	This Reasoning question asks what role the parenthetical statement plays in the story. This means we have to read a few lines back and a few lines ahead to get a sense of the context. When we do this, we find that people are worried about the sudden screaming, but don't have the courage to be the first to bring it up. The parenthetical statement offers a scientific-sounding excuse for their inaction—otherwise known as a *rationalization*—and that makes (C) correct. (A) suggests that the narrator believes that everyone should think in the third person, which goes against common sense. (B) makes it sound as if the author actually believes the parenthetical statement is important advice, when the opposite is true: the quoted thoughts are actually being mocked here. (D) pulls a psychiatric diagnosis pretty much out of nowhere, and (E) is wrong because the passage did not say anything about the people being surprised.

Question	Answer	Explanation
35	E	This question asks with which of five statements the author would agree. Of course, you can't read the author's mind; the only thing you have to go by is the passage. So this boils down to a Main Idea question. In this case, we have a tale of a city that is haunted by a mysterious screaming that everyone is afraid to talk about. Endless disembodied screaming is not very realistic, even if you live in New York, so the screaming is probably symbolic. What does it stand for? You can probably think of all sorts of terrible things that everyone knows about, but few people talk about. (One famous example would be Nazi Germany, where millions of people were carted off in trains and killed, but the people who remained went about their lives as if there were nothing wrong or even strange about this.) The screaming could stand for many things, but they're all bad. That makes the answer (E): The story is about some sort of evil that everyone is well aware of, but won't talk about, and how the fear of speaking out allows the evil to go on. (A) and (B) are the opposite of the lesson the author is trying to teach. (C) is not supported in the passage; the screaming goes on day and night and the author does not indicate that it drives people more crazy at night. (D) might sound like something the author would think, but "never" is too strong of a word.
36	C	This question is a Vocab-in-Context question. It asks about the moment that the foreign visitor arrives in the city and hears the screaming for the first time. He gives a ------- of horror: a squeal? a jump? Something like that. (C) looks good. (B) doesn't mean squeal or jump and (D) doesn't fit, because he certainly wasn't pleased. (A) is too calm to be the stranger's reaction: a sympathetic stare of horror? And (E) is based on a misreading: The stranger is startled by the endless scream, not producing it.
37	E	This looks like a Reasoning question, and it is, but since the narrator explains exactly what the line is intended to mean, in effect it's more of a Go-Fetch question. The line being asked about reads, "The packaging of words with varied intentions is like writing a letter to someone in a foreign land and addressing it to oneself; it never reaches its destination." That is, the message doesn't get through. And that's what (E) says. (A) and (C) say exactly the opposite of the author's intended meaning. (B) is too literal; the stranger doesn't really need a translation, because he speaks the same language as the head of the welcoming committee. (D) can be tempting, because there is a foreign visitor in town, but the author doesn't mention dignitaries and is not advocating the "packing of words with varied intentions" either.

Question	Answer	Explanation
38	A	This is a Go-Fetch question, and lines 68–69 answer this question for us: "He dismissed the thought. The Rest Home was full, and the fees were high. He enjoyed the comforts of civilization." If the Rest Home is full, and fees are high, we can infer that the specialist is making a lot of money. This is confirmed by the next sentence: the "comforts of civilization" are material luxuries—a nice house, a nice car, fine food, that sort of thing. (In line 76 we learn that he drives a Jaguar.) So (A) is clearly the answer, so long as we know that "replete with" means "full of." (B) is too strong, since line 73 indicates that panic is only a possibility. (C) would benefit the specialist, so that's no reason to dismiss the thought. (D) doesn't have any support in the passage, while (E) attributes to him a xenophobia, or fear of foreigners, which also has no support in the text.
39	B	This is another general Reasoning question that asks us to sum up the purpose of the whole passage. We've read enough of the passage to know that this is a story in which one night a city is suddenly filled with the sound of an endless, disembodied screaming. This is surreal enough that we can probably conclude that the screaming is symbolic. What does it symbolize? Whatever it stands for, knowing that the screaming is a metaphor for something means that we can eliminate (D), which is too literal and which also wrongly calls the story a "trivialization." We can also eliminate (C) and (E), since the story may *contain* many metaphors and symbols, but is not itself a metaphor for or symbol of anything. (A) is not completely right; while job security is mentioned (the assistant fears he will be fired), it's not the main theme. This leaves us with (B), which seems right: An allegory is a story based around an extended metaphor, as this one is.
40	A	If we go back and read the lines immediately following the idea that slang is nationwide, we find what Pei means by this: "There are some who think that only poorer and less educated people use slang. This is not necessarily true. A little bit of slang, in fact, is used by practically everybody." That is, slang is used by everyone, both educated people and less educated people. Now we need to find a choice that is a close paraphrase of this idea, which is choice (A). Choice (E) is tempting, but the notion of jargon is not addressed until the fourth paragraph, so it can't be the correct answer to a question about the first paragraph.
41	B	To solve this Vocab-in-Context question, read the sentence, and figure out what the meaning of the word should be from the context. In this case, we'd probably put in a phrase like *has a lot*. The choice that comes closest to this in meaning is (B).

Question	Answer	Explanation
42	E	This question not only gives us the lead words Dizzy Dean and Shakespeare, but also tells us where the answer will be found: in the third paragraph. Let's go back to that part of the passage and see what it says. The first line states that, "In a many good cases, slang words and uses can be traced to one individual." Shakespeare and Dizzy Dean are given as examples, so our answer should be a paraphrase of this line. Thus, (A), (B), and (C) are out. Be careful about (D), which has deceptive wording. Though the passage does say that slang can be traced to one person "in many good cases," the world "usually" is too strong. (E) is best.
43	A	According to line 32, the word *cant* was the "language of the underworld." This has to be our answer; now we need to find the choice that best paraphrases *underworld*, which is choice (A).
44	C	We can use the lead words *François Villon* to find the place in the passage where the answer to this question will be found. François Villon is mentioned in the fourth paragraph, around lines 32–35. The passage states at that point that he "used in many of his poems a type of Paris underworld cant that cannot be understood today." Evidently, the passage cites him in order to show that some kinds of speech can no longer be understood in modern times. Now let's look for a choice that paraphrases this idea. Choice (C) says exactly this: that some kinds of speech are no longer current usage. None of the other choices have evidence to support them from this part of the passage.
45	D	Let's go back to the lines in question and read what the author says at that point in the passage. He says that some examples of cant "are generally understood and even used, though are not the best language in the world." So even if the expressions aren't always appropriate, they are almost always understood. Now we need a paraphrase of that. (A), (B), and (C) find no support in the passage. (E) is too broad and a little too negative. (D) is a good paraphrase.
46	C	Here's another Vocab-in-Context question. If we cover up the word *measure* and use context to put our own word in the blank, we'd probably choose something like *a certain amount*. Choice (C) comes closest to this in meaning.
47	A	Let's go back to the passage, around the middle of the fifth paragraph, where these lines appear. The passage states, "But it is not only the intellectual professions that have jargons; it is also the manual trades and occupations," and then goes on to cite the example of shipboard terminology. This means that shipboard terminology is cited as an example of how jargon has evolved in manual trades and occupations, as well as in other places. Now let's find a choice that paraphrases this idea, which is what choice (A) does.

Question	Answer	Explanation
48	B	According to the blurb, this passage is about the history and significance of slang. Already this should make (B) and (C) look like good choices, but let's see why the others can be eliminated. Choices (D) and (E) are too narrow—cant and important individuals are mentioned only in one paragraph each, so they couldn't be the main idea. Likewise, jargon is only discussed in one paragraph, so choice (A) can be eliminated. Now we're down to (B) and (C). This is a tough choice, but (C) is a little too broad—it's very difficult to do a complete history of slang in only a few paragraphs. But to discuss some of the origins and variations is more feasible, and this what the passage tries to do.

Section 4

Question	Answer	Explanation
21	E	First let's convert minutes to seconds by setting up a proportion: $\frac{1\,\text{min}}{60\,\text{sec}} = \frac{2\,\text{min}}{x\,\text{sec}}$. Cross-multiply to find that 2 minutes is 120 seconds. Next, let's set up another proportion to find the number of files: $\frac{4\,\text{files}}{1\,\text{sec}} = \frac{z\,\text{files}}{120\,\text{sec}}$. Cross-multiply to find $z = 480$.
22	E	Let's draw triangle ABC with equal sides. If it's equilateral, that means all the angles are equal, too. Remember, congruent figures have the same shape and size, so draw triangle DEF to look the same as triangle ABC. Since all three angles in triangle ABC are equal and add up to 180 degrees, they must each be 60 degrees, as are all of the angles in triangle DEF.
23	E	Make a ratio box. The sum of 7, 8, and 10 is 25, and $\frac{1,200}{25} = 48$, so the multiplier is 48. The largest share is 10, and $10 \times 48 = 480$.
24	A	Plugging in $p = 5$, $q = 2$, $r = 6$, and $s = 3$ turns the expression into $\frac{\cancel{2}(5)}{\cancel{2}} - \frac{6}{2(3)} = 5 - 1 = 4$, our target number. Now let's plug in the same numbers for the variables in the answer choices, to see which equals 4. (A) equals 4, but we have to go through all of the answer choices to make sure only one of them equals our target. (B) equals $\frac{1}{3}$, so we can eliminate it. (C) is going to be negative, so we can eliminate it with Ballparking. (D) equals $\frac{1}{2}$, and (E) equals -1, so only (A) is equal to our target.

Question	Answer	Explanation
25	C	Because we have variables in the answer choices, this is a Plugging In problem. The easiest variables to start with are a and b, because they're being used repeatedly and having so many things done to them. Let's plug in $a = 3$ and $b = 2$. Therefore, $c = 3 \times \frac{1}{4} = \frac{3}{4}$ (remember, negative exponents mean to take the reciprocal of the number being raised to an exponent) and $d = \frac{1}{3} \times 2^4 = \frac{16}{3}$. So $cd = \frac{3}{4} \times \frac{16}{3}$, or 4. Our target is 4, so now we need to go through all the answer choices and eliminate anything that doesn't equal 4. We can ballpark out (A), because it's going to be a fraction less than 1. (B) would also be way too small. (C) works, because $2^2 = 4$, but remember we have to keep going until the end. (D) is going to be way too small, and (E) is $\frac{3}{2}$, so only (C) equals our target. Alternatively, you can just say that $c = \frac{a}{b^2}$ and $d = \frac{b^4}{a}$, so $cd = \frac{a}{b^2} \times \frac{b^4}{a}$. Cross-cancel and you're left with b^2.
26	A	Let's plug in our own numbers, starting with x. If $x = 2$, then $a = 9(2^2) + 4 = 40$ and $b = 3(2) + 2 = 8$. The question asks for the value of a, so 40 is our target. (A) equals 40, so we can keep it and work through the rest of the answer choices. We can ballpark (B) out because it's going to be 4 less than (A). (C) equals 64, so it's too large. (D) equals 360 and (E) is even larger, so (A) is the only answer that works.
27	B	From the information provided we know that $\frac{1}{3}$ of the 15 integers are even. That means $\frac{2}{3}$ of the 15 integers are odd. To find a probability we need the relationship of number of things that meet the requirement to the total number of things. Therefore, Roman numeral I can be determined because the probability of selecting an odd number is $\frac{2}{3}$. Roman numeral II cannot be determined; we have no idea how many numbers in the group are not the mode. Roman numeral III cannot be determined because we don't know what the greatest and least numbers in the group are.

Question	Answer	Explanation
28	B	First, let's draw in $\overline{BC}$ and $\overline{AC}$. A line tangent to a circle is perpendicular to the radius at the point of contact. So, $\overline{AB}$ is perpendicular to $\overline{AC}$, and ABC is a right triangle. If you don't recognize it as a 5-12-13 triangle, you could have used the Pythagorean theorem to find the third side: $AC^2 + 12^2 = 13^2$. So, $AC = 5$. That means the radius of the circle is 5. Plug that into $\text{Area} = \pi r^2 = \pi(5)^2 = 25\pi$.
29	139	We don't actually have to know the individual values of x and y to solve this problem. We know that we have two parallel lines in this diagram, so we know that the angle opposite the angle measuring 41 degrees must also measure 41 degrees. Therefore we have an angle of 41 degrees plus the angle marked x and y on the same line —which tells us that their sum must be 180. So we know that $41 + x + y = 180$ and that $x + y$ therefore must equal 139.
30	1 or 2	x is a negative integer but $|x|$ is less than 3. So what values of x could satisfy that inequality? If $x = -1$, then $|x| = 1$ and that would work. If $x = -2$, then $|x| = 2$ and that would work. If $x = -3$ then $|x| = 3$ and that isn't less than 3. Other negative values for x will have the same problem, so the only values of x that satisfy the inequlity are -1 and -2. However, we're looking for the value of $|x|$, and thus the answer is 1 or 2.
31	$\frac{4}{3}$ or 1.33	If the sum of 4 and some number (we can call it x) is equal to $4 + x = 4x$. Now we can solve for x: $$4 + x = 4x$$ By subtracting x from each side we get: $$4 = 3x$$ $$\text{so, } \frac{4}{3} = x$$ That makes our answer $\frac{4}{3}$ or 1.33.

Question	Answer	Explanation
32	90	We know that the angles in a triangle always add up to 180, so we know that $\frac{1}{2}a + \frac{1}{2}a + a = 180$. Now we can solve for a. If we add $\frac{1}{2}a + \frac{1}{2}a + a$, we get $2a$, so we know that $2a = 180$ and that $a = 90$.
33	6,563	The question is really saying that the first term is $2 + 3^1 = 5$, the second term is $2 + 3^2 = 11$, etc. So, the 8th term is $2 + 3^8$. Let's apply PEMDAS and work with the exponent first: $2 + 3^8 = 2 + 6561$. Then, we can add to get 6,563.
34	105	The best way to try to find four consecutive integers whose sum is 414 is to start by finding the average: Each number is somewhere in the neighborhood of 103. So let's just start trying these numbers: $103 + 104 + 105 + 106$ equals 418, which is too large. So let's try $102 + 103 + 104 + 105$. That makes 414, so these are our four consecutive integers. The question asks for the greatest of them, so the answer is 105.
35	9	Remember that an isosceles right triangle (which is the same as half of a square) with a side of x will have a hypotenuse of $x\sqrt{2}$. So to get a diagonal of $3\sqrt{2}$, the sides of the triangle (and therefore of the square) must be equal to 3. If the sides of the square are equal to 3, then its area will be equal to 3 times 3, or 9.
36	8	Let's try Plugging In on this problem. We need to choose a value for n that is a prime number greater then 3, so let's try using 5. The question then reads: How many divisors of 30 are there? The divisors of 30 are 1 and 30, 2 and 15, 3 and 10, 5 and 6, for a total of 8 divisors. For whichever values of n we try, we'll always get the same answer.
37	$\frac{16}{5}$ or 3.2	We know that $x^2 - y^2 = 16$, and since $x^2 - y^2$ can be written as $(x + y)(x - y)$, we know that $(x + y)(x - y) = 16$. The question also tells us that $(x + y) = 5(x - y) = 16$. The question then asks us for $(x - y)$, which we can now solve for: $\frac{16}{5}$, or 3.2.
38	$\frac{2}{9}$ or .222	Since we don't know how many total envelopes there are to stuff, and therefore the question is asking for fractions of an unknown, this is a great Plugging In problem. Let's say there are 120 envelopes to stuff. (120 is a good number because 120 is divisible by 3, 4, and 6.) If Sally could stuff all the envelopes in 3 hours, she works at a rate of 40 envelopes per hour. Abdul can stuff all the envelopes in 4 hours, so he works at a rate of 30 envelopes per hour. Juanita would take 6 hours to stuff all the envelopes, so she works at a rate of 20 envelopes per hour. Therefore, the group can stuff envelopes at a rate of 90 per hour ($40 + 30 + 20$), since they do the whole job together. Juanita will stuff 20 of every 90 envelopes, or $\frac{2}{9}$. We can grid that in as, or divide on a calculator to get .222.

Section 5

Question	Answer	Explanation
1	D	Remember to watch out for misplaced modifiers when there's a phrase followed by a comma at the beginning of the sentence. In this case, *A large predatory snake* modifies *the muscular body,* which is incorrect. Only (B) and (D) put *boa constrictor* in front of the underlined portion, where it belongs, so we can eliminate the other answer choices. (B) doesn't make a complete sentence, though, so (D) is the best answer.
2	C	Be very careful of verbs that end in *–ing* on the PSAT. They often indicate awkward constructions that should be avoided. "Having received" in this case is a good example of this type of problem. In addition to being awkward, it's also passive, so you can cross off (A). (B) and (D) are adding in a lot of unnecessary words. Remember, on Improving Sentences questions, you want simple, concise answers when possible. (E) simply splices two sentences together with a comma. (C) is concise and correctly uses a semicolon to separate the two clauses.
3	B	The split between the answer choices shows that we need to make a decision between *than* and *as*. The correct idiom is *as...as* (e.g., "dancing is *as* fun *as* singing"), so we can eliminate (A) and (D). (C) changes the pronoun *you,* used in the underlined portion, to *one,* so it can be eliminated. (B) and (D) say the same thing, but (B) says it without adding redundant words, so it is the best choice.
4	A	The sentence is correct as written.
5	B	(A) and (D) try to splice two sentences together with a comma, so we can eliminate them. (C) has all the events of the sentence happening at the same time. Furthermore, it's passive, as is answer choice (E). (B) is the only answer choice that fixes the problem without adding new ones.
6	D	As is typical when a sentence starts with a phrase followed by a comma, this sentence has a misplaced modifier. William Faulkner's books weren't famous writers—William Faulkner was. So (A) and (B) are incorrect. (C) and (E) use the word *including* to make it sound like Faulkner was doing something, when in fact he was simply known for certain books. Only (D) is short and direct, so it is the best answer.
7	E	The sentence is passive in two places: *were implied* and *not promised by him*. Only (E) fixes both errors.
8	C	*Cleaning* is not parallel to the other verb in the sentence, *to watch*. Only (C) makes the verbs parallel.

Question	Answer	Explanation
9	C	Here again we have two sentences spliced together with a comma, so the underlined portion needs a conjunction that better connects the two parts of the sentence. Since the second part goes in a different direction than the first part, the conjunction *but* is the best option, and (C) is correct.
10	E	The underlined portion is missing a verb, and only (C) and (E) correct the problem. However, (C) puts *helicopter* before the modifying phrase, *the Italian artist and inventor*, which creates a misplaced modifier. (E) doesn't create a misplaced modifier, so it's the best choice.
11	D	*Couldn't hardly* is a double negative, and only (D) and (E) correct the error. (D) is shorter and more direct, so it is the best answer.
12	C	*Seem…to be* is the correct idiom, so we can eliminate (A), (B), and (E). *Intending to* is another idiom, so (C) is correct.
13	A	The sentence is correct as written.
14	D	*Prevented…to* is an incorrect idiom, so we can eliminate (A). The proper idiom is *prevented…from.* The remaining answer choices are split between *have* and *has,* so we need to decide whether a singular or plural verb is necessary. Subjects joined by *neither…nor* follow the same rule as subjects followed by *either…or;* if they're both singular, the subject is singular. So we need a singular verb, and only (D) fits the bill.
15	B	*Considered* does not require either *as* or *to be* after it, so (A), (C), and (D) can be eliminated. (E) changes the meaning of the sentence, suggesting that Hurston herself was a consideration of some kind, so we can eliminate it. That leaves only (B).
16	C	*Concerned about* is the correct idiom, so we can eliminate (A), (B), and (E). Choice (D) changes the meaning of the sentence, so (C) is correct.
17	C	Here we have two sentences spliced together with a comma, so we can eliminate (A) and also (E), which repeats the error. (B) and (D) are incorrect because a semicolon must connect two independent clauses, which leaves only (C).
18	C	The *natural source of sugar* is not something that can be done, as the sentence states. (A), (B), and (E) all have that error. (A), (B), and (E) are also redundant because the sentence already says that this is an age-old practice, making it unnecessary to also say that it has been done for many years. (D) creates a sentence fragment. (C) fixes the error without creating new ones.
19	B	The word *would* does not belong in the "if" part of a sentence; if-clauses should use the word *were.* For example, "If I *were* rich, I would buy an expensive car," or "*Were* I to exercise more often, I could probably lose weight." So we can eliminate (A), (D), and (E). (C) is out because *taking* is not right. We're not talking about something that is happening right now. (B) is the best choice.

Question	Answer	Explanation
20	E	As written, the sentence says that all the *children* are sharing one big *stamp*. This seems unlikely. They really ought to bring *stamps*, plural. That narrows it down to (D) and (E). And then (D) says that the kids are ganging up to write one huge *letter!* That needs to be *letters*, so (E) is the answer.
21	E	The sentence is correct as written.
22	A	The preposition *with* isn't idiomatically correct when paired with *indebted*. *Indebted to* would be correct.
23	D	The possessive pronoun *its* doesn't agree with the subject, *reference books*. *Their* would be correct.
24	D	The verb *answering* isn't parallel to the verb *to reply*. The correct form would be *to answer*.
25	B	*Peter Straub* is being compared to *the works of Stephen King*, which creates an improper comparison. *To the works of Peter Straub*, *those of Peter Straub*, or *to Peter Straub's* would be correct.
26	B	*Scarcely no* is a double negative. *Scarcely any* would be correct.
27	B	The verb *are* is plural and is paired with a singular subject, *understanding*. *Is* would be correct. Be careful—sometimes a subject can come after the verb.
28	E	The sentence is correct as written.
29	A	The adjective *recent* is being used to modify the verb *conducted*, but an adverb should be used instead. *Recently* would be correct.
30	B	*Or* is not correct when paired with *neither*. *Nor* would be correct.
31	A	The adjective *newest* should only be used when comparing three or more things, and the sentence says that there are two violinists. *Newer* would be correct.
32	E	The sentence is correct as written.
33	C	*Reliant* is a diction error, as it means dependent. *Reliable* would be correct.
34	A	The comparison *less* should only be used when the things being compared cannot be counted. Since Rhodes scholars can be counted, *fewer* would be correct.
35	C	The first paragraph needs a sentence that connects the author's narrative about being afraid of bees to the fact that the author has a garden (that happens to be a good attractor of bees). (A) and (B) do not mention the garden. (D) doesn't mention the bees. (E) mentions both, but doesn't flow well into the second paragraph. (C) flows well from the first paragraph to the second.
36	D	(A) creates a misplaced modifier, as it says the garden is terrified of going outside. (B) creates a change of direction between the two parts of the sentence, which is incorrect because the first sentence is the cause of the second sentence. (C) combines the sentences in a way that shows the causal relationship, but it's awkward. (E) is missing a verb and is constructed awkwardly. Only (D) is combined well.

Question	Answer	Explanation
37	D	(D) best describes what the author does about the garden withering away, as is described in the rest of the passage.
38	D	The pronoun *them* is ambiguous; it's not clear what it replaces. (B), (C), and (E) also contain ambiguous pronouns. Only (D) clearly states what the pronoun is replacing: the bees.
39	B	Because the last part of the paragraph is set in the present, which is made clear in sentence 18, the clearest replacement for the underlined portion should be set in the present tense. Therefore, (B) is the best answer.

Paying For College 101

More Great Titles from The Princeton Review
Paying for College Without Going Broke
America's Best Value Colleges

It's not a long shot to bet that you're reading this book because you're thinking of going to college. We're near psychic, right?! The odds are also good that you understand if you want to get into the college of your choice, you need the grades and the scores, and you need to demonstrate the things you dig outside the four walls of your classroom.

Positioning yourself for college admissions is not gambling; it's an investment. You've been investing your time and effort to be the best candidate for your prospective colleges and now, you've invested a little bit of money—right now by buying and reading this book! We applaud you for it!

But what else do you need to know to go to college?

If you answered, How am I going to pay for it? Then you're not alone and you're solidly on the right track to figuring it out. We think we can help.

Your college education is an investment in your future, and paying for college is a big part of that investment. In the next pages you'll find lots of basic information on that big scary subject—financial aid. While we tried to stick to "need to know" nuggets, the information you'll read about here is powerful because it diffuses frenzy around the aid process and equips you with the knowledge to navigate the process as an educated consumer. We ask that you take a little bit of time right now to learn about what it takes to afford yourself an excellent education.

WHAT ARE THE COSTS INVOLVED?

The first thing that comes to mind when you think about how much it costs to go to school is tuition, right? Well, tuition may be the first thing, but don't make the mistake of thinking that's it. The total cost of a year at college involves more than just the tuition amount that the school lists.

Let's break it down:

- Tuition and fees
- Room and board
- Books and supplies
- Personal expenses
- Travel expenses

All of these things together make up the total cost of attendance (COA) for a year at a particular college. So your tuition might be $20,000, but add on room and board, the cost of books, lab fees, not to mention the cost of travel back and forth for breaks, and miscellaneous personal expenses (you will need to buy toothpaste occasionally), and your COA could be as much as $30,000—that's a big difference.

> According to a study by The College Board, during the 2006-2007 school year, the cost of attending a four-year private college for that year averaged approximately $30,367. The same study found that the total cost of attending a public university for that year was, on average, $12,796.

Paying for college is hard, yes; just about everyone needs some kind of financial assistance. More than 17 million students attend college each year—and only 20 percent manage to pay for it without some kind of financial aid package. That means almost 14 million students receive help.

WHAT'S IN A FINANCIAL AID PACKAGE?

A typical financial aid package contains money, from the school, federal government, or state, in various forms: grants, scholarships, work-study programs, and loans.

Grants

Grants are essentially gifts—free money given to you by the federal government, state agencies, and an individual college. They are usually need-based, and you are not required to pay them back.

Check out the Tuition Cost Calculator
PrincetonReview.com/college/finance/tcc

Check out the Aid Comparison Calculator
PrincetonReview.com/college/finance/acc/calc.asp

Some states have grant programs established specifically to help financially needy students, usually to attend schools within that state. Different states have different standards and application requirements.

Scholarships

Scholarships are also free money, but unlike grants, they are merit-based. Some are also based on your financial need; others are based on different qualifications, and are often need-blind.

Scholarships can be based on anything: academic achievement or test scores (the National Merit Scholarship is a well-known one), athletic achievements, musical or artistic talent, religious affiliations or ethnicity, and so on.

They don't have to come from colleges, either. Corporations, churches, volunteer organizations, unions, advocacy groups, and many other organizations offer merit-based, need-based, or simply existence-based scholarships.

When considering outside scholarships, make sure you know how the college(s) you're applying to treat them. Some schools (but not all!) will count any money you receive from outside sources as income, and reduce the amount of any aid package accordingly.

Check out the Scholarship Search page
PrincetonReview.com/ college/finance

Work-Study Programs

The federal government subsidizes a nationwide program that provides part-time, on-campus jobs to students who need financial aid to attend school. Work-study participants can work in academic departments, deans' offices, libraries, and so on. You get a paycheck, like you would at any job, and you can spend the money however you like—but it's meant for tuition, books, and food.

My Family Doesn't Have $30,000 Lying Around!

You and your family are not alone. In many cases, a school's financial aid package doesn't cover all of your costs, and you might not have the resources to make up the difference. When a school doesn't offer enough in the way of aid to cover the cost of attendance, many families turn to loans.

Let's start with the biggest source of student loans—the federal government.

Last year the federal government gave more than $86 billion in student aid.

Federal student aid is intended to bridge the gap between what college costs and what you and your family can actually afford to pay. The government does this in two ways: It makes money available to colleges, which then, through their financial aid offices, make the money available to students in the form of aid packages; and it helps students get affordable loans themselves, through guarantees to loan lenders and other ways (which we'll discuss in a minute).

How Does the Government Decide How Much to Give Me?

When you're applying for financial aid, you'll be filling out a lot of forms. The most important of those forms will be the Free Application for Federal Student Aid (FAFSA). Basically, the FAFSA will want to know the following information:

- Your parents' available income
- Your parents' available assets
- Your available income
- Your available assets

The federal government will take all this information and apply a complex formula to determine what your family's expected contribution should be.

What Is This "Expected Contribution"?

This is how much of your and your family's income and assets the government thinks you can afford to put toward the cost of attending college. This amount is called the Expected Family Contribution, or EFC.

Your financial need (i.e., the money you need in order to attend college) is defined as the difference between the school's total cost of attendance (tuition, room and board, books, etc.) and your expected family contribution. Or, to put it another way:

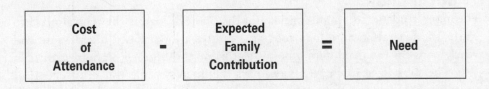

| Cost of Attendance | − | Expected Family Contribution | = | Need |

When you are accepted to a college, the school's financial aid office will then put together an aid package that, hopefully, will make up this difference and cover the cost of your need.

What Do You Mean, "Hopefully"?

The idea is that your EFC will be the same for every school, regardless of the cost of the school. This means that if your EFC is determined to be $9,500, that is the amount you would be expected to pay if you go to State U., where the COA is $14,000, or if you go to Private U., where the COA is $37,000. Ideally, the school will then provide you with a financial aid package that makes up the difference—$4,500 in the case of State U., $27,500 for Private U.

For help filling out the FAFSA, check out MyRichUncle's easy-to-use FAFSA-Assistant tool at MyRichUncle.com/TPR

Chances are you don't have a lot of assets—you probably don't own a house, or even a car, you might not have any stocks or bonds—or do you? Did your parents or grandparents give you any bond certificates? Did they ever give you any stocks, or sign over any of their assets into your name? These are all things the financial aid people will look at when assessing your need.

Ideally?

Yes, in a perfect world, where a school offers to meet 100% of your need, you and your family would pay no more than your EFC, and your EFC would always be exactly what you and your family believe you can afford.

In reality, this doesn't happen nearly as often as we'd like. Some schools have larger endowments for financial aid and can meet your need 100%. Other schools may not.

When that happens, you and your family may want to investigate student loans.

LOANS

The federal government and private commercial lenders offer educational loans to students. Federally-guaranteed loans are usually the "first resort" for borrowers because many are subsidized by the federal government and offer capped interest rates. Private loans, on the other hand, have fewer restrictions or borrowing limits, but may have higher interest rates and more stringent credit-based qualification process—but not always, as we'll see later on.

Federal Loans

For many students seeking financial aid, the Stafford loan is the typical place to start. The federal Stafford loan program features a low capped interest rate and yearly caps on the maximum amount a student can borrow. Stafford loans can either be subsidized (the government pays the interest while you're in school) or unsubsidized (you are responsible for the interest that accrues while in school). Most students who get Stafford loans will end up with a combination of the two. Stafford loans do not have to be repaid until you've graduated or dropped below part-time status.

Here's the thing you might not know about Stafford loans:

Many people assumed that the government sets the rate on student loans, and that that rate is locked in stone. That's not true. The government merely sets the maximum rate lenders can charge (which is 6.8% as of 2007). Lenders are free to charge less than that if they want to.

Historically, however, most lenders have charged the maximum rate because Stafford loans are distributed via colleges' financial aid offices, which maintain preferred lender lists of a limited number of lenders to choose from. Reduced numbers of lenders meant little competition for borrowers, which meant the lenders had very little incentive to offer more competitive rates.

In the last few years, though, a lot has changed. More students now know that they are not required to take a loan from a lender on a preferred lender list. And there are more lenders now willing to compete on price. It's vital that you, as the person making this important and, frankly, expensive investment in your future, educate yourself fully as to all your options when it comes to student loans.

Know Your Rights

You have the right to shop for and secure the best rates possible for your student loans. You have the right to choose the lending institution you prefer. You do not have to use the lenders recommended by your college. All your college must do—and all it is legally allowed to do—is to certify for the lending institution of your choice that you are indeed enrolled and the amount you are eligible to receive.

> **Federal Loans: Advantages and Disadvantages**
>
> **Advantages:**
> Low interest rate
>
> Doesn't have to be repayed until after graduation
>
> **Disadvantages:**
> Yearly and lifetime caps on the amount of money you can borrow
>
> Strict limits on what you can spend it on since the money is disbursed directly to the school

Private Loans

Student loans from private lenders can make it possible to cover the costs of higher education when other sources of funding have been exhausted.

When you apply for a private loan, the lending institution will check your credit score and determine your capacity to pay back the money you borrow. For individuals whose credit history is less than positive, or if you have no credit history, lenders may require a co-borrower: a credit-worthy individual—often a parent—who also agrees to be accountable to the terms of the loan. While private loans do have annual borrowing limits, they are usually higher than government loans, around $40,000; they also have higher interest rates and have floating rate caps, not fixed as in federal loans.

Let's say you have no credit history or a credit-worthy co-borrower. You might consider Preprime™: an underwriting methodology pioneered by MyRichUncle. Instead of focusing solely on credit history, MyRichUncle with its Preprime™ option, also takes into account academic performance, student behavior, and other factors that can indicate that a student will be a responsible borrower. www.myrichuncle.com/PreprimeLoans.aspx

Do Your Research

All student loan lenders are not created equal, so investigate all your options, and look for lenders that are offering loans at rates less than the federally mandated maximum (remember, that's 6.1% for subsidized Staffords, and 6.8% for unsubsidized as of July 2008).

One lending institution that's been in the news lately is MyRichUncle. MyRich Uncle offers federal loans, including subsidized and unsubsidized Stafford loans and private loans. However, MyRichUncle has remembered that the government sets the maximum interest rate for Stafford loans, and has chosen to discount the rate upon repayment. Those discounts will not disappear, like they may with other lenders, unless you default on the loan.

So, Why MyRichUncle?

Well, we here at The Princeton Review think it's important that you have all the information when you're figuring out how to pay for college, and we think MyRichUncle is doing something different—and helpful—with their approach to student loans.

They know that getting a student loan can be a complicated and intimidating process. They believe, as does The Princeton Review, that students should have access to the best education even if they don't yet have a credit history, or at least an opportunity to prove they can be credit-worthy borrowers. They also believe student loan debt can be a serious problem so your loans should be about getting the tools necessary for the best education possible that will position you for the most opportunities when you graduate.

Something else to remember: Your student loan will, ultimately, be your responsibility. When you enter into a loan agreement, you're entering into a long-term relationship with your lender—10 to 15 years, on average. The right student loan, from the right lender, can help you avoid years of unnecessary fees and payments.

THE BOTTOM LINE

College is expensive, period. But if you're reading this book, you're already invested in getting the best education that you can. You owe it to yourself and your future to invest just as much in learning about all your financial options—and opportunities—as well.

Here's a tip: *don't default*. If you ever feel that you are going to be unable to pay off your loans, contact your lender immediately. They will be happy to help you figure out a way to repay your loans, as long as you are upfront and honest with them about the difficulties you may be having.

MyRichUncle was featured in *FastCompany* magazine's Fast 50 and *BusinessWeek*'s Top Tech Entrepreneurs. MyRichUncle and its parent company, MRU Holdings, are financed by a number of leading investment banks and venture capitalists, including subsidiaries of Merrill Lynch, Lehman Brothers, and Battery Ventures For more information, check out

MY RICH UNCLE
STUDENT LOANS

Completely darken bubbles with a No. 2 pencil. If you make a mistake, be sure to erase mark completely. Erase all stray marks.

1.

YOUR NAME: _____
(Print)   Last   First   M.I.

SIGNATURE: _____ DATE: ___ / ___ / ___

HOME ADDRESS: _____
(Print)   Number and Street

_____ E-MAIL: _____
City   State   Zip

PHONE NO.: _____ SCHOOL: _____ CLASS OF: _____

IMPORTANT: Please fill in these boxes exactly as shown on the back cover of your text book.

SCANTRON F-17982-PRP   P3 2803 628 5 4 3 2 1

© The Princeton Review, Inc.

5. YOUR NAME

First 4 letters of last name				FIRST INIT	MID INIT
Ⓐ	Ⓐ	Ⓐ	Ⓐ	Ⓐ	Ⓐ
Ⓑ	Ⓑ	Ⓑ	Ⓑ	Ⓑ	Ⓑ
Ⓒ	Ⓒ	Ⓒ	Ⓒ	Ⓒ	Ⓒ
Ⓓ	Ⓓ	Ⓓ	Ⓓ	Ⓓ	Ⓓ
Ⓔ	Ⓔ	Ⓔ	Ⓔ	Ⓔ	Ⓔ
Ⓕ	Ⓕ	Ⓕ	Ⓕ	Ⓕ	Ⓕ
Ⓖ	Ⓖ	Ⓖ	Ⓖ	Ⓖ	Ⓖ
Ⓗ	Ⓗ	Ⓗ	Ⓗ	Ⓗ	Ⓗ
Ⓘ	Ⓘ	Ⓘ	Ⓘ	Ⓘ	Ⓘ
Ⓙ	Ⓙ	Ⓙ	Ⓙ	Ⓙ	Ⓙ
Ⓚ	Ⓚ	Ⓚ	Ⓚ	Ⓚ	Ⓚ
Ⓛ	Ⓛ	Ⓛ	Ⓛ	Ⓛ	Ⓛ
Ⓜ	Ⓜ	Ⓜ	Ⓜ	Ⓜ	Ⓜ
Ⓝ	Ⓝ	Ⓝ	Ⓝ	Ⓝ	Ⓝ
Ⓞ	Ⓞ	Ⓞ	Ⓞ	Ⓞ	Ⓞ
Ⓟ	Ⓟ	Ⓟ	Ⓟ	Ⓟ	Ⓟ
Ⓠ	Ⓠ	Ⓠ	Ⓠ	Ⓠ	Ⓠ
Ⓡ	Ⓡ	Ⓡ	Ⓡ	Ⓡ	Ⓡ
Ⓢ	Ⓢ	Ⓢ	Ⓢ	Ⓢ	Ⓢ
Ⓣ	Ⓣ	Ⓣ	Ⓣ	Ⓣ	Ⓣ
Ⓤ	Ⓤ	Ⓤ	Ⓤ	Ⓤ	Ⓤ
Ⓥ	Ⓥ	Ⓥ	Ⓥ	Ⓥ	Ⓥ
Ⓦ	Ⓦ	Ⓦ	Ⓦ	Ⓦ	Ⓦ
Ⓧ	Ⓧ	Ⓧ	Ⓧ	Ⓧ	Ⓧ
Ⓨ	Ⓨ	Ⓨ	Ⓨ	Ⓨ	Ⓨ
Ⓩ	Ⓩ	Ⓩ	Ⓩ	Ⓩ	Ⓩ

2. TEST FORM

_____

3. TEST CODE

4. PHONE NUMBER

(columns of bubbles 0–9)

⓪ ⓪ ⓪ ⓪ ⓪ ⓪ ⓪ ⓪ ⓪ ⓪ ⓪
① ① ① ① ① ① ① ① ① ① ①
② ② ② ② ② ② ② ② ② ② ②
③ ③ ③ ③ ③ ③ ③ ③ ③ ③ ③
④ ④ ④ ④ ④ ④ ④ ④ ④ ④ ④
⑤ ⑤ ⑤ ⑤ ⑤ ⑤ ⑤ ⑤ ⑤ ⑤ ⑤
⑥ ⑥ ⑥ ⑥ ⑥ ⑥ ⑥ ⑥ ⑥ ⑥ ⑥
⑦ ⑦ ⑦ ⑦ ⑦ ⑦ ⑦ ⑦ ⑦ ⑦ ⑦
⑧ ⑧ ⑧ ⑧ ⑧ ⑧ ⑧ ⑧ ⑧ ⑧ ⑧
⑨ ⑨ ⑨ ⑨ ⑨ ⑨ ⑨ ⑨ ⑨ ⑨ ⑨

6. DATE OF BIRTH

MONTH	DAY		YEAR	
◯ JAN				
◯ FEB				
◯ MAR	⓪	⓪	⓪	⓪
◯ APR	①	①	①	①
◯ MAY	②	②	②	②
◯ JUN	③	③	③	③
◯ JUL		④	④	④
◯ AUG		⑤	⑤	⑤
◯ SEP		⑥	⑥	⑥
◯ OCT		⑦	⑦	⑦
◯ NOV		⑧	⑧	⑧
◯ DEC		⑨	⑨	⑨

7. SEX

◯ MALE
◯ FEMALE

8. OTHER

1 Ⓐ Ⓑ Ⓒ Ⓓ Ⓔ
2 Ⓐ Ⓑ Ⓒ Ⓓ Ⓔ
3 Ⓐ Ⓑ Ⓒ Ⓓ Ⓔ

---

1 READING

1 Ⓐ Ⓑ Ⓒ Ⓓ Ⓔ
2 Ⓐ Ⓑ Ⓒ Ⓓ Ⓔ
3 Ⓐ Ⓑ Ⓒ Ⓓ Ⓔ
4 Ⓐ Ⓑ Ⓒ Ⓓ Ⓔ
5 Ⓐ Ⓑ Ⓒ Ⓓ Ⓔ
6 Ⓐ Ⓑ Ⓒ Ⓓ Ⓔ
7 Ⓐ Ⓑ Ⓒ Ⓓ Ⓔ

8 Ⓐ Ⓑ Ⓒ Ⓓ Ⓔ
9 Ⓐ Ⓑ Ⓒ Ⓓ Ⓔ
10 Ⓐ Ⓑ Ⓒ Ⓓ Ⓔ
11 Ⓐ Ⓑ Ⓒ Ⓓ Ⓔ
12 Ⓐ Ⓑ Ⓒ Ⓓ Ⓔ
13 Ⓐ Ⓑ Ⓒ Ⓓ Ⓔ
14 Ⓐ Ⓑ Ⓒ Ⓓ Ⓔ

15 Ⓐ Ⓑ Ⓒ Ⓓ Ⓔ
16 Ⓐ Ⓑ Ⓒ Ⓓ Ⓔ
17 Ⓐ Ⓑ Ⓒ Ⓓ Ⓔ
18 Ⓐ Ⓑ Ⓒ Ⓓ Ⓔ
19 Ⓐ Ⓑ Ⓒ Ⓓ Ⓔ
20 Ⓐ Ⓑ Ⓒ Ⓓ Ⓔ
21 Ⓐ Ⓑ Ⓒ Ⓓ Ⓔ

22 Ⓐ Ⓑ Ⓒ Ⓓ Ⓔ
23 Ⓐ Ⓑ Ⓒ Ⓓ Ⓔ
24 Ⓐ Ⓑ Ⓒ Ⓓ Ⓔ

2 MATHEMATICS

1 Ⓐ Ⓑ Ⓒ Ⓓ Ⓔ
2 Ⓐ Ⓑ Ⓒ Ⓓ Ⓔ
3 Ⓐ Ⓑ Ⓒ Ⓓ Ⓔ
4 Ⓐ Ⓑ Ⓒ Ⓓ Ⓔ
5 Ⓐ Ⓑ Ⓒ Ⓓ Ⓔ
6 Ⓐ Ⓑ Ⓒ Ⓓ Ⓔ
7 Ⓐ Ⓑ Ⓒ Ⓓ Ⓔ

8 Ⓐ Ⓑ Ⓒ Ⓓ Ⓔ
9 Ⓐ Ⓑ Ⓒ Ⓓ Ⓔ
10 Ⓐ Ⓑ Ⓒ Ⓓ Ⓔ
11 Ⓐ Ⓑ Ⓒ Ⓓ Ⓔ
12 Ⓐ Ⓑ Ⓒ Ⓓ Ⓔ
13 Ⓐ Ⓑ Ⓒ Ⓓ Ⓔ
14 Ⓐ Ⓑ Ⓒ Ⓓ Ⓔ

15 Ⓐ Ⓑ Ⓒ Ⓓ Ⓔ
16 Ⓐ Ⓑ Ⓒ Ⓓ Ⓔ
17 Ⓐ Ⓑ Ⓒ Ⓓ Ⓔ
18 Ⓐ Ⓑ Ⓒ Ⓓ Ⓔ
19 Ⓐ Ⓑ Ⓒ Ⓓ Ⓔ
20 Ⓐ Ⓑ Ⓒ Ⓓ Ⓔ

3 READING

26 Ⓐ Ⓑ Ⓒ Ⓓ Ⓔ
27 Ⓐ Ⓑ Ⓒ Ⓓ Ⓔ
28 Ⓐ Ⓑ Ⓒ Ⓓ Ⓔ
29 Ⓐ Ⓑ Ⓒ Ⓓ Ⓔ
30 Ⓐ Ⓑ Ⓒ Ⓓ Ⓔ
31 Ⓐ Ⓑ Ⓒ Ⓓ Ⓔ
32 Ⓐ Ⓑ Ⓒ Ⓓ Ⓔ
33 Ⓐ Ⓑ Ⓒ Ⓓ Ⓔ

34 Ⓐ Ⓑ Ⓒ Ⓓ Ⓔ
35 Ⓐ Ⓑ Ⓒ Ⓓ Ⓔ
36 Ⓐ Ⓑ Ⓒ Ⓓ Ⓔ
37 Ⓐ Ⓑ Ⓒ Ⓓ Ⓔ
38 Ⓐ Ⓑ Ⓒ Ⓓ Ⓔ
39 Ⓐ Ⓑ Ⓒ Ⓓ Ⓔ
40 Ⓐ Ⓑ Ⓒ Ⓓ Ⓔ
41 Ⓐ Ⓑ Ⓒ Ⓓ Ⓔ

42 Ⓐ Ⓑ Ⓒ Ⓓ Ⓔ
43 Ⓐ Ⓑ Ⓒ Ⓓ Ⓔ
44 Ⓐ Ⓑ Ⓒ Ⓓ Ⓔ
45 Ⓐ Ⓑ Ⓒ Ⓓ Ⓔ
46 Ⓐ Ⓑ Ⓒ Ⓓ Ⓔ
47 Ⓐ Ⓑ Ⓒ Ⓓ Ⓔ
48 Ⓐ Ⓑ Ⓒ Ⓓ Ⓔ

The Princeton Review
PSAT

4 MATHEMATICS

21 Ⓐ Ⓑ Ⓒ Ⓓ Ⓔ
22 Ⓐ Ⓑ Ⓒ Ⓓ Ⓔ
23 Ⓐ Ⓑ Ⓒ Ⓓ Ⓔ
24 Ⓐ Ⓑ Ⓒ Ⓓ Ⓔ

25 Ⓐ Ⓑ Ⓒ Ⓓ Ⓔ
26 Ⓐ Ⓑ Ⓒ Ⓓ Ⓔ
27 Ⓐ Ⓑ Ⓒ Ⓓ Ⓔ
28 Ⓐ Ⓑ Ⓒ Ⓓ Ⓔ

ONLY ANSWERS ENTERED IN THE OVALS IN EACH GRID AREA WILL BE SCORED. YOU WILL NOT RECEIVE CREDIT FOR ANYTHING WRITTEN IN THE BOXES ABOVE THE OVALS.

Grid-in answer areas for questions 29, 30, 31, 32, 33 (each with fraction-bar and decimal-point ovals, digits 0–9).

Grid-in answer areas for questions 34, 35, 36, 37, 38 (each with fraction-bar and decimal-point ovals, digits 0–9).

5 WRITING SKILLS

1 Ⓐ Ⓑ Ⓒ Ⓓ Ⓔ
2 Ⓐ Ⓑ Ⓒ Ⓓ Ⓔ
3 Ⓐ Ⓑ Ⓒ Ⓓ Ⓔ
4 Ⓐ Ⓑ Ⓒ Ⓓ Ⓔ
5 Ⓐ Ⓑ Ⓒ Ⓓ Ⓔ
6 Ⓐ Ⓑ Ⓒ Ⓓ Ⓔ
7 Ⓐ Ⓑ Ⓒ Ⓓ Ⓔ
8 Ⓐ Ⓑ Ⓒ Ⓓ Ⓔ
9 Ⓐ Ⓑ Ⓒ Ⓓ Ⓔ
10 Ⓐ Ⓑ Ⓒ Ⓓ Ⓔ
11 Ⓐ Ⓑ Ⓒ Ⓓ Ⓔ
12 Ⓐ Ⓑ Ⓒ Ⓓ Ⓔ
13 Ⓐ Ⓑ Ⓒ Ⓓ Ⓔ

14 Ⓐ Ⓑ Ⓒ Ⓓ Ⓔ
15 Ⓐ Ⓑ Ⓒ Ⓓ Ⓔ
16 Ⓐ Ⓑ Ⓒ Ⓓ Ⓔ
17 Ⓐ Ⓑ Ⓒ Ⓓ Ⓔ
18 Ⓐ Ⓑ Ⓒ Ⓓ Ⓔ
19 Ⓐ Ⓑ Ⓒ Ⓓ Ⓔ
20 Ⓐ Ⓑ Ⓒ Ⓓ Ⓔ
21 Ⓐ Ⓑ Ⓒ Ⓓ Ⓔ
22 Ⓐ Ⓑ Ⓒ Ⓓ Ⓔ
23 Ⓐ Ⓑ Ⓒ Ⓓ Ⓔ
24 Ⓐ Ⓑ Ⓒ Ⓓ Ⓔ
25 Ⓐ Ⓑ Ⓒ Ⓓ Ⓔ
26 Ⓐ Ⓑ Ⓒ Ⓓ Ⓔ

27 Ⓐ Ⓑ Ⓒ Ⓓ Ⓔ
28 Ⓐ Ⓑ Ⓒ Ⓓ Ⓔ
29 Ⓐ Ⓑ Ⓒ Ⓓ Ⓔ
30 Ⓐ Ⓑ Ⓒ Ⓓ Ⓔ
31 Ⓐ Ⓑ Ⓒ Ⓓ Ⓔ
32 Ⓐ Ⓑ Ⓒ Ⓓ Ⓔ
33 Ⓐ Ⓑ Ⓒ Ⓓ Ⓔ
34 Ⓐ Ⓑ Ⓒ Ⓓ Ⓔ
35 Ⓐ Ⓑ Ⓒ Ⓓ Ⓔ
36 Ⓐ Ⓑ Ⓒ Ⓓ Ⓔ
37 Ⓐ Ⓑ Ⓒ Ⓓ Ⓔ
38 Ⓐ Ⓑ Ⓒ Ⓓ Ⓔ
39 Ⓐ Ⓑ Ⓒ Ⓓ Ⓔ

The Princeton Review

PSAT

1.

YOUR NAME: _____
(Print)   Last   First   M.I.

SIGNATURE: _____ DATE: _____/_____/_____

HOME ADDRESS: _____
(Print)   Number and Street

_____ E-MAIL: _____
City   State   Zip

PHONE NO.: _____ SCHOOL: _____ CLASS OF: _____
(Print)

IMPORTANT: Please fill in these boxes exactly as shown on the back cover of your text book.

SCANTRON F-17982-PRP   P3 2803 628 5 4 3 2 1
© The Princeton Review, Inc.

2. TEST FORM

_____

3. TEST CODE

4. PHONE NUMBER

(number bubbles 0–9 in columns)

5. YOUR NAME

First 4 letters of last name				FIRST INIT	MID INIT

(letter bubbles A–Z in columns)

6. DATE OF BIRTH

MONTH	DAY	YEAR
○ JAN		
○ FEB		
○ MAR		
○ APR		
○ MAY		
○ JUN		
○ JUL		
○ AUG		
○ SEP		
○ OCT		
○ NOV		
○ DEC		

7. SEX
○ MALE
○ FEMALE

8. OTHER
1 Ⓐ Ⓑ Ⓒ Ⓓ Ⓔ
2 Ⓐ Ⓑ Ⓒ Ⓓ Ⓔ
3 Ⓐ Ⓑ Ⓒ Ⓓ Ⓔ

1 READING

1 Ⓐ Ⓑ Ⓒ Ⓓ Ⓔ   8 Ⓐ Ⓑ Ⓒ Ⓓ Ⓔ   15 Ⓐ Ⓑ Ⓒ Ⓓ Ⓔ   22 Ⓐ Ⓑ Ⓒ Ⓓ Ⓔ
2 Ⓐ Ⓑ Ⓒ Ⓓ Ⓔ   9 Ⓐ Ⓑ Ⓒ Ⓓ Ⓔ   16 Ⓐ Ⓑ Ⓒ Ⓓ Ⓔ   23 Ⓐ Ⓑ Ⓒ Ⓓ Ⓔ
3 Ⓐ Ⓑ Ⓒ Ⓓ Ⓔ   10 Ⓐ Ⓑ Ⓒ Ⓓ Ⓔ   17 Ⓐ Ⓑ Ⓒ Ⓓ Ⓔ   24 Ⓐ Ⓑ Ⓒ Ⓓ Ⓔ
4 Ⓐ Ⓑ Ⓒ Ⓓ Ⓔ   11 Ⓐ Ⓑ Ⓒ Ⓓ Ⓔ   18 Ⓐ Ⓑ Ⓒ Ⓓ Ⓔ
5 Ⓐ Ⓑ Ⓒ Ⓓ Ⓔ   12 Ⓐ Ⓑ Ⓒ Ⓓ Ⓔ   19 Ⓐ Ⓑ Ⓒ Ⓓ Ⓔ
6 Ⓐ Ⓑ Ⓒ Ⓓ Ⓔ   13 Ⓐ Ⓑ Ⓒ Ⓓ Ⓔ   20 Ⓐ Ⓑ Ⓒ Ⓓ Ⓔ
7 Ⓐ Ⓑ Ⓒ Ⓓ Ⓔ   14 Ⓐ Ⓑ Ⓒ Ⓓ Ⓔ   21 Ⓐ Ⓑ Ⓒ Ⓓ Ⓔ

2 MATHEMATICS

1 Ⓐ Ⓑ Ⓒ Ⓓ Ⓔ   8 Ⓐ Ⓑ Ⓒ Ⓓ Ⓔ   15 Ⓐ Ⓑ Ⓒ Ⓓ Ⓔ
2 Ⓐ Ⓑ Ⓒ Ⓓ Ⓔ   9 Ⓐ Ⓑ Ⓒ Ⓓ Ⓔ   16 Ⓐ Ⓑ Ⓒ Ⓓ Ⓔ
3 Ⓐ Ⓑ Ⓒ Ⓓ Ⓔ   10 Ⓐ Ⓑ Ⓒ Ⓓ Ⓔ   17 Ⓐ Ⓑ Ⓒ Ⓓ Ⓔ
4 Ⓐ Ⓑ Ⓒ Ⓓ Ⓔ   11 Ⓐ Ⓑ Ⓒ Ⓓ Ⓔ   18 Ⓐ Ⓑ Ⓒ Ⓓ Ⓔ
5 Ⓐ Ⓑ Ⓒ Ⓓ Ⓔ   12 Ⓐ Ⓑ Ⓒ Ⓓ Ⓔ   19 Ⓐ Ⓑ Ⓒ Ⓓ Ⓔ
6 Ⓐ Ⓑ Ⓒ Ⓓ Ⓔ   13 Ⓐ Ⓑ Ⓒ Ⓓ Ⓔ   20 Ⓐ Ⓑ Ⓒ Ⓓ Ⓔ
7 Ⓐ Ⓑ Ⓒ Ⓓ Ⓔ   14 Ⓐ Ⓑ Ⓒ Ⓓ Ⓔ

3 READING

26 Ⓐ Ⓑ Ⓒ Ⓓ Ⓔ   34 Ⓐ Ⓑ Ⓒ Ⓓ Ⓔ   42 Ⓐ Ⓑ Ⓒ Ⓓ Ⓔ
27 Ⓐ Ⓑ Ⓒ Ⓓ Ⓔ   35 Ⓐ Ⓑ Ⓒ Ⓓ Ⓔ   43 Ⓐ Ⓑ Ⓒ Ⓓ Ⓔ
28 Ⓐ Ⓑ Ⓒ Ⓓ Ⓔ   36 Ⓐ Ⓑ Ⓒ Ⓓ Ⓔ   44 Ⓐ Ⓑ Ⓒ Ⓓ Ⓔ
29 Ⓐ Ⓑ Ⓒ Ⓓ Ⓔ   37 Ⓐ Ⓑ Ⓒ Ⓓ Ⓔ   45 Ⓐ Ⓑ Ⓒ Ⓓ Ⓔ
30 Ⓐ Ⓑ Ⓒ Ⓓ Ⓔ   38 Ⓐ Ⓑ Ⓒ Ⓓ Ⓔ   46 Ⓐ Ⓑ Ⓒ Ⓓ Ⓔ
31 Ⓐ Ⓑ Ⓒ Ⓓ Ⓔ   39 Ⓐ Ⓑ Ⓒ Ⓓ Ⓔ   47 Ⓐ Ⓑ Ⓒ Ⓓ Ⓔ
32 Ⓐ Ⓑ Ⓒ Ⓓ Ⓔ   40 Ⓐ Ⓑ Ⓒ Ⓓ Ⓔ   48 Ⓐ Ⓑ Ⓒ Ⓓ Ⓔ
33 Ⓐ Ⓑ Ⓒ Ⓓ Ⓔ   41 Ⓐ Ⓑ Ⓒ Ⓓ Ⓔ

Use a No. 2 pencil only. Be sure each mark is dark and completely fills the intended oval. Completely erase any errors or stray marks.

4

MATHEMATICS

21 Ⓐ Ⓑ Ⓒ Ⓓ Ⓔ
22 Ⓐ Ⓑ Ⓒ Ⓓ Ⓔ
23 Ⓐ Ⓑ Ⓒ Ⓓ Ⓔ
24 Ⓐ Ⓑ Ⓒ Ⓓ Ⓔ

25 Ⓐ Ⓑ Ⓒ Ⓓ Ⓔ
26 Ⓐ Ⓑ Ⓒ Ⓓ Ⓔ
27 Ⓐ Ⓑ Ⓒ Ⓓ Ⓔ
28 Ⓐ Ⓑ Ⓒ Ⓓ Ⓔ

ONLY ANSWERS ENTERED IN THE OVALS IN EACH GRID AREA WILL BE SCORED.
YOU WILL NOT RECEIVE CREDIT FOR ANYTHING WRITTEN IN THE BOXES ABOVE THE OVALS.

29 | **30** | **31** | **32** | **33**

34 | **35** | **36** | **37** | **38**

(Grid-in response areas with ovals numbered 0–9 and decimal/fraction bars for questions 29–38.)

5

WRITING SKILLS

1 Ⓐ Ⓑ Ⓒ Ⓓ Ⓔ
2 Ⓐ Ⓑ Ⓒ Ⓓ Ⓔ
3 Ⓐ Ⓑ Ⓒ Ⓓ Ⓔ
4 Ⓐ Ⓑ Ⓒ Ⓓ Ⓔ
5 Ⓐ Ⓑ Ⓒ Ⓓ Ⓔ
6 Ⓐ Ⓑ Ⓒ Ⓓ Ⓔ
7 Ⓐ Ⓑ Ⓒ Ⓓ Ⓔ
8 Ⓐ Ⓑ Ⓒ Ⓓ Ⓔ
9 Ⓐ Ⓑ Ⓒ Ⓓ Ⓔ
10 Ⓐ Ⓑ Ⓒ Ⓓ Ⓔ
11 Ⓐ Ⓑ Ⓒ Ⓓ Ⓔ
12 Ⓐ Ⓑ Ⓒ Ⓓ Ⓔ
13 Ⓐ Ⓑ Ⓒ Ⓓ Ⓔ

14 Ⓐ Ⓑ Ⓒ Ⓓ Ⓔ
15 Ⓐ Ⓑ Ⓒ Ⓓ Ⓔ
16 Ⓐ Ⓑ Ⓒ Ⓓ Ⓔ
17 Ⓐ Ⓑ Ⓒ Ⓓ Ⓔ
18 Ⓐ Ⓑ Ⓒ Ⓓ Ⓔ
19 Ⓐ Ⓑ Ⓒ Ⓓ Ⓔ
20 Ⓐ Ⓑ Ⓒ Ⓓ Ⓔ
21 Ⓐ Ⓑ Ⓒ Ⓓ Ⓔ
22 Ⓐ Ⓑ Ⓒ Ⓓ Ⓔ
23 Ⓐ Ⓑ Ⓒ Ⓓ Ⓔ
24 Ⓐ Ⓑ Ⓒ Ⓓ Ⓔ
25 Ⓐ Ⓑ Ⓒ Ⓓ Ⓔ
26 Ⓐ Ⓑ Ⓒ Ⓓ Ⓔ

27 Ⓐ Ⓑ Ⓒ Ⓓ Ⓔ
28 Ⓐ Ⓑ Ⓒ Ⓓ Ⓔ
29 Ⓐ Ⓑ Ⓒ Ⓓ Ⓔ
30 Ⓐ Ⓑ Ⓒ Ⓓ Ⓔ
31 Ⓐ Ⓑ Ⓒ Ⓓ Ⓔ
32 Ⓐ Ⓑ Ⓒ Ⓓ Ⓔ
33 Ⓐ Ⓑ Ⓒ Ⓓ Ⓔ
34 Ⓐ Ⓑ Ⓒ Ⓓ Ⓔ
35 Ⓐ Ⓑ Ⓒ Ⓓ Ⓔ
36 Ⓐ Ⓑ Ⓒ Ⓓ Ⓔ
37 Ⓐ Ⓑ Ⓒ Ⓓ Ⓔ
38 Ⓐ Ⓑ Ⓒ Ⓓ Ⓔ
39 Ⓐ Ⓑ Ⓒ Ⓓ Ⓔ

NOTES

NOTES

NOTES

NOTES

NOTES

NOTES

NOTES

NOTES

NOTES

AP Exams

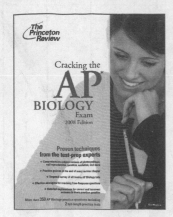

**Cracking the AP Biology Exam,
2008 Edition**
978-0-375-76640-4 • $18.00/C$22.00

**Cracking the AP Calculus AB & BC Exams,
2008 Edition**
978-0-375-76641-1 • $19.00/C$23.00

**Cracking the AP Chemistry Exam,
2008 Edition**
978-0-375-76642-8 • $18.00/C$22.00

**Cracking the AP Economics (Macro & Micro)
Exams, 2008 Edition**
978-0-375-42841-8 • $18.00/C$22.00

**Cracking the AP English Language and
Composition Exam, 2008 Edition**
978-0-375-42842-5 • $18.00/C$22.00

**Cracking the AP English Literature Exam,
2008 Edition**
978-0-375-42843-2 • $18.00/C$22.00

**Cracking the AP Environmental
Science Exam, 2008 Edition**
978-0-375-42844-9 • $18.00/C$22.00

**Cracking the AP European History Exam,
2008 Edition**
978-0-375-42845-6 • $18.00/C$22.00

**Cracking the AP Physics B Exam,
2008 Edition**
978-0-375-42846-3 • $18.00/C$22.00

**Cracking the AP Physics C Exam,
2008 Edition**
978-0-375-42854-8 • $18.00/C$22.00

**Cracking the AP Psychology Exam,
2008 Edition**
978-0-375-42847-0 • $18.00/C$22.00

**Cracking the AP Spanish Exam,
with Audio CD, 2008 Edition**
978-0-375-42848-7 • $24.95/$29.95

**Cracking the AP Statistics Exam,
2008 Edition**
978-0-375-42849-4 • $19.00/C$23.00

**Cracking the AP U.S. Government
and Politics Exam, 2008 Edition**
978-0-375-42850-0 • $18.00/C$22.00

**Cracking the AP U.S. History Exam,
2008 Edition**
978-0-375-42851-7 • $18.00/C$22.00

**Cracking the AP World History Exam,
2008 Edition**
978-0-375-42852-4 • $18.00/C$22.00

SAT Subject Tests

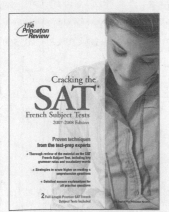

**Cracking the SAT Biology E/M
Subject Test, 2007–2008 Edition**
978-0-375-76588-9 • $19.00/C$25.00

**Cracking the SAT Chemistry Subject Test,
2007–2008 Edition**
978-0-375-76589-6 • $18.00/C$22.00

**Cracking the SAT French Subject Test,
2007–2008 Edition**
978-0-375-76590-2 • $18.00/C$22.00

**Cracking the SAT Literature Subject Test,
2007–2008 Edition**
978-0-375-76592-6 • $18.00/C$22.00

**Cracking the SAT Math 1 and 2
Subject Tests, 2007–2008 Edition**
978-0-375-76593-3 • $19.00/C$25.00

**Cracking the SAT Physics Subject Test,
2007–2008 Edition**
978-0-375-76594-0 • $19.00/C$25.00

**Cracking the SAT Spanish Subject Test,
2007–2008 Edition**
978-0-375-76595-7 • $18.00/C$22.00

**Cracking the SAT U.S. & World History
Subject Tests, 2007–2008 Edition**
978-0-375-76591-9 • $19.00/C$25.00

Death Beam

Death
Beam

A NOVEL BY

Robert Moss

CROWN PUBLISHERS, INC.
NEW YORK

Library of Congress Cataloging in Publication Data
Moss, Robert, 1946-
Death beam.
I. Title.
PR6063.083D42 1981   823'.914   81.7772
ISBN: 0-517-544873   AACR2
Design by Camilla Filancia
10 9 8 7 6 5 4 3 2

To the

DIVA

and the

LEANAN-SIDHE

Death Beam

1

NEW YORK, *September 6*

There was a line at the door to the Café Carlyle, but acquiring a good table was rarely a challenge for the tall Englishman. His steady gaze, his soft, rich voice and sure, understated gestures conveyed a definite air of command. He had the ageless, chiseled good looks that made some of the people waiting for the floor show look twice, uncertain if they had seen the face in a movie or a magazine. The man stood apart, but was not easy to place.

Lean and spare, with wings of gray in his thick brown hair, brushed straight back from a high, broad forehead, he might have passed for thirty-five or forty-five. The silk shirt and impeccably tailored blue suit spoke of money and power. But there was something about the man's military bearing and the ironic set of his mouth that signaled that he did not spend his days contemplating stock-market quotations.

Recognizing him, the maître d' sprang forward.

"Good evening, Mr. Canning. Nice to see you."

"I hope you have room for us tonight." The quiet resonance of Charles Canning's voice, even in a casual exchange, was arresting. It was the kind of voice, women had said, that wraps itself around you.

"For you, any time, Mr. Canning."

The Englishman and his guests were whisked to a large table near the piano where Bobby Short usually held court. New York's answer to Noel Coward was away on tour in Europe. Standing in for him was a rising star from New Orleans, a witchingly beautiful young black diva called Melanie Toussaint. To judge by the critics, she was taking Manhattan by storm. Her photographs and

1

her haunting name intrigued Canning. The Café Carlyle, he had decided, was the perfect place to round out the evening.

His party included two striking and unattached women, one of them an artist who had won notoriety by sculpting wall friezes of plastic and foam rubber, obscenely reminiscent of the female sex organs; the other a model from Memphis, Tennessee, whose sinuous body and huge looking-glass eyes had made her the latest darling of the fashion photographers. There was Howard Pearlman, a financial wizard and dedicated humorist who seemed to know everyone in the city of New York. And there was an earnest, low-key man with glasses who had just escaped from an official banquet for the visiting first lady of the Philippines. His name was Winthrop Gage III, but Charles Canning and his friends addressed him as Trip. He was the National Security Adviser to the President of the United States.

Charles Canning's guests were lively and diverse; they sparked off each other. As for their host, now engaged in sampling a bottle of Dom Pérignon, not one of them could have easily explained what business occupied him on the island of Manhattan. In the space provided for such information on his British passport— which is to say, the passport under which he most frequently traveled—his occupation was described as "landowner." But New York was far removed from Canning's hereditary acres in Norfolk. He was known to engage in unorthodox business deals and in commodity futures. He received telephone calls from places like Muscat, Guatemala City, and Kinshasa. It was said that he had organized a coup in at least one African state. But Canning's past was obscure, and he did not invite questions about it. Trip Gage, who knew more than the others, respected the Englishman's desire for discretion.

Canning's lips grazed the long, perfectly sloping neck of the model from Memphis.

"I hope you enjoyed being had for lunch," he whispered into the shell of her ear. Their "lunch" in his penthouse overlooking Gramercy Park had been protracted into the early evening.

Barbi was not letting herself be easily drawn. But her eyelids dipped and the contours of her lovely face shifted slightly.

"You look as if you're blushing," Canning teased the model as he took his place beside her. "But your color hasn't changed."

2

"Oh, ah *never* blush," Barbi drawled. "Ah just flush all ovah. So it never shows in my cheeks."

Canning was never quite sure whether her responses were a calculated put-on. He had discovered that there was a quick mind at work behind the Southern languors. The girl had a sense of self-parody, and he suspected that part of her style was a mask she assumed to amuse herself as much as those around her.

"Hey, Barbi." Howard Pearlman, who had been flirting with her since they had met for dinner at Elaine's, leaned across the table. "I love the way you talk. You sound just the way good ol' Jack Daniel's sour-mash sippin' whiskey would sound if it could talk."

"Ah know jus' what you mean," she accepted the compliment with the same insouciance. "Awfully smooth."

"Did you see Barbi's picture on the cover of *Glamour?*" interjected the sculptress, Lauren Corder, in her throaty smoker's voice. "The image of the virgin bride." Lauren stabbed toward an ashtray, missed, and left a long charcoal scar across the tablecloth.

"Absolutely." Canning smiled, patting the model's shoulder, reflecting on how she remained disconcertingly silent in the act of love, even while thrashing around like a startled bird trying to escape through a closed window.

"You've gotta watch this guy," Lauren admonished Barbi. "The English are irretrievably decadent. Capable of doing unspeakable things."

"Ah know," said the model. Her hand grazed Canning's knee under the table.

Canning liked Lauren Corder. She was fun, as long as you steered clear of certain sensitive topics. One was drugs. Lauren seemed to think she had a God-given mission to bring about the legalization of all types of narcotics, and tended to get hysterical when people took issue with her. When she had arrived for dinner, Canning had noticed that she was already a little high; he guessed that she had been sniffing coke in her studio. Another taboo subject was Charles's ex-wife, Sally Sherwin. That was harder to avoid, because Sally was a part-time artist who spent many of her weekends sculpting huge stylized animals in the studio she shared with Lauren Corder on Thompson Street in the Village. On workdays, Sally was employed as the personal assistant to Harry Schwab, the New York literary agent who had negotiated the highest advances in publishing history. Lauren talked about Sally as if she were a sainted martyr. This annoyed Canning, even though the pain of the divorce had receded and he and Sally had settled into being good friends.

Howard Pearlman was trying to find out from Trip Gage whether he believed the press reports that the Soviets were getting ready to send troops into Iran to support the Marxist faction in the civil war.

"I've got to tell my broker whether to buy or sell gold," said Pearlman.

"It's hard to read the Soviets right now," the National Security Adviser commented. Trip Gage was being more than usually cautious. "We can't tell who's calling the shots in Moscow. The Soviet leaders are spending so much time fighting each other, I doubt whether they're ready to take on another major foreign adventure. But I can tell you one thing," he added. "If Marshal Safronov emerges as the new Soviet strongman, Iran will be the least of our worries."

"Safronov?" Lauren Corder tested the name. "Is he the head of the army?"

"The Defense Minister," Trip Gage corrected her. "He makes Stalin look like George McGovern."

"I still don't know whether to buy or sell," Howard Pearlman complained.

Canning was now engaged in studying the other patrons of the Café Carlyle. His eyes swiveled from left to right, scanning each table, pausing now and then to focus on an attractive woman or a man who, like himself, could not automatically be placed. His glance lingered on a party of three unaccompanied men who were assaulting a bottle of Chivas Regal. The most voluble of them was a fat, florid man with a red tie. As he cracked jokes, his horn-rimmed glasses kept shooting down his ski-jump nose. He would make a two-fingered stab at them to push them back up. Only one of his companions was joining in the laughter. He was an obvious bruiser, Canning thought. A thickset, bullet-headed tough with fair hair and high cheekbones. The third man, leaner and more elegantly dressed than the others, with black hair receding from a widow's peak, sat silent and reserved. Only his eyes were mobile. They locked with Canning's for a moment, but the stranger hastily looked away.

4

Canning did not need to be in range of the conversation to guess the nationality of the group. He could tell that from their clothes, their bone structure, and the way the fat man clicked his glass in toast after toast, egging his companions on to polish off the first bottle of scotch so they could call for another. Canning had seen identical scenes in the Hotel Rossiya and the Aragvi restaurant in Moscow. The strangers were Russians. And if they had a license to go boozing in the sophisticated Café Carlyle, they must be interesting Russians.

Thoughtfully, Canning took a Havana cigar out of a leather case, circumcised it with his cutter, and flipped open the lid of a handsome red-and-gold lighter. The gesture was out of character for a dedicated cigar smoker who insisted that a gas flame spoiled the savor of tobacco. But a lighter was an ideal place to conceal a mini-camera, and Canning was now occupied in taking a series of snapshots of the Russians on the other side of the room.

Barbi's hand closed unexpectedly on top of his own. Canning clenched the lighter protectively in the hollow of his fist.

"That's real pretty," said the model. "Is it a Tiffany? Let me see."

An imperceptible twist of Canning's thumbnail in the base of the lighter, and the minute lens cover on its side was sealed flush with the surface, hidden from any casual observer. The girl turned the lighter around in the palm of her hand like a Fabergé egg, then amused herself by switching the flame on and off.

"Look, Charles," Lauren Corder suddenly exclaimed. "There's Sally."

A striking blonde in a ruffled black chiffon cocktail dress and a white marabou jacket was taking her place at a table on the other side of the piano. Lauren rushed over and kissed her effusively on both cheeks.

"Excuse me," Canning said to the model. He weaved his way through the tables at a leisurely pace to say hello to his ex-wife.

"We're celebrating," Sally Sherwin said, cool and composed, after Canning had briefly embraced her. She introduced the people at her table. Canning had already met her boss, Harry Schwab. There was a young man at the table with a California suntan and a girl on each arm.

"Meet Alvin Fiedler," Sally introduced him. "We've just sold the paperback rights to his new book for one point five."

"Million?"

"Million."

"Congratulations," Canning said to the young novelist, who had not stirred from his seat. Alvin Fiedler did not seem to be as enthused as everyone else.

"Success isn't what people think," the novelist complained. "I only write when I'm lonely. I got to get lonely again."

"I see what you mean," Canning remarked, admiring the two girls. They looked like twin Lolitas.

"Did you read Alvin's last book?" Harry Schwab asked him. "It's right up your alley. All about spies."

"I haven't got round to it yet." Canning was being polite. He did not read spy fiction. Few thrillers, he considered, bore any resemblance to the pattern of his own life. Even fewer depicted the Soviet secret service, the KGB, in its true colors. The rot had set in, he believed, when Ian Fleming had been persuaded that it was passé to depict Soviet spies as villains, and had sent his unlikely hero, James Bond, to do battle not with the Russians but with a sinister private organization that some readers might confuse with a multinational corporation run by a megalomaniac. Charles Canning believed that there were real villains, and even a few real heroes, and he had had more than average experience with both.

"Are you all right?" he asked Sally.

"Terrific," she said cheerfully. "My social life has really picked up. And I'm going to Paris tomorrow," she went on. "Harry's sending me to wind up a big foreign-rights deal for Alvin's book."

"Will you see Dick?"

"Probably." Sally avoided returning his glance.

"Well, give Dick my best."

Dick Hammond had been Canning's best friend before he became Sally's. Canning had introduced them, back in the old days when the marriage was still strong and he was still officially employed by the Firm, as members of the British secret service familiarly referred to their organization. Now Dick was the Agency's station chief in Paris. And Sally's lover, at least when their paths crossed. Canning felt only an occasional twinge of jealousy. There was no shortage of available women in New York to keep him occupied. But at times, he missed the stability that Sally had been able to give him—and the fact that there had never been secrets between them. He wondered how he would feel if Dick and Sally eventually decided to settle down together.

The pianist struck up a few bars, and Lauren Corder said, "We'd better get back to our table. Bon voyage, sweetie," she gushed to Sally as she flung her arms around her.

"Don't get too lonely," Canning said to the novelist, whose ear was being nibbled by one of his lissome literary groupies.

A surge of applause greeted Melanie Toussaint as she walked onstage. She nodded and waved to the audience, tossing her heavy head of hair. Before the clapping had subsided, her pianist—a living legend who had once played for Billie Holiday—struck up the opening number. The crowd laughed and applauded some more as people recognized the old favorite "When Sunny Gets Blue." Melanie smiled, sharing their pleasure. It was a wide-mouthed grin that set her teeth flashing, illuminating her whole face. Her entire body, generously rounded under the sheath of pink satin, seemed to vibrate with the music and the smile.

Then she started to sing, and the voice was extraordinary in its range and its power. At the end of the first song, her voice seemed to echo in midair, throbbing like a piano wire suddenly drawn taut.

When she took her first bow, Canning found himself clapping as furiously as any other man in the room, his hands raised high, above shoulder height. The photographs had done her less than justice. Her face was dominated by the enormous, liquid eyes, made dreamy by the heavy lids and deep rings of shadow. As she swayed in and out of the light, her skin changed from a honey color to a deep red-gold.

Mostly she sang old blues numbers made famous by Billie Holiday and Bessie Smith, and had the sashay and vocal power to carry them off.

> "You go to my head," she crooned,
> "And you linger like a haunting refrain
> And I find you spinning round in my brain
> Like the bubbles in a glass of champagne."

Then she would switch into a different vein, into a drumming disco beat or nostalgic French ballad. The audience was dazzled.

7

Conversation around the tables was stilled, except in the pauses when the crowd clamored for more. Canning recalled the advice that one of the great divas of the twenties had offered to girls who hoped to make it on stage: "Dazzle 'em, sister. Keep 'em hungry. And never lose your cool." Melanie Toussaint had mastered that lesson. The Englishman approved.

So, he observed, did the Russians. When the show was finished, the last strains of "No Regrets" dying in the air, the fat man at their table kept yelling "Encore." He was so loud that Canning almost expected him to rush up to the singer with a bouquet and an invitation to supper. The taciturn Russian with black hair also seemed fascinated by the singer. Although he was barely applauding, Canning could see that the man's gaze was riveted to Melanie Toussaint, appraising her. It was the quiet Russian who interested Canning most. If the man—as Canning sensed—was responding to the lure of forbidden fruit, that might offer some intriguing possibilities.

Before Melanie had left the stage, the Englishman jumped up from his table.

"Miss Toussaint," he called over the heads of the people who were milling around the piano. He pronounced her name the French way. "You are intoxicating. Can I induce you to join us for a glass of champagne?"

Melanie Toussaint was not easily impressed by men, not since she had been let down in her first serious love affair by a college basketball player. She found it simpler and less emotionally exhausting to go along with her mother's unsentimental philosophy. "Dudes is like a bus," her mother used to say. "Miss one, catch the next." Melanie's reaction to the tall stranger was neutral and analytical. He appeared suave, well-to-do, and possibly humorous. Probably a womanizer, but not tipsy. The party at his table looked safe. Since she had a dry throat, she permitted the Englishman to take her arm and guide her to a seat.

Among the froth of compliments from Canning's guests, only Barbi's seemed faintly contrived. Melanie guessed that the Memphis model came from the kind of family in which blacks are welcome on stage, but not in the front stalls.

Canning saw Sally Sherwin leaving with her friends, and waved to her. Then he summoned a waiter to order another champagne glass for Melanie, but the singer stopped him.

"I'll take a Sazerac," she told the waiter.

"Sazerac." Canning liked the sound of the word. "That's a New Orleans cocktail, isn't it?"

Melanie explained that the drink was a blend of bourbon, Pernod, and bitters, mixed with a little fine sugar.

"The original version was made with absinthe," she continued. "But they outlawed absinthe when some guy went crazy and started hacking up his family under the influence, so we have to make do with Pernod. Most bartenders in this town have never heard of a Sazerac. But I'm slowly spreading the word."

"You come from a place where people really know how to drink," Lauren Corder joined the discussion. "When I was in the French Quarter during Mardi Gras, they had signs in the windows of all the restaurants inviting you in for a pre-breakfast apéritif."

"Sounds like Washington," Trip Gage commented. "Only they don't advertise all their bad habits down there."

When the waiter brought Melanie's drink, Canning asked to try it. He found that the warm, sweet-bitter taste occupied the whole palate.

The Café Carlyle was starting to empty, as people settled their bills. Canning noted that the Russians had lingered at their table, clearly determined to polish off their second bottle of scotch.

"You know something?" Lauren said to Melanie. "I'd like to paint you. Would you come down to my studio sometime? Would you do that?"

"I'd love to." The singer seemed to be flattered by the invitation.

Lauren's behavior sometimes suggested to Canning that, since she had got rid of her last husband, she was getting to like women better than men. She had actually started stroking Melanie's hair. Too much champagne, he decided. On top of whatever she had been taking back in her studio.

"Tell me," Lauren was saying to the singer, "don't you think people in your community would be better off if drugs were legalized? Then we'd get rid of the pushers."

"What are you saying? Are you saying, would it be better if people could just go down to the pharmacy and buy heroin?"

"Yes."

"Come on, Lauren," Canning tried to interrupt. He had seen the sculptress work herself up into paroxysms over the drug issue before. "It's too late to get serious."

But Melanie wanted to get in her reply. "Legalizing hard drugs

9

would just help the pushers," she said. "I don't think that people who live sealed up in nice apartments on the Upper East Side understand just what a power they are in some parts of the community."

Lauren looked wounded. She hated to be reminded that affluence builds its own ghettos. "I'm tired," she said. "Will somebody take me home?"

Howard Pearlman offered to drop her off.

"I've got to go too," said Trip Gage. "I'm taking the first shuttle."

Canning was left alone with Melanie Toussaint and the Memphis model. Even the Russians were at last on their way out. The fat one was swaying and trying to hum the theme from *Mahogany*. He blew a kiss to Melanie.

Barbi inspected her Cartier watch, obviously expecting either Melanie or the Englishman to make a move toward the exit.

But Canning was saying to the singer, "With your looks and your voice, you can go anywhere. I'd love to know where the story begins."

"Oh, singing," she responded. "I've always been a singer. When I was five, I was singing 'The Dark Town Strutters' Ball' at Thanksgiving. If you can sing, where I come from, you can enjoy something good without having to pay for it. I started getting paid for singing on the streets of Dee-troit, when I was trying to work my way through college. You know what I wanted to be? A lawyer. I never figured I would make it big this way. Where I come from, there's lots of people who can sing real good. So I never knew I was different."

"But you are."

She shrugged. "Now a lawyer . . ." she said. "That *would* have been different."

"Husband?" he probed. "Men friends?"

Barbi sighed for their benefit, making a noise like the air rushing out of a balloon.

Melanie said, "Men get left behind." She downed the last of her Sazerac. "I've gotta run. What do you do, anyway?"

"Oh, I mix business with pleasure."

"Lucky you."

They all rose from the table.

"Why don't you have dinner with me one night soon?" Canning

said impulsively. "I'd like to pursue this conversation." He was thinking about the Russians. But not only about the Russians.

"Why?" Melanie studied him with saucer-wide eyes that betrayed nothing of her own mood.

"Because I go on hunches," he said. "Because I like Sazeracs. Because I want to learn about three-card monte."

"Three-card monte!" She burst into a wild, rippling laugh. "Are you putting me on?"

"Certainly not."

It was at that point that Melanie Toussaint decided that the Englishman's quirkiness was not entirely without possibilities.

"Do you go to the fights?" she asked.

"Fights?"

"Shit. Don't you even talk American?" She started pummeling lightly at his chest and stomach.

"Oh. *Fights.*"

"There's a big card coming up at the Garden. You get tickets, you can take me."

She skipped from side to side, still shadowboxing.

"It's a deal."

The wedding-cake clock tower of the old Con Ed building on Irving Place shone through the moonless night, its blue-and-white sheen like icing under floodlights. Charles Canning threw open the french doors of his penthouse and sallied out on the terrace to survey his parish. There was a soft rustle of leaves as a light breeze stroked the oaks and poplars in Gramercy Park, bringing the sudden cold of the last hour before dawn. The streets were deserted, except for a fanatic late-night jogger, the shapeless bulk of a bag lady, almost stationary behind a perambulator loaded up with her pickings from the trashcans, her feet bound up in bandages, and a pair of lovers, their bodies interlaced, straggling back sideways like crabs toward the hospitable seediness of the Gramercy Park Hotel. A solitary yellow cab bucked to a halt at the lights at the bottom of Lexington Avenue, tossing a bright searchlight over the couple, who were exploring each other as they walked. They ran arm in arm, in a gurgle of laughter, into the protective shadows across the road.

Canning loved this leafy, languid quarter of the city, its green-

and-tawny limbo between the exhibitionist bohemia of the Village and the competitive quickstep of midtown. He loved the arthritic hotel that bordered his apartment block, aspiring to remembered gentility but overcome by roaches, new-wave rock hopefuls with dyed hair, and plumbing that hissed and banged in the night like a wrecker's yard. There was a sense of neighborhood around the park, more varied and colorful than in the smart blocks of the Upper East Side where his friends congregated. In Canning's parish, every corner had been staked out by a wino nursing a pint of Thunderbird in a brown paper sack or an inspired lunatic howling imprecations to God. As with the roaches, there seemed to be more of them in summer, helping to ensure that the area could never quite lay claim to propriety. Charles Canning, the restless scion of England's landed gentry, had settled in Manhattan not for the sake of propriety but for a gypsy rhythm that matched his own. Sirens pulsed in the night like valves opening and closing around a beleaguered heart.

He sipped the brandy he had poured himself when Barbi had gone storming out of the apartment, within an hour or so of their return from the Café Carlyle. She maintained that he had insulted her by making a shameless attempt to pick up the black singer. He wondered whether the model's reactions would have been less violent if Melanie Toussaint had been white. He did not regret the timing of Barbi's departure. She was like the *nouvelle cuisine:* beautifully arranged, but you were not encouraged to gorge yourself, and were finally left hankering for something more basic and uninhibited. At the moment of parting, Barbi had displayed more passion than Canning had realized she had in her, while he remained aloof, floating free from the conversation. The biggest explosion came when he advised her to follow the counsel of that supreme courtesan, the Marquise de Sévigné.

"According to the good marquise," Canning had reminded her, "in love affairs it is only the beginnings that are amusing. Therefore you should start over again as often as possible." It was better in the original, he thought, so he added that. *"En amour, il n'y a que les débuts qui sont charmants. C'est pour cela que l'on a envie de recommencer souvent."*

After that, Barbi had abandoned her pose as the languorous Southern belle. "What a crock of shee-et!" she had exploded. "Your problem, Mr. Charles Canning, is that you're too wrapped up in playing some kind of intellectual James Bond to care about anyone's feelings but your own."

Canning had bridled at the accusation, though he thought that Sally might have endorsed it. He did not see his life as a game. He had not been playing at war in the scarred mountains beyond Salalah, on the borders of South Yemen, when, clad in the loose garments of the Dhofari tribesmen, his face blackened by the unrelenting sun, he had led guerrilla *firqas* to ambush Communist raiding parties. He had not been playing at spying when he worked for the Firm in Moscow, running the best agent that the British had ever had inside the KGB. A man whose code name was Hussar.

The way that Hussar had met his end had shaped the whole course of Canning's subsequent life. The agent had been betrayed, arrested, and executed. The anguish and recriminations that flowed from that terrible event had smashed what was left of Canning's marriage and eventually driven him to leave the Firm. Hussar's death had done something more to him. It had left in him a cold hatred toward Moscow Center and the unknown traitor—probably in Washington—who had betrayed Hussar to the KGB. At the same time, it had given him a personal sense of mission that was even deeper than it had been during the years he had spent in government harness. Charles Canning was waging a private war on Moscow Center.

But he was not alone. There were others—Americans, Europeans, Israelis—who were fighting in the same war. Some of them, like Dick Hammond in Paris, were intelligence officers who were officially accountable to their governments but believed that, when a job had to be done, the most effective way was not necessarily through orthodox channels. Together, they formed a secret fraternity that had neither ranks nor organization charts. They called themselves the Club. Some of the Western intelligence chiefs who knew of the Club's existence, like Dicky Prince, the head of the Firm, privately recognized its usefulness. But they also saw the Club as a source of potential danger and embarrassment. They would never formally admit to knowledge of it. Except to disown it if its operations went sour. For this reason, Charles Canning sometimes referred to the Club, with mordant humor, as the "Lost Band." The phrase came from a German mercenary song of the Thirty Years War. The Lost Band—

or *verlorenen Haufen*—was a band of volunteers and condemned criminals who were sent ahead of the main army to undertake hopeless missions. If they succeeded, they were promised the first pick of the enemy's wine, women, and treasure. More often, they were killed.

At 4:30 in the morning, Canning threw himself into bed, and was instantly asleep. That was something soldiers learned: never to miss the chance to snatch an hour's sleep, or a drink, or to take a leak. He dreamed of a black singer and a Russian spy who courted her like a stage-door johnnie.

When it came, the sound did not rouse him at once: the sound of scrabbling feet across the roof. It was repeated before he jerked his head up from the pillow and rolled over to examine the clock on the bedside table. It was not yet 5:00. He lay back, now tense and fully awake, waiting to see if the noise would come again. It might be a cat. But the next sound was a heavy thud, outside on the terrace. Something bigger than a cat had dropped from the roof.

Canning leaped from his bed naked, as he always slept, and grabbed his robe from the hook behind the open bathroom door. He flung it across his back as he darted out into the long hallway, treading lightly on the balls of his feet. He could hear the scrape of wood against the parquet floor of the living room, as if the intruder had collided with a piece of furniture. Canning tried to remember if he had left the french doors to the terrace open. They would not have delayed a serious burglar for long anyway.

Calmly, Canning reached up to a wall rack beside his front door. Mounted there were a pair of 1931 Purdy shotguns that had once been made for his father. The guns were lovingly crafted, with an intricate filigree along the stocks, depicting grouse and pheasants in a rustic glade. Canning angled one of the shotguns out of its cradle and prised open the Chinese lacquered box on top of a console table beneath the gun rack. Inside were several packets of cartridges. He fished out a box of 00 cartridges. Each cartridge contained three layers of three .38 caliber lead pellets. The cartridges, rarely used in England except to bring down deer, were guaranteed to blow a man to pieces at a range of one hundred yards. Deftly, with practiced speed, Canning loaded the shotgun and slammed the breech shut.

But he had not quite completed the operation when the door from the living room burst open. The intruder's silhouette was all black against the somber gray light of the predawn sky. Canning spun on his heel, bruising his shoulder as he threw himself against the wall to dodge the first shot that cracked past. The shadowy intruder dropped to a crouching position, holding his pistol forward with both hands as he prepared to squeeze the trigger a second time. At the same instant, Canning fired from the waist. He heard the obscene *thwack* of metal disintegrating bone and flesh.

Charles Canning was no stranger to the sight and smells of death. But he was most familiar with death outdoors, and above all with death in the desert, where a body left in the sand will soon be stripped of decaying flesh, or buried in the shifting dunes, or simply lost in the vastness, under the sun's lash. He was not prepared for the scene that confronted him in his own hallway when he snapped on the lights, not ready for the particles of flesh and skin that spattered his walls, his pictures, his prized Azerbaijani rug. Fired from a distance of twenty feet, the 00 cartridge had obliterated the intruder's face, as if his features had been hacked away by a chain saw. Canning gagged, and had to spend a long ten minutes in the bathroom before he could bring himself to go through his assailant's pockets.

There was nothing to identify the man. He was black, that was all. His clothes might have been bought in any cheap department store. His gun was an equally anonymous mail-order special. He was not carrying papers, or ID. He had about thirty dollars in cash, which suggested that the break-in was not the act of a terminally desperate man. There was a half-smoked joint in his pocket, but no sign of puncture marks on his arms, which suggested that the motive for the burglary—if that was what it was—was something other than the craving for heavy drugs. If the man had been a simple burglar, Canning reasoned, would he have come at him shooting to kill. Perhaps. There was no way to tell for sure. But it was odds-on that the break-in was a purely criminal act. Canning reminded himself that you were about a thousand times more likely to be done in by a mugger or a burglar in Manhattan than by any kind of political killer.

The first thing to be done was to clean up the mess. He dialed a friend in the intelligence division of the New York police who would be able to ensure that everything was handled discreetly, without awkward questions.

Only when the call had been made, the shotgun stowed away in its cradle, did Canning become fully conscious of the burning sensation across the left side of his chest. The intruder's bullet had dug a shallow trench across his robe and the layers of skin underneath. There was only a smear of blood. The bullet had also neatly clipped the top of one of his omnipresent cigars, in his breast pocket. He took out the cigar, stuck it in his mouth, and lit it with a wooden match.

2

As he hurried past, the man in uniform noted that the queues outside the House of Unions had dwindled away. Since the state funeral in Red Square, tens of thousands of Russians had streamed every day into the ornate, prerevolutionary building near the Bolshoi Theater where the sarcophagus of the late President Brezhnev was on display. Then, abruptly, the Russians had seemed to lose interest. Most of the people milling around outside the House of Unions in the morning sunshine were obviously foreign tourists.

The survival instinct of Moscow's citizens was at work, reflected the man who was passing. A time comes when it is dangerous to display sympathy for a dead dictator. Among all the Soviet leaders, only Lenin's official reputation had survived him. Brezhnev's successors would probably honor his memory for only as long as it took the strongest or shiftiest among them to eliminate his rivals.

The officer caught a snatch of conversation from among the tourists, who were being lined up under the marching orders of matronly guides in severe blue regulation dresses.

"I seen him in Madame Tussaud's in London," said a paunchy American in a fisherman's hat.

"I bet the likeness was better," said the man behind him in line. "And wax dummies don't smell."

The man in deep-blue uniform quickened his stride. He had got a glimpse of Brezhnev's body, close up, during the state funeral, laid out in a black suit, immaculate white shirt, and red tie, with a long row of medals and ribbons pinned to his breast. Only the face

17

and hands were showing. The cosmeticians who had taken over from the embalmers had done their job well, erasing the visible signs of the dead leader's long fight against cancer and old age. Under the wax makeup, Brezhnev looked younger and healthier than he had appeared for more than a decade. Almost unrecognizable. In time, the wax would turn yellow and the cosmeticians would have to go back to work—assuming, of course, that Brezhnev's body, and his name, had not already been condemned to oblivion.

The two stars and narrow stripes on each of the officer's shoulder boards identified him as a lieutenant colonel in the Soviet armed forces. His deep-blue summer uniform was worn by the air force, but his sky-blue collar patches bearing the gold insignia of a winged parachute showed that he was attached to the elite airborne forces. Even without the uniform, you could have told the man was a fighter from the muscular expanse of his chest and shoulders, straining the fabric of his tailored jacket, and his huge, callused hands. With his broken nose and broad, Slavic face, topped by thinning blond hair that was only faintly visible under the peaked cap, he could have passed for a boxer. But the first impression of loosely coiled, animal brutality was qualified by his alert and sensitive gray-blue eyes, a clue that the man had an intellect to match his physique.

Nothing in the man's external demeanor betrayed his true role. Lieutenant Colonel Stepan Ushinsky was the newly appointed deputy chief of the Second Direction of the GRU, Soviet military intelligence. The name of the GRU—the initials stood for Glavnoe Razvedyvatelnoe Upravlenie, the Chief Intelligence Directorate of the Soviet General Staff—was less familiar in the West than that of its ruthless sister service, the KGB. Many of Ushinsky's colleagues in military intelligence resented the way that their KGB rivals hogged the limelight. They knew that while the KGB ruled supreme inside the Soviet Union as an all-powerful secret police, their own service was just as active as the KGB in operations abroad, and could lay claim to some stunning espionage coups.

Ushinsky himself had been elaborately prepared for the sensitive job to which he had just been appointed. He had earned his winged parachute in an intensive training course at the Ryazan Higher Parachute School, famous among the Soviet officer corps

18

for mounting daredevil exercises using live ammunition in which the casualty rates sometimes threatened to equal those incurred in real battle. Later, Ushinsky had graduated near the top of his class from a museumlike institution, garnished with Grecian colonnades, that was located on People's Militia Street in Moscow. It was known to less privileged members of the defense establishment by the cover name Military Department 35576. Shrouded from curious passersby by high walls and thick foliage, its narrow windows masked by string netting and iron grilles, Military Department 35576 was the GRU's school for spies, the spawning ground for the operatives who would be sent out to steal Western blueprints, subvert Third World governments, recruit undercover agents, and run terrorist cells. In the ten years since graduation, Stepan Ushinsky, now in his mid-thirties, had tried his hand at all those things.

The knowledge that his personal file contained details of the secret decorations he had been awarded for important operations that had come right—including the theft of the blueprints for an advanced American space shuttle—did not help Ushinsky to overcome his nervousness about the meeting that he was hastening to attend. For the first time, he would be face to face with the somber men who ruled Russia. The Soviet Defense Council, the secretive committee that now exercised absolute power in Moscow, overshadowing even the Politburo, was conducting an urgent review of Russia's military capabilities. The Defense Council had handed down an unusual request to the GRU. The members of the council wanted a briefing on the capacities of the GRU's networks of "executive agents" (the official euphemism for terrorist saboteurs) to destroy vital communications facilities, command centers, and military installations in the United States, *with special attention to operations that could be mounted against underground headquarters in conditions of intense radiation.* The GRU chief, Leonov, had assigned the job to Ushinsky. He was a former KGB man—like most of his predecessors, also appointed as KGB watchdogs over the military—who was cordially detested by most of his subordinates and referred to behind his back as "Bug-eye."

"This is your province," Leonov had ruled. As deputy chief of the secretive Second Direction of military intelligence, Ushinsky was charged with the day-to-day control of a worldwide network of terrorist cells, and with channeling covert support to the "national liberation movements" the Soviet Union was pledged to patronize under Article 27 of the revised 1977 constitution. The assets of Ushinsky's department ranged from Iranian students and Black Power fanatics to sleeper agents employed in important industrial plants in the West who could be commanded—when the moment came—to cause maximum disruption through sabotage. Among all the so-called national liberation groups, the Palestinians were the favorites of the Second Direction, providing a link between Moscow and many other organizations that would not knowingly have agreed to work in collusion with Soviet intelligence. Out of this exotic menagerie, Ushinsky was now being asked, it seemed, to contrive a plan to paralyze the "main enemy," the United States.

"What's going on?" he had dared to ask Leonov, noting that the pronounced swelling above the GRU chief's eyes, beneath the brows, was even more exaggerated than usual. A doctor might have diagnosed that as a telltale symptom that the spy chief's spleen and lymphatic glands, long besieged by a diet supercharged with fatty dairy foods and vodka, had finally been overpowered. Ushinsky wondered whether the masters of the Soviet state, who pored over medical profiles of their Western adversaries with an intense and prurient interest, paid equal attention to their own physical and mental condition. More than any other, Ushinsky believed, the Soviet Union was a country governed by sick men.

Leonov turned aside Ushinsky's question. "Stock-taking," he said curtly. The heirs to the Kremlin wanted to check how much they were worth.

But there was more to it than that, Ushinsky thought as he showed his pass to a KGB lieutenant at the entrance to the building that housed the Council of Ministers inside the Kremlin walls. Any Moscow resident could sense it. Since Brezhnev's death, there had been endless military parades and maneuvers, gloating displays of Soviet might. The streets of the capital were full of soldiers. Heavily armed patrols of the KGB's private army, the First Dzherzhinsky Motorized Division, prowled around the Kremlin walls, showing off their arsenal of T-72 tanks. Night after night, television viewers were treated to romantic war movies depicting the heroic exploits of the Red Army in combat in World War II, Afghanistan, and Iran. The state-controlled newspapers were full of stirring appeals to Russian patriotism. The tame balladeers of the Writers' Union gave public recitals of new verses exalting the glories of the Great Soviet Motherland, the *Rodina*— a word with an emotional undertone that cannot be translated into English. Official Soviet statements on world affairs had an increasingly bellicose, menacing ring. That very morning, *Pravda* had carried a front-page editorial, signed with a fictitious name that indicated that the text had been approved at the highest level of the Kremlin, which called for the withdrawal of American forces from Europe and the neutralization of Germany.

There was no doubt of it, Ushinsky thought. *War was in the air.* The people in the streets sensed it too. The huge GUM department store had been cleaned out of canned food and cooking oil. Any gold jewelry offered for sale was snapped up immediately, whatever the seller's price. The teahouse gossip was of an impending coup in the Kremlin, or a new Patriotic War, or both.

Ushinsky had to pass through two more security checks before he was admitted to the cavernous conference room that the Defense Council had occupied for its three-day review. The room had been rearranged as a cinema, with enough seats for ninety or a hundred people. The front row was reserved for the ten members of the Defense Council. On the extreme left, Ushinsky could see, from behind, the gray bulk of Manilov, a colorless apparatchik who had climbed the Party hierarchy by clinging tightly to Brezhnev's coattails. Manilov was one of the original Brezhnev Mafia—one of those who had shared in the spoils of running the Party secretariat in Dnepropetrovsk back in the early fifties. The Banda, they were called by envious outsiders in Moscow. But Brezhnev was dead, and the Banda was leaderless, directionless, nerveless. For the moment, Manilov was warming the seat left vacant by Brezhnev as General Secretary of the Party, which also gave him the nominal right to chair the meetings of the Defense Council. But everyone knew that the new General Secretary, who had spent a lifetime taking orders, not giving them, was merely a stopgap. He could expect to fill his present seat for only as many months—or days—as it took for one of the more agile and ambitious intriguers in the front row to emerge as the country's new strongman.

Of all of them, the man that Stepan Ushinsky admired and feared most was the tall, aquiline figure sitting slightly apart from

21

the other members of the Defense Council at the extreme right of the front row, his chair tilted at an angle, his legs nonchalantly crossed. The gray of his uniform contrasted with Ushinsky's blue, and his shoulder boards bore the hammer and sickle and the single large gold star, edged in red, that were the insignia of a marshal of the Soviet Union. As he watched the film clips that were being presented on the huge screen that filled the wall ahead of him, Marshal Ivan Petrovich Safronov made a harsh clicking sound from time to time with his left hand, punctuating the monotone of the briefer's voice. It was the sound of metal striking metal. Analysts of the photographs taken of Russia's military chiefs on the review stands at the big parades could not have identified the origin of the noise, since Marshal Safronov never appeared in public without gloves. In the secrecy of the conference chamber, he had removed his gloves, to reveal that in place of a hand, two steel hooks protruded from his sleeve.

Safronov had lost his left hand, as a twenty-year-old subaltern, to an exploding mortar shell in the battle of Kursk. The splintering metal had ripped into the whole of his left side, leaving a pattern of crisscrossing scars like a mass of barbed wire. The mortar shell had also claimed Safronov's left eye. It had been replaced by a glass eye whose imitation iris perfectly matched the icy blue of the real one, but which never winked or turned. Some nights, even now, Safronov would waken, drenched with sweat, from the appalling, repetitive dream in which he relived the experience of prodding, through the madness of darkness and blood, with the stump of a hand no longer there, to find a useless, obscene jelly where his eye had been. Sent home from the battle of Kursk more dead than alive, he had survived as one of Russia's most highly decorated war heroes. Years after the war, one of the surgeons of the general staff had offered to make him an artificial hand, indistinguishable from the real one. Safronov had declined the offer. There were things he preferred not to forget.

Marshal Safronov was a soldier's soldier, not just another Party hack installed in the Defense Ministry to ensure that the army hewed to the current political line. But because of his physical disabilities, he had spent much of his postwar career in weapons procurement. Thanks to Safronov's success in persuading the Brezhnev regime to loot other sections of the economy in order to accelerate the defense buildup, and the cunning use he had made of the GRU to steal vital secrets from the West, the Soviet Union now had the most formidable war machine in the world. What made Ushinsky nervous was that when Marshal Safronov declaimed that the Soviet Union had developed the capacity to fight and win a global war at the expense of only "acceptable losses," it sounded less and less like a hollow boast. The maimed warrior was spoiling for another fight, and had—almost within reach of his metal hooks—the power to inflict it on the whole of mankind.

Most disturbing of all was that, in the present climate, more cautious men in the Soviet leadership who were vying with Safronov for supreme power seemed to feel obliged to compete with him in hawkishness. This notably applied to the Byzantine plotter Feliks Strokin, the chairman of the KGB, whose gold-rimmed spectacles glinted faintly, under the flicker from the cinema screen, from the middle of the front row. Ushinsky had sensed a growing consensus, in and around the Kremlin, that some kind of new foreign adventure, on an unprecedented scale, would provide the solution to the two most urgent problems weighing upon Brezhnev's heirs. The first was the simmering mood of popular unrest throughout Eastern Europe, spilling over into a now-audible rumble of consumer dissatisfaction inside Russia itself. Ushinsky knew from the secret reports that circulated at GRU headquarters that no less than half the entire Soviet budget was spent on defense and defense-related projects under the supervision of the Military-Industrial Commission, where Marshal Safronov had long been the dominant voice. The people of the Soviet bloc had paid heavily for the policy of guns before butter. Now the shortages of food and essential consumer goods had become so acute that it might require a foreign adventure to rally the Russians' patriotism and give vent to their dangerously pent-up frustrations.

The other problem for the new masters of the Kremlin was the sea change that had come about in the United States after the last presidential elections. The Americans were rearming; their leaders even talked about overtaking the Soviet Union and making the United States number one again. The pendulum of American politics was swinging farther and farther right. The critics of détente who had once been dismissed as alarmists and Red-baiters now found their views echoed in a resounding drumbeat of newspaper editorials and presidential speeches. Weaponry programs that had been scrapped in the heyday of détente had now been revived. There were even plans to reimpose the draft, despite the protest movement that such a step was bound to unleash. Ushinsky knew, from the talk at headquarters, that the new mood of the United States had caused deep alarm among the Soviet leaders. They feared, with reason, that the immense economic and technological resources at the disposal of the Americans could enable them to snatch back the military lead that they had allowed the Soviet Union to steal from them. In the view of Marshal Safronov and his supporters, this led to only one conclusion: Moscow must act *now* to capitalize on the maximum strategic advantage over the United States that it was ever likely to enjoy.

The cinema screen had gone blank, and Safronov was clicking his steel hooks, waiting for the next pictures. Ushinsky had arrived toward the end of a briefing by his counterpart in the KGB, Colonel Zagladin from Department V, which handled "wet affairs"—*mokrie dela*—like assassination. Colonel Zagladin had evidently been ordered to address himself to a theme similar to Ushinsky's. As images of urban violence—looters stripping a supermarket, a mob of black youths overturning a car and kicking at the heads of the passengers through the shattered windows, a city block on fire—filled the screen, Zagladin warmed to his theme.

"These are scenes of race violence in Miami over the past two years," the KGB colonel was explaining. "In the worst case of arson, more than a hundred lives were lost—mostly those of Cuban émigrés, *gusanos.* The mass-transport system collapsed for a period of more than a week during the worst flare-up, and the power and water supply to large quarters of the city was cut off. We must acknowledge the important contribution that our friends in Havana made in intensifying the disruption. The worst incidents were triggered off when a Cuban went into the street and fired on a crowd of black demonstrators with an automatic rifle. The Cuban was never tracked down by the American police. Since most of the Cuban households in Miami contain miniature arsenals, it was generally assumed that the attacker was some rightist cowboy. In fact, he was a Castro agent from the Departamento de America in Havana, who had been infiltrated among the swarm of so-called boat people in 1980. This particular Cuban had studied the arts of provocation in one of our schools here in Moscow. The assessment of the Cuban services, which we share, is that we have the capacity at any time to unleash similar disturbances. With only slight modifications, the formula that worked in Miami can work in the other great conurbations."

For a few moments, the men assembled in the room contemplated the last frames in silence. They showed the burned-out hulk of a huge modernistic hotel and business complex in downtown Miami. Then the spool stopped running, the screen went blank, and a uniformed aide turned up the lights in the conference room.

Ushinsky observed Feliks Strokin, looking toward the General Secretary, Manilov, waiting for verbal applause.

"Very promising," Manilov obliged the chairman of the KGB. "I feel that this particular scenario has tremendous potential." As he spoke, Manilov made the gesture of washing his pale, flabby hands, thus depriving himself of what little image of authority he was otherwise able to convey. "Well," he moved on, "what's next?"

Leonov, the GRU chief, who had been sitting next to Strokin, was already on his feet.

"Comrade General Secretary," said Leonov, "I have the honor to present one of our most capable younger officers, Lieutenant Colonel Stepan Ushinsky. Colonel Ushinsky will brief the Defense Council on the special contribution that the Second Direction of our service can make in the execution of the strategy that is now under review."

Ushinsky, who had been hovering at the back of the room, close to the door, now sprang forward and marched briskly to the podium at the left side of the cinema screen. He cleared his throat, uneasily conscious of the immense power concentrated in the ten men in various conditions of physical decay—none of them younger than sixty-four—whose attention was focused on him.

"Comrade General Secretary," Ushinsky began in a deep baritone that betrayed nothing of his hesitancy. "The film I will show records an exercise that was conducted in the German People's Republic last week under the supervision of my department, following the instructions of Comrade Marshal Safronov." The Defense Minister inclined his head slightly to acknowledge the reference to his name.

Ushinsky paused for the lights to be dimmed again. When the film started to roll, it was apparent that it had not been properly trimmed in the GRU cutting room. For eight or ten seconds, the Defense Council watched a series of numbers, crosses, and whorls.

Then armed men were moving across the screen. Their weird costumes made them look like a cross between Ku Klux Klansmen in their hooded regalia and St. Bernard dogs. Each man's head was encased in a huge triangular hood that extended to below his shoulders. They looked out at the scene around them through goggles sewn into the rubberized fabric of their protective hoods. The St. Bernard effect was the result of the breathing apparatus—a rounded, snoutlike attachment in front of the nose, with an oxygen canister hanging below like the legendary brandy keg. The soldiers' bodies were encased in loose-hanging suits of the same protective material.

"The men belong to one of the special companies of our Spetsnaz forces," Ushinsky explained. Spetsnaz was the abbreviated term for the Special Assignments units of Soviet military intelligence, Russia's answer to the U.S. Green Berets, or Britain's Special Air Service. "As you can see," Ushinsky continued, "they are wearing the latest design in protective clothing. They can survive the effects of intense radiation in those suits for up to twenty-four hours, with only a minimal degree of physical discomfort."

The commandos in the film clip were moving, in five-men bunches, across sloping, lightly wooded countryside. The camera panned to show another assault team, similarly garbed, tumbling down by parachute close to the perimeter fence of what looked like a military airfield.

"The whole area was impregnated with hydrogen mustard gas," Ushinsky commented. "Some of the East Germans who played the defensive role were badly burned."

There was a scraping of metal. This time, Marshal Safronov seemed to be registering approval.

As the Defense Council watched, one man in the last commando team, still swaying downward in midair, was caught in a powerful gust of wind and driven into the spiky branches of a tree. The soldier collided with the tree with such force that the audience, even without a soundtrack, could sense the crunch of bones as a few ribs, and maybe an arm or leg, were broken. The soldier was left swinging limply, upside down, snared by his harness in a forked branch only a few feet above the ground.

The film blurred out of focus for a couple of seconds, and then the audience could see the hanging man's team leader padding toward him, then trying to cut him free. Then the wounded commando was lying flat on the ground, maybe unconscious. The team leader bent over him, shaking him, trying to communicate. The officer crouched lower. Was he trying to revive the man? No. Raising the hood, the team leader went through the motions of stabbing a knife blade through the injured soldier's throat, behind the windpipe.

"Simulation, of course," the General Secretary interjected.

There was a contemptuous snort from Marshal Safronov. "These things are played according to the book," the Defense Minister observed.

"Comrade General Secretary," Ushinsky added, "the Spetsnaz exercises are designed to duplicate the conditions of a real battlefield as closely as possible. Spetsnaz commanders are required to operate according to the principle that, in the event of a strike behind enemy lines, there is no time to tend to your wounded and no justification for leaving men alive who could be taken prisoner and divulge important information to the enemy under interrogation."

"So you killed one of your men," the KGB chairman contributed. "In a game. It seems a little wasteful." Strokin's gold rims flashed again. He clearly thought he had scored a point.

"Comrade Chairman," Ushinsky dutifully carried on. "This particular exercise was not exactly a game. Following the guidelines laid down by the Defense Minister, we were required to test the capacities of our special units to assault highly protected installations in the United States under unusual conditions. I think you will be inclined to conclude from the results of the exercise that it justified the expense."

Marshal Safronov snapped his metal hooks, this time to signify impatience. "Get on with it," he instructed.

"The essence of this exercise," Ushinsky returned to his theme, "was that the attackers were required to identify and locate a secret American command center, in this case similar to the Strategic Air Command headquarters in Nebraska. But the same

27

pattern could be applied to an attack on any underground facility, including the White House bunker, in conditions where ground resistance has been almost entirely removed by intense irradiation."

There was some skirmishing taking place on the screen between the attackers and defending forces clad in almost identical, gray-colored protective suits.

"In the exercise," Ushinsky went on, gesturing toward the screen, "the East German defenders had been issued with the standard equipment for use in a battlefield contaminated by radiation or by chemical and biological agents. They were not informed, however, whether the attack would be purely conventional or not. Despite all their training, many were caught off-guard above ground and neutralized instantly."

The attackers had taken two live prisoners and were seen to be dragging them into one of the control buildings at the military airbase.

"What's happening now?" asked Strokin. "I thought your men didn't take prisoners."

"Battlefield interrogation," Ushinsky responded. "The attackers were issued with detailed plans of the surface installations they were attacking, but not of the underground facilities. To identify their main target, they had to rely on human sources."

The camera zoomed in to follow a grisly scene inside the airport building. The gas mask and hood of one of the prisoners had been ripped away and his captors were engaged in hacking away at his lower teeth with a heavy file. The prisoner started to choke on his own blood and broken enamel.

"It's one of our specialties," the GRU chief interjected proudly. "We maintain that in a combat situation, you need to extract the information you require in the space of less than a minute."

"I doubt whether that prisoner is going to be in any condition to talk," Strokin interjected caustically, motioning at the East German who was writhing in pain on the screen, with one of the masked attackers squatting on his stomach, and another holding his head down by the hair.

"Oh, he's not the one who's going to talk. It's the other one who's going to talk," said Leonov. "It takes far less time to show a man what you are prepared to do with him if he fails to cooperate

28

than to explain to him—especially if there's also a language difficulty."

Ushinsky felt mildly sickened. He recalled a Spetsnaz exercise in which he had taken part during his stint at the Ryazan Higher Parachute School. Filing prisoners' teeth had been practiced then too. There was no doubt that the technique worked. Within minutes, columns of blue and orange flame had erupted on the screen. The Spetsnaz assault team had found its target, and blown it up.

The members of the Defense Council seemed generally impressed with the display. Ushinsky himself did not endorse the view of some of his more complacent colleagues that Russia's special forces were the best in the world. He had a healthy respect for America's special forces, especially the Marine commandos, Britain's SAS, and Israel's Sayeret Motkal, the elite commando unit of Israeli military intelligence that was so secretive that its name had never appeared in print. The Israelis did not believe in the death penalty, Ushinsky had sometimes reflected, but they were second to none at the nonjudicial execution of their enemies abroad.

The Spetsnaz units had still had relatively little experience of special operations. But they had three great sources of strength. What the Spetsnaz forces may have lacked in battlefield experience, they made up for by staging the most realistic (and hence the most lethal) exercises imaginable. Second, they had no shortage of manpower. Spetsnaz brigades were attached to each of the sixteen military districts inside the Soviet Union, to the four army groups deployed in East Germany, Poland, Hungary, and Czechoslovakia, and to the occupation forces in Afghanistan and, most recently, Iran—making a total of some thirty thousand superlatively trained killers and saboteurs. The elite of the elite were the men of the special companies who had been hardened and educated to enter enemy territory by stealth in order to assassinate political and military leaders, neutralize defense facilities, and blow up communications prior to an all-out Soviet attack. In the field, these companies were expected to operate in civilian clothes or enemy uniforms. The files of the KGB and the GRU had provided them with detailed lists of targets.

The final advantage was that, if ordered into battle, these

29

sabotage units would be able to link up with Soviet-controlled networks of terrorist cells, sleeper agents, and Communist supporters throughout the NATO countries—a fifth column of vastly greater proportions than Hitler could ever have imagined in concocting his own war plans. This was the focus for the last segment of Ushinsky's briefing.

The KGB chairman, Strokin, supplied the cue. "These exercises are a lot of healthy fun," he commented. "But I do not see their direct relevance in the immediate future." Strokin paused to shoot a glance at the impassive Marshal Safronov. The KGB chief's expression was a mixture of puzzlement and pure hatred. "I had thought," he resumed, "that our most pressing concern was to examine the instruments we can apply to prevent the new American administration from making any provocative foreign gestures—particularly in relation to the possible evolution of the political situation in Iran and the Federal Republic of Germany."

Listening to Strokin talk, Ushinsky recalled the *Pravda* editorial he had read before leaving his apartment that morning— the article that demanded the withdrawal of U.S. forces from Germany. He knew that a number of prominent West German politicians in key positions had long since reached their private accommodations with Moscow, partly as the result of the fear that had been growing in Bonn for years that the United States could no longer be trusted to keep its promises to its allies. Perhaps things were moving faster on that front than Ushinsky guessed. Perhaps the reason for the Defense Council review was that the Soviet leaders—egged on by Marshal Safronov—wanted to be sure that they could disrupt an American mobilization designed to prevent West Germany from defecting from the NATO alliance.

"Colonel Ushinsky." This time it was not Leonov or Strokin but Marshal Safronov who was addressing him directly, pulling the GRU officer out of his private reverie. "I would be grateful if you would explain to the Comrade Chairman of the Committee for State Security what contribution your department can make to the disruption of the political and military centers of the United States in a situation short of war." The slow precision with which Safronov spelled out the KGB chief's full title was as good as calling him a sonofabitch straight out.

Ushinsky had often heard gossip that it was only a matter of

30

time before the marshal arranged the removal of Strokin and other top KGB officers—especially Krylov, the shadowy chief of the special office that handled top agents in the West. Characteristically, Krylov had stayed away from the briefing session. Even the Defense Council respected his exceptional need for secrecy.

Ushinsky signaled to the projectionist, seated behind a small window at the back of the vast room, like the slit used by archers to fire through a castle wall. The film clips gave way to a series of slides. They showed the faces, and sometimes the whole bodies, of some twenty men and women.

"These," commented Ushinsky, "arc our most effective executive agents in the United States today. Cuban. Vietnamese. Iranian. Black Power. The best of them all"—he gestured to the projectionist to hold the frame—"is this man."

The photograph blown up to forty times life size on the screen showcd a man of Middle Eastern origin seated at a sidewalk café, flanked by two remarkably attractive women, a blonde and a redhead. The man was in his early thirties, perhaps a few years younger than Ushinsky. He was elegantly and expensively dressed in a cashmere jacket, open-necked blue silk shirt, and Gucci loafers. He might have been considered handsome, except that he was starting to run to fat, his skin was badly pockmarked, and there was a sneering, savage curl to his lips.

"Palestinian?" askcd Strokin.

"Palestinian," Ushinsky confirmed. "Born in Jaffa. His name is Sammy Hamad. He has also called himself Abu Gharab. It means the Father of Victories."

"Organization?" Strokin probcd.

Ushinsky shrugged. "He's a mercenary. Arafat, Qaddafi, and the Iraqis have all used him for operations they did not want to be traced back to them. We recruited him on the same basis, and brushed up his training with a specially tailored course at Sanprobal." At Sanprobal military academy, near Simferopol in the Crimea, the GRU supervised annual courses for hundreds of Palestinian and Third World terrorist recruits.

"Recent experience?" the KGB chief's interrogation continued.

"Mostly Iran. He got inside the Ayatollah's inner councils and provided a useful link to the radicals who took over the U.S. embassy. He also had a hand in the assassination of the Shah's

31

nephew in Paris. We have recorded only one operational failure. He was instructed to blow up the main fuel depots in West Berlin when we were protesting the admission of deputies from West Berlin by the European Parliament. It would have been wonderful armed propaganda. But security inside his assault team was lax. The Israelis got wind of the plan and tipped off the West Germans, so they were able to pick up the hit men at the border. As usual, Sammy Hamad got away. We doubt whether his real name or even an accurate description is in the Interpol computers."

Another slide came onto the screen. It showed the same Palestinian, now sporting blue jeans and a newly grown mustache and sideburns, strolling down Fifth Avenue past St. Patrick's Cathedral, between Fiftieth and Fifty-first streets.

"Sammy Hamad is relocated in the United States. He entered under one alias, and has since used a succession of others—"

The General Secretary waved his fat hand, like a loaf of pita bread, cutting Ushinsky off. "We don't require all the details," Manilov said. "Just get to the point."

"The point, Comrade General Secretary," Marshal Safronov intervened, "is that this operative has established a network in the Washington and New York areas that could be mobilized, at the proper time, to disrupt the decision-making mechanisms of the United States."

The General Secretary looked at Ushinsky. "Thank you, Colonel," he said. "I think the briefing has gone on for long enough." He looked questioningly at Marshal Safronov.

"Sufficient for you, Marshal?" Manilov asked.

"Sufficient."

Outside the conference room, Ushinsky was surprised to find himself stopped by one of the Defense Minister's aides.

"Safronov was pleased," the major said in a low voice. "He requests that you join him and a small group of officers for dinner tonight." The location specified was a dacha in the pine groves of Zhukovka, high above the gently rolling Moscow River, some twenty miles from the capital. It was not the type of invitation that Ushinsky could have refused, even had he been inclined to do so. He wondered what was Marshal Safronov's motive for inviting him to enter into a new degree of intimacy with the Soviet elite. His wife's family had been allowed a dacha a few miles from

Zhukovka, in the forests of Nikolina Gora, but he had never set foot inside the hidden world of the village built by Khrushchev—amid a deceptively bland and bucolic landscape—for the supreme rulers of Russia to indulge their secret pleasures.

ZHUKOVKA, *September 7*

Ushinsky marveled at the steadiness of Marshal Safronov—the unruffled evenness of his voice, the sure motions with which he raised one jigger of vodka after another to his mouth with the surprisingly versatile hooks on the stump of his left hand. After all the wine, brandy, and vodka that had washed down the banquet of caviar, sturgeon, and wild boar, Ushinsky was reluctant to speak or even stand up for fear of making a fool of himself. He sat quietly on a sofa close to the open fire that had been lit in the huge pine-walled living room, hung with guns and swords, despite the mildness of the September night, in which the unclouded sky beyond the windows had the light, textured grayness of mother-of-pearl. Safronov, the old soldier, was evidently an assiduous collector of firearms. Among the guns crowded in display cases along the walls was a complete series of Lugers, including the rare 1933 short-barreled pistols produced for the Imperial Persian cavalry, beautifully embossed with Farsi script. In the brief tour of the dacha he had given Ushinsky after his arrival four hours before, the Defense Minister had explained that there were less than fifty of those models left in the world.

Ushinsky had been surprised to find that most of the other dinner guests were men of his age and rank. Only one general was present: the commander of the Kantemirovskaya Armored Division, which, together with the KGB's own troops, composed the Moscow garrison. Twice since Stalin's death, the Kantemirovskaya Division had acted to thwart an attempted palace coup by the chiefs of the secret police. In any power struggle whose outcome depended on force, the loyalty of the division's commander would be a critical factor.

Marshal Safronov positioned himself, ramrod-straight, in front of the fireplace.

"Another toast," Safronov proposed.

Ushinsky watched fatalistically as a steward handed him yet another glass.

"To the immortal words of our great M. V. Frunze." The Defense Minister proceeded to quote the aphorism of the celebrated Soviet strategist that is as familiar to every officer cadet in the Soviet Union as is Abraham Lincoln's Gettysburg Address to American schoolchildren. "In war, victory belongs to those who find in themselves the resolution to attack; those who are merely defensive are doomed to defeat."

The officers downed their vodka with a hearty roar, and their glasses went crashing into the fireplace.

"The stewards will now leave," Safronov ordered. He seemed to be grinning, but because of the surgery that had been conducted on one half of his face, only the right side of his mouth turned up. The Defense Minister, framed by the crackling fire behind him, looked like an apparition in a trick mirror in an amusement arcade.

Alone with his officers, Marshal Safronov began a short speech. "Each one of you," he commenced, "has been selected to be here for a reason. From my observation of all of you, you share a devotion to the security of our socialist Motherland, the *Rodina*. And you are all young enough—at least in spirit—to grasp that our survival may require us to act in the spirit of Frunze's words, rather than in a spirit of bureaucratic caution."

Safronov paused for dramatic effect.

"The correlation of forces in the world today," he resumed, "has never been more favorable for our socialist cause. This was the unanimous conclusion reached by the Defense Council in its review of our military resources, and our political assets, around the world. The moment is rapidly approaching when we will be able to rupture and destroy the NATO alliance, just as we destroyed the two other aggressive alliances founded by the Anglo-Saxons—SEATO and CENTO—in the past.

"However," Safronov was saying, "we also face unparalleled dangers. Washington is bent on an aggressive course. Notorious warmongers like General George Brennan, the Defense Intelligence chief, have the ear of the American President. If we waste any more time, we may forever lose our opportunity to guarantee our own security and the triumph of socialism on a global scale."

He means war, Ushinsky realized. *He is talking about a Soviet first strike.*

"It will not shock any of you to learn," Safronov continued, "that not all my colleagues in the Defense Council or the Politburo have as yet found within themselves the resolution to attack. The General Secretary is befuddled trying to work out where to begin now that he is in a position to line his pockets from the wealth of the whole country instead of that of a single ministry." There was derisive chuckling from several of the others. Manilov's corruption was an open scandal among the Soviet elite; he was even reputed to have demanded—and received—kickbacks from Western corporations in return for arranging contracts that were on a scale worthy of a Saudi middleman. Manilov's venality had not harmed his career in Brezhnev's time, since so many top Party officials were involved in the system of kickbacks and universal graft. But it was now a weapon in Marshal Safronov's hand. In this respect, Safronov was generally considered above reproach. His corruption, Ushinsky reflected, chilled by the logic of the Defense Minister's speech, was of a different kind: a disease of the spirit.

"We have two months," Safronov announced.

Two months? Why two months? Ushinsky mentally counted the days. Of course. It was two months until November 7. The anniversary of the Bolshevik Revolution. Gigantic military parades would be staged, as usual. The leaders of Russia's satellites and client states, and hosts of fellow travelers from the West and the Third World, would flock to Moscow to pay tribute.

"I will ask Chief Designer Berzin to give you some of the details."

Ushinsky had been curious early on about the presence of the self-important, chubby little man in a badly fitting suit of washable olive drab material, the lone civilian in the company. All he knew of Berzin's work was that he was the apparatchik in charge of the development of space weapons—high-energy lasers and particle beams. As early as the fifties, the Defense Ministry had allocated vast sums to the development of this new generation of weapons that had long been dismissed by the Americans, in their smug, self-absorbed complacency, as practicable only in the world of science fiction and the comic strips.

"Some of you," Chief Designer Berzin began in a dry, academic tone, "will be familiar with the project named Razrukha. I can report that our latest tests at Sarova and Saryshagan were entirely successful. We are able to generate a neutron beam with the concentrated force of a giant lightning bolt. It can be fired from a space battle station at approximately the speed of light. It can block out a window in space and destroy any enemy missile entering an area of four hundred square miles through blast or molecular disintegration."

In other words, Ushinsky thought, this beam could deprive the Americans of a second-stike capacity. If Berzin was accurate, it would provide the most efficient system of anti-missile defense ever devised. What on earth could deter Safronov from risking an attack on the Americans then?

"That isn't all," Berzin went on, warming to his topic. "Our latest tests have verified that the new beam weapon could be directed against targets inside the earth's atmosphere from a platform in space. The beam would have the power to deliver intense irradiation over an area of many hundreds of square miles. For example, it could wipe out the population of greater New York without smashing a single window or unsettling a single brick."

"Like a giant neutron bomb," Safronov commented.

"There's really no comparison, Marshal," the chief designer said smugly. "We have evolved the most efficient weapon of mass destruction ever known to man."

My God, thought Ushinsky. *To think our propagandists persuaded the Americans to put off production and deployment of the neutron bomb by caricaturing it as "the perfect capitalist weapon"—"the weapon that kills people without harming property."* If Project Razrukha were to succeed, the blackmail power of the Soviet Union would be irresistible. Assuming the Americans believed in it. If not . . . Ushinsky recalled the film of the hooded men, creatures of nightmare, advancing across a wooded test range in East Germany. That was his answer.

The code name was as terrifying as the vision. In Russian, *razrukha* meant total disintegration, the breakdown of everything into chaos.

"May I ask a question, Comrade Marshal?" Ushinsky ventured.

"Surely."

"What countermeasures could the Americans take against our beam weapon—against Razrukha?"

"Countermeasures?" Safronov's lopsided smile was broader than before. "Would you care to answer that, Berzin?"

"There are no known countermeasures."

KHODINSK AIRFIELD, *September 8*

Stepan Ushinsky divided mankind into the people he liked and disliked, and the vast majority fell into the latter category. He despised the Palestinians with whom he was now obliged to work, regarding most as hopelessly venal and incompetent. Like many of his fellow Russian officers, he detested the Jews, most of whom (he firmly believed) were Zionist sympathizers or Trotskyite saboteurs—although he had a grudging admiration for the Israelis; he could not fathom how pallid ghetto Jews had been metamorphosed into bronzed warriors in the Promised Land.

Too young to remember the devastation of World War II, Ushinsky did not share Marshal Safronov's pathological hatred of Germans; instead, he regarded most of the West Europeans as irretrievably decadent. He despised Western fellow travelers who preached unilateral disarmament and streamed into the Soviet Union for free vacations at the Black Sea resorts. Behind their backs, Ushinsky and his colleagues in the secret services referred to them politely as "shit-eaters." He feared and hated the Chinese with bottomless passion. His nightmare was that the yellow hordes who had defected from Soviet socialism would one day swamp Mother Russia with the massed weight of their bodies. If the beam weapons that Berzin had described were going to be used against anyone, Ushinsky reasoned, it should be the Chinese. Maybe that, too, was part of Marshal Safronov's plan.

Ushinsky's modest store of tolerance for non-Russians extended principally to the North Americans. He had enjoyed his two-year posting in Ottawa, when he had run a notably successful illegal network across the border in the United States. Cleverly, he had arranged for his plain, constantly nagging wife, Ludmila, to remain behind with her family in Moscow. He had thus ensured himself a clear run to enjoy the favors of a female librarian whose buxom physique and bright pink cheeks belied her profession and were, to Ushinsky's taste, the ultimate in sexual appeal. The girl's only drawback was that she believed in nuclear disarmament and the United Nations and was given to telling him, at critical moments in bed, that she believed she was striking a blow for world peace.

Ushinsky's feelings toward the Americans were compounded of contempt, curiosity, and insatiable longing. He felt contempt for a society that had developed the greatest military machine in world history only to abandon its claims to supremacy within the space of a generation. How, he had often puzzled, could a great power not *want* to be number one? He was curious, at the same time, to understand how a society with such fickle, vacillating leadership—blown from one opinion poll to the next—riddled with crime and drugs, divided by bitter conflicts of race and class, could still fuel an economic engine capable of supplying more of the good things of life in a year than the Soviet Union was likely to produce in half a century. Out of that flowed his longing: for the everyday luxuries, unimaginable to the average Russian, that he had briefly sampled in Canada; for the liberated, high-stepping women he continued to admire in the foreign movies imported for delectation of the Soviet elite in their private dachas; for the freedom to kick over the traces without being spied upon, at every turning, by his arrogant, inquisitorial brethren in the KGB.

The KGB, which enjoyed nothing better than cutting the GRU down to size, and employed its own narks inside military intelligence, understood this kind of temptation. The KGB understood that attachment to the great Soviet *Rodina* (and still less, faith in the dogmas of a threadbare ideology) was not sufficient to deter some of Ushinsky's colleagues from occasionally contemplating—in a moment of frustration with their wives, their hopes of promotion, or their chances of foreign travel—the possibility of defecting to the West. All the security apparatus of the Soviet police state had not prevented dozens of intelligence officers from slipping the leash. A fair proportion of these defectors, of course, had been KGB plants, sent to disinform the Agency and other Western services. But many had been genuine. And in a time of political upheavals and changing leadership in Moscow, the risk of new defections was at a peak.

To minimize that risk, the KGB sought, through regular briefings and inspired rumors, to instill a deep dread of what lay in store for Russians who tried to escape to the West. Ushinsky had attended one such briefing, addressed by Krylov, the chief of the most secret office inside the KGB, the office known as the Beacon. Krylov had warned that the chances of a genuine defector's making a safe escape were next to zero, since the Beacon had succeeded in placing a high-level mole inside the Agency. Krylov had recalled the cases of would-be defectors who had been betrayed by Philby when he was head of counterintelligence in the British secret service. He dwelled on the gruesome details of a would-be Soviet defector in the Far East whose body was flown back to Moscow in a rubber body bag after the KGB had been tipped off by its British mole.

Ushinsky was in no doubt about the fate that the KGB had in store for the traitors who were uncovered. One of his colleagues in the GRU—a colonel of his own age who had been working for the British—had been found out. He had been given an exemplary execution. Instead of being shot, Krylov had seen to it that the man was thrown, alive and fully conscious, into the furnace of a crematorium. And in order to ensure that the lesson would not be lost on the colonel's colleagues, Krylov had ordered some of them—including Ushinsky—to attend the execution. Ushinsky still woke some nights hearing the screams.

"We have our Philby at Langley today," Krylov had warned.

Even if a would-be defector succeeded, against the odds, in getting away, Krylov had claimed, his subsequent life would be nasty and brief. The head of the Beacon made out that the Agency would reward Russian traitors with torture and imprisonment while their bona fides was examined. Defectors who managed to pass the endless polygraph tests would be milked dry of whatever information they had to impart and then abandoned to a life of penury and solitude, shunned by all. And that was not the end of it.

"We will hunt down traitors wherever they are to be found," Krylov thundered. Ushinsky knew that this part of the story, at least, was authentic, since the execution of Russian "traitors" abroad was one of the responsibilities of his own Second Direction. Such action did not violate any Soviet law. On the contrary, it was clearly laid down that the laws of the Soviet Union—including a death sentence from a secret administrative tribunal—applied to all Russians living abroad who had been born in the USSR.

Yet Russians still managed to defect and stay alive, and Ushinsky had sometimes been driven to wonder whether the prospects in the society of electric toothbrushes, of video cassettes and panty hose, were quite as bleak as the KGB liked to make out. As one of the select few in Moscow who were permitted access to American newspapers, Ushinsky had read lurid accounts of the life-style of a senior Russian defector from the United Nations in New York: stories of high-class call girls, five-hundred-dollar suits, and limitless expenses that did not quite tally with the tales of hardship circulated by the KGB. On the gossip mill at GRU headquarters, he had heard an even more tantalizing item of information. It was that the going price for a colonel in Soviet intelligence who defected to the Americans had gone up to one million dollars. Even in the country of conspicuous consumption, a million dollars must go a long way toward buying the alluring things displayed in the ads in the glossy American magazines—and the sultry, scantily clad females who decorated them. And Ushinsky had something very valuable to sell.

Ushinsky had left early for the nine-story building, screened by thirty-foot blind walls, out by the old Khodinsk airfield, that housed the headquarters of the GRU. He had left his apartment in a fury, slamming the door behind him to shut out Ludmila's high nasal whine. She was impervious to the fact that he had got less than two hours' sleep after driving back from Safronov's dinner at Zhukovka. He had waked with a black headache and a tongue like flypaper—or rather, she had shaken him awake, howling her suspicions that he had been out with another woman. He had made the mistake of letting her know in advance that he was about to make a short trip to Paris to meet one of Sammy Hamad's agents. She had used the rest of the time before he staggered out of the apartment to ply him with endless shopping lists. In desperation, Ushinsky had sneaked a heart-starter, gulping brandy straight out of the bottle, while Ludmila banged around in the kitchen fixing him eggs he had no desire to eat. The woman handled plates and pans like percussion instruments.

Ushinsky needed time alone, time to work things out. His half-sleep had been ravaged by images of the fruition of Marshal Safronov's schemes. Ushinsky had visualized a great, incandescent beam of light ripping through space. It came from the mouth of a horseshoe-shaped gun the size of a destroyer, mounted on a vast star-shaped battle station orbiting in space. Smaller satellites escorted the main battle station, forming a space flotilla. Then he had seen the beam breaking through the earth's atmosphere and pulsing down into the streets of a great city, with a radioactive force many thousands of times that of the bombs that were dropped on Hiroshima and Nagasaki. He had seen people convulsed and dying, in tens and hundreds of thousands, helpless as insects under a stamping heel, their individual loves and hates, courage and intellect, meaningless against the beam.

Could it really happen?

Did Safronov intend to *make* it happen?

Ushinsky was scared, because while he could not grasp all the technical details, he suspected the answer to both questions was yes.

He dragged out his drive to GRU headquarters. The inside of his own car was about the most privacy he could expect to find. After he had found his parking place outside the hollow square of two-story buildings, windows facing inward, that ringed the main structure, he continued to sit in front of the wheel, trying to make his brain—drugged by liquor and sleeplessness—revolve faster.

Safronov had said they had two months.

In two months' time, on November 7, there would be parades in Red Square and worldwide celebrations for the anniversary of the Bolshevik Revolution.

It was in keeping with Safronov's megalomania, Ushinsky thought, that he would pick the historic date for the fulfillment of Project Razrukha. The date could have a further significance, Ushinsky realized. On November 7, Moscow would be crawling with soldiers. Maybe the marshal had picked the day of the big parades to establish his supremacy over his rivals in the Kremlin, as well as Russia's supremacy over the United States.

The GRU colonel wondered whether this was the reason Razrukha had not been mentioned in the meeting of the Defense Council—at any rate, not during the sesion that he had attended. The marshal might have good reason not to wish to share the full extent of his ambitions with his colleagues.

Ushinsky was disturbed by a persistent tapping against his car window. It was one of the semiretired GRU men who were employed to sit on benches around the headquarters complex, keeping a lookout for any unusual comings and goings.

"Daydreaming," Ushinsky apologized. He flashed his official pass.

He entered the main building with only a copy of *Pravda* and a sheaf of loose papers in his hand. No one was permitted to take in a briefcase, or any kind of metal, not even a lighter or a belt buckle. Security. It would be a problem.

I have twenty-four hours, he reflected, as he marched down a corridor painted the inevitable olive-gray toward his department. *Assuming that the Paris trip is not canceled.* It had occurred to him that Marshal Safronov, having taken the apparently unpremeditated step of including him in his plot, might impose a ban on any foreign travel by those privy to it. The one hope was that no one would think to check. Not until he had boarded his Aeroflot flight to Charles de Gaulle airport.

Even at this point, Ushinsky was too confused, with that iron girder weighing down behind his eyes, to consider what course he was taking. He did not say to himself that he was planning to defect.

He knew only that he could not allow it to happen.

What he was contemplating was not treason, he thought as he nodded good morning to his secretary. If Safronov had his way, who would be left to feed the Soviet people? Who would provide the technology for Soviet industry?

On his desk, there were some developed photographs of the Los Alamos laboratories in New Mexico. The agent who had forwarded them had used a special film, code-named *Schtchit*, or "Shield," that had been developed by Soviet intelligence. It was an ideal means of transmitting secret information. You photographed secret blueprints or installations on negatives that already contained innocuous pictures—holiday snaps, or shots of bogus documents. Anyone who was not in on the secret might develop the film and find only snapshots of the beach.

There was another problem, Ushinsky was thinking. If he got to Washington, would they believe him?

42

He looked at the film.

There could be a way.

When his phone buzzed and he learned that he was being summoned to Marshal Safronov's private office, the pounding inside Ushinsky's forehead intensified, and he broke into a cold sweat. On his way over to the Defense Ministry, he wondered whether something in his behavior at the marshal's dacha the night before had betrayed his inner revulsion over what was being planned.

But, as it turned out, all that Safronov wanted to talk about was the network of sleeper agents that had been established in the United States for future sabotage operations. In particular, the marshal wanted to talk about the terrorist agent called Sammy Hamad. Safronov did not explain what ultimate objective he had in mind for the Palestinian, leaving Ushinsky curious to know the reason for his special interest.

3

PARIS, *September 8*

Sally Sherwin frowned and glared ostentatiously at her watch. She was conscious that she was attracting speculative glances from the two men who were dining by themselves at the next table. One of them—the fattish one with plastered-down hair who had started out using chopsticks but had had to abandon them for fork and spoon—kept turning toward Sally, trying to catch her eye. Give it a few minutes more, and she was sure the man, who reminded her of a well-fed Doberman pinscher, would come over and invite her to join them. He did.

"*Pardon, mademoiselle,*" said Doberman. "*Vous êtes seule ce soir?*"

"Sorry," Sally rebuffed him, making no effort to practice her schoolgirl French. "My husband and my twenty-two-year-old son will be here any second."

She sipped her kir, looking fixedly at the door, until Doberman went away. What she had said was part-true, she reflected. Only her son Jimmy was five, not twenty-two, and was at home in New York. And Charles, her ex-husband, was in New York too—at least he had been a couple of nights ago, when they had run into each other at the Café Carlyle. But it was more than possible that by now Charles would be on a plane, traveling to or from one of the wars or revolutions he seemed to frequent as other men hang out at golf courses or football games. Jimmy had got the picture almost as soon as he started to talk. On a walk in Central Park, he had tugged at her hand and pointed excitedly at a plane cruising overhead. "Daddy! Daddy!" the child had exclaimed, still pointing at the plane. Sally had watched the jet disappear over the sculpted roof of the Dakota building. The kid wasn't dumb, she thought; that was Daddy, all right. But eventually she had become sick of waiting for planes.

She had been seriously involved with Dick Hammond for only a few months, but already he was keeping her waiting too. Thirty-five minutes so far, without even a phone call to apologize for being held up. She should have been forewarned. After all, it was Charles who had introduced them. "We're members of the same club," Charles Canning had said, presenting the tall American with clear, clear blue eyes and a shock of steel-gray hair that flopped boyishly over his broad, commanding forehead. She should have been warned. Charles and Dick Hammond were in the same line of business. For a woman, that meant waiting. And she had decided, after the painful divorce from Charles, that she was not going to spend any more of her life in a kind of permanent transit lounge. At thirty-five, she had all the youth and glamour she needed to start out again on her own terms. She was building a successful career that meant money, adventure, and the right to keep her partners waiting on her. And here she was, stranded in a Chinese restaurant in the grubbiest street in the Quartier Latin, clocking the minutes until Dick Hammond saw fit to show up, when she could have been at Fouquet's with the debonair French publisher who had courted her all afternoon, celebrating the successful conclusion of a foreign-rights deal that would be worth another $200,000 to Alvin Fiedler and $30,000 to Harry Schwab—neither of whom needed it. To cap it all, she wasn't even particularly hot on oriental food. The best thing about the Chinese restaurant, in her view, was that the perenially smiling waiters all called her "Mademoiselle" as if she were sweet sixteen.

Sally looked up as a waiter, unasked, deposited another glass of kir on her table.

"*Vous permettez, mademoiselle?*" Doberman smarmed, indicating that the drink was an offering. The man was more persistent than Sally had anticipated. His attentions made her the more aware that she appeared needlessly dramatic for an out-of-the-way bistro, having swapped the chic navy suit she had worn all day for a flowing Givenchy creation, all lilac and gold.

She nodded curtly, discouraging conversation but wanting the drink. She decided that if Dick Hammond had still not surfaced by the time she finished it, she would leave and treat herself to the excellent room service at the Georges V, where there was no one to stare at her except the gilded caryatid that supported the hall table in her suite. Sally had never enjoyed spending money. She felt the need for stability, not show. She used to make most of her own dresses, and still compared the prices of zucchini with the same studious care as a dealer appraising diamonds. Her boss, Harry Schwab, had joked that that was the legacy of her Puritan forebears. Sally knew it had more to do with the insecurity of growing up in a broken home and of then having to contend with a husband like Charles. The first time she had traveled abroad for Harry Schwab and had signed for the suite he had insisted on booking with her company credit card, the size of the bill had reduced her to a state bordering on catatonic shock. Harry had still not entirely convinced her that in the world of movie moguls, megabucks, and Machiavellian hypes in which she was now operating, conspicuous consumption is often a close cousin to success. But she had less time to shop for zucchini or sew hems.

Her glass was almost empty by the time Dick Hammond finally made his entry, loping between the tables with little regard for the safety of the other diners at the half-run that he normally substituted for a walk. That was another thing Dick Hammond had in common with Charles, Sally Sherwin reflected as she watched the big man in his charcoal suit and striped tie advancing on her. They both seemed to be propelled by a built-in accelerator with the pedal continuously depressed. Maybe it came from constantly rushing to catch a plane. More likely it came from belonging to the same highly unconventional club.

Doberman, observing Hammond's arrival, looked decidedly droopy and called for his check.

"Hey, princess." Hammond leaned over the table to kiss her cheek. "I'm sorry. I got snarled up in something big."

"Just as well you got here," Sally said, finding she could not sustain the frosty expression she had planned to put on. "Strange men were starting to buy me drinks. And you know I'm a cheap drunk."

He reached across the table and caressed her left hand. His hand was scarcely broader than hers, but with much longer, sensitive fingers—the fingers of an artist or surgeon—and a thicket of fine blond hairs that failed to conceal the end of a long white scar that

46

vanished under his immaculate blue cuff. Always look at the hands, Sally's mother had told her. The hands and the eyes. The scar, she knew, ran jaggedly to above the elbow, a memento of the years Hammond had spent in Vietnam; the "lost years," Dick called them. Maybe it was nostalgia for what he had lived through then that had led him to pick a Chinese restaurant for what they had both agreed was going to be a heavy conversation.

Sally did not want to get sucked into Hammond's past. But she waited until he had drained his first scotch before saying, "Let's get out of here. There are thousands of restaurants in Paris, and I've seen enough of this one for one night."

"You don't want to make the chef unhappy," he countered softly. "Our banquet is about to begin."

"But we haven't even looked at the menu," Sally protested.

"The menu is not for beautiful women," Hammond riposted with the overeasy gallantry she knew he employed when his mind was somewhere else.

"I know what it is," Sally announced, alarmed to hear that the wine had already made her speech a little unsteady. "You're still on the job. You've told the station this is where you'll be, so this is where you'll stay until you hear from them. You might as well walk around with a bleeper in your belt."

Hammond raised a finger to his lips theatrically. "A bleeper wouldn't be very discreet in a restaurant," he whispered in a stage hush. "I'm supposed to be cloak-and-dagger, remember?" He did not think it was the right time to mention that he did, upon occasion, go around with a silent bleeper that throbbed rhythmically inside his waistband when the station was trying to reach him urgently.

Sally Sherwin's objections to the restaurant quickly melted away as a succession of exquisite dishes—from a rich, piquant fish soup that captured the whole palate to perfectly crisp Peking duck—materialized before them.

"I got news today," Hammond said at last. "I'm being recalled to Washington. They want me out of here fast."

Sally was surprised. She knew that Hammond had served less than two years as the Agency station chief in Paris.

"It seems I've got my name in the papers," Hammond explained. A forthcoming issue of a radical newssheet called *Whistle-Blower*, which specialized in blowing the cover of Agency operatives around the world, was devoting its lead item to Hammond's alleged activities in Paris. *Whistle-Blower*, the product of a collective of disgruntled former American intelligence employees and New Left radicals, had been published in Canada since Congress imposed legal penalties for exposing the identities of Agency personnel. *Whistle-Blower* claimed that Hammond and his staff had broken the law by bugging U.S. citizens abroad and had violated French sovereignty by operating against terrorist groups in Paris without informing the local security authorities. Though the French government would probably be able to ensure that the article was not replayed in the mainstream Paris press, Hammond was conscious that it cut close enough to the bone to inspire a powerful lobby around the Elysée to press for his withdrawal. In order to sidestep any possible political embarrassment, the Agency wanted him out before anyone asked for him to go. Hammond was not disposed to argue with his new director, for a particular reason that he did not share with Sally. He knew that if the French—or, for that matter, Director Claiborne—should get wind of how he had spent the last few hours before arriving at the Chinese restaurant, he would be hustled out to Charles de Gaulle airport before he even had time to pack.

"It'll give us a good excuse for a vacation," Hammond wound up. "Why don't you stick around in Paris while I clean out my desk? We could go somewhere warm. I've got a friend with a villa in Majorca that he never uses this time of year."

"Dick," she responded, pushing away the last of her food, "you seem to forget that I've got a job too. Harry Schwab needs me back in New York. We've got a terrific new espionage novel we're going to put up for auction. By the way," she added, "that's what you should be doing. Writing fiction. It's a damn sight more profitable and a hell of a lot safer. And it might mean that you'd make your dinner dates on time."

Hammond was looking over her shoulder, at a beaming waiter bearing a huge bunch of roses. The waiter bowed as he presented them to Sally.

"I told you you'd like this place," he said.

She breathed in the heady scent of the flowers. "Where the hell do you find roses at this season?"

In Israel, he thought, but did not say it. "Why don't we leave?" he suggested, suddenly uninterested in the last dishes the Chinese chef had in store. Sally had spent too many years with Charles not to catch the change in mood. The roses were a message for Hammond, not for her. You had to give credit to the Club for one thing. The Club had *style*. Whatever it did to people's lives.

Sally insisted on walking beside the Seine for a bit, to look at Notre Dame and her favorite quarter of Paris—the Ile St. Louis— before the sudden nip in the air drove them back to Hammond's car and the sanctuary of her suite at the Georges V. She was still experimenting with independence, and therefore had to assert it. Why should she go to *his* apartment? Let him come to hers. People needed to reach her too.

They made several calls before retiring to Sally's sumptuous double bed—she to Claire, her ebullient housekeeper, who was looking after Jimmy and her home in Manhattan, he to the duty officer at the station and to room service for champagne. Hammond was a gentle, caring lover who allowed her the time she needed, even when (as she could feel tonight) he needed her urgently. The more they made love, the more her desire grew. It had not been easy to respond at first: the barriers of self-doubt that had been raised over the long, lonely months when Charles, ever more remote, had rejected her were not quick to fall. Disappointed, Hammond had pressed her to tell him what he was doing wrong, to show him how to give her pleasure. To make *him* happy, she had taken to faking orgasm, wondering how realistic the imitation was. Now she no longer needed to pretend.

"I used to be so cold-assed," she mused aloud in the early hours. Hammond, half dozing, stirred awake and reached for the champagne. The lamplight accentuated the deep swell of her breasts. Hammond fondled them tenderly.

"We still haven't had that conversation you suggested," she went on. Hammond had told her, when proposing dinner, that there was something important to discuss.

"I think I'm in love with you," Hammond said, looking directly into her eyes.

Sally reached around him—and his eyes—for the champagne, not sure how she wanted to handle this declaration.

"What are you going to do when you go back to the States?" she said after swallowing some of the wine, now lukewarm.

49

"I'm going to turn forty-six. I could try for early retirement."
Hammond knew this was the answer she wanted to hear. "Sally,"
he added earnestly. "I know one thing. Whatever I do, I want you
with me."

"What will you do if you leave the Agency?" she probed,
avoiding the other implications of what he was saying.

"Private consultancy?" Hammond shrugged. What did twenty-
two years in the Agency prepare you for? "Others have done
okay," he proceeded, trying to reassure himself as much as Sally.
"Look at Charles."

It was the wrong remark to make. Her mouth hardened.
"Charles didn't get out," she said tautly. "He still works for the
Club."

Charles had tried to explain it to her once, quoting a poem by
Cavafy, the brooding, fastidious intellect of Alexandria who had
created in verse a city more haunting and encompassing than any
ever constructed in the real world. Sally's brow furrowed as she
struggled to remember the lines.

" 'You won't find a new country, won't find another shore,' " she
recited, hearing the lines as she spoke them in the rich timbre of
Charles's voice.

"What?" Hammond propped himself up against the brass
bedhead.

"Listen." She went on:

> *"This city will always pursue you . . .*
> *Don't hope for things elsewhere:*
> *there's no ship for you, there's no road.*
> *Now that you've wasted your life here,*
> *in this small corner,*
> *you've destroyed it everywhere in the world."*

Hammond nodded, recognizing the poem. "Cavafy," he confirmed. "Not one of life's optimists."

Charles had once, in a somber mood, suggested that the poem
should be adopted, *in toto,* as a motto for the Club.

Sally understood the Club. In a sense, she belonged to it.
Between her own family and her ex-husband, she knew a lot more
about the secret world than might have been expected of an
assistant to a New York literary agent. Apart from living with
Charles Canning for nine years, she had Max Zimmer for an

50

uncle. For decades, Zimmer had presided over the Agency's counterintelligence staff—until his many enemies managed to stage a purge. Zimmer's endless, and inconclusive, mole hunts through the corridors of Langley were still remembered and resented by Hammond's colleagues. In retirement, the old spy chief was said to have grown more suspicious and introspective than before. Max Zimmer was a subject that Hammond carefully avoided with Sally. He shared the general view that Max had become the dupe of his own overelaborate theories. But Sally's loyalties, he knew, were firmly with her uncle. Her belief that Max had been badly mistreated by the Agency reinforced her hostility toward the profession of intelligence.

Yet she understood the Club, and Hammond knew that her reservations were mingled with the sense that it was something that had to exist. Poetry aside, the philosophy of the Club was, "If there's a job to be done, let's get on with it."

It was in the spirit of the Club—though acting under his own steam—that Hammond had shaped the events that explained his late arrival at the Chinese restaurant six hours earlier. Through an Agency source in the French Atomic Energy Commission, he had learned that France was preparing to ship another consignment of reactor components for the huge nuclear complex—described by some as "a Manhattan Project for the Arab world"—that the Iraqis were building at a desert site heavily defended by batteries of Soviet-made surface-to-air missiles. Since on a previous occasion an Israeli hit team had succeeded in penetrating elaborate French security arrangements and had blown up a reactor core at a heavily guarded warehouse near Toulon, the French had now resolved to take no chances. For one thing, it had been decreed that no one of Jewish extraction should be allowed to know any details of the consignment. The French had a lot riding on the safe delivery of the reactor components and the enriched uranium that went with them: a highly lucrative arms deal, and guaranteed oil supplies. In the view of some advisers around the Elysée, the fact that the Iraqis were ready to pay handsomely—and in "black gold"—for equipment and nuclear fuel that might enable them to make the first Arab bomb was convincing proof that the men in Baghdad had turned into pro-Western moderates.

Hammond did not share this view. Nor did the Israelis. Nor, in general, did the United States. Conscious, however, of the influence of a Washington lobby that believed that Iraq should be cultivated as a "natural ally" against the radicals in Iran, he had decided to move without regard for the formalities of bureaucratic clearance. The roses in the Chinese restaurant were a signal from Moshe Stern, the Paris-based chief of Mossad operations in Europe, that Hammond's leads had paid off. Hammond assumed that somewhere between Paris and the Mediterranean coast the Iraqi consignment had been destroyed—or maybe even hijacked. He wondered how long it would be before the French press got wind of the news, and Paris officials again had to field a volley of embarrassing questions.

Hammond began to massage Sally's back as she lay face down on the pillow, steadily increasing the pressure as his hands flowed back and forth from her shoulder blades to the nape of her neck. He had to concede that she was right. He might leave the Agency, but he had no wish to leave the Club.

"Are you saying you're not prepared to marry another spook?" he challenged her. It was the first time he had broached the question, and she shied away from him as if he had slapped her.

"Aargh," she groaned. "I don't know what to do about you."

"I'm perfectly serious."

"I know. That's what scares me. I don't think I'm ready for this." Just when she was beginning to find herself as an independent person, she thought, another man had to come along and ask her to submerge her life into his. She didn't want to let herself be swamped. Not again.

"You shouldn't confuse the man with the job," Hammond pressed ahead. "It isn't only spooks whose marriages break up. Look at the divorce statistics. I'm not sure that doctors, or brokers, or even literary agents score any better than we do." He reined himself in then, remembering his own first wife, a beautiful survivor of the postwar hell's kitchen of Vienna, drowning herself in a martini glass before her final crack-up.

But already she had rounded on him fiercely, although her voice was half-choked with sobbing. "You talk as if I don't understand what you and Charles are doing," she erupted. "There were times when I thought what Charles was trying to do was the most important thing in the world. Sometimes I still do. I wouldn't ask any man to give that up. It's just . . ." She broke off, furious that tears always seem to make your nose run.

52

Hammond threw his arms around her, trying to draw her to his chest.

"I can't take a repeat performance," she said when she had managed to stop shaking.

"It won't be," Hammond promised.

"I need time," she said. "You have to give me time."

4

Sweat poured in rivulets down from the balding hairline and down both sides of the Irishman's stubby, pugnacious nose. Dark circles had formed around his armpits. Even the front of the man's shirt was damp, noted Adam Claiborne, the director of Central Intelligence, as he eyed the speaker discreetly—his head averted—across the expanse of the oval table where the chiefs of the Washington intelligence community meet, every Thursday morning, to review the state of the world.

It was perfectly in character that the man now working himself into a lather should have been the first of the seventeen around the table to remove his jacket. Lieutenant General George Brennan, USAF, the recently appointed chief of Defense Intelligence and a sworn foe of the old-time Agency, was definitely not a man for the social niceties—or for understatement in any form. Brennan pounded the table as he approached the climax of his peroration. Director Claiborne coughed quietly, covering his mouth with the back of his hand.

My God, Claiborne was thinking. *George Brennan is quoting Dostoyevsky. I don't believe it. Dostoyevsky.*

"Gentlemen," General Brennan was thundering, "I hope you will all recall the immortal words of Ivan Karamazov: 'I want to be there when everyone suddenly understands what it has all been for.' Gentlemen, today I can stand before you and say: I think I have realized Ivan Karamazov's ambition. At last, every one of you knows what it is all about."

Director Claiborne went on coughing. In the old days, one of

54

Brennan's neighbors would have stuck an elbow in his well-padded ribs to indicate to him that the director, chairman, and czar of the American intelligence community had had enough. Since the last elections, things had changed. The Pentagon hawks were stretching their wings, flexing their talons. Brennan, long an isolated Cassandra, clearly believed that his hour had come.

He was still not through. "For two decades," the general boomed, "we have deceived ourselves as to the capacities and the basic intentions of the Soviet Union. Our self-deception has been helped along by arrogant liberal extremists under successive administrations who maintained that the Soviets were too technologically backward to ever steal a march on the United States and were equally incapable of grasping the fact that what Moscow wants is world power. Their closest allies were the people in the intelligence community who were always ready to trim their estimates of the Soviet military threats to the political and electoral calculations of the incumbent administration. I am sorry to have to observe that both types have long prospered in the Agency."

Director Claiborne sought the sympathetic glance of the man facing him at the other end of the oval table, the seat normally occupied by whichever in-house expert he had selected to defend the Agency's position in the debate over a national intelligence estimate. Today, knowing the Agency was under fire, the director had brought two counselors. The man at the other end of the table was Les Winter, the head of the Agency's Soviet Division. Flanking him was an expert from the Agency's nuclear intelligence panel. Winter would not have been included in today's somewhat technical discussions but for the fact that Director Claiborne thought that he happened to be holding the Agency's trump card.

The director decided the time had come to interrupt Brennan's tirade. He cleared his throat again.

"General Brennan," he said, "I think that last remark was uncalled for. I—uh—hope you will reconsider it."

"My remarks are not a personal reference to anyone in this room, Mr. Director," Brennan replied, with the combination of accommodating smile and glassy stare that indicated he was at his most dangerous. "Beyond that, I am not prepared to qualify them.

55

I would remind everyone present that it was the controlling influence of the Agency that led this country into a series of near-fatal miscalculations of Soviet strength."

The director winced, anticipating that Brennan would revive the question of why, for many years, the Agency had understated the true level of Soviet defense spending by a factor of more than fifty percent—and then forced its false assessments into the National Intelligence Estimates and the publications of foreign research institutes subject to Agency influence.

But Brennan chose a different, no less painful, example to score his point. "I recall the occasion," he said, "when, as chief of Air Force Intelligence, I brought to the attention of this board some reconnaissance pictures of a large installation the Soviets had constructed next to a strategic bomber base close to the Chinese border. In the opinion of my analysts, this installation was a huge bacteriological warfare plant. But we were told by the Agency that there was insufficient evidence that that was its purpose and that you had learned from human sources that the Soviets were downgrading their whole program of chemical and biological warfare. I remember vividly sitting in this very room, Mr. Director, when one of *your* analysts—"

"Don't call him *my* analyst," the director interrupted tersely. "I was not sitting in this seat in those days."

"I stand corrected, Mr. Director." Brennan's tone was a further provocation, not an apology. "Let me say then that I was informed by one of the bright young men of the Agency that this installation the Soviets had built might well be an ultramodern incubator for assembly-line poultry production. The Agency only conceded that the Air Force estimate had been right all along when we got a live defector off one of the ships in the Soviet Pacific Fleet. Otherwise, we might still be arguing about whether a bacteriological warfare plant is a poultry farm."

"I don't recall that episode," said Adam Claiborne, studying his agenda. "But in any event, it's all historical. We are wasting time if we're going to start raking over who said what in the mid-seventies."

"I strongly endorse that, Mr. Director," the State Department man from the Bureau of Intelligence and Research chimed in. "If General Brennan wants to take up these . . . well, frankly, somewhat musty episodes, he should go to the National Security

Council. This committee is concerned with current business."

"Agreed," said the man from the Treasury.

"Right." The director moved back a fraction from the edge of his chair. "In that case, I suggest we move right along with the agenda. Did you have anything else you wished to say, General Brennan?"

"With your indulgence, Mr. Director," Brennan resumed. "I suggest that there is no more urgent issue before this board that affects the survival of this nation than the question of whether the Soviets are going to win the war in space."

"Damn right," muttered the admiral from Naval Intelligence.

"At the risk of being accused again of sounding historical," Brennan went on, "I would remind you, gentlemen, that for many years we fought in this room over whether or not it was scientifically possible to produce killer beams that could move at the speed of light to destroy targets thousands of miles away in space. There used to be many people—and I imagine there still are—who could not conceive of the possibility of such weapons outside the world of Buck Rogers and the comic books. The skeptics included some of our most respected nuclear physicists, laureates who would be wheeled out by the Agency to tell us why it was scientifically impossible for the Soviets to develop weapons based on newly discovered principles of physics which, if perfected, could make our nuclear arsenals obsolescent, if not obsolete. Not for the first time, the physicists were wrong. Those of you who have been involved in these matters as long as I may recall that there was a highly respected scientist, Dr. Vannevar Bush, who assured the world in 1945, after Hiroshima, that ICBMs were scientifically impossible."

"I sure do," drawled the Alabama-born major general from Air Force Intelligence, who had inherited the seat once warmed by the speaker.

"I want to pay tribute," Brennan went on, "to the people who mounted the Navy's Chair Heritage program and the Army's White Horse program and proved that the scientific establishment in this country was wrong."

Dammit to hell, the director said inwardly. The Pentagon contingent was advancing in a phalanx, bristling with spears. Or maybe, given Brennan's ancestry, they were brandishing billy-clubs.

"Thanks to the research conducted at the Lawrence Livermore and the Los Alamos laboratories," Brennan marched on, "and at Kirtland Air Force Base, it is now accepted that the Soviets have been working successfully for years on high-energy lasers and charged-particle beam weapons that could enable them to shoot down our space satellites. I believe that even the Agency would now accept that the beam weapons the Soviets are developing could give them the capacity to shoot down our missiles before they leave the earth's atmosphere. In other words, the Soviets are close to establishing an anti-ballistic-missile defense system that would deprive us of the ability to launch a retaliatory strike if they start a war."

Director Claiborne signaled to Lane Hughes, the man from the Agency's nuclear intelligence panel.

"General Brennan," Hughes interjected, "I believe you are presenting all of this in a somewhat alarmist light. We accept that the Soviet objective may be as you state, but they are still several years away from achieving it. In our assessment, ground-based beam weapons would not constitute an effective ABM system. And the Soviets are still way behind us in space-shuttle technology. Especially since the Columbia flight. The Soviets still have to solve the problems of getting these things into orbit."

Brennan snorted. "Who sent up the first Sputnik?" he said. "Who sent up that space station with twelve men on board a couple of years ago? Don't tell me that, having outstripped the U.S. in seven vital areas of beam-weapon technology, the Soviets can't work out how to put their equipment onto a space shuttle."

The bluff FBI director, a former judge, butted in for the first time. "Say, this is getting a bit technical," he complained. "I doubt whether most of us are competent to pass judgment here. Would someone mind telling me what exactly we are supposed to be deciding on?"

"Certainly." Brennan lifted up one of the documents piled in front of him on the table so the FBI chief could see it. "I assume you've taken a look at this?"

"Well, er—"

Brennan knew he had asked an unfair question. The top level of the Washington bureaucracy was swamped with paper, and the FBI director had more useful things to do—like catching Soviet

58

spies, Mafiosi, and Congressmen on Arab payrolls—than puzzling over a report, larded with expressions like "megajoules," "milliradians," and "nanoseconds," that summarized the current view of the Agency analysts of what the consensus of the U.S. intelligence community should be on the threat posed by Soviet beam weapons. Brennan had no wish to embarrass his Bureau colleague. His barbs were directed elsewhere.

"Judge"—Brennan stabbed his heavy forefinger at the Agency's report—"I'll tell you what this brilliant bit of paper says. Number one, the Agency now accepts that the Soviets have been going all out, at least since the early seventies, in developing beam weapons. That is correct, is it not, Mr. Hughes?"

The young analyst from the Agency's nuclear intelligence panel, now sucking on an empty pipe, nodded. Brennan noted the pipe, which fitted in nicely with Hughes's carelessly knotted bow tie and tweed jacket, with a malevolent twinkle. He had observed that the pipe was the perfect prop for a committee man; the laborious mechanics of loading and unloading provided a wonderful pretext for taking extra time to think out an answer, or for dodging one altogether in a cloud of smoke.

"Number two," Brennan proceeded, "the Agency contends that the Soviets still have some major technological hurdles to overcome, especially in the area of pulse-power technology, which they need to fire a neutron beam in space. This is the key reason why the Agency would have us believe it will take another five years before the Soviets can cash in on the investment they've been making over the last two decades. Am I oversimplifying, Mr. Hughes?"

Hughes took his pipe out of his mouth and started prodding at it with a metal scraper. "That is approximately the Agency's position, General," he said, wondering why the director was permitting Brennan to brief the meeting on the views of the Agency. "Of course, we are not all that rigid on the timing of this. You will remember that we suggest some fairly broad parameters."

To Brennan, this was a typical case of the favorite Washington game of CYA—Cover Your Ass. Anyone reading the Agency report would get the clear message that the Soviets were not about to put beam weapons into space next year, or the year after that.

But if it just so happened that they did, it could be proved from the fine print and some of the confusing graphs appended to the report that the Agency had predicted it.

"Well," said Brennan, "I think this assessment by the Agency is outdated. I believe that I have new evidence that the Soviets have overcome all of these supposed technical hitches."

"Would you clarify that?" Claiborne intervened.

"I'll get down to the evidence in just one minute, sir. What I want to say first is that the most monumental error in this document that you want us to submit to the President of the United States as the considered and concerted view of the intelligence community goes beyond the matter of timing. The biggest mistake in this report is that it contends that the Soviets would only use beam weapons for essentially defensive purposes, against targets in space or the upper atmosphere."

Puzzled looks were exchanged around the oval table. The one thing that was generally recognized about beam weapons was that they would give a tremendous advantage to the defense. The side that deployed them first would be able to burn up the other side's nuclear missiles before they could wreak havoc and destruction on their targets.

Some visionaries among the country's strategists had espoused the hope that, for this reason, the United States might one day be able to end the long reign of nuclear terror over mankind. In a prophetic article, the editor of *Aviation Week* had spoken for those farsighted and activist enough to understand the opportunity. "Beam weapons," he had written, "offer the promise of reducing strategic nuclear weapons to a negligible factor in the future. If successfully deployed, beam weapons can end the long reign of nuclear terror introduced by the ballistic missile and its thermonuclear warhead. If the Soviets achieve this capability first, it will give them enormous crucial leverage in imposing their political will on the rest of the world. If the U.S. achieves it first, there will be no need for flimsy SALT agreements, and the threat of Soviet nuclear blackmail will lose its credibility."

When those words had first been published in *Aviation Week* in 1978, their message had been ridiculed by a wide body of opinion in the political, scientific, and intelligence establishment. The knowledge that had since been gleaned, fragment by fragment, from reconnaissance photographs, the occasionally loose tongue

60

of a Soviet physicist, and the fruits of the research going on in U.S. laboratories, had made the skeptics less overbearing. But it was still hard to accept that the Soviets had crossed vast new frontiers in scientific research that the Americans were only beginning to discover. "It wasn't invented here," one prominent American physicist had reasoned aloud in a debate over how far the Soviets had got in developing the complex process of flux compression, "so how could the Soviets have invented it?" The exact capabilities of the Russians remained the focus for passionate debate and speculation, since all the high-resolution photographs taken by the KH-11 and Big Bird satellites might show you every detail of the *outside* of a Soviet military facility—down to car number plates or the expression on a sentry's face—but they only hinted at what was happening *inside*. Still, everyone was agreed on one thing. Killer beams were essentially *defensive* weapons. So what was Brennan talking about?

Adam Claiborne put the question. "Just what are you saying, General?"

"I am saying, Mr. Director, that among the scenarios that are sketched out in this Agency report, describing the way beam weapons could be used in a future war, the most awesome of all has been omitted."

"Well, *I* found what's in there already pretty chilling," said the man from State. The Agency report noted the possibility that the Soviets might use beam weapons to knock out U.S. satellites—blinding American intelligence and disrupting satellite-based communications. The implications of being literally left in the dark on the eve of a possible Soviet nuclear attack were, indeed, awesome.

There was silence around the room as the assembled intelligence chiefs waited for Brennan to explain himself. Relishing his moment of theater, Brennan took his time about extracting a black mock-leather bound folder from the collection of papers he had stacked in front of him.

"You might all like to take a look at these," said Brennan, removing half a dozen aerial photographs from the folder. They were passed from hand to hand around the table. The pictures showed a complex of large concrete buildings, screened by security fences and a large contingent of mechanized infantry, on a strip of barren land. One of the buildings looked like a huge pumping station. Some distance from the main complex there was what looked like a mineshaft. In one of the photographs a pair of giant cranes were lifting a vast metal tube.

The man from Treasury glanced at the photographs and scratched his head. "Could be a sewage treatment plant for all I could tell," he observed.

"Show them to Lane Hughes," said the director, impatient. "Where were the pictures taken?"

"Near Saryshagan, in Kazakhstan."

"You mean that place where the Soviets have been building some kind of weapon that would fire through the atmosphere into space? What was our assessment of that weapon, Lane?"

"Still not confirmed, sir." The pipe seesawed at the corner of his mouth. "It appears to be an electron beam, but it could be a pulsed-iodine laser."

"Why don't you just say that it's a lightning bolt?" Brennan mocked the Agency analysts. "That's the effect it would have if the Soviets fired it at our satellites—a gigantic lightning bolt that can be aimed at targets hundreds of miles away in space, requiring more controlled energy than we derive from the entire Hoover Dam."

"But these aren't pictures of that facility," Lane Hughes commented, now that the photos had reached him.

"You bet your ass they're not," Brennan confirmed. "The Soviets have built something new. They've arranged a little surprise for us."

"We'd obviously need to have these checked out by our photo-analysts," Hughes said, peering at the pictures from a variety of angles, his pipe drooping perilously low. "It's not at all clear what's going on here."

"Sure, we can let the photo-analysts play games for a few months," Brennan said, the sudden softness of his voice conveying pent-up wrath. "And they'll end up telling us that this is another poultry farm. *I'll* tell you what those photographs show. They show that the Soviets are not only ready to put a beam weapon into space, but they are going to be able to use it to attack U.S. territory. The thing they are assembling there would be powerful enough to irradiate an area hundreds of miles square. They would be able to wipe out the population of New York and Boston and everything in between, or kill everyone in the home counties of

England, without breaking one single pane of glass or loosening a single brick."

"Let me see those pictures again," Adam Claiborne sighed. Brennan was famous for exercising poetic license when it came to maximizing the Soviet threat—and thereby maximizing the Pentagon budget. But enough of his forecasts had come true, over the years, for the director to be cautious about trying to slap him down now. Brennan might finally have gone over the top of the hill. Or he could be right. Unhappily, the photographs offered Claiborne no clue as to which was the case. To the director, the pictures were like a psychiatrist's inkblots; you could see anything in them that you wanted to see—anything or nothing. Narrowing his eyes, he tried to practice a little free association. Nothing came. Why couldn't the pictures be clear and unequivocal, like the ones that finally compelled Kennedy to accept that the Soviets had put missiles into Cuba?

"I'm afraid I don't see it," Claiborne stated flatly.

"Allow me to help you, Mr. Director."

Lester Frobisher Winter, head of the Agency's Soviet Division, drummed the pads of his fingers on the tabletop, soundlessly, as General Brennan scraped back his chair, marched around the table, and leaned over Adam Claiborne's shoulder to point out some details in the photographs. Brennan's shoulder, he noticed, was within an inch or two of the director's face. Consciously or not, he had invaded the director's body space. The origin of the words "aggression," Les Winter recalled, was in the two words *ad gradis*, meaning "to step toward." Even in his body language, General Brennan was the consummate aggressor.

Yes, thought Winter, and how he relished tormenting the Agency. It would be ironic if the Agency had survived the bitter years of Congressional inquisition and media muckraking only to succumb to the likes of Brennan.

In the Ireland of his forebears, Winter reflected, George Brennan would have been either an IRA gunman or a Catholic priest. He espoused a creed, and was ready to do battle for it against any odds. Compromise was simply not in the man's makeup. He would have won his third star earlier than he had, and his coveted job as Defense Intelligence chief, if he had been willing to ride

63

with the bureaucratic consensus. Instead he had stuck to his guns, warring with the Agency over its assessments of the Soviet buildup when no one else was willing to give him covering fire.

Winter did not admire Brennan's type of courage—which, years ago, had led him, then an Air Force brigadier general, to go into East Germany on a "black mission" to check the extent of Soviet missile deployments in person. To Winter, that kind of courage was compounded with hubris and self-dramatization. Winter was not a demonstrative man, and he found the theatrical quality in others embarrassing. He had never played John Wayne. In fact, his operational experience was surprisingly limited for a man who now had the task of supervising the Agency's espionage and counterespionage efforts against the Soviets. Much of his Agency career had been spent in the small Reports and Requirements section of Soviet Division at headquarters, processing the raw input from agents into finished reports, telling the field men what the Agency needed to know, and distributing the finished products to the rest of the community. It was not a glamorous job. But it meant that Winter knew where most of the bodies were buried.

Winter was a man of middling height, with the kind of blurred features that blend easily into any crowd, tweedily dressed in the style approved by some of the Old Guard recruited from the better colleges of the Eastern Seaboard. But the eyes were veiled and dangerous behind the pilot-style glasses.

Now returned to his seat, Brennan was haranguing the room again.

"During the Great Plague of London," declaimed the Defense Intelligence chief, "there was a general agreement, by common consent, not to talk about the disease that was ravaging the population. In a way, silence in the face of a natural disaster for which there is no known preventive or cure is understandable. But we are facing *man-made* disasters. We cannot go on chatting as if they were beyond the bounds of polite conversation."

Les Winter maintained, in most situations, a cool, impassive mien in dealings with adversaries. In the case of General Brennan, he tried to affect an Edwardian disdain. But he found his own temper rising quickly to the boil every time Brennan laid claim to a unique store of wisdom and foresight.

"Les," Director Claiborne was saying. "Would you care to comment on General Brennan's position?"

Winter leaned forward into the table, looking at its polished surface as he began to talk in what he hoped was a measured, impartial tone.

"Sir," he began, "like most of us here, I am no expert on the scientific details. Though I am, of course, familiar with the project code-named Four Sevens by the Pentagon that the Soviets initiated at Sarova under the general control of A. I. Pavlovsky and have been running, in recent times, under the supervision of the East German scientist Klaus Milstein. I would agree with General Brennan that if the Soviets have developed the capacity to deploy space-based beam weapons capable of killing hundreds of thousands, or millions, of people many years before us, they will not hesitate to go ahead. But I must also point out that we could easily be the victims of strategic deception."

"What's that supposed to mean?" Brennan interjected. He felt a visceral dislike for Winter, whose attitude seemed to suggest that the peasants ought to repair to the farm and leave high affairs of state to those who were bred to deal with them.

"There are indications," Winter amplified, "that the Soviets, under their new—and probably divided—leadership, are trying to lure our administration into some kind of trap. They are masters of *provokatsiya.* In other words, the art of provocation."

"No need to translate," Brennan growled. "We all know what it means."

"You agreed yourself, General Brennan, that surveillance pictures are susceptible to widely differing interpretations," Winter pursued.

"The Agency demonstrated that in the past by coming up with interpretations that were sophisticated in their incompetence," Brennan sortied.

"Be that as it may," Winter plowed on, "I would hope we could at least agree that human sources are required to inform us, from the inside, of what precisely Soviet capabilities and intentions may be."

"I didn't know that the Agency was still capable of running human sources in Moscow." Brennan's assault was unrelenting.

To Les Winter, Brennan's challenge was the psychological equivalent of a needle pushed under the fingernail. For years, Winter had been engaged in a bitter feud with Max Zimmer—who had presided over the counterintelligence staff for two decades—

over the reliability of the Agency's sources inside the Soviet secret services. It had been a maddening, repetitive conflict. Every time the Soviet Division managed to recruit a Russian agent, Max Zimmer was there to argue that the new source could be a provocateur planted in the Agency by the KGB. In Winter's view, Max Zimmer's paranoia had cast a pall of suspicion over some of the Agency's most successful operations. In fact, he had described the work of the counterintelligence staff in a memo to a previous director as "paranoia with a card index." Zimmer's hypersuspicion had extended beyond challenging the authenticity of Soviet double agents and defectors. He had started hunting through the corridors of Langley in pursuit of a Soviet mole. He never caught one, but his investigations had blighted the careers of a number of Winter's colleagues and driven more than a few of them to the bottle. Winter believed that he had himself become one of Max Zimmer's favorite candidates for the role of "the mole inside the Agency." Max had finally been outmaneuvered and fired. But even from retirement, he kept up his sniping at Winter and Soviet Division. Winter was convinced that the former counterintelligence chief had been the source for press reports that made out that a couple of Soviet double agents recruited in New York had been KGB plants.

Now, in General Brennan's taunt, Les Winter could hear the echo of Max Zimmer. It was as if he were fighting two men across the expanse of the oval table. But he had an answer for both of them with which no sane man—he believed—could quarrel.

"General Brennan," Winter riposted, "the Soviets are not ten feet tall. And I can tell you that our sources in Moscow are better than they have ever been before. In fact, we have a source at an extremely high position inside Soviet intelligence. Naturally, I am not at liberty to give any details around this table."

"Naturally," Brennan said sarcastically.

"I can tell you, however," Winter continued, "that the agent's code name is Martini and that he has provided us with literally priceless information over several years."

"Martini?" George Brennan rubbed his chin. "I guess that shows that the budget cuts haven't affected the Agency's drink allowance."

"Martini," Winter persisted, "has proved himself dozens of times over. His leads have resulted in countless Bureau investigations."

The Bureau chief nodded.

"Did these—leads—result in the arrest of any Soviet illegals, in the United States or anywhere else?"

Listening to General Brennan's question, Winter thought for a moment that he was listening to Max Zimmer.

"Not yet," Winter snapped back. "But he has identified Americans working for the KGB. And he has helped us to recruit other Soviet citizens. I am not at liberty to disclose any further information on that at this time."

Brennan snorted.

"What is relevant to this discussion," Winter went on, "is that Martini has access to Soviet scientific intelligence and has been able to describe to us, at various stages, the tremendous technical problems that the Russians have come up against in their beam-weapons program. Most of this information has been circulated to the Pentagon."

"I don't recall seeing anything from Martini," Brennan interjected.

"For reasons of source protection, General, the code name was not used in dissemination of Martini's product." In fact, one report from Martini—on a failed Russian space-rocket experiment—had been passed on to the Pentagon with a tag that described it as an eyewitness account by a guard at the Baikonur Cosmodrome in Soviet Central Asia. "But I should point out that nobody inside the Agency questions the bona fides of Martini," Winter added.

"What did Max Zimmer say about this cocktail of yours?"

"That is not pertinent, General. Max Zimmer is no longer an employee of the Agency."

But Max Zimmer just won't lie down and die, Winter groaned inwardly.

"What I am trying to say," he concluded, "is that the consensus of everyone who has been briefed—"

"In the present Agency," Brennan cut in.

"—in the present Agency, is that Martini is the best source we have in Moscow. The best we have had since the days of Popov and Penkovsky. And Martini has told us that this Death Beam thing just won't fly."

"Excuse me," Brennan interrupted with quiet menace. "*What* did you call the Four Sevens program?"

"Death Beam." Winter maintained an even smile, but was

conscious of flushing. "Well," he added defensively, "it *does* sound like something from Buck Rogers. You know, this great big killer beam from space . . ."

"Death Beam," Brennan repeated. "So you think it's all a big joke, Mr. Winter."

"General, I didn't—"

"The day may come," Brennan swept on, "when you may come to realize that Death Beam could be an accurate description of this weapon. Whatever your precious double agent in Moscow has been feeding you. It amazes me how little people like you seem to have learned, Mr. Winter. You remind me a lot of the people involved in the Manhattan Project who used to swear blind that it would take the Soviets at least ten years to make their own bomb. In their arrogance and ignorance, they just couldn't fathom what the Russians were up to. It's the same today. You just don't want to believe that the stupid Soviets could have stolen a lead on us."

"George," Adam Claiborne intervened, trying to damp down the argument. "There is room for legitimate disagreement around this table. I agree with you that the Soviets aren't dumb. But I also agree with Les Winter that they aren't ten feet tall."

"I've heard that a few too many times." Brennan slammed the flat of his hand onto the table. "I'll tell you this, Adam. Mr. Winter here could be right. I'll concede that. But if he's wrong, we're going to see some changes made in the way this country's intelligence is being run."

Shit, thought Winter. *The man won't rest until he wrecks the Agency. If Brennan gets his way, it will be just as bad as if Max Zimmer were taken out of mothballs and put in charge.*

"All right, George," said Claiborne, trying to play the pacifier. "We'll keep this under review."

"There's something else we'd better keep in mind," Brennan said.

"What's that?"

"If Death Beam is a reality, then the Soviets have built a weapon against which there are no effective countermeasures. Therefore this country has only one option." He drew breath, pausing for effect. "We'll have to hit them first. We'll have to destroy Death Beam before they get to use it."

The words ricocheted inside Les Winter's head.

Jesus Christ, he thought. *Brennan is capable of starting World War III all by himself.*

Brennan has to be defused.

His thoughts turned to Martini. The only double agent he had ever personally handled. They joked in Soviet Division that you fell in love with your first agent. In a way, it was true. Les Winter had been fortunate. His first agent was a good one. None better.

Martini could settle this thing. And, through benign providence, Martini was visiting New York. Under the cover of a Soviet delegation to the UN whose mission—appropriately enough—was to protest the development of space weapons by the United States.

5

Commander Jim Morton, the assistant naval attaché at the American embassy in Paris, liked to slip away from the office early at least once a week to play tennis. His partner this afternoon was one of the liaison officers from the French Defense Ministry. Morton grinned at the prospect of meeting Jules on the tennis court today. The Frenchman, lean and fit from the months he had spent in the Angolan bush advising the anti-Soviet guerrillas, was a worthy opponent. But they would be playing another game as well. Morton knew that Jules would be sniffing after information on who was responsible for blowing up the latest consignment of French nuclear equipment destined for Iraq. Commander Morton had a pretty good idea about the answer to *that*, but he came from a Charleston family that knew when to keep silence. Jim Morton was so good at keeping his mouth shut that Jules had once complained that he listened so intensely that he exhausted the speaker.

Morton had just emerged from the elevator, his racket under his arm, when he was stopped by the Marine guard.

"Sir, your wife is on the phone."

Morton felt a twinge of alarm as he took the receiver. Marilyn had started getting morning sickness. And she had had one miscarriage already.

"Jim?" Her voice was strained.

"What is it, honey? Is it the baby?"

"There's a man here."

"What man?"

70

Jesus, he thought. Terrorists. Central American revolutionaries had tried to plant a bomb at the embassy only the week before, protesting U.S. involvement in El Salvador.

"I—I don't know. He said he'll only talk to you."

"Now listen," Jim Morton said to his wife. "Just answer yes or no. Can he hear what I'm saying?" Morton remembered the extension in the bedroom.

"No. He's just sitting here. Drinking."

"Is he armed? Did he threaten you?"

"No."

"And there's nobody with him."

"No."

"What nationality? Is he a Latin?"

"I don't—"

Morton heard the receiver clatter against the table.

"Marilyn?" he said. Then louder, almost beseeching, *"Marilyn?"*

A man's voice responded. Thickly accented, it was a strong, powerful voice that made Morton sense the physical presence of the intruder.

"Commander Morton," the stranger said. "We met once in Ottawa. At a reception at the Indian mission."

The naval attaché tried to place the man's accent, and the scene at a cocktail party years before.

"I need to talk to you privately," the man went on. "Please come at once. And please"—the strong voice waivered for a second—"please don't inform anyone at your embassy."

Then Morton remembered a fair-haired Russian built like a heavyweight boxer who had been making a great play for a girl from the Norwegian mission. A man from Soviet military intelligence. Morton groped for the name in his memory, but it stayed just out of reach.

What was the Russian doing at his home? Morton asked himself. He knew that it could be a Soviet trick, some kind of provocation. He also knew that the rules said that he should pass this to the Agency. To Dick Hammond.

But the Russian had Marilyn. And a baby that had gone eight months toward being born.

"I'll come right away," Morton said.

He called his secretary and told her to cancel the tennis match with Jules. Then he ran toward his car, swinging his racket like a club.

When he saw Stepan Ushinsky sprawled on his sofa with a three-quarters-empty bottle of scotch on the table in front of him, Jim Morton remembered the name. But he hugged Marilyn for a long moment before greeting the Russian.

"Why don't you lie down and rest for a while, honey," he said to her.

"Do you want me to make coffee?"

"No." Morton watched the Russian pour himself some more scotch and added, "I guess the sun's already over the yardarm."

"Commander Morton." Ushinsky got to his feet and stretched out his right hand. Morton shook it warily.

"It's Major Ushinsky, isn't it?"

"Colonel. Lieutenant Colonel. Second Direction of the GRU."

Morton cocked an eyebrow. Ushinsky had never referred to his true job during their brief encounter at the Indian mission in Ottawa.

"What can I do for you?" Morton came straight to the point.

The Russian was equally direct. "I want to go to Washington," he said.

"You mean you want to defect?"

"I am ready to cooperate with your government," Ushinsky corrected him. To a man about to change allegiances, the word "defect" has an unpleasant, rasping sound. "There are two conditions," he went on. "First, I must leave here tonight. Second, the Agency must not be informed until I have arrived in Washington."

Morton reached for the bottle, mostly to avoid showing his facial reaction. "I don't have the authority," he said brusquely.

"Go to General Brennan," the Russian prodded him. "General Brennan will give you the necessary authorization. You work for him, don't you?"

"In a manner of speaking," Morton conceded. In fact, his reports from Paris went straight to Brennan's staff at Defense Intelligence. "But I think you've come to the wrong side of the house. You should be talking to the Agency."

"No," Ushinsky said flatly. "Listen, Morton. I picked you

PERT PLUS®

PERT PLUS FOR KIDS
NORMAL OR LIGHT CONDITIONING

EXTRA CONDITIONING FOR DRY OR DAMAGED HAIR

REVITALIZING FOR PERMED OR COLOR TREATED HAIR

COMPLETE CLEANING AND CONDITIONING FOR NORMAL HAIR

EXTRA BODY FOR FINE, THIN HAIR

DEEP CLEANING FOR OILY HAIR

DANDRUFF CONTROL
NORMAL OR DRY HAIR

EXTRA BODY FOR FINE OR OILY HAIR

PERT PLUS®
For Kids

a **tear-free** shampoo and **detangling** conditioner **in one**

ALSO AVAILABLE IN LIGHT CONDITIONING

because I think I can talk to you. We are both from the military. You must deal only with General Brennan. Not with the Agency."

"I still don't get it." The Russian's insistence was making Morton more and more suspicious.

"The Agency is penetrated. By Krylov's section at Moscow Center."

Morton gaped openly at the Russian. "But how—"

"I know," Ushinsky anticipated the question, "because I heard Krylov himself boasting about it. And because I watched a man that I knew being put to death in an exceptionally unattractive way. I won't say more until you get me to Washington."

"You're rushing me," Morton commented as he tried to order his thoughts.

"Of course I'm rushing you. We have no time. My absence from the embassy is going to be noticed. It may have been noticed already. I have no intention of playing games with my own life."

"Well, I don't like being rushed," Morton complained. "Can't you go on as normal for a while while we check this out?" He was thinking that if Ushinsky was on the level, he should try to encourage him to work for Washington as an agent-in-place. In any event, someone should come out of Washington to give the Russian a proper grilling. He couldn't just put him on a plane like a Federal Express envelope.

"No," the Russian said. "You have to get me out tonight. Look," he continued, "I do not expect you to take me with only the clothes I am wearing. I have this." He took what looked like an ordinary packet of negatives out of the pocket of his jacket.

"What is it?"

Ushinsky explained. The film contained pictures of some of the blueprints and experimental tests for a weapon code-named Razrukha. A beam weapon of incomparable power. The Russian believed that Razrukha was going to be sent into orbit on a space battle station on November 7.

Morton was torn between awe and total incredulity.

"How did you get this out of Moscow?" he demanded.

Ushinsky explained the mechanics of the special photographic process developed in the GRU laboratories and code-named Shield, or *Schtchit*. Held up to the light, the pictures of the Razrukha project looked like negatives of harmless family snapshots—and had been accepted as such by the security men at

Moscow airport. Ushinsky then described how the negatives would have to be specially developed to expose the priceless photographs they concealed.

"I'll have to send these to Washington," Morton said. "We wouldn't want to mess around with them here. Our photo-analysts will need time—"

"They're genuine, Morton."

"Tell me one thing," said the assistant naval attaché as he reached for the packet of photographs. But the Russian kept it firmly gripped in his own fist. "What made you decide to get out?"

Ushinsky tapped the packet with a thick forefinger. "Could *you* live with this?" he asked quietly.

The two men studied each other in silence for a moment. Then the Russian added casually, "Of course, you don't imagine that I expect to live like a pauper in the United States. There will be a price. I think your government will pay it."

"How much?"

"Five million dollars."

Morton whistled. "Nobody's going to approve *that*."

"Wait till they've looked at the pictures."

"May I?" Morton again reached for the packet.

Ushinsky again shook his head and put the photographs back in his pocket. "I'll take them to Washington myself. I'll give you only one more thing for now."

"What's that?"

"A name. Sammy Hamad. He is a Palestinian terrorist. And a sabotage agent of my department. He is currently living in your country, preparing a uniquely ambitious operation. Marshal Safronov has taken a personal interest in this man. I can give you his cover name."

"Okay. What's the nature of the operation this—Sammy Hamad—has been assigned?"

"We studied a number of possible scenarios to disrupt military communications in the event of a crisis. The marshal said we should try to ensure that the brain of the United States was not functioning on November 7. He asked specifically whether we could arrange to sabotage the computers on which Strategic Air Command depends."

Morton reflected that, given the highly embarrassing computer malfunctions during recent tests—resulting in unnecessary red alerts—Sammy Hamad's skills might not be needed.

The Russian looked expectantly from the now empty whisky bottle to Morton and back again. With a sigh of resignation, Morton got another bottle out of the liquor cabinet.

"I'll cable Brennan," he said. "I guess you'd better stay here."

His friend Dick Hammond was going to be furious, he reflected, as he put a call through to the embassy to summon a courier. It was bad enough to cut the Agency out of the deal. But Hammond would take it personally. They had both been born into well-to-do old Confederate families, beaten each other up as kids, chased the same girls. Hammond would say that the fact that he had not been consulted about the defector meant that the suspicion Ushinsky was sowing about a mole in the Agency had rubbed off on *him*.

But there was no helping it, Morton told himself. Hammond's anger would be nothing compared with General Brennan's wrath if the Defense Intelligence chief found out that a Soviet defector's demand to deal only with him had been turned down. And the general, not Hammond, was Jim Morton's boss.

PARIS, *September 10*

Dick Hammond was not a product of the technological revolution. He placed more trust in street smarts than computers. In Lisbon in the mid-seventies, when he had been engaged in trying to block a Communist takeover, he had frequently traveled to clandestine meets by public transport, calculating that whoever was interested in his movements would not expect an Agency station chief to be fighting for space on a clapped-out bus during the rush hour. He believed that people were more precious than all the gee-whiz technology at the disposal of American intelligence. All the infrared sensors and satellite cameras ever devised could not tell you what your enemies intended to do; you needed people for that.

Hammond liked to keep his feet on the ground—in the most literal sense. He was boarding the Paris Métro to keep a breakfast appointment at an out-of-the-way bistro with Moshe Stern, the

Israeli operations chief in Europe. He was looking forward to a blow-by-blow account of how Moshe's men had used the tip he had given them to sabotage the latest consignment of French nuclear equipment for Iraq—although he knew that Moshe, true to form, would talk about the episode only in the third person, with an air of utter disinterest. The security men at the embassy had started complaining about Hammond's preferred mode of travel since a radical magazine had printed a photograph of him. He was not instantly recognizable from the picture, which showed only a blurred face, masked by dark glasses, in the back of a car. But it probably meant that he had risen a notch or two higher on the hit lists of terrorist groups that went after American targets—which meant most of them. As a reluctant concession to the times in which he lived, Hammond now traveled around with a mini-transceiver in his belt that was powerful enough to keep him in contact with the station. It did not work down in the cavernous halls of the Métro. But the urgent signal from the station got through to him as he was assaulting, two at a time, the steps leading up into the unsalubrious Place Pigalle.

Commander Morton of the naval attaché's office was trying to reach him urgently. Would the station chief please call Morton at his home number?

Zigzagging through the traffic from the center island to the northern side of the square, Hammond hurried down the stairs of the corner bistro. In his haste, he jostled a tall transvestite, who yelled curses after him in a voice like a drill sergeant's. Downstairs, Hammond slammed a token into one of a bank of public telephones.

Jim Morton's message, delivered in a stilted, embarrassed voice, was urgent enough to make Hammond cancel his breakfast with Moshe Stern and dash—by taxi, not Métro—to the apartment in Neuilly.

Marilyn opened the door. Hammond pecked her cheek, but forgot to make his customary friendly inquiry about how the baby was coming along. There was black thunder in his face.

"So what kind of a going-away present is this?" Hammond challenged the assistant naval attaché. Jim Morton was wearing his uniform today, Hammond noticed. Maybe he felt better-protected under the brass buttons.

"I thought the least I could do was to alert you before Director

Claiborne hears about it and all hell breaks loose at Langley." Morton glanced at his watch. "Ushinsky should be arriving at Andrews Air Force Base in about an hour."

"You gave him a special plane." It was a statement, not a question. "But you couldn't find time to inform your old pals in the Agency."

"Don't think I'm enjoying this, Dick," Morton said. "The defector said we shouldn't tell the Agency, and I got a direct order from General Brennan that we should respect his request. There's no point in you and me fighting over this. The fight's going to be in Washington."

Hammond's eyes moved over the crumpled sofa. "I suppose he spent the evening here," he said.

"Until I got the green light from Brennan to put him on a plane."

"And he just walked in on you," Hammond continued. He had sometimes found that to embark on a rambling narrative was a quicker way to draw people out than to pose direct questions. At the same time, he was trying to work out what he could put in his signal to Adam Claiborne, warning the Agency's director of what was about to break over their heads.

"Right off the street," Morton confirmed. "I met the guy in Canada once."

"And I suppose he told you about how he'd waked up hating the Soviet system after spending the night in bed with a French hooker."

"He was a little more plausible than that."

"Just give me the punch line, Jim. This guy Ushinsky told you some story about a mole in the Agency." This was the only reason, Hammond guessed, why Morton had not called him sooner. He took his friend's silence for confirmation.

"Oh God," Hammond groaned.

Haven't we been through this mill enough times already? he thought. He remembered how Max Zimmer had pounced on a previous defector who had also made allegations about a mole in the Agency and started a witch-hunt that lasted for ten years— without producing a single live mole. At least Max wasn't around anymore to start the chase all over again. But General Brennan was very much in the picture. From what Hammond had learned from Les Winter and other friends at Langley about the bureaucratic bloodletting now going on in Washington, this new defector was just what General Brennan needed. There would be no holding him now.

Hammond stared out the window at a drab panorama of modern middle-class apartment blocks.

With his back still turned to Jim Morton, he said, "You don't suppose that I could be the mole, do you? I figure that's why you didn't call me before you packed Ushinsky onto a plane."

"Oh, *shit*." Morton lapsed into profane incoherence. "You know that wasn't the fucking reason. I was under orders."

"Yeah. I heard that somewhere before."

On the way out, Hammond forgot to say goodbye. He even forgot to give Marilyn her standard peck on the cheek. After he had slammed the door, she patted her cheek as if it had been scratched.

6

HAMILTON, BERMUDA, *September 10*

People in Bermuda had an admirably light touch when it came to handling minor social disturbances, Dicky Prince reflected as the elderly black man who was sitting beside him at the bar of the Hamilton Princess broke into his third rendition of the spiritual "Near to the Heart of God." The man had staggered in drunk, a motorbike helmet under his arm, and flopped down on the nearest stool. When the barman brought him a beer, he attempted to pay for it with peppermints. Nobody seemed to be fussed. No one asked him to leave.

When he finished his song, his head lolled down onto the polished wood of the bar.

"Hey man!" the bartender called out. "No sleeping at the bar."

The drunk hauled himself back up into a sitting position, using Dicky Prince's shoulder for support.

"I'm not sleeping, man," he said. "I'm thinking, man."

Then he struck up again:

> *"There is a place of quiet rest*
> *Near to the heart of God."*

His singing voice was pretty good, Dicky Prince thought. Also, his conversation was lively. Prince quite enjoyed the drunk's descriptions of his life, which had apparently been complicated by four wives, sixteen children, and girlfriends without number. The blue-rinsed ladies at the table of American tourists just behind them did not seem to be quite so amused by the drunk's graphic language. One of them had asked for the manager.

"Hey, Bill," said the drunk. This was addressed to Dicky Prince. "Do you like to eat pussy? I love to eat pussy."

Prince's grunt was noncommittal. He could see the manager hovering at the end of the bar. The complaints from the table behind them became more strident.

"Steady on, old boy," Dicky Prince said to the drunk. "There are ladies present."

Prince saw a familiar figure in the doorway—a tall man in a blazer and cream trousers, carrying an overnight bag. Charles Canning looked quizzically from Prince to his neighbor.

"Hey, Bill," the drunk cried out to Canning. "Do you like to eat pussy?"

"Absolutely," Canning replied, unfazed.

The manager discreetly approached them.

"Time to get home to your four wives," Prince said gently, easing the drunk off his seat. "You've made quite a night of it."

The barman looked forlornly at the two peppermints the drunk had left beside his beer.

"It's okay," Prince said. "He's spoken for."

Dicky Prince had been sufficiently disturbed by the message he had received, via London, from Charles Canning to interrupt his vacation.

Canning had sent him the negatives of some photographs of three Russian visitors to New York. The head of the Firm always tried to get away for a week or two at this time of year, which tended to be an off season in London—at least for the politicians, who consumed as much of his time as the KGB. And his favorite retreat was Bermuda, not just because of the boating and the golf, but because he enjoyed the quiet tempo and the quintessential Englishness of the island, a quality that is always exaggerated in a colonial environment.

"Good of you to come, Charles," said the head of the Firm. It was one of Dicky Prince's favored forms of greeting—even when, as in this case, the other man had asked for the meeting. The head of the Firm maintained his private rituals. They were alone together on the terrace of a suite overlooking the harbor, with a bottle of scotch and a soda siphon on the table between them.

"Any excuse to see the sun is good enough for me," said Canning.

The head of the Firm took a plain brown envelope out of the pocket of his bush shirt. It contained four snapshots. They were the pictures that Canning had taken with his camouflaged mini-camera at the Café Carlyle.

"All right," said Prince. "We've identified your Russians. This one"—he held up a photograph of the fat man, flushed with drink, who had been applauding the black singer most vigorously—"is Miagkov. He's not KGB. He's the head of a Soviet delegation visiting the UN. They're proposing a new treaty to ban the deployment of offensive weapons in space. It's the same old trick, of course. They want to screw up the American program to send up killer satellites, while pulling out all the stops to develop their own. They don't have to respect any treaty they sign, because they can keep what they're doing secret."

"Up to a point," Canning qualified Prince's remark.

"Well, yes, up to a point. Secret from the public, anyway."

"Has this one—Miagkov—got any scientific background?"

"Not that we know about. He's just a front man, sent to read prepared speeches. *This* is the interesting one."

Dicky Prince held up a second shot. It showed a man with thin, aquiline features and black hair receding from a widow's peak. The man who had sat in silence throughout Melanie Toussaint's performance, drinking methodically in pace with his companions but, unlike them, displaying no visible effects.

"Konstantin Alexeyevich Orlov," Dicky Prince recited the name, drawing out the syllables. "He's big, Charles. Very big. One of the top men on the scientific side at Moscow Center. He's using Miagkov's delegation as a cover to make a trip to New York. Probably to meet an agent he's recruited."

Canning leaned forward, excited by the discovery.

"Now hang on," Prince cautioned him. "Major General Orlov is not your game."

"He's a major general in the KGB?" Canning's excitement mounted. The quarry was even more valuable than he had imagined.

"I'm telling you to keep away from him, Charles. You're not on your own turf. We don't want a diplomatic incident."

Canning thought he had heard it all before. When he had moved to New York, the head of the Firm had warned him that because of the special relationship with the Cousins there were very strict limits to what he would be permitted to do in the United States. In Canning's view, a chance to entrap a top KGB operative like Orlov was an excellent reason for bending the rules. He started to say so, but Prince cut him off.

"Listen to what I'm saying, Charles. This particular Russian is Agency property. We got a very clear signal from Washington. Hands off."

"Do you mean they're trailing a bait? Or have they already got him on a string?"

The head of the Firm splashed more soda into his glass. "That, my dear chap, the Cousins did not see fit to tell us. But they've put up a very large sign that says, 'Trespassers Will Be Prosecuted.' And you're going to respect it."

Canning could not argue with a direct order. So he pointed to the third photograph and said, "Who's that?"

The snapshot showed a heavy, fair-haired man with coarse features pouring a tumbler of whisky down his gullet.

"Titov," Prince identified him. "Voldemar Titov. A thug from the local KGB residency. Not much interest for us."

Canning tore the band off a cigar and lit a match. He turned the cigar around and around in the flame so it would draw evenly.

"We don't know this last one, Charles." The head of the Firm smiled as he tossed over the last of the photographs. "But she obviously interests you."

Canning looked at the snapshot of Melanie Toussaint he had taken as an afterthought. Caught halfway through singing "Learnin' the Blues," she looked as if she was pouring her heart out. The singer would not, after all, provide a channel to the Russians, Canning realized regretfully. But that was no reason for failing to keep his date with her.

There was a dampness in the air as the dusk settled.

The head of the Firm sniffed and said, "Good killing weather, as we used to say in Malaya."

The expression reminded Canning of something else that had happened on the night he had seen the Russians in the Café

Carlyle. The fight with the black intruder that had ended with his erasing the stranger's face with a shotgun. He no longer wondered whether the man had been a casual burglar or had been sent. The police had dismissed the episode readily enough; it seemed that two other apartments in the block on Gramercy Park had been broken into the same day, and there was no positive identification.

The two men went in from the terrace, and Prince asked casually, "Did you hear anything about the new defector?"

"Not so far."

"Is the defector KGB?"

"No, the military side of the shop. It might be worth finding out about."

"I'll see what I can do," Canning promised.

7

It was a steamy weekend in Washington, and Director Claiborne had announced that he was taking a couple of days out at his home on Long Island, and did not expect to be disturbed unless the sky fell in. But Les Winter, the head of the Agency's Soviet Division, knew that that was not the reason General Brennan had called him direct, at the unlisted number of the safe house in Arlington. Brennan could have called the deputy director, a man with a military background like himself. Or the duty officer at Langley.

Les Winter was convinced that Brennan was deliberately goading him. Since they had locked horns in front of the entire National Intelligence Board on the issue of what exactly the Soviets were doing in their beam-weapons programs, Winter had no doubt that the general had marked him down as his number-one enemy inside the Agency. Winter had presumed to suggest that Brennan's powers of clairvoyance were not infallible. That the Defense Intelligence chief would not forgive. And he had the longest memory in Washington.

"Where's my defector?" General Brennan bellowed through his scrambler.

"He's where he's supposed to be, General. Being debriefed."

After Stepan Ushinsky had landed at Andrews Air Force Base, General Brennan had spent a few hours with him—long enough to realize that what the defector had to say could be his final vindication in his feud with the Agency—and had then wanted to parade the Russian around the White House and the rest of official

84

Washington like a captive in some Roman triumph. It had been with some difficulty that Adam Claiborne had managed to persuade Brennan that the defector could not be accepted at face value just because he was saying what the General wanted to hear, and that the Agency had the right to interrogate him. The Agency had had precisely three days to grill Ushinsky. And already, it seemed, General Brennan wanted him back.

"You've had long enough," Brennan was saying.

"With due respect, General, three days is *not* long enough to establish the bona fides of a Soviet defector." Winter tried to maintain a calm, reasonable tone.

"How long do you guys want? Three years? Isn't that the amount of time you guys spent putting what's-his-name—Nosenko—through the wringer? And you still couldn't make up your minds whether he was genuine or not. Listen, the world doesn't stop turning while you Agency people try to make up your minds whether it's flat or not."

"Ushinsky is not being cooperative," Winter said.

"I found him to be extremely anxious to cooperate. I don't know what you're talking about. What's your problem?"

"Now look, General." Winter could feel that his pulse was up. And he had been up half the night, monitoring the interrogation through a one-way mirror. But he had to keep cool. Any other response would be seized on by Brennan as an admission of weakness. "You didn't make our job any easier," he went on, "by promising Ushinsky the moon and the stars. He claims you told him you'd get him two million dollars and an interview with the President."

"He'd be cheap at any price. What are you guys giving him? A windowless room and a hypodermic? Why don't you just come out and say it, Les? You don't like what Ushinsky has got to say. That's why you want to keep him on ice."

"We're not happy, General. There are many elements in his story that don't ring true. Things that contradict information we have from proven sources. We can't evaluate all the inconsistencies overnight. We must have a reasonable length of time."

"Now hear this." Brennan's voice rose a few decibels, and Les Winter held the receiver away from his ear. "Ushinsky is *my* catch," the General boomed, "and I want him back *now*."

Winter fell back on a convoluted technical argument about who had legal jurisdiction. Ushinsky had not been formally admitted to the United States. As far as the immigration authorities were concerned, he did not exist. In the past, it had been generally accepted that the Agency would be the custodian of Russians who had defected outside United States territory, until their bona fides was established.

"*If* their bona fides is established," Winter underscored the point.

"What are you trying to say to me?" Brennan broke in impatiently. "Are you telling me you people are thinking of sending Ushinsky back?"

Les Winter made the error of hesitating for a moment to consider his reply.

Brennan pounced. "Jesus Christ," he swore. "I bet that's it. Some of you guys are wetting your pants because this defector says there's a mole inside the Agency. You'd rather send him back to Moscow than have to suffer the embarrassment."

"No one has contemplated sending Ushinsky back to Moscow," Winter intervened. He was not lying to Brennan, he thought, so much as shaping the truth. On the desk in front of him was a draft memo he had prepared for the director that raised the possibility of sending Ushinsky back to Paris, the city where he had defected.

But Brennan was off on his charger. "I tell you," he thundered, "sometimes I think the Agency is the mole. The whole fucking Agency."

"General—"

"I want him back. I want him back *today*."

"General, I don't have the authority to do that. You'll have to talk to Director Claiborne. I can give you his home number in Long Island."

"I've got his fucking number. I'll talk to the President if necessary."

The general banged down his receiver, and Winter was left listening to the dial tone.

Jerry Sarkesian, a roly-poly Armenian from the Office of Security who was helping with the interrogations, ambled in from the adjoining room.

"Trouble?" Sarkesian asked.

"We may have even less time than we thought," Winter said. "Brennan's rattling his cage." Sarkesian, he noticed, was munching a bagel. The three-hundred-pound Armenian had extraordinary stamina. Winter had seen him conduct intensive grilling for more than twenty-four hours without a break. As long as Sarkesian could always lay hands on something to eat. And a six-pack of beer.

"Is Ushinsky asleep?" Winter asked.

"Yeah," Sarkesian mumbled, his mouth full. "I gave him two hours. We've been working him hard."

"But he's holding up."

"Yeah. He's holding up. It's going to be a hard grind. He's giving nothing for free."

Since they had moved him to the safe house, Ushinsky had not departed from his original story. But he responded only to specific questions, and then in as few words as possible. He made it plain that he resented the hostile interrogation, and that he was waiting for General Brennan to come to his rescue. The defector also implied that he understood why his condition had changed overnight from that of a feted hero to that of a prisoner who was denied sleep, made to undergo repeated polygraph tests, and forced to respond to the same questions, over and over, under the glare of a harsh white light trained directly into his eyes. He was no stranger to feuds between, and within, intelligence agencies. He had seen plenty of that in Moscow.

"What's your verdict so far?" Les Winter asked Sarkesian.

"Well, he got through the polygraph. He got a little twitchy when I gave him our routine stuff on his early life. You know, did he play with himself in school. The standard routine. But on the big things—why he defected, where he got his information—the polygraph couldn't fault him. I think the guy is telling the truth."

"Or what he *believes* to be the truth," Winter modified the statement.

"That's your department more than mine, Les."

"I just can't see it." There was a refrigerator in the room, next to the TV. Winter walked over to it, pulled out a tray of ice, and hammered out some cubes on top of the TV. Several rolled onto the floor. Without bothering to pick them up, he filled a tumbler with bourbon and plopped in the remaining pieces of ice.

"Let's summarize," Winter went on, mildly fortified by his first swig. "We accept that Ushinsky is what he says he is. A colonel in Soviet military intelligence. He knows who parks his car next to Leonov's and who does the typing on the sixth floor of GRU headquarters."

"Right."

"We also accept that most of this terrorist stuff is probably on target, although this Palestinian operative—"

"Sammy Hamad," Sarkesian supplied the name.

"Yes, Sammy Hamad. He's vanished off the radar screen. He's supposed to have been smuggled into the United States, but nobody's got a record of his arrival. The Bureau's been trying to run a dragnet, but no results so far. We don't have a photograph, or even a reliable identification, since Ushinsky says the Palestinian is a master at changing his appearance. Even uses colored contact lenses to make his eyes look different. In short, we can't find this Sammy Hamad. So even if Ushinsky is telling the truth about him, the information isn't worth much. It may just be a throwaway. Something to encourage us to believe the rest of the story."

"The Israelis say that Sammy Hamad is a live body," Sarkesian commented. "But they aren't able to confirm whether he's in the United States."

"Okay." Winter swilled more of his bourbon and filled up his glass from the bottle. "Let's look at the sexy part of the story. Ushinsky claims there's a mole in the Agency. He says he personally knew Hussar, the British agent, and that he's sure that Hussar was betrayed by a KGB source at Langley. That contradicts other information that we've developed from sources graded one hundred percent accurate. So how does Ushinsky know different? He says he attended a special briefing arranged by Krylov. I don't buy that, Jerry."

"He didn't waver when we went over that episode during the polygraph tests," Sarkesian commented.

"Shit. The polygraph isn't God, Jerry. Wasn't it you who told me there's a special school where Moscow trains operatives to beat the polygraph by controlling their thought processes? While you were grilling him about Krylov, the defector could have had his mind focused on some roll in the hay."

Sarkesian grunted. "It's not that easy," he said. "To beat our polygraph, you've got to be able to control your heartbeat, blood pressure, breathing and sweat glands. I don't think Ushinsky was lying."

"Meprobamate," said Winter.

"What?"

"You know, that tranquilizer housewives buy. The brand name is Miltown or something like that. One four-hundred-milligram dose reduces the stress signals."

"There's no way Ushinsky could have got the pills. We didn't let him run down to the corner pharmacy, Les."

"All right," Winter plowed on, determined to make his case. "So let's suppose this Krylov briefing really took place. Isn't that awfully strange? I mean, Krylov is the head of the most secret office in Moscow Center, the office known as the Beacon. What is Krylov doing chatting to a bunch of poor relations from the GRU about a mole that he is running inside the Agency? If Krylov really did give such a briefing, it would be for only one reason. It would be because he wanted the story to leak out to us."

"Why would he do that?"

"Because it's a lie, Jerry." Excited now, Winter downed the last of his whiskey and slammed down the glass on top of the TV. "It's all so obvious," he pursued. "Krylov is trying to feed disinformation into the Agency. He wants us to get paranoid about some nonexistent mole and embark on another witch-hunt that will paralyze our operations against Moscow Center. Just as Max Zimmer's brand of sick-think paralyzed our activities in the old days. By building his fabrication around Hussar, a British agent, he wants to get the Brits suspicious of us so they won't cooperate. And on top of all that, he wants to discredit our best source inside Moscow Center. I imagine that he guesses that we have one, though he hasn't yet worked out who. What this defector is telling us is the diametrical opposite of what Martini has told us in the past. They can't both be telling the truth. And I'd rather put my money on Martini."

"What about this Death Beam thing?" Sarkesian asked. "This killer beam he insists the Soviets are planning to send into orbit on November 7?"

Winter snorted derisively. "Science fiction," he said. "Our best scientists say that this weapon is a physical impossibility. General

89

Brennan's hired a few physicists who think differently, but they're in a minority, and anyway, everyone knows they're employed to puff up the Pentagon budget. This Death Beam fantasy is another element in Krylov's disinformation. He probably thinks he can scare the hell out of us and make us waste billions trying to develop something that just won't fly. Maybe he also thinks he can psych this administration into some irresponsible act that would give the Soviets the pretext to kick us in the balls. In any case," he concluded triumphantly, "no one can convince me that a middle-ranking officer from Ushinsky's department would be briefed on something as sensitive as Death Beam—and then allowed to trot off to Paris the next day, where he could sell his information to the West. The whole thing is a tissue of lies. Even if Ushinsky believes he's telling us the truth."

"Is that what you're going to tell the director?"

"You bet your ass that's what I'm going to tell the director."

Adam Claiborne called Winter from Long Island.

"I've talked to George Brennan," he said. "I think he has a legitimate reason for wanting access to the defector. His photographic-evaluation people want to talk with Ushinsky about the pictures he brought of the test facilities at Saryshagan."

"Mr. Director," Winter protested, "we are not being allowed to do our job. And if the Pentagon wants access to Ushinsky, well, then Brennan should send his people to us."

"I don't think this is worth a fight, Les. It's a matter of a few hours. That's all."

"Mr. Director, I'm not sure whether you understand. Brennan talks to Ushinsky as if he's the last of the Romanovs. The defector is difficult enough to deal with anyway. If we let Brennan get his hands on him again, he'll be impossible to handle."

"I think you'd better know," the director's voice crackled over the line, "that Brennan is already threatening to file a formal protest over our handling of the defector. There's no need to go out of our way to give him any extra ammunition."

Adam Claiborne did not feel that he was displaying weakness. He felt reasonably certain that in a frontal confrontation with George Brennan he would win. But he wanted to be sure of his ground before taking a stand. Since he had moved into the director's office at Langley, he had ordered a review of the Agency's analytical record in assessing the Soviet military threat. He had not been impressed with the findings. As long as there was a chance that General Brennan's hunches were right, he was not disposed to meet him head-on.

"Brennan's waiting in his office," Claiborne said. "I want you to send Ushinsky over there. Brennan's agreed you can take the defector back to the safe house tonight."

"All right," Winter accepted the order grudgingly.

But the chief of Soviet Division was resolved on one thing. He was not going to leave the Russian he now believed to be Krylov's plant alone with General Brennan. He would sit in on the Pentagon meeting himself.

Ushinsky walked between Les Winter and Jerry Sarkesian along the yellow-and-dun corridors of the Pentagon to the third-floor office of the chief of Defense Intelligence. At the entrance to General Brennan's private sanctum, they were subjected to what Winter considered to be an unnecessary identity check, calculated to put him on the defensive. Brennan's crewcut aide, Colonel Rice, received them with a neatly pressed smirk that Winter construed as a further provocation.

"I don't believe the general is expecting you, Mr. Winter."

"We are here to accompany Colonel Ushinsky," said Winter. The defector, evidently feeling confident of his ground now he was back in Brennan's territory, had settled himself in an armchair in the outer office and was leafing through Air Force magazines.

"We'll look after Colonel Ushinsky." Brennan's aide smiled. "I really don't believe there's any necessity for you gentlemen to wait."

"My understanding is that I am to be present while the general conducts his debriefing," Winter insisted, endeavoring to contain his anger. "I assume that you know my status."

"We are aware of your rank, Mr. Winter. But *my* understanding is that your attendance will not be required."

"Let me talk to General Brennan." Winter's temper was rising, by degrees, toward boiling point.

"I'm afraid the general is not available."

"Then we'll wait."

Winter flung himself down on the sofa opposite Ushinsky, furious at being made to lose face in front of the defector. Jerry Sarkesian, after a moment's hesitation, sat down too.

The colonel watched them for a moment, then stood up and straightened his tie. "Excuse me." Colonel Rice disappeared into Brennan's inner office.

A few seconds later, the general burst out of his office like a bull from its pen.

"Have you got a problem?" He glowered at Winter.

"No problem, sir. It's just that it is my understanding that Agency representatives are to be present during any debriefing of Colonel Ushinsky, pending a final determination of his case."

"I don't know anything about that," Brennan growled. "How'd they treat you, Stepan?" He turned to the defector, who merely nodded and grimaced. "You mean they didn't put you in a five-star hotel? I'm glad to see you. We need to consult you."

Brennan looked at Winter and Sarkesian. "If you'll forgive me, gentlemen," he said, "I need a little time to myself with *my* defector. Come this way, Stepan."

General Brennan ushered Ushinsky toward his private office.

Les Winter's immediate reflex was to spring to his feet and follow them. Before he had realized it, he had crossed the threshold of Brennan's private office. From the doorway, he could see the framed texts that embellished the laboratory-white walls of the spacious, windowless room. They were excerpts from the National Intelligence Estimates of the past two decades, recording the dissenting footnotes that Brennan had appended to the Agency's assessments on the not inconsiderable number of occasions when he had later been proved right.

Brennan glared at the trespasser from behind his desk. Near to the desk, Winter could see a blown-up photograph of the general on horseback on the President's ranch. Brennan cut an impressive figure in the saddle; the eye was drawn away from his short, thick legs to his sturdy trunk and powerful shoulders.

"Do I have to tell you again?" Brennan said menacingly. "This is my party, Les. You're not invited."

"But—"

"Lew!" Brennan called to his aide. "Get these Agency motherfuckers off my lawn!"

"Yes, *sir!*" Colonel Rice responded cheerfully.

Winter felt his shoulders being gripped in two immensely strong hands. He was spun around to face the door to the outer office and propelled toward it by a less than gentle jab in the back.

"You pushed me!" Winter stuttered, disbelieving. "Take your goddam hands off me!"

He turned to Jerry Sarkesian for support, but the man from the Office of Security tilted his chin toward the exit. They were, after all, on General Brennan's turf. Colonel Rice gave Winter another, harder, push.

"You'll hear from me!" Winter yelled, for General Brennan's benefit. "There'll be a formal complaint."

Brennan stuck his head around his door and replied, in a voice that was silkier than usual, "Kiss my ass."

Director Claiborne did not respond in quite the way that Les Winter had wanted. He did not rush to the President and the Secretary of Defense, Jake Waggoner, to demand that General Brennan should be officially reprimanded and brought to heel. Instead, he had a quiet talk with George Brennan and looked over what his photographic experts had been able to make of the film that Ushinsky had smuggled out of Moscow in his camera. As far as Adam Claiborne was concerned, the evidence remained inconclusive. There was no proof that Death Beam was a reality. Nor was there proof that a mole had burrowed his way inside the Agency. But both allegations were too serious to dismiss on the basis of Les Winter's memo, which developed the theory that the defector had been planted by Moscow Center as part of a devious disinformation plot.

The United States could not run the risk of ignoring what Ushinsky had to say. That was the common ground between Director Claiborne and General Brennan, and they said so to Trip Gage, the President's National Security Adviser. For the sake of avoiding a bush war inside the Washington intelligence community, they also agreed on a division of labor. General Brennan would take primary responsibility for the technical follow-up to the defector's revelations, seeking to confirm, by aerial surveillance, whether the construction going on at Saryshagan and

Baikonur was directed toward deploying weapons of mass destruction in outer space.

General Brennan's brief went further. He won the President's agreement that—regardless of whether Death Beam was fact or fiction—space weapons were likely to be decisive in any future war. Brennan was given a charter by the President to speed up the Pentagon's own program to send up killer satellites. The program had been given the optimistic code name Blue Savior, because the scientists working on it believed that the killer satellites would not only give the United States supremacy in space—if they managed to outpace the Russians—but would provide the most effective anti-missile defense system ever devised. A system that might even help to end the long reign of nuclear terror. Trip Gage expressed the desire to go down to the base in New Mexico where the prototype of Blue Savior was being developed and to learn about it firsthand. In the meantime, Brennan was assured that Blue Savior would have an unlimited budget—despite Secretary Waggoner's cheese-paring habits in relation to other programs—and that he could hire whatever personnel he needed. The space race was on as never before. If the defector was right, it might even be a matter of national survival to get the first of the killer satellites up before November 7.

For his part, Adam Claiborne undertook to organize a full-scale investigation of Ushinsky's claims about the mole at Langley. The outcome of that inquiry might, in itself, serve to resolve whether Death Beam was fact or fiction. If Ushinsky was proved right about the mole, that would mean that Martini had been lying all along and that the Agency had been the victim of a prolonged deception conceived and controlled by Krylov at Moscow Center. And the Agency's disbelief in Death Beam was founded, in large part, on the information that had been coming in from the double agent code-named Martini. . . .

Director Claiborne had resolved that the search for the mole should be the job of the Agency itself. "I wouldn't hire a private detective to check on whether my wife was cheating on me," he had commented. "I'd do that for myself." They would not talk to the British—at least not through official channels—until they had made up their own minds about the Hussar affair.

He needed a man to head the investigation who was respected by all sides within a house that had been deeply divided, a man who had not been involved in the scrapping between Les Winter and Max Zimmer.

Claiborne thought he had found the right man. He was universally regarded as one of the best operations men in the Agency. And he was about to be sent home from Paris. His name was Dick Hammond.

8

The man in the back seat of the big black Zil limousine barely acknowledged the salutes of the Russian and East German guards at the checkpoint. They raised the barrier, and the car rolled on down a road lined with electrified fences. Through the barbed wire, Vadim Krylov could glimpse pine groves and meticulously tended flower beds where no one seemed to walk. Ahead was a cluster of big warehouselike buildings behind a high wall of solid iron. More guards, cradling submachine guns, were patrolling the perimeter. Alsatian dogs bayed at the approaching car.

Krylov was no stranger to Karlshorst. He had first visited the three-story building that formerly housed the St. Antonius Hospital in 1946, when it had been picked by Moscow Center as the headquarters for Soviet secret operations in the German People's Democratic Republic. Today, the Karlshorst apparat remained the largest KGB complex outside the Soviet Union. A short drive away, in the same suburb of East Berlin, was the office of Krylov's most successful protégé. Krylov smiled with pleasure at the thought of the meeting that lay ahead. He had always been fond of Misha. Unlike many of his colleagues at Moscow Center, Misha had subtlety and wit to match the callousness his job required. And even now, thirty years after Krylov had first selected him to head the East German spy service, Misha's healthy tan, spare, athletic build, and full head of light-brown hair still recalled the spectacular good looks that had been part of the initial attraction. Yes, Misha had been beautiful at twenty-nine.

Krylov was one of the few survivors at Moscow Center who had known Misha in the days when he had acquired his Russian nickname. Misha had turned up in Russia at the beginning of Hitler's war, a young man from a Stuttgart family of doctors and musicians who had been forced to flee the Nazi terror. His father was a Communist, and Misha seemed to have no difficulty in understanding Stalin's short-lived truce with Hitler. The Comintern selected him for special training at schools in Kushnarenkovo and Moscow, where Krylov instructed him in the rudiments of running clandestine networks. Karl Meyer, Misha had called himself in those days. But he was soon speaking Russian like a native, and it seemed natural to give him a Russian sobriquet. It stuck. After Hilter attacked Russia, Misha led sabotage teams to blow up Nazi shipping in northern ports. At the end of the war, he returned to Berlin in the uniform of an officer of the Red Army.

Krylov had plucked Misha out, before his thirtieth birthday, to take one of the top jobs in the newly created Hauptverwaltung Aufklaerung, or Main Administration for Espionage. Within a few years, Misha had captured the directorship, with the help of his Russian patron. Krylov had not been disappointed in his protégé. Under Misha's leadership, East German intelligence had become Moscow Center's most prized auxiliary in its covert operations in Europe and the Middle East. Misha had turned the Western half of his divided country into a playground for Communist spies, planting agents in all the key ministries and making recruitment pitches to more than ten thousand West Germans, on average, every year through his networks of illegals. Even Krylov, the unchallenged master of the game, had had occasion to envy Misha's prowess as a mole handler.

These were not Misha's only distinctions. He was also a Jew.

Misha was the only Jew in charge of a spy service inside the Soviet bloc.

Some of Krylov's colleagues at Moscow Center had tried to block Misha's appointment to head the East German service on the grounds that, being a Jew, he could not be completely trusted. Krylov had countered, successfully, that there was no one better equipped to keep a tight grip on the crowd of former Gestapo and SS men who were coerced or blackmailed or bribed into working for East German intelligence. Krylov had never regarded Misha's Jewishness as a problem. On the contrary, Misha had succeeded brilliantly in a number of false-flag operations against Jews, who were duped into working for his service while under the impression that they were helping the Israelis. Misha had been equally inspired in concocting neo-Nazi plots in West Germany in an attempt to discredit the Federal Republic. Misha's Jewishness had not prevented him from lending enthusiastic support to Palestinian terrorist cells, which routinely used East Berlin as a stopping-off point on their way to attack targets in Western Europe. In general, there had never been the slightest question about the firmness of Misha's Marxist-Leninist convictions and his dedication to the Soviet cause, not even during the riots in East Germany and the popular upheavals in other satellite countries.

When Poland's free-trade-union movement ran amok, for example, shaking the Communist regime to its foundations, Misha had sided vigorously with those who favored early Soviet intervention. At a meeting in Moscow, he had quoted the advice sent by Lenin to the Hungarian revolutionaries of 1919: "Be firm. If there is vacillation among the socialists who joined you yesterday in their attitude to the dictatorship of the proletariat, put down the vacillation mercilessly. Shooting—that is their rightful fate." But Misha had also displayed his characteristic suppleness of mind in suggesting how Lenin's advice should be carried out in practice. The solution for Poland, he had argued, was to use secret-police agents inside the free trade unions to push the opposition movement into more and more extreme acts of protest, so that its leaders would become divided, and the authorities would be given a pretext to appeal for "fraternal socialist aid." Misha had recommended that agents provocateurs in the guise of free trade unionists should assassinate a Polish government leader—or better still a Soviet adviser—in order to discredit the unions and provide the justification for the Red Army tanks to move in. That suggestion had been vetoed in Moscow. But Krylov enjoyed the cynical, sophisticated mind behind it. Misha had grasped the essence of *provokatsiya*.

Misha's record, and a drawerful of Soviet medals, showed that the man was invaluable. But his Jewishness would not be forgotten. Marshal Safronov would see to that. Safronov, and the Black Hundreds mentality that those who thought like him were trying to instill in Russia. Safronov was following the same precept that Stalin and the Czars had grasped long before: when you need a scapegoat, when you need to stir up nationalist fervor, attack the Jews. Safronov was capable of starting a pogrom. Perhaps it had started already.

A few days before his trip to East Berlin, Krylov had passed through Kiev and witnessed some of the symptoms firsthand. It was the anniversary of the massacre of Babi Yar, in which more than a hundred thousand people, mostly Jews from Kiev, had been butchered by the Nazis. It was a day when, traditionally, Jews living in other parts of the Soviet Union would make the trek back to Kiev to say a *kaddish* for lost relatives. Not this year. The Jewish Affairs Section of the KGB—acting on Safronov's initiative—had issued an edict that Jews were not to be permitted to travel around the country. In one of the main squares of Kiev, Krylov himself had watched while a group of Jews including a prominent dissident poet who had applied to emigrate to Israel were set upon by a gang of hooligans screaming anti-Semitic obscenities. He knew it was the job of the thugs in the Second Chief Directorate at Moscow Center to arrange "spontaneous" incidents of this kind. The poet was kicked repeatedly in the throat. It would be some time before he gave another public recitation.

There had been other straws in the wind. The notorious anti-Semitic scribbler Valery Emelyanov had been released from jail. It had come as a great embarrassment to Marshal Safronov and his other sympathizers in the armed forces when Emelyanov had been discovered on a building lot in the summer of 1980, attempting to burn the body of his second wife, whom he had apparently murdered. He claimed before the tribunal that his Zionist enemies had framed him, while a claque of supporters—some of them off-duty soldiers—applauded from the benches. Thanks to Safronov, the new masters of Russia had decided to accept Emelyanov's story as the official version of the crime. Emelyanov was again touring garrisons lecturing on how Soviet dissidents were a front for a conspiracy to impose world Jewish domination.

The basic trend had been evident many years before Brezhnev's death. Krylov knew that some of his colleagues at Moscow Center were members of Safronov's faction, mostly for reasons of opportunism. As early as 1979, General Yepishev, the former deputy chairman of the KGB who then headed the political commissariat of the armed forces, had ordered the screening of a viciously anti-Semitic propaganda film to all military units, despite—or because of—the fact that it was so inflammatory that it had been banned from showings in public cinemas. The film, scripted by Dmitri Zhukov, was entitled *What Is Concealed, and What Is Plain to See.* Krylov had arranged a private screening. He found that the film opened with a shot of the "healthy tree of life" covered by a sticky spider web on which Jews were crawling about. The whole thrust was strongly reminiscent of Nazi propaganda. One of Krylov's colleagues in the Jewish Affairs Section confirmed that footage from some old Goebbels-inspired productions was being used in the new documentaries.

Krylov, a realist in all things, fully appreciated that the unwieldy bulk of the Soviet state needed props beyond the secret police and the dubious popular appeal of a threadbare Marxist-Leninist ideology. Resurgent Russian nationalism, with its racist overtones, might provide such a prop. But as an intelligence practitioner, he was appalled by the crudity of Safronov's approach. For one thing, it interfered with the intricate game of wits that he played against the Israelis, whose secret service was one of the few in the West that was able to run important human sources in Moscow. For another, the upsurge in officially sponsored anti-Semitism could imperil Misha. And Misha was critical to the success of a number of Krylov's plans.

Krylov dismounted from the enormous car, submitted to another identity check, and ran up the steps of the building that had once housed the St. Antonius Hospital with a sprightliness that was unusual in a man who was nearly seventy years old. Short and lean, brimming with nervous energy, he looked like an elderly greyhound forever awaiting the signal to start running. Inside the apparat headquarters, he took temporary possession of the office he had once occupied himself in the early fifties. Some changes had been made. A wall had been broken down to enlarge the room, now the size of a hospital ward. In the reception area, what looked like two gigantic doll's houses were on display. They were scale models of the Agency's headquarters at Langley and the main building in the complex occupied by the West German secret service at Pullach. At the flick of a switch, lights went on and off inside the models to indicate the locations of the offices of key personnel. Moscow Center had installed these toys in order to impress the East Germans. The demonstration was wasted on Misha, who took pleasure in pointing out that some of the desks at Pullach had been moved around.

Misha was already there to greet Krylov. The chief of the KGB apparat in East Berlin, Krotkin, kept discreetly in the background, allowing Krylov the deference that his advanced years and his status as head of the Beacon had earned him.

Krylov embraced the German warmly. The few strands of gray hair on top of his head that failed to conceal his baldness barely reached the level of Misha's nose.

"How are things in Moscow?" Misha asked bluntly after the tea had been served. Even indoors, the East German spy chief had not removed his dark glasses. Misha had complained to Krylov of weak eyes, but the Russian guessed that he had taken to wearing dark glasses all the time for the same reason as his former antagonist, General Gehlen: to mask his own feelings and instill fear in his subordinates.

"More or less the same. Everyone's playing the same game. It's called survival."

"But not everyone will survive," Misha observed. He had few inhibitions about talking freely to the man who had been his mentor in Moscow forty years before. They had both survived a series of purges.

"You are right," Krylov acknowledged. "If Safronov comes out on top, it will be like the massacre of the Streltsy. He's already quoting Peter the Great." In order to establish his authority as Czar over the mutinous palace guard, or Streltsy, Peter the Great had slaughtered thousands of soldiers, many of them taken by ambush and hacked to bits with savage brutality.

"Will it affect you?"

Krylov shrugged. "I am merely an instrument," he said, thinking of how he had managed to survive the purge of previous secret police chiefs: Beria, Shelepin, Andropov. Whoever ruled Russia would need him, he believed, and the strings that he held in his hand. But there were no guarantees against lunacy; there was no telling what a madman might do.

"What about the defector? Ushinsky?"

The East Germans had not been officially notified of Ushinsky's defection, and so far the Americans had released nothing to the media. But Krylov was not surprised that Misha was already informed. He had a very special relationship with Moscow Center; after all, he had been a Soviet agent before he became an East German one.

"It's serious," Krylov said. "We've had to roll up a couple of networks, and recall a few people. I don't think any of your agents were compromised. I've been trying to neutralize the total effect. Ushinsky seems to have had more access than he should have been allowed. It's bad."

"But not altogether bad," Misha said casually, not doubting that Krylov would instantly grasp his meaning. Ushinsky came from military intelligence, the rival service to the KGB. On a previous occasion when the high-level traitor Hussar had been detected inside the GRU, the service had been purged and a KGB man installed as director. In Stalin's time, when a conflict between the two spy services had been resolved in favor of the KGB, the unfortunate military intelligence chief had been subjected to an exquisitely protracted process of execution, which involved nailing his genitals to a block of wood. In the normal course of events, an important defection from the GRU would give the KGB a pretext to stomp all over its rival in military intelligence. But at this moment, in the midst of the power struggle inside the Kremlin, more than the long-standing jealousy between the two services was at issue. Ushinsky had defected from Marshal Safronov's camp. There was therefore a chance that his treason could be used against the marshal.

This was not a prospect that Krylov was disposed to chat about in a colleague's office, even though Krotkin had quietly withdrawn to leave him alone with Misha. It was probable that the conversation was being recorded on a hidden tape recorder, and more than probable that if Krotkin thought it was incriminating enough he would not scruple to send a report to Marshal Safronov in order to ingratiate himself with the new Soviet strongman. Many of the most brilliant careers at Moscow Center, as in the other branches of the Soviet bureaucracy, had been founded on stabbing friends in the back at the most opportune moment.

In any event, Krylov had more immediate matters to raise with Misha than the question of how the Ushinsky defection could be used to weaken the gallant marshal. Foremost among them was the problem of how to minimize the damage that Ushinsky might have done to the Beacon itself. As an officer in the GRU, the poor cousin of the KGB, the defector had never had access to the super-secret archives of the Beacon. But Ushinsky knew more about the work of Krylov's section than most people in military intelligence, because he had worked in the same office, for a time, as the British agent called Hussar. After Hussar, also a lieutenant colonel in the GRU, had been detected by Moscow Center, he had been arrested, secretly tried, and sentenced to death. The method of execution prescribed was the firing squad. In fact, Hussar had been pushed, alive and fully conscious, into the oven of a crematorium. Selected secret-police officials and GRU officers had been invited to witness the scene and to listen to Hussar's desperate screams as the flesh was charred from his bones. Moscow Center had wanted the story of how he died to circulate as widely as possible; such anecdotes helped to deter others from working for Western intelligence. Krylov remembered the scene vividly: the strong, handsome officer in prison clothes who had carried himself with such dignity although his face had been bruised and torn from the beatings and one shoulder drooped lower than the other. Hussar's composure had not broken even when they showed him the opening to the oven, like a window into hell with the flames leaping up. Only as they pushed him, feet first, into the furnace, did the screams begin.

All sorts of rumors had circulated within Soviet intelligence about the events leading up to Hussar's arrest. Although the defector had been among those invited to witness Hussar's end, Krylov did not know how much hard information Ushinsky had been able to glean on how his colleague had been detected. It seemed the defector had told the Americans that Hussar had been betrayed by a mole in the Agency. Talk of Soviet moles in the Agency was a common theme for gossip at Moscow Center and at GRU headquarters at Khodinsk airfield, and Krylov had never sought to discourage it, as long as no details were mentioned, or as long as those that were remained false or misleading. The idea that the Agency was hopelessly penetrated by Krylov's section was another deterrent to potential Soviet traitors. The fact that Ushinsky had chosen to defect to the American naval attaché in Paris, and not to Hammond, the Agency station chief, showed that this sort of rumor-mongering served a useful purpose. Ushinsky had been too nervous to go to the Agency direct, fearing betrayal by Krylov's agents in Washington.

Gossip and inspired rumors were one thing; specific leads to the penetration of the Agency by Krylov's section were altogether different. Krylov had learned from sources in Washington that Ushinsky had insisted to the Americans that the Beacon had succeeded in planting a mole in the Agency. There was a serious risk that the resulting investigations could lead to the exposure of Krylov's most valued asset in Washington. He therefore had either to neutralize Ushinsky's information or to point it away from the real target. This was where Misha could help.

Ignoring Misha's oblique comment about Marshal Safronov, Krylov asked an innocent-sounding question. "How's your cousin?"

"Still schizophrenic." Misha's cousin, another refugee from Stuttgart called Judah Klugmann, spent three months a year on a kibbutz in northern Israel, in the shadow of the Golan Heights, and the rest of the year traveling the world first-class, mostly to the United States, where it was widely believed in the intellectual circles that he frequented that he had ties to Israeli intelligence. In fact, Klugmann had tried and failed repeatedly to establish a formal relationship with the Mossad. The Israeli spy chiefs recognized where his primary loyalties lay: with Misha. They came to him only when they wanted to transmit a message to Misha via a back channel.

The fact that Misha's cousin was not an agent of the Mossad did not, however, prevent him from seeking to pass himself off as one whenever this served a purpose. Krylov now had an excellent purpose in mind.

"I think the time has come to bring your cousin in from the cold," he said.

"Leave Israel? Not Judah. He loves the place, even though he hates the Zionists and the politicians almost as much as Marshal Safronov does."

"I'm not talking about where he's going to live," Krylov pursued. "I'm saying that I have a mission for him that will blow his cover. This is so important that that is worth doing. I hope you'll appreciate the need for the sacrifice when I have explained.

Afterward, if Judah wants to live here or in Moscow, fine. He'll have a hero's reputation, the Order of Lenin, all of that. If not, it's his lookout."

"You want me to ask him to betray Israel?" Misha demurred. "I wouldn't want to do that. Judah's a good Communist, but he's also a Jew."

So are you, Misha, Krylov thought. *But you don't like anyone to mention it.*

"No, no." Krylov shook his narrow, elongated head impatiently. "This concerns the Americans. Specifically, Max Zimmer."

The head of the Beacon proceeded to explain what he had in mind. His proposal was that Misha should instruct his cousin to confess, preferably at a press conference in the United States but, failing that, to a well-known and trusted journalist, that he had long been employed as a double agent for Israeli and Soviet intelligence. The first part of the confession would of course be a lie, although it would be believed, readily enough, by many people in America. The second part of the confession, the authentic part, contained the seeds of a very interesting scandal.

"I want your cousin to make a statement on Max Zimmer's relations with the Israelis," Krylov elaborated. The Agency's former chief of counterintelligence had nurtured close ties with the Israelis since he had helped Jews to emigrate to Palestine in the immediate postwar years. The exchange of information between Max Zimmer and the Mossad had been highly lucrative for both sides. The intimacy between the Mossad and the Agency had never quite been the same since Zimmer fell victim to his bureaucratic rivals at Langley.

Misha did not see the point of Krylov's request right away. "Judah never met Max Zimmer in his life," he objected. "And anyway, everyone knows that Zimmer was tight with the Israelis."

"You're forgetting what I asked at the beginning," Krylov said. "What I want your cousin to describe is how, through him, secret intelligence that Max Zimmer was giving the Israelis was being channeled direct to you and to us at Moscow Center. We will supply some original American documents. We can bring in chemical warfare, the Israeli bomb, electronic countermeasures—all the most neuralgic military areas. You see what the net effect would be. We could sabotage relations between the Americans and the Israelis."

"And create the impression that the Mossad is crawling with our agents," Misha interjected. They both knew that, in fact, the Mossad had dealt ruthlessly with Soviet-bloc attempts to penetrate its ranks; Max Zimmer's admiration for the Israeli service had stemmed, in no small part, from the thoroughness with which they had tracked down leads supplied by the famous defector Golitsyn in the early sixties. "I thought you said the Israelis were not the target for this exercise," Misha added.

"The main target is Max Zimmer."

"But Zimmer is retired. Burned out. Discredited. Why bother?" Misha cut himself off, observing the wry twist to Krylov's mouth. "I see," he said. *"Agent-bolvan."*

The Russian phrase that he used was a popular piece of jargon at Moscow Center. Loosely translated, it meant "dummy agent." Misha himself was a veteran practitioner of the art of deploying an *agent-bolvan* to divert the attention of a hostile secret service from a more important agent that his own agency was seeking to protect. For example, when the chiefs of the West German intelligence service had begun to suspect—from a chronicle of disasters—that a mole had burrowed his way into their senior ranks, Misha had deliberately sacrificed a less important agent, a loyal and ideologically committed operative, in order to lead the investigators down the wrong path. To complete the hoax, Misha had made sure that the mole he was trying to protect was able to gain credit for himself by "catching" the dummy.

If Krylov wanted to make out that Max Zimmer had been—consciously or unconsciously—feeding American secrets to Moscow via his Israeli contacts, Misha now reasoned, then the Soviet spymaster's objective must be to cast Zimmer in the part of the *agent-bolvan.*

"Will the Agency believe it?" Misha asked.

Krylov, who had kept crossing and uncrossing his legs since he had sat down on the big sofa that backed onto the scale model of Langley, now got up and started pacing, in high agitation, around the room.

"The Agency will believe what it wants to believe," he said enigmatically.

*   *   *

The bathroom in the suite of rooms prepared for Krylov at Karlshorst was not exactly of socialist proportions. It was more like a sitting room than a mere bathroom, with a tub that was roomy enough for two average-sized people. The lavishness contrasted with Krylov's habitual austerity. The master of the Beacon did not drink or smoke, and his favorite meal was a hardboiled egg with black bread and a little raw herring. A man of his power and advanced years was entitled to some small luxuries. A bathroom fit for a pasha was a trifling thing compared with the life-style enjoyed by most of the Soviet elite in the closed world of their dachas.

Krylov's orderly had measured the temperature of the water. It was precisely seventy-seven degrees, as Krylov liked it. The orderly, a handsome young Georgian who stood fully two heads taller than his master, added a little pine essence. Krylov liked the water of his bath to be aromatic, but clear. Satisfied, the batman went to inform his master that everything was prepared.

Krylov set aside the file he had been studying. It contained the life history of one of the most powerful men in West Germany, a Socialist minister in the ruling Socialist-Liberal coalition. In earlier years, the German politician had sided with the Americans. Then, when he saw the Berlin Wall go up, cutting off the escape route for Germans in the Communist half of his country, and saw that the Americans were unable to prevent the wall from being completed, he concluded that the United States was impotent. If his country was ever going to be reunited, he decided, it would be with the help of the Russians, not the Americans. The trauma inspired by the building of the Berlin Wall had led the minister, Dieter Klages, to welcome a closer and closer relationship with the East. In Moscow and in East Berlin, his hosts had flattered him, praising his idealism, his crusade for détente and disarmament. His hosts had also understood that a man who changes his convictions once, for purely personal reasons, may do so again. They had set out to ensure that Dieter Klages did not change his mind, and his allegiances, again. Little by little, they had drawn him over the fuzzy dividing line between the intimate exchange of confidences and espionage. Now there could be no turning back for Dieter Klages. He was Misha's man. If the West German minister declined to follow his instructions—conveyed to him, of course, in the respectful, diplomatic style that his cabinet rank had earned him—there was enough in Misha's files at Karlshorst and in Krylov's files at Moscow Center to wreck his career and have him put on trial in the Federal Republic as a foreign spy. Klages would play a starring role in Krylov's plans for Germany. Misha would see to that. Misha could always be relied on to do what was required. Tonight, as well.

Krylov rose from the desk. He was wearing a mulberry-colored robe with a quilted satin collar. His sparse hair had been carefully lacquered down across the top of his skull. As he walked, he exuded a faint aroma of eau de cologne.

"Are they here?" he asked the orderly.

"Yes, Comrade General. They have been waiting for half an hour."

The orderly helped to remove the robe, and Krylov lowered himself into the delicious warmth of the tub. His body was withered and blemished, but he was not ashamed of it, and did not fear the judgment of others. It had been two years, at least, since he had had full intercourse, but sex was far from dead.

With the accumulation of years, Krylov had found himself drawn, more and more, to the young. To the very young. As if he rejuvenated himself at their source. Gender was immaterial. To Krylov, boys and girls were equally attractive. Especially those that were still unformed, on the quivering edge of pubescence. He had read, in the writings of Suetonius, about the last years of the Emperor Tiberius on the island of Capri. The aging Tiberius had enjoyed swimming in a limpid pool among young girls and boys. He would dive between their legs, and they would swim between his, nibbling like fish. The image excited Krylov, as the bathwater eddied around his body.

He heard footsteps in the passage as the orderly came, bringing Misha's present to him.

Misha had said they were twins. Eleven years old. A boy and a girl, with an unmarried mother who had been carted off to a psychiatric home because of her antisocial tendencies. Krylov savored the long moment of anticipation.

Only one thought clouded it. Beria, Stalin's secret-police chief, had had the same tastes. When the leadership had changed in Moscow, they had butchered Beria, put him down like a mad dog.

Krylov closed his eyes and concentrated on the mental picture of Tiberius at play in the sunlit waters of Capri.

Then the two children were at the door, naked, eyes downcast. The little girl had her fingers in her mouth. Their sex was like unripe fruit.

"Come to me," Krylov called from the bath, stretching out his gnarled, scrawny arms like dead sticks. "Don't be frightened."

The plump, nervous little faces were almost too beautiful, like faces from a Renoir. Yes, Misha could always be relied on.

9

NEW YORK, *September 18*

"It was a fix," Melanie Toussaint fumed as they fought their way through the mob of fight-goers at Madison Square Garden.

There was a threatening rumble of anger from many of the fans who shared her disappointment with the champion, who had bowed out, with only light injuries, after only nine rounds.

"Fix, fix, fix," they chanted. "Money! Give us back our money!"

"You should go tell them to give your money back too," she said to Canning. "What did you have to pay for those ringside seats, anyway?"

"Come on." Canning propelled her forward. "I didn't come for the fight. I came to have dinner with you. Uptown or downtown?"

"You pick."

He ran out into the street to hail a cab pulling out from Penn Station. Inside the car, which was plastered with yellow stickers—"No Smoking," "No Eating or Drinking"—she was still complaining about the fight.

"Why would Robles do that?"

"You should be happy. Your boy won." The new champion was a handsome young black from Georgia.

"But I knew he was going to lose tonight. I always pick them right. I picked the winner of the Kentucky Derby six years running."

"Well, I hope you'll share some of your sixth sense with me." He studied her, reflecting on the contrast between the Melanie of the Café Carlyle and the screaming and yelling Melanie in the ringside seat. "Am I going to win?"

"I didn't know the fight had been set."

110

"It has been now."

Following Canning's instructions, the cab drove crosstown to Broadway, then south to Union Square.

"Are we going to the Village?" she asked.

"Not quite. Any objection to Burger King?"

The taxi pulled up across the road from the Fourteenth Street Burger King, where a crowd of black youths were passing the time swilling from beer cans. The narrow, somewhat run-down façade of Luchow's gave no hint of the palatial opulence behind its doors. They walked through the vast anteroom and were ushered to the special table that Canning had ordered, set apart from the rest of the diners in the middle of the restaurant within a small gazebo. A string quartet were playing the Viennese waltzes of Johann Strauss.

"I feel like we've stepped back a century," said Melanie as the music eddied around them. "I didn't know there were places like this in New York."

"Pure fin de siècle," Canning agreed. "The place was founded by a young German adventurer in the eighties. The *eighteen*-eighties."

They chose from the house specialties: thick lentil soup laden with sausage, schnitzel, and roast goose, washed down with Riesling.

There was a pause in the conversation as they watched for coffee to be served.

"Ye-es?" said Melanie, making two syllables of the word. "What's on your mind?"

"I was thinking that you're beautiful."

She was wearing red again that night, a swirling dress open at the throat to show the flash of gold chains against her copper skin.

"We-ell?"

The directness of her stare, from eyes that Canning had not learned how to read, made him uncharacteristically timid. He did not express the thought that was uppermost in his mind.

"I was thinking of the first night I saw you, in the Café Carlyle," he said. "I said you were intoxicating. It's true. You were making people drunk. Did you know some of your admirers are Russians?"

"You mean the guy with black hair?" Her eyes clouded. "All I knew is he's foreign. And some kind of diplomat."

"You mean you talked with him?"

"Just a few words. You know. Kissing hands. That kind of bullshit. He asked me to a reception."

"Are you going?"

"I don't know. I don't think so."

For a moment, Canning considered disregarding Dicky Prince's injunction not to get mixed up with the Russians from the Café Carlyle. Melanie offered a delicious variation on the oldest form of entrapment: the honey trap.

The coffee came, and she heaped in sugar, rattling the spoon. Canning was conscious of the glances of other diners, trying to assess their relationship.

"What do you think of the Russians?"

She shrugged. "I guess they're people, like anybody else. Out for what they can get."

"Like Afghanistan, Iran, Poland?"

"So they did that. Look what we did in Vietnam. Who's the good guy? I'm not political, Charles. Except I don't like people left hungry and jobless. I don't like politicians who dream that one day they'll wake up and there won't be any blacks in America."

Canning was conscious that since the last elections, race tension was stirring again in the United States, and that moderate black leaders were under fierce attack by radicals in their community who were saying that nobody would deal with unemployment and the agony of the urban ghettos unless there was a full-scale revolt. Some of the militants identified with Cuba. Canning wondered how Melanie identified herself.

"Were you involved in politics at college?"

"People *tried* to get me involved. You've heard of Ace Samuel?"

"Yes." Ace Samuel had gained prominence as one of the new wave of black radical leaders. In a press conference in Havana after the new President was inaugurated, he had announced that the best thing that blacks could do was go out and buy guns— automatic weapons if they could find them. He had publicly supported Ayatollah Khomeini during the Iran hostage crisis, and had been burned in effigy by the Ku Klux Klan in Montgomery, Alabama.

"Well, Ace was in school with me. Ace had lotsa problems. Starting with that name. It really *was* his name. He was a big, good-looking guy with beautiful teeth, and he was good at sports

112

and girls were falling all over him. He had big ego trouble. He thought he was a real hot dog. And he was into all the Black Power stuff, and would go around campus telling the kids that they ought to do something to express solidarity.

"Ace didn't know how to deal with me," she went on. "For one thing, he had climbed right out of the ghetto, and I came from a much safer home. My mother worked hard. She made us really a middle-class home. And then I was smart. I got better grades than the other kids. And I wasn't interested in sleeping with every member of the football team. All of that made me kind of a nonconformist, and Ace could never quite work out how to cope."

Charles listened attentively, not wanting to break the flow now it had started. In Arab countries, the intelligence service is called the Mukhabarat, "Listening Post"; in all countries, intelligence begins with good listeners.

"One day," Melanie was saying, "Ace stepped up the pressure on me to show solidarity with the Movement. I found him waiting for me outside class with some of his fan club. He told me that from now on I was supposed to sit with him and his supporters at the side of the cafeteria and at the back of the bus. You know, they were staking out their own turf. Only brothers and sisters could sit there."

"Sounds like reverse segregation."

"That's exactly what it was. I said to him, 'Look, Ace, I can understand that if you go into the cafeteria, or if you get onto the bus, you want your own place. But I can't figure out why, after all that the civil rights movement was fighting for, and after we survived George Wallace and Montgomery and all of that, why you want to sit in the *back* section of the bus. Why not take the front? Or at least the middle.' I said to him, 'Why, after twenty years of struggle, are you trying to put us in the back again?'"

"What did Ace say?"

"He wasn't very happy."

"Are you saying that you feel integrated? That you don't feel different because you're—uh—black?"

"No, I'm not saying that." She pushed her coffee cup away impatiently. "I *am* black, and that makes a difference. Look at the way you stumbled over the word. You couldn't say it straight out."

"That's because it seems so inadequate. Anyway, you're not

black. You're a sort of café-au-lait. White Americans spend months on the beach trying to get the color you were born with."

"'High yeller,' they call it down South," she said scornfully. "Look, honey, you still got a lot to learn about this country. Black means where you're from, and mostly it means you're poor and angry."

"Are you poor and angry?"

"Okay, I was lucky. I got into one of the professions that is socially acceptable for blacks. It doesn't mean that I still don't attract a few funny looks when I sit in a place like this with a white man. That couple over there"—she nudged her chin toward a middle-aged couple with tight, hard faces and eyes like dead fish—"haven't stopped staring at us since we arrived."

"They have nothing to say to each other. We provided their entertainment."

Melanie stopped a passing waiter. "Could I have some Rémy Martin? Straight up."

"Make that two."

She looked unsettled, so he took her hand, lifted it, and kissed the palm, allowing his lips to linger there until she pulled away, darting a look at the fish-eyed couple, who were now patently scandalized.

"I'm a little scared of you," she said.

"You have every reason to be. I intend to seduce you."

"God, Charles! You make me feel we're in a B movie. Real people don't talk that way."

He reached for her hand again, and she allowed him to toy with it. Under the table, their knees brushed, and he pressed his leg against hers, as if by accident.

"You said something else in the Café Carlyle."

"Ye-es."

"You said men get left behind."

"We-ell?"

"Did all your men get left behind?"

"You really want it all laid out for you, don't you?"

"Absolutely."

"But Charles, you've told me next to nothing about yourself. You haven't even said if you're married. I'd assume that you are."

"Divorced."

"Children?"

114

"One son. Jimmy. He's lucky. He's just like me."

"You mean humble and tongue-tied."

"I do feel humble toward you," he said, serious again. "You're beautiful, and smart, and somehow unknowable. I would like to know you."

She concentrated on her cognac, ignoring the cue. He shifted gear, dropping the name of a glamorous black female newscaster he had met at Elaine's. She had been accompanied by a pushy Jewish writer from a roughneck neighborhood in Brooklyn who was plugging his book on how to improve your sex life.

"It was bizarre," Canning said. "He kept using these interminable nonsense words. I told him it reminded me of the ancient Egyptian priesthood, which used language not as a means of communication, but as a way to establish and defend a monopoly of knowledge. Since common people couldn't read hieroglyphs, they stayed in their place. I kept wondering what that beautiful girl was doing out with a jerk like that."

Canning thought his remark was innocuous, but it had the effect on Melanie Toussaint of dropping a lighted match into a pool of kerosene.

"You're so damned smart, aren't you, mister hotshot ladykiller?" Melanie flared up. "That jerk may have been the best man she could find."

"But—"

"It's not that easy, you know. Not when you've made it. Black guys get frightened 'cause you're moving places black girls don't usually go. White guys are frightened because you're black. Oh, there are plenty of people who'd like to get into your pants. Especially when you get up there on stage and start shaking your boobs. But try getting beyond that."

"Melanie," he began to protest, but she was off on her own train. As she spoke, he became aware, for the first time, of the possible emotional limbo of the successful, educated black woman, and found himself warming to her even more. He wanted to reach out, to hold her, to show her he understood the words.

"There was a guy called Ray," she said. "He was a three-letter man."

"A three-letter man? What's that?"

"Somebody's gonna have to teach you to talk. A three-letter man is a guy who's got college credits for three sports. With Ray,

115

it was basketball, track, and football. I had a real crush on that guy. When he was out training, I'd go out padding around the field behind him wearing five-pound lead cuffs just to be near him."

"What happened to Ray?"

"Hold on. You gotta understand, I wasn't Melanie Toussaint, the up-and-coming blues singer, in those days. I was just a fat, gawky little girl who got good grades. Ray wasn't scared of me then. In fact, he hardly looked at me. I was the one who was doing the chasing. I'd hang out with Ray and his friends, and to make them take account of me I'd play pool and cards with them—and usually beat them."

"I said I wanted to learn three-card monte."

"Well," she swept on. "I lost sight of Ray for a year or two after college, and the next time we met up, he's got most of the things he wanted, making a lot of money playing basketball, with more girls than he can handle hanging from his ankles. But I'd changed too. I'd lost weight, lookin' good, and I'd landed my first big contract—big for me, anyway. Ray was looking at me like he'd never looked at me before. But the more he looked, the more he started getting scared."

"Why?"

"Competition. Funny, he doesn't have that complex about white girls. But a black girl who's made it comes as some kind of threat to his manhood."

"So you stopped seeing him?" Canning was more anxious about the answer than he wanted to admit to himself.

"We're friends," she said. "Nothing more. Can I have some more brandy?"

"Of course." As he signaled the waiter, Canning felt pleased with the drift of the conversation. It was still fairly jerky, but she was loosening up. It was partly, perhaps, the effect of the alcohol. Her speech was becoming gradually fuzzier.

"The first white guy," she was saying, "was disaster. We went driving around down South, and nearly got ourselves lynched. Do you know the Deep South?"

"I know Africa."

"The Deep South isn't like Africa. It ain't like nowhere. They were ready to cut Mick's balls off because he was out with a black girl."

116

"My God." The fish-eyed couple, Canning noted with relief, were on their way out.

"What do you really want?" she said, when she had got some more brandy inside her. "What are you looking for?"

"I told you." Canning took her hand again. "I intend to seduce you."

"Wouldn't you settle for a flirtation instead of a seduction?"

"No."

"Why not?"

He ran his lips lightly from her palm to her wrist, and up along her forearm. "Because I need to make love to you," he explained, looking up into her impenetrable eyes.

In a sudden, reflex motion, she tugged her arm away and sent both their brandy glasses flying. A pale-brown stain spread across the tablecloth.

"I'm sorry," she said. "I need to go to the ladies' room."

Her exit gave Canning time not only to settle the bill but to brood on the situation he had created. His original intent when he had invited her to dinner at the Café Carlyle had been to form a character assessment, to explore what elements in her personality could be exploited in a play against her Russian admirers. Dicky Prince had ruled that out in Bermuda. But Canning had wanted to keep the date anyway; there was no harm, he thought, in an amusing diversion. What was unexpected was the depth of fascination that he was already coming to feel in the presence of her, the wave of sympathy—in its original sense, of feeling *with* another—that rose within him as she told her stories, shared her hopes and disappointments. Canning was afraid that in the space of a few hours alone with Melanie Toussaint, he was already in danger of losing his objectivity.

"We-ell?" She was back, with those maddening two syllables.

"What about a nightcap at my place? It's just up the road."

"No. Not tonight."

"Why not? It's not late."

"I haven't got your number yet, sweetie."

"I'm an open book." He rose from the table and took her arm. "At least I can give you a lift home."

They went out into the crisp night air and across Fourteenth Street onto Irving Place.

A wino, wandering the sidewalk in intricate ellipses, made straight for Canning. "Shake, partner," he hiccuped.

"I don't know why these people always seem to make for me," said Canning, when they had left him a few yards behind.

"Maybe they know their own kind." She pulled free of his arm to peer in the window of a Greek deli. Ahead, there was a camera crew in front of Pete's Tavern, filming a scene from a detective movie. "Come on, Charles," she whooped. "We'll get your face in the movies."

Instinctively, Canning moved out into the street, skirting the bright circle of the spotlights. Melanie walked straight through the film set.

"So you like the shadows," she said as he was unlocking his Porsche. "I bet you're a British spy. What else would you want with a shy and quiet girl from New Orleans? Why else would you be interrogating me about Russians?"

She got into the Porsche and put a finger to his lips when he tried to argue.

"Sssh. Don't spoil your mystery. I want to know if I'd make a good undercover agent."

"You'd make a great undercovers agent," he said, with the stress on the "s," as he started the engine.

For some reason that, again, he could not comprehend, this remark worked like a detonator. Melanie jumped out of the car, slamming her door, and ran off down the street. He leaped out after her and overtook her just as she was hailing a cab.

"You think you're so fucking smart, don't you?" she spat at him.

"I'm sorry." He fumbled for words. "I don't understand . . ."

But she was already gone. He shambled back to his Porsche, disoriented and uncomprehending, to find he had locked himself out. He had to go back to the apartment to get a coat hanger in order to break in and remove the keys.

Maybe it was just as well that Dicky Prince had told him hands off the Russians, Canning thought. If he couldn't handle a one-night date with Melanie, how could he run her against a KGB major general?

It was definitely the last time he would go out on the town with a blues singer, he resolved.

But he was wrong.

118

Canning awoke to the buzz of the intercom.

"A delivery for you, Mr. Canning," the doorman's voice crackled through the squawk-box, unnaturally loud, drumming in his ears.

"Send it up, please."

When Canning pulled back the drapes, the sunlight hit him in the eyes like a backhanded slap. The bed looked as if it had hardly been slept in. Just a couple of vertical furrows on the side nearest the window. Snatches of last night's conversation drifted back into his consciousness, phrases of Melanie's, some only half understood. "What do you want," she had said, "egg in your beer?" The expression was as incomprehensible to Canning as "egg cream," the name of a soft drink he had seen them selling from carts in the Village, a concoction of syrup, seltzer, and milk that contained neither eggs nor cream. Then he saw Melanie's face, contorted with pain and anger. He must have overstepped an invisible line, violated some taboo that he had not recognized. What was it? He had to try to understand.

The delivery came, a small gray cardboard box tied up with ribbon. Inside was a single red rose, scarcely more than a bud. Canning looked for the card. It contained a single phrase, written in a sloping hand, with great flourishes at the loops. "You go to my head."

He grabbed the telephone so eagerly that the cord knocked over the glass on his bedside table.

Her voice was low and cloudy, hardly more than an exhalation of breath.

"Did I wake you?" he said.

"Ye-es."

"Thank you for the flower. I'll wear it in my buttonhole." The sun brought a pleasant warmth to his naked shoulders as he sat on the edge of the bed, knees tightly pressed together. "I'm sorry about last night," he said.

"So am I. I have a tongue."

"You do?"

"I could always hold my own in playing the dozens, as they say down home."

"Playing the dozens. Is that another card game?"

119

"It's verbal dueling. It comes natural when you're from a big family from the South, you know, when you've got a brother who's a numbers runner, a sister of questionable virtue, a mother who plays ponies and has gold teeth, and a drunk father who runs a poker school in the basement. The insults start with something like 'Your Papa's got false teeth,' and you take off from there."

"That's one thing you didn't say to me last night."

"I don't know why I was like that. You shouldn't give me wine. I can take any amount of spirits, but wine starts me off."

"Can we try again? What about tonight?"

"I have to perform. And I think I'm getting a sore throat."

"That calls for immediate treatment. Let's meet for lunch."

"What's your prescription, doctor?"

"Brandy. And love."

"All right."

They met uptown at Crawdaddy's in the Roosevelt Hotel, dodging the crowds of noisy Madison Avenue executives at the bar to sip Sazerac cocktails at a quiet table in the side room. They lunched on gumbo soup and mammoth hero sandwiches that defeated them both, their eyes on each other, not the food. Her look was frankly appraising. Canning met it, smiling.

"You know," she said, "I look at you sometimes and you look so damn sure of yourself. You've got a sort of off-the-shoulder insouciance."

"I'm not at all sure of myself with you," he said seriously.

"I don't quite understand the attraction. You've got all the fashionable ladies of Manhattan to pick from."

"I've been bewitched."

"This might surprise you, Charles, but I'm not all that liberated. I'm very careful. I call my mother every week. I don't jump into bed with every man who throws a pass at me."

"I'm relieved to hear it."

"Look, we hardly know each other. I don't even know what you do for a living. Other than try to seduce shy girls from New Orleans."

"It's not a question of time. We communicate. We like each other. I think you gave me part of yourself last night." His fingers stroked her palm, her forearm. She was wearing a broad-brimmed

120

straw hat and a long-sleeved blue dress with a white lace collar, as if she were going to an old-fashioned garden party. The modesty of her attire accentuated rather than diminished her sexual magnetism.

"I don't talk that way often," she said. "I hope it wasn't too much for you."

"You're looking beautiful today."

"I look like a cross between Pollyanna and a New York bag lady. I guess that's my style."

He laughed and said, "You have a gift with words. A power. I could be chatting up the great undiscovered American novelist."

Then he suggested that they go back to the Gramercy Park apartment for brandy and coffee, and she said carefully, earnestly, as if tiptoeing over broken glass, "I like you, Charles. I like you a lot. But I feel mixed up. Can't we just pace this out a bit?"

"No."

"Why not?"

"Because I want you. Right now."

He said it without dropping his voice or altering his even conversational tone, and there was a clatter of cutlery at the neighboring table, where three overdressed middle-class ladies were eating dessert.

Melanie stifled a giggle and said, "Look at those women. They're positively scandalized. And probably man-hungry. Two are widows, and the third, the ringleader, is divorced. She's the one with the designer dress and the elaborate hairdo."

"Melanie, how can you tell?"

"Well, the one who's divorced has got the kind of face that tells you she took her husband to the cleaners. And she's obviously got no money problems. She's dripping with jewels. The other two look as if they're on a budget. They've all come in from Long Island, where they used to live in nice suburban cottages with two-car garages and are now maybe living in condos."

"You could be right," said Canning, stealing a glance at the table. "You've got a pretty good eye for detail."

"So I would make a good undercover agent."

"You might."

When he repeated his invitation to go back to the apartment, she did not hesitate. They left to a muted babble of gossip from the Long Island ladies. Sitting together in the back seat of the

121

Yellow cab, Canning could feel her warmth rolling in waves along the side of his body.

Below the windows of Canning's apartment, the park was a small sea of green around the statue of Edwin Booth: emerald green, grass green, lemon and lime. Some of the best-fed pigeons in New York waddled and preened themselves along the railings. Stone knights in armor stood guard outside 36 Gramercy Park East. Bare-chested joggers panted and pounded. A garishly painted van, advertising a rock group, was parked illegally outside the hotel. Oblivious to the scene, Canning and Melanie sat together on the big oatmeal-colored sofa, behind closed drapes, under the perch of a brightly painted papier-mâché toucan, one of the models from Sally's gallery.

They touched each other's faces like blind people, tracing the planes and contours gently, meticulously, as if they needed to touch everything to be able to see it. Then she drew his mouth down to her full, dark lips, and the taste was rich and sweet, like the taste of blueberries. He ran his hand through her hair, so that the tortoiseshell pins that had held it up went flying in all directions, and her face and neck were suddenly framed by a great black halo.

"Wait," she said, gathering up the pins. "These belonged to my mother."

"I want you," he breathed. It seemed to him that all his force, his whole bloodstream, was gathered in one place. His hands roved over her as she leaned over the edge of the sofa, fishing for pins, and he felt the weight of her breasts, the swell of her thighs. His fingertips grazed her inner thigh casually, as if by accident, and then returned there.

She shivered and spun around to look at him, her upper body poised precariously over the edge of the sofa. As she moved, she brushed against the front of his trousers. He nibbled at her neck, her earlobes, pressing her back against the arm of the sofa, so that his body locked into hers, as close and containing as a sculptor's mold around the clay.

"Wait," she again said, and detached herself to go to the bathroom. When she came back, she was wearing only Canning's black silk robe, a gift that Sally had brought for him—eons ago, it seemed—from Hong Kong. The gold chain at her throat, the gold bangles at her wrists, were glinting, in the half-light, like pirate's treasure in a deep cave.

They walked hand in hand to the bedroom. Canning pulled the drapes against the bright sunlight and the windows of the tall red-brick building across the park. He turned on the bedside lamp, and the soft glow from the yellow shade turned Melanie's skin to the warmth of burning embers. He threaded his fingers in her hair and murmured a couplet from Baudelaire:

> "Ma main, dans ta crinière lourde,
> Semera le rubis, la perle, et le saphir."

He nuzzled his face against her neck and shoulder, and her rich natural perfume made him recall the rest of the poem, Baudelaire's tribute to his Dominican mistress, Jeanne Duval, evoking the mingled odors of coconut oil, musk, and tar. He tugged lightly at the sash of her robe, and it slid smoothly from her shoulders. She watched him with great, unblinking, liquid eyes as he folded his arms around her buttocks and lifted her gently onto the big brass bed. He kissed and caressed her for a long time, until he found her moist and giving, her body arching to meet him.

They made love slowly, rhythmically, and in silence until, when he could hold back no longer, he spoke her name, hovering over her like a falcon ready to plunge. Then she kicked out her legs high and wide, her eyes rolled, and the shuddering of her body seemed to match his own. When they were both still, he said to her, "It feels so good to be inside you," and she puckered her lips in a kiss.

"You still taste of blueberries," he said.

When she drew him into her again, restraint was forgotten. She moaned, panted, urged him on with unintelligible half-cries. At the moment of coming, she screamed, not once, but in short bursts, each more penetrating than the last, until she cupped her hand to her mouth, her eyes wide in embarrassed surprise. Laughing, he pulled her hand away and drove deeper inside her.

When they were both spent, she leaned back against the double-piled pillows, her body curved and feline.

"Do that again," she said, "and they'll send in the cops."

"No they won't. It keeps the neighbors amused."

"Some neighborhood."

They rested close to each other, enjoying the luxury of mutual discovery in the middle of a workday afternoon. Later, she lay on her stomach, crooning some of the old torchy songs until he brought champagne and, excited and unsteady, they spilled some on the sheets. They made love again on the floor, slowly revolving in the timeless, weightless sensation of a dream. Finding his own words inadequate, he whispered:

"*Elle était donc couchée, et se laissait aimer,*
Et du haut du divan elle souriait d'aise
A mon amour profond et doux comme la mer
Qui vers elle montait comme vers sa falaise."

Afterward, she said to him, "There's a painting of her, you know."

"Who?"

"Jeanne Duval. Baudelaire's mistress. They're both in that big painting by Cézanne, of the artist surrounded by his friends in his studio, while he shakes his brush at a nude model."

"She must have been good for Baudelaire. They stayed together about twenty years. Even if he did call his poems *Flowers of Evil*. It's funny. I'd never really thought of Jeanne Duval before. I wonder what they thought of her in Paris."

"They would have thought she was exotic," said Melanie. "Like Josephine Baker. If you're classified as exotic, you don't have to take account of social taboos." She didn't say the rest of it: not like being black in America. But Canning guessed at her meaning, and ran his lips over the side of her cheek. Her long eyelashes fluttered like a moth against the side of his face.

"You'd better not recite that stuff to any of your other lady friends," she said. "I have territorial rights over Baudelaire in bed."

124

10

That there had been a changing of the guard at Langley was obvious, in the most literal sense, from the scene in front of the director's private elevator. The previous chief of the Agency, a man of middling height as well as psychic insecurity, had insisted that none of his guards be taller than he. On a visit to the director's office under the old regime, Dick Hammond, who stood six foot four in his bare feet, had felt himself to be surrounded by midgets, and wondered where the Office of Security had found its supply of five-foot musclemen. Adam Claiborne, the new chief of the Agency, was, like his predecessor, a layman—that is, if you discounted his wartime experience running spy networks behind Nazi lines in Europe. But unlike his predecessor, Director Claiborne stood tall in every respect. This was reflected in the fact that the security guard who rode up in the elevator with Dick Hammond was taller than he by about two inches.

On his return from Paris, Hammond had called Claiborne's secretary to request an appointment. He had had no indications of his next assignment, and early retirement was coming to seem more and more appealing, provided the personnel section was helpful about his pension. A woman like Sally Sherwin did not come along more than once, he had been telling himself. Especially at his stage in life. If he had to choose between Sally and the Agency, then the choice had to be Sally. Maybe she would relent. But if not . . .

I've done my share, he told himself. *I've no reason to feel guilty about wanting a life of my own before I'm too old to enjoy it.*

He was startled to find that the director's secretary seemed to be expecting his call. Director Claiborne had asked her to arrange a meeting, she explained. The director wanted to see him right away. Hammond wondered whether he had earned a reprimand not just on one but on two counts. It was quite possible that the French had complained about the help he had given the Israelis in Paris. And then there was the foul-up over the Russian defector. As station chief in Paris, Hammond would have been expected to be able to field a prominent defector, and give the Agency first crack at him before General Brennan or anybody else got in on the act. It was no good blaming his friend Jim Morton at the naval attaché's office for not cutting him in on the deal. Hammond knew he was liable to be held personally accountable for whatever embarrassment was caused to the Agency. He should have had his own feelers out.

To hell with it, he said to himself. If Claiborne carpeted him, he resolved, he would hand in his resignation then and there.

His biggest regret would be that over the past couple of years the mood at the Agency had changed for the better. At one time he had seen some of his friends shrivel up into miserable nine-to-fivers who spent their days pushing papers and watching the clock until they could run home and drink themselves into some kind of private peace, too scared to attempt any serious operation for fear they would become the target of a Congressional inquiry or a press exposé. You had to give the new administration credit for that; it was putting teeth back into the Agency.

But the past kept returning, like the chill from a door to the cellar that wouldn't stay closed.

As he walked with the guard along the corridor to Director Claiborne's office, Hammond had a tightly rolled newspaper in his hand. The headline was depressingly reminiscent of the scandals of the mid-seventies, but with a novel twist. "CIA CHIEF ZIMMER GAVE SECRETS TO ISRAEL, SOVIETS, SAYS DOUBLE AGENT."

The story was based, curiously, on a proof of an article scheduled to appear in a forthcoming issue of a girlie magazine called *Rake*. The author was a well-known investigative reporter called Sol Puig, who had turned freelance after covering the Agency beat for years for a New York paper. Puig quoted an unnamed Israeli source, who claimed that Max Zimmer—described as "the Agency's twisted former counterintelligence mastermind"—had delivered American secrets to Tel Aviv and, via an

126

Israeli double agent, to Moscow. The article might have been dismissed as a fantastic concoction but for the fact that it quoted from top-secret American documents, accurately identified by serial numbers and coding classifications, that had allegedly been part of the material passed on by Zimmer. Sol Puig suggested that Zimmer had knowingly been spying for Moscow Center, using an Israeli channel as a cutout.

Hammond wondered what his Israeli friend in Paris, Moshe Stern, would say about the article. Hammond knew that Israel was no less vulnerable to Soviet penetration than other Western societies. Indeed, given the inflow of immigrants from the Soviet Union, and Moscow Center's unrelenting efforts to hold Jewish families as hostages in the effort to control the actions of relatives abroad, it was remarkable that Israeli intelligence had had so much success in the secret battle with the KGB. Hammond knew, too, that there were Soviet agents who wrapped themselves in the Star of David, just as there were Soviet agents who pretended to be American, British, or West German operatives in their efforts to dupe unsuspecting targets for recruitment. Nonetheless, Hammond was convinced that the Puig article was a disinformation exercise. At one level, it was designed to complicate relations between Washington and Jerusalem. At another level, it was a very professional hatchet job on Max Zimmer. The newspaper piece concluded: "Ironically, the man who for many years paralyzed the Agency by categorizing every Soviet defector as a KGB plant and by seeing moles behind every door at Langley may himself have been a double agent."

Yet Hammond had divided feelings about Max Zimmer. Part of what the article said was true: he *had* paralyzed Agency operations. Hammond had clashed with the former counterintelligence chief himself when he had been based in Miami, running Cuban agents against Castro. Zimmer had wanted to close down Hammond's pet operation on the grounds that some of the Cubans involved were probably double agents for Havana. Hammond had insisted on going ahead anyway, and the operation succeeded.

His train of thought was broken off as he was ushered into Director Claiborne's office.

"Siddown, Dick," the director growled. Hammond found himself facing a photograph of John McCone, the Republican lawyer that President Kennedy had appointed to run the Agency. It was no secret around Langley that of all the previous directors, McCone was the one that Adam Claiborne admired most. McCone had been a dynamic, worldly nonprofessional whose instincts had proved right when the counsel of tame bureaucratic analysts had gone disastrously astray. In the run-up to the Cuban missile crisis, McCone had insisted that the Soviets had smuggled nuclear weapons onto the island, while Agency analysts were protesting that there was no evidence to back up the hunch. McCone, of course, had been proved right; he had known the truth in his bones. It was a style that Adam Claiborne seemed determined to perpetuate.

"I've got a job for you, Dick." Claiborne came to the point at once in the brisk manner that he had perfected while trading commodities in New York.

"I was—uh—hoping to talk to you about that."

"Yeah? Well, I'll tell you what I've got in mind. Has anyone briefed you on what that Paris defector, Ushinsky, has been telling us?"

"Not officially." In fact, rumors about the defector had become the staple topic of conversation in the bars and restaurants and private dinner tables where Hammond's friends in the Agency came together. The most lurid stories involved Les Winter's showdown with George Brennan. According to one account, the general had had Winter physically thrown out of his office, like a drunk getting bounced from a nightclub.

"Well, nobody's happy," said Claiborne. "Except maybe George Brennan. I've had to go to the President on this. As if he didn't have enough on his mind, what with these demonstrations and the state of the economy." Claiborne was one of the men in the new administration who was closest to the President, having helped to run the transition team after the last election. "Not to mention the polls," he went on. "Anyway, I think I may have quieted Brennan down. For a little while. Meantime, we have to get to the bottom of this Ushinsky business and come up with some answers pretty fast. According to this defector, there's a mole in the Agency who has betrayed some of our human sources, and also an agent the British were running in Moscow. A guy with a code name like cossack."

"Hussar," Hammond elucidated.

"Yeah. Now, this is the score. We're going to run our own in-

128

house investigation, and I want you to take charge of it. If the Soviets have an agent at Langley, I want you to catch him. And I'm giving you about six weeks to do it."

Hammond was speechless for almost a minute. Then he said, "I don't understand, Mr. Director. This is a job for the Office of Security and the counterintelligence people. And the Bureau, if things get that far. I'm an operations man. I've got no experience of spying on people inside the Agency. I wouldn't know where to begin. And I'm not sure that I want to learn."

"You weren't the first name on my list," Claiborne said with characteristic bluntness. Hammond saw he had taken out a small pocket notebook and opened it to a list of names. Each name was marked with a plus or a minus sign.

"The guy I would have liked for this," the director continued, "was Max Zimmer. People might have said that would have been like bringing back George Smiley in those British spy novels. I couldn't have cared less. But Max has too many enemies in this building. And anyway, he would have been out after this morning. As far as Agency business is concerned, he might as well be dead. You saw the papers."

Hammond nodded.

"Fact is," Claiborne said, "we're going to have to investigate Max Zimmer too. I don't know how much there is in this Israeli stuff that what's-his-name—"

"Sol Puig."

"Yeah. Well, I'm told this isn't the first time people have made similar accusations against Max. Some people up here think he could be the mole. From what I saw of him in Italy at the end of the war, I just don't buy it. But you'll need to check it out."

"Sir," Hammond protested, "I just don't feel qualified. I don't have the background in counterintelligence."

"Amateurs often do better than pros. Because, coming in from a distance, they can see things that you never get to see from close up. And because their imaginations haven't been fettered by doing the same job day after day. I saw that during the war." Claiborne paused, his mind wandering back. "That's how the British came to work the double-cross system so well against the Nazis. Inspired amateurs. But that's not why I want you for this job." He returned with a jolt to the present. "I want you because you've never been part of these internal Agency feuds. You're respected by all sides of the house. And I want you because there's a foreign dimension to all this and we'll need someone who's top-notch at dealing with the British and the Israelis under the counter. You're that man. From what I hear, none better."

Hammond wondered how much the director had learned about the Club.

"The time factor," he said. "You say we have to come up with answers within six weeks. That's a very tight leash." Even with a routine defector, a typist from the Soviet Foreign Ministry or an interpreter from the Institute of World Economics, Hammond was thinking, months could be required to establish bona fides. The process of checking had to begin with exhaustive interrogation, to wear down the defector's resistance until you were sure he was telling you the truth. In this case, there was an intelligence defector who claimed the Agency was penetrated, and he was being offered six weeks, not just to decide whether Ushinsky was lying but to come up with a live mole, maybe a friend in the Agency who had worked with him, drunk with him, shared a girlfriend, and had all along been living out a lie. The job was not only impossible. It was the last job in the Agency that Dick Hammond would willingly undertake. Better to make the break right now.

"Six weeks. That's all," Director Claiborne confirmed.

"I can't do it, sir. Frankly, I don't think it can be done. But if it's even going to be attempted, you need someone better equipped than me."

"I want you to do it, Dick." It was as if Claiborne hadn't heard anything that Hammond had said.

"Mr. Director," he said, coldly and correctly, "I was hoping to discuss early retirement with you today. I have personal reasons. And I really don't want to take on this assignment." Beyond everything else, there was one more compelling reason, he realized, why he could not agree to become the witch-finder in an investigation involving Max Zimmer. Max was Sally's uncle.

"You'll do it," Claiborne said finally. "I'll tell you why you'll do it. You'll do it because your investigation may decide whether or not this country is at war with the Soviet Union in six weeks' time."

It was then that Director Claiborne proceeded to outline the most scary part of what Ushinsky had brought from Moscow, a story of controlled lightning bolts and an awesome weapon of mass destruction, the Death Beam project whose Soviet code name, Razrukha, meant the disintegration of everything into chaos.

"This could all be a hoax," Claiborne summed up. "Or the Soviets are about to try to spring a technological Pearl Harbor on the United States. If you find the mole, that may help us to know which poker school we're in." The mundane, bathetic metaphor merely heightened the horror of the prospects that the director had spelled out in describing Project Razrukha.

"You'll have all the backup you need," said the director. "You'll have a direct line to me. You can pick your own staff, and you can use whatever private channels you think you require. We're going to bend all the rules on this, Dick, and to hell with anyone who doesn't like it. You have until November 7."

"November 7?"

"The anniversary of the day, in 1917, when it all began."

Director Claiborne did not ask for Hammond's formal consent, nor was he given it. They both knew he had taken the job.

11

Jimmy's toy cars were arrayed in lines, four deep, in the hallway, just in front of the door. He was now engaged in lining up behind them the entire miniature cast of *Star Wars*.

"Hey, Jimmy!" Sally Sherwin called from the living room. "Get all that junk back in your room, will you? How is anybody going to get through that door?"

"I don't want Claire to come tonight."

"You want to sit up by yourself all night? In the dark?"

"No. I want you to stay here, Mommy. You went out last night."

The child's voice was accusing, and Sally felt a surge of guilt. She was not spending enough time with Jimmy. She was out the door by 8:30 most mornings, dropping Jimmy off at the Christian School down the road. She was rarely home before 7:00, her shoulder aching from cradling a telephone most of the day in Harry Schwab's hectic Park Avenue offices. That was when she was able to dip out of the constant round of cocktail and dinner parties that were an unavoidable part of her life as a literary agent in a city that seemed to eat, drink, and dream the printed word. Jimmy spent too many evenings with Claire or with tolerant neighbors who had slightly older kids, and he was starting to make it plain that he was feeling dumped. He had more reason than usual, since she had had to abandon him last weekend to fly down to Atlanta with Harry Schwab to try to persuade a former White House aide to incorporate some sex-and-drug revelations in his turgid, shapeless manuscript to justify the half-million-dollar advance that Schwab had talked out of thin air. Weekends, she tried to stay with Jimmy—either in the studio in SoHo, or at the summer house she shared with friends on Shelter Island. Since his father was never around, the kid had the right to more than a part-time mother.

The doorbell chimed.

"Jimmy!" Her feelings of self-reproach made her sound angry. "Put that stuff away *now!*"

But instead, the boy was opening the door, and there was Claire, round, beaming, and unflappable as always. Now her own children had grown up and left home, Claire had kicked out her husband—who sat in the house drinking beer while she went out to work—and was enjoying herself with a succession of boyfriends. Her main worry, so she said, was that Sally would fire her in favor of a Haitian immigrant who was ready to work ten hours a day for thirty dollars. That had happened to one of Claire's friends. No chance, Sally had reassured her. Claire was one of the few elements of stability and continuity in Jimmy's life. That was worth a lot more than fifty dollars a day.

But Jimmy, instead of welcoming her, was shrieking and stamping his feet.

"Go away!" he yelled. "I won't let you in!"

"Jimmy!" Sally shouted as she rushed for the door, abandoning the pile of bills and invoices she had been trying to sort out. "Stop that at once!"

"You wan' me to tan your hide?" Claire's voice was benign and unperturbed. She scooped up the child and held him over her head, so that he kicked and pummeled helplessly at the air like a beetle on its back. "What's the matter with you, anyway?"

"He's not getting enough of me," said Sally.

The boy used his one available weapon—a piercing, wordless howl—until Claire put him down. Then he started running and stomping over the polished wooden floor of the apartment until he collided with Sally's prized early colonial sideboard and sent a wineglass spinning off the edge. It exploded into dozens of minute fragments.

"Go to your room!" Sally ordered the boy. She stooped to start picking up the broken glass, and promptly gashed her thumb. "Shit!"

"Let me do that." Claire moved in, comforting, competent, taking over. "You go and get ready."

But instead of changing her dress and making up her face, she went into Jimmy's room, determined somehow to make her peace with him. He was lying on his bed, looking at a book about prehistoric animals. He affected not to see her come into the room. His aloof expression was exactly that of his father. So was the hair-trigger temper.

She crouched beside him, looking over his shoulder. "Can you tell me the name of that one?" she said, pointing at the picture.

"Stegosaurus," he rapped out, as confident and contemptuous as if she had asked him to point out a dog or a cat.

"What about that one?" she asked when he turned the page.

"Tyrannosaurus. And that's a pterodactyl."

It was frightening, she thought, how fast the boy was progressing. He was at least a year beyond the others in the preschool class. He could rattle off the capitals of twenty countries, and seemed to be able to follow news headlines on television. He drew pictures of their apartment block and Central Park that looked like primitive art. And the child, brimming over with energy, hardly seemed to sleep. He would come wandering into her bedroom at midnight to show her a drawing or to chat about the events of the day. Although maybe that was because, too often, she got home only late at night. She had to make more room for him in her life, she thought as she stroked his dirty-blond hair. And she had to force Charles to do that too.

The doorbell sounded again.

Jimmy grabbed her leg with both arms as she stood up, trying to prevent her from moving. "Don't go, Mommy," he pleaded.

She picked him up and hugged him. "Listen, darling. We'll spend all weekend together. We'll do anything you want. We can go to the zoo, okay? And we can go on the C-Line ferry, all around New York. Wouldn't you like that?"

But the boy was still crying when Dick Hammond appeared in the doorway, in a suit that looked as if it had just been unpacked from an overnight bag.

"Hi, Jimmy," he said. "Look what I've got for you."

The child's curiosity overcame his wounded feelings, but not until Hammond had laid the packages on the work table, so that Jimmy did not have to receive the peace offerings from the hands of the intruder. One of the Macy's shopping bags contained a bulky plastic laser pistol. When Jimmy pulled the trigger, there was a whirring sound and a red light came on.

"I'm sorry I'm not ready," said Sally. "We're having one heck of an evening."

"I'll take you just as you are."

She felt like asking him to make it another night, but did not have the heart to break the date. Especially after his phone call. He said he wanted to take the shuttle up to New York specially to have dinner with her, and that life would be difficult for a few weeks. He had sounded anxious, even nervous, saying there were important things they had to talk over, things that would not wait. Despite his smile, she could read the lines of tension around his eyes. She had not managed to define her feelings toward him. When he had said "I love you" in bed at the Georges V, she had remained silent, feeling a shutter closing, not opening, within her. She had felt the same way when he used the same phrase on the telephone. She needed tenderness, and loyalty, and companionship. She was not sure she was ready to cope with Dick Hammond's love.

"Give me a few minutes and I'll try to rejoin the human race," she said. "Why don't you fix yourself a drink."

But when she came back, changed into a simple black dress cut deep at the back, Hammond was crouched behind the work table in Jimmy's room, acting out some stellar battle. She was grateful for his patience, his efforts to win the boy.

"Jimmy and I have made some deal," Hammond said. "We're going to watch the Giants play Sunday. And eat hot dogs. You're invited, too, of course."

"Okay." She laughed.

A good companion. Yes, Dick Hammond was that. She felt none of the giddying emotional highs that she had experienced with Charles, but none of the lows either. She had no desire to go through that roller coaster again. Maybe she had what she needed at this point in her life. A man who would cherish her and make her feel safe. She could spend the rest of her life as a single mother, wedded to an office, looking for more than that and ending up in group therapy.

Jimmy started to howl again as they left the apartment.

"I won't be late," she called back.

Dick Hammond kissed her lightly, on the cheeks, then the lips, as they waited for the elevator. He was tall and strong, with the leathery smell of the old wingback chair in her father's study. Perhaps, she thought, this was the way love should be this time around: not a single, blinding light reducing other things to background shadows, but a mellow horizon. Maybe it would work.

As long as he broke with the Agency and the Club. She was not going to marry the Club.

He had picked an overpriced restaurant specializing in the *nouvelle cuisine*, where waiters from Brooklyn rehearsed their carefully honed French accents and catered to the entrenched masochism of New York diners by treating the patrons like bums who should be thrown out on the street. Sally wished she had suggested one of her favorite places: the River Café, down by the water under the Brooklyn Bridge, or the Cuban place, Victor's Café, over on the West Side, or Mary's, the homey little trattoria tucked away in two tiny rooms in the Village. Since she had become an independent, expense-accounted career woman, she had kept a notebook full of restaurants that she used for pampering authors and publishers, while Dick was a foreigner in New York. But she had learned that a man must sometimes be allowed to take the lead, whatever the consequences.

Hammond kept his composure when their surly waiter spilled potage St. Germain over his lap. But when the waiter, clearing away the debris of the first course, removed a fork trailing bits of dressed crab from Sally's plate and placed it, with an air of deliberation, on the tablecloth in front of her, Hammond summoned the maître d'. He pointed out that this was what he expected in a corner bistro, not a four-star restaurant.

"I'm sorry, monsieur," said the maître d' in his Maurice Chevalier accent, "all the waiters here are sixty-three."

"This is surrealistic," said Hammond. "I don't see what the age of the waiter has to do with it. Anyway, our waiter does not look sixty-three. Look, he's got black hair."

"Ah, monsieur, some of them dye their hair to look younger."

He carried the fork away between two fingers, straight-faced;

136

the joke was evidently meant for his private amusement, not that of the guests.

"I came to a place like this with Charles once," said Sally. "The service was so lousy that he decided that he wouldn't give a tip. At the end of the meal, he calls over the waiter and held a twenty-dollar bill under his nose. He told him that normally he might have given a tip that size, but it hadn't been earned. You could see the waiter's nose twitching. Then Charles said he wouldn't want anyone to make out he was a cheapskate, and he took a match and set fire to the twenty, right in front of the waiter. I thought the guy was going to throw a punch at him."

Halfway into the anecdote, Sally realized that she shouldn't have embarked on it. Hammond looked bleak. What on earth had inspired her to mention Charles?

"Have you seen him lately?" Hammond asked.

"He comes to pick up Jimmy sometimes. He seems to enjoy playing the bachelor."

"I talked to him on the phone."

"And?"

"Oh, nothing. Just going over some of the old times. He said he hoped you were happy."

Comparisons, she thought. *I must never make comparisons.*

She gave him her hand, across the table, to reassure him.

To change the subject and lighten the conversation, she started telling him about some of Harry Schwab's latest discoveries.

"You wouldn't believe our latest author. She goes around in a feather boa and a sequined dress slit to the navel. She calls herself Jacqueline Jolie."

"That has to be a pen name."

"It is. She's from Queens. Would you believe, her first book isn't even written, and Harry's already arranged a floor of a quarter million dollars for the paperback rights."

"My God." Then Hammond asked, "What's a floor?"

"A floor is when a paperback house sets the base price in an auction. It gets the right to top the highest bid that is made."

"Okay," said Hammond. "I see that your trade has its mysteries too. What's the book about?"

"Wait for this, Dick. The title is *How to Get It Up and Keep It Up*. She wrote it with her boyfriend."

137

"Are you allowed to sell something like that in a family bookstore?"

"I can't wait to read the whole thing. It's written in this deadpan style, but every paragraph makes me break up. We had just one chapter to show the publishers. It's called 'The Grip.'"

"'The Grip'?"

"Jacqueline makes out she's really writing for the female audience, and she says one of the secrets of a good sex life is getting the right grip on your man. She says the ideal grip is somewhere between your grip on a golf club and your grip on a frying-pan handle."

"Ouch," said Hammond, making an imaginary swing with his hands. "What kind of club does she mean? Is she talking about a putting shot or the grand slam? I'm ashamed of you, Sally. Who buys this kind of stuff, anyway?"

"You'd be surprised. Any title that starts with 'How to' has got a chance of bestsellerdom in this country, especially if it's on sex or money. Look at that runaway best-seller that came out after the last elections, *How to Profit from World War III.*" Charles would say, she thought, that that was because America remained a country of problem-solvers, where people still believed that with a little application there was a rational answer to everything, from incontinence to insolvency.

"I read in one of the gossip columns that your boss has been wrangling with one of the publishers, who said that all these huge advances were driving real literature out of the bookstores."

"Oh, that was Milton Verger," said Sally. Verger was head of an independent family firm whose authors collected a lot of literary prizes but failed to impress the bookstore chains. "He talks as if it's immoral to make money in publishing. As if a book lacks literary depth unless the stores return it by the thousands. I don't think it's wrong to publish page-turners. Even if some of them could do with a little more editing. I don't think Milton Verger has the right to dictate what the public ought to read or what authors ought to earn."

Hammond had stopped listening. He was kneading bread crumbs, evidently trying to work out how to initiate the serious part of the conversation.

"I can't tell you how much I missed you," he said at last. "It seems like months since that night in the Georges V."

She had tied up her long blond hair, and the slope of her neck was like ivory against the black dress. But the wine had brought a rosy flush to her cheeks, and her lips were moist with it.

"I missed you too, Dick."

"We've both been through the hoops," he said. "We're not teenagers."

"Speak for yourself."

"What I mean is, I've led a pretty full life, and I've played the field, and I could have become cynical. I guess I *was* fairly cynical about women before I met you."

Oh God, she was thinking, *why does he have to sound so trite and clumsy?* And then she was concerned about her own reactions. Sensing what he was building up to, why did she feel like a detached observer? Was it that she did not feel enough for him, or that she could not feel enough for any man?

"You're what I need, Sally. I'm not interested in other women. I know you have your own life, your job, your son. I understand that you'll need your own breathing space. But I want you to marry me."

Even then, she felt no rush of excitement. The words passed by her, like a poster viewed from a car along the motorway.

"Sally?" He was waiting. The big man looked boyish, so vulnerable to what she would say.

"There's something you haven't explained," she said. She fingered the intricate gold cross, inlaid with precious stones, that hung from a chain around her neck. It had been fashioned for her by her uncle, Max Zimmer, who had copied it from a Byzantine original in the workshop in a corner of his garage where he sought relief through the goldsmith's art from insomnia and the terrifying irresolution of his work at the Agency. In his pastimes, Max Zimmer sought the joy of the finite—the fish that could be landed, the piece of jewelry sufficient unto itself, the rose that would blossom and die. It was a necessary compensation for a vocation in which it was rarely possible to draw a line across the page and say that there was an end of the affair; one mystery opened into another. For the service of this vocation, Sally reflected, the Agency had rewarded Max with a pink slip and public disgrace.

"When I came back from Paris," he said, "I was determined to leave the Agency. I meant everything that I said to you. But I can't pull out. Not yet."

"When do you think you'll be ready, Dick? When you're sixty? I don't think you'll ever break with the Agency. Not unless they treat you the way they treated Uncle Max. It's in your blood."

"It's not that way, Sally. There's a very major crisis that I've been asked to field."

"There usually is."

"This one is so big that frankly—well—I'm awed by it. I just can't stand apart from it. And if you knew what it was you wouldn't respect me for one minute if I were to back away."

"Tell me about it."

"I'm sorry." He reached for her hand, but she moved it away. How could he tell her that he was engaged in an investigation of the penetration of the Agency by a Soviet mole, and that the leading suspect was her uncle?

"What do I have to do to get a clearance—marry you?" She sounded bitter, remembering how Charles, in the name of official secrecy, had kept her in the dark about things that affected their personal lives.

"I promise I'll tell you when it's all over. It's not a matter of years. It's a matter of weeks. Sally, don't look away. Look at me. Please."

She gave him a depthless glance, her mind focused on a scene in a Moscow park four years before, when Charles had sent her, confused and uncomprehending, with baby Jimmy in a pram to meet a Soviet agent.

"Sally, don't let this come between us. You know you are the most important thing in my life."

"That's not true. If it were true, you'd break with the Agency."

"You'll understand, Sally. Later. I promise you'll understand. This is something that affects all of us."

"That's what you all say. You, Charles, Uncle Max. It's what you'll always say."

12

BAIKONUR COSMODROME, KAZAKHSTAN,
September 28

Marshal Safronov looked down over the gray-brown steppes of Central Asia as the Tupolev 134 began its slow descent toward the landing strip, near the village of Tyuratam. Away to the west was the misty blue of the Aral Sea. Farther away, to the east, was the secret center at Saryshagan where the seminal discoveries in the beam-weapons program had been successfully tested. It was from Saryshagan that the weapon the marshal called Razrukha had been carried to the Cosmodrome on a special armored train, the precious components carefully camouflaged on their platform cars to hide them from the spy cameras of the Americans' orbiting satellites, thousands of miles above.

Here, in the wilds of Kazakhstan, in a province of the Russian Empire that the czars stole from China, Soviet scientists had been working for decades to turn the unthinkable into usable tools of war. Shut up in secret laboratory complexes whose names were never published, working under semi-monastic conditions, the best graduates of the scientific academies had been assigned to extend the frontiers of the possible, not for the sake of knowledge or to improve the human condition, but to enable the Soviet Union to inflict total defeat on the United States. Some of their research involved weapons that still existed only in the pages of fantasy magazines: antigravitational devices, reverse lasers designed to create a darkness that no light would penetrate, a method of decomposing photons that would make a military target temporarily invisible. Some of the major experiments had literally blown up in the scientists' faces. But there had been uncontested triumphs as well. At Saryshagan and at Semipalatinsk, the marshal's scientists were perfecting ground-based particle-beam weapons intended to shoot down American missiles and planes. From Baikonur Cosmodrome, where he now headed, small killer satellites had been put into orbit and successfully tested in space. They were designed to destroy their targets by converging on them and exploding into a thousand fragments. They were no match for the Americans' Blue Savior program. Blue Savior was no secret to Safronov—or to any serious newspaper reader in the United States. A report on the acceleration of the American space-weaponry program had appeared on the front pages of the East Coast press, and well-meaning columnists had been fulminating against the "militarization of man's last frontier." But in a matter of weeks, Blue Savior would be only a memory, a scrap of paper torn from the drawing board. Razrukha was the vindication of an excursion along the wilder shores of science that had lasted for decades and cost billions of rubles. After November 7, when it was put into orbit, Razrukha would change the world. Marshal Safronov had no doubt of it. Safronov mentally rehearsed the ultimatum he would issue to the United States. He would order the Americans to dismantle their own Blue Savior project and withdraw their forces from West Germany. That would be the first installment. If the Americans submitted, further, more difficult demands would follow. Adding up to total surrender. If the Americans refused the demands, he would demonstrate what Razrukha could do to the population of the Eastern Seaboard.

The marshal had not discussed all of his plans with his colleagues on the Politburo. They knew about Razrukha, of course. His rival Strokin, the chairman of the KGB, had actually helped—indirectly—in the project. Disinformation spread by KGB double agents in Washington had helped to keep the Americans in ignorance about Razrukha. However, Safronov saw no need to consult the other members of the leadership on how he would use the Razrukha weapon once it was deployed. By that stage, he calculated, he would be strong enough to hire or fire them at will.

He frowned at the thought of the one event that could still interfere with his design. Ushinsky's defection meant the Americans were now alerted—if they believed what the traitor had told them. It had also had the effect of making Safronov more dependent on the KGB, for the moment, than he found comfortable. Krylov's section at Moscow Center had taken on the task of trying to discredit the defector and deflect his information. And the marshal knew that Krylov was not among his admirers. Even less so than Strokin. Furthermore, many GRU agents had been recalled from the United States because of fears that Ushinsky might betray their identities. This meant that communications with the terrorist Sammy Hamad were now being handled by a KGB agent, a New York bookseller. This was another source of vulnerability, the marshal felt—especially since Sammy Hamad had a role in his plans that he had not, so far, seen fit to confide to the chairman of the KGB. Or to the gathering of trusted officers that the traitor Ushinsky had attended. The marshal could at least be thankful for *that*.

But these were all transient problems, Safronov reassured himself. Everything would be resolved after November 7.

The marshal and his entourage—which included a squad of Spetsnaz commandos, a personal bodyguard he insisted on maintaining, over the mild protestations of some of his colleagues on the Politburo—deplaned and boarded a fleet of waiting olive-drab cars. The Baikonur Cosmodrome was a vast complex, the Soviet answer to Cape Canaveral, and had been the launch site for most of the famous Russian space flights, including the voyage of the world's first cosmonaut, Yuri Gagarin, on April 12, 1961. From the back seat of his staff car, the marshal watched a gray-green bus pull up in front of a massive concrete buiding. Two men in bright-red spacesuits, with black boots and matching white helmets with the initials CCCP painted in bold letters above the clear face-masks, got out. They were cosmonauts on their way from their barracks to submit to simulator tests, perhaps on the whirling, terrifying centrifuge that duplicated the effects of the acceleration of gravitation during takeoff and landing.

Over to the left, Safronov could see the tall green work towers, like colossal oil derricks, where the new launch site was being prepared. According to his plan, there would be two independent launches from the Baikonur Cosmodrome on November 7. The satellite containing the beam weapon would be carried up into orbit, three thousand miles above the earth's surface, by a Lenin X booster, an enormous silver-gray monster, with a thrust three times as powerful as the Americans' Saturn 5 that now lay concealed in an underground bombproofed shelter. At the same time, a three-man crew would be sent up in a winged, reusable spacecraft, a primitive but serviceable version of the American space shuttle. The cosmonauts would rendezvous with the Razrukha satellite in space and oversee the process by which it would be coupled to a permanent, manned station that the Russians had sent into orbit the previous year. The space station already contained the extra fuel tanks that Razrukha required to become operational. The Americans, in conceding a clear lead to the Russians in the development and deployment of permanent manned space stations, had apparently ignored their military-support potential. With modules docked around a central core, the space station that was to become the home of Razrukha resembled a wheel without a rim.

Safronov's driver followed the lead car along a road that led away from the launch pad toward a cluster of anonymous, heavily guarded buildings. They stopped before a pair of huge, twelve-inch-thick steel panels that slid noiselessly back on rails at the push of a button by someone inside once the visitors' identity had been verified. Inside was an asphalt-covered forecourt, surrounded by blank walls, with no visible exit once the steel panels had slid shut behind the visitors' cars.

"The Mousetrap," Safronov murmured.

An unwanted visitor who somehow managed to bluff his way past the steel gates would get no further. The forecourt was a perfect killing ground. The thirty-foot walls around it were as smooth and polished as glass. And there was no sign of a door.

Then a panel in the wall ahead slid open—downward, into the ground, not sideways—and Chief Designer Berzin appeared.

Berzin led the marshal and his aides into a modest, airless room with bright-green walls and cheap, cream-upholstered furniture that was the headquarters of the final phase of Project Razrukha. The only decoration on the walls, apart from the obligatory official portraits of Lenin and General Secretary Manilov, were photographs of some of the Soviet inventors and apparatchiks whose work had paved the way for Razrukha: Tsiolkovsky, the legendary rocket designer; Korolev, who organized the first space flights; and Kapitsa, the scientific adviser to Khrushchev who had first won the Kremlin's approval for a huge secret budget for

144

beam-weapons development. All of them, the marshal briefly reflected as he sat down on an uncomfortable straight-backed chair, had been Soviet. Impeccably Soviet.

That could not be said for the fidgety old man in a mauve cardigan and baggy brown pants who was waiting for them in the chief designer's office. Klaus Milstein. The senior adviser to Project Razrukha. Milstein was .a native of Germany. And as if that were not bad enough, the marshal thought as he curtly acknowledged the scientist's awkward greetings, Milstein was a Jew.

There was no denying Milstein's genius. The superweapon that would go into orbit on its space station on November 7 was the direct result of the research that Milstein had done with M. S. Rabinovich at the Lebedev Institute in Moscow in the early sixties. Milstein had proved to be equally pathbreaking when it came to developing the practical applications of the early equations in which he had proved the theoretical possibility of generating the incredible quantities of pulsed energy that could drive a killer beam through space to wipe out whole populations without breaking a single window. Chief Designer Berzin would get the medals, but it was Milstein who had made the project happen, supervising the tests of his beam accelerator at Saryshagan. Even now, it was Klaus Milstein, rather than Berzin, who was in charge of the final delicate operation of readying the huge killer satellite for the launch.

Marshal Safronov accepted the need for Klaus Milstein. But he did not like this nervous, mousy, self-effacing man. And he did not trust him. How was it possible to trust a German Jew who was naive enough, after all his years in the Soviet Union, to believe that the Razrukha project was designed to bring peace to the world? Two years before, in an address to the Pugwash group, Klaus Milstein had fervently argued the need to free the world from the fear of mass destruction in nuclear war. The marshal had not the slightest doubt that Milstein had honestly believed what he had said. The scientist, then deeply engaged in beam-weapon experiments, had really been convinced that the discovery of an entirely new generation of armaments would make the Bomb obsolete. In his abstracted way, he had probably never considered that the engine of ultimate terror that he had constructed might actually be used. Nor, in all likelihood, had he given much thought to what it could mean in Marshal Safronov's hands. The marshal did not intend to enlighten him

"I want to see the control center," Safronov announced.

They entered the room adjacent to the chief designer's office. The entire wall on the left looked like the door of a safe. In order to open it, Berzin had to insert an identification card into a computerized scanner, submit to a voice check, and finally punch out a combination on a panel beside the wheel that took the place of a handle. The whole process, Safronov noted, took seventy seconds. Too long, he judged.

The huge armored door gave access to a stark, boxlike elevator that carried them a tenth of a mile underground. At the exit, they boarded a monorail train that sped them along in the general direction of the main launch pad.

As Marshal Safronov entered the control center, followed by Chief Designer Berzin and Air Force General Osipov, the chief of staff of Strategic Rocket Forces, there was a general clatter as technicians jumped from their stools and stood to attention. The marshal waved them back to their places. The room was only dimly lit. There was a soft blue flow from the dozens of video monitors that filled one wall. The marshal peered at one of the screens. It showed a slate-black sky, blacker than he had ever seen from the ground, the blackness of outer space. Farther along, a bank of monitors showed the star-shaped space station, and cosmonauts moving about between the command satellite and the outlying modules.

"This is the tracking room," Berzin commented gratuitously. From here, we'll be able to monitor every detail of Razrukha's docking procedure. The pictures are relayed instantaneously from our tracking stations at Talsi and Kirzhach."

They moved on into the launch-control room. Operators dressed in black coveralls were rehearsing at a long bank of monitoring instruments. Colored lights flashed red, green, and yellow. "Bleed-off," recited a man wearing headphones. "Hold. . . . Ignition. . . . Switch to launch. . . . Lift-off." He checked each rehearsed command against a chronometer and the gauges on his command console, while pictures of the launch pad were flashed onto a large screen via a periscopic videocamera.

It was the last room that interested Safronov. The sanctum

146

sanctorum of Project Razrukha. There was no air of bustle in this room. Its only occupants, apart from the security men at the door, were two communications technicians manning what looked like a futuristic switchboard. There was a single large video monitor on the wall. The dominant item of furniture was a big semicircular desk, fitted with a battery of telephones and a miniature television. Inset at the center of the desk, under a shield of unbreakable plastic, was an eight-button command console.

Marshal Safronov gestured toward the empty swivel chair behind the desk.

"That's your seat, General," he said to Osipov. "Why don't you try it out?"

Obedient, General Osipov lowered his heavy frame into the chair. Then, with the chief designer as his instructor, he practiced the procedures he would follow if the order came from Moscow to unleash the weapon called Razrukha.

"We should all be scared of you, Osipov," the marshal joked. "No man before you will ever have held so much power under the tip of his index finger."

Safronov noted that one man in the neon-lit, surgically white room did not appear to approve of his casual remark. Klaus Milstein shuffled and twitched and tugged at his carroty wisp of a beard.

"Is something wrong with you, Milstein?"

The marshal looked into Milstein's frightened, watery eyes and knew. The scientist, watching General Osipov's sausagelike finger poised over the button, had finally begun to understand that what he had invented was not a laboratory toy. Nor the white dove of peace.

Razrukha was ultimate terror, and was made to be used.

Marshal Safronov resolved that the German Jew would have to be removed before November 7.

13

Following Trudy Cook along the brightly lit corridors of what had once been Max Zimmer's domain, it struck Dick Hammond that she had the gait of a vastly overgrown Pekingese. He had always disliked the breed. His grandmother in Charleston had kept one, and it had terrorized him as a schoolboy until one day his father, grown comfortable and portly since his retirement from the Navy, had plopped down onto a chintzy sofa by the window overlooking the bay. There had been an ominous crunch that did not sound like protesting springs, and that was the end of Taipan. Fortunately, Hammond's grandmother had been out of the room at the time. The rear admiral, who lived in awe of her, pressed a finger to his lips, enjoining the boy to silence, while he hastily concealed the remains inside a big vase of gardenias. Dick Hammond grinned to himself at the memory and wondered what sound Trudy Cook would make if you jumped on her.

Poor Trudy. She was not born to be one of the beautiful people. Her square, shapeless trunk wobbled along on little stubby legs. She wore thick, moon-shaped glasses on a peg of a nose that looked as if it had been struck on her flat, saucerlike face as an afterthought. She trotted around in nondescript tentlike dresses that exaggerated her girth instead of concealing it, her hair tied up carelessly in a bun that always seemed to be unraveling. How old was she now? Hammond wondered. Forty-two, forty-three? Trudy had never found her man, and was not likely to find him now. Trudy was the bride of the Agency, one of those indispensable spinsters with a memory as reliable as a computerized data bank and another quality for which no computer could substitute: the

148

ability to smell out the hidden connections between seemingly unrelated facts.

Trudy stopped in front of a sealed door and inserted a plastic card in the combination lock before punching a series of numbers. There was a short electronic beep, and the door clicked open.

"After you, Don Ricardo." Trudy waved him through into the top-security vault. As Hammond walked in, Trudy playfully pinched at the seat of his trousers, and he heard her stifled giggle.

Trudy Cook was unlikely to marry, but she was certainly not a nun.

Hammond remembered vividly the scene at Langley a few years before when she had calmly announced that someone had to drive her to a hospital immediately, because she was about to give birth to a baby. The first reaction was general disbelief. Those tentlike dresses had protected Trudy's secret for more than eight months. They called in someone with paramedical experience, and he confirmed that she was indeed pregnant, and the baby could arrive within an hour. Panic ensued. Trudy's boss, Les Winter, had piled her into his own car and driven like Mario Andretti to the nearest hospital. They almost made it.

According to the story that circulated around Langley afterward, Trudy's contractions started in the car, and the baby was starting to come by the time Les Winter pulled up, in a screech of burning rubber, in front of the hospital. The baby was actually born on the greensward in front of the main entrance, while Winter ran inside screaming, "Baby, baby!" The delivery was astonishingly effortless, and a midwife appeared in time to cut the umbilical cord and remove the placenta. Afterward, when the Agency received a bill from the hospital that included the cost of a delivery room, Winter responded with a curt note recalling the circumstances of the birth. The hospital sent back a revised bill that included a four-dollar charge for "greens fees."

Trudy had been entirely calm about the whole episode, and studiously vague about the identity of the father of her newborn son. It was only after she christened him Lester Frobisher—as in Lester Frobisher Winter—that her boss insisted that she must come clean. It was evident to all of Winter's colleagues that Trudy idolized him. In all the years they had worked together in the Reports and Requirements section of the Agency's Soviet Division, it had seemed that in Trudy's eyes Les Winter could do no wrong; anyone who crossed him earned her bitter enmity. This, combined with her decision to call her baby by not just one but *both* of Winter's Christian names occasioned the inevitable flow of gossip. Trudy finally owned up to a one-night fling with a Marine guard in Bonn, in the course of a working trip when she had gone with Winter to inspect a double-agent operation. She did not want the Marine to be informed; and he—a married man with a couple of kids already—most certainly would not have been overjoyed to hear from *her*. Trudy insisted on her right to exist as a single mother, and her record was such that after a little head-scratching in Soviet Division she was permitted to return to work after three months' leave.

"How long have you worked with Les?" Hammond asked her as they walked past the computer terminals into the arc-lit bays where raw files were kept.

"Twelve years, seven months and—uh—seventeen days. Since Les was first assigned to Soviet Division."

"You remember to the exact day?"

"Sure. I've got a good memory for details."

When she grinned, he thought, you could almost forget she was ugly.

"You were never in the field, were you?"

She shook her head. "Only on special assignment."

"You've traveled quite a bit with Les, though, haven't you?"

"Oh yes. London. Bonn. Melbourne. We're not quite as sedentary in Reports as some of you guys out on station seem to think."

Trudy had the file that Hammond had asked for. The file on Hussar. He was surprised at how slender it was. It contained routine liaison material from the Firm, and a note recording Ushinsky's allegations about how Hussar had met his end, and that was virtually all. One of the British documents mentioned Hammond's friend, Charles Canning, as the case officer who had handled Hussar in Moscow, and described their clandestine meets, mostly on public buses and in the men's rooms of popular restaurants. There was nothing on the case that had been compiled by Max Zimmer, not even a handwritten note. That struck Hammond as particularly odd, since as chief of the counterintelligence staff at the time, Max would have been expected to review the Hussar affair. His commentaries on similar cases had sometimes run to book length.

"Is this all?" Hammond asked.

"That's it," Trudy Cook said offhandedly. She was squatting on the edge of a table, swinging her heels in the air.

"It can't be," Hammond insisted, disbelieving. "Where is Max Zimmer's report on the case?"

"You better ask Max."

"What do you mean?"

"Where were you during the Christmas Massacre?" The phrase was in-house slang for the purge of Max Zimmer and his close lieutenants.

"Down in Miami. Chasing Cubans."

"Well, I don't think it's an overwhelming secret," she went on. "Les saw it coming. He tried to persuade the director to seal off Max's archives to make sure nothing went missing. But the director wouldn't hear of it. We're supposed to be honorable men, aren't we? The result was that when Max moved out, we found that his files had been cleaned out too. Especially liaison stuff from London and Tel Aviv. Max didn't believe that anyone could be trusted with our allies' secrets except him. At least, that's one explanation."

"Meaning?"

"That's what Director Clairborne is paying you to find out, isn't he, sweetie? But I don't think you're going to find it in here."

The first thing Dick Hammond did when he got back to the temporary office that had been rigged up for him on the seventh floor was to check out his messages. He had been trying to reach two men for the past twenty-four hours, but had only been able to get through to their answering services. Charles Canning, he found, had at last returned his call. Max Zimmer had not.

Hammond's secretary managed to track Canning down at the 21 Club in New York.

"All that high living in Manhattan can't be healthy for you," Hammond told the Englishman. "Why don't you come see how poor workin' folks live in the nation's capital?"

"Sally told me she saw you," Canning said. Mindful of what Dicky Prince had told him in Bermuda about the new defector, he was glad of the chance to see his Agency friend. "Have you got something special going?" the Englishman asked obliquely.

151

"It concerns an old friend of yours."

"Right. When and where do we meet?"

Hammond nominated a smart French restaurant called La Fleur.

When he had finished his call, he buzzed his secretary and asked her to try Max's number again.

"I tried five minutes ago, Mr. Hammond," she said. "All I'm getting is that recorded voice."

"Do we know if Mr. Zimmer's left town?"

"Not so far as we're aware."

Dammit, Hammond thought. Why didn't Max return his calls?

He glanced at the newspapers, which he had not had time to digest all morning. There was a photograph on an inside page of some Russians at Kennedy Airport. A Soviet official called Miagkov was grinning at the cameraman. He had delivered a speech at the UN attacking the United States for developing space weapons and calling for an international ban on killer satellites. Looking more closely at the picture, Hammond could see the back of the head of a dark-haired man in dark glasses who was trying to hide his face from the cameraman. The Russians were about to board an Aeroflot flight back to Moscow.

The direct line from Director Claiborne's office purred, and Hammond picked up the red phone.

"How are you making out?" Claiborne barked.

"I'm just trying to bone up on the files," Hammond replied. "That is, what's left of them."

"I don't want to hassle you, Dick. But things are starting to hot up. I want you to come over to my office right away."

To his surprise, Hammond found that Les Winter was already ensconced in the director's office.

"When the statements of that Israeli double agent started to appear in print," Claiborne began, "I didn't think much of them. This Agency has had its fill of press smears, and Max Zimmer seems to attract them like a magnet attracts pins. But I'm starting to worry that what we've got here is more than just another piece of irresponsible reporting. Tell him, Les."

"Martini has made contact again," Winter said, coming straight to the point.

"When?" Hammond had learned that there had been a gap of several months since the agent called Martini had reported. He refused to maintain contact with the Agency while he was in

Moscow, so meetings could be arranged only when he was traveling abroad.

"This week?"

"Where? In Europe?"

"No." Les Winter looked at Director Claiborne, who nodded. Then he added, "In New York."

"Did he know about Ushinsky's defection?"

"Martini did not know the name of the defector. But he said that one of Krylov's people at Moscow Center had been indiscreet, boasting about the hoax they were going to pull on the Americans. He said he had heard that Krylov was sending us an empty vessel." The phrase was spy jargon for a defector who was only carrying the information that his masters wanted to pass on to his new hosts, and had no significant knowledge of his own. "But Martini did not know any of the details."

"Well, that doesn't prove much," Hammond observed.

"No, but Martini gave us a couple of other things that may impress you more." Winter had adopted the professorial tone that he always affected when he thought he had the winning argument. "He gave us some more material from Department T. It includes current intelligence requirements for Soviet scientific espionage in the United States—a shopping list issued by Moscow Center to agents in the field. We're still having it processed and evaluated. But we've reached one very significant conclusion."

"What's that?"

"If the Soviets are still trying to steal our space-shuttle technology and other technical secrets that are listed in Martini's shopping list, then it's extremely unlikely that they have developed the skills to construct this Death Beam thing or to put it into space."

"Does that necessarily follow?" Hammond spoke cautiously, putting his half-formed thought in the form of a question. "Couldn't they be interested all the same in what stage we've reached? Surely they would want to know how closely we are to catching up to them in the space-weapons race."

"Perhaps," Winter conceded. "We'll leave that to the scientific experts. Let's stick to what you need to know. Here's what that is, Dick. Martini says that Krylov had a source inside the Agency."

Hammond held his breath, waiting for the rest.

"Martini says," Winter resumed, "that this source had good

153

access to the British and particularly the Israelis. He laid a lot of stress on the Israeli angle. He says that some reports from this source reached Moscow via Israel."

The parallel with the press accounts of the allegations of the Israeli agent, Judah Klugmann, were already obvious to Hammond.

Winter paused for dramatic effect before delivering the coup de grace. "And what about this, Dick," he said. "Martini also states that reports from this source inside the Agency dried up about the time Max Zimmer left the Agency."

Winter beamed at Director Claiborne. "I think that just about wraps it up," concluded the chief of Soviet Division.

"Well, Dick?" Adam Claiborne asked. "What do you think?"

Hammond put his fist under his chin, concentrating hard as he tried to rearrange the handful of facts—if they were facts—that Les Winter had presented.

"Do we bring the Bureau in on this?" Claiborne prodded him. "Do we pull Max in for questioning? You tell me. You're supposed to be in charge of this investigation."

"No," Hammond said, responding belatedly to the director's questions. "Let's take it bit by bit. Les," he went on, turning to the chief of Soviet Division, "if I'm right, Martini never talked about a mole in the Agency before now. Or did he?"

"No."

"And in fact, Martini told us that Hussar had been detected by routine KGB surveillance."

"Right."

"Then how come Martini is spouting about a mole—for the first time—just a few days after we got a defector who was talking about the same thing?"

Winter shrugged. "Coincidence," he suggested. "Martini doesn't work in Krylov's office. He didn't know about a mole before. He only found out because of a colleague's indiscretion."

"Do you believe in coincidences, Les?"

"It happens."

"Now listen," Director Claiborne broke in. "I want some action. I want to know who's going to do what. And I want you to know, Dick, that in my book Max Zimmer now ranks as the number-one suspect in this investigation."

"Okay." Hammond could not argue with that statement. "But let's remember that we have no evidence as yet. And we can't just kidnap Max and lock him up in a safe house to undergo hostile interrogation."

"Well, I'm waiting to hear how you want to handle it."

"First, I want to go see Max. Talk to him. See whether I can persuade him to part with those files he borrowed from the archives. Then I want to go to Israel and check out this supposed Klugmann connection."

Hammond did not mention that he also intended to talk to Hussar's British case officer.

"Well, get moving," Director Claiborne said.

ALEXANDRIA, VA., *September 30*

Jerry Sarkesian drove Hammond out to the rambling house outside Arlington where Max Zimmer had been living, alone with his cats, since he was purged from the Agency. Jerry had pushed the driver's seat in the little Volkswagen back as far as it would go, but Hammond still marveled at how he had been able to settle his formidable girth behind the wheel. Jerry, resplendent in a bright-pink shirt, floral tie, and check sport coat, looked as if he would have been more at home selling rugs in an Istanbul bazaar.

There had been no answer from Max Zimmer's phone, though Dick Hammond had called repeatedly. Each time, he got the same recorded answer: "We are not at home. . . ." Max had not returned his calls. But as far as anyone knew, he had not left town. So Hammond had decided simply to drop by uninvited.

He realized before they pulled up in front of the house that it had been a mistake to bring Jerry along. The arrival of the two of them would make the interview look too official, especially since Jerry was from the Office of Security. But Hammond had wanted someone with him who was more familiar than he was with the handling of the previous investigations into alleged leaks from the Agency, and Jerry had the advantage—like Dick Hammond himself—that he was respected by all factions. Anyway, it was too late to turn back now. As they pulled up in front of the old shingled

155

house with its wide porch, Hammond saw a curtain move in one of the front windows. As he climbed out of the Volkswagen, a neighbor's dog started yapping.

Though it was late morning, Max opened the door in his robe and carpet slippers, peering at his unwanted visitors through thick bifocals that magnified his eyes to twice their real size, his massive head lolling on his narrow shoulders as if it were about to roll off. In his hand he was clutching a large plastic cocktail shaker, half filled with black coffee.

"Sorry to roust you out, Max," Hammond apologized.

"I was working most of the night." Max Zimmer did not specify what he had been working on. He might have been crafting gold jewelry, one of the hobbies to which he resorted during his frequent bouts of insomnia, or translating the sonnets of Rainer Maria Rilke, or puzzling again over the cases he had failed to solve in all his years of counterintelligence.

Max Zimmer did not invite his visitors to come in. He merely turned on his heel and walked back into his living room, assuming they would follow. A fat white cat arched its back and bristled as Hammond entered the house.

An old tea chest, full of books, was in the middle of the living-room floor. Hammond noticed that several of the shelves of the bookcase that lined the walls had been completely cleaned out.

"Are you moving, Max?"

"I've had my dose of Washington," said the retired spymaster.

Hammond glanced at Jerry Sarkesian. Max did not offer them coffee. The room reeked of stale tobacco. Max, a chain smoker, was taking deep pulls on a Lucky Strike, spilling cigarette ash down the front of his robe. He had long given up taking care of himself and had no one to care for him. *Except his sister, Phyllis,* Hammond thought. Sally's mother.

"Are you going down to Miami?" Hammond asked.

Max Zimmer responded with an indeterminate grunt.

"Look, Max," Hammond continued, "you know about the defector." It was well known at Langley that Max Zimmer still had a network of old-timers inside the Agency, loyalists who kept him briefed on what was going on. "You know what he told us about Hussar. What you believed all along. That Hussar was betrayed by someone inside the Agency."

Zimmer grunted again.

156

"You were the first man in the Agency to be briefed by the British."

Zimmer stubbed out his cigarette in an ashtray that was already overflowing. A small cloud of ash rose in the stuffy room.

"Max," Hammond persevered, "I think you should know that some very disturbing allegations have been made."

"I read the newspapers."

"If that were all, we wouldn't be taking it so seriously. But we're getting the same kind of stuff from one of our own agents. He claims that Moscow Center had a source on the counterintelligence staff that dried up when you left the Agency."

Hammond paused for a reply, but none came.

"Well?" he said at last.

"I didn't realize that you'd asked a question," said Max. "May I know the identity of this agent you're quoting?"

"His code name is Martini."

"Martini is a cocktail," Zimmer said derisively. "A cocktail of lies. People who don't know how to handle their liquor get drunk on that kind of thing."

"Max, I have an open mind," Hammond appealed to him. "I'm not here to pass judgment. I'm here to ask for your help. There are files that are missing. We need them to get to the bottom of this business."

"And you think I've got them?" Max got up and started pacing the room, visibly angry now, waving his narrow, tubular arms around like a scarecrow blown by the wind. "Take a look around. You can tear the roof off for all I care. You're not the first to ask. Jerry's asked." He nodded to Sarkesian. "Others have looked without asking. Les Winter has sent contract thieves in here to rip out the floorboards."

Hammond's face registered his surprise, and Max Zimmer said, "Oh, there's a lot you have to learn about Les Winter. But you'll have to do your own homework. I'm through. Finished. Retired. Kaput. Have you got it?" Zimmer started to cough, a horrible liquid cough from far down in his chest, but he recovered himself and added, "And if you and Jerry want to grill me, you can come back here with a cop and an arrest warrant. I'm not volunteering a damned thing."

Max Zimmer did not ask them to leave. He just walked out of the room. Hammond heard a door slam inside the house.

157

Sarkesian said, "Don't push it too far. Not yet."

So they left without saying goodbye, and the fat cat darted away in front of Hammond as if it feared it was going to be struck.

"I don't know why the Agency picked *you* for this," Max called out. "But I'll offer you just one piece of advice. You'll never finish the puzzle until you get inside the mind of Krylov at Moscow Center and see it through his eyes."

"How do you recommend that I do that?"

Max Zimmer, the poetaster, quoted William Blake: "If you would know the devil, find out his system."

As Dick Hammond stood, mystified, in the driveway, Max dragged down his venetian blind. The white cat watched them from the porch until the Volkswagen drove off.

As he wandered his unruly house, throwing books into packing cases, Max Zimmer brooded on the mission of his unwelcome visitors. How Krylov in Moscow must welcome his discomfiture, he thought. The Agency had turned on him, Max believed, because he had persisted in telling unpalatable truths. Winter had led the pack in the old days, and Max was convinced that Les Winter was leading the pack again. There were plenty of people who would join in. Dick Hammond might mean well enough, but he did not grasp the first principles of counterintelligence. Few people did.

The counterintelligence staff are unpopular inside any intelligence service. That is in the nature of their calling, which is to second-guess their colleagues, and to ferret out signs of hostile penetration and deception. No case officer out in the field who has just succeeded in smuggling out a Soviet defector or recruiting a valuable double agent wants to be told that he has merely fallen victim to a KGB plant. No station chief who has just learned of a glittery opportunity to channel covert support to a secret resistance movement in a Communist country wants to be informed that he is actually dealing with a network of agents provocateurs. No secret servant enjoys having his private life and his operational record raked over for evidence that he may himself have been compromised or recruited by a foreign power. Within the Agency, few people outside Max Zimmer's staff believed that the Soviet spy chiefs were as complex and devious as he made them out to be. Many resented the counterintelligence staff as a cabal behind locked doors whose paranoid suspicions prevented others from getting on with their jobs. Some talked as if Max had exceeded his brief as the Agency's institutional devil's advocate and become the devil incarnate. Max's personal style only added to such complaints. He had refused to share his files with other sections of the Agency, but insisted on his right to go through theirs. His mole hunts through the corridors of Langley became notorious; the careers of more than a dozen Agency staffers were blighted when his suspicion fell on them like a spring frost, yet he failed to come up with conclusive proofs of treason. On his own initiative, he went to the head of the French secret service and told him not to share sensitive information with the Agency's station chief in Paris, since the man was a possible Soviet mole. So the scores mounted up, and some members of the old-boy network of operations officers decided to settle them. First they conspired to keep the details of their own agents and operations secret from Max, cold-shouldering his staff and drying up his sources. They tried to exclude the counterintelligence staff altogether from the Agency's unsecret war in Vietnam, with the result (as Max later argued) that Hanoi was able to run no fewer than forty thousand double agents inside the South Vietnamese administration, negating American efforts to prop up the crumbling Saigon regime. Then Max's bureaucratic rivals started leaking to the press, scoring a lethal hook when they helped publicize his involvement in a program of domestic mail intercepts.

The fact that the letter-opening had been carried out under direct presidential mandate since the early fifties did not save Max. The public embarrassment was used by his enemies to remove him from the office he had controlled, as a virtual fiefdom, for two decades.

In the name of economy and reform, a hatchet was taken to the old counterintelligence staff. Its veterans were scattered; its wide-reaching prerogatives were stripped away; some of its most closely guarded secrets—including its ultrasensitive manuals on allied secret services—became coffee-table reading throughout the Agency. An extensive review that Max had initiated of how the KGB might have fed disinformation to Washington via false defectors was unceremoniously trashed. The "can do" mentality had taken charge; there was no longer time to agonize over the reliability of human sources, no longer need to pore over the secret archives to infer occult connections between twenty-year-old cases and what was happening today. To many, it seemed that a cleansing wind was sweeping through Langley. To others, it seemed that the wind was throwing all the doors open to Soviet deception and penetration.

Ignorance of history, Max Zimmer had once declared, was at the root of the impatience and alarm with which Agency colleagues viewed his activities. The American vice: ignorance of history, and contempt for it. That alone, in Max's view, could explain how a previous director of the Agency, tossing aside a multivolume study of Soviet double-agent operations that had been painstakingly compiled by Zimmer's research staff, could exclaim: "I don't understand what those people think they are doing down there—running a history class?" Learning of his unloved director's remark, Max had sent him a one-line memo, quoting T. S. Eliot: "History may be servitude; history may be freedom."

In Zimmer's view, the strength of the Soviets in the secret war with the United States lay not only in the vast concentration of power and resources in a leadership that was answerable only to itself, uninhibited by Congress, the media or the courts, and in the secrecy that enveloped the operations of Moscow Center. The KGB's strength was found also in tradition and continuity: in other words, regard for history. In the early years after the Bolshevik Revolution, as Zimmer reminded his acolytes, Feliks Dzherzhinsky, the first chief of the Soviet secret service, had set up the special office called Mayak, or the Beacon, that was responsible for recruiting and running high-level agents in hostile countries. The Beacon was an evocative name for a department concerned with searching out, as under the beam of a spotlight, the secrets and the plans of the enemy.

After his dismissal from the Agency, Max had tried to explain it all to the apprentice Sovietologists at the Defense Intelligence School by quoting a statement of Dzherzhinsky. Reporting to Lenin, the first Soviet spy chief had said, "We are following your advice, Vladimir Ilyich, penetrating deeper and deeper, into the enemy's plans."

For Max, the word "plans" was the guts and heart of it. Krylov's section of Moscow Center did not simply recruit moles in the West in order to steal secrets or capture foreign agents within the borders of the Soviet Union. The Beacon tried, through its penetration agents, to shape, or rather misshape, the whole pattern of Western policy and intelligence operations.

His obsession with the minutiae of cases dating back to the twenties, and even to czarist times, wearied many Agency people. In vain he would argue that the biography of a service is as important as the biography of a man, or that those who do not understand history are condemned to repeat it. He came up against a sullen wall of incomprehension.

Krylov, Max Zimmer had concluded long before receiving his pink slip, was the key to it. For decades, Krylov had been the guiding hand behind the Beacon. Krylov had bobbed in and out of the most famous cases. He had been active in the expansion and strengthening of the KGB's Service A, charged with disinformation and other "active measures" against the West, including not only the planting of false stories in the media but the drip-feeding of deception—via false defectors—to hostile governments and secret services.

Krylov knew history. And who was to say that where Krylov and the Beacon had succeeded against the British and the French and the Germans—despite all *their* worldly wisdom and tradition—it had been unable to succeed against the Americans? Max Zimmer had reason to believe that Krylov had planted a mole at Langley. And that the Beacon had gone one better, by ensnaring the Agency in a sticky web of false double, or treble, agents who made it impossible to distinguish true information from false, real defectors from controlled plants. The history said it could happen.

But the beauty of it all, Max said to himself sardonically as he opened a can of pet food for his cat, was that when the Agency had finally been brought to accept that this was so, it had rounded on *him*. That was the penalty, he thought, for being right too soon.

14

La Fleur, a smart French restaurant on the corner of Embassy Row and Wisconsin Avenue, was almost deserted when Canning arrived. He surveyed the handful of predinner drinkers at the soft-lit tables and opted for a seat at the bar. The pretty bargirl wore bright-scarlet lipstick, a frothy white blouse with embroidered armbands, and a hip-hugging skirt. She served him his Manhattan, straight up, and returned to her conversation with two sleek regulars at the other end of the bar.

"How's your sex life?" Canning overheard her purring to one of the customers.

"Next to nothing."

"Oh, I wouldn't complain," said the girl. "You can get exhausted, you know? Like, you need some time off. I spent last weekend with this guy on a boat and I'm ready to goof off."

"Well, the only time I use it these days is when I go to the bathroom."

There was a hiss of cold air as the heavy front door to the restaurant swung open. Canning swiveled on his barstool to watch Dick Hammond make his entry, ripping off his trenchcoat as he hurried forward.

"Sorry I'm late," Hammond apologized.

"No problem. I'm always happy to broaden my sociological research." He nodded toward the bargirl.

"I see what you mean. Are you ready for the other half?"

"Always."

"Okay. Two more," Hammond said to the girl. "But we'll take them back there, all right?"

In the penumbra of the salon beyond the bar, Hammond wasted no time in explaining why he had asked the Englishman to fly down to Washington.

"We've landed a big one."

"A defector." Canning's tone was not interrogatory. Dicky Prince had told him already.

"Yes. But listen, Charles. This is just for you. The liaison people have not been informed. Fact is, we can't make up our minds about him."

"Tell me something new." It was common knowledge that many Soviet defectors came under suspicion as double agents planted by the KGB. Back in the early days, the Agency had conducted an exhaustive counterintelligence review of Soviet-bloc defectors who had crossed over to the Americans between 1945 and 1960 and had concluded that three-quarters of them were probably fakes.

"But this case is really tearing us apart. People are at each other's throats. And the fight is not just inside the Agency. It's an interagency battle too."

"How can I help?"

Hammond scanned the bar area before reaching into his pocket and pulling out a single piece of paper. "You're involved," he said.

"You mean I know this Russian? Or he knows me?"

Hammond shook his head. "No. But he's been talking about a friend of yours, Hussar, Moscow. Four years ago. Right?"

Although he had been expecting to hear that code name, after what the head of the Firm had told him in Bermuda, it brought back a swamping flood of memory that altered his physical reactions so that for a moment Canning felt the same clammy fear, the same tightening constriction of his chest over his lungs that made his breath come hoarsely and painfully, the same pounding behind his forehead that he had experienced at his last meeting with Hussar in the sordid setting of the men's room of the Aragvi restaurant in Moscow. For a moment, he could see the condemned man's face, white with terror, and hear the gurgle of water as someone flushed the cistern in one of the cubicles.

"Hussar," the Englishman repeated softly. "He was one of the best. Perhaps the best we ever had."

"Look at this now and then I'll get rid of it." Hammond's eyes were roaming the restaurant again as Canning unfolded the paper on which his Agency friend had typed a rough summary of Ushinsky's allegations about the betrayal of the agent called Hussar. With only the flicker of the candle on their table to read by, Canning had trouble making out all the words.

"Why does our profession suffer from negative phototropism?" the Englishman complained.

"Come again?"

"Fear of the light. Like bats."

Canning heaved a deep sigh as he finished reading the summary and then started going over it again, making sure that he had memorized every detail.

"Got it all?" Hammond asked when he finally refolded the paper.

"I've got it."

"Okay. I'll be right back." Hammond went out to the men's room and destroyed his notes.

"Is it possible?" Hammond asked, when he had returned to his place.

"It's possible."

MOSCOW. *Four years earlier*

Hussar.

The instant that Dick Hammond had pronounced the code name, Canning had heard, echoing inside his head, the phrase the Russian agent had whispered twice, in the guttural accent of fear.

"My life rides with you." And again, as he walked off across the shiny, scrubbed floor, "My life rides with you."

The loss of the agent called Hussar had nearly broken Canning. For a time, he had blamed himself. Then he had blamed others, hunting possible traitors in London or Langley, turning and slithering in a sticky spiderweb of suspicion. But proof was elusive. Each trail that he followed seemed to end in a blind corridor. His chiefs were indulgent. They sent him on leave, saying he needed time to get over the strain. Away from the office, he started drinking to kill time and memory, until one night he fell down from the table at four o'clock in a dead stupor. The incident caused him to reorder his life. To escape the drink, and the suspicion, he transferred out of the Firm and went soldiering for two years in Oman. The sheer difficulty of surviving in the desert, among people who spoke a different language and followed different gods, had been all-absorbing. And the desert had served as an airlock between life in the Firm and the new life Canning had made for himself in New York.

Now Dick Hammond was taking him back. To the men's room in a Moscow restaurant.

To arrange a safe meeting in Moscow was about as simple as frying eggs on an electric light bulb. The resources of the Soviet secret police, in manpower and technology, were almost limitless. No casual tourist escaped scrutiny; an innocent holiday-maker who left the stifling cocoon of a group tour was instantly placed under tight surveillance by the Second Chief Directorate of the KGB. To control its own citizens, the regime had created a vast network of informers. Failure to report on "antistate" activities was itself considered a crime against the Soviet state. Nevertheless, the control of the KGB was less than watertight, and there were many Russians who remained willing to risk their lives to overthrow the system.

The most precious of them all, as far as the Firm was concerned, had been Hussar. Then a major in military intelligence, he had surfaced first in Algiers, approaching a frightened and disbelieving Foreign Office man with a banal little tale of how he had dipped into his operational funds to pay for an affair with a local woman, and was alarmed that his masters would find out. The Firm's man in Algiers was away on tour at the time, and they had nearly lost Hussar before his message got through. The Foreign Office man had a pinstriped mind, and treated the Russian with a froideur bordering on rudeness, as if to suggest that it was not the done thing for anyone—even a Soviet—to rat on his government. Luckily, the man the Firm sent from London to establish contact, Dicky Prince, had a reassuring, avuncular manner as well as an assayer's eye for the exact karat value of an item of intelligence. Dicky Prince saw instantly that what Hussar had to offer was real gems.

Once the trade began, they came in abundance. From a series of foreign postings, Hussar exceeded the expectations of even Dicky Prince. He provided the latest field manuals of the Red Army. He was the first to warn of the construction of a new generation of giant Soviet missiles far exceeding the predictions of most Western analysts. He identified the routes by which Soviet-made arms were being smuggled to dissident groups in Saudi Arabia and to terrorists in Western Europe. He supplied clues to illegal Soviet espionage networks operating under deep cover in the West. One of those clues, passed on to the Americans, had led to the arrest of an important spy posing as a garage owner in Yonkers.

Then the blow had fallen. Abruptly, Hussar had received his summons to return to Moscow, almost a year before his tour of duty in Bern was supposed to end. Dicky Prince had flown to Switzerland to urge him not to go back; the risk was too great. "I am a Russian," Hussar had said. "I must go back." It had long been plain that Hussar's essential motivation was not mercenary, though it had taken a little financial embarrassment to make him turn to the Firm at the outset. In all the years he had been risking his life for the British, he had refused to accept any money beyond the modest amounts that allowed him to buy presents for girlfriends. When Dicky Prince had told him that the Firm was setting aside a thousand pounds a month and holding it in escrow for him, against the day when he might eventually feel driven to defect, he had evinced absolute uninterest. No, what drove Hussar was something other: a borderless contempt for the men guiding the destiny of Russia. That contempt, welling up out of a personal sense of patriotism, had made Hussar secure in his own mind that, by collaborating with the Firm, he was helping to prepare the way for the overthrow of the Soviet regime. Such men, Charles Canning knew, are not recruited; they recruit themselves. Hussar did not want to live in the West. He wanted a new life for Russia, and the Russian people. That was why he accepted the recall signal from Moscow. And walked, open-eyed, into the jaws of the trap.

At their last meeting in the safe house in Switzerland, Dicky Prince had made the proposal in a diffident, tentative way, knowing it was more than a man can reasonably ask of another, his big, balding, egg-shaped head nodding as he talked. Would Hussar be prepared to go on reporting to the Firm from Moscow? The Russian treated the request as the most normal thing in the world, like an invitation to an outing in Battersea Park. He wanted merely to know the mechanics. Personal meetings, they understood, would be hopelessly dangerous, and must be avoided except in an emergency. An occasional brush contact, the quick passage of a message from hand to hand in a crowded bus or subway station, might be risked, perhaps. Beyond that, communications would be confined to a system of dead drops. To act as Hussar's personal case officer in Moscow, Dicky Prince was assigning one of the Firm's high fliers, Charles Canning.

After Hussar's return to Moscow, there was a silence that was prolonged through several months. Canning, brushing up on his Russian at a desk in the British embassy, had no way of ascertaining whether the agent had been secretly imprisoned, or shot, or assigned to Siberia. Then Hussar gave his contact signal: a simple chalk mark beside a doorway. The flow of information started again. Hussar's material was less sexy than before, suggesting that he had less access to highly classified documents in Moscow than he had enjoyed at foreign embassies, a possible indication that he had indeed fallen under suspicion. Canning exercised his imagination to vary the system of pickups as much as possible, avoiding using the same dead drop more than once. He even roped in his wife, sending Sally to the park with one-year-old Jimmy and another embassy spouse. Hussar, strolling by, dropped a tiny package into the pram on the pretext of admiring the baby. Sally was not amused, later accusing Canning of recruiting his son for the Firm before he had even learned to talk. Canning was not amused either when he studied the message. Hussar wanted a personal meeting. Urgently.

A famous restaurant like the Aragvi is a perfectly natural place for a foreign diplomat to be seen at lunchtime, and it is equally unexceptional for him to answer the call of nature after drinking half a bottle of Bulgarian wine.

Canning had done just that when, at 3:30 on an oppressive August afternoon, he made his excuses to his luncheon guest—an embassy secretary—and headed for the men's room. There were a couple of Russians at the urinals, and two of the booths were occupied, so Canning took his time washing his hands and combing his hair until the room had cleared. Except, that is, for the anonymous occupant of one of the cubicles. Then Canning stuck his hand in his pocket and dropped a coin, as if by accident, on the floor. Before it had stopped rolling, there was the clank and roar of a flushing cistern, and Hussar emerged from the cubicle. Without looking at Canning, the Russian made straight for a washbasin and began to rinse his hands. The face, which Canning had studied only in photographs, was white and damp. The Russian's civilian suit hung loose and shapeless, as if he had lost a lot of weight. His collar was deeply wrinkled where he had knotted his tie tightly against his neck—suggesting that the shirt, too, belonged to a much heavier man. Hussar breathed in raspingly, as if his nasal passages were blocked. As Canning walked by him, into the booth he had just left, he inhaled the sour odor of cold sweat. He paused for an instant, to look back at Hussar in the mirror above the washbasin. The Russian raised a finger to his lips.

Inside the cubicle, Canning found what he was looking for under the lid of the cistern. Hussar had not troubled with the normal techniques of concealment. The brown corner of a tightly rolled wad of paper stuck out. There were eight sheets in all, of coarse lavatory paper, the sort that might be used in a barracks. Or a jail. Each sheet was covered in minuscule Cyrillic print, laboriously and neatly penciled so as not to waste a centimeter of space. Canning's Russian was too primitive for him to get more than the general drift. Something about detection. Torture. KGB control. To be sure that his meaning would not be mistaken, Hussar had printed one sentence in ungrammatical English. "If you value my life, you must not stop to collaborate." The sense of it was clear to Canning. Hussar had been discovered by the KGB, imprisoned and tortured, and ordered to go on reporting to the Firm—no doubt in order to lure the British into a subtly laid trap. They would have Hussar under surveillance at this moment. In all probability, he was wired for sound. Somehow he had managed to find a moment of privacy in a top-security cell in order to pencil his warning to the Firm, and his plea for help. The man's courage, and his loyalty, were stunning.

When Canning emerged from the booth, Hussar was still standing where he had been before, soaping his face roughly, as if to bring color back to the cheeks. Under the cruel, antiseptic glare of the lights, Canning could find no trace of hope in his eyes. The stare was that of a dead man before his eyelids are drawn shut.

Pointing at his chest, perhaps to warn that microphones concealed under his coat were the main source of danger to them both, Hussar said, "People are leaving Moscow for the summer."

168

"There will be many cars on the road," said Canning in his awkward Russian.

"I will go by bus."

The Russian had named his choice for the next rendezvous, which would take place, according to the rules agreed with Dicky Prince, at the same time next week, minus a day and an hour. As he spoke, Hussar made a sudden movement with his wrist and transferred a small package into the hollow of Canning's palm. This was the form in which the bulk of the material he had been smuggling to the Firm in Moscow had been supplied. Now, however, Canning knew that the contents of the latest package had been put together by the KGB. Maybe that was true of the previous packages too. The answers must lie in the hand-printed note.

Another Russian made a noisy entry into the men's room and locked himself into the cubicle that Hussar and Canning had used. Hussar, who had looked at the Englishman only obliquely, with darting glances toward the mirror, now swiveled to face him directly.

"My life rides with you," he said almost inaudibly.

Canning stretched out his hand, but the Russian ignored it.

"My life rides with you," Hussar repeated. As he strode toward the door, Canning saw he was limping, one shoulder raised higher than the other.

Canning sensed then, and said so later in their postmortem sessions in London, that something was even more terribly wrong than the fact that Hussar had been detected by the KGB. It was not that the Russian's parting words communicated his terror and pain as completely as if their nerve ends had touched, so that the Englishman stood anchored to the floor as the big swing door hissed open and shut, feeling winded and clammy. It was the incomprehensibility of Hussar's speaking as he had done. His words must have alerted the people who were monitoring their exchange that he had departed from the KGB's plan—so ruining the elaborate attempt he had made to warn Canning that he was now under Soviet control without tipping his hand to the eavesdroppers. Why should Hussar have run the incalculable risk of writing an eight-page note on toilet paper, only to betray its basic content in a single phrase, faithfully recorded on a KGB tape machine? Was it the desperate, flailing gesture of a drowning man, serving only to drag his would-be rescuer down with him? That did not accord with Hussar's character, so far as Canning had been able to fathom it. The Russian knew fear, as other men did. But, more than most, he had consistently displayed an extraordinary capacity to calculate each step even as the earth was crumbling underfoot along the narrow ledge above the abyss. Either they had broken him so completely in the cells of the Lubyanka that he had lost his instinct for survival, or there was some hidden meaning in Hussar's final outburst, something Canning was intended to puzzle out.

Dicky Prince flew out from London, and, in a safe room at the embassy—defended by soundproofed, windowless walls and the low hum of electronic interference devices from the probing monitors of the KGB's long-range surveillance equipment and the bugs that peppered most of the building—they pored over the contents of Hussar's letter. His story was simple enough in outline, but remarkably full of details. More details, both Englishmen agreed, than a condemned man would normally find time or inclination to include in a note that must have been written under the most dangerous circumstances conceivable. Hussar revealed that the KGB had uncovered his relationship with the Firm through routine surveillance after his recall to Moscow. He described the methods the KGB had used to monitor Canning's movements discreetly. They had arranged to have a chemical smeared on his shoes that left an invisible trail, so that he could be tracked from a great distance by trained dogs to a dead drop he had set out to service. What had finally allowed the KGB to nail Hussar, according to his letter, was the meeting with Sally in the park. Untroubled by staff shortages, the Second Chief Directorate routinely set a watch on all persons connected with Western embassies, deploying up to twelve men to cover targets of special interest like an identified member of the Firm. The brief encounter between the young English mother strolling her baby and the colonel from Soviet military intelligence had not passed unnoticed. And nothing passed for coincidence in Moscow. After that, Hussar had been arrested before dawn and taken to the Lubyanka for interrogation.

Knowing the variety of methods of physical and psychological torture in use by the KGB, Hussar had quickly made his confession. This had not deterred his questioners from subjecting him to some of the forms of physical abuse that do not leave external marks. Canning knew the repertoire ranged from beating the soles of the feet to applying electrodes to the genitals to sticking a steel bar up the rectum. The KGB had never been overtender in its treatment of traitors—real or invented—in the rival service. Finally, as Hussar's note recounted, he had been offered his choice. Either he would agree to be played back against the Firm as a KGB-controlled double agent, or he would receive an immediate death sentence from a secret tribunal and be sent to the wall—in other words, the firing squad. His letter concluded with an appeal to his British friends to go on meeting with him as if nothing had happened.

"Of course, we have to do it," Dicky Prince said. "Or rather, *you* have to do it. Where's the next meeting?"

Canning mentioned a bus station in a residential district of Moscow.

"All right. We'll try to cover you. Just be careful."

"Dicky, can we get him out?"

"I don't think so. Not now. We'll try to let it run, and see. If it seems to be working, we could try to provide some reason for them to let him out of the country to meet us abroad. It would have to be juicy. We'd have to be prepared to burn an operation, or another agent. Even so, I don't believe they'd let him go. Not ever."

"A trade?"

Dicky Prince sighed. "We'll let it run," he repeated. "As long as they want to let it run."

Both men sat glumly in silence, knowing they were clutching at broken straws.

"He was the best, you know," Prince said at last.

"I know." Canning swallowed and said, "I'm sorry. About using Sally. That was stupid."

"Don't blame yourself. They were bound to catch him. It was merely a matter of time." Prince took off his glasses and polished them with his thumbs. "Anyway, they were probably on to him long before that."

It was what both of them were thinking. The note simply did not ring true. It was too pat, for one thing, as if the lengthy account of KGB surveillance techniques had been concocted to divert the Firm's attention from some other, unmentioned, factor, that had led to Hussar's downfall. It was too long, too meticulous. How would a prisoner under constant observation in the Lubyanka find the time and the privacy to write a message that ran to almost a thousand words? Would the guards leave him unwatched for ten or twenty minutes, even in the latrines? How would he have been able, after the repeated strippings and beatings, to conceal a pencil, or to acquire it in the first place? Above all, would he have been permitted to attend a controlled meeting with a British operative without first being subjected to a thorough body search?

"Is it possible that the note is authentic?" Canning said bluntly.

"It's possible. I'd say the odds are ten to one against. But it's possible. This is no ordinary man."

"All right, let's assume the note is genuine. Then why did he speak to me as he did in the lavatory?"

"Panic?" Prince speculated. "Despair? Despair would be a realistic reflex for a man in his position. He was always that. Realistic."

"And if he was trying to warn us? That the note is a fake? What would that say to us? What is the KGB trying to hide?"

Dicky Prince straightened his bulk, slumped in the embassy chair, and rammed his glasses back onto his nose. "Play the game, Charles," he said, in the tone of a commanding officer addressing a subaltern. "That's your role here. I'm going to mull all of this over in London."

"His recall to Moscow," Canning pursued, now that he saw the isolated facts rushing together into a pattern. "That's it, isn't it? That's what he was trying to tell us. He wasn't detected by the KGB in Moscow. He was betrayed before they brought him back to Moscow. Which means"—he weighed the rest of the sentence before speaking it—"by someone in London."

"Stop it, Charles. You're not in counterintelligence. Just do the job you've been assigned."

"But I'm not wrong, am I?" Canning, excited now, got up and started pacing round the room. "There's a mole, and Hussar was trying to warn us."

"It doesn't follow."

"What?"

"That the mole would have to be in London. If there is a mole."

"You mean—"

"We briefed the Cousins. I was there myself. Now there's an end of it, Charles." Prince started pushing buttons on his watch, a huge American-made chronometer with a map of the world on the dial on which different areas lit up in red according to the time zone selected. It was a clear signal that the conversation was at an end. "You already know more than you need to know. Just keep your appointment with Hussar, will you? Poor bastard."

Poor bastard was right. They were both poor bastards, Hussar and Charles Canning. The KGB waited until they had exchanged messages from palm to palm, jammed together among the crush of stocky Muscovite housewives on board the bus, before moving in. As Canning got off the bus at the next stop, three burly men jumped him. When he tried to protest that he had diplomatic immunity, one of the secret policemen threw an arm around his throat, jerking his chin upward, while twisting his left arm behind his back until he could feel the joint beginning to crack. He got a parting glimpse of Hussar's pale face, the features stoic and immobile, through the window of the bus as they wrestled him into a waiting car. The watchers that Dicky Prince had posted were helpless to intervene as the driver took off, tires screeching, in the direction of Dzherzhinsky Square.

"You have no right to hold me," Canning told the officer seated behind a bare wooden table in the interrogation room.

The KGB man nonchalantly removed the black cigarette from his mouth with two fingers and blew smoke into Canning's face. The interrogator had penetrating, close-set eyes, ears that jutted out like radar discs, and a mouth full of yellow, ruined teeth that he displayed too often for Canning's comfort.

"You made quite a cock-up, old boy," the man said in an appalling parody of an English accent. "I'm sure the Firm will be far from pleased when they see your face on the front page of the newspapers. Your career will be finished. As dead as a doornail." Pleased with the passé expression he must have memorized in some orientation course, he displayed his rotting teeth again. "Meanwhile, your Russian friend will be dead. You should consider an accommodation. We are both civilized adults."

"What kind of accommodation?"

173

"You could cooperate with us. That way, we can avoid diplomatic unpleasantness, and there would be no need to proceed with—er—formalities here. You understand that we employ very thorough questioners."

"You can't threaten me. You have no right. I have diplomatic immunity."

"What a stickler for protocol," the KGB man mocked him. "I know we will be hearing from the British consul in due course. But you know how slowly bureaucracies work. It will take time for the protest to be processed by our Foreign Ministry, and it will take more time for it to be communicated to the Committee of State Security. And I doubt whether your government will be disposed to make a public issue of your treatment here."

Canning knew it was bluff. The suggestion that he should collaborate with the KGB had no depth of menace to it. His interrogator was following a weary routine, without conviction. If they had wanted to scare him, or seriously compromise him, they would have taken a different route. What was obvious was that they had decided to wind up the Hussar affair as neatly and convincingly as possible.

"I want to speak to my consul," said Canning.

"We can arrange for you to talk to Mr. Prince in London," said the KGB man, patting his desk telephone. "I imagine he is not very happy with you."

"Let me ask you one question," said Canning, deciding he had nothing to lose by putting it. "How did you catch him?"

"Come, come, Mr. Canning. This is not the place for party games. A responsible family man like yourself."

Family man. It was the same message as Hussar's penciled note. The meeting with Sally in the park. Was that how the KGB had caught him? Was Canning himself to blame? Or was that simply what Moscow Center wanted him to believe?

Four years later, these remained open questions. The KGB had released Canning within a few hours, declared him persona non grata without public fanfare and quietly booted him out of the country the following day. There was no information on Hussar's fate until after Canning had already left for Oman, when an article in a Red Army newspaper obscurely referred to the treason of a certain "Lieutenant Colonel H," who "received the treatment from the Russian people that such vipers within our bosoms deserve." For its own reasons, Moscow Center had avoided turning the Hussar affair into a media event—in striking contrast to the big show trial that had been organized for an earlier Western mole, Colonel Oleg Penkovsky. On the south bank of the Thames, at the headquarters of the Firm, the directors were relieved that a curtain had been drawn over a bad piece of business.

This was in part because the prolonged inquest in London had not resulted in any agreed verdict. Canning, torn between gnawing feelings of guilt over his apparent mishandling of Hussar and suspicion that the agent had been betrayed by a mole in the West, was admitted to only a few of the discussions; most of what he was able to glean came from his friend and protector, Dicky Prince. It was from Prince that he learned the names of those who had been privy to the Hussar case—or at any rate, to enough details to have been able to identify the existence of a British agent in Soviet military intelligence who had once served in Algiers and Bern. The Foreign Office man who had first been approached in Algiers had been elevated to a knighthood and an ambassadorship in a minor Commonwealth country, and was soon ruled out as a suspect. The number of people inside the Firm who had known about Hussar had been strictly limited to two of the directors and a special handling section responsible to Dicky Prince in U.K. Station. There was a universal disinclination to bring in the Security Service on any investigation; members of the two sister services referred to each other, with indiscriminate cordiality, as "the shits across the river." The Firm's own security section ran some checks, and came up with nothing beyond the predictable incidence of a romantic liaison inside the office and a man who liked boys as well as girls.

This left the problem of the Cousins.

"We brought them in late," Prince told Canning. "About six months before Hussar was ordered back to Moscow. Of course, that was before the Melbourne fiasco."

Everyone inside the Firm knew what had happened in Melbourne. At a gathering of Western service chiefs hosted by the Australians, a top Agency official had turned up tired and emotional and delivered a rambling speech in which he warned the astonished allied directors that his service could no longer be trusted to keep its secrets. He spoke as a man who had been bloodied and exhausted by the constant inroads into official secrecy that had been made in Washington by a group of congressional and media witch-finders who talked and behaved as if the Agency were a greater threat to democracy than the Soviet KGB. But his remarks, recorded on the official tape of the proceedings, had a profoundly disturbing effect on his audience. One Canadian participant had whispered to Dicky Prince that the Agency was committing public hara-kiri. Prince and his colleagues felt no sense of *Schadenfreude* over the misfortunes of the Cousins; the directors of the Firm remained vigorous proponents of a special relationship with the United States, to be defended against all comers. But the timing of the "Melbourne fiasco" could hardly have been more unfortunate. It had followed a visit to London by the Agency's then director, a blue-water sailor who displayed ostentatious contempt for traditional tradecraft, who had insulted the head of the Firm by informing him that the British were only "minor league" spies because they relied on human sources instead of technological wizardry. After Melbourne, the Firm had decided to cut back on the supply of sensitive intelligence to the Agency and to rely on informal contacts with trusted individuals rather than the institutional flow of paperwork.

"Who was briefed on the Agency side?" Canning was asking.

"There were two stages," Prince explained. "First, our man in Washington was passing on some of the Hussar product to Max Zimmer, with clear instructions to camouflage the source."

Canning nodded. Max Zimmer, as the Agency's counterintelligence chief, was the natural conduit. And much of Hussar's military information had far more immediate relevance for the Americans than for the second-rank power that Britain had become.

"Then Les Winter came to London," Prince continued, "and virtually demanded to be given the whole story. He said they couldn't assess Hussar's product properly without a better idea of the source. Of course, he was right. So I laid on a full briefing for him."

"Was anyone else there?"

"A girl from his division. Trudy Cook. Ever come across her?"

"Yes." Canning vaguely remembered a short, homely spinster with glasses, built like a brick.

"I trust you were wearing your chastity belt."

"Not quite my type."

"I gather she doesn't always leave it up to the man to decide. Quite a nympho. I suppose that's the style of the modern American woman."

"I wouldn't have guessed."

"My dear Charles, I'm surprised. A man of your worldly experience."

"What about back at Langley?" Canning pursued. "How did they handle the Hussar information?"

"I don't have the ghost of an idea."

Canning had kicked the names, and the possibilities, around for weeks. He had little else to do, since the Firm had put off any decision about his next assignment while waiting to see whether the Russians would try to whip up some kind of furor over his activities in Moscow. He had applied for leave to go to Washington, but that had been firmly ruled out. "We don't spy on the Americans," the head of the Firm told him flatly. And he was far too personally involved. He was made aware that in some quarters his persistent inquiries were seen as a clumsy attempt to vindicate himself for his shoddy performance in Moscow. "Incompetence costs us more than treason," he overheard a colleague saying pointedly in the smoking room of the Travellers' Club.

In the end, it seemed easiest to accept Hussar's view of events: the version hand-printed on lavatory paper. That, at any rate, was tangible, and inherently probable. Beyond that, there was nothing to go on but intuition, and the head of the Firm was not disposed to confront his counterpart at Langley with a tissue of theories that corresponded to no proven facts. Many of Canning's colleagues felt, too, that the Agency had suffered enough already—through the divisive and inconclusive mole hunts of the sixties and early seventies, as well as through public exposure and political vendettas—and should be left to lick its wounds. Dicky Prince, one of the few who shared Canning's suspicions, was also one of the many who maintained that another mole hunt that would tear the Agency apart and subject it to new public embarrassments could serve the purposes of the KGB just as well as the existence of a real mole in Washington.

"Don't rock the boat," Prince advised Canning. "You can't bring Hussar back. Go away and make love to your wife. Forget Moscow."

The advice was easier to give than to follow. A week alone with Sally in the Portuguese Algarve, Jimmy left behind in the care of his grandmother, did not kill the memories, and brought them closer to divorce than in all the months when the tension building between them could be evaded in a swirl of work and other people. Mating doves left alone in a cage too small for them will eventually rip each other apart. By the end of a week in the Algarve, Canning and Sally were shouting and clawing at each other. In an effort to smooth things over, he drove her north for a day, to the beach suburbs of Lisbon, to a hotel in the aristocratic demesne of Sintra with the haunting name Palacio de Seteais, the Palace of Seven Sighs. The hotel, standing in its formal, manicured gardens, with sculpted figures rising from the rooftops, recalled the setting of the film *Last Year at Marienbad*. The day began well, in a blaze of sunlight. They strolled through the flowering arcades, laughed, told jokes, made love in the suite that Canning rented with the sudden abandon of a young lover. But the mood did not last. The sight of a family with small children walking in the gardens that looked like a checkerboard under the tilting shadows of the late afternoon touched a raw nerve in Sally. "You don't want a family," she accused him. "You don't want to be a father. Or a husband. All you can do is use people. Like you used us in Moscow. You were even ready to use your own baby." He had rounded on her then, shouting into the wind that blew in squally gusts from the sea, and keened through the trees of the Palace of Seven Sighs. Then he had left her, and sat drinking at the bar until it was late enough to go to the casino. She ran behind him as he staggered and lurched toward the borrowed Maserati, begging him not to drive, fighting her way into the front seat and trying to take the wheel. His voice, as usual, was steady, his speech unslurred, as he said, "I'm perfectly capable of driving a fucking car." On the short stretch of coast road, he gunned the car up to a hundred miles an hour before braking, in a whine of burning rubber, outside the casino. He opened the door, said, "You see?" to Sally, still shaking under her seat belt—and fell flat on his face on the bitumen. She had to help him into the casino, where he collapsed onto a seat at the closest roulette table and bet steadily on the nearest number he could see on the board. The number was eight. After the wheel had spun ten or eleven times, and eight had still not come up, Sally tried to pull him away. Then the croupier turned the wheel again, and the little bouncing ball stopped at eight. Canning collected his chips, and put them all on eight again, ignoring Sally's tugging at his shoulder. And eight came up again.

"You're lucky in some things, Charles," she had conceded as they made their way out of the casino, Canning more composed, with a glazed but triumphant look on his face. She added, "It's a pity they're not the important things."

Although he could not remember the details of the conversation the next day, that was the night that Sally said she was going to leave him. It would be better, she said, for Jimmy to grow up without a father than to have to witness his parents mauling each other.

"Don't worry," she had said. "I won't embarrass you. I won't damage the Firm. It will be very decorous, very amicable. A two-year separation."

Except that it was not at all decorous. They had both started weeping, until Canning made love to her again in the early dawn, and found her body as trembling-cold and light and fragile as a wounded sparrow. The act was like reaching a hand from the window of a train that is picking up speed to someone who is running along the platform: the fingers brush, but the hands cannot clasp.

Canning had felt he was losing everything that had given his life coherence—his family, his faith in the Firm, his self-respect. It had all come tumbling down with the loss of Hussar, and his failure to account for it. It was easier to go and make war in the desert than to cope with the phalanx of doubts that surrounded him in London. With the passage of time, fresh tissue had grown over the scar. Now Dick Hammond had torn it open again.

The notes that Hammond had just destroyed summarized the allegations of the Agency's new defector. Charles Canning now knew that Ushinsky had been a personal friend of Hussar's. The defector had even been one of the officers ordered to witness Hussar's appalling death in the secret crematorium.

Ushinsky's account of how Hussar had been detected by the KGB confirmed what Canning had suspected all along. It flatly contradicted what Hussar had penciled on the lavatory-paper letter. The defector claimed that as soon as he had been recalled to Moscow, Hussar had been interrogated, tortured, and forced to play a double game for Krylov. If Ushinsky was telling the truth, it meant that—in all the time that Canning had been in Moscow—Hussar had been a puppet dancing on a string. But what gripped Canning's consciousness was the final part of the defector's story. Ushinsky claimed, on the authority of none other than Krylov himself, that Hussar had been betrayed by a mole in Washington.

"Yes," Canning said slowly. "It's more than possible. It's what I always believed." He looked at Hammond speculatively. "Tell me," the Englishman said, "how do you come to be mixed up in this? I didn't think this was your normal line of country."

"Adam Claiborne wanted someone who wasn't involved in the Wars of the Roses. Also, he wanted some quick answers. I suppose that's another reason why he picked an operations man instead of a counterintelligence type. Some of Max's inquiries used to proceed at the speed of preparing a doctoral dissertation. And were no more conclusive."

Then Hammond leaned over the table and explained in whispers the consuming reason why he had to wind up his investigation within a matter of weeks.

"Death Beam," Canning repeated the name.

"The Soviets call it Razrukha. It means the destruction of everything, disintegration into total chaos. At least that's what the defector says."

"If he's telling the truth, Razrukha sounds like the right name." Canning chewed on the end of an unlit cigar. Then he said, with a kind of solemnity, "I'm sure you understand that there's no one alive who has a stronger personal interest in getting to the bottom of the Hussar affair than I. I want to be involved. Tell me how I can help."

"Look, I told you that Claiborne has ruled that we are not going to brief the Firm at this stage. Not officially, anyway."

"I hear you," Canning said enigmatically.

"If you want to go to Dicky Prince privately, that's okay with me. But nothing on paper. No liaison reports."

"What do you need?"

"I need to know who in the Agency was briefed on Hussar by your side. And the dates."

"I can tell you that myself. God knows I've brooded over it long enough." Canning told him. "There were three people from the Agency who were told about Hussar," he summed up. Max Zimmer. Les Winter. And Trudy Cook. "Of course," Canning added, "I don't know how tightly the material was held inside the Agency. We assumed it was going to be sealed up in some very special vault. But the way secret papers have been wafting around Washington like confetti, who knows? That's something for *you* to check into."

Dick Hammond took the maraschino cherry out of his Manhattan, ate it, and started stirring the dregs of the glass with the stem.

"You know Max is in trouble," he said.

"I've read the story in the newspapers."

"It's a lot worse than that, Charles. We're convinced that he stole files from the Agency."

"He wouldn't be the first," Canning commented. "Or the last. Anyway, I'm sure Max believes that there's no one left in his old shop who would be able to decipher his reports."

"There's worse, Charles. We got a report from a double agent that Moscow Center had a source inside the Agency—on the counterintelligence side—that was current until about the time Max left. According to this double agent, some of the material was shipped to Moscow via Israel. Because of the dates and the Israeli connection, the report points to Max. Add to that Ushinsky's claim and the fact that Max was briefed on Hussar—"

"This double agent," Canning interrupted. "Can you trust him?"

"If we can't, then I'm not sure that we've even got the name of the Soviet General Secretary right."

"He's that important?"

"Did you ever hear the code name Martini?"

Canning shook his head.

"I don't think the Firm was ever briefed," Hammond went on. "I never heard of Martini myself until I got back to Washington. The general opinion is, he's one of the best sources we ever had at Moscow Center. He's supplied countless leads to Soviet agents and some priceless information on the technology stuff. And he's been reporting for more than ten years."

Canning was so surprised that he nearly dropped his glass. It rattled against the edge of the table. "Ten years," he murmured. Hussar had survived for less than four. And that was already remarkable longevity for a Western agent inside Soviet intelligence.

"Martini has even risen to the rank of a KGB major general," Hammond went on. "And he made contact within the last month."

Canning suddenly realized that he might already know Martini's true identity. He visualized a scene at the Café Carlyle, when three Russians were paying court to a black singer from New Orleans. One of them, the one with black hair, had been a KGB major general.

"Konstantin Alexeyevich Orlov," Canning said, reciting the name Dicky Prince had given him.

"What?"

"That's your man, isn't it? Martini?"

"I'm not . . . I don't have the real name," Hammond fumbled.

"Then try that one out on Les Winter." Canning described the evening at the Café Carlyle. "I don't know," he concluded. "But I think that that particular Ivan was a bit too sure of himself—and too mobile—to be a double agent who was reporting to the Agency for ten years. Unless he had a license from Krylov."

Hammond weighed the possibility for a long moment.

Then he said, "I feel I'm still at sea with a lot of this, Charles. But as things now stand, Max Zimmer is under active investigation. He is the number-one candidate for the mole in the Agency."

"I see." Canning sounded less than convinced. He had had numerous dealings with Max during his time in the Firm, and liked the old spymaster, for all his eccentricities. Quite apart from the fact that Max was Sally's uncle.

"Max isn't helping himself by clamming up," Hammond went on. "I went out to his place in Alexandria to try to find out about the missing files, and he virtually slammed the door in my face. Now he's holed up in Miami and doesn't want to talk to anyone from the Agency."

Hammond paused to study the Englishman's reactions, and Canning knew at once what he wanted to ask.

"All right," Canning said. "I don't mind a few days in Florida,

182

even if it is off season. I'll go and talk to Max. Tell me just one thing."

"Yes?"

"Have you talked to Sally about this?"

"Not in so many words." He avoided Canning's inquiring gaze. "All right," he conceded. "I was gutless. I put it off."

"Do you want me to tell her?"

"That I'm investigating her uncle as a possible Soviet agent? Thanks but no thanks. I'll tell her myself. I'll call her today."

15

The store with the sign that read "Geo. Mallaby. Rare & Antiquarian Books" was tucked away on Thirteenth Street, off Broadway, not far from the celebrated Strand bookstore that advertised ten miles of secondhand volumes. The bins outside Mallaby's shop contained prints and movie posters and blown-up photographs of famous people, not all of them old. At the top of one pile was a well-preserved portrait of the President in cowboy garb on which some passerby had doodled a handlebar mustache with a felt pen.

Inside, Mallaby's bookstore had the comfortable, musty, leathery smell that immediately defined it as the genuine article. Books of all conditions, shapes, and sizes spilled out of shelves and cupboards. The serious bibliophile in search of something special—a 1922 edition of *The Waste Land* with a dropped letter on page 9, perhaps—could ask one of the elderly, nearsighted attendants for access to the locked cabinets where the real prizes were stored. One of them was a lady called Bertha, of uncertain origin and even less definable age, who presided majestically in a wheelchair, gripping her cane like a scepter. She seemed to hold the entire inventory of the store in her head.

Some days, the owner himself could be found on the premises, darting in and out of the back room, jerking his head up and down with rapid, nervous motions like a woodpecker. His name was not Mallaby, but Malinovsky. Zhores Malinovsky. He had anglicized it for the sign above his windows. He told the inquisitive that he felt that this was a small and natural gesture to make in return for the pleasure of being an adopted citizen of the United States, a

184

sort of affirmation of loyalty. Also, it meant that fewer of his mail-order clients misspelled the name of his store on their checks.

Nobody entering the shop on Thirteenth Street, or the new branch of Mallaby's that had opened in Washington, near Dupont Circle, felt the presence of the cash register. The atmosphere was more like that of a library, or even a cloister, than that of a place of commerce. Patrons were permitted to browse for hours without interruption. But there were some who came and left in a hurry, as if they were rushing to keep a pressing appointment elsewhere. They would go diving into the back room, often clutching a book they had brought with them, and emerge with a different book, as if they had made a barter exchange. They were a cosmopolitan crowd, some of them obviously foreigners. But they had one thing in common. They all came at times when the owner was in the cluttered back room.

Sally Sherwin had come to Mallaby's in search of a present for Uncle Max. It would be his birthday soon, and he had had such a dismal year so far. The ridiculous stories in the papers that made out that Max Zimmer was the mole in the Agency were bad enough. What made it worse was that the Agency itself seemed to be joining in the spirit of the witch-hunt. Even Dick seemed less than totally convinced that the accusations against Max were all lies. Sally, knowing both men intimately, could imagine what the confrontation between them must have been like. She could imagine Dick, starting out by pleading with Max to open up in order to clear himself, and ending by losing his temper as the old spymaster, deeply offended at being called on to account for himself, retreated into a stony, unyielding rage. She could understand, too, why Max, pushed beyond the limits of his endurance, had decided to uproot himself from Washington and to seek privacy in the beach house in Miami. At least Max could be with someone there who would never doubt him: his sister Phyllis, Sally's mother, lived in the house next door, overlooking the backwaters of the bay. They had bought the houses at the same time, with the inheritance they shared from Sally's grandfather, a local banker who had once run for governor of Florida.

Sally had decided to follow Max south for a week in the sun. She deserved a break from the New York rain and the pressure at the office, she had told herself, and it was high time that Jimmy had a proper holiday with at least one of his parents. Charles was always promising to take him somewhere, and finding a pretext to cancel at the last moment. Maybe she would be able to find a day or two to take Jimmy up to Orlando to visit Disney World. Then, too, she wanted time away on her own to work out whether there was any future in her relationship with Dick. While he was away playing mole catcher in Europe and Israel seemed a good time to start working on that. And finally, she thought it would do both Max and Jimmy good to have some time with each other. Max, who had become so tight-mouthed and withdrawn with adults, seemed to let go of his reserves with the five-year-old boy. And for Jimmy, the deepening relationship with his great-uncle seemed to be partial compensation for the lack of a full-time father.

Max was a true bibliophile, Sally was thinking as she pushed open the jangling door of Mallaby's. His main interest, of course, was in the arcane literature of espionage, reaching back to Elizabethan times and before. But he had parallel—and perhaps not altogether unrelated—interests in occult philosophy and poetry, especially the poetry of the early French surrealists. Sally wondered whether she might be able to find a first edition of André Breton in Mallaby's. She remembered a strange novella by the French master of the surreal, about a couple who meet, fall in love, but can encounter each other only by chance, against the most unlikely backdrops. They can find each other only when they are not looking for each other.

"Oo-ooph," Sally gasped as a youngish man, hurrying out of the store, collided with her, sending her shopping bag flying. Apples and a packet of animal crackers rolled across the floor.

The young man did not stop to help Sally pick them up.

"Sorry," he muttered, pushing his way out the door.

He was expensively dressed, Sally noticed, wrapped up in a cashmere overcoat with a fur collar. She even noticed his hand-tooled shoes. They were either crocodile or a remarkably good imitation.

The man in a hurry was definitely not American, and all in all he seemed an improbable client for Mallaby's rare-book store. He had oily black hair, a fleshy nose, and a swarthy, pockmarked complexion. He might have been Latin. But to Sally he looked more like an Arab. His face reminded her of some of the men she had seen at Abu Dhabi, en route to Oman.

186

She wondered what he had purchased at Mallaby's bookstore. He had been carrying a small oblong package tied up with string, tightly clutched to his chest.

Sally was soon absorbed in perusing the shelves, and quickly forgot the incident. On a table by the entrance to the back room, she found a pile of books that were apparently waiting to be sorted and mailed out. She picked one of them up at random. It was an 1849 London edition of a book entitled *A Manual of Scientific Energy, Prepared for the Use of Her Majesty's Navy, and Adapted for Travellers in General*, edited by Sir John Herschel, Bart. She leafed through it, and found that the author of the chapter on "Geology" was Charles Darwin. The book contained precise instructions as to what the intelligent traveler should be observing in the scientific and technical fields in the course of his peregrinations. It did not take Sally long to realize that what she was examining was a mid-nineteenth-century manual of intelligence requirements, prepared by British Naval Intelligence to instruct loyal subjects of the Crown on what information they should seek out in the course of their travels in order to sustain England's technological lead over other countries. It was just the right sort of literary curio to delight Max. But there was a slip of paper in the book full of meaningless initials that might mean that someone had already laid claim to it. All Sally could make out were the letters "D.C.," which presumably meant that the book had either come from Mallaby's Washington branch or was being sent there.

"Excuse me."

Sally looked up at a frail, white-haired man, wearing a brown cardigan under the jacket of his gray suit, and a red polka-dot bow tie whose floppiness demonstrated that it was not the clip-on variety. The half-moon reading glasses that hung from his neck were suspended by a carelessly knotted length of black cord.

"That volume is not for sale." The echo of the steppes in the man's accent was very distant. His diction was clipped and precise, and the vowel sounds were English rather than American.

"Mr. Malinovsky." Sally recognized him from a recent Christie's auction.

He blinked myopically and said, "I believe you have the advantage."

"Sally Sherwin," she introduced herself. "I work for Harry Schwab, the literary agent."

"Ah, yes." He shook hands, but took the book away from her so brusquely that, in a different context, Sally might have taken his action for deliberate rudeness. But the rare-book trade breeds eccentricities.

"I'm sorry," she said. "I didn't realize that the books on this table were not for sale."

"Mail orders," Malinovsky said, holding the *Manual of Scientific Energy* as if he feared it would break if he dropped it. "We do a lot of mail-order business. Perhaps I can help you with something else." He looked at the title of the book. "You are interested in science? In Darwin, perhaps?"

"Not particularly." She mentioned the surrealist poets, the general area of the occult.

Malinovsky pinched his nose. "No, I don't think so," he said. "Nothing in that line. But wait . . ."

He went back into his private office and came out with an old morocco-bound volume embellished with arabesques in gold leaf.

"Perhaps this would interest your friend."

Sally turned the book in her hands. It was an old edition of the *Oracles of Nostradamus*, with a rather unwieldy English translation. Sally leafed through and stopped, at random, at the eighth quatrain of Book V:

> *Unending fire will bring hidden death*
> *Horrible and fearful within the globes;*
> *The fleet will destroy the city by night*
> *The city will burn, the enemy rejoice.*

The commentator's note suggested that the Renaissance seer was conjuring up the prospect of a weapon of destruction "beyond our imagining." Sally closed the book.

"This will do," she said. "I'll take it."

Rushing with Jimmy through the Eastern Airlines terminal that afternoon to catch the flight to Miami, Sally Sherwin did not notice the swarthy young man who was loitering at the cocktail bar, the man who had bumped into her in Mallaby's bookstore.

Booked on a later flight, Sammy Hamad was in no particular hurry now. He recognized the attractive blonde with the small child and too many bags. Sammy Hamad followed them with his eyes as they passed through the automatic scanners at the security checkpoint.

16

"Atari!" Jimmy took the black stone from the board, and clapped his small hands in excitement.

"Very good," said Max Zimmer. "Excellent. But what do you think is going to happen next?"

Jimmy surveyed the board, partially covered by vertical and diagonal columns of black and white stones. It was no child's game, Go. The war game devised more than three thousand years before Christ had been studied throughout centuries by the warrior class in China and Japan; it was part of the foundation of oriental strategy. General Giap, the architect of Hanoi's victory in the Vietnam War, was said to have been a keen student of Go. It was eccentric, at the least, for Max Zimmer to be seated at a table with his five-year-old great-nephew, coaxing him in a game of skill that had defeated generals. But the boy was no ordinary child. His mind seemed to sum a problem and vault to a solution, without having to run through all the laborious intermediary steps. He had already beaten his mother at Othello, a simplified version of Go.

"Bugger," said Jimmy. "I didn't see that." The boy, by seizing Zimmer's piece, had allowed a zigzag column of seven of his own white stones to become encircled. With his next move, Max Zimmer would be able to capture all of them.

"You must learn, Jimmy, that in life it is often necessary to accept a small sacrifice in order to make a great gain. Come on, we'll call it a draw."

"No, Uncle Max." The child shook his head obstinately. "You're not the winner yet."

190

"You've got plenty of spunk." Max Zimmer tousled his hair, which Jimmy hated because it made him feel like a baby. Jimmy pulled away, out of his mother's uncle's reach. "Who taught you to say 'bugger'?" asked Zimmer.

Jimmy said nothing, leaning his chin between his fists as he brooded over the board.

"I bet it was your father. Come on now, we've got to get ready. He'll be here soon."

"Oo-oh." It was when he complained that you remembered that Jimmy was barely more than a toddler. Max Zimmer wondered what troubles lay in store for him, with a brain that already so far outstripped his physical and emotional capacities.

There was the sound of a car in the drive. Jimmy ran to look.

"It's Daddy, it's Daddy!" he shouted, hurrying toward the door so fast that he slipped and bruised his knee. He had tears streaming down his cheeks by the time he got the door open to let Charles Canning in.

"Have you been in the wars again?" his father asked, lifting him up to kiss his cheeks. "Never mind. Look what I've brought for you."

Jimmy soon forgot his accident, rapt in contemplation of a toy space battle station.

"Max." Canning shook the older man's hand. "It's been too long. How have you been?"

"Surviving." It seemed barely true. Max Zimmer looked paler and thinner than Canning remembered him, as if he never stepped out from the shade of his porch into the sunlight of Miami Beach. When he rose from the table where he had been playing Go with the boy, he used a cane to steady himself. Despite the heat, he wore a funereal black jacket and tie with his gray trousers.

"Is Sally here?" Canning asked.

"She'll be back soon. Do you want to go next door? Phyllis is in the garden. She can look after Jimmy." Max called out to his sister. "Phyllis!"

Charles Canning looked toward the door, made nervous by the imminent entry of his former mother-in-law. What made the woman most formidable was that she had been studiously civilized since the divorce. Now in her late fifties, Phyllis remained a beautiful woman, the skin of her neck and shoulders still smooth where it was displayed by her strapless sundress.

"Hello, Charles," Phyllis cried out cheerfully. "You're putting on weight. It's that decadent life you lead in Manhattan. Can I get you a drink?"

"No thanks, Phyllis." He pecked her cheek, turning uncertainly toward Zimmer.

"We were just going next door," Max came to his rescue.

"Daddy," the boy called out. "Can you play Go?"

"You'll have to teach me."

"Atari! Atari!" The child pursued them with an imaginary samurai sword as they stepped across the garden and through the gate in the picket fence. Max stumbled on a loose stone in the path, and Canning caught his arm, nervous that he would fall. Max shook off his effort to help with sudden petulance.

"I'm not dead yet," he spat.

Max's living room had the look of a bachelor don's apartment—unkempt, with bottles, papers, and books lying about at all angles, on the floor as well as the furniture, contending for space with saucers spilling over with cigarette ash.

"I don't let Phyllis come in here," said Max, by way of explanation, not apology. "Drink?"

Charles accepted a generous slug of bourbon. Max poured himself a sickly pineapple soft drink, a sign that he was under doctor's orders.

"They came through here the other day. When I was out," said Max.

"Who?"

"Who do you think?" the old spy chief said contemptuously. "The Agency opens my mail and bugs my phone. For all I know or care, there are bugs in these walls. So what's a little black-bag job?"

Canning chewed on the question in silence. He did not need to ask what Max's former Agency colleagues were looking for.

"So what brings you to Miami, Charles?"

"Hussar."

The code name set wheels turning in Zimmer's mind. His memory functioned like one of those mechanical data banks in which you turn a handle to bring the right bank of index cards to the front, then select the right alphabetical stack, and then flick through, stumbling over similar names and topics before finding the correct one. Memory was the basic tool of counterintelligence; no computer could take the place of a master analyst's ability to draw together superficially unrelated fragments of information gleaned over decades of experience. But the years and the sheer weight of facts had overwhelmed Max Zimmer's memory. The wheels revolved slowly.

"Hussar." Max tasted the word. "I never got to the bottom of that."

"Nor did the Firm." Canning wanted to ask him point-blank whether the missing papers from the counterintelligence archives contained Zimmer's findings on the Agency people who had been briefed on the Hussar case. But a direct question was the slowest way of eliciting information from Max Zimmer. So instead, Canning said, "The Agency has a new defector."

"I know."

Max would, Canning thought. He still possessed his private Mafia of unconditional loyalists. Had he been a mobster, he was the kind who would have been able to go on running his rackets from inside a jail cell.

"The defector says Hussar was betrayed from inside the Agency."

"I know." Zimmer was volunteering nothing.

"I have an interest, Max. You know that."

Max gave no sign of acknowledgment, busying himself with the mechanics of rolling and lighting a cigarette. The black tobacco gave off a sour, pungent aroma.

"Les Winter doesn't believe the defector."

Now Max looked up, and there was unalloyed hatred in the huge eyes behind the bifocals.

"Have you talked to Winter?"

"No," Canning admitted. "But you know, there's a big investigation going on. Dick Hammond is handling it on the Agency side."

"Dick is a good operator," Zimmer conceded. "But he should stick to overthrowing foreign governments. He knows as much about counterintelligence as I know about quadrupole accelerators. I suppose that's why they picked him."

Canning knew that Max was bitter that nobody had invited him back, after the change of presidency, to advise on the rebuilding of counterintelligence. A number of top Agency people had threatened to resign if he was given any official role, even as a consultant. The newspaper story that he had been a double agent had destroyed any remaining hope.

"Anyway," Canning pursued, "the argument seems to revolve around Martini. Winter says the Agency can't be penetrated if it's able to run such a valuable agent-in-place as Martini."

"Nonsense. The case is closed down. Wound up. Kaput. Whatever Martini really amounted to."

"I don't understand." Canning was genuinely puzzled. "Martini made contact with the Agency in New York within the last four weeks. After Ushinsky's defection. And he's still secure in Moscow. In fact, he's a KGB major general."

"*What?*" Zimmer gasped so painfully, out of a constricted throat, that Canning was afraid he was in the process of choking. "It can't be," he said almost inaudibly, in the voice of a man who had been gassed.

"Martini was in New York. I saw him myself, at a table in the Café Carlyle. I'm told his real name is Orlov."

Max sat mouth agape, limbs dangling slackly over his sofa, in a state that seemed to Canning to approach catatonic shock. The Englishman waited for some response, and when none came, he said, "Max? Are you all right?"

Max still did not move, his eyes glassy, staring into space.

"Max? Can I get you something?"

When Zimmer spoke, his words seemed to come from far away, addressed to himself, not the Englishman who had divorced his niece. "Krylov knows they never learned the history," he said.

"What's that, Max? The history?"

"Tell Dick Hammond to read the history. I can't help you." The bitterness inside him drew lines on his face like cracked ice. He seized his cane and tried to haul himself to his feet, stabbing at the floor.

It was then that Canning risked the direct question. "The files," he said. "I have to know about the handlers, Max. You have to help me."

"I don't know what you're talking about."

"I have a right to know, Max. Because of Hussar."

"Go to the Agency," Zimmer spat. "They've got the files. Go to

Les Winter. If anything's missing, it's because they've been shredding paper to cover their ass."

"Max . . ." Canning pleaded.

"I'm tired," said the old spymaster. "I need to lie down for a bit. It gets to the point where all you have to look forward to in the day is an afternoon nap."

17

MIAMI, *October 13*

"I'm in a pay phone." Max Zimmer spoke so fast that he sounded as if he were gargling his words.

"Hold on, Max." Canning switched off the television news, and a shot of a memorial service in Chicago in honor of the workers who had died when Soviet tanks rolled into Poland slowly faded from the screen.

"I think I've got something," said Zimmer, still swallowing the ends of his words. "Can you meet me later? Say around nine?"

"Of course." Canning looked out through the eighteenth-floor window at the Coconut Grove Hotel over the panorama of hundreds of yachts and skiffs bobbing about in the Dinner Key Marina. "Do you want me to come out to the house? Or we could meet at Arthur's," the Englishman suggested. "That's about midway between us."

"No. Meet me at Vizcaya. It's just up the road from you. Do you know Vizcaya?"

"I haven't been there in years." Canning recalled an improbably Italianate limestone palace, set in formal gardens, looking out over Biscayne Bay.

"Meet me in the casino."

"Where?"

"The summerhouse at the back of the place. You'll find it okay."

"I'll try. But Max . . . " The phone went dead.

Why the dramatic shift in Zimmer's tone? Canning wondered. Earlier, when he had got to his real questions, the former counterintelligence chief had clammed up, displaying at first

196

shock, then icy reserve. Now, Max sounded desperately anxious to talk.

Canning took a last swim before sunset. Girls in skimpy shorts ferried cocktails in plastic cups to people lounging around the pool. A middle-class New York couple were soaking up the last rays on lounges by the poolside. The man held a reflector under his chin, while she read him extracts from a how-to book on improving your sex life. "Gee, honey," Canning heard her say as he came up for air, "a book like this can really help you with your life."

Back in the suite, he put on a light linen jacket over his cream trousers, to conceal the 9mm Smith & Wesson he slipped into a shoulder holster. He rarely wore a gun in New York, even though nearly two thousand people a year got killed there, often enough the victims of random murders. But the same intuition that made Canning strap on a gun in Miami led him to check under the front suspension and the hood of his rented Mustang, which he had left parked in the street, before settling into the driver's seat. In proportion to the population, Miami ranked as one of the murder capitals of the United States, especially since the latest influx of Cuban and Haitian immigrants, and in the underground wars between drug racketeers and political factions, booby-trapping cars had become the favorite way of disposing of enemies. Canning was not part of the Miami scene, but had been there often enough to develop a profile.

As he swung north along South Bayshore Drive, he recalled his last visit to Vizcaya. One of the most active Cuban émigré groups had been pleading with the Agency to renew support for seaborne raids into the island. The Agency had been officially banned from supporting these dangerous maritime missions from the start of 1973; more recently—to the horror of the South Florida Cuban community and old Agency hands—the Bureau had been ordered by a previous administration to turn over intelligence on "terrorist" activities planned by émigré organizations to Castro's secret service. Against this backdrop, the exile group's hopes for Agency backing in a fairly half-baked scheme reflected a touching naiveté about the condition of American politics and the American intelligence community. However, it had transpired that the man in charge of the Agency's Miami base at the time, operating under cover of one of the beach clubs, was not a demoralized nine-tofiver, but Dick Hammond. He had listened sympathetically to the argument that resistance inside Cuba would eventually flicker out unless there were constant demonstrations that rebellion was possible. Instead of filing a report to Langley, he had turned to the Club. In the elaborate gardens of the Vizcaya Palace, he and Canning and a former Cuban naval officer with the sobriquet Captain Blood had plotted a seaborne landing in Oriente province that had resulted in the overnight occupation of a large village, under the noses of Castro's army and secret police. They handed out leaflets, transistor radios, and toys. Canning had insisted, as a private citizen, on going all the way, and landing with the rebels. Hammond, straining at the leash, had finally said, "Screw it. I'm going too." If they had been caught, they both knew, they would still be sitting in one of Castro's jails. But the Club was not caught out. Not that time.

Canning pulled off Miami Avenue and wound up the sinuous driveway through an untamed tropical jungle. A steamy heat huffed at him like a forge bellows through the open window of the car. Remembering the rendezvous with Captain Blood on a narrow bridge over the backwaters of the bay, framed by twisting oriental columns surmounted by stone peacocks, Canning reflected that the Vizcaya Palace was the perfect locale for a clandestine meeting. Dick Hammond and his predecessors must have held hundreds there in their day, in the shadowed privacy of the walled gardens, grottos, and wooded clearings.

He gently braked to a halt in front of the exposed roots of an ancient banyan tree, gnarled and tortured like arthritic limbs. The humid air coated his face like a hot towel. He could hear the shrill of cicadas, the twittering and hooting of birds concealed among the dense foliage, a distant cacophony of voices. Another sound provided a steady chorus: the sound of running water. It became stronger as he walked, in the clear light of the half-moon, toward the circular plaza in front of the main entrance to the house. On either side of the road, water spouted from jets and splashed in little cascades through a series of shell-shaped basins in a finely graduated descent toward the two big fountains in the plaza. There was never stillness in the grounds of Vizcaya: at every turning, there was the sense of constant movement, the rippling of a fountain or a man-made stream.

198

Vizcaya. It was a Basque word, meaning a high place. The people of Miami had given the same name, in a corrupted form, to their bay. The house and its splendid gardens—comparable with Versailles, or the Villa d'Este—had been constructed by a bachelor millionaire, James Deering, in the first quarter of the century to serve him as a winter palace. He used his fortunes to import Roman baths, Egyptian urns, Italian marbles, and French tapestries, and to simulate the architectural flourishes of the Renaissance and the baroque schools. In 1952, his heirs had sold his magnificent folly to Dade County, and it was thrown open to the public and borrowed for mayoral receptions. At night, spotlights were turned on and the main house, with its dramatically contrasting facades, became the theme of a *son et lumière* entertainment.

Canning dutifully paid his admission fee at the gate, and side-stepped the straggle of tourists outside the entrance loggia, turning instead through a gateway on the left that supported a seahorse carved from coraline rock. Farther left, over away to the north, he could see the causeway that linked the mainland to Key Biscayne. He walked parallel to the northern wall of the palace, built in a heavy, solemn seventeenth-century style that contrasted with the open, airy facade of the front of Vizcaya, decked out with jaunty blue-and-yellow hangings. The eastern facade, overlooking Biscayne Bay, was different again; viewed from the seaward side, the palace, with its tall corner towers and parapets, looked like a fortress armed to repel intruders. James Deering's great house suited the multilayered complexity of the man that Canning had come to meet. Within its walled gardens, nothing could be taken for granted; appearances altered abruptly, radically, if you shifted your vantage point by even a few feet.

The scene that confronted the Englishman, as he looked out toward open sea, might have been lifted from one of Canaletto's canvases. A terrace of broad flagstones ended in wide steps leading down into the water. The tall mooring posts along its edge were painted in stripes, like barbers' poles. Rising out of the bay, only twenty or thirty feet from the shore, was a great stone barge, designed by Stirling Calder to serve as a breakwater that would guard the palace against squalls and storms. Disporting themselves on its upper decks were stone figures of noblemen and

199

Venetian doges; midships were sculptured porters and women bearing baskets on their heads.

Adjusting his stride so as to make the rendezvous at the stroke of nine, Canning continued his walk into the landscaped gardens. Clipped hedgerows and shrubs were laid out in the shape of a fan. He strolled between statues of nymphs and fauns, Olympic gods and nameless presences of the night. Leaving the bright lights of the palace behind, he walked on into deeper shadows, where the thicker vegetation blotted out the moon. He skirted the rim of a deep grotto, lined with shells, presided over by the threatening images of grimacing giants. Ahead were the muddy backwaters of the bay, which swallowed the moonlight instead of reflecting it. Upstream, the channel's course was lost in a sprawling mangrove swamp.

Canning paused in front of a flight of winding steps leading up to the garden casino that James Deering had built, on its artificial hill, according to the conventions of baroque design. From the other side of the mound came the sound of muffled voices, gradually rising in volume. Two people, he guessed. Soon there were footsteps, accompanied by gusts of laughter. Probably young lovers, coming from the direction of the Peacock Bridge.

He had already climbed three or four steps when he was arrested by the sight of something that glinted at the water's edge. He retraced his steps, checking both ways to make sure that no one was in sight of him along the path. He had not been mistaken. The object was a gun. An old Beretta, semiautomatic. Fitted with a silencer. And—stranger—some kind of weight attached to the butt. The barrel was still warm. Canning looked up, over his shoulder, at the open facade of James Deering's casino on the hill. The meeting place. Yes. The gun could have been thrown—or fallen—from there, maybe intended to land in the backwaters of the bay. Max Zimmer.

Canning had his hand on the butt of his own gun, under his jacket, as he leaped up the steps toward the garden pavilion. He was not fast enough. He was only halfway up when a scream knifed through the summer night. A scream, followed by a woman's cry—"Oh my God!"—and then the pulpy sound of retching.

Canning came over the edge of the mound, crouched low, his Smith & Wesson stretched out before him.

200

"Get down, Suzie," said a nervous, adolescent voice. "Don't look."

Cowering in a corner of the open pavilion, under a fresco of gamboling nymphs and minor deities in the style of Tiepolo, Canning saw a teenage girl and boy, identically clad in T-shirts, Levi's, and sneakers. Closer to him on the tiled floor was the huddled body of a man. He looked as if he had fallen forward from a sitting position, perhaps from the wide sill of the open, arched window behind him. There was a rust-colored pool around his head, which was buried face-down on the floor, spattered with gray. Canning knew the man at once from his spare, bony limbs and his old black jacket.

"You're okay. Just stay put," he said to the kids, as he inserted the toe of one suede shoe under the dead man's chest, spinning his body sideways, so that his face would be clearly seen in the moonlight.

"Are you a cop?" asked the boy, still edgy.

"Sort of."

The bullet had been fired from the level of Max Zimmer's mouth or jaw, tracing a red welt all the way up his cheek to where it had exploded into the socket of his left eye, leaving a raw, oozing jelly. The bullet had exited through the top of his head, spattering specks of flesh and brain matter over the walls and floor of the casino.

There was a grayish splodge on Canning's shoe.

He looked away, willing himself not to see the columns of tiny ants that were converging around the corpse. The body was still warm. Zimmer could not have been shot more than ten or fifteen minutes earlier. Maybe less.

"Did you see anyone?" he addressed the teenagers. "Anyone leaving here?"

"Only you," said the boy. "We saw you down by the water."

"You'd better go and tell one of the attendants to call the cops."

"I thought you said you were a cop."

"Only sort of."

Staring at Canning, the boy guided his girlfriend backward down the first few steps, as if scared of what the Englishman might do if he turned his eyes away.

Canning took the Beretta out of his coat pocket and looked at the curious metal attachment that had been fitted to its butt.

Some kind of weight, and a spring. Canning had seen a similar contraption used only once before, by a man who had committed suicide. In order to make sure that his family would be able to claim on his insurance policies, he had shot himself on top of a high cliff, using a weighted gun in the hope that the suicide weapon would vanish from sight in the scrub in the valley below him. For Max Zimmer, a man of mercurial mood changes and black, nihilistic depressions, suicide was not an impossibility.

But Canning found it difficult to accept that the man who had phoned him with an urgent message a few hours before would have decided to take his own life in the interim. And if his aim was indeed to kill himself while hiding the evidence, why pick such a clumsy way of going about it, in a public place where he might easily have been observed?

There were no clues in Max Zimmer's pockets, which were empty apart from car keys, a few dollars, and basic identification: driver's license, social security registration, a couple of credit cards. Oh yes. And a book of matches from the Tel Aviv Hilton.

Sally, he thought. How was he going to explain her uncle's death to her? Or to Jimmy, who had been playing an oriental board game with the old man the day before? In Max's barren, loveless life, tenderness for the boy had blossomed like a single flower in an asphalt prison yard. The child had sensed that, and responded.

A stone satyr mocked Canning as he walked back toward the main house.

18

Fuck it, Sergeant Tom Ryan of Homicide had said to his chief, *I want to grill this limey.*

No way, he was told. *The Bureau's taking over this one.*

I say it stinks, Ryan had said. *This is our bag.*

Leave off, the chief had warned him. *Ain't you got nothing else to do?*

So Tom Ryan sat there and glowered at his desk, munching on an onion roll, while a procession of worried outsiders traveled in and out of the chief's office. He could pick the Agency guys at a glance: the short, Latino type in a dressy blazer, with a pencil-thin moustache; the lean, waspy one who looked, in his gray suit, as if he'd just come off a commuter train from Wall Street. He wondered what they were all hatching in there.

A cover-up. He could smell it. They wanted to make sure everyone got his story straight and called it suicide. *Well,* he thought, *they better not ask me. It weren't no suicide.*

Tom Ryan got up, tucked in his shirttail, and reached for the report he had made out earlier that day on another murder case. He'd been called out to the bank of a canal in southwest Miami to look at what a couple of Cuban fishermen had hauled in. It was the naked, decomposing trunk of a white male. Someone had hacked the dead man's legs off just above the knees, maybe using a saw. The arms were missing too, severed at the shoulders. The sawblade must have broken when they tried to cut off the man's head, because they hadn't quite finished the job. The butchery had been carried out four or five days earlier, since the fish—or maybe the rats—had had time to strip a lot of the flesh away from his

203

face. And his genitals. There was no sign of the missing limbs. But someone had called in from Monroe County to say that some tourists had come across a pair of severed and rotting legs out on Duck Key. Maybe they would fit. *Hell, what did it matter,* Tom Ryan said to himself. The guy had no use for them anyway. "Victim unidentified white male," his report noted. "Perpetrators unknown. Case is open pending." There were plenty of murder cases in the files marked "open pending." Eight or nine out of ten. It helped to depersonalize them, to use words like "victim" and "perpetrator" inside your head as well as when filling out forms. You got less angry that way.

Ryan, with his face like a slab of raw beef, looked like a man who could get pretty angry. Years of frustration had trained him to get a bridle on his temper, not to get angry every time a case had to be marked down as "open pending" or a junkie knocked someone off for the price of a fix. More and more, his anger was focused on the big things that made his job impossible, things he was so powerless to change that they were almost abstractions. Like the government, which had let in a tide of new immigrants from Castro's jails and other hellholes around the Caribbean without finding them jobs and homes and a place in the community. Like the mob, which got away with peddling the hard drugs because, when the payoffs are fat enough, people think it's respectable to be on the take. Like the bigotry of fellow cops who saw the county's black community as an undifferentiated, hostile mass and had given up trying to work it for the kind of sources and cooperation you need to solve cases. Like the big media, which played up stories of police brutality and made that schism even wider.

At this moment, Tom Ryan's temper was slowly coming to the boiling point because he perceived that some very powerful interests were conspiring to come between him and a case that he thought, for once, he might be able to crack. The death of the Agency's former head of counterintelligence was not like the identikit murder of one of a hundred nameless Colombian drug pushers who'd got knocked off in Dade County in the last few years. You had names. Enemies. Motives. And you could start with the question of what that unexplained Englishman was doing with Max Zimmer after dark in the grounds of Vizcaya.

But there was the Limey, leaving the chief's office in a huddle with the Latino spook. Ryan scowled at them, noting the bulge of Canning's pistol under his light summer jacket. That was a pretty big cannon for a tourist.

"Good evening, Sergeant," said Canning pleasantly.

Ryan groped around in a paper sack from the grocery store for a sandwich, pointedly ignoring the Englishman. You didn't lose weight on night shift. That made him angry too.

"Can I give you a lift?" Canning's swarthy companion asked him when they were outside.

Morales was a tiny mulatto built like a steel spring who had fought in the Bay of Pigs and almost everywhere else that had given him an opportunity to fight Castro. No longer on the Agency payroll, he seemed to have contacts everywhere and could play the Miami Cuban community like a harp. Morales and Canning had been friends since they had sailed together on an insane maritime raid into Oriente province.

"Thanks," said Canning, "but I've got a car." He looked at his watch. It was nearly midnight. Sally and Phyllis had probably gone to bed, but he decided it was better to drive over to the Beach and tell them what had happened now, instead of waiting. By breakfast time, the news could be on TV. "We'll talk in the morning. All right?"

"Listen," said Morales. "You need anything, you call that second number I gave you. Not the home number, okay? My wife thinks I'm in Panama."

"Okay." Canning smiled. Morales had a reputation as a dedicated womanizer.

The Englishman walked up the street, toward the rented Mustang that he had left parked in a pool of shadow between two street lights.

He stopped short before he reached the car. Something was different. Or else he must have been so preoccupied by Max Zimmer's death that he'd forgotten to turn the headlights off. Yes, that must have been it. An easy thing to do. But . . . it was not the fact that the Mustang's lights were blazing, or even, as he now noticed, that the door on the driver's side had been left ajar, that caused the chill sensation along his spine. *The engine was running.*

Could he have left the keys in the ignition?

Canning thrust a hand into his trouser pocket and felt the heavy loop of his monogrammed key ring. He had his keys, so he must have turned off the engine.

There was his car, door open, lights on, engine running, as if someone had made it ready for him to drive away. He asked himself who would have done that. A thief who had been surprised at the last minute and fled? Or someone who meant to warn him off?

The Mustang could be booby-trapped, he realized. He called out to Morales, who was getting into his own car. Morales immediately grasped the situation.

"Okay," said the Cuban. "I'll fix it. Take my car."

"It's all right," said Canning. "I'll get a cab." He walked down to the corner and one stopped almost immediately.

The driver was a cheerful beach-boy type who was heading for forty but not admitting it. He came complete with a deep tan, surf-rinsed blond hair, a set of flashy gold charms around his neck, and a relentless patter. He did not seem to be put off by Canning's silence in the back seat.

"I wasn't always a cabbie," he announced, getting into his stride.

Canning made no response, staring fixedly at the office blocks along Biscayne Boulevard.

They must have followed me from Vizcaya, he was thinking. *But how did they know the meeting was going to be there? They must have followed Max from the Beach. But he's an old pro at dodging surveillance. It must have been the phone call. Max was using a phone booth. So either they bugged me at the hotel, or . . . they knew Max used that phone booth for special communications, and bugged it as well as his house. But who was They?*

"Care for a smoke?" the cabbie persisted, determined to draw Canning into conversation. He half turned, waving a pack of Marlboros.

"No thanks."

The state of his car could not have been a coincidence, Canning was thinking. Whoever had killed Max must have been trying to scare him away. They were not going to succeed.

"I used to be in show biz." This time, the cabbie didn't wait for a comment from his passenger. "I tell you, though, taxi driving can be quite a ball. You wouldn't believe the women I get in this hack. One of them offered me a big bill to do it right there on the back seat. She wasn't too old, either. Said her husband kept her on a chain."

Canning grunted. *Max said the Agency had been spying on him. And the Agency man with Morales, at the police station, was very eager to write Max's death off as suicide. Too eager. As if that was already Company policy. As if . . . No.* Canning's mind buckled away from the thought. The Agency did not murder its own, not even those who switched sides or went public to denounce its supposed crimes. *But the information that prompted the killing could have come from inside the Agency. If there's a mole.*

"I picked up this chick earlier tonight," the driver was saying. "She was a real fox. You know what she said to me? She says, 'Do you want a blow?' I couldn't believe my luck. I turned around, pulled off the road, stopped the cab. You know what she meant? She was snorting coke there, right in the back. She was asking if I wanted some. I guess she was pretty embarrassed."

Canning let the stream of anecdotes, each raunchier than the last, wash over him like background Muzak. *It can't be suicide,* he told himself again. Max had wanted to tell him something, something that held the key to Hussar's end. That was what he had to find. He had to make a dead man speak.

When he got to the house, he found Phyllis sitting up, watching the late show. She came to the door in a flowing silk robe, the color of ripe apricots, her ash blond hair hanging loose. The woman was ageless, he thought.

"Sally's asleep," Phyllis said. "She caught too much sun at the beach today. I don't sleep much myself anymore. I suppose it's the effect of creeping senility."

He lingered by the door until she said, "It's Max, isn't it? I sensed it when he didn't come back tonight."

There had always been a certain telepathy between Phyllis and her close family. The rapport that she had had with her brother, Canning had noticed, was even more intense between Phyllis and her daughter. When Sally was in a hospital bed, about to give birth to Jimmy, Phyllis had called Canning, imploring him to warn the doctors about possible complications. She had dreamed that the child would be born with the cord wound twice around his neck, threatening to choke him. Canning had been too embarrassed to say anything to the hospital staff. But the scene had been enacted exactly as Phyllis had seen it in her sleep. Only the deftness of a veteran midwife had saved Jimmy from strangulation or possible brain damage.

Now Phyllis accepted the news of her brother's death calmly and fatalistically, as if she had known all along.

"Poor Max," she said. "At least there's nothing more they can do to him now. He didn't kill himself, did he?"

"We can't be sure. But I don't believe it."

They agreed not to wake Sally. Phyllis could tell her in the morning. They would explain to Jimmy that Uncle Max had been called away on business.

"Look at that." Phyllis pointed to the corner of the living room where the Go board had been set up on a coffee table. "They were playing that game again after lunch. Jimmy refused to leave off. That boy just won't say die."

The mask cracked then, and Phyllis began to sob. Canning put his arms around her, folding her gently to his chest.

"Max wanted to tell me something," he said to her. "I have to find out what it was, and I don't know where to begin. Will you help me?"

"Of course. But how can I help?"

"There were papers, Phyllis. Agency files. They were important enough to kill for. Everyone will be looking. We have to find them first. Do you know anything?"

"Let me think." She sat up straight, still dabbing at her eyes, but composed now that there was a practical problem to be dealt with. "I don't know."

"Did he give you anything of his to keep for him?"

"No."

"I don't think I'll find what we're looking for in his home. Everyone's looked there already. But there may be some clue they've all overlooked."

"I'll give you the spare key."

The air in Max Zimmer's living room, overlooking the water, was acrid with stale tobacco. Canning threw open a window and lit up one of his own cigars. The house was full of old books and memorabilia. Max had stored in a glass cabinet part of his famous intelligence library. Canning inspected a few of the volumes. He recognized a copy of the memoirs of Matthew Smith, a seventeenth-century English spy who had infiltrated the Jacobite movement in Versailles on behalf of William of Orange; his autobiography, first published in 1699, was the first book in the English language entirely devoted to the art of spying. There were still more exotic tomes on Max's shelves. Canning gingerly removed an elaborately morocco-bound volume and found it was the original Latin edition of the *Steganographia* of Abbot Trithemius of Sponheim, published in Frankfurt in 1606. The book had been the inspiration of the famed Elizabethan magus and arch-intriguer John Dee, who, centuries before James Bond was conceived, had used the number 007 as his personal cipher. The *Steganographia* was a guide to secret writing in code; it also contained the occult instructions according to which the magus could summon up the angels and the demons of earth, time and the planets, and make them work to do his bidding. As Canning leafed through the magical tome, a slip of paper covered with Max Zimmer's minute, spidery scrawl slipped from between the covers. Canning scooped it from the floor. The note contained a translation, evidently by Zimmer himself, of a letter of advice that Abbot Trithemius had sent to one of his disciples in the occult. "This one rule I advise you to observe," wrote Trithemius, "that you communicate vulgar secrets to vulgar friends, but higher and more secret matters, only to higher and more secretive friends."

That was the spirit in which Max Zimmer had conducted his life. To be admitted to his secrets was to be admitted to a hermetic cabal. But how could Canning gain admission now that Max was dead?

He ransacked the house, from the near-empty refrigerator to bathroom cabinets full of pills, finding no clue. He explored the garage, and saw that Sally had been borrowing space in the corner that Max used to fashion his gold and silver jewelry. Canning found the parts of a small copper monkey, not yet soldered together.

Then he walked around the garage and looked out over the water. He could hear the engine of a small boat coughing and rumbling as it nosed south, toward Fisher Island. He stared at the small private jetty that ran out from the foot of Zimmer's lawn. There was no sign of the motorboat.

Canning did not need to call Phyllis. As if drawn by instinct, she was standing by the picket fence.

"Max took the boat out after lunch," she said. "I never saw him come back."

Maybe that was the clue. Max had gone by boat, not car, to keep his rendezvous at Vizcaya. The boat might hold what Canning was looking for. If someone else had not already found it.

"Do you mind if I take your car?" he said.

Max Zimmer had sometimes remarked that you are rarely as private as you can be in a popular meeting place. He had tied up his motorboat, with no effort at concealment, at the yacht landing near the great stone barge in front of James Deering's winter palace. Canning could see under the moonlight, before he even snapped on his torch, that his search was wasted. There was a small metal box in the belly of the boat, the size of a small suitcase, the sort of thing that a camera crew might use to transport film. The box had been waterproofed. Canning could see that because it was wide open. Whatever Max had been carrying in the box was gone.

That could not be the end of it, Canning thought later as he lay on his back on the big bed at the Coconut Grove Hotel, watching the glow of his cigar ash. Max must have carefully weighed the risk that he would be followed or intercepted. It was impossible to accept that, having hidden his secrets so successfully for so many years, he would risk losing everything now. He must have taken out an insurance policy. He might have left copies of the files with a lawyer, with instructions to release them—to the White House? to the media?—in the event of his sudden death. But it was more likely that the man who had studied Abbot Trithemius would want to ensure that his secrets were passed on to someone close to

210

him who would know precisely what use to make of them. Who would that person be?

The Café-Brasserie on the ground floor was still closed when Canning took the elevator downstairs. He had already taken a couple of swallows from his traveler's flask of brandy to wash the burr from his mouth. When he stepped out through the swing doors of the hotel into the drive—walled in by a line of spreading banyans, magnificent survivors from a previous era—the morning was already dank and warm. His reflex movement was to throw off his jacket, but he stopped himself, remembering the pistol strapped to his side.

The traffic was still light on the road to the beach, but there were a few refugee families straggling along on foot, their worldly goods tied up in bundles on their backs. Like Los Angeles, Miami was not a city for pedestrians; sidewalks were rare. Futuristic shopping malls took the place of a town center, a space where people could stroll and shoot the breeze. That was why, for all the delights of long sandy beaches and all-year sun, Canning thought Miami alien, governed by quadrupeds, not bipeds.

At the house at the beach, he found Sally and Phyllis red-eyed, sitting up drinking coffee from big steaming mugs.

"The police came by," Phyllis explained. "And a guy from the Bureau. They asked a few questions."

"About what?"

"Max's psychological state, mostly."

"What did you tell them?"

"I told them I hadn't seen Max so at ease with himself for a long time. Mostly because of Jimmy."

"Where is Jimmy?" Canning looked around for his son.

"He's playing by the pool," Sally said.

Canning kissed her cheek. She looked gray and wan, as if the Miami tan had faded away overnight. "I'm sorry," he said. "You know how I felt about Max. I loved him too."

Phyllis studied him interrogatively. "Did you find—"

"No. Only the boat. We can drive out to Vizcaya and bring it back later if you want."

211

"Oh." Phyllis withdrew into brisk practicality. "We have to plan the funeral."

Jimmy came running into the living room in his swimsuit. He grabbed Canning around the waist, dripping water over his trousers. "Daddy," he said, "why did Uncle Max have to go away?"

"He couldn't help it, Jimmy. I'll explain when you're bigger."

"That's what Mommy's always saying," the child protested. "I don't understand. Uncle Max said he was going to take me to Monkey World. And we never finished our game."

The Go pieces were still laid out on the coffee table, as they had been the night before. Most of the board had been overrun by black stones.

"Which color were you playing?" Canning asked his son.

"White."

"Well, it looks to me as if Max had this game sewn up."

"He didn't! He said I could be the winner."

"Uncle Max was being nice."

"*No*, Daddy," the boy insisted. "He said the game isn't over until the box is empty."

"That's a funny thing to say." Canning swilled the words around in his head. Then he moved over to the coffee table and examined the antique ivory box, engraved with oriental court scenes, that held the Go stones. Phyllis had said that Max had not given her anything of his to keep, Canning reflected. But that wasn't entirely true. There was the game. The box, he noticed, seemed deeper than was necessary to accommodate the shallow trays that held the players' black and white stones. Canning removed the trays and turned the box around in his hands, exploring its surface with his fingertips.

His thumb touched a tiny indentation in the underside of the box. He pushed, and a hidden catch snapped free, so that he was able to slide back the bottom panel to reveal a secret cavity. Inside, sealed up in light-tight metallic containers, were four spools of microfilm. So Max had left his message after all. He had bequeathed his secrets not to a lawyer, or a former colleague, but to a five-year-old boy.

"Let's make a deal," he said to Jimmy. "You let me keep these, and I'll finish the game with you later."

*   *   *

The simplest course of action, Canning knew, would be to board the next plane to Washington and turn Max's microfilm over to the Agency. It was not just the fatigue and the pain clogging the Englishman's brain that made him act differently. Max had wanted to reach *him;* even after an assassin's bullet had stopped their meeting, Max had managed to reach him through the child. Canning had the right to know *first.* Because Max had wanted it that way. And because of Hussar.

So he called Morales and asked if he would arrange to have some microfilm developed and screened quickly without officially involving any government organization.

"I'll call in a favor," Morales said. Morales always seemed to be able to do that. Whatever problem needed to be solved, there was always a man in the community who owed him.

Within an hour, Morales had installed Canning in a private office at the back of a photoprocessing company near Calle Ocho in Little Havana, with a machine of the sort that is routinely used for browsing through old newspaper files that are stored on microfilm.

As he studied the first few documents that were blown up on the screen, the Englishman sucked in his breath. They were not what he was looking for, but they were dynamite. Already enough to kill for. There was an assessment, in Max Zimmer's own near-illegible scrawl, of the damage that might have been done by a Soviet agent on the National Security Council. There was a long report on the career of Max's favorite *bête noire* in the media, Sol Puig. According to Max, the celebrated investigative reporter had come from the same stable as a Polish-born Communist who had been Moscow's main recruiter in Havana before the revolution. There was a copy of a field directive from Krylov at Moscow Center to the KGB residency in Bonn, outlining the ground rules by which double agents were to be recruited and run in the West. Krylov's directive reiterated the basic philosophy of the Beacon. "Without planting our agents in the enemy services," it stated, "we cannot hope for success in our operations." In the frame following the Krylov directive, Max had included a roughly drawn organizational chart headed "The Beacon." Like branches of an upside-down tree, growing from top to bottom, Max had sketched a network of KGB controllers and agents fanning out from Krylov's office in Moscow Center over a period of more than thirty years. The dates checked off along the left-hand side of the chart enabled you to see, at a glance, what assets had been available to the Beacon in a given year, and to guess at how Krylov's agents in different Western services had been used to support each other.

It was the right-hand, downward-sloping branch of the tree that interested the Englishman most. It contained the names of a number of people in the Agency. Some of the names appeared between brackets, suggesting that the individual had retired, or died. Some were qualified by question marks, indicating that Max had not been able to resolve his suspicions.

One name that frequently appeared with a question mark had Canning peering forward into the viewer in disbelief. He read it again: Lester F. Winter.

He switched frames hastily, looking for supporting documentation. But it was clear that whoever had made the microfilm copies of Max's key papers had grouped the material together in random fashion. The next document was an evaluation of the harm that a Cuban double agent might have done to Agency operations while he was employed in Caracas as one of the chiefs of the Venezuelan secret service.

Canning made a mental note to come back to the next document: a study of double-agent cases originating in New York, with Max's evaluation of how disinformation could have been fed to the administration through contaminated channels.

Les Winter's name leaped at him from the middle of a page, and he read it carefully. In a commentary on the work of the double agent code-named Martini, Max observed that the man at the Agency who had been mainly responsible for handling the case—and for disseminating the intelligence product to consumers in the Washington community—had been Les Winter. The dead spy chief noted that Krylov and the Beacon had spared no effort, over the decades, in trying to advance the careers of their agents in Western services by supplying them with apparent intelligence successes that could be used to advance their careers. Had this been Martini's role? Had Moscow Center used a fake double agent to help build the career of a mole at Langley?

The next frames were again unrelated to the main questions in Canning's mind. His eyes were becoming sore from poring over the viewer under the harsh, surgical light in the office. The air in the room was cold and stale from the air conditioning. The desktop was littered with photographs of grinning children, the family of the proprietor, an old *brigadista* who had fought with Morales in the Bay of Pigs. A smiling Cuban girl who might have been one of his kids in the photos popped her head around the door to hand Canning a tiny cup of black coffee.

He had exhausted the first two spools before he found what he wanted: Max's personal notes on Agency colleagues who had fallen under his suspicions. There were notes on twelve cases, some of them dating back to the early fifties, in which Max had brought in the Bureau to investigate the possible disloyalty of Agency personnel. Canning recognized some of the names. Two of the suspects had been cut out of classified work and put in windowless box rooms without telephones until they got the message and sought early retirement. Canning remembered a third suspect from his time in Moscow. Lacking time to savor all the details, Canning flicked on from sheet to sheet with gathering impatience.

Then he had it. "Memo to Self: Lester F. Winter" read the title of a handwritten report in which Max's minuscule script shrank to near-invisibility. Canning looked around the office for a magnifying glass to help him make out some of the more obscure words. The memo had been couched by Zimmer in the form of a question-and-answer session with himself.

Q: What is the ideal job for an American Philby?

A: Moscow Center wants continuity of access. There are relatively few jobs in the Agency where a man (or woman) can retain access to highly classified counterespionage material over a long period of time, without being shuttled around from one foreign post to another. One post where this is possible is the Reports and Requirements section of Soviet Division. It's a small section with a fairly permanent staff—i.e., once you've got a penetration agent in there, you've got a permanent fix. Access is far-reaching as a result of the two specific functions of R&R section. It takes in raw reports from Soviet Division's sources in the field and processes them into finished products for distribution to the rest of the community. So if Soviet Division recruited a new agent, R&R section would know about it. (Was there ever a case when this wasn't so? I believe not.) The requirements function of R&R section means that it has a need to know what types of information the Agency—and other U.S. services—are looking for in order to task agents in the field. Someone in R&R would know what we had, in terms of human sources, and what we do *not* have, in terms of intelligence from Moscow. It's an ideal slot for a Philby. That or the CI staff. Winter worked in R&R section for seven—or eight?—years. (Check bio.)

Q: What went wrong after Winter took charge of Soviet Division?

A: Nearly everything for which he could not take personal credit. Witness: a series of human sources blown or doubled back against us. (Note: one major leak may have been from NSC.) To the extent that Winter had access to allied operations, their agents were burned too. Witness: arrest of Hussar. By contrast, Winter's own prize agent, Martini, appeared to be indestructible. This fits the pattern of Beacon operations. Once Krylov maneuvers a mole into a key position, he takes care not to close down all the agent networks that the mole is able to betray. He leaves some channels and networks open. Ones he can control. That way, the victimized service is duped into thinking that everything is okay, and that the mole is its star performer. Irony: the mole *looks* like the most successful operator in the service. That's why it's so hard to get backing for an investigation. You'll be accused of sour grapes, or worse: of doubting the service's most prized achievements.

Q: What other damage did he do?

A: Winter helped destroy our mechanisms for monitoring Soviet deception/penetration, by (1) emasculating the counterintelligence staff, and (2) circulating reports from Soviet-controlled double agents under misleading labels, so the rest of the Washington intelligence community was gypped.

216

This led to some of our most serious errors in assessing Moscow's intentions and military capacities.

Q: How did Krylov get to him?

A: Through the wife, Katya. Daughter of Zhores Malinovsky, bookseller, trades under name of George Mallaby, White Russian émigré involved with Blake in Korea. See separate memo. Additional motivation: professional jealousy and spite.

Canning's eye ran on, through Max's chronicle of the intelligence failures for which he believed Winter to be responsible. It all seemed circumstantial, or merely speculative, or, worse still, the accumulated bile of an intra-Agency feud in which Max had been bested. The Englishman looked for the "separate memo" on Winter's ex-wife, Katya. He failed to find it. He switched off the viewer, sunk in a deep depression. Max's files, at the end of the hunt, seemed to amount to little more than the written equivalent of a confidence whispered, behind a sheltering hand, in the smoking room of the Army and Navy Club. There was nothing firm enough to stand on.

Canning pocketed the four spools of microfilm and walked out, to find that the sun was about to be hidden behind a gray cloudbank massed as far to the west as he could see. He felt cheated.

19

ISRAEL, *October 14*

Dick Hammond smiled at the olive-skinned hostess standing just inside the forward door of the El Al airliner and stepped out into the white, dry heat of Lod airport. The bus was parked just beyond the steps. So was a slightly battered cream Fiat.

As Hammond bounded down the steps, a small, balding man with a fringe of bright-ginger hair, built like a teddy bear, jumped out of the Fiat. He was wearing dark glasses, an open-necked shirt, and shapeless gabardine trousers.

At the foot of the steps, the Israeli caught Hammond in a warm embrace.

"Shalom, Dick," said Moshe Stern. "Welcome back."

Moshe's smile was unfeigned, but the American could read deep concern in his intensely blue, slightly disconcerting eyes.

"Shalom, Moshe. It's good to be back."

"Luggage?" Moshe Stern looked at Hammond's black overnight bag.

"Just what I'm carrying."

"Good. Let's get moving."

As they sped off in the Mossad car, Moshe said, "You're staying at the embassy?"

"No. I thought I'd check into the Hilton. I want to hang loose."

"*Beseda*. I hope your flight was okay."

"Fine, fine." Hammond pushed away the memory of the minor inconvenience of having to fight his way through a mob scene at Rome's Leonardo da Vinci airport to catch the connecting flight to Tel Aviv.

"Good. If you're not tired, Arik would like to see you right away."

"That's great." Arik was the deputy chief of the Mossad. His name had never appeared in print but was a household word throughout the spy world. Arik had also been a lifelong friend of Max Zimmer's. Since the days of the Haganah, when Max had helped Jewish refugees to escape to Israel.

"It's terrible news about Max," Moshe said when they were out on the open road, heading toward Tel Aviv.

"Yes," the American said distantly, looking at a pair of girl soldiers in their sand-colored uniforms, waiting on the other side of the highway to hitch a ride to Jerusalem.

Moshe Stern studied his expression as he shook a couple of Lucky Strikes out of a crumpled pack.

"Of course," Moshe said softly. "With the time difference, and the planes, you wouldn't have heard yet. We only got the flash from Washington this morning."

"What's happened?"

"Max is dead. He was killed, or killed himself, in Miami last night."

The air conditioning in the small car suddenly made the American feel cold and damp under his light poplin shirt. He rolled the window halfway down.

"This whole business bears Krylov's signature." Arik's English was only faintly accented. He spoke at least seven languages with the same precision, including Arabic and Russian. He was most fluent in the Polish that his family had spoken in their native Gdynia.

They were sitting, Hammond and Arik and Moshe Stern, looking out over the Mediterranean from an isolated table at an Arab restaurant in the Old Town in Jaffa. Half a mile out to sea, a spotter plane flew low along the coastline, on the lookout for terrorists who might try to penetrate Israel's defenses in small boats or one of the submarines that Libya's erratic strongman had promised the Palestinian movement.

Arik wore an indefinable sadness about his sensitive features. The sadness of a man who had lost most of his family to the Holocaust and knew that in every generation his people were destined to an unending war for survival. Today, which had begun like every other day when he said goodbye to his wife at 4:30 in the morning and drove to the tall building, bristling with powerful antennas, that housed the headquarters of the Mossad, had brought a new sense of loss. The first batch of cables had brought good news, the news that the chief of Fatah's special operations group had been gunned down in the street in the al-Adawi district of Damascus, on his way to a meeting with his Soviet advisers. But Arik's momentary elation over the death of the man who had masterminded the latest wave of terrorist attacks on Israeli civilians was canceled out by the knowledge that one of his own best agents had been killed in the operation. Terrorist chiefs were struck down, but sprang up again like dragon's teeth. An agent like Binyamin, who had fought for Israel without heed for his own life, was not so easily replaced.

Then Arik had received the message from Washington.

Arik remembered vividly the first time that Max Zimmer had visited Israel, and they had stood together watching an exchange of gunfire between the Syrians and the youthful Israeli army across the Golan Heights.

"Do you recall," Max had asked, peering about through those thick, ugly glasses, "that passage in Herzl's diaries where he describes his first visit to the Holy Land? He was standing with his guide when he saw a group of horsemen riding fast across the desert in his direction. Thinking they were Bedouin, Herzl wanted to flee, but his guide told him to stay. The riders were Jews. Herzl, astonished, said that he had never thought to see Jews on horseback. That is the marvel of Israel." He gestured toward a pair of young men reloading a mortar. "A nation of Jews on horse-back."

Max had been a unique friend, to Arik and to Israel. For many years before he was purged from the Agency, he had personally taken charge of the Israeli Account: the exchange of sensitive information with the Mossad. It was Arik who had gone to Max, back in the fifties, bearing the text of Khrushchev's secret speech denouncing Stalin—an acquisition that was later regarded as one of the Agency's greatest coups. It was Max who had come to Arik when a Soviet defector brought news of a mole inside the Israeli administration, and Arik had moved with ruthless expedition to deal with the traitor. Both men believed in the essential truth of the saying from the Torah: "He who would kill you, get up early and kill him first." In that understanding, Arik had brought Max priceless intelligence from inside the darkest recesses of the Soviet Union, and Max had helped to forewarn the Israelis of the plans of their Arab enemies.

That very special relationship had never been quite so intimate since Max had been purged from the counterintelligence staff. Since then, Arik had watched his old friend being smeared, harassed, and driven to ground. What satisfaction Krylov, at Moscow Center, must have derived from the humiliation of the American who had been his foremost antagonist! Krylov's fingerprints were all over the disinformation exercise that had been mounted against Max Zimmer before his death. Arik knew the devious workings of the Russian spymaster's mind. When a genuine Soviet defector fled to the West, Krylov exercised himself to sow doubt about the defector's bona fides and deflect his information so that it would be useless to those who gave him sanctuary. It was characteristic of Krylov to attempt not one but several overlapping deception operations. So after Ushinsky had crossed sides to the Americans, Krylov had tried to convince the Agency that he was a fake, hoping that the defector's revelations would not be believed. But at the same time, recognizing that an investigation might begin that could result in the exposure of a Soviet agent at Langley, Krylov had mounted a parallel operation to frame Max Zimmer.

When Arik narrowed his eyes, his whole appearance changed. The heavy, hooded lids gave him the look of a goshawk. You could see that this man who at first appeared in the guise of a world-weary philosopher was also eminently capable of killing. Arik narrowed his eyes now, as he thought of how Krylov had even dared to use Max's Israeli connections to discredit him.

Few Americans were capable of folloing the convoluted mental processes of a man like Krylov, who was the product of a wholly alien tradition. It required more than training and experience. It required the intuitive power to feel into the mind of an enemy, even across a vast cultural divide. Arik and most of the men and women who worked for him had cultivated that power to a remarkable degree. Binyamin, the young agent who had been shot in the streets of Damascus, had been capable not merely of passing himself off as a Palestinian terrorist or a Syrian officer or an agent of the KGB, but of *thinking* like one. Within the Agency, Max

Zimmer was one of the few men known to Arik who had had the faculty of psychic self-transposition that the Israeli spymaster believed to be the key to perfecting the art of human intelligence. Now that extraordinary American was dead.

Arik's eyes narrowed still further.

Dick Hammond was asking to meet someone. "I need to talk to Judah Klugmann," he said. "The man who told the American media that Max was a mole."

Arik studied the big, open-faced American now draining his cup of sweet Turkish coffee. He knew that Hammond was a friend. Just how much of a friend he had discovered from Moshe after their agents had blown up the latest consignment of nuclear equipment destined for Iraq. Arik believed that friendship must be tested. But once proved, he returned it with a fierce loyalty.

"Of course you can talk to Klugmann," Arik said. "If you need to. But I'm sure you'd rather talk to Rael."

"To Rael?" Hammond could hardly believe his ears. He saw Rael Halevi as vividly for a moment as if she were standing in front of him, her hands outstretched, her long black hair borne aloft by the wind as it had been that day years before when they had stood together at Masada, on the spot where the zealots had fought and died. He had loved Rael Halevi once. Perhaps she had been moved by an answering love. But Rael was not only a spectacularly, unjustly beautiful woman. She was one of the most professional operatives in the Israeli secret service.

"Go to Rael," Arik was saying. "Judah Klugmann is her father."

Hammond now experienced a real sense of shock. "How is it possible?" he questioned. "She never told me—"

"There may be many things Rael never told you. There are things Rael does not share. Not even with me." Arik contemplated the American's reactions, following Hammond's facial expressions with his hooded eyes. And it crossed Hammond's mind that perhaps Arik had loved Rael too.

"Go to her, Dick," Arik repeated. "She's in Jerusalem. Moshe will take you."

Hammond had calls to make from the embassy in the morning, so they left around 11:00 and arrived in Jerusalem shortly before lunch. They pulled over to a roadside stall en route and Dick

Hammond watched Moshe and their driver wolfing down their falafel with a mounting sensation of queasiness.

"You're not hungry, Dick?"

"Not just yet. I'll stick to a beer. Thanks all the same."

In the car, Hammond went on thinking about the guarded conversation he had had with Charles Canning. The Agency already seemed determined to sweep Max's death under the rug. Les Winter was happy to accept the suicide theory. That figured, since the most probable reason Max would take his own life was that he was harboring a guilty secret. But Canning seemed convinced Max had been murdered. If so, Hammond asked himself, then who was the hit man? He recalled the Palestinian terrorist that the defector, Ushinsky, had talked about.

"Moshe," Hammond said to his friend, "do you remember anything about a Palestinian called Sammy Hamad? We put in a request for a trace to your service a few weeks ago. I gather you were able to oblige on some of the background, but had no information on his current whereabouts."

"Hamad is a common name," said Moshe Stern. "But we have information on one terrorist who may be your man. We captured a prisoner who was trained by the Soviets at the Sanprobal school in the Crimea a few years back. He mentioned that several of his classmates were singled out for special training in clandestine warfare. One of them was called Hamad. We believe he was recruited as an executive agent for the Soviets, reserved for special operations under direct control from Moscow. The same man was active in Central America a couple of years ago, helping to organize the guerrillas down there. Which means he must be able to pass himself off as a Latin. We also have him identified as one of the instructors at the Lahej camp in South Yemen before the attack on the Grand Mosque in Mecca in 1979. You'll remember that some of the ringleaders of that Saudi uprising got their military training at Lahej, under the supervision of the Soviets and East Germans. So Sammy Hamad, if that is his real name, seems to be a very well-traveled young man."

"Ushinsky said that Sammy Hamad was a key figure in a plan for major sabotage in the United States."

"Why not?" Moshe was weaving his mobile hands. "It makes perfect sense. He's a Palestinian. If he gets caught out, the Soviets can easily disown him. Your President has declared himself to be a friend of Israel, so any action orchestrated by a Palestinian against the United States can easily be explained away in terms of wounded Arab nationalism."

Moshe Stern must have guessed what was on Hammond's mind, because he added, "Max Zimmer was a good friend of Israel too."

Moshe led the way to a modest office in an anonymous building near the Plaza Hotel. He opened the door without knocking, and was greeted familiarly by a man who was running a tape through a telex machine.

Moshe headed straight for the glass door at the end of the corridor and flung it open.

"Enter," he invited Hammond.

"My God!" Hammond exclaimed, frozen in the doorway. "What's happened?"

Rael was stretched out full-length on the floor. Her skirt, bunched up around her waist, revealed a long expanse of her temptingly rounded thighs. Her face was pillowed on her left arm.

"Is she . . . is she . . .?" Hammond stammered, unsure if she had fainted. Or if something worse had happened.

His answer came in laughter, from Moshe, standing behind him, and from Rael, as she picked herself off the floor and rushed to fling her arms around him.

"I was sleeping," she told him, still grinning broadly. "I always try to take a catnap around noon. I arrived at the office at four this morning."

Hammond studied her. He saw that her body had ripened in the years since they had been lovers. "You're more beautiful every time I see you," he said, meaning it.

When they were all sitting down on the simple wooden chairs in the room, Hammond said, "You know why I've come."

"I know. You want to ask about my father."

"I never realized—"

"There was no reason why you should have known Judah Klugmann was my father," she anticipated his thought. "He was never a father to me. He left my mother before I had learned to talk." She spoke of Klugmann with indifference rather than bitterness.

"This newspaper story about how he was a double agent—"

"Is partly true. My father believed in Moscow all his life. He was run via East Berlin. We never talked about that either. My father and the chief of the East German service came from the same family in Stuttgart. It means that Misha and I are cousins too. But I've never met Misha." She glanced at Moshe Stern, who nodded. "The story about Max Zimmer was a lie," she went on. "My father was ordered to say that. Misha told him to do it. Misha and Krylov wanted to frame Max. My father was never told why."

"You sound very sure of your facts," Hammond observed.

"I talked to my father after the newspaper story appeared," she explained. "Arik asked me to do it. I hadn't seen my father in ten years or more. He's a very old man, Dick. Much older than his years. Old and weak. He confessed everything. And you know why he confessed?"

"Because his daughter was asking the questions," Hammond suggested.

"That wasn't the main factor. Misha ordered him to tell lies that hurt Israel, and its friends. My father wasn't prepared for that. He finally had to choose between being a Communist and being a Jew. He's finished now. He won't do any more harm. He wants to bury himself on a kibbutz for however much time he has left. You can tell that to the Agency. Moshe can confirm it." Moshe Stern nodded again.

20

Sally Sherwin curled her toes and dropped the back of the lounge chair to stretch out full-length beside the pool. The late sunlight sprinkled through the vines that half-covered the sloping glass roof above her head and fell across the paving slabs like wheat sheaves. She needed the moment of stillness, the private space in which to start piecing things together again. "We cannot look squarely at either death or the sun," she had read somewhere. She was trying to look squarely at Max's death. The sudden shock of it made her feel, more than ever, that she was right to try to create a normal, happy environment for herself and Jimmy, right to have gone through the divorce, right not to put herself absolutely at any man's disposal—least of all a man from the secret world that had swallowed up Max. Everything was so provisional; you had to enjoy and fulfill yourself in whatever time was given.

The sunlight was cut off as if a curtain had been drawn. Sally shivered at the thought of what might be awaiting her in New York after the funeral. She had left on a day of torrential rain, under the lash of the winds that had built up to gale force in the steep canyons between the Manhattan skyscrapers, shredding umbrellas and driving pedestrians into sodden huddles in doorways.

She thought about Dick Hammond, and how difficult it was for him to understand what she needed. The shadow that fell between them was not just the shadow of the Agency. It was that there was a point beyond which she could not, or would not, give herself to a man. As a mother, an artist, and a professional woman, she was

226

obliged to defend her private space, the space from which Dick was excluded.

Sally jumped up with a start as cold water splashed over her stomach and thighs.

"Hey, cut that out!" she yelled.

Jimmy giggled. His nose, just visible over the edge of the pool, disappeared as he kicked off again and swam toward the far side with short but determined strokes. The boy had already outgrown the water wings she still made him wear. That was one of her ex-husband's contributions to Jimmy's education. Charles's idea of teaching his son how to swim had been crude but effective, he had thrown him into the deep end and told him to get on with it.

"Mommy," the child called out, "when is Uncle Max coming back?"

"He's not coming back, darling."

"Where's he gone?"

"He's gone to heaven, sweetheart." How did you convey the absoluteness of death to a five-year-old?

"Is heaven a long way?" Jimmy asked.

"Yes. It's a long way."

Phyllis popped her head out the back door. "I'm just going down to the supermarket," Sally's mother said. "Is there anything you need?"

"No, Mother. Thank you."

"Can I have some animal crackers, Grannie?" Jimmy called out.

"Okay," Phyllis said indulgently. "Sally, will you do something for me? Will you give Christophe ten dollars when he's finished out back?"

Christophe was an elderly Haitian refugee—one of those who were streaming into Miami at the rate of seven hundred or so every week—whom Phyllis had taken under her wing. She gave him odd jobs to do around the house, communicating with him, it seemed, by some form of telepathy. The neighbors were scared of the new immigrants, blaming them for the rising crime wave in southern Florida. Phyllis maintained that now that the immigrants were here it was no use bewailing the fact that they had been allowed to come; the community had to absorb them. She had nothing but scorn for nervous friends who talked about moving out into the white fortress suburbs in Broward County.

When Phyllis had gone, Sally got up and walked to the door of the greenhouse. Phillis's latest protégé was wearing only a ragged pair of gray pants, suspended by a bit of rope, and a straw hat as he hacked about in the garden with a machete. The blade flashed, the man bent forward, and then he straightened up, with a large clump of greenery in his hand.

That doesn't look like a weed, Sally thought.

She opened the door, to see clearly. There was no doubt about it. The Haitian was chopping down her mother's prize gardenias.

"Stop!" she yelled at him.

Christophe turned to her with a gap-toothed grin.

"Christophe, on ne doit pas couper les fleurs." Sally switched into uncertain French, remembering that the Haitian did not speak English.

Christophe appeared not to understand. He doffed his straw hat with a flourish.

"Bon jou', Maman," he said in his patois. And returned to assaulting the gardenias.

"Arrêtez ça!" Sally screamed. She leaped forward and grabbed Christophe's hands, physically arresting the fall of the machete on the last of her mother's flowers.

The Haitian looked at her as if she were crazy.

"Moi pr'aller," he said in a tone of wounded reproach, and shambled off around the side of the house.

"Jimmy," Sally called. "Come out here and help Mommy." Together they picked up the sorry heap of savaged gardenias and ferried the debris to the trashcan. It was just as well, Sally thought, that Phyllis had gone out and did not have to witness the price of her philanthropy firsthand.

"Where's heaven, Mommy?" Jimmy asked as she crammed the last of the greenery into the bin, keeping aside the prettiest of the flowers to put in vases inside the house.

"Up there," she said helplessly, gesturing toward the western sky, where the sun had sunk behind some tall apartment blocks on the other side of the water.

The boy's question, the dead flowers, the approach of nightfall filled her with unutterable sadness.

"Why are you crying, Mommy?" The child was standing next to her, peering up into her eyes.

"I'm not crying."

"Poor, poor Mommy." Jimmy was hugging her legs, pressing his head against her lower thigh. "Don't be sad. I'm going to marry you."

She picked him up and cuddled him. The boy's expressions were pure Charles: the smile that dimpled his chin, the black scowl, the look of dogged, unyielding determination that now molded the round face under the shaggy mop of hair.

"I'm hungry," the boy said as she carried him back into the house.

"Okay. Go watch television for a little while, and I'll fix us some hamburgers. Then it's time for bed."

"Can I go swimming again?"

"It's too late for swimming. Look: the sun's going down." There was a long orange glow in the western sky.

"Can I play by the pool?" he persisted.

"All right," she conceded. "But don't go in the water. Is that a deal?"

"Yeah."

Sally went into the back bedroom, overlooking the water, to try to repair her face. She had caught too much sun for her sensitive skin, and was afraid that it would dry out and peel. As she dabbed on cream, she heard the sound of light engines on the water. There was a constant traffic of small boats, mostly pleasure crafts along this stretch of the shore, but sometimes a suspect *navioneta* that might belong to drug runners or one of the anti-Castro groups that still attempted maritime infiltrations into the island. She heard a boat slowing close to the jetty behind Max's house. Maybe it was Charles, bringing back the motorboat that Max had left at Vizcaya.

Sally peered through the slats of the venetian blinds. It was a different boat, bigger, more powerful, painted a crimson that glowed dully in the failing light. She saw two—no, three—men on board.

"Jimmy," she called, instinctively troubled. "Are you okay?"

"Yeah." The pitch of the child's voice suggested that grown-ups are always worrying for irrational reasons.

Sally smoothed more cream into the bridge of her nose.

Then her day exploded into splinters of glass.

The burst of machine-gun fire probably lasted no more than ten or twelve seconds. But it sounded to Sally as if hundreds of bullets were fired and as if every window in the house had been shattered.

229

A daggerlike fragment of glass from the bedroom window slammed into the pot of cream from which Sally had just raised her fingers to her face. The jar went careening off the dressing table. Smaller slivers of glass powdered Sally's hair and pricked the skin of her neck and shoulders like myriad insect bites.

Her first reflex when the shooting started was to fling herself onto the floor, arms raised to protect her face and eyes. Before it had stopped, she was on her feet again, and running. She heard her own voice, detached and terrified, screaming her child's name.

When she threw open the door to the greenhouse, her knees weakened and she had to grab hold of the lintel to prevent herself from falling. Not a single pane of glass in the walls or roof remained intact. The vines and creepers that Phyllis had carefully trained to grow along a latticework screen overhead were dangling over the pool like torn streamers at the end of a riotous party. The paving slabs were covered with broken glass that crunched underfoot. Sally, wearing open sandals, gashed the side of her left foot with her second step. On the cream-and-lime lounger where she had been relaxing earlier she saw more glass and a fresh stain that looked like blood.

And there was an ugly cloud of blood in the chlorinated water of the pool. It was slowly spreading.

Sally mouthed the word a couple of times before she heard herself say it, first in an asphyxiated whisper, then from the top of her lungs.

"Jimmy. Jimmy!"

His small body was floating on its stomach in the middle of the pool. The face was turned away from her. Blood was still pouring into the water from the boy's side.

It can't be, she told herself. Whoever the men in the red boat had come to destroy, it could not be Jimmy.

She sank into a crouching position, unmindful of the glass, tugging at the sash of her robe as she prepared to jump into the water to bring back her child.

Then the impossible happened. She saw the little moon-round face turned toward her, pale under the tan, blood gushing from above the right eye.

"It's all right, darling," she said. "I'm coming."

The boy had had the presence of mind to duck underwater when the bullets started to fly. When he paddled over to Sally at the edge of the pool, she could see that the cuts were fairly minor, apart from the nasty, jagged slash along his side. She bound it up hastily with the sash of her robe. As she did so, she kept her eye on the water for any sign of the red boat. It did not reappear. It seemed their attackers had not waited to see the results of their attack.

"We have to call Daddy," the child said in a strangled voice.

"Yes, darling. But first we have to call the doctor."

"Daddy will be very angry."

The sound of the gunfire traveled clearly downwater to where Charles Canning was testing the controls of Max's boat. The steering seemed to be off; he had narrowly avoided a collision with a harmless dinghy not far up the coast from the Vizcaya landing. He was almost within sight of the house when he made out the shape of a powerful red motor launch, lunging toward him through the dusk. He might not have made the connection between the red boat and the shots he had heard but for the fact that a man in the stern of the launch was holding something that looked like a submachine gun.

Canning did not hesitate. He jerked the wheel of Max's boat, steering straight for the red launch, hoping to force it over to starboard and maybe run it aground. But the steering fault exaggerated the motion, so that he swung too far over, under the bow of the heavier, more powerful boat. Canning barely had time to throw himself into the water before the two boats collided. There was a crunch of fiberglass and a clang of metal as the red launch, without slowing its speed, sawed Canning's boat in two. He watched it begin to subside for only an instant before diving deep underwater to escape the deliberate machine-gun fire from the man in the stern of the bigger boat, now heading fast toward the open sea. When the red boat was out of range, Canning pulled off his shoes, tied them with their laces around his neck, and began swimming toward the shore. After a few strokes, he pulled off his jacket to make better speed, uncaring that his gun in its shoulder holster was now exposed. He had no doubt about where those shots had been coming from.

Canning called Morales before he drove Sally and Jimmy to the hospital to have some stitches put in Jimmy's side. He was dressed in some old clothes belonging to Max; the cuffs were a bit too long and the jacket was too narrow to button across Canning's broad chest. There was a hole burned by cigarette ash in the lapel. Morales confirmed to Canning that things had not changed much in Miami since he and Dick had been helping to stir up trouble for Castro a few years earlier. There was one man who would almost certainly know what Canning wanted to know, and his hangouts were still in Little Havana. Eddie Machado still owned the local Mob. If a professional hit was to be made, the odds were that he would know about it. Drugs, gambling, gunrunning, girls: Machado had a hand in all of it. He was not political. That is to say, he did business with everyone. He supplied hit men for rightist death squads in Guatemala and traded guns for dope with Colombian leftist guerrillas.

"Si," Morales reiterated. "Machado debe conocer."

Canning's requests were simple and precise. Morales would meet him at the hospital. And he would bring something more lethal than a 9mm pistol.

"¿Qué quieres? ¿El magnum?"

"No." Canning explained what he wanted.

Morales handed it to him in a mock-leather briefcase when they were both installed in the front seat of the Cuban's sky-blue Cadillac.

"You asked for an Uzi," Morales said. "But you'll like this even better."

The machine pistol looked like an Israeli-made Uzi, the dream weapon of the close-quarters killer—of urban guerrilla and counterterrorist alike—because of its featherweight lightness and the high velocity with which it spewed out bullets. But, testing the weight of the weapon, Canning found it was even lighter.

"Shoots faster too," Morales commented. "It's a Swedish copy. Some friends of mine locally are mass-producing them for the export trade."

Canning knew that a couple of leading gun shops in the Miami area were the hub of a lively and highly lucrative gunrunning traffic to Central America, and that Morales had more than a nodding interest in one of them.

"Fine," said the Englishman. "Where do we find Machado?"

232

"I checked around. He's in a poker game at the Bodegón Sevilla."

"Can we get in there?"

"No problem. Those guys know me."

They would know Morales's record as a fighter, too, the Englishman reflected, glancing at the bulge in the waistband beneath the trim Cuban's guayabera shirt. Pantera Negra, they called him in the community. Not just because of his dark skin.

The Bodegón Sevilla was a popular Spanish-style restaurant on South-West Eighth Street, the main drag in Little Havana. From the outside, it looked like a tourist trap. The place had been tarted up to look like a Spanish castle, complete with mock battlements and a fake drawbridge in place of a door. Inside, the dining rooms had a musty, airless smell and were furnished with uncomfortable, high, narrow-backed chairs and an improbable assortment of swords and armor on the walls. But the place served excellent *filete de cerdo a la criolla* and good locally rolled Camacho cigars.

Morales let a valet park the car. Inside the restaurant, there was the normal mix of customers: a high proportion of Cuban émigrés, a couple of pretty Nicaraguan girls in floppy gray hats, a sprinkling of gringos who were probably suffering from the highhanded manner of the waiters, elderly *mignons* who had fled from Havana with the owner the day after the revolution and affected not to understand Spanish unless it was spoken by a fellow Cuban.

Canning followed Morales through the tables to the private room at the back. A young Cuban was sitting by the door, sipping a beer. He got up as they approached, barring the way.

"*Privado,*" he rasped. "*Los servicios están por allá.*" He pointed toward the men's room, down the corridor.

"*Soy amigo de Eddie,*" Morales countered, with an easy smile on his lips. "*Dígale que Morales le espera.*"

The guard looked them over slowly. Then, without turning his back, he opened the door and whispered to someone inside.

He shut the door and said, "*Eddie está ocupado.*"

The guard, who was too ignorant to have heard of Morales, was also too inexperienced to cope with his next move. Morales's hands shot out like pistons. Before the young Cuban could react, Morales had him pinioned against the wall, one hand over his

233

mouth, the other twisting his right arm up toward the base of his neck. With the toe of his hand-tooled boot, Morales kicked the automatic pistol he had extracted from the guard's belt over toward Canning.

"Comando Zeta," Morales hissed. The young Cuban blanched and stopped trying to struggle. Comando Zeta was the name of the most extreme of the Cuban émigré organizations. Canning knew from Dick Hammond that Castro's secret service had managed to penetrate it and had encouraged some of its most lunatic operations in the hope of discrediting the anti-Communist cause in general. Comando Zeta's assassins had gunned down a Cuban diplomat in New York and sent death threats to Cuban-Americans they accused of "collaboration" with the regime in Havana. The name inspired fear throughout the community. Even the Mob was nervous of Comando Zeta.

Tossing the young guard aside like a crumpled tissue, Morales threw open the door into the private room.

Machado was in shirtsleeves, his tie loosened, a coarse, heavy man whose hairy stomach showed through the gaps between the straining buttons of his shirt. He was clutching a fistful of cards, surrounded by cronies who included several fairly prominent citizens; Canning recognized one of them from posters that had been put up during the last municipal elections. The stakes they were playing for were impressive. Most of the money on the table was in hundred-dollar bills. Canning saw only a few wads of twenties.

"*Buenas tardes, Eddie,*" said Morales, still with that thin, dangerous smile that looked as if it had been etched with a razor.

"*Espere un ratito nada mas,*" said the gangster. "I'll see you," he said in English to the politician with the familiar face. The man showed three nines and a pair of aces with a smirk of triumph.

"*Lo siento mucho,*" Machado said in false condolence as he displayed a straight flush. He scooped up his winnings in his pudgy arms. "Ten-minute break," he announced to the table. "Drinks are on me."

His friends filed out obediently except for a solid, bullet-shaped man who was an obvious Machado soldier. The younger guard loitered sheepishly in the open doorway. Machado bellowed at him to shut the door, and then turned to the intruders with a show of bonhomie.

"It's been too long," he said to Morales, patting his shoulder. "You remember that time in Panama, eh? That night you made it with those two incredible girls?"

"Three," Morales corrected him.

"I tell you, this guy is some *faldista*," Machado said to Canning. The Englishman sat on the edge of a chair that he had pulled back from the table, between the guard and the door, cradling the mock-leather briefcase on his lap.

"My friend needs some information," said Morales.

"I think you probably know what happened," Canning said to the mobster. He described the attack on the beach house. "My son could have been killed. I'm very angry about that."

"Yeah," said Machado, offering them scotch, straight up, in small tumblers. "I'm a family man myself."

"What do you know, Eddie?" Morales pressed him.

Machado rubbed his armpit. "Well, I heard something from a friend," he said. "I don't think nobody was supposed to get hit. This wasn't a hit job. Someone just wanted to put the frighteners on."

"Who might that be?"

Machado shrugged. Morales burst into a stream of voluble Spanish, from which Canning was able to extract only a phrase or two. The name of a local bank and some account numbers. Morales seemed to be threatening that unless the mobster opened up, he would release some information on how Machado had been laundering drug money for Castro to the rightist paramilitary groups. That would guarantee that Machado's name would appear on a political death list. The threat seemed to have the desired effect.

"I might have heard something from this friend," Machado remarked. "There was a guy down here from New York. He told my friend that the lady—your ex," he said to Canning—"is shacked up with a guy who's sticking his nose into things down here that he didn't oughta know about. *Este tipo de Nueva York* made it sound, you know, like the boyfriend could cause big headaches for all of us."

"What did he say, this man from New York?" Canning took

over the questioning. "Did he say this was political? Did he say it was connected with the Agency?"

"No, no, nothing political. We don't touch politics."

"Drugs, then? Did he say that Sally's friend was investigating the drug rackets?"

"Something like that."

"And this man from New York issued a contract. Is that right?"

"Listen, it wasn't anything heavy. It wasn't a hit." Machado drew his sleeve across his face, mopping up the beads of sweat that had started to form there.

"Tell me about this man from New York who saw your friend." The Englishman was increasingly convinced that Machado himself had supplied the hoodlums who fired on the beach house. "Was the guy an American?"

"No, not American."

"Cuban, then?"

"He said he was *colombiano.* A dark guy, *sabe.*"

"As dark as me?" Morales asked.

"*Más o menos.* He could have been from Colombia. They get a lot of *indios* down there. But there was something wrong about the accent. And my friend got word nobody heard of this guy down in Medellín."

Not a Latin, then. But dark. "Could he be an Arab?" Canning asked.

"Beats me," said Machado. He started shuffling cards with a professional dealer's flick of the wrist.

The gesture released the force of pent-up anger that Canning had felt welling up since he had nearly been drowned by the gunmen in the red boat. He leaped forward out of his chair, clutching the briefcase with his left hand. With his free hand, he seized the heavy gold chain that Machado wore around his neck, twisting it tight until the mobster was gasping for breath. The guard jumped up to help his boss, but Morales waved him back with the Smith & Wesson he had pulled from his belt.

"You're holding back," Canning growled into Machado's damp, puffy face. "Do you own a red motor launch?"

Machado could not get the words out until the Englishman loosed his grip on the chain. "*¿Qué dice este loco?*" he appealed to Morales. "*¿Qué lancha?*"

"Talk in English," Canning commanded.

236

"I don't know nothing about a red boat."

"You're lying," said Canning. "We both know it."

"Look," said Machado. "Nobody knew this was political. And nobody knew there were kids involved. I wouldn't do that. I'm a family man. I got a wife and six kids."

"And a dozen whorehouses," Morales added. "And that piece of ass you keep out on Key Biscayne."

"I want a name," said Canning. "The guy from New York has got to have a name."

"Names is like poker hands. Win some, lose some. This guy calls himself Sammy."

"That's all?"

"Sammy. Just Sammy."

Not so much to go on so far, thought Canning. Except the pattern. A stranger from New York, possibly Arab, had issued a contract to the Mob to scare him off by threatening his family. Whoever was behind this had studiously avoided using people who were known to be involved with identified intelligence networks or terrorist groups. The Agency had done deals with the Mob in the past, he remembered. The Agency had even tried to use the Mob to assassinate Castro. But it was a game that others could play too. Who was the Arab? Was he also behind Max Zimmer's murder. He did not expect Machado to answer *that* question.

"Did this guy from New York ask for anything else?" Canning tried nonetheless. "Did he put out a contract for a hit?"

"No. No hits."

Impossible to tell if the man was lying.

"All right," said Canning. "There's just one more thing for now." He opened the flap of the cheap briefcase and took out the machine pistol. Then he pushed the barrel up under Machado's nose. "I am not a violent person," he said. "But I am capable of violence, and I am trained for it. We don't know each other, but you can ask Morales about that. I don't work for your government or any other government, so I don't have to play by any rules. Except the ones I make for myself." He swung the barrel of the gun so that it grazed the side of Machado's fleshy nose.

"I swear to you," said the Englishman, "that if any further attempt is made to harm my son, or my ex-wife, I am going to come down to Little Havana and a few people are going to be sorry that they ever left Cuba. Including you. I hope we understand each other."

"Es auténtico," Morales commented.

"Okay," said Machado. *"Entendido.* You got my word. This won't happen again. Not here in Miami. I tell you, I'm a family man."

21

Canning's suite at the Coconut Grove Hotel was clean. He had left the microfilm with Morales's friend at the photoprocessing company to have it copied before he carried the original to Dick Hammond in Washington. Old habits of caution, nonetheless, had induced him to leave the "Do Not Disturb" sign on his hotel door, with a hair glued across the chink at the top right-hand corner. When Canning got back to the eighteenth floor, he saw that neither—apparently—had been disturbed. The scene in the corridor was also reassuringly familiar: in front of the elevators, there were two trolleys piled up with dirty plates and wineglasses from adjoining rooms. There was the recorded boom of gunfire from some war saga on television, less powerful than the voices of two of his neighbors raised in anger.

"I'm as good as you, you secondhand bitch," the man in room 1814 bellowed.

Canning lingered outside his door, taking in the sights and sounds of the eighteenth floor. Something had changed. He was trying to place what it was. Then he had it. There was no glow of light from under his door. If a light had been on inside, he would have been able to see it in the soft penumbra of the corridor. Yet he always left a light on wherever he was staying; the habit had been born of trying to scare the roaches back into the woodwork in New York.

Standing to one side of the door, Canning slipped his key into the lock. It turned easily. He held the machine pistol in his free right hand, his finger on the trigger inside the mock-leather briefcase that concealed it. Without exposing his body to the line of sight of anyone inside the room, he flung back the door with his left hand. There was no sound from inside, except for the low hum of the air conditioning.

From behind him, back along the corridor, Canning heard the whirr and bump of the elevator returning to his floor. He paused for a moment, then leaped forward into the room, swinging the machine pistol in an arc in front of him, letting the flimsy briefcase drop to the floor. The big open-plan reception area was deserted, the drapes pulled back to expose the breathtaking view over the Dinner Key marina. Lights twinkled on the rigging of some of the bigger boats like Christmas trees.

He leaned back against the door with his shoulder, gently pushing it closed, and suddenly knew he was not alone.

"Excuse me," said the voice from behind him. He wheeled, but instinct made him drop the gun to his side, out of sight. It was a woman's voice.

"Night maid," said the short, attractive brunette in a thick Hispanic accent. "You need anything tonight?"

"No, not tonight. Thank you."

"You need fresh towels?"

"It's all right. Where I come from, we take a bath only once a week." Relief made it easy for him to joke.

But when he closed the door and double-locked it, the sensation returned again. He was not alone.

He looked around the apartment. The doors to the bathroom and the kitchenette were open. But the door to the bedroom, down a short corridor, was only slightly ajar. Stepping lightly on the balls of his feet, Canning ran to it, dropping to his knees as he flung it open, the gun extended before him.

Before his eyes could focus inside the bedroom, the door was slammed back into the muscles of his forearm. Canning gasped at the pain. But worse than the pain the sudden absence of sensation in his right hand. The machine pistol slipped from his nerveless fingers.

The intruder behind the door wrenched it back. Canning propped himself against the doorframe for support. From his crouched position, the man looming out of the shadows seemed huge, twice life size. Metal glinted in the attacker's hand. Canning rolled over to the right, expecting a switchblade knife. Instead, a solid shaft of steel lashed forward. It only scraped the edge of

Canning's shoulder, but the shock of the vibrations made him feel as if a drill were being forced through his bone marrow. The intruder had some kind of steel whip. As the man raised it high above his head, ready to bring the weapon down with full force against the side of Canning's neck, the Englishman struggled not to swoon. Thrusting back with his arms against the wall, he kicked upward, toward the blurred face of his attacker, with all his remaining strength. The toe of his shoe cracked against the side of the intruder's chin, hard enough to send the man reeling back across the king-size bed. There was a crunch of splintering wood and the center of the mattress bellied down onto the floor.

Canning grabbed the machine pistol with his left hand and threw himself at the writhing heap on the bed. He swung the butt at the man's head, but could not control his aim, striking only a glancing blow off the rocklike expanse of the intruder's chest. Then the man was lashing at Canning again with the steel whip, and the Englishman went rolling and weaving off the far side of the bed and through the plate-glass window that opened onto a narrow terrace.

The man grabbed him from behind, grasping for his windpipe as he pinioned Canning against the railing with an irresistible weight. *He must weigh at least three hundred pounds*, Canning thought as he wriggled in a vain effort to break free. Now his attacker had him bent nearly double over the railing. Eighteen floors below, he could see the hotel pool, as unnaturally blue under the floodlights as the pools in David Hockney's canvases. The end nearest to Canning was seventeen feet deep. Not deep enough to break a fall from eighteen stories. Assuming that he did not land on the paving slabs instead. With his massive paws still gripping Canning's throat, the intruder was now trying to hump his body upward over the edge of the railing. One of the Englishman's feet was already off the ground. His right arm hung limp and useless. A red film was spreading in front of his eyes, changing the scene below into shades of mauve and vermilion.

Like slides on an old-fashioned, crackling projector, scenes from the past returned to him. He saw Hussar and heard him whisper, "My life rides with you." And then a scene around a campfire in the bone-dry Hadhramaut, with Dhofari tribesmen who had tested their courage, and his own, by thrusting their hands, one after another, into the flames. "A man is not a man until he has overcome not only the fear of pain, but pain itself," their leader had said. In his nostrils, it seemed to Canning, he could again smell the sweet, sickly aroma of charred flesh.

He forced the fingers of his nerveless right hand into a fist and gripped the railing. Then he brought the heel of his shoe up into his attacker's testicles. The man flinched, and Canning could breathe more freely. The red mist subsided a little. He kicked up again, harder, and the man relaxed his grip, groaning and reaching toward his genitals. Canning was able to slip sideways, along the railing.

His attacker went for him like a stampeding bison. This time the Englishman was too fast for him. He went down, ducking the charge, and as the man went careering into the railing, he pushed upward with his shoulder, sending the angry mass into a surprisingly graceful dive over the edge of the terrace. Canning heard screams from a floor below before he had hauled himself back up, breathing in short, rasping swallows through his open mouth, to survey the scene around the pool.

Canning had been right. Seventeen feet of water is not a sufficient depth to save a man from breaking his neck after a fall from eighteen floors up. The body floated, arms spread wide, legs together, like a parody of the crucifixion played by Sidney Greenstreet.

Sergeant Tom Ryan was in a rebellious mood. The Miami papers had syndicated a sensational article by Sol Puig, that high-paid muckraker, on Max Zimmer's death. According to Sol Puig, Zimmer had been the Soviets' top mole inside the Agency, and the Agency—in an effort to avoid public embarrassment—had had him bumped off. Ryan had told his chief that he believed the story could be true. There were some very dirty people out at Langley, he had said. Tom Ryan knew all about that from his years in Homicide in Washington. But they were still keeping him off the Zimmer case. He wondered whether he ought to call Sol Puig and tell him about the cover-up.

He was off-duty, stewing over a few beers in his regular bar, when they told him about the death at the Coconut Grove Hotel. The dead man was an out-of-town hood who had dodged a manslaughter rap in Vegas thanks to tricky lawyers. There was no evident connection with the Zimmer business. Except that Charles Canning just happened to be staying at the Coconut Grove Hotel and had left right after the death in the swimming pool. Tom Ryan had checked on that. No one at the desk had seen the Englishman go. His bill had been settled and his bags collected by his friend Morales. He had not been around to answer the routine police inquiries. Nothing could be pinned on him, of course, since it seemed that no one had witnessed the dead man fall. But Canning's pattern of behavior was suspicious. Like everything else about him. Ryan wanted to pull the Englishman in for questioning. But they gave him the same answer as before: keep your nose out of it.

It was by chance that he ran into Canning again. He had gone out to the airport to pick up his wife's sister, a snotty-nosed bitch who talked as if cops were social untouchables, when he spotted the Englishman, dapper in a midnight-blue silk suit, heading toward the Eastern Airlines counter.

"So you're leaving us, Mr. Canning," Ryan addressed him.

Canning squinted at him, not immediately recognizing him in his sport clothes. "Sergeant Ryan, isn't it?" he said eventually.

Ryan saw the Latino, Morales, hurrying in from the door. Bringing up the rear.

"I'm not happy, Mr. Canning," he said. "I think the Zimmer case stinks. That was no suicide."

"I think you may be right."

"Oh yeah?" Ryan cocked a skeptical eyebrow. "Then who did it?"

"That's what we'd all like to know."

"I don't know about that. I've been involved with these so-called Agency suicides before."

"What's that?" Canning stared at the policeman with sudden interest.

"Is everything okay?" Morales asked, coming up alongside him.

"Yes, yes. What were you saying about Agency suicides, Sergeant?" Canning moved his bags out of the way of a stream of people making for the Eastern ticket counter.

"I used to be stationed in Washington," Ryan explained. "I came down here for my wife's health. And my own. I got into trouble up there because I didn't believe in another Agency suicide. Ever hear of a guy called Winter?"

Canning looked nervously around, feeling terribly exposed, before he nodded. Lester Frobisher Winter. Chief of the Agency's Soviet Division. And Max Zimmer's candidate—according to the microfilmed documents that Canning was now carrying in his slim black attaché case—for the role of the American Philby.

"He had a wife," Ryan went on, apparently untroubled by the risk of being overheard. "She had a Russian name. Katerina, or Katya."

The confirmation that Les Winter had had a wife with a Russian name did not startle Canning. He knew several Agency people who had married East European émigrés. And quite a few Russian exiles had been hired by the Agency as contract employees. He had seen Katya's name in Max's notes. It was the other part of what the cop was saying that made Canning feel more and more nervous.

"This Katya," Tom Ryan went on, "the story was, she got depressed over too many Manhattans in a house in Georgetown and killed herself. It wouldn't be the first time that an Agency wife did that. Or a cop's wife, either. I just didn't like the way she was supposed to have committed suicide. People kill themselves in all kinds of ways. With guns and knives and sleeping pills and gas ovens and a cord tied to the ceiling. They drown themselves. They eat powdered glass. They jump in front of cars and under trains. They even jump out of eighteenth-floor windows into pools."

Ryan paused to register the Englishman's reaction, but none was visible.

"But let me ask you this, Mr. Canning," he continued. "What percentage of suicides would you say were committed by people who asphyxiated themselves by holding a piece of plastic over their nose with both hands until they died? Like this, huh?" He held the paper he was carrying—the one with the Sol Puig story—up in front of his face.

"I don't see how it's possible," said Canning. Surely, he was thinking, the would-be victim's hands would weaken. The suffocating plastic would slip away, and air would reach the lungs. Was that really how Katya Winter had died? If so, it was almost impossible that she had taken her own life. *That* must be the clue that Max Zimmer had wanted to give him.

"You try it sometime," said Ryan. "Let me know whether it works."

"Hey, look at the time," Morales prodded the Englishman. "You're gonna miss your plane."

"Excuse me," Canning said to Ryan.

"You got any plans to come back to Miami?" Ryan asked.

"Well, I certainly don't plan to spend the whole winter in New York."

"I'll be seeing you, then. I'd like to talk some more about suicide."

Exhausted, Canning drank a couple of Bloody Marys on the plane and tried to catnap. But he woke up again almost immediately from a midmorning nightmare. He saw a woman's features, horribly distorted like melting wax, the mouth opening and closing in a soundless scream under a sheet of clear plastic. In the dream, the woman was not the unknown Katya Winter, but his ex-wife, Sally. Babies killed themselves that way, he thought as he rubbed the dry seeds of sleep from his eyes. By accident. But not adults. It was even less likely that Katya had killed herself like that than that Max had put the gun to his own head in the gardens of Vizcaya. It was more than probable that the two mock suicides were connected, that the person who had destroyed Katya Winter had also destroyed Max Zimmer in order to hide his appalling secret. One man was clearly visible to Canning, standing in the center of a vast web of murder and deception. That man was Les Winter, who had helped to task Dick Hammond—and thereby, ironically, Canning himself—to hunt for the mole in the Agency. More than likely, Winter had taken that initiative in order to divert attention from his own guilt. And then he had been ready to kill to suppress Max's evidence of his past. Could it all be proved?

Canning felt cold, and pulled his jacket from the overhead rack. Proving his suspicions would mean detonating a bomb that would blow a gaping hole in the old Agency. But the road from suspicion to proof was already more dangerous than any he had traveled in the rocky wilderness of the Dhofar.

22

October 18

Trip Gage, riding with General Brennan in the back seat of the Buick, heard the yelling long before the demonstrators came in sight around the last bend in the dusty access road. The Air Force driver swerved to avoid a small object on the road, and the National Security Adviser shuddered involuntarily. From a distance, the tiny shape was only a plastic doll, blackened and twisted as if it had been on fire. The eyes were missing, and the bland features had buckled and contorted into a horrible leer.

Then the protesters were in view, maybe three hundred of them, milling around outside the main gates to a compound defended by an electrified fence and blue-uniformed guards toting M-16s. The sign beside the entrance read, "Prohibited Area: Unauthorized Personnel Enter at Own Risk. U.S. Air Force."

"I thought this was supposed to be a secret facility," Gage observed to General Brennan.

"Nothing stays secret from Rent-a-Mob." The general stuck out his jaw, chewing the edge of his upper lip. "Now look at that," he said. "Isn't that beautiful?"

The crowd had opened out, and a group of a dozen or so girls were snaking across the road like a conga line. They were dressed in identical white smocks, their faces concealed by white death's-head masks. Each demonstrator cradled a baby doll, gruesomely mutilated like the one Gage had seen farther back down the road.

Above the heads of the protesters bobbed a forest of banners and placards. Gage noted some familiar slogans, like "No Nukes," and some less familiar ones, like "Save Man's Last Frontier," "Kill the Killer Beam," and, most puzzling, "Stop the Baby-Killers."

246

As the masked women weaved back and forth for the benefit of television cameras and a gaggle of press photographers, the crowd struck up a new chant. "Save the babies!" Gage heard them shout.

"Save the babies?" He turned to Brennan. "Baby-killers? What the hell do these kids think is going on here?"

"They think we're irradiating babies to test the fallout from a particle beam."

"That's absurd."

"Oh, yeah? You tell her." Brennan gestured toward a lank-haired girl in dungarees who had pressed her face against the rear window of the car, on Gage's side, as it inched forward toward the gates. Catching sight of the general's uniform, other protesters started pounding on the hood and the windshield of the Buick. A couple of pebbles pinged off the chassis. Brennan, apparently unruffled, stuck a greenish cigar in his mouth and started gnawing on it without lighting it. "One of these United Nations gurus put out the story," Brennan explained. "I regret to say that he's of Irish descent. The Albuquerque papers quoted him as stating that the United States has done a deal with the generals in Seoul to import forty thousand South Korean babies to use as guinea pigs in some new experiments on radiation. Of course, it figures nobody was quite sure where all the babies had ended up. So some of these radicals had the bright idea of pinning the story to a secret Air Force facility out here in New Mexico. The next step was to bus in no-nuke kooks from all over the country to create a media event."

The Buick had slowed to a stop, its forward progress blocked by the solid wall of screaming, gesticulating demonstrators that had now formed. Pushed from both sides, the car started to rock back and forth. Gage's briefcase shot off the seat and onto the floor. He could see Air Force guards and state police shoving through the crowd, brandishing rifle butts and billyclubs, trying to clear a corridor for Brennan's car.

"I must say I've got to hand it to whoever dreamed this up," Brennan went on. "It's a highly professional job. Just think about this Korean-babies story. You whip up antinuclear and antidefense frenzy by dragging in the most emotive issue there is. You manage to pile more dirt on a friendly government in Asia at the same time. And you get the public concerned about a research facility that nobody ever heard about before."

"But surely this is just a one-day wonder," Gage commented.

He pulled away from the window as a gob of spit settled on it, inches from his face. "Nobody's going to buy the Korean-babies story. Anybody who tries to run with it in a serious media outlet is going to look like an idiot."

"It's not for me to teach *you* about psychological warfare, Mr. Gage. But I think you're missing the point. Sure, Jake Waggoner up there at the Defense Department will be issuing denials, and sure, anybody responsible is going to accept them. But look what else is happening. We've got kids here who were ready to get on a Greyhound bus and come in from Washington or San Francisco. We've got a lot of little old ladies who worry about clean air who are going to go on believing that Strangelove types have taken over the Pentagon, whatever the papers print by way of denials. And we've got the media focusing in on our most sensitive defense project, something we wanted to keep well away from the public eye. Next thing you know, we'll have a team of Congressmen down here demanding a guided tour of the whole installation."

One of the masked girls slid her skinny body between two guards and started bashing her baby doll against the car window on Brennan's side. The general, still chomping on his cigar, smiled and blew her a kiss. The gesture seemed to throw her into a paroxysm of rage.

"*Murderer,*" she shrieked. "Infanticide!"

"Hope she doesn't grow up treating her own kids that way," Brennan commented as the mangled doll thudded against the glass.

A soldier tried to drag the girl back, but she fought him, kneeing and kicking at his groin, until he backed away in pain. A second guard grabbed her by the throat, and she collapsed on the ground. A watching network cameraman zoomed in for a close-up, then panned to catch General Brennan's satisfied expression as the scene unfolded a few feet away from the car.

"You see?" said Brennan. "They create events. What are people going to remember? The fact that some kids were sold a propaganda lie, or the videotape of military brutality?"

Gage looked on, faintly disgusted, as the general pulled some wet pieces of tobacco off the end of his disintegrating cigar. "I'd bet there'll be shooting before we're through," Brennan continued. "Of course, that would make the people who are behind this very happy. What they want is war in the streets. Takes you back some, doesn't it?"

Trip Gage nodded solemnly. The scene was familiar, all right. It took him back to the era of Nixon's first years in the White House, the era of the Vietnam vigils and the mass demonstrations in Washington. He recalled one of the first 9:00 briefings he had given the new President, in which they had talked over intelligence reports of a meeting of American radical leaders in Havana. Leftists who had tried to work for their ideas inside the system under the previous administration had resolved to take the battle back to the streets. The aim was to make the country ungovernable. Vietnam had been the umbrella cause in the Nixon years, when Gage had last worked in the White House. Today, the radicals were mobilizing a broad spectrum of support around a different umbrella cause: the campaign against nuclear energy and nuclear weapons. The campaign had already been well under way before the last elections, when pop stars raised millions by singing at antinuclear beachside festivals, and a large sector of the public was induced to believe that an accident at a nuclear power plant at Three Mile Island, in which no one was killed or even seriously injured, had been the greatest threat to civilization since Hiroshima. Under the new administration, each new defense project or nuclear-power development had been targeted for demonstrations, picketing, and scare reporting. The administration countered that nuclear power was the only viable alternative to oil imported from highly unstable areas as a source of energy in the eighties and that the defense buildup was occasioned by the aggressive designs of the Soviet leadership. But the arguments broke against the concentrated passion of the Movement like spray against a reef.

"I think we're almost there, sir," said the driver.

The guards had finally managed to form a cordon, holding back the demonstrators so the car could get through.

There was a rapping on the back window, and Trip Gage heard his name being called.

"Mr. Gage!" the voice shouted again. "I'm Mike Masters, Southwest TV. Have you got any comment for us?" The reporter was hurrying along beside the car, quickening his stride as it picked up speed.

"No comment," Gage shouted back.

"General Brennan?" the reporter persisted.

"Why don't you ask these guys who put up the money to have them bused in here?" Brennan boomed, lowering his window a fraction so the words would carry.

They drove about half a mile across the stony, desert plateau, between red, vertical cliffs where the road had been driven straight through the natural contours of the land. The countryside was bare apart from the cactus and a few low, xerophytic shrubs. Their destination was a stark, barracklike, windowless building.

"Welcome to the home of Blue Savior," Brennan said to Gage. "If we're gonna beat the Soviets, it will be because of what we've been able to do here. I hope you remind the President about that when we get back to Washington."

Gage cocked his head. "Blue Savior," he repeated in a quiet voice.

"It fucking could be," Brennan confirmed profanely.

The name, like the man who had dreamed it up, was visionary, and therefore liable to arouse skepticism in those of a less messianic cast of mind. Trip Gage was a skeptic. Until they knew for certain that the defector Ushinsky was authentic, there was no guarantee that the Blue Savior project was not merely an exercise in futility. However, being descended from God-fearing Puritan forebears, Gage was not wholly immune to conversion. He settled his briefcase protectively on his lap.

As they got out of the car, a man in the uniform of an Air Force major came running out of the building. He snapped smartly to attention and saluted in front of Brennan.

"Got a problem, Major?"

"Sir. I don't know how it happened. A TV crew got inside the perimeter."

"*What?*"

"They must have got in through the southern gate. We had trouble over there too. Some demonstrators tried to break through. I guess the camera crew just slipped by."

"Did they get up the mountain?"

"About halfway, sir."

"Where are they now?"

"Sir, we're holding them under guard."

"Have you got their film?"

"Yes, sir."

"Okay," said Brennan. "What we do is this. They have committed a breach of federal law by entering a restricted defense establishment without authorization. So you call the special agent in charge of the Bureau office in Albuquerque and get him to come out here with some of his people and put these guys through the wringer."

"Sir, they're asking to call their producer."

"No calls. Just sit on them. Make sure they don't see anything. Shit. This isn't reporting. This is espionage. I want those guys charged."

"What network are they from?" Trip Gage asked.

"They're not from a network, sir. They work for a public TV station out in California. The reporter's name is Steve Dunn."

"Okay," said Brennan. "We'll do our rundown. And you make sure the base commander sits in on the Bureau interview and reports to me afterward."

"Yes, *sir!*"

Brennan returned the major's salute, and the officer strode, stiff backed, ahead of them into the building.

"The mountain?" Gage queried.

"Yeah," said Brennan. "We've set up our prototype ground-based defense system there."

Gage looked up at the scarred slopes of the mountain that overshadowed the research center.

"If you think about this kind of thing for too long, you go nuts," Brennan complained to Gage as he walked the National Security Adviser inside. "Here we are, trying to get close enough to whatever Marshal Safronov's building out there in Kazakhstan to get a picture of it that even your pals in the Agency can't argue about. And we can't seem to get an agent within hundreds of miles of it. Now *that's* what security means. Do you think this country understands it? You can bet your ass we don't. This is supposed to be a top-security facility, right? And we've got a mob at the front door and reporters sneaking in the back door. If a sergeant or a lab assistant goes down for a drink, the Soviets will have a hooker ready to try to pick him up, or an agent ready to wave a fistful of hundred-dollar bills in front of his nose. We held a conference out on the West Coast when this project was just picking up steam, and do you know what the genius in charge of booking arrangements did? He sent a complete list of participants, military and civilian, to the manager of the hotel where the meeting was being held, complete with office or home addresses. What do you think it takes the Soviets to get hold of a list like that? And what do you think they do with it?"

"They check everyone out and see who's vulnerable."

"Right. So this prof's a fag, or this contractor has a lady friend he wouldn't want his wife to know about, or this colonel plays the ponies. I'd like to see us try to operate the same way inside Russia. Sometimes I wonder whether we've got any secrets left."

"We have Blue Savior," Gage ventured.

"Oh, the Soviets know all about Blue Savior," said Brennan as they penetrated the security checks inside the main building. "What I hope they don't know—until we're ready to let them know—is how close we are to completion. And whether we have the guts to use it."

There was a buzz of frantic activity from the offices as they were passing. Young men in casual shirts or white lab coats scurried back and forth, some of them pausing to greet General Brennan.

"My Young Turks," he observed to Trip Gage. "See that guy there?" He pointed at a pink-faced young man in a yellow turtleneck sweater who looked like a college kid. "I hijacked him from RAND. When the Agency's analysts were telling us that the Soviets didn't have the technology to aim lasers against space satellites over long distances, that kid proved that the Russians had adapted the computer we sold them back in 1972—the one that was supposed to handle Intourist reservations, remember?— to provide themselves with the necessary guidance system. When the Agency analysts told us that the Soviets didn't have cables that were capable of carrying the tremendous power pulses involved in beam weapons, the same guy established that the Russians were using pressurized gas lines, invented right here in the United States, that they had bought from one of our biggest corporations."

"You're saying that we supplied the technology for these Soviet beam weapons?"

"I'm saying that the Soviets could never have solved all their technical problems without the stuff that they bought or stole from us. That we can live with. It shouldn't have happened— never would have happened if we'd been able to make the business community and the State Department understand the connection between technology transfers and the military balance. But that doesn't worry me as much as the fact that the Soviets, through conscripting their best scientists to work in this

252

field, have been able to make some tremendously original break-throughs on their own. In many areas, they were plowing virgin soil, or rather, icebound tundra. We've got to give them credit for that. And we've got to live with the consequences."

"Okay. Where does my tour begin?"

"With a man. A most unusual man." Brennan rapped on the door of the office at the end of the corridor and flung it open without waiting for a response. Inside, a shy, awkward man with a metal-stemmed pipe and a crewcut so short that you could see his scalp through the hair was scribbling equations in chalk on a blackboard that might have been borrowed from the local school.

"Trip," Brennan made the introductions, "I want you to meet Professor Ed Greenhouse. Ed was the first goddam scientist in this country who was ready to stick his neck out in public and say that I was right to contend that directed energy weapons will decide the wars of the future. He was the first nuclear physicist who was prepared to break with the establishment and acknowledge that Soviet beam-weapons research and development could turn out to be more decisive than the Manhattan Project, and that the United States should be in the race. I drafted him from California. Ed, you know who Mr. Winthrop Gage is. For a change, I've got you someone down here from the White House who's going to listen to you."

"You'll need to go slowly," said Gage with a smile.

Ed Greenhouse looked at the floor, and then at the wall, as if peering through an imagined window, as he shook the National Security Adviser's hand. The scientist was more at home with his equations than with people. But like many of the physicists engaged in thinking the unthinkable about weapons of mass destruction, he was a dedicated humanist. One of the things that excited Ed Greenhouse most about the project code-named Blue Savior was that it held out the prospect—still distant, but shimmering on the horizon—that one day the grim shadow of nuclear holocaust that had terrorized mankind for two genera-tions might be finally removed.

"I should say one more thing about Ed," Brennan resumed. "Something he's far too coy to tell you for himself. More than anyone, he's responsible for the scientific breakthrough that's gonna give us an answer to the killer beam the Soviets are developing. Ed's developed a negative-hydrogen beam that we can fire from space battle stations. It will take out Soviet missiles within seconds of a launch."

Greenhouse said, "I'm really only an editor, arranging other people's contributions. Mostly, of course, the Russians'. Berzin's people are still several laps ahead of us. Especially Klaus Milstein."

"Chief Designer Berzin and Special Adviser Milstein." General Brennan underlined the names. "They had a few advantages we never enjoyed here, Ed. Don't let's forget it. With Marshal Safronov behind them, they never had any trouble squeezing the money and manpower they needed out of the leadership. And the Soviet leadership has been extremely farsighted. Khrushchev understood, as long ago as the early sixties, that whoever controls space will be able to dictate what happens on earth. Of course, Khrushchev talked too much and nearly gave the game away when he started boasting about it. You remember that interview Khrushchev gave back in 1964, Ed?"

Greenhouse nodded. "It had all of us speculating like hell," he commented. "It was a funny situation. Khrushchev was playing host to a crowd of Japanese reporters, who expected him to launch the routine attack on the United States. Instead, he went into a strange kind of dramatic rhapsody and started telling how he'd visited a scientific establishment in the Moscow suburbs and seen something so terrible that he dared not talk about it. He even said he was afraid of what the scientists carried with them. We weren't sure what he meant in those days. Now I'm afraid that we do. Khrushchev's scientists were already working on space-launched weapons of mass destruction."

"And some people in Washington don't want to believe it even now," added Brennan. "What Ed says is right, Trip. We have to credit the Soviets with some truly astonishing scientific innovations in this field. That's one reason why it's been so hard to persuade our own people about the viability of these weapons. In their arrogance and complacency, many of our scientists, not to mention our friends in the Agency, just did not want to believe that the Russians could have developed something that wasn't invented here. By injecting protons into a stream of electrons, the Soviets have produced a beam that is as powerful as a lightning bolt—a lightning bolt that can be aimed against a target. It's a beam that travels at close to the speed of light."

"One hundred and eighty-six thousand miles per second." Trip Gage injected one of the few scraps of scientific lore he had retained from his high-school days.

"Right," Brennan said, warming to his audience. "Accelerated to that speed, the stream of protons acquires a staggering mass. Each proton pulse generates between ten billion and a hundred billion electron bolts at energy levels of ten to the fourteenth power. You can imagine what will happen to anything that gets in the way of a killer beam like that. And that's just one of the weapons in their arsenal. Our pundits were saying for years that they didn't believe the Soviets could produce a beam like that, because it would require solutions to at least seven major problems that our scientists hadn't figured out at that stage. Right, Ed?"

"Yes. The first step was to generate the pulsed power for a particle beam or a high-energy laser from a nuclear explosion. Ironically, the Soviet inventors of the explosive accelerator were Andrei Sakharov, the leading dissident, and Andrei Terletsky, who was chief of the Soviet intelligence network in Sweden during World War II. Then the Soviets had to develop giant capacitators capable of storing unthinkable amounts of power for fractions of a second, a flux compression system to convert explosive energy into energy to power the beam, and a collective accelerator to produce streams of electron pulses and to accelerate other subatomic particles. The United States was ten to twenty years behind them in some of these areas. But we did get the occasional clue. Remember when that physicist who had been working with Berzin came out to the Livermore laboratories in California, George?"

"I sure do." Brennan chuckled. "I always thought the Soviets milked us for more than we got from them in these scientific exchanges. But that get-together was an exception to the rule. Berzin's man got carried away and started scrawling diagrams and equations on a blackboard, just like Ed's there. When the Russian had left and we took a closer look at what he'd written down there, we classified the blackboard. It helped Ed to copy the Soviets' RFQ."

"RFQ?" Trip Gage queried, already floundering among unfamiliar technical expressions.

"Radio Frequency Quadrupole," Greenhouse spelled it out. "It's a way of focusing particles into a concentrated beam by using tremendously powerful radio-frequency electrical fields."

"Look," Gage appealed to Brennan, "I'm afraid I'm already seriously out of my depth."

"Don't worry," the general assured him. "You don't have to understand how it all works. It's enough for you to get a picture of the end results. If I can summarize what Ed is saying, it's like this. The Soviets already have a beam weapon. Let's think of it as a controlled lightning bolt. We have every reason to think that they can fire this thing from ground bases against low-flying satellites and aircraft. It's only a matter of time before they put the thing on board a space battle station and take the war a few thousand miles up into space. They may have done so already. We also have the strongest possible reasons to believe that the Soviets have developed an offensive beam weapon capable of irradiating huge areas on the earth's surface, something that would make Hiroshima look like a picnic in Central Park. Are you with me so far?"

"Sure."

"Now, where is poor old Uncle Sam left? We're lagging badly behind the Soviets in the whole field. Thanks to Ed and my Young Turks, we've been closing the gap. We are not in the business of mass extermination, so we have no equivalent for Death Beam. And we have zero—but *zero*—defensive capacity against it. There's just no way known to us that you can stop a beam as powerful as the ones that Berzin and company have devised. Which all leaves us up shit creek." For once, Brennan's language seemed ridiculously mild.

"So what's the answer?" the general asked rhetorically. "We need a quick fix. We may just have time to get one. I don't believe in miracles, but some writer said that this is a country where miracles happen all the time. And I do believe in Ed Greenhouse."

The physicist, Gage noticed, actually blushed.

"Ed is the man who's gonna make Blue Savior fly," Brennan wound up. "Ed, let's show our National Security Adviser what we've got in the big top."

What General Brennan described as the big top was an enormous auditorium in the center of the research complex, the size and shape of an aircraft hangar—which, Gage guessed, it had been in some previous incarnation.

"This is our quick fix," Brennan announced. As the dimmer

lights were turned up in the auditorium, Gage could see that it was dominated by a huge scale model of the planet earth, being orbited by spacecraft of differing shapes and sizes, with both American and Soviet insignia. Brennan took a pointer and tipped it toward one of the satellites.

"That," he said, "is a pretty good replica of one of our Cosmic Interceptors." He moved to the control console and flipped a switch. A narrow beam of bluish light shot out from the model spacecraft, was bent through a thirty-degree angle by an orbiting mirror, and shone on another miniature satellite—a model of a Soviet Salyut.

"What you are looking at is only a flashlight," Brennan observed. "In practice, the Cosmic Interceptors will be armed with a deuterium-fluoride laser. We've tested the lasers, and they work. In fact, we've got up one on the ground, atop that mountain you were looking at on the way into the laboratories. We think the laser will work better in space, because there won't be interference from clouds or changes in the earth's atmosphere. Maybe you'd like to fill in some of the details, Ed."

"We've perfected a continuous-wave chemical laser," Greenhouse began. "We use thermonuclear combustion to produce atomic fluorine that is expanded through a set of supersonic nozzles and mixed in with deuterium when it flows into an optical cavity. There is a device like an inverted telescope at the aperture through which the laser exits that expands it into a wide beam capable of traveling huge distances. Our prototype laser guns have a power of ten megawatts, an aperture twelve meters wide, and a jitter of about a hundred nanoradians. In other words, we think we can aim them with an error of only four feet over a distance of 7,575 miles."

"This thing isn't a flashlight," Brennan said. "It can kill a hostile spacecraft or missile with a pressure pulse that drives a hole through the skin of the target, punching through anodized aluminum like a blowtorch through cardboard. It delivers photon bullets at the speed of light, and can shoot again and again until its nuclear fuel is used up. We calculate it could knock out Soviet ballistic missiles, launched from the ground bases or submarines, at the rate of one a second."

"What does it take to get the thing up into the air?" asked Gage.

"Two space-shuttle flights," Brennan replied. "One to take up

257

the Cosmic Interceptor and its battle equipment, the second to take up the fuel tanks. The laser gun itself is about twenty-five feet long."

They all stood in silence for a moment, contemplating the model spacecraft spinning around the globe. Trip Gage counted twenty-five of the miniature Cosmic Interceptors. They were arranged in three rings, following each other at precisely graduated intervals on separate polar orbits.

"Why twenty-five?" the National Security Adviser asked.

"We estimate," Brennan explained, "that that is the number we would need in order to screen out a Soviet missile attack as well as cope with any attempt the Soviets might make to knock out our reconnaissance and communications satellites. At present," he digressed, "our KH-11 and Big Bird satellites are completely vulnerable to a surprise Soviet attack with beam weapons. We could be blinded without warning, left in the dark trying to figure out whether or not World War III had started."

"May I?" asked Gage. He took Brennan's place at the control console and pressed some of the buttons. Crisscrossing red and blue beams of light gave the impression of a duel between American and Soviet satellites in space.

"I suppose the lasers could also be used against manned aircraft," the National Security Adviser reflected aloud.

"A high-energy laser would turn the window of a plane incandescent," General Brennan confirmed. "Everything inside the cockpit would be melted like butter."

The Defense Intelligence chief studied the expression forming on the aristocratic face of the National Security Adviser. Had Trip Gage grasped fully what was at issue? Year after year, Brennan had fought to make Washington understand that the next war would probably be won or lost in space. At the start, even his fellow generals had not wanted to believe it; like most generals, they had preferred to go on fighting the previous war.

Brennan had never bent to pressure from his colleagues or superiors to dilute his opinions. Among the other photographs that littered the walls of his office in the Pentagon, he kept a picture of the view from the window of his house in Maine. The new Secretary of Defense, Jake Waggoner, had been foolish enough to ask what the photograph was. "It's what I have to look forward to if I get thrown out of this office," Brennan had triumphantly replied. For the rest, he had memorized a line from the writings of the poet Hafiz: "The heart of the most powerful tyrant trembles before the man who wants nothing for himself." That, even Brennan's most bitter critics were obliged to acknowledge, summarized the root of the man's strength; he wanted nothing for himself.

But he wanted to best the Soviets.

Trip Gage turned from the model to Brennan and Ed Greenhouse. His face looked gray and deeply lined; he removed his gold-rimmed glasses and rubbed his eyes.

"How long?" asked the National Security Adviser. "How long before we get the first of these killer satellites up?"

"We were hoping to launch the first Cosmic Interceptor by the end of December," said Greenhouse. "We're now shooting for the first week of November, following the President's directive. I can't promise that we'll meet the deadline. Nor can I promise that the laser is going to work according to plan once we put the Cosmic Interceptor into orbit. We've never tested one of these things in space."

"Get it up," said Gage. "You know there are no restrictions on this. Right now, nothing has higher priority than Blue Savior."

"I know," said the scientist, fidgeting with the row of pens in the pocket of his lab coat.

"But it's good to hear it again," said Brennan.

When the scientist had gone back to his blackboard and Brennan was alone with Trip Gage, the National Security Adviser said, "Suppose Ushinsky is right about this Death Beam launching on November 7?" Gage's tone implied that he did not share Brennan's absolute belief in the defector. He went on, "What happens if we can't meet the deadline?"

"In that event," Brennan said, sinking his heavy jaw into his chest, "we wouldn't have but one option. We'd have to go in first. And destroy Death Beam on the ground."

23

"Oh, *shit*." Dick Hammond's somber expression brightened as he sized up Charles Canning's surroundings. "You look like a commercial for soybeans." Hammond grinned.

"You chose the place, not me," the Englishman reminded him. "We could be in some friendly hostelry. *And* you're late."

Canning was puffing a cigar in front of the Band Shell on the east side of Central Park, not far from the zoo. He was standing beside an elaborate poster display with a big multicolored sign that read, "Cow Protection." There were photographs of sacred cows roaming loose in India, and leaflets explaining how man takes the good things of life from the milk of the cow, and therefore has no right to kill it.

They had walked into the middle of a Hare Krishna festival. Hammond stared around, bemused by the strange assortment of believers in their saffron robes. A hulking man who might have passed for a professional wrestler with his shaven head and pigtail was conversing with an older woman who looked as if she had just been to the hairdresser and wore her sari with such natural elegance that it could have been a cocktail dress. Inside the Band Shell, a grossly obese oriental guru was reclining in state among grimacing idols, fanned by four young American acolytes. Other devotees of the cult marched back and forth in single file, beating drums and droning their monotonous chant.

"Do you think we can find somewhere quieter?" asked Hammond.

They passed some stalls where the disciples were selling vegetable curries and slices of watermelon. They strolled on, dodging the joggers and skateboarders and bikers, until they came to the Bethesda Fountain. Usually a favored haunt of drug pushers and hippies, the area around the fountain was almost deserted today.

"Closed for repairs," Canning commented tersely, pointing to the scaffolding around the fountain. The place was curiously silent, apart from the lapping of the oars of boaters on the fetid waters of the lake. The two men wandered along its edge.

Canning began, in staccato sentences, to brief his friend on what had happened in Miami. Hammond did not interrupt, except to curse under his breath when Canning described the attack at the beach house, until the Englishman reached the final part of the story: his encounter with the police sergeant at Miami airport.

Then Hammond said, "I guess it has to be Les Winter."

"That's what Max had decided," said Canning. "Someone was ready to have killed to stop him using his evidence. And to try to scare *me* off."

"Max didn't have *evidence*, Charles," Hammond corrected him. "Call it suspicions, guesswork, inspired sleuthing. But not proof. We don't have proof that Les Winter is a Soviet agent. Not the kind of proof that sends a man to jail."

Hammond was already considering how he would put it to Director Claiborne. Max Zimmer had been framed, and then murdered. That seemed to clear *him*. Now suspicion centered on Max's longtime adversary, Les Winter, the man who claimed that Death Beam was a KGB fiction. But they had to be sure. Far more was at stake than catching the mole who had betrayed Hussar. If Winter was working for the Soviets, it meant that the Agency's best source in Moscow—Martini—was a KGB plant. It meant that the defector had been telling the truth. It meant, in all probability, that the weapon called Death Beam was a reality. And that all the resources of the United States would need to be deployed to prevent it from being launched.

Hammond needed more than the statement of a Miami cop and the bits and pieces of microfilm that Charles Canning had been able to salvage from Max's files to be sure that he had the right answers.

"What's the next step?" the Englishman asked him as he stood absorbed in his thoughts, swinging the toe of his boot against the side of a grassy knoll.

"I'll talk to the director," Hammond said. "We'll put Les Winter under round-the-clock surveillance. We'll go back through the files on the death of his wife."

"Don't forget the father-in-law. The bookseller. He could be the key."

"Malinovsky. Yeah. He sure has the right name." The bookseller's namesake, Roman Malinovsky, had been one of the leaders of the Bolsheviks before the Russian Revolution. Lenin, frequently warned that Roman Malinovsky was a double agent employed by the Czar's secret police, had refused to believe the allegation until after the revolution, when captured documents had proved it was true.

Hammond looked up the hill, to where a group of folk dancers were frolicking to recorded bouzouki music under the trees.

"For Chrissake," he said, "I'll talk to him face to face."

"Malinovsky?"

"No, no." Hammond shook his head impatiently. "To Les. I've worked with him for a long time. I owe it to him. And I think I can tell if he's lying."

Canning considered the possible outcome of a face-to-face confrontation between Hammond and Les Winter.

"Isn't it a bit dangerous?" he suggested. "You might only succeed in alerting him to the fact that now he's the one under investigation. Wouldn't it be more sensible to play things quietly for a while and see whether he makes a slip?"

What Canning proposed was standard tradecraft. But Hammond said, "It won't work that way, Charles. This isn't a normal situation. We just don't have the fucking time."

Hammond visited Sally that night and ended up staying over in her apartment. They played Roberta Flack records, and Hammond brought Jimmy what the boy regarded as the supreme gourmet supper—burgers and fries from McDonald's. Hammond played Monopoly with Jimmy and was astonished, as he had been before, by the child's precociousness. He had not mastered the complexities of all the rules, but he knew enough to want to grab the properties at the upper end of the price scale and to slap hotels on them. When Hammond had been cleaned out of all his money

262

through having to pay Jimmy's colossal rents, the boy clapped his hands in delight.

"It's long past your bedtime," Sally then said. In fact, it was nearly 10:00.

Jimmy said something at that point that made both Dick and his mother bend down and kiss him.

"I hope Darth Vader is sleeping here tonight," he said.

If Hammond had had some remaining inhibitions that prevented him from talking candidly about the investigation, the boy's statement somehow helped him to overcome them. He had resolved when he got back from Israel and heard the full details of Max's death from Canning that Sally deserved to be told more than he had so far been prepared to reveal to her. Now that he was convinced that Max had been murdered and framed by people who wanted to shift the suspicion away from a real mole in the Agency, he was no longer shackled by the fear of appearing before her as her uncle's accuser. But Jimmy's sudden trust in him—after the earlier resentments and jealousy—gave Hammond a total sense of release. He suddenly felt that there was no need to keep up any barriers between him and Sally. Though her anger against the world of the Agency and the Club had been deepened by Max's death, she appeared to be as determined as he was that it should not be meaningless, that they should find the killers and trace the thread that Max Zimmer had left trailing through the maze that he had only begun to explore.

"Yes, darling," Sally said to her son. "Darth Vader's going to stay with us tonight."

They stayed up for several hours, drinking wine and endless cups of coffee, while Hammond explained the possible background to Max's death and the reasons why his suspicions had shifted from her uncle to Les Winter, his bitter antagonist. Sally seemed especially interested when he mentioned Winter's father-in-law, the antiquarian bookseller Zhores Malinovsky.

"I've met Malinovsky," she said thoughtfully. "He has a store down on Thirteenth Street. I was in there not long ago, just before I went to Miami." She shuddered at the thought of Miami and what her vacation had brought, and Hammond enclosed her in his arms and held her for a long time, in perfect stillness, before they went into the bedroom.

263

In the morning, Hammond woke up to find himself staring into the glass eyes of a big fluffy toy dog, Jimmy's favorite play animal.

"I want Darth Vader to stay here all the time," Jimmy said.

As Sally scrambled the eggs for their breakfast, she found that her eyes kept watering.

"What's the next step?" she asked Dick after they had dropped Jimmy off at school.

"I've got to confront Les Winter," he said. "After I've talked to the director."

"Please be careful," she said, remembering Max. "If they've killed once, they won't hesitate to kill again."

24

Dick Hammond poured more soda into his whisky. It was after midnight, and he felt the evening had just begun.

From the noises coming from the bathroom down the corridor, it sounded as if Les Winter was throwing up. Then there was a thud, as if Winter had collided with a door.

"Les," Hammond called out. "Are you okay?"

For a moment, there was perfect silence in the little brick house fronting onto the Georgetown canal. Hammond felt a slight singing sensation in his ears as he strained to pick up some sound of movement. In that moment, it crossed his mind that Winter might have taken something—an overdose of sleeping pills, or some more reliable poison.

"Les?" he yelled. The uncertainty in his voice came from the sudden fear that he had pushed Winter too far, hustled him back against a blind wall from which he saw only one possible way of escape.

Then Winter croaked, "I'm coming."

Hammond went out to look.

The door to the bathroom was open, and Les Winter was sprawled like a limp scarecrow on the floor, his back propped up against the edge of the lavatory bowl. There was an acrid smell of sick in the room, and Hammond noticed a grainy smudge over Winter's shirt and pants.

"Let's get you cleaned up," Hammond said as he grabbed him under the armpits and hoisted him to his feet.

" 'S all right," Winter said thickly. "Just let me alone for a minute."

The head of the Agency's Soviet Division turned on the cold tap and started splashing water over his face from his cupped hands.

Hammond went back into Winter's living room to wait for him, a room decorated with Japanese silk prints and Korean lacquered screens that must have been part of Katya's legacy. Under different circumstances, Hammond would have left Les Winter to sleep off his drunk. But there was no time to let Winter sleep.

"It's not the way you think." Les Winter stood swaying in the doorway, gripping the frame for support. "I swear to you, Dick. You've got it wrong." He looked like a derelict from the Bowery, with his tie hanging loose, an ugly stain across the front of his shirt, and his face turned the color of unbaked pastry. Hammond noticed that he had not even managed to buckle his belt. Yet his speech was better. His voice was reedy-thin, but unslurred. If you did not look at him, you might almost say he was sober.

Now he was leaning over the armchair where Hammond was sitting, hands pressed to the big man's shoulders, entreating with his washed-out, red-rimmed eyes. His breath reminded Hammond of the fish market in Saigon at the end of the day's trading.

"I never killed her," Winter said. "God knows I wanted to. I had the right. You can't conceive how that woman treated me." And it came spewing out of him, a sorry, sordid tale that made Dick Hammond want to turn away, embarrassed at the shame of this man who had been a friend. Except he could not look away, because he had to read the eyes. You could learn more from the eyes, Hammond believed, than from any polygraph. Except in a man so hardened that he had managed to burn guilt and shame out of himself. Les Winter did not appear to be that kind of man.

Winter had met Katya at the end of the Korean War, in Tokyo, where he had been trying to run agent networks in the Soviet Far East.

"You can't imagine," he said, "how beautiful she was then. Wait. There's a picture."

Winter fumbled in the cabinet beyond the bar and produced a faded snapshot that showed a slender girl with bobbed hair in a kimono. Her figure, Hammond observed, could almost have been that of a boy. Her features were delicate, but she had glared into the camera with what might have passed for defiance—or hatred—of whoever was taking the shot.

"Pretty girl," Hammond said diplomatically, handing back the picture. "When did she find out?"

266

"On vacation." Winter swallowed and reached for the whisky bottle. Dick Hammond grabbed it first and held it away from him. "We were in San Francisco," Winter went on, eyeing the bottle disconsolately. "On vacation," he repeated. "I was always very careful, Dick. I never thought about it for long stretches at a time. I tried to suppress it altogether. I read books, Dick. I even went to see an analyst. Under a false name, of course."

"Sure." Feeling sorry for him, Hammond relinquished the bottle.

Winter seized it gratefully and poured himself another slug.

"That California trip was a disaster from the beginning," he resumed. "Katya was a demanding woman, Dick. Hungry. I couldn't satisfy her. Maybe no one man could. But certainly not this one. That time in San Francisco, Dick, I couldn't get it up. Not once. Jesus." He choked on the words and started sobbing into his glass. "I should never have married her. Never."

"Well?"

"She started mocking me. She had a cruel tongue, that woman. I couldn't repeat the things she said to me. First I started hitting the bottle. Then I hit her. She threatened to call the cops. I went out, rode cable cars, found a bar or two. You know those bars in San Francisco."

"Yeah." Last time Hammond had been in San Francisco, he had run into two men in cutaway leather outfits cruising the streets right next to Union Square. He had looked twice, because the bigger of the two men had been holding a leash chained to a dog collar around the other one's neck.

"Well, I cruised a few bars. Had a few more drinks. I met this kid. A nice kid. Not a weirdo. Not a druggie. He'd been working as a grease monkey."

Oh my God, Hammond repeated inwardly. *A grease monkey.*

"I spent the night with him." Winter looked up at Hammond with a flash of defiance. "I couldn't go back to Katya that night. Not after what she'd said. And I had to remind myself that I was still a man."

"I assume you succeeded," Hammond said drily.

"It wasn't dirty," Winter insisted.

"Did you pay this kid?"

"*No*," Winter whipped back, obviously stung by the question. "We were friends."

"But there were times you paid, weren't there?" In order to hide his secret from the Agency, Hammond knew, Les Winter must have had to deny himself regular boyfriends, confining himself to furtive encounters in gay bars and public men's rooms.

"Yes." Winter seemed to be asking, with those hopeless eyes, how far his humiliation had to go.

As far as is necessary to get to the truth, Hammond said to himself. *I'm sorry, Les.*

"So what happened after your night with the grease monkey?" Hammond pursued.

"She saw us."

"What?"

"Katya saw us. It was midmorning, and the kid and I had gone out to get some coffee and an eye-opener. I guess Katya was just roaming around town, doing some shopping and trying to work out what had happened to me. We rounded a corner and there she was, coming down one of those steep, sliding streets that run down from Nob Hill."

"In the whole of San Francisco, she just happened to be at that particular corner." Hammond was no great believer in coincidence. The whole scenario sounded like something that Katya and her father, Malinovsky, might have contrived.

"Yeah. Some luck," Winter commented. "She knew, of course. She never let me forget it, either. We started sleeping in separate rooms back here in Washington. Then she started drinking too, and popping pills, and she'd come in and wake me up in the middle of the night, hitting and screaming, saying she wanted a man in her bed."

No wonder most of us never met Katya, Hammond was thinking. *No wonder Les never invited people from the Agency around for dinner at home.*

"So Katya died—what?—three, four months after your trip to San Francisco?"

"Thereabouts." Winter chewed his lip and then said, "She paid me back, Dick. She got a man in her bed. Quite a few of them."

"So you killed her." Saying it point-blank was a gamble. In his distraught condition, Winter might have reacted any way at all. He did not react the way that Hammond expected.

"Maybe I did," Winter said. "Maybe I drove her to it."

"I meant literally."

"I'm sorry you said that, Dick. I went over all of that with the police at the time."

268

"Did they tell you the statistical odds against a woman's killing herself by holding a bit of plastic over her face until she was smothered?"

"Now look." Winter was trying to sound angry, but his voice quavered. He was now standing behind his corner bar, propping himself up with his forearms as he leaned over the polished surface. "I don't know," he tried again, "why she picked that— horrible, horrible way to do it. I don't know how she managed to kill herself that way. Maybe it had something to do with all those pills she was popping. Pills to wake her up and put her to sleep. Uppers and downers. Pills to make her forget about sex and pills to make her remember. They found Quaaludes in her pocketbook after she died. All those pills. She'd get them mixed up, and then she'd wash them all down with booze. That was probably what killed her."

Winter is tied in with two dubious suicides, Hammond was thinking. Katya and Max Zimmer. The pattern was the same in both cases.

"I wasn't even in the house the night Katya—uh—killed herself," Winter was protesting. "You can check that out with the cops too."

"Where were you?"

"I was with George."

"You mean your father-in-law? Zhores Malinovsky?"

"Yes."

Now we're getting closer, Hammond thought. *What better basis for blackmail! Les killed his wife and her father supplied him with an alibi.*

"You were always close to Malinovsky, weren't you?"

"Sure."

"You know what Max Zimmer believed about your father-in-law, don't you?"

"That George was a Soviet agent? Sure. Zimmer even managed to get him taken off the Agency payroll."

"I've been back through the files, Les. I found that a remarkable number of the operations that your father-in-law was running out in the Far East just blew up in our faces. Agents were parachuted into North Korea or infiltrated along the coast in rubber dinghies, and they'd just be swallowed up without trace. Seems there was always a reception committee to greet them. They were always expected. Then we got refugees coming down from the North who

269

said that everyone up there knew that Malinovsky was bad, that his story about being a White Russian playboy who fled south when the commies took over was a fabrication, that he'd been working for Soviet intelligence since before the end of the war."

"I know," said Winter. "A lot of what you say is true."

"You're admitting you *knew* that your father-in-law was a Soviet agent?"

"Not when I married Katya. I found out later."

"I don't understand, Les. The records show that *you* took the initiative in getting Malinovsky rehired as an Agency consultant after Max Zimmer had been fired and there was no one around to stop you. Now why would you want to do that if you knew Malinovsky was working for Moscow Center?"

Unless you yourself were a KGB mole, Hammond finished the thought inside his head.

"It's a long story, Dick."

"Then you'd better take a deep breath and start telling me."

The time, Hammond noticed, was just after 1:30. As good a time as any for a confession.

Hammond switched on the wafer-thin cassette recorder concealed in his breast pocket. Each side of the tape recorded up to two hours' conversation. It could be switched on and off by a simple button at the top without exciting the attention of onlookers. Ten or fifteen years ago, the machine might have been thought an example of gee-whiz spy technology; today one like it could be bought at any good electronics store.

"One more drink," Winter pleaded.

Hammond poured for him. Les Winter had reached the point where an extra drink seemed to stabilize the water table, rather than making him drunker.

"The story begins with Martini." Winter paused to take a long swallow. He wiped his mouth with the back of his hand before asking Hammond, "Were you at headquarters when Martini first came to us?"

"When was that? Nine, ten years ago? I guess I was in Saigon. If I'd been at Langley, nobody would have told me back then anyway. Compartmentalization. Need to know."

"Okay." Winter gulped down his scotch. "Well, you've been briefed. You've seen the files. You know how it started."

"Martini was a walk-in, right?"

270

"Yeah. The Bureau had followed standard procedure. Here was this new KGB guy in New York under United Nations cover, so they put a twenty-four-hour tail on him and they also assigned him a companion." The job of a Bureau companion was to make himself visible to the Soviet agent to whom he was assigned, to the point of trying to strike up conversation, in the hope that his mark might decide one day to cross sides. "The companion's name was Larry Webster," Winter continued. "For the first couple of weeks, Larry had a pretty routine job, walking Martini back and forth to the Soviet mission, watching him snooze away his afternoons behind dark glasses in some boring United Nations committee, you know the form. Larry tried to talk to him a couple of times, but the guy pretended he didn't know English. Then one morning, on the corner of Forty-fifth and Second, Martini turned around and said he wanted to be introduced to Larry's director. Of course, the director never met him, but the Bureau assigned some top people to handle him, and it turned out that Martini was the head of the science and technology section in the KGB *rezidentura* in New York. He then held the rank of colonel. He was the right man in the right place to tell us what the Soviets could and could not do in the field of new-weapons development. But the Bureau fumbled him. We nearly lost Martini right then and there."

"What went wrong?"

"Well, Martini was required to work to a quota system, just like any other operative that Moscow Center assigns to a foreign post. If he failed to recruit his quota of American agents, and to fulfill a set proportion of the assignments that headquarters gave him, he was liable to be hauled back to Moscow with his ass in a sling. So to run him as a double agent, the Bureau had to help him satisfy his bosses that he was up to snuff as a spy."

"You mean they had to arrange to give him feeder material."

"Sure. That's where I first came in. The Bureau eventually came to us to coordinate the flow of information to and from Martini. At Reports and Requirements section, we were not only pushing on his product, under disguised sourcing, to the rest of the community, we were also collecting material, from the Pentagon as well as the Agency, that we could feed to Martini to send back to Moscow."

"How much of the stuff was genuine?"

"Seventy, maybe eighty percent. The rest, of course, was disinformation. We knew we had to give away some real secrets in order to save Martini from getting blown. We figured that was worthwhile in exchange for the treasures that he was giving us. Plus the fact that we had the chance to deceive the Soviets, especially in relation to some of our defense research projects."

"But you say that Martini nearly was blown early on in the game. That the Bureau fumbled him."

"Right. Here was Martini, collecting all this terrific stuff. But sooner or later, Krylov or someone else at Moscow Center was bound to start looking very carefully into the question of where he was getting it. Who was the superagent Martini was running? The Bureau people just hadn't thought about that problem seriously enough. They gave Martini some half-assed academic who did contract work for the Pentagon, and he was supposed to be the source of the feeder material. No one would have believed that. If Krylov had started an investigation, Martini would have been dead from day one."

"But Martini, according to you, is very much alive. After ten years or so."

"Yeah. And I'll tell you why." Winter was no longer defensive and self-pitying. He spoke with the subdued, arrogant snarl with which his adversaries were familiar from debates at headquarters. "You and Max Zimmer and Director Claiborne may all think you've got me taped as a Soviet mole or whatever." He was talking, Hammond noted, as if Max were still alive. "But I'll prove to you why that is absurd. It's sick-think, Dick," he digressed. "I must say, I never thought I'd find *you* seeing eye to eye with that paranoid Max Zimmer."

"Go on."

"Martini is alive today because of me. And Martini is the only clear window we have into Moscow Center. He's the most valuable agent we've ever had. He's fucking good, Dick. You didn't handle his reports, month after month, over these years. You can smell it when they're good. Martini is the best."

"So how come he's alive?" Hammond knew that the main reason that Max Zimmer had been convinced that Martini had been a plant had been that he had survived so long, against all the odds, first in New York and later in Moscow.

"I'll give it to you straight from the shoulder, Dick. Martini is alive because I gave him a source that Moscow Center had to believe was real. Larry Webster and the Bureau guys didn't know how to do that. They were just pissing around. When we were brought in on the case, I insisted that they had to let me take over on this front. I created a superagent for Martini. He was able to take credit for that at Moscow Center. It was beautiful, Dick. While Moscow Center believed that Martini had pulled off a tremendous espionage coup in the United States, he was turning over the KGB's secrets to us."

"I get the picture," said Hammond, not letting his skepticism show. "So who was this superagent you invented for Martini?"

"You can figure that out, Dick. Out of the entire American intelligence setup, what section do the Soviets most want to penetrate? What is Krylov's top priority?"

"Your own section," Hammond replied without hesitation. "Soviet Division." The answer was obvious, because Soviet Division was directly responsible for operations against the KGB. A Soviet mole inside that section would be well placed to paralyze the Agency's operations, worldwide, against its main target.

"Right. And what's the ideal job for a mole inside Soviet Division?"

"Reports and Requirements."

Where you spent most of your career, Hammond thought. The trend of the conversation gave Hammond the uncanny feeling of déjà vu. It was as if he were watching one of Max Zimmer's counterintelligence briefs being mimed out. One of the reports in which Max had concluded that Les Winter was, in all probability, the mole in the Agency.

"You're on track," said Winter. "I gave Martini a source inside Reports and Requirements." He said it proudly, almost as if he expected applause.

"You mean—" Hammond began.

"No," Winter cut him off, shaking his head. "I know what you're thinking. It wasn't me, Dick."

Hammond remembered the shapeless, oversexed girl with the prodigious memory who worshiped the ground on which Les Winter walked.

"So it was Trudy Cook," he said.

Winter nodded.

"You're telling me that the Agency itself created a mole for the KGB."

"Exactly."

It was 3:45 when Hammond started making coffee in the kitchen. The coldest, hollowest part of the night. The time when, if you've been out drinking, you wake up feeling dehydrated. The time when you start questioning the whole meaning of your life. The time when self-negation and thoughts of suicide are hardest to resist.

Hammond made Winter drink two big mugs of black coffee, one after the other. The man's eyes were like open wounds. But the questions had to go on.

"All right," Hammond summarized. "So while Martini was in this country, he was in contact with Trudy Cook, with your knowledge and approval. What happened when he was recalled to Moscow?"

"We did not seek to maintain contact with Martini in Moscow," Winter responded. "It was far too risky. Look at what happened to Hussar."

Yes, thought Hammond. *I'd like you to explain that.*

"Martini would resume contact when he was traveling abroad. The signal was usually a postcard to one of a number of dead-letter drops in Switzerland."

"You said you were going to explain why you got your father-in-law rehired by the Agency. I don't see how Malinovsky fits into this Martini story."

"Well, Martini's departure for Moscow left a pretty visible loose end just trailing there," Winter explained. "Trudy Cook. Martini was supposed to have recruited her as Moscow Center's super-agent in Washington. If Trudy had just broken off contact with the KGB after Martini was called home, Krylov would have been very suspicious."

"You're saying that Trudy kept up the relationship with the KGB even after the cause of it—Martini—had gone back to Moscow."

"We had to do that, Dick. Martini himself was very insistent

274

about it. He said that if we tried to cut Trudy's relations with Moscow Center, we would be putting his head on the block."

"How did Trudy feel about it?"

"She accepted the need. She had a good rapport with Martini. I think she liked the guy a lot."

I wonder if she tried to screw him, Hammond was thinking. He pictured the tubby spinster from Reports section in bed with the Russian agent in a safe house in the Washington suburbs.

"This is where my father-in-law came in," Winter continued. "It was a stroke of luck, really. Martini arranged it before he flew back to Moscow. He managed to get Moscow Center to agree that Malinovsky should take charge of communications with Trudy. He was ideally placed, what with the bookstores both in Washington and New York."

"Let's see if I've got this straight. Your father-in-law was working for the Soviets all along, right?"

"Yes."

"So you turned over Trudy, the mole you had created for Martini's benefit, to Malinovsky. At the same time, you got Malinovsky reemployed by the Agency on a contract basis. So your father-in-law was also a double agent. You thought you controlled him too."

"Absolutely. All the threads were in my hands, Dick. I never doubted that."

No, thought Hammond, *you probably never did.* But in this intricate dance of double agents—Martini, Trudy Cook, Malinovsky—which loyalties had really been uppermost? Hammond recalled the enigmatic advice of the dead spymaster Max Zimmer. "Read all messages as in a glass," Max used to say. "Read them backward." If the game of double agents had really been working according to the rules that Winter had described, then surely Max would have been alive today. Max had been convinced that Winter himself was the mole. Max had been close enough to the truth for someone to have killed him in an effort to suppress the evidence that he had acquired. But had Max Zimmer been right? Damning though it was, the evidence that had built up against Les Winter did not make him a Soviet mole. His closet homosexuality, the suspicion that he had murdered his wife, Katya, the fact that his father-in-law was a Soviet agent: none of this resolved the

275

question, Hammond now felt, his earlier certainties breaking up and reforming like the colored patterns of a kaleidoscope. Four in the morning is not a time for certainties.

"The heart of it all," Winter now said, "is Martini and what he gave us. You can argue everything else back and forth, but you can't argue with that. The information that Martini brought us is priceless. It proves that he was our man, not Krylov's."

"General Brennan doesn't think so."

"Brennan hasn't had access to the files."

But maybe Brennan is right all the same, Hammond said to himself. *Maybe the Agency has been sold a pup.* Les Winter was clinging to his belief that the relationship with Martini had worked the way that he intended: that the Agency had been able to feed Moscow Center disinformation, sugared with a few secrets, while receiving priceless Soviet secrets in return. To conclude otherwise, after more than a decade, would be to suffer irretrievable loss of face. It would also force the Agency bureaucracy as a whole to rethink many of the counterespionage operations of the past ten years or more. It would provide the clinching argument for those, like General Brennan, who wanted to clip the Agency's wings. Yet the possibility now had to be faced that the Martini case had gone disastrously wrong. That, via Martini, Moscow Center had drugged the Agency with graduated doses of deception. In that event, Les Winter need not have been a conscious agent for the Soviets. Merely an unwitting dupe, willing himself to believe a living lie.

But there's more to it, Hammond thought. He imagined Charles Canning's agent, Hussar, being pushed alive into the oven of a crematorium. And he pictured the scene in the grounds of the Vizcaya Palace in Miami that Charles had described, of Max Zimmer lying in a summer house with the top of his head blown away. Whoever was responsible for those deaths was not merely a dupe. And they were deaths that had to be atoned for.

So he said to Winter, "Who killed Max?"

And Winter merely flapped his hands in the air and said, "Maybe Max killed himself."

At which point something in Hammond snapped. Maybe it was fatigue after the long, winding course of the all-night interrogation, the piling of one doubt on top of another, blended with the scotch they had consumed. Maybe it was the angry frustration that can overtake despair after 4:00 in the morning, when those who cannot sleep find a black hole has been drilled through the heart of the night.

Whatever it was, Hammond heard himself yelling, "Like your wife! Max killed himself like your wife!" and was shaking the smaller man like a rag doll.

When he had recovered himself, he apologized.

Les Winter had his hands on top of his head in the posture of a victim waiting to be struck.

It was astonishing, Hammond told himself as he poured both of them coffee, that Les Winter had been able to keep his secret for so long. He wondered whether Katya and her father, the bookseller, had known that Winter was a closet homosexual before the marriage. Maybe they had guessed at the truth and maneuvered him into the wedding, knowing they would be able to blackmail him later. Or Maybe Katya had not found out until that time in San Francisco. Hammond could picture what must have happened after that. He could see Winter driving home from Langley night after night, drinking himself into insensibility while his wife mocked him as a useless fag. One night, maddened beyond endurance, Winter had rebelled. In a fit of blind hatred, he had assaulted Katya with the first weapon that had come to hand, a simple sheet of plastic, clamping it over her mouth and nose until she suffocated.

At what point, Hammond asked himself, had the blackmail started? When Katya found out he was a homosexual? Or after he killed her and his father-in-law offered to help him construct an alibi so he could escape criminal prosecution? Or not at all?

It had occurred to Hammond at several points during the interrogation that Winter might not, after all, be the man who had betrayed Hussar. On the surface, the pieces all seemed to fit. Winter had been briefed by the British on the Hussar case. He had several possible motives for working for the Russians. There was not only the fear of exposure as a homosexual and a murderer; there was also the tremendous career advantage he had garnered from handling the fake double agent called Martini—an agent who had been planted, Hammond was now convinced, by Krylov's section at Moscow Center. Possibly Winter had also taken pleasure in the daily betrayal of colleagues he disliked. Especially Max Zimmer.

And yet there was no proof. Nothing to nail him. And Hammond found the insistent denials from a man who had taken enough liquor to break down most inhibitions curiously convincing.

Equally significant was that by Winter's own account there was a second person who was just as deeply embroiled in the whole Martini affair and had equal motivation for playing the Russians' game. Trudy Cook. The more he thought about it, the more Hammond was convinced that she had been Martini's lover.

"What happens now?" Winter asked, on his return from one of his many trips to the bathroom.

Hammond looked at his watch. Nearly 8:00. Late enough to call Director Claiborne.

"I have to use your phone," Hammond said. "Do you mind if I do this in your study?"

"Sure."

Adam Claiborne's reactions were terse and practical. Winter would be subjected to intensive grilling by Jerry Sarkesian and the Office of Security. Both Winter and Trudy Cook would be placed under physical surveillance.

"We can't prove anything about either of them without a confession," Hammond reminded the director. "Or even about Malinovsky. Unless someone makes a false move." Hammond did not need to express what both of them also knew; that there was still no final confirmation that the defector had been telling the truth.

"We're not taking any risks," Claiborne growled. "As of this moment, Winter's clearances are lifted and he's suspended from duty. You can tell people it's for health reasons if you want. Even if he's not working for the Soviets, we can't have a fag running Soviet Division."

"What about Trudy Cook?"

"She'll stay where she is. We'll keep an eye on her."

Hammond broke the news to Winter.

"So this is the end of the line," Winter said. He was close to tears as he looked at Hammond. "It's been a long time, Dick," he said. "I don't know what there's left for me to do now."

278

Hammond stared at the floor, not wanting to witness his emotions.

"You're making a mistake," Winter said with sudden defiance.

"You're the one who made a mistake, Les."

25

ZHUKOVKA, *October 23*

"Stalin shot his generals."

The blond colonel sitting nearest the fire in the vast living room of Marshal Safronov's dacha laughed politely. The sound shrank to a nervous waver as the colonel corrected himself, noting that the marshal's expression had hardened.

"This is no joking matter," Safronov reproved him. "History can be repeated."

The marshal was a dedicated student of the history of power struggles as well as of battles. He had learned that whatever the complexion of the regime, a change of leadership in the Kremlin had most frequently been brought about by a coup.

"Stalin butchered most of his high command in the thirties," he reminded his audience. "Heroes were led like cows to the slaughtering block because they did not comprehend the nature of power in Russia. The purge of *your* service, Yuri Ivanovich"—his cold eyes rested on the blond colonel, a senior officer in military intelligence—"was so thoroughgoing that they even shot the cooks and the lavatory attendants. Imagine that scene, comrades. The secret police went through the latrines, shooting the poor illiterates who were mopping up the shit. After the purge of 1937, there was only one solitary survivor in the ranks of military intelligence. He was a young captain, still wet behind the ears, who had had the good fortune to be far away from Moscow, studying in an academy. I remember him well. I was that captain."

His guests were now perfectly immobile, as if frozen in a movie still.

"We should learn from Stalin," he continued his historical disquisition. "Stalin understood that the successful exercise of power in Russia requires maximum ruthlessness. Also, he had a supreme instinct for survival. Do you remember why he started shooting his generals? He had learned that Marshal Tukhachevsky—yes, the great Tukhachevsky—had got his hands on documents that proved that, in the old days, Stalin had worked as an informer for the czarist secret police. But sooner or later, he would have shot the generals anyway."

Marshal Safronov proceeded to elaborate. Power in Moscow, he explained, rested on three pillars: the Party, the army, and the secret police. Whenever the army or the KGB became overmighty, the two other members of the triad had combined to bring it to heel. So, after Stalin's death, the Party and the army had joined forces to strike down Beria, the dreaded chief of the secret police. Four years later, the KGB and the Party had combined to destroy the war hero Marshal Zhukov, whose soaring ambition and freewheeling style had inspired fears that he aspired to the role of a Soviet Bonaparte. And now, Safronov believed, an unholy alliance was being formed in the shadows to eliminate *him*.

"I have positive proof," he told the assembled military men. "There are traitors in high places, in Dzherzhinsky Square and in the Politburo itself. Men who do not share our vision of the historic destiny of the Soviet *Rodina*. Men who do not understand the responsibilities of greatness and are willing to forsake our chance to bring the United States to its knees. Men who are even willing, in their self-seeking jealousy and ambition, to play the game of our enemies and to collaborate with Western intelligence services."

"Give us the names of the traitors, Comrade Marshal!" The irruption came from the blond colonel, anxious to make up for his earlier faux pas.

"The worst of them," Safronov indulged him, "is that geriatric pedophile Krylov."

There were audible gasps of astonishment. Among the few men in Moscow who were privileged to know the true role of the head of the special KGB department known as the Beacon, Krylov's name inspired awe. He was widely believed, within that narrow circle, to have been the mastermind behind the greatest coups of Soviet espionage over a period of many decades.

"There is irrefutable evidence," the marshal assured his listeners, "that Krylov has betrayed Russia to the Zionists and to American intelligence. In the interests of our enemies, he has conspired to weaken state security and to jeopardize the success of Project Razrukha. I have proof that over many years, Krylov has been transmitting our secrets to the Americans through a member of his service employed by the Beacon."

There was now a rumble of anger around the room. It satisfied Marshal Safronov. He had not selected his dinner guests this evening because of their powers of reasoning. He had no need of intellectual skeptics to execute the plan that he had in mind. Rather, he needed men who would follow his instructions unquestioningly, because they looked to him as the natural leader of the *Rodina* and because their careers depended directly on his favor.

"Krylov is not alone," the marshal went on, clacking his steel hooks against the carved mantelpiece for dramatic effect. "There are men more powerful than Krylov who are involved in this anti-Russian plot, men whose names are household words. We will deal with them in the fullness of time. For the moment, we must act with caution. We will commence with Krylov."

With his surviving eye, the right one, Safronov scanned the faces of the eight men in the room. They were all hewn from the same oak: vigorous, athletic young officers from elite units. Superlative killers. There was no need to share with them the reason why he had decided that Krylov had to be dealt with immediately, before the rest of Safronov's plan had come to fruition, and the marshal had no intention of doing so.

He believed that in politics, as in war, the only effective form of defense was the offense, and that best of all was the preemptive strike. He knew that in Moscow he was surrounded by men who were only waiting for a suitable opportunity to have him shot like a mad dog. Since that morning, he had known that of all of them Krylov was the most dangerous. Safronov had learned from a sympathizer inside the KGB that Krylov was the moving spirit in a conspiracy against him. Safronov had only contempt for his informant, an opportunist who hoped to grab Strokin's job as chairman of the KGB once the marshal had consolidated his power as the new Soviet strongman. But he had no reason to doubt the veracity of the information.

Krylov had concocted a scheme to brand *him*, Safronov, as a traitor to Russia. The enormity of the lie was breathtaking. But that would not prevent the lie from being used by those who had a personal interest in bringing about Safronov's downfall. And if they got their way, the lie would soon be upheld as established truth. The marshal, honored today as a war hero and the foremost champion of the *Rodina*, would see his name excised from the history books and the honor rolls, while officers of the Red Army, even those assembled in his dacha, would revile him as a renegade—if he survived the firing squad. That was the way of dictatorship.

The defector, Stepan Ushinsky, was at the center of the scheme that Krylov had spun from his convoluted, arachnid brain. The marshal recalled with bitterness that only two months before, he had played host to Ushinsky in his own dacha. He himself had singled out the broad-shouldered young GRU officer as one of the select band who had been made privy to the secret of Project Razrukha. For once his instinct about men had failed him; it had been the worst error of judgment the marshal had ever made. He had expected that Ushinsky would feel exalted by his vision of a Soviet empire greater than any the world had known. Instead, Ushinsky had fled from it as a man hides his face when he has looked into the eye of the midday sun.

Marshal Safronov's misreading of a man had given Krylov the tool for which he had been searching. The marshal had been informed that a secret report, prepared by Krylov, had reached Strokin's desk at the headquarters of the KGB. The report accused Safronov of being personally responsible for the defection of his protégé, Stepan Ushinsky. Worse, the document made out that the marshal and his Russophile supporters were themselves a threat to state security. Krylov claimed, with fabricated evidence of the kind that he was skilled in manufacturing, that Safronov's faction was heavily penetrated by the Agency and other organs of Western intelligence. The implied conclusion was that Marshal Safronov should be removed from the Defense Ministry immediately. Safronov could imagine the rest. On a dark night—perhaps a night like this, when he was isolated in his dacha outside Moscow—KGB gunmen would push through the door and he would hear the shout that was feared by all of Russia: "Hands behind your neck!"

But the marshal did not intend to allow his enemies the time to carry through Krylov's plot. His great strength, in this new contest for power, came from their irresolution. Krylov's explosive report was sitting there on Strokin's desk, while the chief of the KGB discreetly sounded out members of the Politburo and the Defense Council to see whether they had the guts to use it as a pretext to drive the marshal from office or actually have him seized and dragged off to prison. Safronov pictured them as fat, greedy rodents who could smell the cheese but feared being caught in a trap. He had no doubt that most of the Politburo would endorse Krylov's scheme—once they were certain that it was going to succeed and they would not be required to risk anything themselves. Even Manilov, the timorous apparatchik now warming Brezhnev's old seat as General Secretary of the Party, would cheerfully sign for the marshal's arrest once he was sure there was no danger that the army would dispose of *him*. They were all of them the same, thought the marshal: quick to conspire, but slow to act. Except Krylov.

"Krylov's the only one who's got balls," he said aloud. This tribute to his enemy was felt. In drafting his accusations against the marshal, Krylov had knowingly placed his own head on the block. Safronov wondered what had inspired the veteran spy chief. He'd always been a Jew-lover, of course. Witness Krylov's relationship with that *jid* Misha in East Berlin. It would be no surprise if Misha was somehow mixed up in this conspiracy too. When he had made himself master of Moscow, the marshal resolved, the last vestiges of Jewish influence would have to be rigorously weeded out. For now, there was Krylov to attend to.

He had briefly considered dealing with all his rivals with a single stroke. He would use the Kantemirovskaya Division, the Moscow army garrison, to surround the KGB troops in their barracks and disarm them while Spetsnaz squads were sent to scour the city and arrest or liquidate those members of the Party leadership who were known to the marshal to sympathize with the conspiracy against him. He had a list. It included five members of the Politburo as well as the KGB chief, Strokin. Marshal Safronov had derived a certain pleasure from the thought of Strokin's being arraigned before a show trial of the sort that he had arranged for others, his loose flesh wobbling like jelly between the constraining arms of his jailors.

But a successful coup depends on exactitude of timing more

284

than any other factor. It would be premature to risk everything now, the marshal had decided, so close to the success of Project Razrukha. His moment would come after November 7. No one would be able to stand against the man who had finally brought the United States to its knees. That would be the time to settle all the outstanding accounts.

The Krylov account, however, would not wait. The elimination of Krylov would accomplish two ends: it would remove the brain and the driving force behind the conspiracy, and it would terrorize and divide the rest of the conspirators.

The marshal explained to his young officers, their faces flushed with vodka and brandy, what he had in mind for the rest of the evening's entertainment.

Krylov spent the weekends when he could detach himself from the grueling demands of his special department in a lodge barely a mile away, through the woods, from Marshal Safronov's country retreat.

That night he was suffering from a diffuse melancholia. It came, in part, from the sense that his body was failing him. The KGB doctors had diagnosed angina and warned him to give up his horseback rides and his hunting expeditions.

It was mostly the effect of waiting. Since he had placed his bombshell on Strokin's desk that morning, nothing had happened. *Nothing*. Perhaps instead of using Strokin he should have gone higher, direct to Manilov himself. But things would probably have moved the same way. They all hated Marshal Safronov, but were paralyzed by fear.

After dinner, Krylov called his Georgian valet, Vissarion, into the library.

"You've been a good friend," Krylov said. "There is something of mine that I want you to have." He pulled off his heavy gold watch, a Swiss Rolex, inscribed on the back with a dedication from Misha. "Take it," he ordered his valet.

The man held back, puzzled and embarrassed.

"Go on, take it," Krylov urged him.

Vissarion held out his palm and felt the heaviness of the gold watch.

"I don't understand," he protested.

"I won't be needing it anymore."

At that moment, they both understood. The handsome young Georgian looked as if he were about to burst into tears. Krylov, who had offered the present from a man who was close to him to another who had served him loyally without considering the meaning of the gesture, now realized what he was doing. He had understood, in those ancient, instinctual layers of the brain that men have in common with the lower orders of animal life, since he had left his office that afternoon. It had taken several more hours before the higher part of his brain, the neocortex, had been able to accept the knowledge and turn it into verbal form. In many situations, delay is tantamount to defeat. Krylov's plot would not survive a country weekend.

He felt no panic; merely weary resignation. He did not even consider the possibility of flight. If he had been a drinking man, he would have asked Vissarion to bring him the brandy bottle.

Instead, he said, "I'd be grateful if you'd run me a bath."

Relieved to have a straightforward order to follow, the Georgian valet hurried out of the library, still clutching the Rolex awkwardly in his big peasant's fist.

Krylov watched him go, thinking of the boys and girls—children, many of them—that Vissarion had discreetly procured for him over the years to help him slake his thirst to recapture his own youth. Now the passage of time had overwhelmed him; he felt older than he had ever been. As he rose to his feet, the spymaster felt not only the stiffness of the joints that had bothered him all week, but an exquisite pain in his chest, around the heart. He felt that his heart was floating inside a molten ball.

A boy whom Krylov had never seen before was standing in the corridor to the bathroom. He was very young, younger than any of the children that Vissarion had brought to him in the past.

"What's your name, boy?" asked Krylov.

"Sasha." The boy looked straight up into his face, without any sign of fear or deference.

Vissarion appeared from the doorway to the bathroom.

"It's Vera's grandson," he explained. Vera was Krylov's cook at the dacha. "He's just here for the weekend." He was suddenly nervous as he watched Krylov staring wordlessly at the boy. This was not the child of a deportee or a whore. This was Vera's property. Vissarion cleared his throat.

"I'm coming," said Krylov. "Run along then, Sasha." But he stopped the child, adding, "Would you like to learn how to shoot?"

The boy nodded, shaking his mop of straw-colored hair in all directions.

"Vissarion will teach you how to shoot," said Krylov. "You can use my hunting rifle. I hope the kick isn't too much for you. Now I'm going to take my bath. I'm very tired, and it's past your bedtime."

The small boy solemnly shook hands with him before running off in the direction of the kitchens.

Krylov had fallen asleep in his enormous tub, and he was dead to the world until the door to the tiled bathroom burst open. He was dreaming of the translucent blue waters of Capri, the island he would never see, and his deeply lined face almost seemed at peace. But a shadow was passing in and out of the dream, like the belly of a shark above him in the water.

Krylov had only two bodyguards at Zhukovka. When Marshal Safronov's men came stealing through the trees, in pairs, they had found the first of the guards smoking a cigarette in the driveway in front of the house. A Ukrainian lieutenant garroted him swiftly and silently, using the piece of piano wire that Spetsnaz commandos on special assignment wore coiled around their left wrists to meet just such a contingency. The blond colonel ground the dead man's cigarette into the loose gravel of the drive with the heel of his boot.

The second guard, who doubled as Krylov's chauffeur and had driven him out from Moscow that afternoon, was more fortunate. He had been given the evening off and had gone to visit a girl in a neighboring village.

That left Vissarion, who was listening to records in his room at the back of the house, and Vera, the cook, who was snoring upstairs after partaking generously of the Grand Marnier she kept to garnish one of her special desserts, and her grandson, Sasha. The boy was the only one who heard the crack as the front door was broken open, and the light padding of rubber-soled boots inside the house. He tiptoed downstairs in his pajamas to inspect the new visitors.

He saw armed men, their heads covered by woolen masks with holes cut for the eyes and mouth, like the headgear his mother made him wear in the depth of winter. He hunched down, making himself as small as he could, and slipped barefoot down the stairs, hugging the banisters, to conceal himself in the deep shadow of the stairwell. He stayed there while the first two men raced up the stairs, heading toward Krylov's bedroom. Other men fanned out to search the rooms on the lower floor.

In Krylov's dream, the menacing shadow was clearer now. He saw the great jaws open and close with a click. But they were not the jaws of a shark after all. They were Marshal Safronov's steel hooks.

Krylov awoke with such a start that his shoulders slid off the back of the bath and for a moment his mouth and nose were submerged. He dragged himself back up, gasping for air, and found himself looking into the snout of a big Stechkin 9mm APS automatic pistol. His heart boomed and heaved in his chest like a volcano about to erupt.

The man with the gun had no face. Only the eyes and mouth showed through the black mask.

"Who are you?" Krylov gasped, trying to adjust his scrawny limbs to conceal his genitals.

"Traitor," hissed the man behind the Stechkin. "Pervert."

Only inches away from his nose, Krylov could see the man's finger begin to tighten on the trigger.

"*Nyet*," a shouted command came from someone standing further back. "Not that way. Like this."

A broad, leather-gloved hand slammed into Krylov's face, gouging at his eyes, blocking off his mouth and nose. At the same instant, another hand seized his throat, squeezing at the windpipe, pushing him down into the bathwater. He tried to wrestle back, but he seemed to have no control of his body. At first he gagged on the water flooding into his throat as they pushed him down, but then a kind of calm descended. For an instant he could see the whole course of his life unfurled like the Bayeux tapestry. He could even see Misha in his cadet's uniform in the summer of 1942. The scene was suffused by a wondrous blue light, like the light in the emperor's grotto at Capri. Then the black shadow passed over him again, and swallowed up everything.

"No!" The piercing scream from the doorway caused the blond colonel, taken by surprise, to loosen his grip. He saw a small boy, maybe eight or nine. Quite a pretty boy, with fine, almost feminine, yellowish hair. It was perfect. Marshal Safronov would be delighted. No one in the KGB or the Kremlin would have the guts to dispute the physical evidence that Krylov had drowned in his bath in the midst of a disgusting orgy with a minor. It didn't matter whether they believed the story or not.

"Bring that boy here."

Sasha wriggled, trying to escape from the grip of the sturdy Ukrainian lieutenant. It was useless. The lieutenant folded him under his arm like a trussed chicken.

Vissarion, in his narrow back bedroom, was indulging a taste in classical music that was most unusually developed for a valet, even the personal servant of the head of the Beacon. He had been playing Schoenberg on his hi-fi. As usual, the discordant notes left him feeling somber and deeply disturbed; Schoenberg's subversion of conventional harmony could make you feel that there was a howling wind at the center of the universe. Only when the record stopped did Vissarion become aware of discordances that had nothing to do with the troubling composer. He looked at his bedside clock and realized that his master had been in the tub for only about forty minutes, a modest length of time for Krylov on the weekend. So what were those noises around the house, the footsteps, the shutting of doors?

Cautiously, Vissarion crept upstairs in his slippers toward Krylov's bathroom. He was in time to see a masked man overpower Vera's grandson. Unthinking, Vissarion hurled himself at the stranger's back. The man went down. But before the valet could get a proper grip on the man's throat, a crushing weight descended on the back of his neck. It was the butt of a Stechkin pistol.

With the practiced, impersonal skill of a man employed in a slaughterhouse, the colonel broke Sasha's neck, stripped the body, and threw it into the bath, where it lay in an obscene huddle on top of Krylov, whose bluish face now seemed to have no blood in it.

"What about him?" asked the Ukrainian lieutenant, pointing to the body of the valet sprawled on the floor.

"Get the others to bury him somewhere he won't be found."

The colonel stopped to inspect the gold watch on Vissarion's left wrist. It was a pretty fancy timepiece for a valet. He pulled it off and looked at the inscription on the back. The watch was a gift to Krylov from Misha. The *jid*. He put the Rolex in his pocket. The marshal was going to enjoy *this*.

"The purpose of terror," Safronov quoted Lenin, "is to terrify. Comrades," he addressed his chosen company of assassins, "I think tonight we have succeeded in that. Nothing will stand in our way. We will teach men the meaning of terror."

26

Harry Schwab's regular table at the Four Seasons restaurant, the mecca of New York publishing mavens, was a curving booth against the wall with a commanding view of whoever entered the Grill Room up the open flight of steps from the basement entrance on Fifty-second Street or through the glass doors from Park Avenue.

Sally Sherwin was sipping Dry Sack on the rocks, sitting between her boss, who looked tanned and prosperous after a long weekend at La Semana, the celebrities' Caribbean resort, and a short, beefy man with many chins whose eyes rarely strayed above the top buttons of Sally's sheer blouse of crêpe de chine. Its provocative effect was enhanced rather than diminished by the low-cut camisole she wore underneath. The blouse was the perfect match for Sally's black velvet suit, set off by a wide black leather belt with a lion's-head clasp.

The guest who was admiring her outfit so frankly was Lloyd Wallace, a good ol' boy from the Deep South who had enjoyed his brief moment of glory as personal aide to the former President. Lloyd had grown attached to the Washington singles scene and the culinary pleasure of the Pavillon and Lion d'Or. He felt not the slightest temptation to spend his evenings showing off to the locals who rolled up in their pickup trucks to the barroom of Lenny's Motel in Dixietown, Alabama. Since he had no money of his own and not even his bank in Alabama was ready to put him on its board, Lloyd Wallace had decided to write his memoirs. Hell, he had said to Harry Schwab. If his former boss could pick up a million bucks by finding a ghostwriter to hack out some flimflam about how the Israelis and the Egyptians had been made to talk peace, then why couldn't he pull the same trick?

"Kiss and tell," Harry Schwab was saying. "It's got to be kiss and tell. Nobody wants to read another book explaining what the last administration did or failed to do. People already look back on those years as the years of the Missing Presidency. When the record is that insignificant, there's no point in trying to set it straight. Give the public the breath of scandal. That's what will sell."

"I was thinking more about the Iran story," Wallace said. "All the behind-the-scenes stuff. You know, I was heavily involved in some of the negotiations."

Harry Schwab drained the last of his Perrier and said, "I don't know that I could sell it. Not for the kind of bucks you want, Lloyd. The story's been told too often. There was even that TV mini-series that Ham Jordan got involved with. It's getting to be like Vietnam. People just want to forget."

"There are some things I still don't understand about what happened in Iran," Sally chipped in, recalling something Dick Hammond had told her about the origins of the embassy seizure. "Is it true that the embassy gates were opened so the militants could get in? I was told the embassy gates were made of super-reinforced metal, and that it might have taken the radicals hours to blast their way through. If the gates hadn't been opened for them, there might have been time to fly in some Marines from Ankara. In any event, if the Iranian regime had just stood by for a few hours while our embassy was besieged, it would have been clear to everyone from day one that we weren't just dealing with a bunch of students. We were dealing with the Ayatollah. I'd be interested in a book that explained how those gates came to be opened up."

Lloyd Wallace coughed into his martini glass, obviously embarrassed. "I—er—don't know about that," he said.

Sally, afraid she had come on too strong, returned to picking at her striped bass. She liked the luncheon menu in the Grill Room: light, simple things rather than the rich, creamy French dishes that were served in the other part of the restaurant. Her attention turned to the scene around the captain's desk. Among the throng—mostly men in conservative business suits, with a sprinkling of confident career women—she recognized people who had published, written, promoted, or sold the rights to half the titles on the *Times* best-seller list. In the discreet jungle of the restaurant, garnished with plants and leafless trees, the most powerful among them had their territorial space clearly demarcated. From their regular tables, they glanced speculatively, sometimes hungrily, at each new face. As Sally herself was doing.

The glass doors swung open, and Sally recognized a man she had never expected to see in the Four Seasons, an old man with a cane and a floppy bow tie. It was the antiquarian bookseller, Zhores Malinovsky. He stood stooped over the captain's desk for a moment, consulting one of the owners of the restaurant. Then he was ushered to an empty table on the other side of the room. Sally wondered who Malinovsky was meeting. Maybe he wanted to publish his memoirs too. She knew that in some way the bookseller was involved in the chain of events that had resulted in Max's murder and the disgrace of Les Winter.

On a sudden impulse, she said to Lloyd Wallace, "I'm very sorry, but I clean forgot that I have another appointment with an author back at the office. I do hope you'll excuse me."

Harry Schwab cocked an eyebrow as she slid out from behind the table, abandoning the remnants of her striped bass, but said merely, "See you later."

Sally claimed her raincoat from the checkroom and hurried down the stairs to the Fifty-second Street exit, where she hailed a cab.

"Thirteenth and Broadway," she told the driver.

If she had paused to ask herself what she was doing, she could not have come up with any coherent answer. She simply felt driven to revisit the chaotic little bookstore where she had bought the *Oracles of Nostradamus* for Max Zimmer. While the owner was away at lunch, she did not know what she could expect to find. In fact, she did not even know what she was looking for.

Inside Mallaby's bookstore, a black delivery man was unloading crates while Bertha, propped up in her wheelchair, made notes in a tattered school exercise book. Bertha seemed annoyed at being interrupted when a young man came in to buy an old movie poster he had fished out of one of the bins outside. Sally noticed that the poster showed Humphrey Bogart and Katharine Hepburn steaming through the jungle in the decrepit riverboat from *The African Queen*. Bertha paid no attention to her as she walked quickly toward the biography section at the back of the store. No one else was in sight. Sally guessed that the emaciated old man she had sometimes seen arranging books on the shelves must be out to lunch too. It appeared that Malinovsky had left Bertha alone in charge.

The door marked Private was out of the line of sight from the cash desk where Bertha was now presiding. Sally pressed her ear to the wood panels. She could hear no sound of movement inside the back room. Cautiously, she tested the handle. The door was unlocked. But it creaked loudly on its hinges as she slowly swung it open, and she drew back, ready to slip away if someone challenged her. There was still no sound from inside. Decisively, she pushed the door wide open, stepped into the private office, and closed the door behind her.

She found the room in even greater disorder than the main part of the bookstore. It looked like a dispatcher's room more than an office. Books were piled in crazy heaps on the floor. The desk was a sea of paper, rising more than two feet above the surface. Newspapers, letters, and invoices were all jumbled up together. Sally even saw a couple of checks pigeonholed in the fold of an old copy of the *New York Times*. There were thick wads of letters, tied up with rubber bands, that had not even been opened. The general confusion suggested one thing to Sally: that the proprietor of Mallaby's bookstore did not devote much of his time to attending to routine business.

She pulled open one of the desk drawers. She found a bulky sheaf of paper held together by a bulldog clip. Each sheet contained ten or twelve names and addresses, run off from an automatic addressograph machine. Sally guessed that they must be the names of people who received catalogues from Mallaby's through the mail. The lists were surprisingly diverse. The addresses ranged from San Francisco to Toronto, from Nassau to Seattle. She remembered what Malinovsky had said about running a big mail-order business, and the bookseller's testiness when he had found her looking through a volume that was going to be sent out. Her eye lingered on one name in the lists: "Ms. Gertrude Cook, 2020 Massachusetts Ave., Washington, D.C."

One thing Sally had learned during her years with Charles Canning was that one of the most secure forms of secret communications is a one-time code, often enough based on two identical editions of a book that are in the hands of both the sender and the receiver. She looked from the list of names to the teetering piles of books on the floor. She now observed that there were two copies of some of the editions. Was this Malinovsky's secret, staring her in the face—the method by which a network of secret agents was controlled?

Sally had barely begun to pose the question to herself when she was startled by the sound of footsteps approaching the door. They were heavy, confident steps, not the scuffling sound she associated with Malinovsky or his elderly male assistant, and certainly not the wheeze of Bertha's wheelchair.

There was just enough room to hide behind some cartons stacked in front of the far wall. Sally crouched down behind them, making herself as small as she could. She had to hold her nose for an instant to avoid sneezing as the dust rose from the litter of forgotten books and magazines on which she was kneeling.

She heard the door open and then slam shut. The same heavy footsteps echoed inside the room, weaving among the piles of books, circling around and around. From her hiding place, Sally could see nothing. She felt another sneeze coming on and put a finger to her nose, desperately afraid she would betray her presence.

Then she heard a second set of footsteps. They made a lighter, shuffling sound. The door opened again, and she heard two men's voices raised in argument. For an instant she thought they were talking in Portuguese. Then she realized her error. It was strange how two languages as far removed in structure and vocabulary as Portuguese and Russian could sound similar to someone familiar with neither.

Sally could understand only the tone of what was being said. The newcomer's voice was petulant and complaining. He sounded like a man who had been imposed upon—perhaps by being called away from his lunch. The other man's voice was deep and commanding. He sounded as if he was issuing orders.

She risked taking a peek around the corner of the boxes.

She darted her head back quickly, but not before she had caught a glimpse of Zhores Malinovsky face to face with an ugly, fair-haired man whose neck looked like an extension of his shoulders. The stranger was wearing a navy-blue raincoat and a gray hat.

Their conversation was brief. Sally heard desk drawers being hastily opened and closed, and a noise like the tumblers of a combination lock falling into place. Perhaps there was a hidden safe in the room that she had missed.

Then the two men left the office together. She heard the door snap shut, and their footsteps retreating through the bookstore.

She waited one full minute before she moved from her hiding place, watching the second hand on her watch.

Then she slipped back into the store. There was no sign of Malinovsky or the unknown Russian. Bertha was still behind the cash desk, pouring tea as she held court before a plain, bespectacled girl with frizzy hair who might have been a librarian.

Sally hurried out of the bookstore. To her left, shambling along down Thirteenth Street toward Fifth Avenue, she could see the hunched figure of Malinovsky. She looked the other way, and saw the Russian in the navy-blue raincoat on the other side of Broadway. He was walking westward, with brisk, military strides.

Sally ran across Broadway, dodging a taxi. She saw a phone booth and began fumbling in her purse for a dime. She knew she had witnessed something important, and that someone—Dick or Charles—should be told. But when she looked again, she could see the Russian rounding the corner of Third Avenue, heading south. She was scared of losing him. If he vanished, they might never know the meaning of the scene she had just witnessed.

She quickened her pace and followed him, wishing that her heels were two inches lower.

The Russian kept up his long, loping stride down Third Avenue, and Sally had trouble keeping up as she passed huddled pawnshops, dealers in nostalgic bric-a-brac—postcards of long-dead baseball idols, yellowed comic books—and serious drinking establishments advertising chilled mugs. The Russian never looked back, not even as he crossed the street at the corner of Ninth Street. Sally crossed over a block farther back. She glanced down the leafy side streets that angled off into the Bowery, and saw ragged groups of men sitting, standing, or sprawled full-length on the sidewalk, as seemingly immobile as Siegel's life-size sculptures. But more dangerous.

The man in the navy-blue raincoat had stopped at the corner of

Eighth Street. His hands were steepled as he lit a cigarette. Sally hesitated for a second. The man discarded a match but still did not move.

Sally breathed in deeply and walked on, past the Russian.

On the corner of Seventh Street, as she waited for a car to go by, she stole a quick look backward, over her shoulder.

The Russian was walking behind her. Thirty yards farther back along the road, she saw two other men, in trenchcoats, advancing with the same determined stride.

Crossing the street, she broke into a half-run.

She heard the footsteps behind her coming faster and faster. The Russian was not following her. He was coming after her.

Sally's ankle buckled as she tried to run in her high-heeled shoes, and she almost fell. She stared around wildly, looking for someone to whom she could turn for help, a doorway through which she could find shelter. The first man she saw was a wino, slouched on the sidewalk with a bottle in his lap. His boots were missing, no doubt stolen by one of his companions of the night. A blackened big toe showed through a hole in his socks.

Sally panicked.

Her only weapon was a tube of Mace, the shape and size of a Cricket cigarette lighter, that she had bought in Miami. She could not stand on the sidewalk with that and fend off three men. Men who were probably armed.

Ahead of her, just short of Sixth Street, she saw a gap in the inhospitable line of houses. Without thinking, Sally ripped off her shoes and scrambled down, five or six feet below street level, where the ground of the vacant lot was being hollowed out for future construction. The broken, rocky earth cut into the soles of her feet.

It was then that Sally realized she had done the most stupid thing in the world. Ahead of her was a high brick wall. The Russian was still pounding after her, closing the distance fast. There was no way out.

Except up.

Sally threw herself at the wall, willing that there should be sufficient handholds and toeholds in its scarred and pockmarked surface. Halfway up, she grazed her left knee badly as she tried to propel herself higher, over to the right, to grab hold of a ventilation pipe. Her polished fingernails scraped and tore against the rusted metal. Then her hands got a purchase on it, and she was able to haul herself up onto the roof in a few jerky motions.

She could hear a man grunting and panting from below as he tried to climb up after her.

Her heart seemed to rise into her throat as she slithered and stumbled over the roof of the neighboring house and down the fire escape on the other side. The view she found below her was amazing. The building across Sixth Street, with its dome and brightly colored mosaics, looked like a Byzantine church transplanted, brick by brick, from Istanbul. Except that it was all new. The mosaic tiles blazed in the sunlight as if they had been fired the day before. As Sally half ran, half fell down the fire escape, she glimpsed a street sign that read "Taras Shevchenko Place," a name as improbable as the church. As she hit the last landing, her arm snagged in a piece of linen—washing or a torn curtain—trailing from a second-floor window. She heard voices raised shrill in anger as she tumbled the last few steps into Sixth Street.

She saw a car idling at the end of the street, a white Lincoln. She picked herself up and hurried across the road. The mosaic above the colonnaded portico of the church, she saw, depicted St. George slaying the dragon.

Inside the church, Sally inhaled the sickly sweet smell of incense as she skirted the pews, looking for a means of escape. She felt winded and nauseated. The great wooden door of the church swung open behind her, and she forced herself on. She stumbled around the side of the altar and found an exit at the back. Peering around the door, she could see the back of the white Lincoln, apparently parked in front of the church. Gulping the air painfully through her mouth, she staggered on down toward Fifth Street, seeking a hiding place.

The broken-down brownstones ahead housed an antiquated hardware store and a tiny greengrocer's store that appeared to sell only tomatoes. There were steps to the cellars below each store, barred only by a loose chain. Sally hesitated, uncertain whether to run into one of the shops or bolt down the steps, into shadows that might mean safety or blank, exitless walls.

A delivery van, built like a crackerbox on wheels, was parked in front of the greengrocer's. The back door was partly ajar, and Sally could see crates of tomatoes inside. On a sudden instinct, Sally jumped inside and pulled the door shut, hunching herself down among the boxes of fruit.

The minutes dragged until the delivery man emerged from the store. He was singing—a passable impression of Frank Sinatra performing "I Did It My Way." Without even a glance into the back of his van, he started up the engine and drove off. Through the chink in the back door, Sally could see the man in the navy-blue raincoat walking fast up the street. He was looking at the van.

Sally did not move until the van slowed to a stop on University Place, just north of Washington Square. Then she pushed open the door and jumped out. The delivery man spun around in surprise, the last bars of the Sinatra song swallowed up in a gargling sound.

Sally ignored his shouts, walking quickly south, toward her studio gallery on Thompson Street. There was no sign of the white Lincoln or the man in the raincoat.

She hurried through the roller skaters on Washington Square. A blue-and-white Sixth Precinct squad car was cruising slowly through the park, offering improbable protection to its floating population of derelicts, sidewalk musicians, and girls with Bo Derek hair and white shorts, walking their dogs. Across the square, Sally saw a tall, patriarchal figure, a man with a beard and flowing locks, with a heavy coat and a shopping bag under his arm. As he paced, the man would pause from time to time to scribble lines in a notebook. From a distance he might have passed for an eccentric writer. But as Sally approached him, the man turned on her with the red, unfocused eyes of the hopelessly insane, and she could see that his clothes were rags, the shopping bag the probable home of everything he possessed.

"Kill the Christians!" the tramp screamed. "We gotta kill all the Christians!"

"Hey, lady!" a young black on roller skates, earphones strapped to his head, called out to her. "What happened to you?"

Sally looked down and saw that her clothes were spattered with red from the tomatoes in the delivery van.

"Who cut you, lady?"

"It's nothing," she said. "I'm a messy eater."

"Hey, look at this," the black called out to his friends. "A walking pizza."

She was already on Thompson Street, barely two blocks away

from the studio, when the man's hand fell on her shoulder.

She turned and recognized one of the men in trenchcoats who had been following her, in the wake of the Russian, down Third Avenue.

She tried to pull away, but his firm hand restrained her.

"It's okay," he said. "FBI. Special Agent Hedges. You led us quite a chase."

She looked at his badge, to be sure. It was real.

When Charles explained it to her later, the pieces began to fall into place. The Russian she had thought was pursuing her was Voldemar Titov, a KGB officer working on special assignments under cover at the Soviet mission to the United Nations. He was one of the three Russians whom Charles had seen in the Café Carlyle, the first night he heard Melanie Toussaint sing. What Sally had witnessed in the back room of Mallaby's bookstore, so the Bureau and the Agency had concluded, was Titov delivering an urgent summons to Zhores Malinovsky to drop everything and run. The reason for the KGB's alarm signal, they assumed, was that the interrogation of Les Winter had suggested to Malinovsky's controllers that the net was finally closing in. That, and the signs of Bureau surveillance that the Russians must have detected.

"So I was never really in danger?" she asked Charles. They were sitting in the studio she shared with Lauren Corder, among the huge stylized animals—whales and toucans, lions and tortoises—that she fashioned from copper and brass and German silver at odd weekends in the style of the Mexican artist Sergio Bustamante.

"You were only in danger of falling off a roof," said Canning.

"But why was the Russian—Titov—chasing me?"

"Was he chasing you, or trying to get away from the watchers the Bureau had set onto him?"

"He was definitely chasing me."

Canning still looked skeptical, but he didn't want to tax her after what she had put herself through. So he said, "Well, it may have been a diversion."

"A diversion from what?"

"A diversion from Malinovsky. The bookseller has disappeared. Slipped his tail and disappeared. He hasn't gone back to his apartment. He's gone to a foxhole somewhere. Or he's on the way back to Russia."

Canning said it with a kind of relief. Malinovsky's contact with Titov, and his subsequent disappearance, had suppressed the last doubts about the Martini network. By saving its agent, Moscow Center had finally showed its hand. If Malinovsky was controlled by the KGB, then the others were too: Martini himself, Les Winter, Trudy Cook. It only remained to establish whether Les and Trudy had been conscious agents or unconscious dupes. The whole deception was at last unraveling.

27

"What do we tell the President?"

Director Claiborne, slumped in his swivel chair, looked up at the framed photographs of his predecessors on the wall, speculating about how each of them might have handled the problem that now confronted him. On his desk was a report from the Bureau on the meeting between a contract employee of the Agency called Zhores Malinovsky and a KGB man called Titov. The report detailed how Malinovsky, in a display of sprightliness unexpected in a man of his advanced years and frail appearance, had slipped his FBI markers and vanished.

Dick Hammond, seated in the chair on the other side of the desk, waited for Claiborne's lead. He had already given part of his reply, in his own report. He could see the corner of the green file in which it had been presented peeping out from under the Bureau report on the director's desk. He had wasted no time in bureaucratic evasions. His conclusions were terse. Malinovsky's disappearance, he contended, was the final proof that the Agency had been systematically conned by Moscow Center in a deception operation designed to mislead the United States about the military capabilities of the Soviet Union. From beginning to end, Hammond concluded, the double agent known as Martini had been controlled by Krylov's office at KGB headquarters. The Soviets had collected a remarkable bonus when Martini had succeeded in seducing and recruiting his Agency case handler, Trudy Cook. Her involvement was, admittedly, the one weak link in the chain of connections that Hammond had managed to establish. There was no hard evidence that Trudy Cook had betrayed the Agency's secrets. As a mole, she had the perfect cover: she had had a license to feed secret material first to Martini and later to Malinovsky, because Les Winter had convinced the Agency that the whole operation was under American control. Maybe nothing would ever be proved against her unless she broke down and confessed—just as the British were unable to prove anything definitive against Philby before his flight to Moscow. But in his report, Hammond shot from the hip. He accused Trudy Cook of betraying American networks behind the Iron Curtain. And the British agent called Hussar.

"We've been had," Adam Claiborne was saying. "And we've lost precious time because we went on refusing to accept that possibility. It's my duty to tell the President the truth about that. I have to advise him that in the considered view of this office, the defector Ushinsky is for real. Which means, in all probability, that Death Beam is for real. Now he's going to ask me what we propose the United States should do about that. Have you got any suggestions?"

Dick Hammond was not unprepared for the question. He had now had access to the stream of TECHINT—technical intelligence, mostly aerial-surveillance photographs—on the progress of the weapons testing at Saryshagan, in Soviet Central Asia, and on possibly related construction work at the Baikonur Cosmodrome. He knew that General Brennan's assessment, supported by the leads the defector had provided, was that the Soviets were preparing to launch Death Beam from the Baikonur facility. He had studied the possibility of sending in a sabotage team, overland from China, or dropped in by parachute. It was a very long shot.

But there was an alternative, Hammond believed. The odds in favor of its success were not much better, but were good enough to risk a throw of the dice.

"The one thing we have going for us," Hammond told Claiborne, "is that the Soviets are at each other's throats. Maybe we can use that."

"How?"

"Our information—confirmed by British and Israeli sources—is that Krylov has been assassinated as part of a Kremlin power play. You can't take a player as good as Krylov out of a side without badly damaging its performance. I think the haste with which the Soviets pulled Malinovsky out of New York must be connected with the loss of Krylov. The networks he controlled have lost their central direction. The people who were loyal to him are confused, maybe fearful for their own lives. I expect we'll find that Trudy Cook feels like that, left hanging on a limb now her control has disappeared. If she's handled properly, she'll crack."

"Okay. We'll put our best interrogators onto it. But what about Death Beam?"

"One of the men who was closest to Krylov is the head of the East German service. He's a Jew, though he doesn't like people to mention the fact. He has every reason to hate Marshal Safronov. And it just so happens that one of his boyhood friends is the top scientific adviser on the Death Beam project."

"Have we got a line out to him?"

"Not directly. But I know how to do it."

Hammond explained.

"Do it," Director Claiborne said. "Jesus, I just hope it works. We can order up an Air Force plane and you can leave today."

"That won't be necessary," Hammond replied. "If I get moving, I can make the El Al flight from New York."

28

"There is no more important function for intelligence than to forewarn a nation's leadership of an impending attack by its enemies. The Agency has failed this country in the performance of that most basic function."

General Brennan was standing rock-solid in the center of the Oval Office, among the men on whom the President would reply in deciding how to handle the most momentous crisis of his administration. The others present were Trip Gage, the National Security Adviser; Henry Peyton, the Secretary of State; Jake Waggoner, the Defense Secretary; and Adam Claiborne, the director of Central Intelligence.

Director Claiborne had reddened slightly as General Brennan got into the swing of his attack on the Agency. He cleared his throat. "Mr. President," he interjected with deceptive mildness.

"Why yes, Adam."

"I enjoy listening to George Brennan's speeches, but I think he should temper his rhetoric to the circumstances that actually confront us. First off, the Agency did *not* fail to warn this administration of an impending Soviet attack. We insisted on acquiring sufficient evidence of Moscow's intentions, and the precise form such an attack might take."

"You had evidence two months ago," Brennan rebuked him, "and you damn well tried to suppress it."

"I will concede that in the course of our investigations we uncovered some—uh—vulnerabilities inside the Agency," Director Claiborne carried on, his voice reedy-thin, almost inaudible, the result of lack of sleep and a persistent throat condition.

305

"These deficiencies have been attended to with the resoluteness that is one of the goals of this administration, Mr. President."

They all knew what that meant: the Agency's Soviet Division was being turned inside out. Its chief, Les Winter, had been suspended, and Trudy Cook, his long-term assistant, was being held under conditions of house arrest while the Justice Department prepared a formal indictment on charges of espionage. Short of seizing the printing presses, there was no way that they would be able to keep an Agency scandal of these proportions out of the newspapers for more than a couple of days.

"Why don't you come out and say it, Adam?" General Brennan baited him. "The Agency went looking for moles, and found the mole was the Agency itself."

"General Brennan." Henry Peyton's strong baritone rang out across the Oval Office. Peyton was an old soldier himself, and though his rapid ascent up the promotion ladder had led envious colleagues to call him a political general, the Secretary of State had Brennan's respect. "I think it is inappropriate to take up the President's time with recriminations about who was right and wrong at what point in time. I think everyone here concedes that you were substantially right about this Death Beam project long before we had convincing proof that it was a reality. That's what comes of having a good nose, George." Peyton lapsed into a more familiar tone. "Furthermore, we've all been made more aware of to what point Soviet disinformation, melded with institutional self-deception, has blinded us in the face of developments that threaten our national security, if not our survival. I hope we won't fall prey to the same infirmities again. We're now here to decide our next move. As I understand it"—Peyton consulted his watch— "the Soviets are due to launch Death Beam in just over a week, taking account of the time difference."

"Let me clarify something." The President leaned over his desk. The strains of office and the months away from his California ranch had aged him, but his face was still ruddy, his shoulders unstooped under the fabric of the morning coat in which he had just hosted a public reception for the Prince of Wales. "Now, as it's been presented to me," the President continued, "if the Soviets succeed in getting this new weapon—Death Beam—into space, the only way we could stop it is to send a killer satellite up to shoot it down."

"That's correct, Mr. President." Jake Waggoner made his first contribution to the discussion. "We have not yet devised counter-measures—frankly, our scientists have barely begun to think about them—that would stop a beam of this kind from reentering the earth's atmosphere. The best we could hope for is that climate and atmospheric conditions might disperse the radioactive fallout, and even drive some of it over Soviet territory."

"What about civil-defense measures? Population dispersal?"

Waggoner shook his head. "Hardly worth thinking about. We couldn't even predict the area of impact within a radius of a hundred miles, unless the Soviets were good enough to tell us. But suppose we knew that the beam was going to be targeted on our Eastern Seaboard—say against the New York–Washington–Boston triangle, the most likely target zone. We can all imagine the panic if we tried moving even essential personnel out to protected areas. The roads would be jammed solid with traffic. I can foresee mass looting, whole city blocks in flames. And we just don't have safe areas to relocate even a tenth of the population of Greater New York. What the Soviets have built is truly the ultimate weapon."

"Just what Khrushchev boasted they were going to build in the early sixties," said General Brennan. "Except we didn't want to listen."

"All right, George," the President addressed him. "This is where you come in. Can we shoot this thing—this Death Beam—down once they get it up?"

"Eventually, yes."

"I don't like that word 'eventually.'" The President studied Brennan with his calm blue eyes, the blue of faded denim.

"Well," Brennan explained, "you know we've been going hell for leather on the Blue Savior program. I took Mr. Gage down to New Mexico to take a look at it a coupla weeks ago."

"Very impressive," the National Security Adviser chimed in.

"The trouble is that with these space programs, you don't count delays in hours, you count them in months," Brennan went on. "Remember what happened to NASA with the space-shuttle program."

"The space shuttle was never given the top-priority status that you've been given for Blue Savior," the President observed drily.

"Absolutely, Mr. President. But whereas Soviet scientists have been working full-blast in this area for three decades or more, with the full backing of the political establishment, our scientists have been given the money and the green light they needed only under your administration. And now they've been ordered to catch up and overtake the Soviets in the space of a couple of weeks. High technology just doesn't work within those parameters."

"It sure doesn't," Peyton agreed. The Secretary of State had sat for a brief time on the board of a large corporation manufacturing high-technology weapons systems.

"I'm still waiting for an answer, George," the President said. "If the Soviets send Death Beam into orbit, can one of your space cruisers—what do you call them?"

"Cosmic Interceptors."

"Yes. Can one of your Cosmic Interceptors shoot it down?"

"Mr. President." Brennan clasped his hands behind his back and bent his neck as if an intolerable burden were straining his back. "I have to report that as of this moment I cannot give you a firm date for the first launch of Blue Savior. As you know, we were hoping to make it by November 7, the same day as the Soviet launch. But we are still working to resolve a technical hitch—I understand that it has to do with the fuel tanks—and I cannot give any guarantee that we will be able to send Blue Savior up before Death Beam is sent into orbit."

"Which we can't allow to happen," said Secretary Peyton.

"Excuse me?"

"I said, we can't allow the Soviets to put Death Beam into space," Peyton explained. "The blackmail power it would give them is almost unthinkable. They could order us to withdraw our forces from Europe—and if you've been watching political trends in West Germany, you'll see they've been building quite a lobby for that anyway. They could force us to stand by while they stage a nice little revolution wherever they like, or while they take out the Chinese. They could even tell us to start dismantling our own weapons systems. And if we refused, they'd have the option of staging a little demonstration of what their superweapon can do."

"Well," said the President. "All that may be as you say. But what options have we got. Jake?" he turned to the Secretary of Defense.

Jake Waggoner, like several of the men in the room, was a long-time personal friend of the President who had made his reputation

308

as a sober conservative who eschewed novel solutions. "I would point out, Mr. President," he responded, "that we are in no position to invite a full-scale war with the Soviet Union, on either the conventional or the nuclear plane."

No one in the room was inclined to dispute this statement. They had all seen the charts showing the relative defense preparedness of the two superpowers, and knew that in many categories—manpower, conventional hardware, missile size—the Soviets were in the lead. Even if Soviet inefficiency and the untested friendship of the Chinese might partly compensate for the disparities of size, they knew, too, that the Russians had made a huge investment in civil-defense programs designed to minimize the casualties that would be inflicted in a full-scale nuclear war. In the entire Western world, only Switzerland had pursued a comparable program for nuclear survival. In the estimate of the Soviet leadership, the proportion of the Soviet population that would be wiped out in a nuclear war could be limited to fifteen or twenty percent—a frightening figure still, but not awesome enough to deter a man like Marshal Safronov when he knew that American losses would be vastly greater. It would still be a couple of years, according to Jake Waggoner's estimates, before the United States managed to restore real strategic parity.

"All right, Jake," the President said. "None of us is contemplating pushing the button that starts World War III. So where does that lead us?"

Jake Waggoner sat silent, nibbling the cap of his fountain pen.

"Trip?"

"I was just thinking, Mr. President. What if we sent agents in and tried to blow the launch vehicle up while it is still on the ground? We at least know that the launch is scheduled to take place from this new cosmodrome near Baikonur."

"And how do you propose that we get these agents in?" Director Claiborne, who had been containing his impatience with difficulty throughout most of the meeting, now intervened.

"Parachute?" the National Security Adviser reflected aloud. "I read somewhere that secret agents used to be infiltrated into these parts of Soviet Central Asia where the secret scientific cities and launch pads are located on camelback, over the Persian or Afghan borders."

Adam Claiborne snorted. This, he considered, was a prize example of the danger of appointing academicians to high places in government.

"Or maybe the Chinese could help out," Trip Gage pursued his theme. "The border can't be all that tight, and we know the Central Asians aren't in love with the Russians."

"It's still a helluva long way from Sinkiang to Baikonur," Secretary Peyton commented.

"May I say something, Mr. President?" It was George Brennan, as usual, jumping his turn. He would not normally have been included in this inner circle of counselors, but nobody questioned his right to be there today. Like the man or not, they all accepted he had earned it.

"Go ahead, George."

"We can shoot down Death Beam, either while it's still on the ground or before it has left the earth's atmosphere. As long as our intelligence about the location and the timing of the launch is accurate, this doesn't present any insuperable problems. We can hit it with a missile, preferably launched from a sub tucked away out of sight somewhere in the Pacific. Or we can send in our new Stealth bomber and sneak in under the Soviet radar." Brennan, in his excitement, started marching up and down, but, suddenly recalling his august surroundings, he corrected himself and stood stiffly erect, his arms crossed.

"What about the radioactive fallout?" Jake Waggoner challenged him. "What effect will it have if this thing is detonated on the ground or a couple of miles up?"

"Our guess is the fallout would be very limited in range and intensity," Brennan replied. "And if not, well, it would be happening over the Soviets' territory, not ours."

"I don't think the Soviets would just sit back and let us get away with it," the President observed.

"There is one reason why they might want to play it low-key, Mr. President." Trip Gage had been studying the treaties on outer space that had been signed by Moscow and Washington. "The Soviets have signed a couple of treaties that explicitly forbid the deployment of weapons of mass destruction in space. The text of the 1969 treaty is particularly forthright."

"I doubt whether a scrap of paper is going to tie Marshal Safronov's hands," Secretary Peyton commented. "What you're

310

saying, Trip, is that the Soviets might not want the world to know what this Death Beam project is all about. Therefore they might not be inclined to go public if we manage to blow it up. That far, I think you're on the right track. But that doesn't mean that Marshal Safronov isn't going to retaliate if we wreck his pet project."

"If we do what George Brennan advises," the Defense Secretary summmmarized, "we would be risking World War III."

"What other choice have we got?" The President glanced around his circle of advisers. Outside, beyond the White House precincts, people were strolling about in the street in their shirtsleeves, coats casually draped from their shoulders. It was one of those remarkably warm fall days that reminded you that Washington was part of the South, with a subtropical climate.

The President straightened the corner of the white handkerchief that was displayed from the breast pocket of his morning coat and said, in the homespun style that he had made famous on television, "Seems to me that we're damned if we do and damned if we don't."

Director Claiborne was rubbing the skin of his throat as if he hoped to loosen something that was clogging his vocal cords. But when he spoke, his voice was even more strained than before.

"I don't think we've exhausted the available options yet, Mr. President," said the director of the Agency. "There is an outside chance that we can destroy Death Beam without having to run the incalculable risks of going in there and bombing the hell out of that cosmodrome in Kazakhstan. Of course, under either scenario, we would merely succeed in wrecking the space vehicle the Soviets have built. We can't deprive them of the technology they now have just by blowing up a prototype weapon. But we can delay their program for long enough to give the Defense Department time to put Blue Savior into orbit and give us the capacity to slog it out up there"—he gestured toward the chandelier—"without having to have a war down here."

"Let's hear your idea, Adam."

"It hinges on a man called Misha."

"Misha?"

"The head of the East German service."

The others looked puzzled. Step by step, Director Claiborne began to explain. "The Kremlin power struggle is far from being

311

played out," he said, "but we have learned that it has already claimed one prominent victim. Krylov." He paused to make sure they had all registered the name. "Krylov," he repeated, "was one of the most brilliant and subtle spymasters at Moscow Center."

"The man who managed to put a mole inside the Agency," General Brennan interjected.

"That is unfortunately correct," Claiborne conceded. "In some way that our sources have not yet been able to explain, Marshal Safronov came to perceive Krylov as a threat to himself, and had him eliminated."

"You mean executed?" the President asked.

"'Murdered' would be a more accurate term, Mr. President. By taking this step, Marshal Safronov scared a lot of people who can now feel the noose tightening around their own necks. One of the men who has most reason to be scared is this Misha in East Berlin. For one thing, he was Krylov's protégé from way back, from the war years, when they met at a training school in Moscow. Krylov was always Misha's friend and protector. If Krylov is out, given the way these games are played in Moscow, it's only a matter of time before Misha is out too. For another thing, Misha just happens to be a Jew. As far as Marshal Safronov is concerned, that alone would be reason enough to stew him. Safronov is preaching undiluted anti-Semitism to the troops in Russia, and I think the guy believes his own propaganda."

"What are you saying, Adam?" Secretary Peyton chipped in. "That this East German might be ready to defect?"

"He might be. I think we could scare him off if we went to him directly. We're trying a more roundabout approach. Misha has a cousin in Israel. Dick Hammond—you may remember, Mr. President, he's the officer who led our in-house investigation of the defector's allegations about a mole in the Agency—Dick Hammond, as I say, is on his way to Israel now to see what understanding we might be able to reach with their service."

"Let me see if I've got this straight," the President said. "You've sent Hammond to Israel to ask for Israeli support in encouraging the head of the East German service to defect."

"Right. The Israelis may ask for a quid pro quo. In which case I would ask that you authorize Secretary Peyton, and maybe myself, to fly out to negotiate."

"Okay. We'll face that hurdle when we come to it. What I'd like to know is what connection this Misha has with the Death Beam project."

"That is the best part, Mr. President. We have learned that the key scientist involved in the Death Beam program is a Jew. His name is Milstein, like the famous Soviet general, but his family came from Stuttgart, like Misha's. In fact, his path first crossed with Misha's in the forties, during the war."

"A Klaus Fuchs type," Brennan commented.

"We know that Milstein was one of the scientists who was involved in applying the secret formulas that Fuchs and his circle took to Moscow after the war. But for fifteen years or more, he was employed by the Institute of Space Research in Moscow. And over the past couple of years, he's spent the bulk of his time in Central Asia, at Baikonur and the test sites where the Soviets have been developing Marshal Safronov's popgun."

"So what are you saying, Adam?" the President asked.

"I'm saying that if we can get to Misha, we can get to Milstein. And Milstein could make it possible for us to destroy Death Beam before it lifts off the ground. In such a way that our role in the sabotage could never be proved." The irony, he thought, was that if the plan worked, it would have been through Safronov himself, who had supplied the means of his own undoing through his precipitate action against Krylov.

Secretary Peyton was bending back the fingers of his left hand, counting the number of separate moves involved in Director Claiborne's scheme. "It's very pretty, Adam," he said, looking up over half-moon reading glasses, "but I don't see how you can pull it off in little more than a week, even if all the whiz kids in the Mossad sign up."

"We can try," said Claiborne.

"We have to try," the President said softly. There was finality in his tone. He was announcing his decision. "We'll go with Adam's plan, but we'll simultaneously prepare our fallback position." He nodded toward General Brennan. "If Adam's scheme doesn't work, we'll send our best pilot into Russia on a Stealth bomber and blow that thing up on the ground. That about rounds it up for now."

As they began to disperse, Trip Gage whispered in the President's ear that Colonel Masters, the head of the White House Military Office, was waiting to give an update on emergency procedures—the escape routes the chief executive would use, and the places he could hide, if the balloon went up and the Russians launched a missile attack. In the event of World War III, the United States could be governed for a few hours from an airborne command center—a plane bristling with communications equipment—or, for a few weeks, from a bunker headquarters buried deep in the side of a mountain. The contingency plans no longer seemed farfetched. Trip Gage wondered what the place would be like where Marshal Safronov would conceal himself to ride out the storm he had created.

"How did we get to this point?" the President said, shaking his head, as Colonel Masters came in to give his briefing.

Euphoria and horror, Trip Gage said to himself. It was a phrase that Max Zimmer had used to describe how the Soviets dealt with their intended victims. They sought to lull them into a false sense of security. Then, when a victim's guard was sufficiently lowered, the Soviets made an overwhelming show of force that inspired a paralyzing terror. It was extraordinary how thoroughly these tactics had taken hold of the American psyche in the past, Gage thought. On the one hand, the Americans had told themselves that there was no need to mobilize against the Soviet buildup because Russia's motives were essentially "defensive," having to do with fear of China or paranoia inherited from World War II. Even the Agency had contributed to the mood of psychological disarmament with its failure to report accurately on the full extent of Russia's military capacities. On the other hand, when it came to reacting to Soviet initiatives, the Americans, like their European allies, had been stealthily overcome by dread of the horrors that a confrontation might bring—by fear that the Soviets, at the end of the reckoning, were stronger.

The President heard Colonel Masters through to the end of his quickfire briefing. Then he said, "I think we might all do better to pray."

29

"At this hour of the morning," she said, "Jerusalem is the most beautiful city on earth."

"At any hour of the day," he said, "there is no place like it."

Dick Hammond took her arm as they walked the rough ground around the brow of the hill called the Mount of Olives. Behind them, above the road and the car park, rose the modern bulk of the Intercontinental Hotel. In front of them, down in the folds of the valley of Kidron, they could see twinkling lights. In the darkness before dawn, they could hear cocks crow, and the trilling and warbling of other birds that rose with them, and the chanting of prayers in several tongues, and the noises of the great city stirring and starting to rub the sleep from its eyes. Then, when the sky was still black, came the high wail of the muezzin's call from the minaret of the al-Aksa mosque: *"Al-salat khayr min al-naum,"* "Prayer is better than sleep."

In all the city, this corner, solitary in the moments before dawn when the faithful were making their first prayers of the day elsewhere—at the Western Wall, and the Dome of the Rock, and the Church of the Holy Sepulchre—was to Rael a private sanctuary, a place for self-knowledge in communion with the miraculous, undying city. It was a place that bore one of the city's scars: the road that led up to the hotel had been plowed, in the time of Jordanian rule before the Six-Day War, through the ancient Jewish cemetery. The Hasidim still came to mourn the desecration. Rael had not been raised in a religious family. But at this hour, listening to the lilting whispers of the city's rival faiths, she felt attuned to a history of anguish and overcoming that reached back further than the four thousand years of Jerusalem's recorded history, to the age, perhaps, of the massive stone on the Temple Mount, revered by Moslems as the spot where the Prophet began his night ride to heaven but believed by some religious Jews to be the *Even Shetiyyah*, the rock on which the world was created.

It was a mark of her trust in the American, the depth of her feeling for him, that she wanted to share this place with him. She could not find words to communicate the complex of emotions it evoked. But holding her tenderly against him as the wind gusted about them and the birdcalls sounded from below, Hammond knew.

"I'm sorry it has to be you," he said.

"It has to be someone." She leaned against him, hugging his waist. "I have all the qualifications. Fluent in German and Russian. Trained in special operations. And with a father called Judah Klugmann."

"Do you trust him?"

"He's my father." She released his waist and clasped her arms tightly under her breasts, feeling the chill through her light cotton blouse. She had left her sweater in the car.

Klugmann hadn't been much of a father, Hammond thought. He had ditched Rael's mother soon after Rael had been born, leaving his child to grow up fatherless in the communal crèche at the kibbutz. Rael had had to master the habits of independence early. Now Arik, the deputy chief of the Mossad, had decided that she would accompany her father to East Berlin to meet Misha. And, if things went well, to help arrange Misha's escape.

"Your father," Hammond pursued. "Has he really chosen his loyalties?"

"Arik thinks so."

"I'm asking you, Rael."

When she turned on him, she looked fierce, as if Hammond had violated some unspoken rule he had been expected to observe in that strange, windy place she had shown him.

"You're not a Jew," she said. "That may be why you ask so many unnecessary questions."

"I'm sorry," he said, still not understanding.

"You know my father's history," she said. "When he was a young man, his heroes were people like Trepper, the head of the Red Orchestra. He was a socialist, and he believed that the Soviet

Union was the mainstay of a war against fascism that did not end with Hitler's defeat. He believed in Misha, at least until very recently. But he also believed in Israel, not as a Zionist, but as a socialist who was convinced that a new kind of society could be built here where Jews would be at home. When the Soviets assisted in the birth of Israel, my father's loyalties were not divided. For many years, he continued to believe that there was no contradiction between being a loyal Israeli and a loyal socialist— the sort of socialist, that is, who thought that defending the Soviet Union, with all its defects, was a primary duty."

She paused to light up a menthol cigarette. The wind blew out the match, and Hammond lit another for her, cupping his hands to protect the flame.

"I don't know why I'm giving you this speech," she said.

"Please go on."

"There were Jews like my father in the worst days of Stalin inside Russia," she went on. "Jews who couldn't believe that the great socialist motherland could reject them and devour them. Jewish socialists who ended up singing the *Ha-Tikvah* alongside Zionists, penned up in the same cattle trucks en route to forced labor camps in Siberia." She shivered, and he put his arm around her shoulders again. "My father didn't go through that experience. It took him a lot longer to understand that there was a basic conflict between his feelings as an Israeli and his loyalty to the Soviets. He could shrug off what Stalin did because, after all, Stalin died and the Soviet leadership was supposed to be reformed. He could try to ignore the fact that the Soviets were helping our worst enemies among the Palestinians and the radical Arab regimes. He could even turn a blind eye to Marshal Safronov and the rebirth of organized anti-Semitism in Russia. Misha was always there to reassure him."

She stubbed out the half-smoked cigarette against a rock, but immediately shook another from the pack.

"It was Misha who forced him to understand," she concluded, squatting on the edge of the rock, looking out toward the orange-flecked, lightening sky. "Misha asked him to do something that hurt Israel. Or could have hurt Israel. Something broke in my father at that point. He was forced to face the reality of choosing between two commitments."

"But he obeyed Misha," Hammond commented softly.

"Never again," she said. "Now it's Misha's turn to make a choice. It will be easier for him than it was for my father."

"Why are you so sure?"

She studied him with her almond eyes. She said, "Because Misha knows he could be put on a cattle truck."

The whole scheme hinged, Hammond knew, on a fragile chain of ifs and mights. The only solid link in the chain was that Klugmann and Rael would be able to get to Misha. With an offer of unlimited cash, and a safe existence under an assumed identity in Israel, the United States, wherever he chose. Plus the warning that his days of power in East Berlin would end as suddenly as Marshal Safronov's plan came to fruition. Misha would know that already, because of what had happened to his protector in Moscow, Krylov. These were the only certainties. Would Misha accept the offer relayed by the Israelis? If so, could he move Klaus Milstein, the chief scientist on the Death Beam project, to help arrange its sabotage? Was Milstein even accessible, or was Safronov keeping him locked up and incommunicado at the secret base in Kazakhstan? They would have the answers, the American hoped, within the next twenty-four hours. If they got the wrong answers, they would be reduced to General Brennan's alternative: to bomb the hell out of the Death Beam site, and invite world war.

He took Rael back to the King David Hotel for breakfast. She ordered only coffee and orange juice.

"You're not hungry?" he asked.

She shook her head. Lack of sleep had made dark circles around her eyes.

"Shouldn't you take a nap?" he asked, feeling guilty that he had let her stay up all night, following her whim to be taken to a late supper at a run-down Arab restaurant in the Old City, and then on to the Mount of Olives after their meetings with Arik and her father. "You could use my room here. I do mean a *nap*," he added hastily, seeing her inquiring glance.

"Tell me something, Dick," she said. "We were close to each other once, weren't we?"

"We were very close." He had fallen in love with Rael and with Israel at the same time, he realized.

"Do you still feel something for me?"

"Of course." He reached across the table and took her hand. "You can't just cut something like that out of your life." *Nor could you just return to it casually*, he thought. They had talked about that on his last trip, when he had told her about Sally. When you felt deeply for someone, you couldn't reduce them to a sexual convenience. By doing that, you diminished yourself as well as the other. Then he thought of Rael among the harsh concrete blocks of East Berlin, and felt fear for her, entering that prison city.

"I have to leave for the airport in two hours," she said. "And I'm frightened. I need to be held. Please hold me, Dick."

He helped her to her feet and kissed her gently on the lips in the almost-empty restaurant. They found the elevators, and in their shared sleeplessness and nostalgia and fear, the next hour slipped away as weightlessly as in a dream.

30

EAST BERLIN, *November 3*

"You told me you had a daughter, but you never told me she looked like this! You old crow," Misha laughingly chastised Judah Klugmann, "it's just not possible. I wish I had known her mother."

They were together, Rael and her father and their cousin, the head of the East German service, in Misha's apartment in the Johannisthal quarter of East Berlin, not far from his office in the modern building on the Gross-Berliner Damm. The apartment was large and expensively furnished, but had the unlived-in, un-cared-for look of a place that belonged to a man who was rarely there and was wedded to his job.

Misha was breaking the ice. Rael guessed that he was also playing a game with them. Misha was far too meticulous and much too well-informed not to have briefed himself fully on her association with Arik and the Mossad.

"Your father and I are old sinners," Misha said to her, pouring white wine into her glass until it was full to the brim, so she had to bend over it in order to sip without spilling the wine.

Rael and her father had made their journey in three stages: from Lod airport via Zurich to Prague and thence to East Berlin, where Misha—alerted by Klugmann through his usual contact, an Israeli stringer for East German television—had had a car waiting on the airport runway. Their reception contrasted very favorably with the somber greeting that awaits the average tourist, who has to run the gauntlet of laborious immigration checks and customs searches, all closely supervised by the Ministry of State Security.

"Can we talk?" Judah Klugmann looked nervously around the room.

Misha threw back his head and laughed, a high unnatural laugh that made Rael feel nervous too.

"Whatever's the matter, Judah?" Misha challenged him. "Do you think we're bugged, already? Who's going to bug me in East Berlin?"

They all knew the answer to *that*. The Soviets were not averse to spying on their poor relations. And since Krylov's demise, Misha was especially likely to be under scrutiny.

"Oh, *all right*," Misha said, seeing that neither Rael nor her father had joined in his show of good spirits, "I'll put on some music. It doesn't necessarily make it impossible to eavesdrop electronically, but it gives anyone who tries an earache."

It was characteristic of Misha, the closet Jew, that he put on Wagner.

They were well into the first act of *Tristan und Isolde* before Klugmann summoned the courage to say, "You've got to get out, Misha."

"What the fuck are you talking about?"

"They killed Krylov. They're going to kill you too. Unless you get out. Don't tell me you don't know what Marshal Safronov is doing."

"You're insane. I don't know what happens to you people under that Palestinian sun." Misha tried laughing again, as if he had made a joke, but trailed off in a sickly falsetto.

"Don't push me too far, Misha," said Klugmann. Rael noticed that her father's unease had been overtaken by anger. "We've come to help you," he went on. "We may be the only friends you have left."

"When I need help, I'll ask for it." Misha affected a cold sneer as he reached over to light Rael's cigarette. "Are you interested in opera?" he said to her. "Our state opera may not be up to Bayreuth standard, but I fancy it's not bad compared to your Israeli product."

"Next time, perhaps," she said coolly, watching the smoke rings climb. She was conscious of Misha's appraising glance. His cold eyes ranged over the lush contours of her body, stripping her to a thing of flesh with the same impersonal lust, she imagined, that he would exercise on a paid whore. Maybe he was testing her poise, seeking to elicit some sign of anger or embarrassment. She was determined not to give it. When Misha's eyes returned to her face, she met his stare with her own, looking just above his pupils to an imagined middle distance beyond his head, the smile on her lips as static and brittle as if it had been set in plaster.

"You're not drinking enough, little cousin," Misha boomed at her with forced jocularity. "We should be celebrating."

"We did not come with empty hands," she said to him, cutting off the banter. "We came with an offer."

"Wait a minute," said the East German spy chief. "The next bit is too good to be ignored." He strode over to the hi-fi and turned up the volume. The strains of Wagner became deafening.

Naturally, Rael thought, Misha's neighbors—no doubt service colleagues or high Party officials—would never presume to complain. But the privilege he enjoyed was of the kind that could vanish between night and morning. Surely he must sense that. She recalled the scene that had greeted them at the airport: columns of banner-waving Youth Pioneers from the Wilhelm Florin training camp at Prebelow, formed up in their cadet uniforms as an honor guard for the East German army chief. The scene recalled the rallies of the Hitler Youth, as well as Marshal Safronov's appeals for military preparedness, "ideological vigilance," and patriotic fervor. What Safronov represented for Russia was coming to pass in East Germany too, and there were many who would welcome its return. Then the tables would truly be turned on Misha. As Krylov's pupil, he had mastered the arts of using old Nazis who could be blackmailed or threatened or bought to serve his own purposes. With Marshal Safronov's triumph, the beast he had harnessed would round on him and rip him to shreds.

Misha sat next to her on the sofa, so they could hear each other's words through the Wagnerian thunder.

"What kind of an offer?" he asked. His eyes were veiled and opaque now. He was no longer appraising her. He was concealing himself.

"My father is right," she said. "If you stay here, Safronov's people will eventually get around to killing you. All he has to do is give the order to your puppet government. No one in Moscow is going to protect you now Krylov is gone."

"So?"

"So we've come to offer you sanctuary. In Israel."

Misha's lips puckered as if he were making a raspberry.

"Or in the United States, if you prefer. The Americans will talk to you anytime you nominate. Our understanding is that the President will personally guarantee your physical security and whatever conditions you require. Money is no object. If that interests you, you can name any price you want."

"How about twenty million dollars?" Misha asked playfully.

She frowned slightly. "I don't think even that would be impossible," she said seriously.

Misha patted her knee. "You don't understand, little cousin. There is no price for a man like me, whatever your rich American friends may think. I am the chief of my service. I have given my life to this. Chiefs of service don't defect."

"The chief of the Rumanian service did."

This time he made an audible raspberry.

"Rumanians," he spat out derisively. "I'm not a Rumanian. Anyway," he went on, "I've tried exile once before, when Mr. Hitler was running this country. I don't plan to live in exile again."

Rael paused, exasperated.

"Misha, you're a Jew." It was Klugmann who spoke. "Are you crazy or something? Don't you remember people like your grandfather who didn't believe in the gas chambers until they were led right up to the door? There's no future for people like us here. Not anymore."

Now the mask broke. Misha reddened and clenched his fists. "I should have you both arrested," he hissed at them. "You are provocateurs. I'm going to deport you on the first plane that takes off tomorrow morning. You should be grateful that you're family. Otherwise things would go worse for you."

"Misha—" Klugmann tried again, but the spy chief cut him off.

"I'll tell you what it all comes down to," Misha said. "And then maybe you'll leave off with these fantastic proposals. You're asking me to join up with the losers. You hear that?" he repeated. "The losers. You're asking me to leave here and run away to America or your little pocket-handkerchief Jewish state. I'm telling you that after November 7, there won't be anywhere to run to. The world is going to look very different. And I intend to be on the winning side."

He drew breath, and though she could feel her heart pounding, Rael said evenly, "We know."

"What do you know?"

"We know about Project Razrukha. The Americans call it Death Beam."

For the first time, Misha looked scared. "Then you understand what I'm saying," he responded. "There's really no point in running away. Whatever comes to pass, I prefer to face it here, on my own ground."

She swallowed and said, "There's a better alternative."

"What is that supposed to mean?"

"You can help to stop Razrukha. You can stop Safronov."

"You're out of your mind." He was thinking that the beautiful Israeli agent really must be possessed. Here they were sitting in his apartment in Johannisthal, and she was talking about destroying the most closely guarded project in the Soviet Union, many hundreds of miles away in the wastes of Kazakhstan. Even he, the head of the East German service, had no more chance of being admitted to the Razrukha site than an American holidaymaker on a package tour.

"There is a way," she continued, steeling herself to say the next part. Fear is infectious, and Rael was more nervous than she had been at the start; his fear, she sensed, was greater than her own. "There is your friend, or your former friend, Klaus Milstein. He helped to create Death Beam. He could help to destroy it."

Misha pictured the mild-mannered scientist, always unkempt, with burn holes in the pockets of his jackets where he would thrust a pipe, unthinking, without knocking out the tobacco. Klaus Milstein, who had chosen to live in the Eastern bloc when the Americans would have given him millions to set up his own laboratory, because he believed in peace.

"Klaus Milstein," he repeated the name. "Why would he want to wreck his own project, the crowning achievement of his whole career?"

"Because he still believes in peace," she suggested. "Because he knows the fable of the sorcerer's apprentice. Because he doesn't want to live in the world that Marshal Safronov wants to give us."

Misha's eyes, she saw, were almost closed. He had drained the last of his wine.

She pushed her half-smoked cigarette into the ashtray, and it lay there like a worm cut in two by the spade.

324

"And Klaus Milstein will do it," she said, "because you were his friend and you are going to tell him to do it."

This time Misha did not get angry. For a long time, he rested against the sofa as if he had dozed off.

Then he said, "It's still impossible. Klaus Milstein is here, in East Berlin. Under guard. Safronov was happy enough to let him build Razrukha, but he doesn't trust him enough to let him stay around the countdown. After all," he commented sardonically, "Klaus is a fucking *jid*."

It was the first time that Rael or her father had heard Misha concede, even obliquely, that the Soviet motherland had a "Jewish problem."

Rael wrestled down her sense of total despair.

"There may still be a way," she thought aloud. "There has to be. Klaus Milstein has the master plan in his head, doesn't he?" She took stock for a moment, considering the next step. Milstein could tell them how to get into the site, and how to sabotage the launch. She could go herself. With Misha's help, it should not be impossible to obtain the appropriate documentation; Department K of his service was recognized internationally as the most proficient forgery factory that existed. She would need help. She would need to contact Arik and Dick Hammond. But Misha could help there too. If he chose. They would need explosives, demolition equipment. She wondered for a moment how difficult it was to blow up a space rocket with dynamite or plastique. Maybe not difficult at all. The most complex technology, she had learned, is vulnerable to the most primitive weapons of terrorism. Then something blindingly simple occurred to her, and she liked the idea because it is usually the simplest schemes that work best.

"Listen," she said. "Klaus Milstein is the father of this project. He knows more about it than any other scientist on the Razrukha staff. Suppose he conceives of a last-minute hitch, something that could go wrong when the satellite is put into orbit, something that requires his personal attention. So they would have to let him back into the base." *With me as his personal assistant,* she added mentally. The old scientist would need to have his hand held. If Milstein agreed to the plan, someone would have to be there to ensure that he did not lose courage.

"You're talking crap," Misha dismissed her rudely. "They've been testing this weapon for months. Everything has been covered."

"Is that ever true? That *everything* has been covered?"

Misha flapped his hands in the air. "They've finished with Milstein," he said. "Forget it."

"Milstein could scare them," she said. "There've been accidents before. Terrible accidents. You remember in 1969, when the Soviets were racing to get the Super Booster into space so they could beat the Americans to the moon? The Super Booster blew up in a great ball of fire just after takeoff. They thought they had everything covered then too. Until the explosion. If Klaus Milstein tells them now that they've got a problem, they've got to listen to him. They can't take the risk of doing anything else."

"Persistent bitch, aren't you?" Misha stared at his lovely cousin, astonished by the boldness of what she was proposing. His mind returned to Krylov, who had plucked him out of the anonymous stream of refugees from Hitler's Germany and turned him into what he was today, and to the imagined scene of Safronov's thugs drowning Krylov in his bath. In the system to which Misha belonged, you had to be ready to forget personal friendships and cling to the hairpin bends of political expediency. But he could not forget Krylov. And Judah Klugmann was right: if Krylov's killers were allowed to get their way, he was a dead man.

"You're going to get us all shot," Misha said, resting his forehead in the palm of his hand as if the weight had become too much for him.

"You mean you will do it?" she asked, suddenly daring to hope.

"I will talk to Klaus Milstein," he confirmed. "If I were Judah, I would say I must be *meshuggeh*."

Rael threw her arms around the spy chief's chest and kissed him.

"*Todah rabah*," she whispered.

Misha hastily disengaged, straightening his tie.

Compared with other would-be defectors, the head of a country's spy service is in an enviable position. His subordinates are unlikely to challenge his plans, however eccentric they may appear. For Misha, the main danger in an attempted flight to the West came from the big brothers, the Soviets. When Rael and her father retired to their bedrooms in the guest apartment that the service provided for Misha's personal use on the floor below, the East German spy chief began sweeping his living room with a compact bug-detection device. He had done so before Rael and Klugmann had arrived, and once a week, he had a couple of trusted men from the technical-services department around to make a more thorough check. They had once caught the Americans trying to bug him. But he was less worried about eavesdropping by the Americans than by the Soviets. In the view of Moscow Center, nobody was above suspicion. Krylov had drilled that into him. So when he had finished sweeping the living room, he went on into the bedroom, the bathroom, even the kitchen and the linen closet. No precaution was excessive. Especially now.

31

"You keep reminding me of the daughter I never had," the old man kept saying to her. "It's hard to believe you're a relation of Misha's."

Rael found herself liking Klaus Milstein. Physically, he reminded her vividly of an elderly immigrant she had once encountered at Qiryat Arba, on the West Bank, a spindly stick of a man who was newly arrived from Russia. Once in the middle of the night he had roused the whole settlement by switching on the alarm sirens. When people gathered with guns in their hands, expecting an Arab attack, the crazy old man had explained that he had been alone on watch, thinking about what a terrible plight the Jews were in. "It just wasn't right," he had insisted, "to let all of you lie asleep in bed when we Jews are in such a terrible state."

Klaus Milstein was far from crazy, but he had been having visions in the dead of night. Since the day he had accompanied Marshal Safronov and General Osipov on their inspection of the Razrukha control center at Baikonur, he had often lain awake trying to compute the likely area of radioactive fallout from the relativistic particle beam that he had perfected, and the numbers of people who would die if it were targeted on a densely populated area like the Eastern Seaboard of the United States. The fallout, of course, would be distributed in concentric waves. The more intense the dosage of radiation that the victims received, the less likelihood that they would recover from it. For those in the least-affected areas, radiation sickness might be confined to feelings of nausea, reddening of the skin, throat infection, and diarrhea. Those exposed to two hundred rads would experience severe

328

disorders of the lymphatic glands, and their red blood cells would begin to decay and die. Exposure to three hundred rads would attack the genitals; men would become sterile, and women would give birth to children with horrible deformities. Three-quarters of the people exposed to eight hundred rads would die. Over twelve hundred rads, everyone would die within a week after convulsion and coma.

Milstein's best guess was that Razrukha, if it functioned according to plan, would deliver more than five thousand rads to an area of some ten square miles, with the dosage decreasing to two thousand rads over a circle of a hundred square miles, and to one thousand rads across a wider circle of two hundred square miles. Within that largest circle, most forms of life that were not in protected shelters would die.

Cockroaches, he decided, would be an exception. The humble Paleoblattidae dated back 350 million years, to the carboniferous era, before dinosaurs appeared in the pattern of evolution. All that they had that resembled a brain was a concentration of nerve ganglia in their heads. But they were the earth's greatest survivors. Milstein had heard that there were a lot of roaches in New York. He found this an interesting datum, since he was certain of one thing: the roaches would be all that would be moving above ground in Manhattan, and within a radius of a hundred miles, if Marshal Safronov gave the order to push the button and fire the beam.

The enormity of the weapon's death-dealing power and the defenselessness of the victims were not its only unique qualities. It would also make it possible for a conqueror to occupy the cities and towns of a target country without reducing the property value of a single house. Radiation does not last forever. As a general rule, it drops to one-tenth of its initial strength after each time factor of seven: in other words, the risk from fallout will have dropped to a tenth after seven hours, and after two weeks it will have dropped to one-thousandth of what it was after one hour. If Razrukha was used, it might be only a matter of days before the marshal's soldiers came to claim the ownerless real estate and to pick off the survivors.

Milstein had agonized over the possible consequences of his scientific work long before his encounter with Marshal Safronov in the Baikonur control room. But the mood he had sensed that day had brought home to him the reality of unleashing the most hideous instrument of mass destruction that man had devised—an instrument which he, more than anyone else, was responsible for bringing into the world. He had seen men who loved war, who even sniffed after it, with their fingers poised above the button.

Then Misha had told him things that had sharpened his fear into a knife that twisted among his entrails. Misha, the callous spy chief who was unrecognizable as the handsome, open youth he had grown up with in Stuttgart before the war, had suddenly revealed something of his former self in explaining why the marshal had to be stopped.

"Razrukha is your child," Misha had said to him, with a strange, fleeting smile plucking at his mouth. "That gives you the right to kill it."

When he had said he would do it, Klaus Milstein found that for the first time in years, his hands had stopped shaking and he could hold himself upright, as if he had reason to be proud.

The mechanics of arranging his return to the Baikonur Cosmodrome were easier than Misha or Rael had imagined. He sat down in his study and drafted, overnight, a memorandum expressing some last-minute doubts about whether the flux-compression process by which the energy generated by a mini-thermonuclear explosion would be converted into electrical power to produce the beam had been accurately adjusted to the conditions of outer space. His art was to couch the memo in a succession of impenetrable scientific formulas. A senior physicist who specialized in advanced beam technology would probably have recognized Milstein's memo as the scientific equivalent of a nonsense rhyme. But it was addressed to Chief Designer Berzin, who was essentially a political apparatchik who had compensated for a third-rate, derivative mind by stealing the research discoveries of the scientists who had to answer to him. Klaus Milstein calculated that the chief designer would not wish to put his ignorance on show by consulting the specialists at the Lebedev Institute in Moscow. And that at the same time Berzin would feel that he could not run the risk of a failure for which he would be held personally accountable by ignoring an urgent warning from the man who created Death Beam.

Milstein had accurately assessed the psychology of his former boss.

Though Marshal Safronov had instructed him to "get rid of that *jid*," Chief Designer Berzin thought it was clear that the marshal had meant this to be done as soon as Milstein's usefulness was exhausted. Within two hours of his receipt of Milstein's memo, a message from Berzin arrived in East Berlin demanding the scientist's return to Baikonur the same day on a special military flight.

"It will be like Telemark," Milstein whispered to Rael as they sat, in solitary splendor, on board the Ilyushin turbojet. Since Misha had briefed him on the full extent of Marshal Safronov's ambitions, the old scientist had been polishing the analogy between the intended sabotage of the Razrukha project and the daring commando mission that had destroyed a Nazi heavy-water plant in Norway and so helped to prevent Hitler from acquiring the Bomb.

"Telemark," he repeated, rubbing his chin against the shabby collar of his ancient Harris-tweed jacket.

"But not quite so violent, I hope," Rael whispered back, patting his arm.

The most extraordinary element in the scene was her presence.

Misha had objected violently at the outset, insisting that her desire to go to Baikonur with Milstein could jeopardize the whole mission. To provide her with plausible documentation to travel inside the Soviet Union was easy enough. But the number of people admitted through the zealously guarded perimeter of the Razrukha project was tightly restricted; there was no way that Misha could provide her with clearances that would stand up to any degree of scrutiny. And there was another constraining factor on Misha's side. He did not intend that the trail of the saboteurs should lead back to him. Why burn his boats?

If they failed, well, escape to the West might be the only course left to him. But if they succeeded, there would be other, more appetizing, possibilities. The destruction of the Razrukha project might finally arm Marshal Safronov's rivals with the courage to move against him. In that event, Misha might be able to emerge stronger than ever. As long as whatever happened at Baikonur could not be laid at his door. Which was a very good reason for doing nothing to facilitate the entry of an Israeli secret agent to Russia's most protected military facility.

But Rael insisted on going. "He needs to be looked after," she had said, patting Milstein's arm.

To Misha's surprise, it was the habitually reticent, unworldly scientist who solved the problem. It was plain that Klaus Milstein, for many years a widower, had fallen in love with Rael at first sight. A benign, paternal kind of love, to be sure. Milstein was sufficiently smitten to recall that he had once had a girl assistant at the Lebedev Institute called Lena Aldrich, who had since married and was leading a quiet life as the wife of a university professor in Leipzig.

"But did she look like *this?*" Misha had asked skeptically. At the time, Rael was wearing an eye-catching red turtleneck sweater that clung to her bust, with her long black hair hanging free.

"Not exactly," Milstein had conceded.

But in the end, they did their best to make Rael look the part. Even in owlish glasses, her hair tied back in a bun and thoughtfully streaked with gray, and wearing a drab maroon suit that made her look fatter, her feminine attractions were not completely disguised. But equipped with the false papers that a trusted man in Department K was ordered to prepare, she might just pass muster—assuming that Milstein was right when he said that neither Chief Designer Berzin nor anyone else at Baikonur had ever met the real Lena Aldrich.

It was in this guise that Rael joined Klaus Milstein on the special flight to Baikonur.

At their last meeting, after her father had been packed off back to Israel, Misha had returned her parting kiss. He had also said, "If you blow it, don't come running back to me."

Chief Designer Berzin sometimes found his attention drifting away from the reports on the acrylic surface of his work table and into a recurring and extremely pleasant daydream. He saw himself at a mass ceremony inside the Kremlin walls, standing a dozen paces or so in front of the mass of technicians and scientists who had been engaged in Project Razrukha. The galleries were lined with the entire membership of the Supreme Soviet and the Academy of Sciences. While anthems played, Berzin saw himself marching up the red carpet to the podium where the members of the Politburo were seated. He saw the whole auditorium rise to its feet in a standing ovation as General Secretary Manilov pinned the Order of Lenin to his chest, already covered with the ribbons of other decorations. He heard Manilov announce that in recognition of his services to the Soviet *Rodina*, he had been declared a Hero of the Soviet Union and would take up the office of chairman of the State Commission of Science and Technology. He saw himself enjoying the spoils of success: country dachas, Zil limousines, lissome secretaries who could refuse him nothing. And, at the end of it all, he saw his name commemorated on a plaque on the Kremlin Wall beside that of Korolev, the famous former chief of the space rocket program.

The message from Klaus Milstein had punctured Berzin's comforting daydream. The chief designer could make neither head nor tails of Milstein's equations. Maybe the old man had finally cracked. They had run endless tests, and everything appeared to be functioning according to plan. Milstein could not have picked a worse time to develop the jitters. The day before, they had mated the Razrukha satellite to the thirty-story-tall Super Booster rocket that would carry it aloft, after carrying out a twenty-second test firing of the rocket engines. Workers on the launch pad had just completed the laborious task of clamping back the steel scaffolding that would protect the delicate silica tiles that lined the satellite's skin until the launch. Razrukha and its rockets were safely concealed from overhead surveillance in a huge man-made crater half a mile deep, protected by a reinforced shield that would withstand anything except a direct missile hit. It would be no joke if they were obliged to dismantle the rocket assembly at this late stage in order to examine Razrukha all over again.

It had occurred to Chief Designer Berzin that Milstein might be fantasizing deliberately, in order to prove that his presence was indispensable to the success of the project, and thereby steal some of the credit away from Berzin himself. Befuddled by Milstein's message, he could have sent it to Moscow for evaluation by the experts at the Lebedev Institute. But Berzin had rivals there who might have seized on an appeal for consultation at this point as evidence that he was incompetent. The competition between the directors of the Soviet scientific establishment was just as vicious as the infighting among their political masters. The easiest thing to do, Berzin decided, was to bring Milstein back, let him state his case, and pack him off again as quickly as possible. After all, Klaus Milstein could pose no threat to the chief designer. The marshal had already said that they should get rid of the *jid*.

Berzin was pleasantly surprised by Milstein's female companion, and made a great fuss of kissing her hand. It was a pity she didn't use makeup and wear more fashionable clothes, he thought. The girl was really quite pretty.

"It's strange we never ran into each other at the Lebedev Institute," Berzin said to Rael with over-oiled charm. "Milstein must have been hiding you away from me."

"I was only involved in the theoretical phase of the project," Rael said, looking at the ground with a show of modesty that she felt was in keeping with the character she was trying to represent.

"Ah, but all the fun is in the practice," Berzin smirked, with a plodding attempt at humor. Lena Aldrich. The girl's name rang a distant bell. Milstein had had a succession of female assistants in Moscow. Berzin remembered one of them, a pallid bluestocking type with a bad skin and a limp, clammy handshake. But he had certainly never seen a girl like this in Milstein's office. He studied the movement of her hips as he ushered her ahead of him into the room with the bright-green walls.

"You'd better explain yourself, Klaus," the chief designer said when they were all seated as comfortably as the stark office furniture permitted.

Milstein sailed off into a squall of scientific jargon. Berzin, diverted by the ripe figure of the girl, who was trying to hide her looks behind the ridiculously unflattering glasses, soon stopped trying to follow him. The chief designer began to picture what the girl would look like if she took off the granny glasses and let her hair down. The mental image he formed was extremely inviting. If she was so useful to Milstein, he thought, he could not be faulted for offering her a job on his own staff. Milstein did not know how to appreciate her anyway. It was probably years since Milstein had had a woman.

"Get to the point," Berzin ordered the old scientist, masking his distractedness in a display of authority.

And Milstein was off again. All the chief designer could grasp was that there might be a problem with the flux-compression system.

Berzin groaned. "Do you mean we have to open the thing up again?"

"Unless you want to run the risk that if Razrukha is ever fired, it will explode on itself and destroy the space battle station instead of its target."

It took a crew of two hundred men using robot decoupling devices over three hours to disengage the scaffolding and lower the Razrukha satellite to rails on the floor of the underground launching pad.

Rael, watching from a command platform, was awed by the scene. The Super Booster rocket towered up through the gloom like a platinum-gray cathedral. Lying on its side, the Razrukha satellite looked like a monstrous wingless insect. She saw Milstein, mounted on the platform of a vehicle like an enormous fork-lift truck, supervising the technicians who were working to open the side panels.

Long before Milstein had completed his inspection, the chief designer came to take her away to the canteen for dinner.

"Naturally, the base is dry," he said. "But tonight, we are making an exception." A steward brought sweet Russian champagne, the sort that has to be drunk in gulps before the bubbles disappear.

Rael fenced with Berzin's questions about her scientific qualifications, wishing she had had more time to memorize her legend. She thought that she had been caught out at one point, when the chief designer looked at her quizzically after she had said something about her supposed work at the Lebedev Institute. But it soon became apparent that Berzin's mind was on other things.

"How come you're back with Milstein?" he asked.

"I got bored with being a housewife," she lied. "And he needs someone to look after him. He's a brilliant man, a genius. But you know how vague he can be."

Berzin snorted, and fished in his lentil soup for a chunk of thick peasant sausage.

"Milstein is too old," he said. "He's finished. When we've seen this project through, you'd do better to come to Moscow and work with me. I'm going to be a very important man, you know. One of the most important men in Russia."

"I'm flattered, Comrade Berzin."

335

The chief designer mopped his mouth with his napkin. "Your Russian is excellent," he complimented her. "But of course, you've still got a German accent. It will go, with enough practice."

Rael was inwardly grateful that her mother had insisted that her children master her native tongue.

"You shouldn't wear those glasses all the time, you know," Berzin went on. "They age you."

"I'm afraid I can't see where I'm going without them." Rael did not dare to take off the offending spectacles for fear that he would see that the lenses were clear glass.

Her situation was relieved by the arrival of a thickset man in military uniform. The angry expression that molded his coarse features softened only a little at the sight of Rael.

The newcomer nodded curtly to the girl before challenging Berzin, in the tone that a self-important headwaiter might use to a busboy.

"What the hell is Milstein doing back here?" General Osipov thundered.

The chief designer nervously crumpled his napkin into a ball. "Just a last-minute check," he explained. "I thought it would be useful to have a second opinion."

"I've just talked to the marshal," said Osipov. "He wants Milstein off the base right away. The mood the marshal's in, I'm surprised he didn't order me to put both of you under arrest."

The color had drained from the chief designer's face. He got up hastily from the table and said, "I'll see to it immediately." He turned to Rael, his other plans forgotten under the menace of Marshal Safronov's displeasure. "You'd better come too."

Despite the late hour and the fact that he had not eaten all day, Klaus Milstein had a beatific expression on his face on the flight back to East Berlin. A couple of Russian army officers had hitched a ride—perhaps to keep an eye on the passengers, Rael reflected— and it was only when she was sure that they were not within hearing range that she whispered to the scientist, "Well?"

"It's done," he said, folding his hands over his stomach. He did not feel like a man who had just strangled his child. He felt cleansed.

336

"But how?"

"The basic source of energy for the weapon is supplied by fusion," he murmured into her ear. "A controlled, mini-thermonuclear explosion. I've tinkered with the device so that it will go off when they test the rocket engines again. I managed to find out that there is going to be another test tomorrow. No time for detailed explanations now," he added hastily.

They both fell silent at the sight of one of the Russian officers walking deliberately toward them down the aisle. Rael tensed, wondering if they had been found out.

The Russian smiled at her appreciatively and said, "I thought perhaps I could bring you some coffee from the galley. There is no steward on this plane."

"You're very kind." She smiled up at him. "We would love some coffee."

Rael took off her glasses.

32

"I suppose I should congratulate you."

Misha's chin nestled in the upturned collar of his overcoat. It was black, like the shapeless hat he had jammed onto the crown of his head against the brisk morning breeze that gusted across the exposed tarmac of the military airfield. It was just after 4:00 A.M., and Misha had not gone to bed. That was not unusual. Misha was a creature of the night.

He looked from Rael, bundled up in a sheepskin coat, to Klaus Milstein.

"How long?" the East German spy chief asked.

Milstein consulted his watch. "Maybe five hours," he said.

The expression on the old man's face, Misha thought, was reminiscent of a schoolboy who has just got away with raiding a neighbor's apple orchard. He would never understand scientists. So much abstract intelligence, combined with so little common sense.

"You understand that I can't let you go," he said to Milstein.

"Go?" The scientist sucked on the stem of his briar pipe, blackened with use. "Where should I go?"

"You're going home, Klaus," Misha said firmly. "There is a car waiting to take you." It was incredible, Misha thought. The man had no sense of survival, absolutely no concern for himself. Perhaps it took such a man to create Death Beam. And then destroy it.

"Klaus," the Israeli girl said, her face lined with worry. Then her eyes searched for Misha's. She began, "Can't you—"

"No," Misha snapped. "I can't."

338

Milstein was startled by the spy chief's abruptness. He still didn't get it.

Rael put her hands against the scientist's narrow, hollow chest, as if she were feeling for his heartbeat. Then she gently removed the pipe from his mouth and kissed him on the lips. "You were magnificent," she said. "You are one of the just."

Milstein was still trying to stutter some reply when Misha said harshly, "This way." He did not enjoy prolonged farewells. Least of all in their present situation.

Two cars were waiting. Milstein was put in the first—a sleek black official limousine with an armed guard as well as the driver.

As it sped away through the early drizzle, Rael said to Misha, "What will happen to him?"

"It depends." Misha was opening the door of the second car for her. It was an anonymous, unmarked sedan, dirty gray like the sky above them.

"Depends on what?"

Misha ignored her question until he was strapped in behind the wheel.

"It depends," he then explained, "on whether what happened at Baikonur is traced to him. It probably will be. It's all a little too obvious, isn't it? The great Klaus Milstein returns to inspect his superweapon, and a few hours after he leaves, it blows up. It won't take an investigative genius to make the connection."

As he started the engine, she asked, "And what about Lena Aldrich?"

"*This* Lena Aldrich"—he glanced sideways at her—"is going back to Israel. Going back the way she came. We'll collect your things, and I'll drop you off near the airport. There's a flight leaving for Prague at seven-thirty."

"What about you?"

"What about me?" he mimicked her.

"You can't mean that you're staying here."

"Certainly I'm staying here. Did you ever seriously suppose otherwise?"

"I'm—I'm confused," Rael said. They had cleared the perimeter guards and were speeding back into the city. "If the Russians connect the sabotage with Milstein, then they're going to come for you. You're in more danger than you were before."

"Why?" The confidence of his tone gave Rael the sensation that she was playing a game in which he changed the rules whenever it suited him. As if just when she had assembled a good poker hand he told her they were actually playing euchre. "How can I be blamed?" Misha went on. "I am responsible for Milstein's security and good behavior. The Russians wanted him to go back to Baikonur, so I followed instructions and put him on a plane. They sent him home again, so I played the faithful watchdog and made sure he was put back safely under lock and key. I simply did my job. I didn't let him run away."

"Aren't you forgetting something?"

"What?" Again, the cheerful insouciance he affected both astonished and infuriated her.

"Lena Aldrich," she said. "How do you explain me? How do you explain the girl who went to Baikonur and then disappeared?"

"You do manage to get things muddled up," he commented, whipping through a red light at a deserted crossroads flanked by identikit apartment blocks. "You are not Lena Aldrich. You are—" He mentioned the assumed name that was in the fake passport she had used for her trip to East Berlin. "The real Lena Aldrich is a housewife living in Leipzig who was formerly Klaus Milstein's assistant at the Lebedev Institute. Her husband is a woolly academic who will confirm, if anyone asks, that she left home on an important government assignment on the same day that Milstein flew to Baikonur. He will also verify that Lena Aldrich has not returned home since. The poor man must be starting to get quite alarmed."

"What did you do with her?" Rael was starting to understand Misha's confidence. "The real Lena Aldrich?"

"It's of no consequence."

At that moment, Rael knew that the price of destroying Death Beam had included the life of an obscure Leipzig housewife.

"And what about you?" she asked him directly as he pulled up near the passenger terminal.

Misha shrugged. "I'll be here, as always. Leading a quiet life."

"Do you really think you can outlast Marshal Safronov?"

"I've survived worse."

The upper part of his face was in shadow, the eyes masked by dark glasses.

"*Auf Wiedersehn*," he said. "Look after your father."

They shook hands solemnly. Misha's thoughts were already

turning on the next stage of the game, which would be played out in Moscow. It was still a gamble, but he considered that the odds had improved.

She paused, her hand on the handle of the car door. "The offer remains open," she said.

"Goodbye," he repeated, reaching across to open her door. "If we meet again, it will be as enemies."

33

"Bleed-off," the launch controller intoned into his microphone. They had started the countdown for the final test of Razrukha's engines. On November 7, flight day, the Super Booster would burn for six minutes before dropping away. Then Razrukha's own engines would carry it up into orbit.

Like the American space shuttle, Razrukha had three main engines, powered by the combustion of liquid hydrogen and oxygen at temperatures of up to six thousand degrees Fahrenheit—hot enough to turn steel into steam.

"Hold," the launch controller recited, checking his clocks and gauges.

It was not a moment of high tension for the Baikonur launch controller. The engines had performed perfectly in the last static firing, and he knew that if a fault had developed, his computer systems, interacting with the computers on board the spacecraft, would automatically close down the test.

In his inner sanctum, General Osipov was observing the scene unfolding in the underground launch site on his big video monitor.

"Ignition," came the launch controller's voice.

The countdown to the simulated launch had reached 4.3 seconds before zero when the first of Razrukha's engines ignited. On his color screen, General Osipov saw the blinding flash of orange flame, followed by great billowing clouds of white vapor.

At the instant of ignition, red lights started to flash on the launch controller's instrument panel, and a hooting klaxon began to sound.

"I don't understand," the controller muttered to himself. If there was a fault in the system, the computerized monitors should automatically have aborted the test. Unless someone had triggered the override mechanism.

"Abort," he commanded.

But Razrukha's other two engines were already spewing gas and flame.

"Abort," he repeated, his voice high-pitched and strident. The engines began to throttle down, six seconds after ignition.

He could not understand why the computerized monitor was still flashing red alert.

General Osipov, alarmed by the klaxons, came marching out of his lair.

"What's happening?" he demanded of Chief Designer Berzin, who was now standing beside the launch controller, staring in disbelief at the signs of imminent disaster being flashed out by the colored lights on the command console.

"It's a minor systems dysfunction, General," he said, willing that the statement should be true. "I think—"

Chief Designer Berzin did not have the chance to elaborate.

The vibrations from the blast shook the underground control room like an earthquake taking place directly underfoot. Berzin caught a glimpse of the launch pad, swallowed up in an angry sheet of flame that filled the video screen, before the screen exploded and General Osipov fell heavily against him, sending both men crashing to the floor. Even through the ten-foot-thick concrete roofing of the bunker, Berzin could hear an ominous rumble from somewhere overhead. As if the moving earth were about to fall on them.

MOSCOW, *November 6*

Feliks Strokin, chairman of the KGB, was inclined to agree with Marshal Safronov that the disaster at the Baikonur Cosmodrome was sabotage, although proof was lacking and it was impossible to get a coherent account of what had happened from the survivors. The survivors did not include General Osipov or Chief Designer Berzin.

At the same time, Strokin's basic reaction to the episode was rather different from the marshal's. The marshal had appeared before the Defense Council in a state of high agitation, calling for instant retaliation against the Americans, whom he deemed responsible for the sabotage. Those who wished to rule, Strokin believed, could not afford to become agitated—or, at the least, they could not afford to display it.

When Safronov had finished his heated diatribe, Strokin asked, as lightly as if he were inquiring about the menu for lunch, "What are you proposing that we should do, Comrade Marshal? Launch a preemptive strike against the Americans?"

"That is *exactly* what I am proposing." There was a crunch of metal against wood as the marshal brought the stump of his left hand down hard, scarring the edge of the walnut table with his hooks. "Listen," he went on. "It will take us nine months, perhaps a year, before we are ready to attempt a second launch of Razrukha. In the meantime, our intelligence suggests that the Americans will be able to send up killer satellites of their own, capable of giving them ascendancy in space. I remind you all of the words of the great Sokolovsky—'It would be a terrible mistake to allow the imperialist camp to achieve superiority in space.' If we fail to act now, we will miss an unrepeatable opportunity. Water does not flow under the same bridge twice."

"Permit me to observe," Strokin quietly interrupted, "that the reason that most of us agreed to support Project Razrukha was that, as you eloquently argued, Comrade Marshal, it would have given us the ability to compel the United States to agree to strategic surrender without the necessity of incurring the risks, and the casualties, of a world war. You are now telling us that we must embark on a nuclear war."

"We have to move *now*, while the correlation of forces is in our favor," the marshal said passionately. "When the Americans were stronger than we were, they abdicated the chance to use their power to hold us in check. That was because their society is decadent. A bourgeois democracy does not understand the role of violence in the evolution of history. While we have the upper hand, we must exercise it."

Before Safronov could embark on another harangue about the reasons why the Soviet Union was bound to win a nuclear engagement if it struck before the Americans had fulfilled their new defense program, Strokin cut in again. The caution that had prevented the KGB chairman from openly confronting the marshal in previous debates around the oval walnut table had vanished since the disaster at Baikonur Cosmodrome. Everyone in the room sensed the change. General Secretary Manilov, in particular, was relishing the developing confrontation between the two men. The marshal's spell had been broken.

"I do not question," Strokin was saying, "that the statistics of the Defense Ministry are accurate. I do not doubt that we will defeat the United States if we go to war tomorrow and have the advantage of surprise. But would the victory be worth the cost? Tens of millions of Russians would die. Moscow and Leningrad would be reduced to foul, smoking ruins. And our reward would, in turn, be a heap of rubble. Going into battle is the least intelligent way of making war, even if the odds are overwhelmingly in our favor. We have won many victories in the last decades, but the ones that were most important were not achieved by the direct involvement of our armed forces. They were achieved by subtler, more intelligent means. I think the Committee of State Security can claim to have made a leading contribution to the achievement of those victories. Through deception and penetration, we attacked the *psychology* of our enemies. We helped, not least through media operations, to make them uncertain of their own goals, to make them question their governing institutions and their national interests. We kept them in ignorance about our own capacities and intentions. We exploited the divisions in their societies, sharpening the conflicts of race, religion, and class. We played on their guilt complexes to prevent them from coming to the aid of controversial allies, as in Angola, Iran, and Central America. It is true that our military strength helped to paralyze resistance to our plans. But we did not need to *directly* invoke our military power in order to expand our influence throughout the world. In fact, when we did use our armed forces, in Afghanistan, we succeeded only in shaking the Americans out of their torpor. That, and the excesses of the Ayatollah's regime in Tehran, helped to mobilize anti-Soviet feeling in the United States on a scale that we have not witnessed since the fifties. The change of mood among the American people brought to office a right-wing administration with a mandate for rearmament."

"What are you suggesting?" General Secretary Manilov asked.

"I am suggesting that we revert to the tactics that have worked in the past. Democracies quickly forget. A bourgeois democracy cannot sustain continuity in its leadership or its strategy. The present mood of war hysteria in Washington will pass. This administration will find itself besieged by the revolt of the unemployed, by racial upheavals, by the campaigns of antidefense and anti-intelligence lobbies, by scandals and press exposures. We can help to make it progressively more difficult for the American President to govern, while widening the gulf between the United States and its European allies. We do not need to risk everything in a head-on confrontation, let alone the war that Marshal Safronov is proposing. We can win by indirect means, through attrition, just as we have been winning in the past."

"You seem to be forgetting about Blue Savior," Marshal Safronov objected. "We can't allow the Americans to seize the lead in space."

Strokin sighed, an unpleasant sigh, like the hiss of dry ice suddenly exposed to the air. "We can protest the Blue Savior program in the United Nations," he said, "and call for a ban on military weapons in space. Many well-meaning Americans will support that. We can announce that the program violates our arms-control agreements, and that Washington is putting détente in jeopardy. We can help to mobilize the antinuclear lobby. And of course," he concluded, "we can try to sabotage the program. If it's possible to infiltrate the Baikonur Cosmodrome, then it is presumably not hard to infiltrate a U.S. Air Force base in New Mexico or California."

"I think Comrade Chairman Strokin is far too blasé," Safronov appealed to the room. "We are dealing with an aggressive leadership in Washington. With the success of their Blue Savior program, following on the destruction of Razrukha, the Americans may be tempted into a belligerent course. They might attack Cuba. They might even intervene more directly to support subversive elements in Eastern Europe. We cannot predict the actions of this group in the White House."

"I beg to differ, Comrade Marshal," Strokin countered. "It is not at all difficult for us to predict the actions of the Americans. We can read their newspapers. And the unfortunate loss of Comrade Krylov did not entirely deprive us of highly placed sources in Washington."

At the mention of Krylov's name, Marshal Safronov recoiled as if he had been slapped. Strokin's statement, he knew, was a deliberate provocation. It was the first time that anyone had dared to refer to the murdered spy chief in a meeting of the Defense Council. It was also the first time in recent memory that Marshal Safronov had failed to lash back at an implied criticism.

The chemistry of the exchange was not lost on the other members of the Defense Council. Power in the room had shifted, and the sense that they were adjusting their positions accordingly was as tangible as if they had been moving their chairs.

Formal votes were never taken in the Defense Council. A consensus was allowed to emerge.

As other ministers spoke up, it became clear that the consensus was running strongly against Marshal Safronov. By the end of the meeting, no one remained in doubt that his views had been crushingly rejected.

Feliks Strokin toyed with the cover of a slim white folder as he addressed the four men who were assembled in his office in the forboding building on Dzherzhinsky Square that housed the headquarters of the Committee of State Security. Three of them wore the uniforms of generals: General of the Army Pavel Ryumin, the commander of the Border Guards, the KGB's 200,000 strong private army, responsible for the security of the frontiers; Lieutenant General Vadim Khlestov, the chief of the Kremlin Guards, charged with the protection of the members of the Politburo; and Major General Marius Boiko, the commander of the First Dzherzhinsky Motorized Division, Moscow's praetorian guard. The fourth man, black-haired and dapper in his Italian-style civilian suit, also held the rank of general. His name was Konstantin Orlov, known to the Americans by the code-name Martini.

"We are about to change the history of Russia," Strokin announced. He opened the folder on his desk. "I am holding three documents that spell the epitaph of Marshal Safronov. The first"—he held it up—"is a copy of the indictment of Safronov that was originally drawn up by Krylov. It was this document that led directly to Krylov's assassination by the marshal's thugs. In it, Krylov exposed how Safronov's intrigues imperiled state security.

In particular, Krylov held the marshal personally accountable for the defection of Colonel Ushinsky to the Americans. I am certain that we all agree that Krylov's accusations have been amply vindicated by the course of events that led to the destruction of the Razrukha project."

There was a rumble of agreement from the KGB generals. They were Strokin's appointees, all of them, although he had suspected at one time that Ryumin had had secret dealings with the marshal. He was sure he could trust them fully now it was clear which way the wind was blowing.

"This document"—Strokin held up a closely-typed transcript—"is the deposition of one of the army officers who took part in the murder of Krylov. It is incontrovertible proof that Marshal Safronov was personally responsible for the assassination. The officer is being held in the Lubyanka under close guard. I am grateful to General Khlestov, who arranged to make the arrest quietly before dawn this morning."

"How did you manage to extract a confession?" asked the chief of the Border Guards.

Strokin allowed himself to smile. "We promised him clemency," he explained. "And we pointed out the possible consequences for his family if he refused to cooperate. He had a pretty young wife and two small children. We allowed him to call his apartment, and one of our men answered the phone. His attitude changed immediately. He was even prepared to call his own office to make his excuses for not appearing there today."

Strokin replaced the transcript in his file and took out the final document, a single sheet of stiff paper embossed with the Communist Party seal. He handed it to General Ryumin, who scanned its contents quickly and passed it on to the others. The familiar signature at the foot of the page was that of General Secretary Manilov. The document formally expelled Marshal Safronov from the Communist Party of the Soviet Union and authorized his arrest, to face charges of antistate crimes.

"Manilov signed this warrant immediately after the meeting of the Defense Council today," Strokin continued. "It is up to us to execute the General Secretary's directive before he loses his nerve."

General Boiko snickered. The KGB chiefs had little respect for

Manilov, who had displayed Hamlet-like powers of indecision at each stage of the Kremlin power struggle.

"Khlestov." Strokin turned to the commander of the Kremlin Guards. "You will make the arrest. The task of the Border Guards and the Dzherzhinsky Division will be to neutralize any armed resistance by military units in the Moscow region."

"Where is Safronov now?" Khlestov asked.

"He went from the meeting to the Defense Ministry," said Strokin. The KGB was kept well informed on the movements of senior military personnel by its own network of agents, especially inside the Main Political Administration of the armed forces, which supplied commissars to all units.

"What if the marshal himself resists arrest?" Khlestov went on.

"He won't." It was curious, Strokin thought, how, throughout the long and bloody history of Moscow purges, even the most ruthless and ambitious leaders had gone tamely like lambs to the slaughter once they had been outmaneuvered.

"But if he does?" Khlestov pursued.

"Then shoot him." Strokin sniffed as if there were a bad smell in the room. Then he said, "Any more questions?"

No one spoke.

"Well then, let's get on with it."

The four generals rose to leave.

"Not you, Orlov," Strokin ordered the man in civilian clothes. "We have something more to discuss."

The man the Americans called Martini took out a slim red-and-gilt cigarette case and offered Strokin a Winston.

"No thanks," said the chairman of the KGB. "They're too mild for me."

"I got into the habit of smoking Virginia tobacco in the States," said Martini. "You're too noticeable there if you insist on black tobacco."

Alone with the KGB chairman, Martini seemed completely at ease. He strolled about the office, exhaling clouds of smoke, then sat down again in a big leather wingback, his legs nonchalantly crossed.

"Such a waste," Martini commented. Then he quoted an old

349

Russian proverb. "You shouldn't spit into the well you may have to drink from later on."

Strokin grunted approvingly. Then he took a bottle of vodka and two small tumblers from the cupboard behind his desk. It was Strokin's favorite variety—pepper vodka, flavored with pimientos that gave the liquor more bite and alcoholic effect. Whoever invented pepper vodka probably had the same thing in mind as the Bowery drunks on Manhattan's Lower East Side who used to be seen sprinkling red pepper into their rotgut gin.

Martini accepted the vodka without comment. Both men drained their glasses, and Strokin refilled them.

"You will have to take up where Krylov left off," Strokin said to the man who had duped the Americans for more than a decade. "I want you to take charge of the Beacon."

Martini began, with a show of modesty, to protest his lack of adequate qualifications to run the most secret office at Moscow Center—the one responsible for recruiting and handling Soviet agents inside Western intelligence services. Strokin brushed his protestations aside.

"You're the man I want," the KGB chairman told him. "Because you are the man who made possible the most successful operation that Krylov ever planned against the Americans. I wonder if even now the Agency has taken the measure of what we did to it. I am sure that but for that madman Safronov and Ushinsky's defection, our operation would still be continuing undetected and the intelligence chiefs in Washington would still be debating whether or not the weapon they call Death Beam could really exist. It's staggering what you and Krylov achieved. For ten years, playing the role of the double agent code-named Martini, you told the Americans what they wanted to believe—that the United States was superior to the Soviet Union in military technology, that the Agency was running a top-level agent inside Moscow Center. The longer the operation went on, the more the Americans *had* to believe. Because of the incredible loss of bureaucratic and individual self-esteem that would have been involved in reevaluating all the intelligence estimates and operations that they based on the deception that we were feeding them. Oh yes"—Strokin interrupted himself to replenish their glasses—"I understood what Krylov was doing. I understood the mission of the Beacon. We must never lose sight of it. Remember what Dzherzhinsky said?

That we have to penetrate deeper and deeper into the enemy's *plans*? There is the key to it all. To be able to deceive the enemy to the point where we not only shape his view of the world but actually control his decisions. We did that, didn't we, Orlov? How amazing that it took the Americans so long to understand. Will they ever recover from Martini?"

"They won't forget him," said the man whose *klichka* was Martini. "And they won't forget the agents they lost because of Martini, now that they finally understand what happened. They won't forget Hussar."

"I wonder," Strokin mused aloud. "There weren't many men who have the imagination, the concentration span, the memory to grasp how these things work. And such men do not appear to be appreciated in Washington. Look what happened to Max Zimmer before we had him killed."

"Look what happened to Krylov," Martini observed mildly.

"It's not comparable," Strokin said testily. "We've been undergoing a palace revolution since Brezhnev died. Krylov was one of the victims. By contrast, Max Zimmer's demise was the consequence of the Americans' failure to understand how we operate. All right." He reverted to his main theme. "The resources of the Beacon are now at your disposal. Including Max Zimmer's personal files."

Martini cocked an eyebrow.

"Oh yes." Strokin confirmed. "We succeeded when the Agency failed. We've got Zimmer's memory. Well," he went on, "where do you want to begin?"

"With the loose ends that Krylov's death left trailing in Washington. Where is Malinovsky?"

"On a freighter, heading from San Francisco to Hong Kong." Strokin explained that the antiquarian-bookseller who had served as the contact man for Trudy Cook after Martini's recall to Moscow had been ordered to go to ground as soon as the Agency's investigation had begun to home in on the real mole. "Malinovsky is as remarkable, in his way, as you are," the KGB chairman said to Martini. "He seems to have as many lives as a cat. He always lands on his feet. I think it's partly because he enjoys it so much. He loves the adventure."

"What about Trudy Cook?"

"Oh yes. The girl. Perhaps I should say *your* girl." The KGB chief was fully briefed on how Martini had seduced the spinster from the Reports section of the Agency's Soviet Division. "We did not consult you," Strokin said bluntly, "because you might have been less than entirely objective. Also"—he waved his Russian cigarette at the chairs where the other KGB generals had been sitting—"you will appreciate that we have been quite preoccupied here at headquarters."

Martini showed no external sign of emotion. But he walked to the window and looked down for a moment through the bulletproof glass into the drab expanse of Dzherzhinsky Square. There were hundreds of soldiers milling about in the street. But they were the KGB's troops—men of the Dzherzhinsky Motorized Division—not Marshal Safronov's.

"We thought of trying to get her out," Strokin went on, "when we learned that her superior, Lester Winter, was under interrogation. At that point, Malinovsky reported that suspicion was inevitably bound to fall on Miss Cook. And on Malinovsky himself."

"So?" Martini rounded on his chief. "So why didn't you get her out?"

Strokin understood the thrust of the question, beyond Martini's personal concern for a female agent he had recruited by the oldest means in the world—sexual entrapment. The KGB had gone to considerable lengths in other situations, as in the case of the Philby spy ring in Britain, to help agents who had come under suspicion to escape from the Western authorities. This was deemed essential in order to reassure Soviet operatives all over the world that their safety was highly prized by Moscow Center, and that they would not be abandoned in time of trouble.

"There was an element of confusion with Krylov gone," Strokin apologized. "There was also a feeling in some quarters that it might actually be helpful if Miss Cook was arrested and subject to a public trial. That would demoralize the Agency and weaken public confidence in it. The information she can give the Americans now is stale. With Krylov and Max Zimmer both dead, and with Martini exposed, we have moved into a completely new situation."

"You were prepared to have Max Zimmer murdered in order to protect Trudy Cook's identity," Martini countered. "And yet you were not prepared to help her get away. There seems a certain . . . disproportion."

"Perhaps." Strokin chose to sound accommodating. "But remember that we were also still trying to prevent the Americans from believing in the reality of Project Razrukha. There was a lot more than Trudy Cook at stake."

"You said something about it being helpful if she is brought to trial. What does that mean?"

"It means that a public inquisition could seriously embarrass the Agency at the moment when it is trying to—how do they say it in American?—*got their act together.*" The KGB chief said the last phrase in English, in an atrocious parody of a Texas accent.

"There's one more thing," said Martini.

"Yes?"

"About Malinovsky. He was not only the control for Trudy Cook. He was also the control for the assassin who killed Max Zimmer. That was a mistake. We should have used separate channels."

"You may be right," Strokin conceded. "But I assume that Krylov knew what he was doing." He paused, considering whether to go further. "You may as well know," he added decisively. "We borrowed the executive agent—the assassin—from the military side. He is a Palestinian. He was available, competent. And I suppose that Krylov calculated that if something went wrong, our tracks could be more easily covered that way."

"What happened to him? The Palestinian, I mean?"

"He's still in place. Marshal Safronov had further uses for him." Strokin hesitated again. He had only just discovered through Malinovsky the ultimate assignment that Marshal Safronov had entrusted to Sammy Hamad. The Palestinian had been ordered to prepare the assassination of the President of the United States. The marshal apparently believed that this would cripple the Americans' ability to retaliate to a Soviet first strike. The assassination was to be timed to coincide with an attack.

"Is it wise to leave the Palestinian in place?" Martini challenged Strokin. "I mean, shouldn't we recall the man? The Americans are bound to catch up with him in the end."

"Give it time," the KGB chairman cautioned. "We have to deal with some unfinished business in Moscow first. Why don't you take this." Strokin gave Martini Krylov's draft indictment of Marshal Safronov. "See what you can add to it." His tone implied that the discussion was over.

Martini rose to leave, but, on an impulse, Strokin stopped him.

"The girl," Strokin said. "Trudy Cook. You didn't feel anything for her, did you?"

Martini revisited in his mind his evenings with Trudy. The remarkable energy the little roly-poly woman had displayed in bed, grinding her pelvis like no Russian woman he had ever slept with. And he thought of a child, a boy who had been named after Lester Frobisher Winter, but had black hair and high cheekbones. Like Martini.

"No," he replied. "It was just part of the job."

General Vadim Khlestov of the Kremlin Guards did not find Marshal Safronov in his office at the Defense Ministry. A nervous woman, a junior secretary, was the only person on duty there apart from the guards. Whatever loyalty she felt for the Defense Minister wilted under Khlestov's glare. She knew what this man with bristling eyebrows represented. The chief of the Kremlin Guards not only represented the power of the secret police; he embodied the will of the Party leadership. She also noticed that unlike army generals on staff assignment in Moscow, General Khlestov was wearing a pistol at his hip.

"The marshal has gone to the Bunker," she told him.

A reserved, taciturn man, Khlestov revealed an unsuspected richness of vocabulary when he started to swear. He started swearing now, indifferent to the sensitivities of the junior secretary, who listened in wonderment as he suggested various ways in which Marshal Safronov's mother should be sodomized by certain farmyard animals.

The Bunker—in effect, the largest of many such boltholes—was the underground headquarters of the Defense Ministry, a buried city, with buildings up to four stories high, capable of housing some fifteen thousand key officials. Located ten miles east of Moscow, the Bunker was the command center where the marshal and his staff would take refuge in the event of a nuclear war. Similar underground facilities existed for the Politburo and other government ministries. Over the years, the Soviet Union had made a colossal investment in civil defense, to the extent of stockpiling grain, even in years of bad harvests and international embargoes, in buried silos three times the size of a football field, protected by reinforced surfaces like those that were used to defend missile launchers.

Khlestov used one of the phones on Marshal Safronov's desk to call Strokin.

"The wild boar has gone to its cave," said Khlestov. "And you thought the marshal wouldn't resist."

Strokin rapidly assessed the possibilities. One dominated all the rest. It was that Marshal Safronov, alerted to his own peril, had decided to disregard the decision of the Defense Council and launch a nuclear attack on the United States on his own authority, calculating that in the ensuing chaos, it would not be difficult for him to dispose of his enemies in the Kremlin. Fortunately, thought Strokin, the Soviet Union was not a banana dictatorship. A carefully structured system of checks and balances had been devised by the Party and the KGB to prevent the military from running amok. Under standing orders, military commanders were not permitted to carry out instructions that were not approved by the commissars appointed by the Main Political Administration of the armed forces. These commissars answered to the Party and the KGB, not to Marshal Safronov.

"Your orders stand," Strokin said to General Khlestov. "Go after the marshal. And do it fast."

For his part, the KGB chairman got his secretary to track down the deputy chief of the Main Political Administration. His superior, curiously, was nowhere to be found. Strokin's instructions were crisp. Any orders coming from Marshal Safronov were to be disregarded. The marshal had been dismissed from his post and was a wanted criminal.

Next, Strokin called General Secretary Manilov. The man sounded edgy. He wanted to know why the marshal had not already been placed under arrest. Strokin fudged his answers, fearful that the timorous General Secretary might do an about-face and rescind his own orders.

Only then did the KGB chief return to his bottle of pepper vodka, and a list of Marshal Safronov's closest military associates

355

that he had had drawn up by the Third Chief Directorate.

Strokin settled in to wait.

It took precisely twelve minutes and fourteen seconds to close tight the steel-and-concrete doors to the Bunker. They were seventy feet wide and just over thirty feet high, and ran on rails. Once they were closed, Marshal Safronov would be effectively sealed off from the outside world. It would take more than blowtorches or a laser gun to penetrate the three-foot-thick shield. It would take a bomb.

The doors were closing as General Khlestov's Chaika limousine sped toward them down a winding road lit by overhead neon flares. Three more cars followed behind, carrying a total of eighteen men from the Kremlin Guards, a hand-picked elite composed of men selected for their outstanding physical and intellectual prowess. They all stood over six feet tall, and were permanently forbidden to travel abroad. They knew too many of the secrets of the men they protected for the Kremlin to run the risk that one of them might defect or be kidnapped.

There was barely space left between the doors for Khlestov's car to pass. Unhesitating, he ordered his driver to go through. As he looked back, he saw that the car behind was jammed between the huge doors like a broken-down jalopy between the presses at a wrecker's yard.

It didn't matter, Khlestov decided. What he had to do did not depend on the number of armed men at his disposal. It depended on deeply ingrained habits of obedience, and the awe inspired by a warrant signed by the General Secretary. And the uniform of the Kremlin Guards.

General Khlestov informed the officer in charge of the gatehouse what he thought of his mother's morals, and the doors slowly ground open again.

No one inside the Bunker challenged the commander of the Kremlin Guards until he reached the marshal's outer office, where a fair-haired young colonel demanded to know his business. Several Spetsnaz soldiers with automatic weapons were in the room.

"The commander of the Kremlin Guards does not answer to a

colonel," Khlestov informed him. "I am here to see Marshal Safronov, on the orders of the General Secretary."

The fair-haired colonel continued to bar the way to the marshal's private office. Khlestov concluded that he was either drunk or a fanatic. The thought crossed his mind that the young officer might have been one of the men who murdered Krylov.

Alone with only a handful of guards inside the Bunker, Khlestov knew that his position was hopeless if he permitted his authority to be challenged, even for a moment.

"Stand aside," he commanded.

The colonel's glance wavered for a moment. But he did not budge.

"Very well," said Khlestov.

The general calmly unholstered his heavy Stechkin pistol, and, with the same absence of haste, leveled it at the colonel's face and put a 9mm bullet through his forehead. As the colonel's body rolled on the floor, the men in the room could see that the skin at the back of his head had exploded in the shape of a ragged star where the bullet had exited. Nobody moved.

Except Khlestov, who strode forward and opened the marshal's door.

Safronov was sitting alone at his desk, with his service pistol on top of the papers in front of him.

"So it's over," the marshal said.

"It's over."

Safronov looked from the pistol on his desk to Khlestov, and back again.

"Will you give me a minute to myself?" the marshal appealed to the commander of the Kremlin Guards. "I think you understand."

General Khlestov understood.

He stepped backward two paces, clicked his heels, and closed the door.

He did not reopen it until they all heard the shot from inside.

34

The bell captain at the Hay-Adams noticed that the group from Rome TV were carrying unusually bulky equipment. The leggy girl reporter with the inviting smile was actually apologetic about it, explaining that they were planning to erect a mobile stand to get some good shots over the heads of the crowd during the big antinuclear march that was expected to sweep past the White House around the middle of the day. Claudia Fiorella was the name on the elegantly printed card that she left at reception. She laughed and nodded when they explained that, yes, they had reserved a room for her overlooking the White House on the other side of Lafayette Square, but, no, the management would definitely prefer that filming not be done from inside the hotel. She had an engaging manner. And the way she moved her hips under her daringly cut tunic dress of pink suede did not escape the attention of the men who happened to be standing about in the hotel lobby.

The Italian television crew were not the last guests to check into the hotel before the first shouts of the antinuclear protesters began to be heard as they tramped along Pennsylvania Avenue toward the White House. An exorbitantly long pearl-gray limousine with blacked-out windows pulled up the drive just after noon. The distinctive baggage checks on the passenger's luggage suggested that he had recently flown the Concorde to New York, presumably coming from Paris or London. He wore an expensive tailored suit whose stripes were too bold, and a tie that was rather less subdued than a peacock's tail. This was clearly a man on whom Beau Brummell's admonition that elegance was invisible

358

would have been wasted. Yet he had had the good taste to choose the reserved, decorous Hay-Adams over some of the more showy hotels favored by moneyed Middle East visitors to America's capital. He signed the register as Mr. Kamal, from Riyadh, Saudi Arabia. He left the porter a tip that was big enough to win an effusive show of gratitude, but not so big as to invite disrespect.

The Arab visitor's facade of urbane confidence cracked as soon as he had double-locked his door. He tore off his dark glasses, tugged loose his tie, and splashed water over his face and neck in the bathroom to wash away the sweat that had been accumulating since he had decided to claim his reservation at the Hay-Adams. Then he fished around in one of his bags for the bottle of Black Label he had packed. He swigged the liquor straight from the bottle, which did not bear any duty-free seals. The man with the Concorde tags had bought his whisky at a discount liquor store in Bethesda, Maryland. He had been in need of it that morning.

He turned on the television set in his room to catch the end of the news bulletin. As if in hope that something that appeared on the screen might contradict the reality of what he had watched on the TV news at breakfast time. The newscaster was summarizing the day's headlines. The main story, as at 8:00 that morning, was from Moscow. The screen was filled again with banner-waving women and Youth Pioneers, strutting Red Army soldiers, rocket launchers and motorized artillery. It was the traditional show of strength that the Soviet leaders organized to commemorate the anniversary of the Bolshevik Revolution. "But the big news from Moscow," the announcer's voice came over the videotape, "is that one of the most familiar Soviet leaders is missing from the podium. He is Marshal Safronov, the Defense Minister. His absence is all the more remarkable because today's parade is normally regarded as one of the most important occasions in the entire year for the Soviet armed forces, the day when they put their muscle on display and exhibit their latest hardware. Marshal Safronov's absence from the parade, for which no official explanation has been given, has intensified speculation that he may have fallen victim to a palace coup. Diplomatic observers say that the power struggle that has been raging in the Kremlin since Brezhnev's death may have been resolved in favor of General Secretary Manilov and KGB chief Strokin." The camera zoomed in to show the two men's faces as they stood, shoulder to shoulder

359

with the other members of the Politburo, on the podium. Strokin looked as if he was greatly enjoying the parade. His gold-rimmed glasses actually appeared to twinkle.

Sammy Hamad switched off the TV set in disgust. He sat down, but jumped up again immediately and started pacing back and forth across the room, from the door to the window. He would pause for a moment, each time, at the window that faced the White House. There would be no rest for him until he had seen this thing through.

Sammy Hamad had not been initiated into the secret intrigues of the men who ruled Russia and had only a hazy conception of what the fall of Marshal Safronov would mean. But he strongly suspected that it was somehow connected to the communications problems that he had experienced in recent days. When he had first been called into action, the message had come from the bookseller, Malinovsky. It had been through Malinovsky that he had received his instructions to kill Max Zimmer and to scare off the English spy, Charles Canning. Similarly, it had been Malinovsky who had passed on the order to act on November 7 according to the agreed plan. Sammy Hamad had been told to check back at regular intervals right up until the last moment for confirmation that the order was still valid. But then his contact had vanished. No one at Malinovsky's bookstores admitted to knowing where he had gone. Malinovsky himself had omitted explaining his disappearance to the Palestinian or producing someone to take charge of communications in his place. He had simply vanished, and left Sammy Hamad running loose.

Until he received the abort signal. He had picked it up that morning on his transceiver in the safe house in Bethesda—a squirt transmission relayed direct from Moscow via one of the orbital satellites that told him, in the space of less than one second, that the operation that he had been preparing for months had been called off. All teams were ordered to leave the United States by the safest route available. On no account was contact to be made with any Soviet diplomatic mission. The style of the message was different from those that Hamad had received through similar channels in the past. He was not practiced enough in espionage to be able to recognize the signature of an individual operator when he had slowed down the recorded message and replayed it, carefully translating the code. But he knew that whoever was his ultimate control in Moscow had changed.

Perhaps that was the reason for the revealing slip in the message, which referred not merely to his team but to "*all* teams." That phrase had severely wounded Sammy Hamad's pride. Prior to receiving the new signal, it had never occurred to him that he was not alone in his mission—alone, that is, apart from those he selected to work under him, whether they were contract killers like the ones he hired in Miami, or an old girlfriend he had first picked up in a training camp outside Aden. Sammy Hamad had not been pleased to discover that Moscow had arranged for him to have competition in carrying out the biggest assignment of his career. It implied a lack of confidence. He had deserved better of his employers. The media had built a mythology around terrorist leaders like Carlos. But compared to himself, Sammy Hamad believed, Carlos was a pop entertainer.

It was not in the Palestinian's character to ignore, or forgive, an affront to his dignity of this proportion. So he did not acknowledge the abort signal. Let his faceless controllers in Moscow—whoever they now happened to be—imagine whatever they liked. He would go ahead with the operation alone. The others in his team would obey without question, because he would not inform them that the original orders had been countermanded. He would show Moscow that he could succeed on his own, without the benefit of other people's planning or operational intelligence.

Besides, he believed, an American President who had openly pledged his support for Israel and the Zionist cause deserved to die.

If Sammy Hamad had been privy to Marshal Safronov's broader plan and the reasons why it would never be carried out now, his mind would probably have been the same. He was moved by a sense of fatality. He could no more turn back than a bullet that has already left the barrel of a gun.

They made a curious foursome, Sally Sherwin thought as she intercepted the stares from other diners in the restaurant of the Hay-Adams. Those who found their mere appearance fascinating, like the new Senator from Mississippi at the corner table, would be still more intrigued if they knew the actual relationships between them. Melanie Toussaint, who maintained that Washington was part of the South, had dressed outrageously for the occasion in a butterfly hat complete with a veil of antique lace, long gloves, and a billowing dress with a pattern of tiny roses. Charles was fussing over her, pointing things out on the menu.

Sally had not yet adjusted sufficiently to the surprise of her first meeting with the black singer to decide whether or not she felt jealous of her. Could you be jealous when it was so hard to begin to make comparisons between yourself and the object of that jealousy? Watching her with Charles, Sally felt an electricity that passed between them. She had to admit that she liked Melanie: the girl was quick and bright and uninhibited, radiating a spontaneous warmth to her as well as to the men. But she could see, too, that men felt a live sexuality in her presence. Even Dick Hammond was sensitive to it, sitting there at her elbow with a martini in his hand, looking as if he hadn't been to sleep for a week.

It was a sort of celebration that they had all made it through. If it was strange for Sally to be sitting there with her lover, her ex-husband, and his current mistress, well, that was less odd than what all of them had had to live with over the past two months. Between them, she realized, they might have helped to prevent a war. She trembled inwardly at the thought of what today, November 7, might have brought to their world.

Charles was in an ebullient mood, proposing toasts.

> *"Here's to you as long as you live,"* he recited,
> *"As long as you live may you want to,*
>   *May you want to as long as you live."*

It was in crashingly bad taste, given the situation, but Sally found herself joining in the second stanza that Charles had taught her in London years before.

> *"If I'm asleep when you want to, wake me.*
>   *If I don't want to, make me."*

Melanie giggled, Dick perked up a bit, and the Senator from Mississippi looked distinctly shocked.

"I want to go and ask the Senator for his views on sex," said Melanie in a stage whisper.

"Don't you dare!" Sally said.

"Why not?" Charles encouraged his girlfriend. "I think it's a wonderful idea. The Senator seems to believe that extramarital sex is a greater threat to civilization as we know it than Marshal Safronov." At the mention of the marshal's name, Canning's expression became suddenly grave. "Is it confirmed that Safronov has been executed?" he asked Dick Hammond.

"Nothing definitive yet," Hammond responded. "We're expecting to hear any minute. Behind that circus show in Red Square, Moscow is being turned inside out."

None of them paid any attention to the pretty girl in pink suede who hovered at the entrance to the restaurant for a moment before darting downstairs into the basement arcade.

The fiberglass tube was almost five feet long, but was so light that even with the trigger mechanism attached, Sammy Hamad could lift it with his thumb and forefinger. When he fitted it to his shoulder, most of the tube projected over his back.

"Now the rocket," he said to the curly-haired man who was in charge of Claudia Fiorella's sound equipment.

Gingerly, they fitted the rocket into the tube, which was about as thick as Sammy Hamad's sturdy forearm. The weapon was complete.

"Now we wait," said the Palestinian.

The SAM 7 rocket, described in NATO manuals as the Grail missile, a "man-portable antiaircraft heat-seeking device," was the dream of every terrorist organization. A dream that was attainable for many, thanks to the large number of SAM 7s that the Soviet defense industry had exported to pro-Moscow regimes in countries like Cuba, Libya, and South Yemen. Handling the SAM 7 had been one of the shortest lessons in Sammy Hamad's course at the Sanprobal military academy in the Soviet Crimea. Firing the rocket was so simple that even a child or a mental defective could hardly flunk the first attempt. All that was required was the patience to wait the six seconds required for the rocket's heat-detection system to lock onto the engine of a target aircraft.

The rocket that Sammy Hamad held in his hands could attain a speed of more than twelve hundred miles per hour. Roughly one and a half times the speed of sound. It could be fired at a plane flying as low as fifty feet, or as high as fifteen hundred feet. Once the trigger was pulled, a capsule of liquid gas was released, bringing about a sudden and extreme reduction in the temperature of the heat-sensing device installed in the nose cone of the rocket. This would enable the tracking system to home in on the heat emanating from the engine of an aircraft. Once the heat-sensing device had locked onto its target—which normally took about six seconds—the rocket would automatically be launched. Its two-stage propulsion system would allow it to develop a speed of five hundred yards per second in less time than it would take to say, "The President of the United States is dead."

Sammy Hamad had not had to trouble with the mechanics of smuggling the weapon into the United States. It had come in the diplomatic bag. But if the rocket was captured—as it was almost certain to be—nobody would be able to prove that it originated in the Soviet Union. Moscow had seen to that. The weapon was secondhand. It had been reclaimed from the Libyan stockpiles. It even had Arabic markings on it. The operation would look like the work of Arab terrorists. And so, in a sense, it was.

Hamad was surprised that SAM 7s had not been used more frequently by terrorist groups. During the Rhodesian war, Nkomo's guerrillas had used SAM 7s to bring down two civilian airliners. There had been some fumbling efforts by Palestinians in Italy and in Kenya to use the rockets against Israeli planes. But the true potential of the weapon had yet to be exploited. Sammy Hamad would demonstrate what it was.

Carefully, as if he were moving rare porcelain, he laid the launcher with its rocket across the arms of the chair by the window in Claudia's suite. A breeze stirred the drapes, which had been pulled tightly shut against the possible curiosity of anyone on the other side of Lafayette Square who might happen to be scanning the area with binoculars.

The Palestinian lifted the edge of the drapes and peered out through the narrow chink he had made. He saw the crowd of milling antinuclear protesters, held back from the White House fence by a thick cordon of policemen. The crowd was not large, but it was angry. Scuffles had already broken out. Over to the right, on the corner of the Executive Office Building, it was easy to pick out Claudia in her pink suede tunic dress from among a

364

gaggle of reporters. Mario, the last member of the team, was out of sight from the hotel window, down the road toward the back of the White House. He would be the first to see the President's helicopter lift off the lawn. Then Claudia would relay the signal.

Sammy Hamad was sure he had guessed right. According to the President's schedule, as published in the morning paper, he was due to fly to the West Coast at 2:30 in the afternoon. The demonstration made it almost certain that he would travel to Andrews Air Force Base on one of the green-and-white Presidential helicopters, instead of by car.

What a country, he thought. You did not need spies to find out the movements of the head of state. All you needed was a couple of dimes for a newspaper.

The first duty of a new ruler, wrote Machiavelli, is to destroy the family of the old prince. Strokin, the head of the KGB, had enjoyed reminding Manilov, the General Secretary of the Party, of this useful aphorism. Marshal Safronov had had a large family, although the remarkable changes that had taken place in Moscow over the past twenty-four hours had resulted in many of his former intimates swearing blind that they had been his dedicated opponents all along. It was for Strokin to decide who should be transferred to a Siberian border post or jailed as a member of the marshal's Bonapartist plot, and who should be reprieved. Conducting the purge gave him the delicious sensation of omnipotence. But it had also cost him a night without sleep, and after several hours of standing on the podium in Red Square like a stuffed dummy in order to leave no one in doubt about who now controlled Russia, Strokin was ready for a nap.

But a purge is a demanding business. There were still too many ends trailing loose for Strokin to allow himself the luxury of going home to his private apartment. There were still generals in command posts who would need to be quietly replaced. Members of his own secret service who had conspired with the marshal and would have to be liquidated. And there was possible fallout from Safronov's Project Razrukha that had urgently to be assessed and, if possible, contained.

It was the head of the First Chief Directorate who reminded

Strokin of how serious that fallout might prove to be when the KGB chief had returned to his cavernous office in Dzherzhinsky Square as soon as he was able to slip away from the parade.

Sammy Hamad had slipped his leash. In Washington. His final mission had been to prepare an assassination attempt against the President of the United States. Marshal Safronov had planned to eliminate the President, the Vice-President, and the Defense Secretary simultaneously in order to paralyze the command process in Washington as he launched Soviet missiles in a preemptive strike. Safronov's insane scheme—his effort to lash back after his secret weapon was sabotaged—had died with his fall from power. Two of the three terrorist teams that had been deployed in the United States had responded to the urgent recall signals sent from Moscow Center. But the third team, headed by the Palestinian, had not.

Strokin considered the possibilities. It was possible that Sammy Hamad had simply gone to ground or, sensing the change in Moscow, had taken the initiative and left the United States. It was possible that the Americans had arrested him. It was also possible that he had not received the recall signal and was going ahead with the original plan.

In which case, lacking support facilities and crucial operational intelligence on the President's movements and security arrangements, the Palestinian would most likely fail. But what if he succeeded?

For a moment, Strokin's plump hand rested on the special red telephone that he kept in the bottom drawer of his desk. He was tempted to call Washington, to talk in person to Director Claiborne, a man he had never met, or perhaps to Trip Gage, the National Security Adviser. To warn them. But what could he say? That a Soviet agent, assigned to Washington to murder the President, intended to do just that, even though his orders had been changed? No, of course not. He would have to camouflage the information, merely telling the Americans that he had received a tip that a crazy Palestinian was hoping to kill the President. A wild card.

There was not much to be gained from *that*. Whatever gratitude the Americans might express would be counterbalanced by the fact that they might interpret his approach as further proof that Moscow Center was involved in international terrorism.

"Tell our people in Washington to find this Palestinian," he instructed the head of the First Chief Directorate. "Make him obey orders."

"And if they can't find him?"

Strokin reflected for a moment. Would it be such a bad thing, he asked himself, if the Palestinian succeeded? The American President was aggressively anti-Soviet. Yet nobody would be able to pin his murder on Moscow Center.

On the other hand, if the Soviets warned Washington of the intended assassination, that would prove that they were not involved and might help to undermine the U.S. administration's claims that Moscow was promoting international terrorism.

Strokin realized that it was possible to have it both ways.

"This is what we'll do," he said. "We will warn the Americans. Unofficially. Nothing on paper. What's the name of that Agency man who ran the investigation of Martini?"

"Dick Hammond."

"Yes. Put one of our people in contact with Hammond. On a private basis. He probably won't know what to make of the information. If he fumbles it, that might even put an end to his career. The chances are the Americans won't be able to find this Palestinian anyway."

The mention of Marshal Safronov had cast a pall over the conversation at Sally Sherwin's table in the Hay-Adams. At least three of them, she knew, were thinking about a piece of unfinished business. The killer of her uncle, Max Zimmer, still had to be found.

Melanie, alone among them, did not catch the undertow. At least initially. She kept on poking fun at the Senator from Mississippi until, sensing the shift in the mood of the others, she too fell silent. Sally wondered how much Charles had confided in the black singer about the secret dimension of his life. Maybe not at all. But she had little doubt that if Charles found a use for Melanie beyond the amorous ones, he would end by recruiting and initiating her too. That was Charles's way. There was no insulation between his personal life and his wars.

The maître d' came up and said to Dick Hammond, "There's a call for you, sir."

"Excuse me, princess," Hammond said to Sally.

There was no more chance of defending the private space that she had tried to stake out for herself against Dick, Sally thought, than there had been against Charles. Something would always obtrude: the Agency, the Club, or some more obscure crusade. Of course she admired them, these two tall men who were too alike, both directed by some hidden gyroscope that was more powerful than family, or social pressures, or orders from on high. But you would have to be a masochist to let your life revolve around either one of them.

Dick Hammond looked moody and preoccupied when he returned from the phone booth.

"I think I'll have to get back out to Langley," he said. He glanced at the table, littered with the remains of their main course and a half-consumed bottle of Muscadet. "Don't let me break anything up."

"I'm coming too," Sally said firmly. "I'm going over to the National Press Club to talk to a reporter friend. I want to be able to tell Harry that this trip wasn't pure vacation."

Charles stood up and kissed her cheek. "I think we'll linger for a bit," he explained. "How long are you staying in Washington?" he asked Sally.

"Just overnight." She winked conspiratorially at Hammond, for Charles's benefit.

"I'll call you later today," Hammond said to the Englishman. He bent over the table to give Melanie a kiss.

"You're a million miles away," Sally whispered to Dick as he ushered her through the lobby. "What's wrong? Has something happened?"

"I'm afraid so." Deep lines of worry creased his forehead, and his hair looked grayer. The last weeks had aged him.

"Was it your phone call?" she persisted, wanting to understand.

"Not now, princess. Please."

They hurried out through the main door of the hotel, and Hammond looked around for the valet who had parked his Volvo.

"No nukes! No nukes!" came the chant of the protest marchers. The police were trying to keep the straggling crowd moving along Pennsylvania Avenue.

"It reminds me of the anti-Vietnam demonstrations," Sally remarked. Among the banners and clenched fists, there were a few people strumming on guitars.

"Yeah," Hammond agreed. "If it's not one slogan, it's another."

The press seemed to be all over the place. Among a knot of reporters and cameramen over on the corner outside the Executive Office Building, Hammond noticed a striking girl in a short pink dress who seemed vaguely familiar. As he watched, she raised her hand in the air, waving to someone he could not identify. The way she was facing, she might have been waving at *them*.

The chanting suddenly stopped. The comparative silence that descended abruptly over Lafayette Square was eerie. Then a threatening roar began to well up out of the crowd, slowly gathering force and shape.

"There he is!" a woman's banshee shriek rose above the roar.

"He's running away!" someone else yelled.

The protesters were all staring in the same direction. Hammond followed their gaze, and saw a helicopter rising from the lawn at the back of the White House. It was painted in the distinctive green-and-white colors of the Marine Corps Helicopter Squadron, based at Anacostia for the personal use of the President of the United States. A hundred feet or so off the ground, the chopper hovered for a moment, as if the men on board were surveying the demonstration.

"Come down and talk to us, you bastard," someone shouted at the helicopter.

"No nukes! No nukes!" the monotonous chant resumed.

"Is it him?" Sally asked Hammond. "Is it the President?"

Before he could answer, something beyond imagining took place.

A gray blur shot out from somewhere close by them, picking up speed as it homed in on the green-and-white chopper.

The helicopter was already climbing fast, its big blades whirring as it headed east. Then it looped around, as if the pilot was trying to dodge the trajectory of the thing that was pursuing him.

The rocket overtook him.

The heat sensors in its nose cone guided it, with unerring precision, to the engine of the chopper. In the instant of impact, so it appeared to Hammond, the presidential helicopter erupted in a ball of blue-and-crimson fire. Metal debris flew out in all directions from the incandescent core of the chopper. A thick column of black smoke rose from the dead body of the aircraft as it crashed onto the roof of the National Theater, between F Street and Pennsylvania Avenue.

Only then did Sally Sherwin scream.

For a long moment, thousands of spectators had been frozen in shock or horror. Now animation returned. Sally's scream was drowned in the general uproar. People started running in dozens, then hundreds, toward the National Theater.

A solitary protester started to applaud.

A policeman in a riot helmet hurled himself through the mob at the man who was clapping and started laying into him with his nightstick. It looked as if the cop meant to kill him.

Colonel Ted Masters, the head of the White House Military Office, led the way through the tunnel. Approached through a thick steel door in the blastproofed basement of the East Wing, it ran under the Treasury Building to a secret exit on the other side. It was the first time, so far as Masters knew, that the tunnel had actually been used by the Commander in Chief; most Presidents had been only vaguely aware of its existence.

Behind Masters, flanked by Secret Service agents, the President maintained a brisk pace, glancing from time to time at the bunks and caches of canned food and medical supplies that had been stowed along the sides of the tunnel. Limping along at his left elbow was Trip Gage, the National Security Adviser, who had damaged his ankle in a riding accident. Bringing up the rear was a warrant officer carrying the Football—a black leather briefcase with a combination lock, chained to his wrist, that contained the black-bound briefing books that explained the options available to the President of the United States if the Soviets launched a nuclear attack.

"At least we're getting a little exercise," the President quipped to Trip Gage. "But I don't understand why we couldn't leave by the front door. This feels, well, a little furtive."

"I hope it was just a false alarm, Mr. President," said Gage. "But we couldn't afford to take the risk. Not today."

It had been less than fifteen minutes since he had received the call from Dick Hammond. His Agency friend had told him that he had received an extraordinary warning that a Palestinian called Sammy Hamad was planning to assassinate the President that same day. The call had come from Voldemar Titov. Hammond knew the name, because the same KGB man had given Malinovsky his orders to get out—and pursued Sally through the streets of New York. Hammond was unsure whether he could believe information coming through a KGB "back channel," but he had pleaded with the National Security Adviser to persuade the President not to stick to his prepared schedule. Hammond had been right on too many things before for Trip Gage to dismiss the warning. He had called in Ted Masters and asked him to arrange alternative transportation from the White House to Andrews Air Force Base. Masters had welcomed the assignment as a chance to test one of the possible escape routes that might have to be used in the event of a full-scale nuclear alert. Mercifully, the President had not objected to an underground walk to the armor-plated limousines awaiting them on the other side of the Treasury Building.

The ruse would be pointless, Masters had observed, unless it were made to appear that the President was keeping to his advertised program. So they had sent a pilot up in the presidential helicopter with a Secret Service agent posing as the head of state. They could only guess at where or how the attack would come—if it came at all.

None of them had foreseen what actually happened.

Charles Canning forced a way for himself and Melanie through the crush of diners and waiters fighting to get out of the restaurant. Word had already spread among the people swarming through the hotel lobby. Canning heard someone say, "The President's been killed." Before they got to the door, he saw Dick Hammond, towering above the throng as he pushed his way back inside.

"Rocket," he spoke to Canning in telegraphese. "Downed a chopper. Must have been fired from inside the hotel."

Hammond grabbed a distraught-looking assistant manager.

"Stop the elevators," he said.

"What?"

He flashed his Agency identification. It carried no legal force, but under the circumstances, it would have to suffice. "I said, stop the elevators," he repeated in the calm voice that carries more authority, in conditions of panic, than a shouted command. "There are killers inside the hotel."

Uncertainly, the assistant manager obeyed.

"Service exit?"

The manager pointed the way downstairs. Uniformed police and Secret Service agents were now pressing into the lobby, against the human tide.

"Block off the exits," Hammond said authoritatively to a sergeant in riot gear. "Make sure nobody leaves."

They were too late to stop an expensively dressed Middle Eastern gentleman who had whisked out the door and into a waiting pearl-gray stretch limousine in the first minutes after the helicopter exploded. Even as the police started to throw up makeshift cordons around the area, they did not think to challenge the VIP car. Conspicuous wealth, Sammy Hamad had long believed, was one of the most effective forms of camouflage.

The Palestinian did not favor kamikaze operations. At least not when his own life was involved. He was less scrupulous about the lives of those he employed. The Italians were expendable. Even the succulent Claudia. Let them make their own getaway if they could. If not, they knew nothing that would lead the Americans to him. Within twenty minutes, he would have changed his appearance and his identity. He would no longer be Mr. Kamal from Riyadh, but Señor Herrera from Caracas, a businessman with interests in Florida. From Miami it was an easy jump to Mexico City and from there, via Cuba, to his old sanctuary in South Yemen.

He was sure the Americans would not catch up with him. But he felt a moment of fear, on the drive back to the safe house in Bethesda, when he considered the possible reactions of Moscow Center. By rights he should be made a Hero of the Soviet Union. But he had disobeyed orders. And the knowledge inside his head, if ever released, would be explosive for the Soviet leadership. He thought for a moment about the fate of Lee Harvey Oswald, Kennedy's assassin. And wondered if there was any safe place on earth for the assassin of an American President to hide.

When they got to the house in a quiet cul-de-sac in Bethesda, the driver of the hired limousine was surprised by the Arab's request that they should put the car in the garage for an hour while he sorted out some papers inside. But the Saudi gentleman had already been generous with his tips, and the driver was not disposed to question his wishes. Perhaps he wanted to avoid ostentation in view of the neighbors in this quiet, middle-class neighborhood.

As they drove into the garage, the metal door automatically closed behind them. At the same moment, Sammy Hamad fired a single bullet, at point-blank range, through the silencer of his Walther P-38 into the back of the driver's neck.

Charles Canning was first up the emergency stairs. Bounding three steps at a time past a startled maid loaded up with towels, he collided with a short, swarthy man on the second landing. The man was toting a television camera. The shock of the impact sent it skimming off his shoulder. Charles managed to catch it, like a basketball, before it went crashing down the stairs.

"Sorry," he apologized.

The Englishman was in the process of handing back the camera when he noticed there was something odd about it. There was no film in the camera. It was the first time he had seen a television cameraman rushing to film a violent scene without preloading his camera.

"Are you from one of the networks?"

"Rome TV." The man's voice was heavily accented.

"Never heard of it." Canning was wondering why the cameraman would have been inside the hotel, instead of outside, filming the antinuclear demonstration, when the rocket was fired. He stood across the stairs, still holding onto the camera, blocking the man's path.

At that point, the man made an elementary mistake. He reached for the knife that was strapped to the side of his right leg, under his jeans. He just had time to get it out before Canning felled him with a karate chop.

The Englishman jumped to one side as the Italian fell heavily down the stairs.

Dick Hammond, racing up behind them, reached him just as he rolled onto the first landing.

"Shit," the American swore softly as he kicked the Italian over onto his back. He had fallen onto the blade of his own knife.

The hotel register told them the rest of the story. Two more Italians accredited to "Rome TV" had checked in, one of them a girl reporter called Claudia Fiorella. The police found the rocket launcher in her room, hastily concealed under the mattress. Also, a Mr. Kamal from Saudi Arabia had checked in that morning but subsequently vanished. The police searched his elegant bags, and found they were stuffed with newspapers.

Dick Hammond remembered the sexy girl in pink suede and gave the description to the police. He was sure she must be Claudia.

The two Italians ran into a police roadblock on the way to Dulles Airport. They tried to drive through it, and a police sniper shot the man at the wheel through the back of the head. Claudia tried to grab the wheel, but the car swerved off the road, rolling over and over. They got her out of the wreckage, but she died on the way to the hospital before they could extract more than one word from her. The name "Sammy" mumbled over and over.

That was enough to clinch it for Hammond and Canning.

They made a pact between themselves that night.

Wherever Sammy Hamad went to ground, they would seek him out and kill him.

35

Every Western secret service and police organization was brought in on the worldwide manhunt for Sammy Hamad. Even Moscow Center was consulted. But, as expected, the Soviets expressed complete ignorance about the whereabouts of the man who had tried to kill the President. Dick Hammond tried to reach Voldemar Titov, the KGB man who had supplied the tip that Hamad was gunning for the President. He was told that Titov had been recalled to Moscow.

In the end, it was Dicky Prince in London who had called Charles Canning, the day before Thanksgiving, with the news that a man who matched the description of the assassin had turned up in his old sanctuary in South Yemen.

"I think you'd best come home and talk about it," Dicky Prince said in a guarded fashion over the transatlantic line.

Canning and Dick Hammond both canceled their dates for the Thanksgiving weekend. The Englishman had planned to fly to New Orleans to spend the holiday with Melanie in her home town. "I promise we'll make it for Mardi Gras," he said to her. Melanie took the news philosophically. "My mother wouldn't approve of you anyway," she said. Sally Sherwin was less relaxed. She saw their self-appointed mission as a stupid, and possibly suicidal, vendetta. Even if they caught up with the Palestinian, they could not compensate for the horror he had already inflicted. It would not bring back Uncle Max. Or justify Dick and Charles risking their own lives.

"Just give me time enough to get there and back," Hammond entreated her. "This is one date I intend to keep." And he showed her photographs of the lovely old inn at East Hampton where he had made reservations for their post-Thanksgiving vacation.

They met Dicky Prince at the Army and Navy Club on Piccadilly, known to its familiars as the "In and Out" because of the big signs painted on the pillars at the entrance and exit of the circling driveway. The martinis served in the bar were big enough and stiff enough to satisfy even Dick Hammond, although they were served at a lukewarm temperature that would have brought down the wrath of any New York bartender. After lunch they sat outside in the wan sunlight of the flagstoned courtyard, sipping port at a table set apart under the trees.

"We have a man at al-Gheidda," Dicky Prince explained. "He worked for the Firm in Aden in the old days, before we handed over power to the terrorists. Somehow he has managed to stay alive. Even more exceptional, he hasn't sold out. So far as we can ascertain."

That was exceptional for a Yemeni, Canning agreed. He remembered the first South Yemeni defector he had picked up during his time in Oman, a captain in the security police. The man had heard that the pickings were better on the Sultan's side of the border, and had seized his moment to walk across. When asked about his wife and children, left behind in a dusty frontier village, he had shrugged his shoulders and said, "I can always get another wife."

Dicky Prince took a pinch of snuff from the silver box attached to the watch chain that girded from the broad expanse of his waistcoat. His doctor, to his considerable chagrin, had forbidden him cigars. He knew that some of the American Cousins regarded his snuff-taking, like the monocle that dangled, unused but always visible, from a black cord around his neck, as a sign of foppish eccentricity. It was a mistake from which those who had seen him in action quickly recovered.

"Our chap in al-Gheidda," Prince continued, "managed to get a signal out this week. It seems there's been great excitement over a new arrival. They've got him shut up in the officers' quarters in the camp outside the town in the restricted area where the East German instructors live. He's got special protection. It's not altogether clear whether that's to keep other people from getting to him or to keep him from getting out."

"Has our chap actually seen him?" Canning asked.

"Yes. Our man works in the canteen. On several occasions he's been ordered to serve special meals in the officers' quarters, and he got a good look at this new fellow. Says he's definitely a Palestinian, and that he remembers seeing him a year or two back, when he was helping to train terrorists from other places. Our man says that he recalls this Palestinian vividly, because he had a particularly vicious temperament. Seems he shot some trainee who answered back to him. Also, our chap says this Palestinian always seemed to be on especially close terms with the Slavs and the Krauts."

Canning and Hammond looked at each other.

"It sounds like Sammy Hamad, all right," the American commented.

"How do we get to him?" asked Canning.

"I'm afraid that's your lookout," said Dicky Prince. "Naturally, HMG could in no way be involved in any act that might violate the sovereignty of the People's Democratic Republic of Yemen."

"Naturally," Canning observed acidly.

"However." Prince gave the two men at his table a conspiratorial wink. "It's not all that difficult to travel around in South Yemen if you've got a strong pair of boots. I would have thought that you knew rather a lot about that, Charles, after your Omani stint. You could try going in from the Saudi side." He glanced at Hammond. "But, for my money, I'd be inclined to start out from the sultanate. Al-Gheidda isn't far from the Omani border. And you've got quite a few IOUs outstanding down there, Charles. And if you need a chit from me, you'll have it. Nothing on paper, of course."

"Of course."

MUSCAT, *November 27*

Pushing the bay stallion forward at full gallop, Charles Canning rode across the path of the player in blue. Leaning low from the saddle, so his head grazed the neck of the straining horse, he intercepted the ball and hammered it back toward the blue team's goal. It was a perfect pass. The ball was neatly fielded by a player whose shirt, like Charles's, bore the crossed daggers and palm trees of the Sultanate of Oman, embroidered in red and gold. His full black beard and jeweled turban set him apart from the other riders on the field. Whooping with pleasure, he pummeled the ball on with his mallet to make the last score of the game. The winning goal.

"Well played, Charles!" shouted the turbaned polo player as he came riding up to the Englishman at the close of the game. His accent was pure Sandhurst. Between the words, you could almost hear the sound of smartly drilled cadets springing to attention.

"Thank you, your majesty," Canning acknowledged the young Sultan's salutation.

"I can't say the same for your American friend." The Sultan gestured toward Hammond, who was awkwardly dismounting from his palomino mare. "He sits a horse as if it were a tractor. I bet he'll be sore tonight."

"I don't think they play much polo in Washington."

When they had showered and changed, Canning and Hammond joined the Sultan in the pavilion, where white-robed attendants brought them thimble-small cups of strong, sweetened coffee, tall glasses of fruit juice, and trays of candied delicacies. On the flight from London, Canning had tried to explain to his American friend the uniqueness of the tiny sultanate that stood guard over the oil routes of the West through the Strait of Hormuz, and of Oman's ruler. The Omanis, looking southward to the Indian Ocean and the African coast instead of northward or westward to the Mediterranean, had always stood apart from the rest of the Arab world. Fiercely independent, they had their own proud and often bloody history as colonizers and privateers. Skilled in the arts of war, they looked on their Arabian neighbors with aloof disdain. Like the other Gulf rulers, the Sultan had turned to foreigners— Europeans, Pakistanis, South Koreans—to supply the skills and the labor to build the new cities and highways and to run the new businesses that were the visible signs of his country's oil wealth, only modest by Saudi standards. But, unlike the others, he had refused to admit radical Palestinians, whom he saw as the agents of future revolutions in the fragile neighboring sheikhdoms. He apologized to no one for his deep emotional attachment to the British, who had helped to install him in place of his brutishly repressive father, had defended him in his war against Communist guerrillas backed by South Yemen, and still supplied contract officers and advisers for his security forces. The Moslem ruler of a backward and still mostly illiterate people, he had declined the temptation to win easy applause in the Arab world by attributing all the problems of his troubled region to Zionist maneuvers. For years he had been warning all who would listen that the main challenge to the stability of the Gulf states came from the Soviets and their proxies.

It was to this man that Canning now turned in his quest for Max Zimmer's killer.

"You should have seen Charles in the old days," the Sultan was saying to Hammond. "He not only rode like one of us, he looked like a Dhofari. Killed like one, too. Mustafa remembers well. Don't you?"

The Sultan turned to a wiry man with a clipped mustache. He was the player from whom Canning had stolen the ball in the last chukka.

"Charles saved my life," said Mustafa Ghazi, who was now, as the Sultan's personal military aide and constant riding companion, one of the most powerful men in Muscat. He recounted how a small border post that he had once commanded had been surprised by a guerrilla attack, mounted from across the Yemeni border. Canning had come down from the hills with his *firqa*—a unit composed of defectors from the rebel camp and enthusiastic cutthroats from the hills—and beaten off the attack. His eyes shone as brightly as the curved ceremonial dagger that he now wore from the sash around his robe.

"Well, Charles," said the Sultan when the story was finished. "This is your home. Tell us what you need."

Canning explained. It did not take long to state his request. He mentioned several men by name, men who had fought with him in the *firqas* of the old days, and were bound to him by the memory of shared danger. One of them, Canning learned, had been killed, racing around town in a car he had never learned how to drive.

"You can have the others," the Sultan said. "If you can find them. Mustafa will take you."

"With your permission, your majesty," Mustafa intervened, "I

379

would like to accompany Charles and Mr. Hammond on their mission."

The Sultan considered the request.

"Begging your leave, your majesty." The new voice was that of a handsome Englishman who used too much hair oil and looked the part of an old-fashioned lady-killer in his tailored fawn safari suit. Canning had met him before. His name was Peter Hill-Waring, a former member of the Firm who was employed as one of the Sultan's advisers and kept up his membership at White's Club in London.

"I believe it would be extremely inadvisable to allow Colonel Ghazi to enter Yemeni territory. If he were to fall into enemy hands, that would provide the Aden government with evidence of direct Omani intervention, sanctioned at the highest level. It would even supply the South Yemenis and their Soviet friends with a *casus belli*, if they happen to be looking for one." Hill-Waring smoothed the crease on his starched trousers.

"But the Yemenis do not respect our border," Mustafa protested. "They are still infiltrating terrorists all the time."

"He's right, Mustafa," Canning said quietly.

"Yes," the Sultan pronounced. "Mustafa will take you to the border, but no farther. We will be reunited soon. *Inshallah*."

NEAR AL-GHEIDDA,
PEOPLE'S DEMOCRATIC REPUBLIC OF YEMEN,
November 29

After the long trek through the rugged Hadhramaut with its dizzying gorges, moving mostly by night to avoid the South Yemeni spotter planes, it was pleasant to have wheels for the last stage of the journey. It had been providential, Canning thought, that they had run into the security patrol. They had spotted the old Russian-made armored car from the brow of a hill in the glow of early dawn that made the contours of the rocky landscape, monotonous under the midday sun, leap to the eye in a jagged, dramatic contrast of light and shade. Canning recognized the cumbersome vehicle, rattling along on six huge wheels, as a

380

BTR-152, an armored monster mass-produced in the fifties that the Russians had taken to passing on as a hand-me-down to their Third World protégés. It was moving along a rough track two miles or so away. Through his field glasses Canning could see clearly the heavy machine gun mounted at the front of the open-roofed vehicle, and counted twelve men on board. Two of them, in distinctive uniforms, appeared to be Europeans.

"Couldn't be better," the Englishman whispered to Dick Hammond. "The East Germans are out on the warpath. I can see one who's about my size. I'm not so sure about you." He glanced dubiously at the big American, improbably decked out in the purplish robes and headgear and swinging cartridges of a Dhofari tribesman. Clustered around them were four lean, sun-blackened men on whom the traditional garb looked like anything but fancy dress. The remnants of Canning's best *firqa*.

"How do we get to them?" asked Hammond.

"Ambush?" Canning rapidly assessed their chances. In plain view from their hilltop perch, a few hundred yards over to the west, was a narrow ravine through which the armored car would have to pass. "I don't know if there's time," he reflected aloud.

"No problem," said Hammond, who had borrowed the field glasses. "Look."

The armored car had stopped down the road. Several men climbed down and wandered off among the boulders, fumbling at their flies.

"Let's move, then," said Canning. He rapped out his orders in passable Arabic to Abdullah, the oldest and toughest of his Dhofari fighters. Surefooted as mountain goats, the Arabs raced toward the edge of the ravine.

"Like shooting ducks in a bathtub," Hammond commented when they were crouched on the cliff, looking down on the winding stretch of dirt road. From their snipers' positions above, the men in the open-roofed armored car would be defenseless targets. "Just one hitch," the American added. "How do we do it without breaking radio silence? If they put out an alarm, the whole mission could be blown right here."

Canning studied the terrain. Thanks to the zigzag course of the dirt road, this stretch was out of sight from the present position of the armored car. The edge of the road was littered with boulders

381

that had rolled down the sides of the ravine. There were several big freestanding rocks scattered about them on the clifftop. Canning was squatting behind one that vaguely resembled a helmet.

"Landslide," he said. "Come on, it's worth a try."

He signaled Abdullah, and they all started heaving and pushing at the biggest of the loose boulders. The first to crash down rolled to a stop at the side of the dirt road, leaving plenty of room for a vehicle to pass. The next two rocks, carrying smaller ones in the train, landed closer to the middle, but there was still room to get by.

Hammond paused to take a look over at the other side of the hill.

"They're moving," he announced.

"This one has to do it," Canning said. Together, he and the American had failed to budge the helmet rock. Now Abdullah and another of the Dhofaris lent a hand. The boulder began to sway back and forth. It finally tumbled down, blocking the road as neatly as if it had been placed by a crane, moments before the armored car came in sight.

The men waiting on the clifftop flattened themselves to the ground as the Yemeni driver braked to a halt. One of the East Germans, the one wearing a lieutenant's uniform, nervously scanned the ridges above him. The other swung the heavy machine gun in a slow arc.

Then the East German lieutenant barked an order, and the armored car reversed quickly back down the road, out of the ravine.

"Have we blown it?" Hammond whispered.

They had their answer within a couple of minutes.

The East German lieutenant and six of the Yemenis came walking back up the road, their Kalashnikovs cradled at the ready. When they saw no sign of life, they formed up a work party. Five of the Yemenis started trying to shift the rocks, while the lieutenant and another soldier kept watch.

"Take them when you hear my signal," Canning whispered to Hammond. "Abdullah and I will take the others."

Hammond nodded, readying his compact MP5 submachine gun. Canning took his short-barreled pump shotgun in one hand and a six-inch fighting knife in the other. Hammond noticed that Abdullah was bristling with knives.

On the other side of the ridge, the East German sergeant was still manning his heavy machine gun, and the Yemeni driver was still at his seat. The remaining men were slouched by the roadside, sunning themselves. No one seemed to be paying any attention to the radio. Abdullah's first knife, thrown from a distance of thirty feet, caught the sergeant just below the chin. He collapsed almost soundlessly, with the low noise of the last sink water going down the drain. As the driver turned, mouth agape, Abdullah's second knife thudded into his chest, just below the collarbone. The other Yemeni soldiers, shaking from their stupor, had not had time to aim their weapons before Canning downed two of them, pumping shells from his shotgun. The third dropped his gun and started running. Abdullah took aim with the new M-10 rifle the Englishman had given him as a token of friendship—and an inducement to join the mission—and shot him between the shoulder blades.

The sound of automatic fire from back along the road, in the ravine, stopped a few minutes later.

As Canning later observed, they had earned themselves a first-class ticket to the Camp of the Martyrs.

He was sitting in the front seat of the armored car, wearing the uniform of the East German lieutenant. It had only one bullet hole, too low down to be noticed from outside the vehicle, and, as he had predicted, it fitted fairly well for something off the hook. Hammond's uniform, with its sergeant's stripes, was without bullet holes. But the trousers were about four inches too short and he had left the tunic partly unbuttoned for fear that the seams might burst.

CAMP OF THE MARTYRS, NEAR AL-GHEIDDA, SOUTH YEMEN, *November 29*

The small man with the fixed smile and a napkin over his arm hovered by the center table in the officers' mess after serving the *mezze*. The Russian in civilian clothes seemed to be irritated by the waiter's attentions. He muttered something to Langemann, the East German camp commandant. The East German shooed the waiter back into the kitchen.

Most of the conversation at the table was in English, a language that the waiter understood well. He had a quick mind, this particular waiter, to match the rapid movements with which he darted about on his short legs. His friends called him Lizard. His British employers had adopted the nickname as his working cryptonym. The Lizard noted that the Russian's English was stilted, the product, no doubt, of a crash course in a language laboratory. When the Russian had trouble communicating, he would switch back to his native tongue. The third man at the table, the Palestinian, obviously understood some Russian, but appeared to be embarrassed at being required to sustain conversation in it. But the Lizard, a quick judge of character, had gauged that this was not the root cause of the Palestinian's nervousness. From the moment the three men had entered the canteen, it had been plain that the Palestinian was terrified of the Russian. From the few phrases that the Lizard had been able to catch, he had learned only that there was some question about whether the Palestinian would be taken to Moscow. That, and the name he had just heard mentioned. Sammy Hamad. That confirmed that this was the man that the Lizard's British employers were seeking. Tonight, he thought, he would try to sneak out of the camp to the radio transmitter he had secreted in a niche at the base of the fieldstone wall around his house.

The hour was early for lunch, and the officers' mess was almost deserted. A couple of East Germans were sitting in the corner of the canteen, as far away from the Russians' table as possible. Everyone, even Langemann, seemed to live in fear of the new arrival. He must be a powerful man at Moscow Center, the Lizard concluded. His presence would also interest the Firm. On the pretext of delivering another round of the fizzy local beer, served up in tall brown bottles, he reentered the mess. Behind him, the smell of sizzling lamb kebabs wafted out of the kitchens. The East German instructors at the camp ate a lot better than their trainees, who came not only from all over the Arab world, but from Latin America, Italy, Holland, Ireland, and even the United States.

The Palestinian seized the beer gratefully, but the Russian

roughly took the bottle away from him. Noting the gesture, the Lizard decided he had been correct in his guess that the special security precautions that had been arranged for Sammy Hamad meant not that he was a VIP guest, but that he was a prisoner. This Palestinian whom he had seen swaggering about a couple of years before, secure and self-important in his special relationship with the Soviets, had somehow fallen under a cloud.

Langemann ordered the waiter to hurry up with the lunch service, and he scurried back out to the kitchens. He relayed the order to the fat, oily Yemeni cook, who had run a cheap whorehouse down by the docks in Aden before the British left and the new regime, in its early flush of revolutionary puritanism, had the establishment closed down. The cook slewed the saliva around in his mouth and ceremonially spat once on each of the kebabs that he was now removing from the grill. The skewers were like long, narrow steel knives.

As the Lizard returned to the canteen with the nine kebabs tastefully arranged on a large salver, he saw that the room was beginning to fill up. He frowned slightly as he assessed the two new arrivals, an East German lieutenant he had never set eyes on before and a sergeant. They must be bearing a dispatch, he thought, since NCOs were not admitted to the officers' mess. Furthermore, this sergent was improperly dressed. His jacket was not correctly buttoned, and his trousers looked as if they had shrunk in the wash. Worst of all, he still had his automatic rifle slung from his shoulder.

Langemann, the commandant, got up from the table so fast that he almost collided with the tray of food that the Lizard had been preparing to serve. Langemann glared balefully at these unfamiliar soldiers whose breach of protocol had embarrassed him in the presence of his most important Russian visitor.

The lieutenant's eyes flicked from one face in the room to the next, taking in the two East Germans sitting by the far wall. His gaze came to rest on the Palestinian.

"Sammy Hamad?" the unfamiliar lieutenant inquired coolly.

The Palestinian's reflexes were quicker than those of his lunch companions. Langemann stood frozen in rage as Charles Canning pulled out his heavy service pistol and Dick Hammond unslung his rifle. The Russian had his beer stein halfway to his mouth. But Sammy Hamad slid off his chair, scampered between Langemann's legs, and ran, ducking and weaving, toward the kitchen.

Dick Hammond, covering the far table, shot one of the East Germans while he was still fumbling at his holster. The second had time to fire back, but the shot went wild. Hammond fired again, aiming for the stomach, and the man dropped to the floor.

Langemann had even less chance. As he groped for his own gun, Canning put a 9mm bullet between his eyes with the same impersonal exactitude he would have applied to hitting the center of a bull's-eye.

The Russian put his hands up.

"All right, tovarich," said Canning. "Just stand quietly against the wall over there, will you? Keep an eye on him, Dick."

Canning was already running toward the kitchen, after Sammy Hamad.

"Look out, Charles!"

Hammond's shouted warning came too late. A bullet clanged against the barrel of Canning's automatic, knocking it from his hand. So the Palestinian still had a gun. As Hammond crouched down, trying to cover the Englishman from behind, a second bullet zinged past. The American gave a short cry of pain. A dark-red stain began to spread on his left arm, just below the shoulder, as he tried to steady the rifle with his other arm.

As the shooting began, the Lizard had dropped his salver and remained hunched down below one of the tables. He now saw the action unfolding jerkily, almost in separate frames, as in an animated cartoon that is being wound too slowly. While Canning was scrabbling around on the floor, the Russian, who had been pressed motionless to the wall, was now reaching for his own gun, unnoticed by either of the strangers wearing East German uniforms. In the next frame, the Lizard assessed, the Russian would shoot the man who had had his gun blown out of his hand. The Lizard was sure that the two intruders must have been sent by the Firm. By his own employer.

The Lizard had not survived through futile acts of heroics but by skulking, unnoticed, in the shadows. He now did something that was thoroughly untypical. He scooped up three of the swordlike skewers in one hand and two in the other and ran, full-pelt, at the Russian. There was a hiss like escaping gas as the Lizard drove the five steel points into the well-padded Russian's chest and stomach. The Russian screamed, and blood began to spurt from him in all directions. He bled, the Lizard thought philosophically, exactly like a stuck pig. He savored the short moment of dreamlike objectivity that comes to a man who has chosen the circumstances of his own death. His hands were still on the skewers when the East German security guards burst through the door of the canteen and pumped so many machine-gun bullets into him that his corpse was still writhing and dancing on the floor after life had expired.

In the kitchen, the cook had flattened himself, trembling, against the open door of the pantry. Crumbs from the baklava he had been munching while preparing lunch for the East Germans were visible on his stubbly chins. Sammy Hamad ignored the Yemeni. He was aiming his pistol at the hollow between Canning's shoulder blades as the Englishman stooped on the linoleum-covered floor, redolent of the disinfectant with which Commandant Langemann had insisted it be swabbed three times a day.

Canning could not see his pistol. But he could see the toe of one of Sammy Hamad's desert boots.

"Move, Charles!" he heard Hammond yell as the shooting erupted from behind them, in the dining room.

There was nothing else, the Englishman realized, that he could do.

Weaponless, he hurled himself at the Palestinian, his fingers tensed into claws that were reaching for Sammy Hamad's throat, his eyes.

The Palestinian pulled the trigger of his Makarov automatic before Canning reached him.

And his gun jammed.

Sammy Hamad ran back into the kitchen, looking for an exit.

Canning clutched at the handle of the heavy butcher's knife on the chopping block beside the oven. The cook had been using it to slice the lamb for the kebabs.

The Englishman caught up with Sammy Hamad before he had managed to unfasten the heavy bolts on the kitchen door. He pulled the Palestinian's head back by the hair. And cut his throat in the style approved by the Dhofaris, slipping the blade in smoothly behind the windpipe.

"This is for Max," Canning breathed.

Hammond, sniping at the East German guards who had overrun the canteen from the cover of the kitchen doorway, glanced back at the scene behind him and turned quickly away, slightly nauseous.

36

Jerry Sarkesian turned off the engine of his rheumatic Volkswagen in the Rosslyn parking lot and decided that he was
disgusted with his life. His wife was nagging at him to get rid of
the car, which had developed an ominous banging sound somewhere inside the motor. She had vetoed his plan to go out to
dinner at the Orleans House, where he could load up with as
much bread and salad, smothered in creamy dressing, as he could
eat, on top of a man-sized plate of prime ribs. Instead they were
going to a Japanese eatery where the chefs played at being Zorro
with the food right under your nose. If she disliked having a fat
husband, he had told her, she should marry somebody else. He had
long passed the stage when he was likely to be converted to bean
shoots and jogging. Anyway, she was not much of a clothes hanger
herself. She had probably been stocking up on chocolate-chip
cookies all afternoon to get through the evening meal.

The dismal prospect of dinner with his wife had deepened Jerry
Sarkesian's gloom. But it was not its main source. That was the
funny thing. The man from the Agency's Office of Security
normally felt a sense of euphoria when he had finished a
successful interrogation and closed the book on a case. Not this
time.

He kept thinking about the lonely, dumpy little woman he had
been grilling every couple of days for almost three weeks. And
about her kid, who looked so unlike her, with his black hair, his
fine, sensitive features and dark, intelligent eyes. He felt as
virtuous about breaking Trudy Cook as he would have felt about
stealing from a collection box. She had no anchor in her life,

nothing to hold on to. The Russians, she knew, had abandoned her. Martini, the man who had bedded her, recruited her for the KGB, and, in all likelihood, fathered her child, was back in Moscow. If he cared what happened to her, he had not bothered to send a message. Her control, Malinovsky, had run out on her as soon as the investigators started to close in, without even taking the trouble to send her a warning signal.

Would she have taken the boy and gone to Moscow if they had asked her? Jerry Sarkesian was not sure of the answer to that. Trudy Cook might be a traitor, but she was not a Communist or an admirer of the Soviet system. Despite all that she had brought to the KGB—including the life of Hussar, and the lives of other Russians who had made contact with the Agency—she had not done it out of conviction. She was not cast in the mold of the agents the Soviets recruited in the thirties, true believers who were convinced that Moscow held the secret of the perfect society. The damage she had been able to do was out of all proportion to her character and her motives. She had been inspired by emotions no more exalted than those that led a bored housewife in a midafternoon soap opera into the arms of a handsome stranger: by loneliness and hope. The hope of finding real passion, perhaps even love. Trudy Cook made the mistake of choosing a Russian spy instead of a traveling salesman. That meant signing a contract with no escape clause.

She had not stood up to Jerry Sarkesian's insistent questioning for long. He suspected that that was not only because she felt no loyalty toward the Russians, who had callously ditched her, but because of her anguish over what had happened to Les Winter. The head of the Agency's Soviet Division had been more than her boss over many years. He had been almost her idol. Why else would she name her child—Martini's child—after Les Winter? Ironically, over an amazingly long period of time there had been no direct contradiction between her work for the Russians and her fierce loyalty to her Agency boss. On the contrary. The material supplied by Martini had strengthened Les Winter in the Agency's internal feuds. Martini had been Winter's trump card in his contest with Max Zimmer. In many ways, Winter's career had been built on the webs of deception spun by Krylov in Moscow Center.

That had all changed after Max Zimmer's murder. Then the

webs had begun to unravel. Suspicion turned on Winter, and, although he was cleared in the end of the charge of being a Soviet mole, enough of his past came crawling out of the places he had tried to bury it to destroy his Agency career. He agreed to accept premature retirement. That, more than the knowledge that she had caused the death of Hussar, was the root of the intense feeling of guilt that had undermined Trudy Cook's will to resist interrogation. Sarkesian felt that Les Winter, more than he himself, had been responsible for her confession.

Sarkesian wondered what would happen to the boy. Martini's boy. He doubted that the father would ever send for him. Someone had said Trudy Cook had an aunt living in Salt Lake City. Maybe Martini's son would grow up a Mormon.

37

On the video monitors in the control room at the specially prepared launch site at Vandenberg Air Force Base, the President watched the orange flash and the rising clouds of vapor as the rocket engines ignited.

"Lift-off, Mr. President," General Brennan murmured as the twin booster rockets carried the first of his Cosmic Interceptors upward into space. "There was a time when I thought we weren't gonna make it."

The President shook hands, one by one, with the men gathered around him in the control station: the scientist, Ed Greenhouse; the Defense Secretary, Jake Waggoner; the Secretary of State, Henry Peyton; his National Security Adviser, Trip Gage. And George Brennan. It was odd to find them all together without a press camera in sight. It was not an occasion for the media, the President had flatly ruled. But it was an occasion that none of them had wanted to miss.

"This is a proud day for the United States," said the President. "And I am proud that the launch took place in my home state. The step we have taken today makes it possible to hope that mankind can end the long reign of nuclear terror."

"The Soviets will try again, of course," Secretary Peyton observed. "But for the first time in years, we have the edge. The commanding edge."

"The only reason we ever lost it," General Brennan chipped in, "is that we allowed our nerve and our judgment processes to be eroded. Mr. President, you may be familiar with the story of the three men who were shipwrecked on a cannibal island."

392

"As a matter of fact, I'm not." It was a day to indulge George Brennan, the President thought, even if he was going to lapse into folk humor.

"Well, a Frenchman, an Englishman, and an American were all shipwrecked on this cannibal island," Brennan pursued, needing no further encouragement. "The cannibal chief told them that they were all going to be slaughtered and cooked for lunch the following day. He also told them that by way of compensation, he was ready to grant any reasonable request as to how they wished to spend their last twenty-four hours."

The President stood patiently in the middle of the control room, hands clasped behind his back, his head slightly inclined.

"The Frenchman pointed to a beautiful cannibal girl," Brennan went on, "and said he wanted to spend his last day with her. The Englishman demanded pen and ink so he could write to the United Nations and Her Majesty the Queen to protest such treatment of a British subject. Their requests were instantly granted. But the American had a more unusual request. He asked to be taken into the village clearing, bent over, and given a good hard kick in the rear end.

"The cannibal chief was astonished, but he agreed to do what the American wanted. So the next day, they took the American into the village clearing, and the chief administered a forceful kick to his backside. As soon as this had been done, the American whipped out a tommy-gun he had had concealed in his pants all along and mowed down all the cannibal warriors.

"As soon as they heard the shots, the Frenchman and the Englishman came hurrying out of the bushes. Needless to say, they were delighted by the way things had turned out. But they demanded to know why the American had not used his weapon at the very beginning, and saved them from all the distress and humiliation.

"The American explained that he would not have felt morally justified in using his gun unless he had first been kicked in the rear end. Even though he knew he was on the menu for lunch that day."

The President chuckled, and some of the others joined in.

"That, Mr. President," General Brennan moralized, "is the condition in which this country has languished when it came to dealing with those who were hostile to us. In fact, we were in an even worse condition, since we refused—thanks to the Soviets' skill in exploiting our endless capacity for self-deception—to believe we were going to be cooked for lunch even when the pot was simmering. In the meantime, we agonized over the moral justification for acting to defend our legitimate interests, and neglected to maintain the resources that are indispensable to our national survival. No wonder our friends in Moscow concluded that we were irrational and terminally effete.

"This time," Brennan concluded, "we have been granted a reprieve, after we came closer to going under than at any previous stage in our twentieth-century history. But the situation will be repeated unless we remain psychologically prepared to recognize Moscow's intent and to contain it. Blue Savior may live up to its name, at least for a time, until science comes up with a further generation of weapons. But the conflict in which we are engaged is not just a question of hardware. Its outcome will be determined by men, not weaponry—by their intelligence and foresight and nerve. Or the lack of it."

"I couldn't agree with you more," the President said quietly. "I said in one of my first speeches that I intend to make America strong again. I said that I don't care if some people think it's old-fashioned to want to live in a country that's fit for heroes and recognizes their worth. We don't need to be kicked in the rear end anymore to persuade us to maintain our strength, and to use it. What do you say, Henry?"

The President turned to Secretary Peyton.

"I really wouldn't want to caveat that," said the Secretary of State.

38

November 29

The way home is always shorter than the outward journey. So it seemed to Sally as she regained the point, on the beach at East Hampton, where the sandpipers had left their tracks. Their feet had imprinted winding trails of arrows, like clues to buried treasure on a chart in a children's book. Sally turned her face to the wind and the choppy waters of the Atlantic, empty and magnificent, gleaming in places where the ocean reflected the slanting afternoon sun like old polished brass. She picked a thin, perfectly rounded pebble from the water's edge and flicked it with thumb and forefinger into the slack, calmer water between the waves. The stone skipped three, four times. It reminded her of how Jimmy had clapped his hands in excitement the first time he had watched a pebble dance on the water.

Drawn by the cries of whirling seagulls, Sally walked inland, over the brown stalks of a wheatfield and the manicured greens of the golf course, to the narrow wooden bridge over Hook Pond. By Christmas, she thought, the pond would be frozen over and the skaters would come out and another year, more difficult and taxing than any she remembered, would be almost at an end. She wondered whether instead of spending the holidays in the Florida sun, as in previous years, she would come back to the Hamptons to build snowmen with Jimmy this Christmas and bike across the back-country paths. It would depend so much on Dick, and on what she wanted of him. If Dick was safe. He should have reached East Hampton already.

They might have killed him, she thought, and felt the chill of someone passing over her grave. *They might have killed them*

395

both. Dick and Charles. The two men in her life, men who did not know when to lay down their arms.

Oh God, she prayed inwardly. *Don't let them be killed. Not now, when the war is over.*

She walked on across the bridge and along paths that led back between the sprawling summer ranches of the rich, with their wraparound sundecks and profligate pools, to the main road. She almost turned into an Episcopal church, built of old stone in the style of Victorian England, but something about its ugly, incongruous glass doors, framed in black aluminum, deterred her. Nor did she stop when she came level with the pretty white-shingled facade of the 1770 House, where she had taken the big room on the upper floor with a canopied four-poster bed. She could not wait passively for the phone to ring or the door to open, not with the fear and restlessness that were seething inside her. She wandered on past the hotel to the old windmill on the village green, and over a humped stone stile into the tiny cemetery that lay in its shadow.

The ragged rows of tombstones brought back to her the scene in the Miami graveyard when men sweating heavily under their black clothes had lowered Uncle Max's coffin into the ground.

Why do men insist on vengeance? she asked herself. Nothing that Dick and Charles had accomplished in their pursuit of Max's killer could bring her uncle back.

She began to look more closely at the blurred inscriptions on the gravestones. Most of them, she saw, were more than a century old, many dating back to the turbulent times of the revolution. She read names that had already become familiar to her from the street signs of East Hampton and Amagansett: Daytons, Strattons, Millers. Here and there were clumps of headstones cut to a miniature scale. Puzzled, she peered down at them and deciphered the names or simple initials of children who had died in their first years.

She came to a row set apart. The first of the big, square-cut gray stones recorded the passing of S. Hedges Miller, aged seventy-four, in the year 1888. Next to him was buried his wife Elizabeth, daughter of David and Esther Edwards, who had died in 1882. Her age at the time of death was recorded down to the last day:

65 yrs, 2 mos & 5 d's

Beside Elizabeth's tombstone stood that of her sister Hannah, the second wife of S. Hedges Miller. She had passed on in 1888, a few months before her husband. The duration of Hannah's life was inscribed with the same care for detail:

57 yrs, 3 mos & 26 d's

At the foot of her headstone was a banal rhyme about hope eternal. But in addition, there was a quotation from the Psalms of a freshness and oddity that moved Sally. Silently, she mouthed the words: "Precious in the sight of the Lord is the death of his saints."

She stood, arms folded under her bosom, in front of the graves of S. Hedges Miller and his two wives, reflecting on the meaning of the mundane yet implacable statistics of human mortality. Here was a man who had married two sisters, one after the death of the first, in the style of the patriarchs of the Bible. Hannah, the second, had been fourteen years younger than Elizabeth. Sally wondered what depth of passion, jealousy, and lust the stark inscriptions on the tombstones must conceal. Farther along was the memento of tragedy in the same family. The gravestone bore the name of Abraham, brother of the two wives of S. Hedges Miller,

whose Death was occasioned by a Fall from the Mast Head on board the Ship Thorn at Sag Harbor,

in the year 1836, when the seafarer was just twenty-two years old. Sally roamed the cemetery, searching for the graves of the parents, David and Esther, who must have been raised, loved, and married in the era of the American Revolution. Their graves were not to be found. Sally felt a vague disappointment that these pieces of the puzzle were missing. She had become strangely absorbed in the imagined drama of this family of unknown, long-dead people. It brought her a sense of the continuity of the human condition. Their world, too, had been tormented by violent change, the order of their family life buffeted by squalls of emotion, random fatality, wars within and without. Yet their seed had survived. She felt a certain community with these villagers whose names had meant nothing to her.

Walking back toward the stile, she scuffed her shoe against a minute, ruined brown headstone, and squinted down to read the

397

inscription. Time and the seasons had removed the traces of all but one word: "D I E D." The letters were spaced wide, in block capitals.

Let them be safe, she prayed to a God to whom she had not consciously turned since Jimmy had contracted pneumonia at the age of two.

The smell from Miriam Perle's kitchen permeated the whole of the 1770 House, a rich smell, that afternoon, compounded of garlic and thyme and basil and baking pastries and puffed crepes. It was a quarter to six, and the library room was deserted, although Sid Perle, the owner of the inn, bobbed his big, friendly face around the door to the sunporch that he used as his office to ask Sally if she needed a drink.

"No thank you," she said. "I think I'll just sit quietly for a bit and watch the fire. There haven't been any calls for me, have there?"

There hadn't.

Sally curled up on the sofa under the windows, facing the big open fireplace framed by wood paneling whose recesses recalled the shapes of the tombstones in the village cemetery. Sid had told her that he thought the stripped wood might be pecan. Funny. She had never thought of pecans growing on trees.

5:48.

The library was a beautiful room, like the rest of the restored eighteenth-century house, full of things to touch and explore. Like the other public rooms at the inn, it was above all a room of clocks, dominated by two handsome Morbier pendulum clocks. The one that hung between the windows, just behind Sally's head, was embellished with fanciful patterns of flowers and fruits in repoussé brass and blue enameling. The other, by the far wall, was an ancient granddaddy encased in walnut, with a tiny bull's-eye window through which she could watch the motion of a small bob pendulum.

Sally, who never wore a watch and for that reason was more punctual than most people, constantly asking others for the time, felt most at ease on working days when a clock was somewhere in her line of sight. Today, however, the incessant swish of the pendulums and the steady ticking unsettled her.

5:53.

Her thoughts shifted to Charles. He would have taken the lead in this stupid vendetta. That was his nature. She would have been angry with him, but anger was swamped by stronger emotions. Fear, mostly, for both men's lives. And something more, that came from the understanding that the assassin Charles and Dick were tracking was not only her uncle's killer, but the man who had narrowly failed to murder her son in that night of shattering glass on Miami Beach.

5:59.

A noise broke into Sally's thoughts, and she sat up with a start. She realized, with relief, that it was only the granddaddy clock chiming the hour of six. The chimes had barely stopped when the clock behind her took up the refrain. Sally relaxed, feeling foolish that she had been thrown off balance by something so commonplace.

6:02.

She jumped up from the sofa with a startled cry. The granddaddy clock had started to chime again. No sooner had the chimes stopped than the clock behind her began again to sound the hour.

My God, she said to herself. *My nerves must really be shot. Now I'm starting to hear things happening twice.*

Hearing her cry, Sid Perle came out from behind the antique bank teller's grille that divided his corner office from the rest of the sunporch.

"How are you doing?" he asked.

"I'm sorry," she said. "I'm feeling a little strange. I thought I heard the clocks chime twice."

"You did. They're Morbier clocks. The mechanical action makes them sound the hour twice within three minutes. It's very useful if you have trouble waking up or if you missed counting the number of chimes the first time around."

"Oh."

"Are you ready for a drink?"

"Later, I think. I'm going to take a long hot bath."

The clocks were everywhere, she thought, as she went out into the narrow hall and began to mount the stairs. Through the glass door to the elegant restaurant, decked out with pre-Raphaelite maidens in stained glass, candles inside huge glass bells, and an imposing brass chandelier from the Schiff family mansion, she glimpsed more clocks: a big nautical timepiece made by C. G. Symons of Kettering and an even bigger one rescued from the Long

Island Railroad. Below her, above the stairwell that led down to the cellars, she saw the Roman numerals on the solemn marble face of the biggest clock of all, salvaged from a building on Wall Street that had long since been torn down. Its ticking sounded darkly ominous to Sally, like a heavy, unhealthy drip inside an old lead pipe.

It was strange, she thought as she ran the bath upstairs, how the shapes and sounds of everyday life can change totally in significance according to mood. She had felt an odd sense of security among the mementos of death in a graveyard; yet the harmless sounds of the clocks had filled her with foreboding.

NEAR AL-GHEIDDA, SOUTH YEMEN,
November 29

It was Abdullah who got Dick and Charles out of the canteen in the Camp of the Martyrs. He drove the old BTR-152 armored car through the barrier that divided the officers' quarters from the rest of the camp, and used the heavy machine gun to pin down the East German guards as Canning and Hammond made their break out the kitchen door. Total confusion reigned in the camp. The alarm sirens wailed, but most of the trainee terrorists were uncertain whether this was just one more emergency drill. On board the armored car, Canning assumed the accent of authority, ordering anyone who seemed likely to question them to get to the parade ground. His air of confidence, and the borrowed uniforms, seemed to work. Until Langemann's deputy received a firsthand report from one of the guards inside the canteen and ordered a full-scale pursuit. He also called up the garrison commander in al-Gheidda to block off the main road.

The BTR-152 is not the ideal vehicle for a high-speed getaway. And a single heavy machine gun was hardly adequate defense against the thousands of South Yemeni soldiers and foreign advisers who were now massing to cut off the route to the border.

"I think it was worth it," Canning commented to Dick Hammond, whose left arm was hastily bound up with a torn strip of cloth, as they rattled back the way they had come. The American understood the calm finality in his friend's voice.

As a betting man, Charles Canning would not have quoted the odds against their getting through at less than a hundred to one.

"It was worth it," Hammond agreed, thinking of Sally and the assignation in East Hampton that he would not now be able to keep. One of so many rendezvous he had missed. Then he thought of Max Zimmer and the trail of blood the man who had almost killed the President had left across the United States. "It had to be done," he added. His voice was strong and vibrant.

Then Canning started to sing, and after a few bars the American joined in. It was the song made famous by Edith Piaf, "Je ne Regrette Rien." Canning had once observed that it had been the song that was sung by the paratroops in Algiers as they marched off to make their abortive coup against de Gaulle in 1960, and the song they had sung as they were carried off to jail afterward. Abdullah looked at the two men booming out offensive sounds in a tongue that was neither English nor Arabic as if their brains had melted in the Yemeni sun.

This was the spirit in which they would almost certainly have been taken and killed. Except that Colonel Mustafa Ghazi of the Omani Sultan's personal household decided not to obey orders. There was a debt of honor where Charles Canning was concerned, and Mustafa knew that his master—whatever had been said in the presence of his prim English adviser—understood what a man owed to a brother who had saved his life. News travels fast among the nomadic tribesmen of the Hadhramaut, and it was carried to Mustafa, waiting at his border post, by one of the oldest methods in the world: primitive semaphore.

Mustafa took a single helicopter, flying low to escape South Yemeni radar. He found Canning and Hammond before the armored units that were converging on them from three sides. The pattern of their advance was like three pointing fingers, guiding him to his target.

When Canning was strapped into his bucket seat, he yelled into Mustafa's ear, "You know you could be cashiered for this, don't you, old son?"

"We both know there's another law," Mustafa yelled back. "Though we may call it by different names."

Canning nodded. "The law of the Club," he said, too softly for Mustafa to hear above the clamor of the engine.

Over the narrow neck of Georgica Cove and along the straight white shoreline beyond it, Charles Canning followed the shadow of the Bell helicopter as it raced ahead of him, over to his left. In the passenger seat, Dick Hammond craned forward, peering through the glass bubble, trying to make out the 1770 House among the neat white and gray buildings of East Hampton.

"I can see it!" he said with excitement. Next to the white house with its shutters and gabled roof, he recognized the Clinton Academy, the first high school in the state of New York.

When Charles had rented the helicopter at Kennedy Airport, showing the pilot's license that he had kept current since his time in Oman, Dick had assumed that they were going to land at the East Hampton strip and take a car to the village from there. But Charles wouldn't hear of it.

"That's no way to treat a cripple, old son," the Englishman had said, pointing to Hammond's left arm, now bound up in a sling. Just above the elbow, Hammond had taken the last bullet that Sammy Hamad had fired before Canning had cut the assassin's throat. No, Charles Canning had wanted to land on the village green, in plain sight of the inn where Sally was staying.

"You'll get us locked up," Hammond had protested. "They'll take your pilot's license away. This isn't the rural wilds of Norfolk, Charles."

They made a compromise.

Canning set the helicopter down on the golf course, a few hundred yards away from the spot on the beach where Sally had found the sandpipers' tracks in the sand. In the early dusk, the beach had emptied. But the two men could see people coming to their doors in nearby houses, alarmed by the noise of the whirring chopper blades.

"Give Sally my love," said Canning, reaching over to shake his friend's hand.

"Aren't you coming too?"

"'Fraid not," Canning shouted over the roar of the blades. "I've got a date of my own. Besides"— he grinned—"I suspect this is a no-parking zone."

"Give my love to Melanie then," Hammond shouted back, now

crouched on the ground, bending his tall frame to avoid the blades. "I'll do that."

Dick Hammond leaned over her as they sat close together on the wooden bench beside the open hearth of the taproom. With his good hand, he stroked her cheek where the firelight touched it.

"You're more beautiful each time I see you," he murmured. "I hope you'll always be there for me."

Sally let her head slump back against his chest, watching the red glow as the fire ate into a pine log.

The cheerful, bearded bartender hovered beside them. "You guys okay?" he said.

"Philadelphia," Hammond responded. The bartender had told him about a pub in Philadelphia where they mixed martinis in a silver goblet that held enough for two glasses.

"The other half?"

Hammond nodded, holding out his empty martini glass. "You know the recipe for the perfect dry martini?" he said. "You pour the gin while studying a portrait of Count Rossi, the inventor of Italian vermouth."

Sally angled her back into the comfortable groove between Hammond's chest and shoulder. The firelit room swirled gently before her eyes. She felt her eyelids drooping.

"Sleepy?" Hammond whispered. "We can always skip dinner."

"Let's stay here for a bit," she mumbled. "While the fire is strong." It was a pleasant sensation, the warmth from the hearth and the warmth of his body against her, as fatigue washed over her in waves like the flow of hot water into a deep, delicious bubble bath. But even as she let herself sink luxuriously into it, something pulled her back. Just as, upstairs in the canopied bed, some force had reined her in, tugging her away when she had been about to give herself fully to the strength of his lovemaking and his need, so that she had been distant, apart from him at the moment of his coming, as in the first days of their affair. The depth of her relief that he was safe, and that the horror of the last months was behind them, had not served to overcome that block. Even now it stopped her from simply flowing along with the tide of sensation.

The sudden clamor of loud voices shook her fully awake. She opened her eyes and watched a party of four couples filing into the bar. The men, in blazers and check sports coats, looked at if they had all gone to the same school, then the same Brooks Brothers store, and the same barber. They talked in constricted voices that emanated not from their diaphragms but from somewhere high up in their throats. They sounded as if someone were holding their noses. Their women were more varied, and seemed to Sally to be more alive. One girl, in particular, stood out from the rest. Clad in a lacy, diaphanous white blouse and a simple, hip-hugging black skirt, she seemed sexier and more sure of herself than her peers. Marianne, Sally heard someone call her. She studied the men again, curious to see which one was attached to Marianne. It was hard to judge. The men might almost have been clones.

"Waiter, I'm buying bubbly for everyone. Lots of bubbly."

Sally looked at the man who was stridently calling for champagne. He was good-looking in a way, but unformed. Fresh-razored skin gleamed pinkly behind his ears. He puffed on a large cigar, mechanically, for show rather than pleasure. Mentally, she contrasted the voluptuous way that Charles would suck and chew at a cigar. She watched with a voyeur's fascination as the man with the cigar discreetly fondled the trim rump of a tall, leggy brunette as the group settled themselves around a couple of tables on the other side of the taproom. The tall girl was attractive, but she carried herself like a marionette, with a stilted, unnatural curvature of the spine.

The voices of the people in the new group were still raised, as if they thought they were the only occupants of the room. She could sense that they were annoying Dick. The big man shifted in his seat, and she squeezed his right hand.

"You're so dear to me," she said.

"I love you," he breathed, kissing the edge of her lips. He smelled of leather.

I love you, she responded inwardly. *But I can't say it to you. I just can't seem to get the words out.*

He looked at her expectantly, and she turned her head away. *I won't let myself be hurt again*, she thought. *Don't ask me to make myself vulnerable. I can't let myself relive what I went through with Charles.* It had been her fault then, not just Charles's. She had given too much, laid herself open. For all the difference of character between Charles and Dick, the new situation was just too similar to the old one for her to risk making the same mistake again. Whatever Dick had resolved to be for her, he belonged, like Charles, to the secret world—to the world of the Agency and the Club and of never-ending war fought out in lonely places beyond the frontiers of normal experience or understanding. That world had formed Dick, and he would never escape it. Especially after what he had just been through. Dick carried that world within him. If she was honest with herself, she knew that that was part of his attraction for her. There are women, Charles had once remarked, who are turned on by the smell of cordite. So she was drawn, even now, to the kind of men that he described as the Lost Band, the men who would never be at peace. But she did not want to be a prisoner of their world again; she wanted peace.

"Those guys must think they own the place," Dick said quietly.

The volume had actually increased. Apparently some kind of fight was in the making.

"It's like a play," Sally said, her attention again riveted on the new group.

"More like a soap opera."

The man with the cigar was leaning over the table where Marianne was seated beside a young Wall Street type with sloping shoulders and an upturned nose, wearing a club tie that clashed with his check sports coat.

"You'd better stop coming on to him!" the cigar smoker yelled at Marianne. "You'd better stop doing that, or else we're gonna get out of here right now."

Marianne sat sullen and silent. The expression on her face, Sally noticed, conveyed boundless hatred and contempt. So the cigar smoker was Marianne's husband.

"What was going on?" she whispered to Hammond. "Was Marianne touching up that other man?"

"She just had her arm around him. Like this." Hammond put his right arm around Sally's shoulder, softly caressing her.

"Hey, Tom!" someone called out.

The cigar smoker had stormed across the taproom and stood sulking in the gangway beside the bench that Sally and Dick were sharing.

"That's what comes of marrying an insecure man," Marianne announced to the room, loud enough for everyone to hear.

All other conversation in the taproom was silenced as two of the cigar smoker's friends came over to him and started reasoning with him. They were standing so close to Sally that she could have touched them without shifting from her place.

"Hey, Tom," one of the men was saying. "You shouldn't feel threatened by your wife socializing with George. It doesn't make you any less of a man. It's nothing personal, Tom. If I'd been sitting next to Marianne, I might have been doing the same thing. It was just an accident that George happened to be sitting there. It could have been any of us."

"Oh, yeah?" The aggrieved husband's forearm still carried the cigar back and forth to his mouth with the mechanical regularity of a pendulum. "Would you want somebody climbing all over your wife?"

"Now, Tom," the friend persisted. "Marianne's a very social person. That's just the way she is. Don't take it personal. You wouldn't want her hanging all over you all the time. You've got no worries, Tom. I have to tell you that my wife, and she's young, Tom, she was saying to me today how attracted she is to you. She's always been very attracted to you, Tom. You're a very attractive man."

"I think you're taking this too seriously," the second male friend chimed in. "Let's get this straight. When we all came in here, I could have got upset when you had your arm around my wife."

That must be the tall brunette, Sally thought. *The one who looks as if she's being moved by strings.*

"I really mean it, Tom," the second friend was insisting. Sally noted his bright-red pants. "I could have got mad when you started feeling around Peggy. But I'm glad. I think that's wonderful."

Jesus, Sally said to herself. *This guy is saying that he thinks it's wonderful that someone was patting his wife's ass.*

Meantime, she noted, the women in the group had segregated themselves from their men and were sitting in a huddle. Some kind of herding instinct was at play.

"Shall we go?" said Dick.

"Wait just a second." The group was again rearranging itself, with much hubbub. People were getting up from the tables and preparing to leave. They made a ragged exit. Marianne left with some of the women; Tom and his men friends brought up the rear. As the cigar smoker walked out, he gave a vicious twist to an old wooden lottery wheel that was hanging by the door, uncaring whether it might fall apart. Sally saw that the pointer came to rest at number eight. The number Charles had played in the casino at Estoril.

When they had all gone, spontaneous laughter erupted from the people who remained in the taproom.

"Better than *Dallas!*" someone said.

"Is there an entertainment tax?" Dick Hammond quipped to the bartender.

They went upstairs to the restaurant, just in time before the kitchen closed, and dined on homemade tortellini and flounder Nob Hill, stuffed with smoked salmon and encased in strudel, in a corner next to one of the stained-glass maidens who looked as if she had been born in the mind of Burne-Jones. Their conversation was light and undemanding. They steered away from the events that had marred their lives over the weeks before: Max's murder, the shooting at the Miami beach house, the near-slaying of the President, the terror of a world slithering and tumbling toward Armageddon like a slalom careening out of control toward a sheer cliff. They laughed a lot about the scene in the taproom, and over Sally's greedy pleasure in the chocolate cake. Then she fell silent, thinking about the gulf that separated the lives of those—like the loud group in the bar—who were cushioned from the savage undertow of history even at the moment when it might have swallowed all of them up, and men like Dick and Charles who lived immersed in those treacherous currents. The insulation of money and social ritual had not brought happiness to the Toms and Mariannes.

She pushed aside her coffee.

"Can we take a walk on the beach?" she asked. "It's not too cold." Then she looked at his arm in its sling and remembered. "I'm sorry. You must be in pain."

"It's okay," he assured her. "Let's take that walk. It may be the last moonlight walk before the winter sets in."

She led him back to the place on the beach where she had seen the arrowlike tracks of the sandpipers. The incoming tide had washed most of them away. The tracks that remained led to a clump of rocks. She felt a sort of inevitability as they sat there, holding hands, looking up at a clear night of stars and the full moon. Somewhere up there, in the tideless oceans of space, the first of General Brennan's Blue Saviors was orbiting the planet. She shivered, thinking of the danger that had passed.

"You can't see it," he said, intuiting her train of thought. "It's thousands of miles up."

"Does it mean the end of war?" The wind blew her long blond hair across his face. Tenderly, he smoothed it back into place.

"No," he said. "So long as we survive on this planet, it will take men to stop others from fighting."

"The Lost Band," she murmured.

"What's that?"

"Nothing." She looked up into his strong, weather-beaten face. This man who would never be at peace could bring the gift of peace to others. She kissed his chapped, salty lips and said, "I love you."